Human Resource
MANAGEMENT

GLOBAL EDITION

TWELFTH EDITION

R. WAYNE MONDY, SPHR

In Collaboration with
JUDY BANDY MONDY
McNeese State University

Boston   Columbus   Indianapolis   New York   San Francisco   Upper Saddle River
Amsterdam   Cape Town   Dubai   London   Madrid   Milan   Munich   Paris   Montréal   Toronto
Delhi   Mexico City   São Paulo   Sydney   Hong Kong   Seoul   Singapore   Taipei   Tokyo

Editorial Director: Sally Yagan
Editor in Chief: Eric Svendsen
Director of Editorial Services: Ashley Santora
Senior Acquisitions Editor, Global Edition: Steven Jackson
Editorial Project Manager: Meg O'Rourke
Editorial Assistant: Carter Anderson
Director of Marketing: Patrice Lumumba Jones
Marketing Manager: Nikki Ayana Jones
Marketing Manager, International: Dean Erasmus
Marketing Assistant: Ian Gold
Senior Managing Editor: Judy Leale
Production Project Manager: Ilene Kahn

Senior Operations Supervisor: Arnold Vila
Operations Specialist: Cathleen Petersen
Creative Director: Christy Mahon
Sr. Art Director & Design Supervisor: Janet Slowik
Cover Image: © Bobo Ling-Fotolia.com
Interior Designer: Integra-Chicago
Cover Designer: Jodi Notowitz
Editorial Media Project Manager: Denise Vaughn
Media Project Manager: Lisa Rinaldi
Full-Service Project Management:
   Integra Software Services, Inc.
Cover Printer: Lehigh-Phoenix Color/Hagerstown

Pearson Education Limited
Edinburgh Gate
Harlow
Essex CM20 2JE
England

and Associated Companies throughout the world

Visit us on the World Wide Web at: www.pearsoned.co.uk

© Pearson Education Limited 2012

ISBN: 978-0-2737-5299-8

British Library Cataloguing-in-Publication Data
A catalogue record for this book is available from the British Library

10 9 8 7 6 5 4 3 2 1
15 14 13 12 11

Typeset in 10/12 Times by Integra Software Services, Inc.
Printed and bound by Courier/Kendallville in the United States of America.

The publisher's policy is to use paper manufactured from sustainable forests.

To Judy Bandy Mondy,
my love, my inspiration, and
my travel partner.

Brief Contents

PART 1 Introduction 28

Chapter 1 Strategic Human Resource Management: An Overview 28

PART 2 Ethical, Social, and Legal Considerations 48

Chapter 2 Business Ethics and Corporate Social Responsibility 48

Chapter 3 Workforce Diversity, Equal Employment Opportunity, and Affirmative Action 70

PART 3 Staffing 106

Chapter 4 Job Analysis, Strategic Planning, and Human Resource Planning 106

Chapter 5 Recruitment 136

Chapter 6 Selection 162

PART 4 Human Resource Development 198

Chapter 7 Training and Development 198

Appendix Chapter 7 Career Planning and Development 222

Chapter 8 Performance Management and Appraisal 234

PART 5 Compensation 262

Chapter 9 Direct Financial Compensation 262

Chapter 10 Indirect Financial Compensation (Benefits) and Nonfinancial Compensation 290

PART 6 Safety and Health 318

Chapter 11 A Safe and Healthy Work Environment 318

PART 7 Employee and Labor Relations 346

Chapter 12 Labor Unions and Collective Bargaining 346

Appendix Chapter 12 History of Unions in the United States 378

Chapter 13 Internal Employee Relations 384

PART 8 Operating in a Global Environment 408

Chapter 14 Global Human Resource Management 408

Contents

PART 1   Introduction   28

    Chapter 1   Strategic Human Resource Management: An Overview   28

    HRM in Action: Employer Branding Helps Attract the Best and Makes Them Want to Stay   28

    Chapter Objectives   29

    Human Resource Management   30

    Human Resource Management Functions   30

        Staffing   30

        Human Resource Development   31

        Compensation   32

        Safety and Health   32

        Employee and Labor Relations   32

        Human Resource Research   32

        Interrelationships of HRM Functions   32

    Dynamic Human Resource Management Environment   33

        Legal Considerations   33

        Labor Market   33

        Society   34

        Political Parties   34

        Unions   34

        Shareholders   34

        Competition   34

        Customers   34

        ■ TRENDS & INNOVATIONS: The Many HR Uses of Social Networking   35

        HR Technology   36

        Economy   36

        Unanticipated Events   36

    How Human Resource Management Is Practiced in the Real World   36

    HR's Changing Strategic Role: Who Performs the Human Resource Management Tasks?   36

        Human Resource Manager   37

        HR Outsourcing   37

        HR Shared Service Centers   38

        Professional Employer Organizations (Employee Leasing)   38

        Line Managers   39

    Human Resource Designations   39

    Evolution of Human Resource Management   40

    Evolving HR Organizations   41

    Scope of This Book   42

        ■ A GLOBAL PERSPECTIVE: Managing Human Capital in a Borderless World   43

    Summary   43   •   Key Terms   44   •   Questions for Review   44   •   HRM Incident 1: HR after a Disaster   45   •   HRM Incident 2: Downsizing   45   •   Notes   46

PART 2 Ethical, Social, and Legal Considerations 48

Chapter 2 Business Ethics and Corporate Social Responsibility 48

HRM in Action: Satyam: The case of the vanishing million 48

Chapter Objectives 49

Ethics 50

The Bad and the Ugly; Now Comes the Good 51

A Model of Ethics 51

■ ETHICAL DILEMMA: A Selection Quandary 53

Legislating Ethics 53

Code of Ethics 54

Linking Pay to Ethical Behavior 55

Human Resource Ethics 56

Ethics Training 56

Professionalization of Human Resource Management 58

Society for Human Resource Management 58

Human Resource Certification Institute 58

American Society for Training and Development 58

WorldatWork 58

Corporate Social Responsibility 59

■ TRENDS & INNOVATIONS: Strategic Corporate Social Responsibility 60

Stakeholder Analysis and the Social Contract 60

Obligations to Individuals 62

Obligations to Other Organizations 62

Obligations to Government 62

Obligations to Society in General 63

Implementing a Corporate Social Responsibility Program 63

■ A GLOBAL PERSPECTIVE: Can Corporate Social Responsibility Succeed in the Global Environment? 64

Summary 65 • Key Terms 65 • Questions for Review 66 • HRM Incident 1: An Ethical Flaw 66 • HRM Incident 2: "You Can't Fire Me" 66 • Notes 67

Chapter 3 Workforce Diversity, Equal Employment Opportunity, and Affirmative Action 70

HRM in Action: Do-it-yourself diversity in times of recession 70

Chapter Objectives 71

Workforce Projection: 2050 72

Diversity and Diversity Management 73

Components of the Diverse Workforce 74

Single Parents and Working Mothers 74

Women in Business 74

Mothers Returning to the Workforce 74

Dual-Career Families 75

Workers of Color 75

Older Workers 75

People with Disabilities 76

Immigrants 76

Foreign Workers 76

Young Persons with Limited Education or Skills 77

Equal Employment Opportunity: An Overview 77

Laws Affecting Equal Employment Opportunity 78

Civil Rights Act of 1866   78
Equal Pay Act of 1963, Amended in 1972   78
Lilly Ledbetter Fair Pay Act of 2009   78
Comparable Worth   79
Title VII of the Civil Rights Act of 1964, Amended 1972   79
Pregnancy Discrimination Act of 1978   81
Civil Rights Act of 1991   82
Age Discrimination in Employment Act of 1967, Amended in 1978 and 1986   83
Age Can Actually Be a Bona Fide Occupational Qualification   83
Rehabilitation Act of 1973   84
Americans with Disabilities Act of 1990   84
Americans with Disabilities Act Amendments Act of 2008   85
Immigration Reform and Control Act of 1986   85
Illegal Immigration Reform and Immigrant Responsibility Act of 1996   85
Uniformed Services Employment and Reemployment Rights Act of 1994   86
Veterans' Benefits Improvement Act of 2004   86
State and Local Laws   86

Significant U.S. Supreme Court Decisions Affecting Equal Employment Opportunity   86
■ ETHICAL DILEMMA: What Was the Real Message?   87
Griggs v Duke Power Company   87
Albemarle Paper Company v Moody   87
Phillips v Martin Marietta Corporation   87
Espinoza v Farah Manufacturing Company   88
Dothard v Rawlingson   88
American Tobacco Company v Patterson   88
O'Connor v Consolidated Coin Caterers Corp.   88

Significant U.S. Supreme Court Decisions Affecting Affirmative Action   89
University of California Regents v Bakke   89
Adarand Constructors v Pena   89
Grutter v Bollinger   89
Gratz v Bollinger   89
Ricci v DeStefano   90

Equal Employment Opportunity Commission   90

Uniform Guidelines on Employee Selection Procedures   90

Concept of Disparate Treatment   91

Concept of Adverse Impact   92

Additional Guidelines on Employment Selection Procedures   93
Guidelines on Sexual Harassment   93
Guidelines on Discrimination Because of National Origin   95
Guidelines on Discrimination Because of Religion   96

Affirmative Action: Executive Order 11246, as Amended by Executive Order 11375   96
■ TRENDS & INNOVATIONS: Caregiver (Family Responsibility) Discrimination   97

Affirmative Action Programs   98
■ A GLOBAL PERSPECTIVE: Multinational Whistle-blowing   100
Summary   101 • Key Terms   102 • Questions for Review   102 • HRM Incident 1: I Feel Great   103 • HRM Incident 2: So, What's Affirmative Action?   103 • Notes   104

PART 3   Staffing   106

Chapter 4   **Job Analysis, Strategic Planning, and Human Resource Planning   106**
HRM in Action: Strategic Talent Management Systems   106

Chapter Objectives 107

Job Analysis: A Basic Human Resource Management Tool 108

Reasons for Conducting Job Analysis 109

Staffing 109

Training and Development 109

Performance Appraisal 110

Compensation 110

Safety and Health 110

Employee and Labor Relations 110

Legal Considerations 110

Types of Job Analysis Information 110

Job Analysis Methods 111

Questionnaires 111

Observation 111

Interviews 111

Employee Recording 111

Combination of Methods 111

Conducting Job Analysis 112

Job Description 113

Job Identification 113

Date of the Job Analysis 113

Job Summary 113

Duties Performed 113

Job Specification 113

O*NET, the Occupational Information Network 114

Standard Occupational Classification (SOC) 115

Job Sculpting 115

Timeliness of Job Analysis 115

Job Analysis for Team Members 115

Job Analysis and the Law 116

HR as a Strategic Business Partner 117

Strategic Planning Process 118

Mission Determination 118

Environmental Assessment 119

Objective Setting 119

Strategy Setting 120

Strategy Implementation 120

Human Resource Planning 121

Forecasting Human Resource Requirements 122

Zero-Base Forecasting 122

Bottom-Up Forecast 122

Relationship between Volume of Sales and Number of Workers Required 123

Workforce Planning Software 123

Forecasting Human Resource Availability 123

Human Resource Databases 124

Shortage of Workers Forecasted 124

Innovative Recruiting 124

Compensation Incentives 124

Training Programs 124

Different Selection Standards 124

■ ETHICAL DILEMMA: Which "Thinker" Should Go? 125

Surplus of Employees Forecasted 125

Succession Planning: A Component of Strategic Planning   125
■ TRENDS & INNOVATIONS: Layoff Alternatives   126

Disaster Planning: A Component of Strategic Planning   127

Manager Self-Service   128

Employee Self-Service   128

Job Design Concepts   129
Job Enrichment   129
Job Enlargement   129
Job Rotation   129
Reengineering   129
■ A GLOBAL PERSPECTIVE: Global Job Rotation as a Unique Fast Track Benefit   130

Summary   131   •   Key Terms   132   •   Questions for Review   132   •   HRM Incident 1: A Degree for Beauty Therapists   133   •   HRM Incident 2: Strategic HR?   134   •   Notes   134

Chapter 5   Recruitment   136

HRM in Action: Recruiting by Promising an Interview   136

Chapter Objectives   137

Recruitment Defined   138

Alternatives to Recruitment   138
Outsourcing   138
■ TRENDS & INNOVATIONS: Are Contingent Workers the Workforce of the Future?   139
Professional Employer Organizations (Employee Leasing)   139
Overtime   139

External Environment of Recruitment   140
Labor Market Conditions   140
Active or Passive Job Seekers   140
Legal Considerations   140

Promotion Policies   141

Recruitment Process   141

Internal Recruitment Methods   142
Job Posting and Job Bidding   142
Employee Referrals   143

External Recruitment Sources   144
High Schools and Vocational Schools   144
Community Colleges   144
Colleges and Universities   145
Competitors in the Labor Market   145
Former Employees   145
■ ETHICAL DILEMMA: Unfair Advantage?   146
Unemployed   146
Military Personnel   146
Self-Employed Workers   146
Ex-Offenders   146

Online Recruitment Methods   147
Internet Recruiter   147
Virtual Job Fair   147
Corporate Career Web Sites   147
Weblogs (Blogs for Short)   148
General-Purpose Job Boards   148
NACElink Network   148
AllianceQ   148

Niche Sites 148

Contract Workers' Sites 149

Hourly Workers' Job Sites 149

Social Network Recruiting 149

Job Search Scams 151

Traditional External Recruitment Methods 151

Media Advertising 151

Private Employment Agencies 152

Public Employment Agencies 152

Recruiters 152

Job Fairs 153

Internships 153

Executive Search Firms 153

Professional Associations 154

Unsolicited Applicants 154

Open Houses 154

Event Recruiting 154

Sign-on Bonuses 154

Competitive Games 154

Tailoring Recruitment Methods to Sources 155

■ A GLOBAL PERSPECTIVE: Our Company Headquarters
Has Been Outsourced! 156

Summary 157 • Key Terms 157 • Questions for Review 158 •
HRM Incident 1: A Problem Ad? 158 • HRM Incident 2: "The Grass is Greener
on the Other Side" or Is It? 159 • Notes 159

Chapter 6 **Selection 162**

HRM in Action: From E-Verify to Biometrics 162

Chapter Objectives 163

Significance of Employee Selection 164

Environmental Factors Affecting the Selection Process 164

Other HR Functions 165

Legal Considerations 165

Speed of Decision Making 165

Organizational Hierarchy 165

Applicant Pool 165

Type of Organization 166

Probationary Period 166

Selection Process 166

Applicant Tracking Systems 166

Preliminary Screening 167

Review of Applications 168

Review of Résumés 168

Sending Résumés via the Internet 170

Selection Tests: Advantages and Potential Problems 170

Advantages of Selection Tests 170

Potential Problems of Selection Tests 170

■ ETHICAL DILEMMA: Employee Selection Criteria? 171

**Characteristics of Properly Designed Selection
Tests 171**

Standardization 171

Objectivity 172

Norms 172

Reliability   172

Validity   172

Test Validation Approaches   172

Criterion-Related Validity   172

Content Validity   173

Construct Validity   173

Types of Employment Tests   173

Cognitive Aptitude Tests   173

Psychomotor Abilities Tests   173

Job-Knowledge Tests   174

Work-Sample Tests   174

Vocational Interest Tests   174

Personality Tests   174

Online Assessment   175

Assessment Centers   175

Unique Forms of Testing   175

Genetic Testing   176

Graphoanalysis (Handwriting Analysis)   176

Polygraph Tests   176

Employment Interview   177

Interview Planning   177

Content of the Interview   177

Candidate's Role and Expectations   178

General Types of Interviews   178

Unstructured Interview   178

Structured Interview   179

Behavioral Interview   179

Methods of Interviewing   180

One-on-One Interview   180

Group Interview   180

Board (or Panel) Interview   180

Multiple Interviews   180

Stress Interview   180

■ TRENDS & INNOVATIONS: Interviewing Through Crowd Sourcing   181

Realistic Job Preview   181

Potential Interviewing Problems   182

Inappropriate Questions   182

Permitting Non-Job-Related Information   182

Premature Judgment   183

Interview Illusion   183

Interviewer Domination   183

Contrast Effect   183

Lack of Training   183

Nonverbal Communication   183

Concluding the Interview   184

Pre-Employment Screening: Background Investigations   184

Continuous Background Investigation   185

Background Investigation with Social Networking   185

Remembering Hiring Standards to Avoid   185

Pre-Employment Screening: Reference Checks   186

Automated Reference Checking   186

Negligent Hiring   187

Selection Decision 187

Medical Examination 187

Notification of Candidates 188

Candidate Relationship Management 188

Human Capital Metrics 188

Metrics for Evaluating the Effectiveness of Recruitment /Selection 189

Quality of Hire 189

Time Required to Hire 189

New Hire Retention 189

Hiring Manager Overall Satisfaction 189

Turnover Rate 189

Recruiting Costs 189

■ A GLOBAL PERSPECTIVE: Leadership Effectiveness in the Global Environment 190

Selection Rate 190

Acceptance Rate 191

Yield Rate 191

Cost/Benefit of Recruitment Sources and Methods 191

Summary 191 • Key Terms 193 • Questions for Review 193 • HRM Incident 1: A Matter of Priorities 194 • HRM Incident 2: The Best Person for the Job: A Matter of Fit! 194 • Notes 195

PART 4 Human Resource Development 198

Chapter 7 Training and Development 198

HRM in Action: Executive Integration, the Sink or Swim Approach Does Not Work 198

Chapter Objectives 199

Strategic Training and Development 200

Learning Organization 200

Factors Influencing Training and Development 201

Top Management Support 201

Technological Advances 201

World Complexity 201

Lifetime Learning 201

Learning Styles 201

■ ETHICAL DILEMMA: Tough Side of Technology 202

Other Human Resource Functions 202

Training and Development Process 202

Determine Specific Training and Development Needs 202

Establish Specific Training and Development Objectives 203

Training Area: Employment Compliance 203

Training and Development Methods 204

Instructor-Led 204

E-Learning 204

Case Study 205

Behavior Modeling and Twittering 205

Role-Playing 206

Business Games 206

In-Basket Training 206

On-the-Job Training 206

Internships 207

Apprenticeship Training 207

Training and Development Delivery Systems   207
   Corporate Universities   207
   Colleges and Universities   207
   Community Colleges   208
   Online Higher Education   208
   Vestibule System   208
   Video Media   208
      ■ TRENDS & INNOVATIONS: Telepresence—High-Tech
        Videoconferencing   209
   Simulators   209

Management Development   209
   Mentoring and Coaching   210
   Reverse Mentoring   211

Orientation   211

Implementing Training and Development Programs   212

Metrics for Evaluating Training and Development   213
   Participant Reaction   213
   Level of Learning Achieved   213
   Changes in Learner Behavior   213
   Business Results Derived from Training   213
   Return-on-Investment from Training   213
   Benchmarking   214

ISO 9001 Quality Assurance Training Standards   214

Workforce Investment Act   214

Organization Development: A Strategic HR Tool   214
   Survey Feedback   215
   Quality Circles   215
   Team Building   215
   Sensitivity Training   216
      ■ A GLOBAL PERSPECTIVE: Buddies Across the Globe   217
   Summary   217   •   Key Terms   218   •   Questions for Review   218   •
   HRM Incident 1: Training at Keller-Globe   219   •   HRM Incident 2: Career versus Job
   Security?   219   •   Notes   220

Appendix Chapter 7   Career Planning and Development   222
   Job Security versus Career Security   222
   Career and Career Planning Defined   223
   Career Planning   223
      Career Planning: Self-Assessment   223
      Using the Web for Self-Assessment Assistance   225
      Using the Web for Career-Planning Assistance   226

   Career Paths and Career Development   226
   Career Development Methods   227
      Manager/Employee Self-Service   227
      Discussions with Knowledgeable Individuals   227
      Company Material   227
      Performance-Appraisal System   228
      Workshops   228

   Career Paths   228
      Traditional Career Path   228
      Network Career Path   229
      Lateral Skill Path   229
      Dual-Career Path   229
      Adding Value to Your Career   229

Demotion   229
Free Agents (Being Your Own Boss)   230

Developing Unique Segments of the Workforce   230
Baby Boomers   230
Generation X Employees   230
Generation Y Employees   231
Generation I (Google Generation) as Future Employees   232
Multigenerational Diversity   232
Key Terms   232   •   Notes   232

Chapter 8   Performance Management and Appraisal   234

HRM in Action: Employee Engagement as a Strategic HR Tool   234

Chapter Objectives   235

Performance Management   236

Performance Appraisal   236

Uses of Performance Appraisal   237
Human Resource Planning   237
Recruitment and Selection   237
Training and Development   237
Career Planning and Development   238
Compensation Programs   238
Internal Employee Relations   238
Assessment of Employee Potential   238

Performance Appraisal Environmental Factors   238
■ TRENDS & INNOVATIONS: Integrating Learning and Performance
Management   239

Performance Appraisal Process   239

Establish Performance Criteria (Standards)   240
Traits   240
Behaviors   241
Competencies   241
Goal Achievement   241
Improvement Potential   241

Responsibility for Appraisal   242
Immediate Supervisor   242
Subordinates   242
Peers and Team Members   242
Self-Appraisal   243
Customer Appraisal   243

Appraisal Period   243

Performance Appraisal Methods   244
360-Degree Feedback Evaluation Method   244
Rating Scales Method   245
Critical Incident Method   247
Essay Method   247
Work Standards Method   247
Ranking Method   247
Forced Distribution Method   248
Behaviorally Anchored Rating Scale Method   248
Results-Based System   249

Problems in Performance Appraisal   249
Appraiser Discomfort   249
Lack of Objectivity   250
Halo/Horn   250

Leniency/Strictness   250

Central Tendency   251

Recent Behavior Bias   251

Personal Bias (Stereotyping)   251

Manipulating the Evaluation   251

■ ETHICAL DILEMMA: Abdication of Responsibility   252

Employee Anxiety   252

Characteristics of an Effective Appraisal System   253

Job-Related Criteria   253

Performance Expectations   253

Standardization   253

Trained Appraisers   253

Continuous Open Communication   254

Conduct Performance Reviews   254

Due Process   254

Legal Implications   254

Appraisal Interview   255

Scheduling the Interview   255

Interview Structure   255

Use of Praise and Criticism   255

■ A GLOBAL PERSPECTIVE: Two Cultures' Views of Performance Appraisal   256

Employees' Role   256

Concluding the Interview   257

Summary   257   •   Key Terms   258   •   Questions for Review   258   •
HRM Incident 1: These Things Are a Pain   258   •   HRM Incident 2: Performance
Appraisal?   259   •   Notes   259

PART 5   Compensation   262

Chapter 9   Direct Financial Compensation   262

HRM in Action: Are Top Executives Paid Too Much?   262

Chapter Objectives   263

Compensation: An Overview   264

Equity in Financial Compensation   265

Determinants of Direct Financial Compensation   266

Organization as a Determinant of Direct Financial Compensation   266

Compensation Policies   267

Organizational Level   267

Ability to Pay   267

Labor Market as a Determinant of Direct Financial Compensation   267

Compensation Surveys   268

Expediency   268

Cost of Living   268

Labor Unions   268

Economy   269

Legislation   269

Job as a Determinant of Direct Financial Compensation   270

Job Evaluation   270

Ranking Method   271

Classification Method   271

Factor Comparison Method   271

Point Method   272

Hay Guide Chart-Profile Method (Hay Plan)   272

Job Pricing   272
Pay Grades   272
Pay Ranges   273
Broadbanding   274
Single-Rate System   274
Adjusting Pay Rates   274

Employee as a Determinant of Direct Financial Compensation   275
Job Performance—Performance-Based Pay   275
Skills—Skill-Based Pay   276
Competencies—Competency-Based Pay   277
Seniority   277
Experience   277
Organization Membership   277
Potential   277
Political Influence   278
Luck   278

Team-Based Pay   278
■ TRENDS & INNOVATIONS: Salary Compression, Why Is the
New Guy Making What I Am Making?   279

Company-Wide Pay Plans   279
Profit Sharing   279
Gainsharing   280

Professional Employee Compensation   280
■ ETHICAL DILEMMA: Creative Accounting?   281

Sales Representative Compensation   281

Contingent Worker Compensation   282

Executive Compensation   282
Base Salary   282
Bonuses and Performance-Based Pay   282
Stock Option Plans   283
Perquisites   283

Golden Parachute Contract   283
■ A GLOBAL PERSPECTIVE: Executive Compensation in the Global
Environment   284

Clawback Contract Provision   284
Summary   285   •   Key Terms   286   •   Questions for Review   286   •
HRM Incident 1: A Motivated Worker!   286   •   HRM Incident 2: The Controversial
Job   287   •   Notes   288

**Chapter 10   Indirect Financial Compensation (Benefits)
and Nonfinancial Compensation   290**
HRM in Action: Two in a Box   290
Chapter Objectives   291
Indirect Financial Compensation (Benefits)   292
■ TRENDS & INNOVATIONS: Total Rewards Are Much More
Than the Money that Jingles in Your Pocket   293

Mandated (Legally Required) Benefits   293
■ ETHICAL DILEMMA: A Poor Bid   294
Social Security   294
Unemployment Compensation   294
Workers' Compensation   294

Discretionary Benefits   295

Payment for Time Not Worked   295
Paid Vacations   295
Sick Pay and Paid Time Off   295
Sabbaticals   296
Other Types of Payment for Time Not Worked   296

Health Care   296
Managed-Care Health Organizations   297
Consumer-Driven Health Care Plans   297
On-Site Health Care (Work-Site Clinics)   298
Major Medical Benefits   298
Dental and Vision Care   298

Life Insurance   298

Retirement Plans   298
Defined Benefit Plans   299
Defined Contribution Plans   299
Cash Balance Plans   299

Disability Protection   300

Employee Stock Option Plans   300

Employee Services   300
Child Care   300
Educational Assistance   301
Food Services/Subsidized Cafeterias   301
Scholarships for Dependents   301
Relocation Benefits   301
Unique Employee Services Benefits   301

Premium Pay   302

Voluntary Benefits   302

Customized Benefit Plans   303

Health Care Legislation   303
Consolidated Omnibus Budget Reconciliation Act   303
Health Insurance Portability and Accountability Act   303
Employee Retirement Income Security Act   303
Older Workers Benefit Protection Act   304
Family and Medical Leave Act   304
Pension Protection Act   304
Patient Protection and Affordable Care Act   304

Communicating Information about the Benefits Package   305

Nonfinancial Compensation   305
Job Itself as a Nonfinancial Compensation Factor   305

Job Environment as a Nonfinancial Compensation Factor   306
Sound Policies   306
Capable Managers   307
Competent Employees   307
Congenial Co-workers   307
Appropriate Status Symbols   307
Working Conditions   308

Workplace Flexibility (Work–Life Balance)   308
Flextime   308
Compressed Work Week   309
Job Sharing   309
Examples of Executive Job Sharing   309

Telecommuting   310

■ A GLOBAL PERSPECTIVE: Global Customized Benefits   311

Part-Time Work   311

Summary   312   •   Key Terms   313   •   Questions for Review   313   •
HRM Incident 1: Flextime   314   •   HRM Incident 2: A Benefits Package Designed
for Whom?   3114   •   Notes   315

PART 6   Safety and Health   318

Chapter 11   A Safe and Healthy Work Environment   318

**HRM in Action: Smoke-free Workplaces: Dealing with the
Low Hanging Fruit   318**

Chapter Objectives   319

Nature and Role of Safety and Health   320

Occupational Safety and Health Administration   320

Safety: The Economic Impact   322

Focus of Safety Programs   322

Unsafe Employee Actions   322

■ ETHICAL DILEMMA: Illegal Dumping   323

Unsafe Working Conditions   323

Developing Safety Programs   323

Accident Investigation   324

Evaluation of Safety Programs   324

Repetitive Stress Injuries   326

Ergonomics   326

Workplace Violence   327

Vulnerable Employees   327

Legal Consequences of Workplace Violence   328

Individual and Organizational Characteristics to Monitor   328

Preventive Actions   328

Domestic Violence   329

Laws Related to Domestic Violence   329

Nature of Stress   329

Potential Consequences of Stress   330

Stressful Jobs   330

Managing Stress   331

■ TRENDS & INNOVATIONS: Identity Theft as a Major Stressor in Today's
Environment   332

Burnout   333

Wellness Programs   333

Physical Fitness Programs   334

Substance Abuse   335

Alcohol Abuse   335

Drug Abuse   335

Substance-Abuse-Free Workplace   335

Implementing a Drug-Testing Program   338

Employee Assistance Programs   338

■ A GLOBAL PERSPECTIVE: Global Healthcare for Expats   339

Summary   340   •   Key Terms   341   •   Questions for Review   339   •
HRM Incident 1: What a Change!   341   •   HRM Incident 2: I'm Just Stressed
Out!   342   •   Notes   343

PART 7   Employee and Labor Relations   346

Chapter 12   Labor Unions and Collective Bargaining   346

HRM in Action: The Two-Tier Wage System Returns   346

Chapter Objectives   347

Union Objectives   348

Why Employees Join Unions   348

    Dissatisfaction with Management   348

    Social Outlet   349

    Opportunity for Leadership   349

    Forced Unionization   349

    Peer Pressure   350

Organized Labor's Strategies for a Stronger Movement   350

    Strategically Located Union Members   350

    Pulling the Union Through   350

    Political Involvement   350

    Union Salting   351

    Flooding the Community   351

    Public Awareness Campaigns   351

    Building Organizing Funds   351

    Unions Partnering with High Schools   351

    ▦ TRENDS & INNOVATIONS: Organizing Younger Workers, A Strategy Seriously Needed   352

    Organizing Through the Card Check   352

    ▦ ETHICAL DILEMMA: A Strategic Move   353

    Employee Free Choice Act   353

Union Structure   353

    Local Union   353

    National Union   354

    American Federation of Labor and Congress of Industrial Organizations (AFL-CIO)   354

    Change to Win Coalition   354

Establishing the Collective Bargaining Relationship   355

    Signing of Authorization Cards   356

    Petition for Election   356

    Election Campaign   356

    Election and Certification   357

Collective Bargaining   357

Collective Bargaining Process   357

Bargaining Issues   357

    Recognition   358

    Management Rights   359

    Union Security   359

    Compensation   360

    Grievance Procedure   360

    Employee Security   360

    Job-Related Factors   360

Preparation for Negotiations   361

Negotiating the Agreement   361

Breakdowns in Negotiations   363

    Third-Party Intervention   363

    Union Strategies for Overcoming Negotiation Breakdowns   364

    Management Strategies for Overcoming Negotiation Breakdowns   365

Reaching the Agreement 366

Ratifying the Agreement 366

Administration of the Agreement 366

Grievance Procedure in a Union Environment 366

Recent Labor/Management Legal Trends 368

Collective Bargaining in the Public Sector 369

Union Decertification 370

Unions Today 370

■ A GLOBAL PERSPECTIVE: Union Organizing in the Global Environment Can Be Dangerous 371

Summary 372 • Key Terms 373 • Questions for Review 374 • HRM Incident 1: Break Down the Barrier 374 • HRM Incident 2: You Are Out of What? 375 • Notes 375

Appendix Chapter 12 History of Unions in the United States 378

Labor Movement Before 1930 378

Labor Movement After 1930 379

Anti-Injunction Act (Norris–LaGuardia Act), 1932 379

National Labor Relations Act (Wagner Act), 1935 379

Labor Management Relations Act (Taft–Hartley Act), 1947 380

Labor-Management Reporting and Disclosure Act (Landrum-Griffin Act), 1959 381

Key Terms 382 • Notes 383

Chapter 13 Internal Employee Relations 384

HRM in Action: Worker Retention: It Costs Less to Keep Qualified Workers than to Replace Them 384

Chapter Objectives 385

Internal Employee Relations Defined 386

Employment at Will 386

Discipline and Disciplinary Action 387

Disciplinary Action Process 388

Approaches to Disciplinary Action 389

Hot Stove Rule 389

Progressive Disciplinary Action 389

Disciplinary Action without Punishment 390

Problems in the Administration of Disciplinary Action 391

■ ETHICAL DILEMMA: To Fire or Not To Fire 392

Termination 392

■ TRENDS & INNOVATIONS: Emotional Intelligence Needed in Disciplinary Action 393

Termination of Employees at Various Levels 393

Termination of Nonmanagerial/Nonprofessional Employees 394

Termination of Executives 394

Termination of Middle and Lower-Level Managers and Professionals 394

Demotion as an Alternative to Termination 395

Downsizing 395

Negative Aspects of Downsizing 396

Downsizing Software 396

Worker Adjustment and Retraining Notification Act (WARN) 396

Outplacement 397

Severance Pay 397

Ombudspersons 398

Alternative Dispute Resolution 398

Transfers   399

Promotions   399

Resignations   400

    Analyzing Voluntary Resignations   400

    Attitude Surveys: A Means of Retaining Quality Employees   401

    Advance Notice of Resignation   401

    ■ A GLOBAL PERSPECTIVE: Disciplinary Action in the Global Environment   402

    Offboarding   402

Retirements   402

Summary   403   •   Key Terms   404   •   Questions for Review   404   •
HRM Incident 1: Should He Be Fired?   404   •   HRM Incident 2: It's the Best
Thing to Do   405   •   Notes   406

PART 8   Operating in a Global Environment   408

Chapter 14   Global Human Resource Management   408

HRM in Action: Getting Tougher to Bribe in the International Arena   408

Chapter Objectives   409

Evolution of Global Business   410

Global Strategic Human Resource Management   411

Global Staffing   412

    Types of Global Staff Members   412

    Approaches to Global Staffing   413

    Selecting Expatriates   414

    Background Investigation   414

    ■ TRENDS & INNOVATIONS: Cyberwork in the Global Environment   415

    Hiring Temps in Japan   415

Global Human Resource Development   415

    Expatriate Training and Development   416

    Pre-move Orientation and Training   416

    Continual Development: Online Assistance and Training   416

    Repatriation Orientation and Training   417

    Global E-learning   417

Virtual Teams in a Global Environment   418

Global Compensation   419

    Compensation for Host-Country Nationals   419

    Expatriate Compensation   420

Global Safety and Health   421

Global Employee and Labor Relations   422

NAFTA and CAFTA   422

Global Legal and Political Factors   423

    ■ ETHICAL DILEMMA: Mordita   424

Global EEO and Sexual Harassment   424

Summary   425   •   Key Terms   426   •   Questions for Review   426   •
HRM Incident 1: The Overseas Transfer   426   •   HRM Incident 2: Was There Enough
Preparation?   427   •   Notes   427

Glossary   430

Name Index   440

Company Index   445

Subject Index   447

Preface

Human resource management (HRM) is arguably the most exciting area within the field of business. It is constantly changing and evolving. In fact, much has happened in the world since the writing of the 11th edition. Certainly the national elections and the recession of 2008/10 have affected many aspects of human resource management. In recent years, my hometown has been hit by two major hurricanes and I have seen how these unanticipated events can affect the practice of human resource management. You will see how these changes have affected human resource management as you study the information in the book. Major technological changes appear to be increasing geometrically with no end in sight. Social networking trends such as wikis, blogs, LinkedIn, and Facebook and other tools such as Twitter have worked their way into human resource (HR) use. I have personally had to learn how to use social networking to write about it successfully.

New to This Edition

- **HRM in Action** features are provided at the beginning of each chapter and present current topics in human resource management that set the tone for a discussion of major topics included within the chapter. New or completely rewritten HRM in Actions to the 12th edition are: Employer Branding Helps Attract the Best and Makes Them Want to Stay; No Age Discrimination Here, Strategic Talent Management Systems; Recruiting by Promising an Interview; From E-Verify to Biometrics; Executive Integration, the Sink or Swim Approach Does Not Work; Employee Engagement as a Strategic HR Tool; Are Top Executives Paid Too Much?; Two in a Box; Smoke-free Workplaces: Dealing with the Low Hanging Fruit; The Two-Tier Wage System Returns; Worker Retention: It Costs Less to Keep Qualified Workers than to Replace Them; and Getting Tougher to Bribe in the International Arena.
- **Trends & Innovations** that highlight current developments in the field of human resource management section are included in each chapter. New or completely rewritten Trends & Innovations to the 12th edition are: The Many HR Uses of Social Networking; Strategic Corporate Social Responsibility; Caregiver (Family Responsibility) Discrimination; Layoff Alternatives; Are Contingent Workers the Workforce of the Future?; Interviewing Through Crowd Sourcing; Telepresence—High-Tech Videoconferencing; Integrating Learning and Performance Management; Salary Compression, Why Is the New Guy Making What I Am Making?; Total Rewards Are Much More Than the Money that Jingles in Your Pocket; Identity Theft as a Major Stressor in Today's Environment; Organizing Younger Workers, A Strategy Seriously Needed; Emotional Intelligence Needed in Disciplinary Action; and Cyberwork in the Global Environment.
- **A Global Perspective** that highlights HRM in the global environment is included in all but the last chapter. New or totally rewritten global perspectives to the 12th edition are: Managing Human Capital in a Borderless World; Can Corporate Social Responsibility Succeed in the Global Environment?; Global Job Rotation as a Unique Fast Track Benefit; Our Company Headquarters Has Been Outsourced!; Leadership Effectiveness in the Global Environment; Buddies Across the Globe; Executive Compensation in the Global Environment; Global Customized Benefits; Global Healthcare for Expats; and Disciplinary Action in the Global Environment.

  In addition to the Global Perspectives identified above, new global information is provided in virtually all chapters.

- **Social Networking** topics included in this edition include sections on: The Many HR Uses of Social Networking; Social Network Recruiting; Background Investigation with Social Networking; and Behavioral Modeling and Twittering. In addition, social networking is included in the discussion of numerous topics.

- **Laws, Supreme Court Decisions, and Executive Orders and EEOC** changes that are new to the 12th edition are: Lilly Ledbetter Fair Pay Act, Americans with Disabilities Act Amendments Act, Patient Protection and Affordable Health Care Act, Troubled Assets Relief Program (TARP), Restoring American Financial Stability Act, Supreme Court decisions of *Ricci v DeStefano, CBOCS West Inc. v Humphries,* and *Vicky S. Crawford v Metropolitan Government of Nashville and Davidson County, Tennessee.* Caregiver (Family Responsibility) Discrimination is described in considerable detail in Chapter 3, Workforce Diversity, Equal Employment Opportunity, and Affirmative Action. Four executive orders that will greatly affect federal government contractors are included in the labor unions and collective bargaining chapter. I also point out potentially significant HR legislation that if passed will have a major impact on human resource management.

- **The importance of technology,** both hardware and software, was a major focus of the 12th edition revision. For example, HRIS topics are discussed throughout the text. Some examples include: Talent Management Systems; Workforce Planning Software; Human Resource Databases; Applicant Tracking Systems; Online Recruiting; Online Assessment; Automated Reference Checking; Relationship Management; and Downsizing Software.

- **Additional new topics** for the 12th edition not included in the above list include: Foreign Workers; Job Sculpting; Active or Passive Job Seekers; AllianceQ; Job Search Scams; Interview Illusion; Lifetime Learning; Multigenerational Diversity; Clawback Contract Provision; Unique Employee Services Benefits; Voluntary Benefits; Laws Related to Domestic Violence; Employee Free Choice Act; Unions Partnering with High Schools; and Offboarding.

- **Thoroughly updated.** The recession of 2008/10, the election of 2008, and the use of technology for HR-related tasks created a need to take a fresh look at many traditional HR topics and how they were discussed. The 12th edition of HRM provided me the opportunity to incorporate more than 900 new sources in the development of this edition.

- **Suggestions from reviewers** revealed that certain material from Chapter 1 would be more appropriate in other chapters. I agreed! The need for the human resource manager to be a strategic partner was moved to Chapter 4 where I address strategic planning and strategic human resource planning. I now describe human capital metrics in Chapter 6, Selection, along with the metrics for recruitment and selection. Grievance handling in a union environment, previously in the Internal Employee Relations chapter, is now discussed in Chapter 12, Labor Unions and Collective Bargaining. Downsizing, previously presented in the Job Analysis, Strategic Planning, and Human Resource Planning chapter, is now discussed in Chapter 13, Internal Employee Relations.

What This Course Is About

This course is about human resource management, the utilization of individuals to achieve organizational objectives. Basically, all managers get things done through the efforts of others. Consequently, managers at every level must concern themselves with HRM. The major topics covered include staffing (human resource planning, recruitment, and selection), training and development, performance appraisal, compensation, and internal employee relations. You will also be shown how health and safety topics affect HR. In addition, you learn the basics of how to deal with a union should your firm have one. Throughout your text, dealing with human resource management in the global environment will be explained as well as the importance of technology in HR.

Why It's Important to Management Majors and Nonmajors

No matter what your major, there will always be managers in your chosen career and all managers need to have an understanding of human resource management. For instance, if you are majoring in marketing, or finance, or any discipline and ultimately wish to be a manager in that field, you need to know how human resource management affects that field. All managers need to know how to recruit and select their employees; they need to know how to pay them (compensation); and they need to know how to train and evaluate them. I have noticed over the years that students in my HR course come from majors across campus because the information provided in this course is just as important to them as it is to business majors.

My Approach to the Writing of This HRM Book

I approach the study of human resource management in a practical, realistic manner. I focus on showing how HRM is practiced in the real world. Throughout the book, you will see examples of how organizations practice human resource management. In explaining a concept, I often quote HR professionals yet all HR discussion is based on sound theoretical concepts. Throughout this book, the strategic role of HR is apparent in the discussion of each major human resource function. In addition, I also show how HR topics relate to other HR topics. For instance, a firm that emphasizes recruiting top-quality candidates but neglects to provide satisfactory compensation is wasting time, effort, and money. A firm's compensation system will be inadequate unless employees are provided a safe and healthy work environment. If a firm's compensation system pays below-market wages, the firm will always be hiring and training new employees only to see the best leave for a competitor's higher wages. This interrelationship will become more obvious as these topics are addressed throughout the book. Further, global human resource management is woven throughout the course to show how HRM is altered in the global environment.

What's Expected of You in This Course

I have told undergraduate students many times over the years that the guiding principles for receiving a good grade in this course are coming to class, paying attention to the material presented, and studying the material presented. You can usually tell from the material highlighted by your professor what the most important points are.

Just what prerequisites are needed to succeed in the course? Certainly you must follow the prerequisites provided by your professor and the requirements in your chosen major. Some may require you to be a junior before you can take the course; others may require a basic management course to be taken as a prerequisite. However, I believe that your dedication to succeed in this course is the most important prerequisite of all.

Using Your Text to Be Successful: How to Get a Good Grade in This Course

One of my goals when I wrote the first edition many years ago was to provide an HR book that was realistic, practical, interesting, and stimulating to read. Here is my advice as to how to begin studying for the course. First, notice that there are *Learning Objectives* at the beginning of each chapter. Look those over because they identify the major topics to be covered in the chapter. Second, look at the *Summary* at the end of the chapter. The *Summary* provides a synopsis answer to the *Learning Objectives* provided at the beginning of the chapter. Review the *Summary* to get a good idea of chapter content. Third, read the chapter, paying attention to the *Key Terms* in the page margin. Key terms usually are excellent questions that you might see on a test. Fourth, after reading the chapter, go to the *Questions for Review* at the end of the chapter. Answering them will give you a quick appreciation of your understanding of material in the chapter. If you cannot answer a question, reread the material and try again.

I have worked very diligently to provide you with information that is both exciting and informative to read. At the beginning of each chapter, there is an *HRM in Action* that focuses on current interest topics related to the chapter. These range everywhere from Bernard L. Madoff's $65 Billion Ponzi scheme in my discussion of ethics to questioning whether top executives are paid too much in the compensation chapter. *Ethical Dilemmas* are included in all but the first chapter to see how you would react in an ethical situation. You will quickly discover that it is quite easy to make an ethical decision in a classroom environment. But, then I will show you how other factors may make you want to "bend the ethics rules." A *Trends & Innovations* is included in each section to highlight current developments in the field of HRM. Some examples are: the many uses of social networking and understanding why unions need to organize younger workers. A *Global Perspective* is included at the end of each chapter that highlights HRM in the global environment. I make the point that your first job may not be with a firm headquartered in the United States but with a company headquartered in another country. Two *HRM Incidents* are provided at the end of each chapter to highlight material covered in the chapter. These are real-life situations experienced by real people. Some were based on experiences I personally encountered. Perhaps you can identify the cases that are based on my experiences.

I have included *HR Web Wisdoms* in each chapter to provide you with the opportunity to go further in-depth in your understanding of the covered material. All *HR Web Wisdoms* are tied to a topic close to its placement.

Finally, I provide a model in Chapter 1 (see Figure 1.2) that gives you a vehicle for relating all human resource management topics. Studying it first will provide you with an overview of what you will be studying in this course.

Now go to class, listen to your instructor, and enjoy the lecture and the information provided in the course.

Student Resources

mymanagementlab

www.pearsonglobaleditions.com/mymanagementlab is an easy-to-use online tool that personalizes course content and provides robust assessment and reporting to measure individual and class performance. In each student chapter, mymanagementlab contains a study plan activity, a video activity, a critical thinking activity, and end-of-chapter assessments. Further, student PowerPoint files and flash cards help students quickly review and prepare for class. Further, instructors will also find access to their supplements, including an extensive video library featuring clips that illustrate the most pertinent topics in human resource management today.

Acknowledgments

As with the previous editions, the support and encouragement of many practicing HRM professionals have helped to make this book possible.

I especially appreciate the efforts of the professionals who reviewed this edition. These individuals are:

Jason Coleman, Wesley College
Diane Galbraith, Slippery Rock University of PA
Bobbie Knoblauch, Wichita State
Debbie Mackey, University of Tennessee—Knoxville
Fred Dorn, University of Mississippi
Laurie Giesenhagen, California State University—Fullerton
Thomas Zagenczyk, Clemson University
Tracy Porter, Cleveland State University
Scott Warman, ECPI Technical College
Mark C. Butler, University of Dubuque

Pearson would like to acknowledge and thank the following people for their work on the Global Edition:

Dr. Kwame R. Charles, Director, Quality Consultants Limited, Adjunct Faculty, Arthur Lok Jack, Graduate School of Business, University of the West Indies.

Evangellos-Vagelis Dedoussis Ph.D. Associate Professor of Management, American University in Dubai

Roger Fullwood, Associate Lecturer, Business & Management, Manchester Metropolitan University, UK

Dr. Elham S. Hasham, Associate Professor, Department of Management and Marketing, Faculty of Business Administration & Economics, Notre Dame University, Lebanon.

Evelyn Toh Bee Hwa, Taylor's Business School, Taylor's University, Malaysia.

Prof. Dr. Anja Karlshaus, Cologne Business School (CBS), European University of Applied Sciences (EUFH), Germany.

Drs. François de Kock, Department of Industrial Psychology, University of Stellenbosch, South Africa

Dr. Roberta Wong Leung, Community College of City University of Hong Kong, Hong Kong

Dr. Pei-Chuan Wu, Senior Lecturer, Department of Management & Organization, NUS Business School, National University of Singapore.

About R. Wayne Mondy

I have always had a strong interest in business practices as evidenced by my many years of academic and professional experience. I believe that managing people is the crucial side of business because a firm's human resources are the foundation upon which everything is accomplished. Prior to entering academics, I had business experience with such companies as Peat, Marwick, Mitchell, and Co. (now KPMG); General Electric Corporation; Gulf South Research Institute; and Houston Data Center. In addition, I served in the Air Force as a management analysis officer. Several examples in your text relate to my business experience.

I received my DBA from Louisiana Tech University and have enjoyed many years of teaching and administration, having served as professor, department head of the Department of Management & Marketing, and Dean of the College of Business. I retired from teaching in 2008 but still enjoy my writing and research. I have authored or co-authored seven college textbooks in a total of 31 editions, 54 articles, and 20 papers. The textbooks are: *Human Resource Management* (twelfth edition); *Management: Concepts, Practices, and Skills* (eighth edition); *Personal Selling: Function, Theory and Practice* (fourth edition); *Supervision* (third edition); *Management Concepts and Canadian Practices* (second edition); *Staffing the Contemporary Organization*; and *Management and Organizational Behavior*. In addition to the 12th edition of *Human Resource Management*, the HR book has been translated into Spanish (*Administración de Recursos Humanos* Prentice Hall, 1997, 2001, and 2005), and Chinese (Prentice Hall, 1998, 2002, and 2005). A special international edition of the tenth edition was prepared for India, Bangladesh, Bhutan, Pakistan, Nepal, Sri Lanka, and the Maldives and an international edition was prepared for the 11th edition. Articles have been published in such journals as *Business Journal, Journal of Education for Business, HRMagazine,* and *The Journal of Business Ethics*.

I am also Life Certified as a Senior Professional in Human Resources (SPHR) by the Human Resource Certification Institute. During my career at various universities, I have had the opportunity to charter three Student Chapters of the Society for Human Resource Management. In one instance, about 20 students wanted to take the Certification Examination. I was excited about their enthusiasm until they informed me, "Dr. Mondy, you have to take it, too." I have never studied so hard, but we all were successful in achieving our objective. That is how I received my SPHR designation; I earned it.

R. Wayne Mondy, SPHR

CHAPTER

1 Strategic Human Resource Management: An Overview

HRM in Action: Employer Branding Helps Attract the Best and Makes Them Want to Stay

I remember as a child that my mother would always buy a certain brand of canned fruit even though it was more expensive than the others. The brand name itself caused her to buy a product that while higher priced was, I suspect, the same or similar quality as another brands. The company had created a positive image that permitted it to charge more for its product. As with the canned fruit my mother purchased, companies want a brand that will entice individuals to join and remain with the firm.[1] **Employer branding** is the firm's corporate image or culture created to attract and retain the type of employees the firm is seeking.

"Employer branding is an extension of product or business branding," says Jeffrey St. Amour, national practice leader for PricewaterhouseCoopers' HR Services strategic communication group. "They're both trying to create the same thing, which is product loyalty or a feeling that this is a high-quality company." Employer branding has become a major recruitment and retention strategy.[2] With employer branding, everyone in the company works to promote the image of the firm. Toni Kaski, employer branding consultant at Magnet Communications said, "It's an ongoing, systematic process that necessitates continuous investment as well as a logical approach to reach a main goal: to have a strong appeal on current and future ideal employees."[3]

An employer brand embodies the values and standards that guide people's behavior. Through employer branding, people get to know what the company stands for, the people it hires, the fit between jobs and people, and the results it recognizes and rewards. "Every company has a brand," says Joel Head, president of Headwinds Ltd., a human

After completing this chapter, students should be able to:

1. Define *human resource management*.

2. Identify the human resource management functions.

3. Identify the external environmental factors that affect human resource management.

4. Explain who performs human resource management tasks.

5. Describe the various human resource classifications, including executives, generalists, and specialists.

6. Describe the evolution of human resource management.

7. Explain the evolving HR organization.

resources consulting company in Independence, Ohio. "The brand could be from the company of choice to the company of last resort."[4] Kaski further states, "Strong consumer brands might sell goods and services but strong employment brands attract people and make them want to stay."[5]

Jane Paradiso, national practice director for workforce planning at Watson Wyatt Worldwide defines employer branding as "spending money up front to attract the right people in the beginning. If [a company can convey] that 'We're a great place to work' concept, [it] can attract the right people."[6] Brands imply what employees will get from working there, and why working for the company is a career and not just a job.

An employer's brand is known for such things as, "it's fun to work at this company," "we have a passionate and intelligent culture," or "there is a strong team feeling here." These employer brands are quite important in getting the highest-quality applicants to join the firm.[7] Larry Ellison, founder of Oracle, said, "your brand is what people say about you when you've left the room. So, if you've already got a brand, shouldn't you make it the one you'd like?"[8] Being recognized as a great place to work is a strategy that makes a difference.

Achieving acknowledgment by an external source is a good way for a brand to be recognized.[9] Being listed on *Fortune* magazine's 100 Best Companies to Work For is so desirable that some organizations try to change their culture and philosophies to get on the list.

Think about how being on the following lists might assist in a company's recruitment and retention programs:

- *Working Mother* list of 100 best companies
- *Fortune* magazine list of 100 fastest-growing companies in the United States

- *Money* magazine list of 100 best places to live
- *Business Ethics* magazine list of 100 Best Corporate Citizens
- *BusinessWeek* list of 100 best small companies
- *Computerworld* list of Best Places to Work
- *Black Enterprise* list of Best Companies for Diversity

In the first part of this chapter, employer branding is discussed. Next, human resource management and the human resource management functions are described. Then the dynamic human resource management environment is presented and the many HR Uses of Social Networking are discussed. Next, the changing role of HR is described and human resource designations are discussed. The evolution of HRM and the evolving HR organization are described, and a description of the scope of this book is provided. The chapter concludes with a global perspective entitled "Managing Human Capital in a Borderless World."

Human Resource Management

Human resource management (HRM) is the utilization of individuals to achieve organizational objectives. Basically, all managers get things done through the efforts of others. Consequently, managers at every level must concern themselves with HRM. Individuals dealing with human resource matters face a multitude of challenges, ranging from a constantly changing workforce to ever-present government regulations, a technological revolution, and certainly the recession of 2008/10. Furthermore, global competition has forced both large and small organizations to be more conscious of costs and productivity. Because of the critical nature of human resource issues, these matters must receive major attention from upper management.

Human Resource Management Functions

People who are engaged in the management of human resources develop and work through an integrated HRM system. As Figure 1.1 shows, five functional areas are associated with effective HRM: staffing, human resource development, compensation, safety and health, and employee and labor relations. These functions are discussed next.

Staffing

Staffing is the process through which an organization ensures that it always has the proper number of employees with the appropriate skills in the right jobs, at the right time, to achieve organizational objectives. Robert Half Management Resources recently surveyed 1,400 CFOs and the top business concern among these executives was finding skilled staff.[10] Staffing involves job analysis, human resource planning, recruitment, and selection, all of which are discussed in this text.[11]

Job analysis is the systematic process of determining the skills, duties, and knowledge required for performing jobs in an organization. It impacts virtually every aspect of HRM, including planning, recruitment, and selection. Human resource planning is the systematic process of matching the internal and external supply of people with job openings anticipated in the organization over a specified period. The data provided set the stage for recruitment or other HR actions. Recruitment is the process of attracting individuals on a timely basis, in sufficient numbers, and with appropriate qualifications, to apply for jobs with an organization. Selection is

Figure 1.1

Human Resource Management Functions

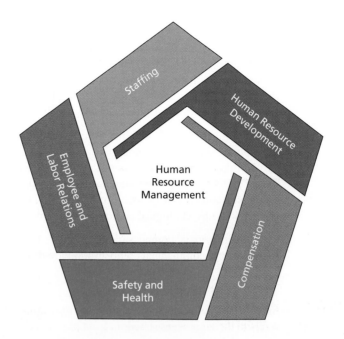

the process of choosing from a group of applicants the individual best suited for a particular position and the organization. Successful accomplishment of these three tasks is vital if the organization is to effectively accomplish its mission. Chapters 4, 5, and 6 are devoted to these topics, which are collectively often referred to as staffing.

Human Resource Development

human resource development (HRD)
Major HRM function consisting not only of training and development but also of individual career planning and development activities, organization development, and performance management and appraisal.

Human resource development is a major HRM function consisting not only of training and development but also of career planning and development activities, organization development, and performance management and appraisal. Training is designed to provide learners with the knowledge and skills needed for their present jobs. Development involves learning that goes beyond today's job and has a more long-term focus. Training and development is covered in Chapter 7.

Organization development (OD) is planned and systematic attempts to change the organization, typically to a more behavioral environment. OD applies to an entire system, such as a company or a plant. A number of interventions are discussed that serve to improve a firm's performance.

Career planning is an ongoing process whereby an individual sets career goals and identifies the means to achieve them. According to the Bureau of Labor Statistics, today's employees will work for approximately nine companies during their careers.[12] A survey conducted by NYU's School of Continuing and Professional Studies showed that on average, individuals will change careers (not merely "jobs") three times in their life.[13] Employee loyalty loses its meaning in this environment.

Career development is a formal approach used by the organization to ensure that people with the proper qualifications and experiences are available when needed. Individual careers and organizational needs are not separate and distinct. Organizations should assist employees in career planning so the needs of both can be satisfied. Career planning and career development is discussed in the appendix to Chapter 7.

Performance management is a goal-oriented process that is directed toward ensuring that organizational processes are in place to maximize the productivity of employees, teams, and ultimately, the organization. Performance appraisal is a formal system of review and evaluation of individual or team task performance. It affords employees the opportunity to capitalize on their strengths and overcome identified deficiencies, thereby helping them to become more satisfied and productive employees. Performance management and appraisal is discussed in Chapter 8.

Compensation

The question of what constitutes a fair day's pay has plagued management, unions, and workers for a long time. A well-thought-out compensation system provides employees with adequate and equitable rewards for their contributions to meeting organizational goals. As used in this book, the term *compensation* includes the total of all rewards provided employees in return for their services. The rewards may be one or a combination of the following:

- **Direct Financial Compensation:** Pay that a person receives in the form of wages, salaries, commissions, and bonuses.
- **Indirect Financial Compensation (Benefits):** All financial rewards that are not included in direct compensation, such as paid vacations, sick leave, holidays, and medical insurance.
- **Nonfinancial Compensation:** Satisfaction that a person receives from the job itself or from the psychological and/or physical environment in which the person works.

Direct financial compensation is discussed in Chapter 9 and indirect financial compensation (benefits) and nonfinancial compensation are discussed in Chapter 10.

Safety and Health

Safety involves protecting employees from injuries caused by work-related accidents. Health refers to the employees' freedom from physical or emotional illness. These aspects of the job are important because employees who work in a safe environment and enjoy good health are more likely to be productive and yield long-term benefits to the organization. Today, because of federal and state legislation that reflects societal concern, most organizations have become attentive to their employees' safety and health. Chapter 11 is devoted to topics related to safety and health.

Employee and Labor Relations

Businesses are required by law to recognize a union and bargain with it in good faith if the firm's employees want the union to represent them. In the past, this relationship was an accepted way of life for many employers, but most firms today would rather have a union-free environment. When a labor union represents a firm's employees, the human resource activity is often referred to as industrial relations, which handles the job of collective bargaining. Chapter 12 relates strictly to labor unions and collective bargaining; Chapter 13, internal employee relations, comprise the human resource management activities associated with the movement of employees within the organization such as promotions, demotion, termination, and resignation.

Human Resource Research

Although human resource research is not a distinct HRM function, it pervades all functional areas, and the researcher's laboratory is the entire work environment. For instance, a study related to recruitment may suggest the type of worker most likely to succeed in a particular firm. Research on job safety may identify the causes of certain work-related accidents. The reasons for problems such as excessive absenteeism or excessive grievances may not be readily apparent. However, when such problems occur, human resource research can often shed light on their causes and offer possible solutions. Human resource research is clearly an important key to developing the most productive and satisfied workforce possible.

Interrelationships of HRM Functions

All HRM functional areas are highly interrelated. Management must recognize that decisions in one area will affect other areas. For instance, a firm that emphasizes recruiting top-quality candidates but neglects to provide satisfactory compensation is wasting time, effort, and money. In addition, a firm's compensation system will be inadequate unless employees are provided a safe and healthy work environment. If a firm's compensation system pays below-market wages, the firm will always be hiring and training new employees only to see the best leave for a competitor's higher wages. The interrelationships among the HRM functional areas will become more obvious as these topics are addressed throughout the book.

Dynamic Human Resource Management Environment

Many interrelated factors affect the five previously identified HRM functions. Factors outside an organization's boundaries that affect a firm's human resources make up the **external environment.**

The firm often has little, if any, control over how the external environment affects management of its human resources. As illustrated in Figure 1.2, external factors include the legal considerations, labor market, society, political parties, unions, shareholders, competition, customers, technology, the economy, and unanticipated events. Each factor, either separately or in combination with others, can place constraints on how HRM tasks are accomplished.

Legal Considerations

A significant external force affecting HRM relates to federal, state, and local legislation and the many court decisions interpreting this legislation. In addition, presidential executive orders have had a major impact on HRM. These legal considerations affect virtually the entire spectrum of human resource policies. Chapter 3 highlights the most significant ones, which affect equal employment opportunity. Laws, court decisions, and executive orders affecting other HRM activities will be described in the appropriate chapters.

Labor Market

Potential employees located within the geographic area from which employees are normally recruited comprise the *labor market*. The capabilities of a firm's employees determine, to a large extent, how well the organization can perform its mission. Since new employees are hired from outside the firm, the labor market is considered an external environmental factor. The labor market is always changing, and these shifts inevitably cause changes in the workforce of an organization. In turn, changes in individuals within an organization affect the way management must deal with its workforce. This topic will be discussed later in Chapter 3, in the section on "Diversity and Diversity Management."

Figure 1.2

Environment of Human Resource Management

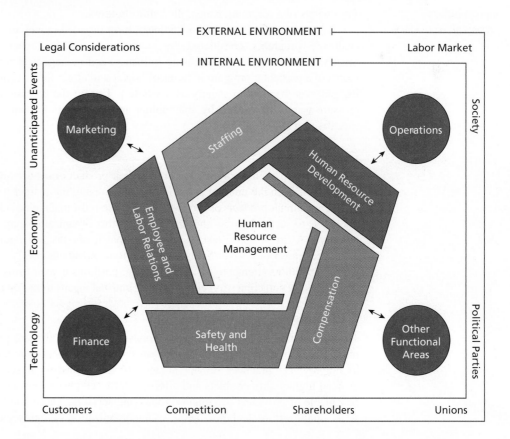

Society

Society may also exert pressure on HRM. The public is no longer content to accept, without question, the actions of business. Huge corporate executive salaries have caused many in society to question their value to the firm. To remain acceptable to the general public, a firm must accomplish its purpose while complying with societal norms.

Chapter 2 is on "Business Ethics and Corporate Social Responsibility." Ethics is the discipline dealing with what is good and bad, or right and wrong, or with moral duty and obligation. Corporate social responsibility is closely related to ethics. Corporate social responsibility is the implied, enforced, or felt obligation of managers, acting in their official capacity, to serve or protect the interests of groups other than themselves.[14]

Political Parties

Closely related to society, but not the same, are political parties. There are two major political parties in the United States. These parties often have differing opinions on human resource topics. Such was the case of the presidential election of 2008 in which the Democrats came to control both houses and the presidency and numerous laws and executive orders were signed into law over the objection of the Republican minority. As you move through this text, you will notice some of the impact of the 2008 election on HR. On a global perspective, countries change governments from time to time which may affect how human resource management is practiced.

Unions

union
Employees who have joined together for the purpose of dealing with their employer.

Wage levels, benefits, and working conditions for millions of employees reflect decisions made jointly by unions and management. A **union** is comprised of employees who have joined together for the purpose of dealing with their employer. Unions are treated as an environmental factor because, essentially, they become a third party when dealing with the company. In a unionized organization, the union rather than the individual employee negotiates an agreement with management.

Shareholders

shareholders
Owners of a corporation.

The owners of a corporation are called **shareholders.**

Because shareholders, or stockholders, have invested money in the firm, they may at times challenge programs considered by management to be beneficial to the organization. Stockholders are wielding increasing influence, and management may be forced to justify the merits of a particular program in terms of how it will affect future projects, costs, revenues, profits, and even benefits to society as a whole.[15] During the recession of 2008/10, considerable pressure was being exerted by shareholder and lawmakers to control the salaries of corporate executives, a topic of Chapter 9.

Competition

Firms may face intense competition in both their product or service and labor markets. Unless an organization is in the unusual position of monopolizing the market it serves, other firms will be producing similar products or services. A firm also must maintain a supply of competent employees if it is to succeed, grow, and prosper. But other organizations are also striving for that same objective. A firm's major task is to ensure that it obtains and retains a sufficient number of employees in various career fields to allow it to compete effectively. A bidding war often results when competitors attempt to fill certain critical positions in their firms. Even in a depressed economy, firms are sometimes forced to resort to unusual means to recruit and retain such employees.

Customers

The people who actually use a firm's goods and services also are part of its external environment. Because sales are crucial to the firm's survival, management has the task of ensuring that its employment practices do not antagonize the customers it serves. Customers constantly demand high-quality products and after-purchase service. Therefore, a firm's workforce should be capable of providing top-quality goods and services. These conditions relate directly to the skills, qualifications, and motivations of the organization's employees.

TRENDS & INNOVATIONS

The Many HR Uses of Social Networking

A social networking site is a "Web site that serves as a virtual community, where a group of people use the Internet to communicate with each other about anything and everything."[16] It is a broad term that encompasses such sites as LinkedIn, Facebook, and Twitter. Ninety-five percent of electronic communication is via social networking sites while e-mail accounts for only five percent.[17] One author uses the metaphors whereas Twitter is like a cocktail party; Facebook, is more like a reunion; and LinkedIn, is more like a job fair.[18] They are ideal for facilitating interactions between people who cannot easily meet in person.[19] In just over two years the number of users has increased from 10 million, to upwards of 140 million.[20] The tip of the iceberg has only been seen regarding uses of social networking and there are many potential benefits to the use of social networking in business.[21]

When BIMA's chair, Paul Wash, was recruiting for a new public relations agency, he looked to Twitter, to help identify the best candidate. He would not accept application forms or résumés. Rather, Walsh wanted prospective candidates to get in touch via Twitter. By doing so he believed he could weed out applicants who were not capable of communicating quickly with the new communication technology. He received quick response to his recruitment tweet, which he blogged and posted on BIMA's Facebook group. Three agencies were immediately interested. When asked why he required applicants to tweet him, he replied, "Why? Well, if you need me to answer that you're not right for the job."[22]

Serena Software Inc., based in San Mateo, California, sent out a press release that quoted CEO Jeremy Burton as saying, "Social networking tools like Facebook can bring us back together, help us get to know each other as people, help us understand our business and our products, and help us better serve our customers."[23] Burton encouraged his 800 employees to sign up for Facebook, and to use it to network with one another. He also urged employees to take time each Friday getting to know fellow workers at different locations. Employees call it Facebook Fridays. Mary Helen Waldo, Serena's vice president of global HR, says, "From a cultural standpoint, bringing together a lot of disparate corporate cultures can be a challenge, and we see Facebook as helping that effort." Effective communication is often difficult when you never see coworkers or see them only perhaps a couple of times a year. If employees know each other as real live individuals they are likely able to work better together. Facebook might be considered the virtual water cooler.[24]

Social networking has even been used successfully in training and development.[25] It can help employees locate others who are applying new skills and share best practices, discuss obstacles and solutions to application, and foster collaboration. Millennial workers have adapted quite easily to the use of social networking. Jeanne C. Meister, founding editor of *New Learning Playbook* said, "Organizations that want to effectively reach out to this group, whether for recruiting or learning, have to use the tools that they are already comfortable with. Social networking is a natural way for people to learn, especially among the Millennials."[26]

Social networking has also entered the performance appraisal arena. Gen Y workers want feedback on their performance in real time and know how to get it using social networking tools such as Twitter and Facebook. Instead of waiting months for a formal review from their bosses, they are asking people in their online networks to help them learn how to improve right away. Social networkers "have figured out how to shorten the 'learn and do loop' and are using tools that are part of their daily lives."[27] Marcia Conner, co-author of *Creating a Learning Culture* and a social media analyst and commentator for Pistachio Consulting said, "Performance reviews have been an event, not a reflective process. Social networking tools make it more mindful."[28]

Social networking is also available to assist students in their preparation for tests. A social-networking Web site called GradeGuru, is for student users to upload papers, class notes, and study guides for sharing and collaborative thinking. Emily Sawtell, founder of GradeGuru said, "GradeGuru is essentially the Web 2.0 version of a study group." The site gives students the chance to get help from peers across the world, not just in their class. Many students find it useful to consult before tests.[29]

The rapid growth of social networking has caused companies to consider whether or not to implement policies to control their use. One study commissioned by Robert Half Technology found that 54 percent of U.S. companies have banned workers from using social networking sites on the job.[30] In another study, half of employers still lack policies addressing their employees' use of social networking Web sites at work, even though one-quarter have already disciplined an employee for improper activities on Facebook, Twitter, or similar sites.[31] A public relations executive recently upset FedEx Corp., one of the agency's clients. As he was visiting Memphis, headquarters of FedEx, he tweeted: "True confession but I'm in one of those towns where I scratch my head and say 'I would die if I had to live here!'"[32] Some professional football teams have forbidden the use of Twitter to comment on any of the team's activities. In 2009, an NFL player was released from the team for Twittering unfavorable comments about his coach.

HR Technology

The world has never before seen the rapid rate of technological change that is occurring today. The development of technology has created new roles for HR professionals but also places additional pressures on them to keep abreast of the technology. In a survey of more than 1,000 CEOs worldwide, 83 percent ranked change as the most important issue confronting their organization.[33] Joe Rotella, chief technical officer for Delphia Consulting LLC, and heads Delphia Consulting's usability practice said, "HR needs to learn and embrace technology."[34]

human resource information system (HRIS)
Any organized approach for obtaining relevant and timely information on which to base human resource decisions.

With the increased sophistication of technology has come the ability to design more useful human resource information systems (HRIS). A **HRIS** is any organized approach for obtaining relevant and timely information on which to base human resource decisions. Think of an HRIS as an umbrella for merging the various subsystems discussed throughout this text. For example, in Chapter 6 (Selection), I have included HRIS topics entitled "Applicant Tracking Systems," "Online Assessment," "Automated Reference Checking," and "Candidate Relationship Management." Today, mainstay HR responsibilities such as recruitment, selection, oversight of legal and regulatory compliance, benefits administration, and the safeguarding of confidential employee information cannot be carried out effectively without an HRIS.[35] Throughout your text, I will highlight topics that are part of an HRIS.

Economy

The economy of the nation, on the whole and in its various segments, is a major environmental factor affecting HRM. As a generalization, when the economy is booming, it is more difficult to recruit qualified workers. On the other hand, when a downturn is experienced as with the recession of 2008/10, more applicants are typically available. To complicate this situation even further, one segment of the country may be experiencing a downturn, another a slow recovery, and another a boom.

Unanticipated Events

Unanticipated events are occurrences in the external environment that cannot be foreseen. Perhaps I have been influenced to identify unanticipated events as an external environment factor after personally seeing the impact of Hurricanes Rita (2005) and Ike (2008) on human resource management in my hometown (see HR after a Disaster at the end of this chapter for a real-life case). The 2010 gigantic oil spill off the Gulf coast caused major modification in the performance of many of the human resource functions. I would venture a guess that every disaster, whether manmade or natural, requires a tremendous amount of adjustment with regard to human resource management. On a global perspective think of the many different ways HR was affected when earthquakes struck Haiti and Chile.

How Human Resource Management Is Practiced in the Real World

At the beginning of each chapter, there is an *HRM in Action* that focuses on an important topic related to the chapter. Features entitled *Ethical Dilemma* are included in all but the first chapter to test how you would react in an ethical situation. A *Trends & Innovations* feature is included in each section to highlight current developments in the field of human resource management. *A Global Perspective* is included at the end of each chapter that highlights HRM in the global environment. Two *HRM Incidents* are provided at the end of each chapter to highlight material covered in the chapter.

OBJECTIVE 1.4
Explain who performs human resource management tasks.

HR's Changing Strategic Role: Who Performs the Human Resource Management Tasks?

The person or units who perform the HRM tasks have changed dramatically in recent years, and today there is no typical HR department. Many of these changes are being accomplished so that HR professionals can accomplish a more strategic role, a topic discussed in Chapter 4. Also, the economic climate of 2008/10 forced HR departments to accomplish more with less.[36] Some

HR Web Wisdom

The Hackett Group

**http://www.
thehackettgroup.com**

Students can visit this Web site to get information about The Hackett Group, which is a leader in best practice advisory, benchmarking, and transformation consulting services, including shared services, offshoring, and outsourcing advice.

**human resource
manager**
Individual who normally acts in an advisory or staff capacity, working with other managers to help them deal with human resource matters.

HR outsourcing (HRO)
Process of hiring external HR professionals to do the HR work that was previously done internally.

companies downsized the HR department in order to keep production-oriented people.[37] This restructuring often resulted in a shift in who carries out each function, not the elimination of the previously identified five HR functions. Some organizations continue to perform the majority of HR functions within the firm. However, as internal operations are reexamined, questions are raised, such as: Can some HR tasks be performed more efficiently by line managers or outside vendors? Can some HR tasks be centralized or eliminated altogether? Can technology perform tasks that were previously done by HR personnel? One apparent fact is that all functions within today's organizations are being scrutinized for cost cutting, including HR. All units must operate under a lean budget in this competitive global environment, and HR is no exception.

Today, the HR profession continues to evolve. The recession of 2008/10 caused HR departments to deal with such areas as hiring freezes, reduction in force, and planning large-scale terminations.[38] HR departments continue to be asked to do more with less, and others are now accomplishing certain HR functions. Many HR departments continue to get smaller because others outside the HR department are now performing certain functions. HR outsourcing, shared service centers, professional employer organizations, and line managers now assist in the accomplishment of many traditional human resource activities. Let us first look at the role of the traditional human resource manager.

Human Resource Manager

Historically, the human resource manager was responsible for each of the five HR functions. Traditionally, a **human resource manager** was an individual who normally acted in an advisory or staff capacity, working with other managers to help them deal with human resource matters. Often, large HR departments were created, with the central figure being the HR manager or executive. The human resource manager was primarily responsible for coordinating the management of human resources to help the organization achieve its goals. There was a shared responsibility between line managers and human resource professionals. Frequently, the line manager went to HR for guidance in topics such as selection, training, promotion, and taking disciplinary action. The traditional distinction between human resource management and the human resource manager is illustrated by the following account:

> Bill Brown, the production supervisor for Ajax Manufacturing, has just learned that one of his machine operators has resigned. He immediately calls Sandra Williams, the human resource manager, and says, "Sandra, I just had a Class A machine operator quit down here. Can you find some qualified people for me to interview?" "Sure Bill," Sandra replies. "I'll send two or three down to you within the week, and you can select the one that best fits your needs."

In this instance, both Bill and Sandra are concerned with accomplishing organizational goals, but from different perspectives. As a human resource manager, Sandra identifies applicants who meet the criteria specified by Bill. Yet, Bill will make the final decision about hiring, because he is responsible for the machine operators' performance. His primary responsibility is production; hers is human resources. As a human resource manager, Sandra must constantly deal with the many problems related to human resources that Bill and the other managers face. Her job is to help them meet the human resource needs of the entire organization.

HR Outsourcing

HR outsourcing (HRO) is the process of hiring external HR professionals to do the HR work that was previously done internally. In this chapter, I discuss the impact of HR outsourcing; outsourcing of all company positions will be addressed briefly in Chapter 5. The key to HR outsourcing success is to determine which functions to outsource, the extent to which they should be outsourced, and which ones to keep in-house.[39] HR outsourcing focuses primarily on routine, transaction-oriented processes and clerical work.[40] This permits HR to focus on strategic areas.[41] However, tasks such as strategic human resource management topics (a focus in Chapter 4) are better handled by HR. HR outsourcing is done in three ways: discrete services, multiprocess services, and business process outsourcing.

With discrete services, one element of a business process or a single set of high-volume repetitive functions is outsourced to a third party. Benefits have been the HR task most likely to be outsourced.[42] "Benefits administration has become so complex that it really takes someone who works with it every single day to keep track of all of the different laws and changes that are going on," said Dan Thomas, president of Trivalent Benefits Consulting Inc.[43]

Multiprocess services involve the complete outsourcing of one or more human resource processes, such as training. Procter & Gamble has outsourced its entire training operations.[44]

Business process outsourcing (BPO) represents the transfer of the majority of HR services to a third party. Typically the larger companies are involved with BPO. The largest HR outsourcer is IBM with more than $96 billion in revenue.[45] Kraft Foods Inc. and IBM signed a multi-year BPO agreement in which IBM took over workforce administration, compensation, and performance reporting for all of Kraft's 98,000 employees spread across 72 countries. The agreement with IBM comes with Kraft in the third year of a three-year turnaround strategy to fix its business. Lisa Gibbons, a Kraft spokeswoman, said, "HR roles within Kraft will be more strategic, less transactional." However, for larger countries, including the U.S., Canada, Austria, Belgium, France, Germany, Switzerland, the U.K., Brazil, and Mexico, IBM will also provide call center support, employee data management, parts of recruitment administration, and learning administration, as well as payroll.[46]

Major outsourcing firms have evolved to accomplish many of the HR tasks that were formerly done in-house. For example, Accenture is a global management consulting, technology services, and outsourcing company, with net revenues of $21.58 billion. Accenture has 176,000 employees (including more than 4,600 senior executives) with offices and operations in more than 200 cities in 52 countries.[47] Accenture is capable of handling the outsourcing needs of a single HR activity or the HR activities of an entire company.

HR Web Wisdom

Accenture

http://www. accenture.com/

Information about Accenture, a global management consulting, technology services, and outsourcing company.

HR Shared Service Centers

shared service center (SSC)
A center that takes routine, transaction-based activities dispersed throughout the organization and consolidates them in one place.

A **shared service center (SSC),** also known as a center of expertise, takes routine, transaction-based activities dispersed throughout the organization and consolidates them in one place. For example, a company with 20 strategic business units could consolidate routine HR tasks and perform them in one location. Shared service centers provide an alternative to HR outsourcing and can often provide the same cost savings and customer service.[48] Fewer HR professionals are needed when shared service centers are used, resulting in significant cost savings.[49] The most common HR functions that use SSCs are benefits and pension administration, payroll, relocation assistance and recruitment support, global training and development, succession planning, and talent retention.

Professional Employer Organizations (Employee Leasing)

professional employer organization (PEO)
A company that leases employees to other businesses.

A **professional employer organization (PEO)** is a company that leases employees to other businesses. When a decision is made to use a PEO, the company releases its employees, who are then hired by the PEO. The PEO then manages the administrative needs associated with employees. It is the PEO that pays the employees' salaries; it also pays workers' compensation premiums, payroll-related taxes, and employee benefits. It is the PEO that is responsible to the IRS if, for example, the payroll taxes go unpaid.[50] The company reimburses the PEO, which typically charges a fee of from 2 to 7 percent of the customer's gross wages, with percentages based on the number of leased employees. Since the PEO is the employees' legal employer it has the right to hire, fire, discipline, and reassign an employee. However, the client company maintains enough control so it can run the day-to-day operations of its business. Although PEOs have been available since the early 1980s,[51] they have recently become a $68 billion industry with more than 400 PEO companies.[52] PEOs permit business owners to focus on their core business while the PEO handles HR activities. Companies using a PEO are provided with a high level of benefits and greater HR expertise than they could possibly have had on their own.

PEOs have advantages for employees. Because they provide workers for many companies, they often enjoy economies of scale that permit them to offer a wider selection of benefits at considerably lower cost, because of the large numbers of employees in their pools. In addition, workers frequently have greater opportunities for job mobility. Some leasing firms operate throughout the nation. The relocation of one employed spouse in a dual-career family may be more satisfactory if the leasing company offers the other spouse a job in the new location, too. In addition, if a client organization suffers a downturn, the leasing company offers job security. The PEO can transfer employees to another client, avoiding both layoffs and loss of seniority. Finally, according to the Small Business Administration, business owners spend up to 25 percent of their time on employee-related paperwork. Since smaller companies are less likely to have a dedicated human resources specialist, the PEO can handle the compliance requirements of programs such as 401(k) programs.

A potential disadvantage to the client is erosion of employee loyalty because workers receive pay and benefits from the leasing company. Regardless of any shortcomings, use of employee leasing is growing.

Line Managers

line managers
Individuals directly involved in accomplishing the primary purpose of the organization.

Individuals directly involved in accomplishing the primary purpose of the organization are **line managers.** As the traditional work of HR managers diminishes, line managers are stepping up and performing some duties typically done by human resource professionals. Automation has assisted greatly in this process. Managers are being assisted by manager self-service, the use of software, and the corporate network to automate paper-based human resource processes that require a manager's approval, record-keeping or input, and processes that support the manager's job (discussed further in Chapter 4). Everything from recruitment, selection, performance appraisal, to employee development has been automated to assist line managers in performing traditional HR tasks.

OBJECTIVE 1.5
Describe the various human resource classifications, including executives, generalists, and specialists.

Human Resource Designations

Various designations are used within the human resource profession; among these are HR executives, generalists, and specialists. An **executive** is a top-level manager who reports directly to the corporation's chief executive officer (CEO) or to the head of a major division. A **generalist,** who may be an executive, performs tasks in a variety of HR-related areas. The generalist is involved in several, or all, of the five HRM functions. A **specialist** may be an HR executive, manager, or nonmanager who is typically concerned with only one of the five functional areas of HRM. Figure 1.3 helps clarify these distinctions.

The vice president of industrial relations, shown in Figure 1.3, specializes primarily in union-related matters. This person is both an executive and a specialist. An HR vice president is

executive
A top-level manager who reports directly to a corporation's chief executive officer or to the head of a major division.

generalist
A person who may be an executive and performs tasks in a variety of HR-related areas.

specialist
An individual who may be a human resource executive, a human resource manager, or a nonmanager, and who is typically concerned with only one of the five functional areas of human resource management.

Figure 1.3

Human Resource Executives, Generalists, and Specialists

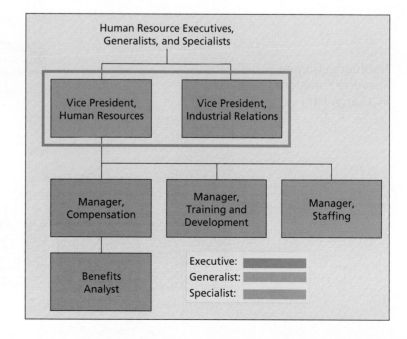

both an executive and a generalist, having responsibility for a wide variety of functions. The compensation manager is a specialist, as is the benefits analyst. Whereas a position level in the organization identifies an executive, the breadth of such positions distinguishes generalists and specialists.

OBJECTIVE 1.6
Describe the evolution of human resource management.

Evolution of Human Resource Management

It seems appropriate, as the 12th edition of *Human Resource Management* is published, to see how HR management has evolved over the past 30 years. Traditionally, separate functions such as staffing, training and development, compensation, safety and health, and labor relations (if the firm was unionized) were created and placed under the direction of a human resource manager or executive (see Figure 1.4). Large firms might have had a manager and staff for each HR function that reported to the HR executive. The HR vice president worked closely with top management in formulating corporate policy.

The title of the book says much about the HR evolution. In the first edition, this text was titled *Personnel: The Management of Human Resources,* and the focus was more on personnel as a staff or advisory function. By the fourth edition, the title of the book had changed to *Human Resource Management,* and a more general management focus was evolving. This was about the same time that the journal *Personnel Administrator* changed its name to *HRMagazine.* The journal entitled *Personnel* changed its name to *HR Focus,* and the journal entitled *Personnel Journal* changed its name to *Workforce Management.* Moving from the more narrow focus of personnel suggested the more important role that human resource management would play out in the business world.

We wrote in the first edition:

> Not many decades ago, people engaged in human resource work had titles such as welfare secretary and employment clerk. Their duties were rather restrictive and often dealt only with such items as workers' wages, minor medical problems, recreation, and housing.[53] Personnel, as human resources was most commonly called, as a profession was generally held in low esteem, and its organizational position was typically near the bottom of the hierarchy. As one personnel director said, "the personnel executive was the 'glad hander' or 'back slapper' who kept morale up in a company by running the company picnic and making sure the recreation program went off well."
>
> These days are over in many organizations. The personnel director's position is no longer a retirement position given to managers who cannot perform adequately anywhere else in the organization.

Figure 1.4

Traditional Human Resource Functions in a Large Firm

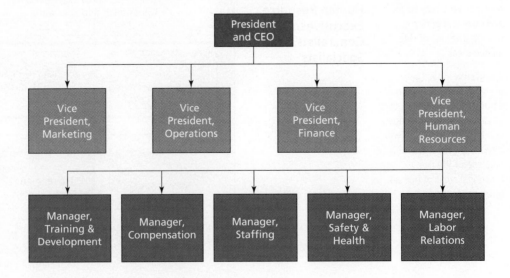

Today, the person or persons who perform HR tasks are certainly different than they were even a decade ago. As more and more companies use alternative means to accomplish HR tasks, the role of the traditional HR manager is diminishing. HR is now entering into the business of strategic HR, focusing more on the bottom line of the organization, and leaving the more administrative tasks to technology or others. HR leader Libby Sartain, who sits on the board of directors at retailer Peet's Coffee & Tea said, "I can remember when the Society for Human Resource Management.changed its name from the American Society for Personnel Administration, because we were part of *management*. Now we've moved from part of *management* to part of the senior leadership team. We're that person who is part of the leadership team—some people are fighting to get that seat at the table—there to manage the return on investment in talent or human capital."[54]

OBJECTIVE 1.7

Explain the evolving HR organization.

Evolving HR Organizations

In previous editions, the manner in which human resource tasks changed as the firm grew was presented. HR functions in small businesses, medium-sized businesses, and in a large firm were described. These days the HR organization is much more difficult to describe. As previously discussed, line managers, HR outsourcing, HR shared service centers, and professional employer organizations are now handling many of the traditional HR tasks. In discussion with numerous human resource managers in organizations of various sizes, the conclusion was that there is no pattern for how human resource tasks are now achieved. The only certainty is that the five previously identified HR functions must still be accomplished. Each company must choose the appropriate vehicle for doing these tasks based on its specific needs and goals.

A possible example of an evolving HR organization is presented in Figure 1.5. Here, the company has outsourced training and development, a function previously performed by the Training & Development Department. The compensation function is now performed at a shared service center. Safety and health has been removed from HR and, because of its importance in this particular firm, reports directly to the CEO. Staffing activities remain under the strategic vice president for human resources but many activities have been automated and line managers are now more involved in the selection process. Since the firm is nonunion, there is no Industrial Relations Manager. In this example, as the title suggests, the HR vice president is now more concerned with the strategic human resource matters. Because of the many changes that have occurred in HR in recent years, it is not realistic to show a typical HR organization. Some firms have chosen to totally outsource their HR function; others choose different options. The organization of HR in today's environment is truly a work in progress.

Figure 1.5

A Possible Example of an Evolving HR Organization

Scope of This Book

Effective HRM is crucial to the success of every organization. To be effective, managers must understand and competently practice HRM. This book was designed to give you the following:

- An insight into the role of strategic HRM in today's organizations, the strategic role of HR functions, and the impact of technology and global competition.
- An awareness of the importance of business ethics and corporate social responsibility.
- An understanding of job analysis, human resource planning, recruitment, and selection.
- An awareness of the importance of human resource development, including training and development, for employees at all levels.
- An understanding of performance appraisal and its role in performance management.
- An appreciation of how compensation programs are formulated and administered.
- An understanding of safety and health factors as they affect the firm's profitability.
- An opportunity to understand employee and labor relations.
- An appreciation of the global impact on HRM.

Students often question whether the content of a book corresponds to the realities of the business world. In writing and revising this book, the comments, observations, and experiences of HR practitioners are integrated throughout, along with extensive research efforts. HR practices of leading business organizations are provided to illustrate how theory can be applied in the real world. The intent is to enable you to experience human resource management in action.

This book is organized in eight parts, as shown in Figure 1.6; combined, they provide a comprehensive view of human resource management. As you read it, hopefully you will be stimulated to increase your knowledge in this rapidly changing and challenging field.

country's culture
Set of values, symbols, beliefs, language, and norms that guide human resource behavior within the country

Figure 1.6

Organization of This Book

HUMAN RESOURCE MANAGEMENT, 12TH EDITION

PART ONE. INTRODUCTION
Chapter 1: Strategic Human Resource Management: An Overview

PART TWO. ETHICS, SOCIAL, AND LEGAL CONSIDERATIONS
Chapter 2: Business Ethics and Corporate Social Responsibility
Chapter 3: Workforce Diversity, Equal Employment Opportunity, and Affirmative Action

PART THREE. STAFFING
Chapter 4: Job Analysis, Strategic Planning, and Human Resource Planning
Chapter 5: Recruitment
Chapter 6: Selection

PART FOUR. HUMAN RESOURCE DEVELOPMENT
Chapter 7: Training and Development
Appendix Chapter 7: Career Planning and Development
Chapter 8: Performance Management and Appraisal

PART FIVE. COMPENSATION
Chapter 9: Direct Financial Compensation
Chapter 10: Indirect Financial Compensation (Benefits) and Nonfinancial Compensation

PART SIX. SAFETY AND HEALTH
Chapter 11: A Safe and Healthy Work Environment

PART SEVEN. EMPLOYEE AND LABOR RELATIONS
Chapter 12: Labor Unions and Collective Bargaining
Appendix Chapter 12: History of Unions in the United States
Chapter 13: Internal Employee Relations

PART EIGHT. OPERATING IN A GLOBAL ENVIRONMENT
Chapter 14: Global Human Resource Management

A GLOBAL PERSPECTIVE

Managing Human Capital in a Borderless World

Chrysler Corporation employees have gone through major cultural changes in the last several years. First, they were merged into a German firm, Daimler-Benz, then they were resold back to an American company, and they are now merged into Fiat, an Italian firm. Each ownership change brought new cultural rules. Certainly the Germans and Italians have two distinct, but different cultures.[55]

Throughout this text, cultural differences between countries will be identified as a major factor influencing global business. This borderless world adds dramatically to the difficulty of managing human capital. Cultural differences reveal themselves in everything from the workplace environments to very divergent concepts of time, space, and social interaction.[56] Culture differences are often the biggest barrier to doing business in the world market. A **country's culture** is the set of values, symbols, beliefs, languages, and norms that guide human behavior within the country. It is learned behavior that develops as individuals grow from childhood to adulthood. Companies operating in the global environment recognize that national cultures differ and that such differences.cannot be ignored.[57] The cultural norms of Asia promote loyalty and teamwork. In Japan, most managers tend to remain with the same company for life. In the United States, senior executives often change companies, but the Japanese believe strongly that leaving a job is to be avoided out of respect for the business team. A businessperson who travels from Switzerland to Italy goes from a country where meetings tend to be highly structured and expected to start on time, to one where meetings can be more informal and punctuality is less important.[58] Recognizing the cultural differences present in a workplace can help managers achieve maximum effectiveness.

Eric Rozenberg, CMM, CMP, president, Ince&Tive, of Brussels, Belgium, stated, "Even though people are aware that there are cultural differences between various nationalities, they're still uncomfortable with it and are afraid of making mistakes." Rozenberg provides an illustration in which there are two opposing views to an issue based on culture. He stated, "Monochronic people go from point one to point two to point three; and polychronic people don't necessarily go in a straightforward manner. For them, the importance of context is more important than what you say." According to Rozenberg, North Americans are more likely to be monochronic in that they take deadlines seriously. On the other hand, polychronic people may be more easily distracted, and their commitment to deadlines may not be as important. "The cultural differences barrier is not something that is easily overcome," adds Rozenberg.[59]

It is not just that U.S. companies need to understand the culture of the countries where they are operating. Companies who want to do business in the United States are doing the same thing. As a step in becoming a major global supplier, Hyundai Mobis, headquartered in Seoul, Korea, is attempting to foster a global culture among its employees. Teams of three employees design their trip to study the culture in countries where they may be doing business, and write a proposal explaining what they can learn. Then they compete for company sponsorship of a 15-day expedition. Itineraries have ranged from going to Peru to visiting cultural sites in Egypt, Turkey, and Greece. In the United States one team studied the culture of Alabama, where Hyundai Mobis was building a plant.[60]

Recognizing the importance of employees understanding the global environment, KPMG member firms are encouraging their people to take short- and long-term international job rotations through a revitalized rotation program called Global Opportunities, or GO. Aidan Walsh, partner-in-charge, International division, said, "Living and working in another country gives you an in-depth understanding of how the rest of the world works. You develop a greater appreciation for different cultures and the different ways in which people manage and grow their business. Generation Y wants to explore the world. Our international assignment programs make KPMG a more desirable place to launch and build a career."[61]

Highly educated foreigners are coming to the United States and U.S. managers must be attuned to the cultural differences they bring to the workplace. U.S.-born managers often make the mistake of thinking that they need little help assimilating into the U.S. business culture. In teaching foreign students, I had to "Play the name game,"[62] and often had to work to pronounce some of their names.

Summary

1. *Define human resource management.* Human resource management is the utilization of individuals to achieve organizational objectives. Consequently, all managers at every level must concern themselves with HRM.

2. *Identify the human resource management functions.* The HRM functions include staffing, human resource development, compensation, safety and health, and employee and labor relations.

3. *Identify the external environmental factors that affect human resource management.* External factors include legal considerations, the labor market, society, political parties, unions, shareholders, competition, customers, technology, economy, and unanticipated events. Each factor, either separately or in combination with others, can place constraints on how HRM tasks are accomplished.

4. *Explain who performs human resource management tasks.* Human resource managers are individuals who normally act in an advisory or staff capacity, working with other managers to help them deal with human resource matters. HR outsourcing is the process of hiring an external provider to do the work that was previously done internally. HR shared service centers take routine, transaction-based activities that are dispersed throughout the organization and consolidate them in one place. A professional employer organization is a company that leases employees to other businesses. Line managers in certain firms are being used more frequently than before to deliver HR services.

5. *Describe the various human resource classifications, including executives, generalists, and specialists.* Executives are top-level managers who report directly to the corporation's CEO or the head of a major division. Generalists (who are often executives) are persons who perform tasks in a wide variety of HR-related areas. A specialist may be a human resource executive, manager, or nonmanager who typically is concerned with only one of the functional areas of HRM.

6. *Describe the evolution of human resource management.* It seems appropriate as the 12th edition of this text is published to view HR as it has evolved over the past 30 years. The title of the book says much about the HR evolution. In the first edition, the book was titled *Personnel: The Management of Human Resources,* and the focus was more on personnel as a staff or advisory function. By the fourth edition, the title of the book had been changed to *Human Resource Management,* and a more general management focus was evolving.

7. *Explain the evolving HR organization.* The HR organizational structure of firms changes as they outsource, use professional employer organizations and shared service centers, and involve line managers more in traditional HR tasks. Regardless of an organization's design, the five previously identified HR functions must still be accomplished.

Key Terms

employer branding   28
human resource management
   (HRM)   30
staffing   30
human resource development
   (HRD)   31
external environment   33

union   34
shareholders   34
human resource information
   system (HRIS)   36
human resource manager   37
HR outsourcing (HRO)   37
shared service center (SSC)   38

professional employer
   organization (PEO)   38
line managers   39
executive   39
generalist   39
specialist   39
country's culture   43

Questions for Review

1. Define human resource management. What human resource management functions must be performed regardless of the organization's size?
2. What are the external environmental factors that affect human resource management? Describe each.
3. This chapter describes HR's changing role in business. Describe each component that is involved in human resource management.
4. What are the various designations associated with human resource management?
5. What has been the evolution of human resource management?

HRM INCIDENT **1**

HR after a Disaster

After Hurricane Rita struck Lake Charles in southwest Louisiana, on September 24, 2005, many businesses wondered if they would ever return to their former selves. Massive destruction was everywhere. Lake Charles, known for its large and beautiful oak and pine trees, now had the job of removing those downed trees from homes, businesses, and lots. You could see for miles through what used to be thick forests. Huge trucks designed for removing massive tree trunks were everywhere. While driving down a street, downed trees could be seen stacked two stories high, waiting to be picked up. The town grew rapidly in size because of the large amount of debris and the increased number of repair crews working on recovery operations. The noise created by chain saws could be heard from daylight until dark. The sounds of hammers were everywhere as homeowners scrambled to get their roofs repaired. Often repair crews would just find an empty lot and set up tents for the night because all motels were full. Traffic was unbelievably slow, and it appeared as if everyone was attempting to get on the road at the same time. Just driving from Point A to Point B could often be quite an adventure. As might be expected in conditions such as these, accidents were numerous. Often police did not have the resources to ticket every fender bender, so unless there were injuries, insurance cards were exchanged and the police went on to the next accident.

Months after Hurricane Rita struck, large and small businesses were still frantically trying to find workers so they could start up again. It appeared that every business in the town had a "Help Wanted" sign out front. Individuals who wanted a job could get one and could command a premium salary. Walmart, known for remaining open 24 hours a day, could only stay open on an abbreviated schedule. It even bused in employees from Lafayette, Louisiana, 70 miles away, each morning and returned them at night because there were not enough workers available in the local area. Restaurants that normally remained open late into the evening closed at 6:00 p.m., if they opened at all. Compensation scales that were in use prior to the hurricanes had to be thrown out and new plans implemented. Minimum-wage jobs were nonexistent. Employees who earned minimum wage before the storm could now command $10 per hour just for being a flagger (a person who directs traffic). Fast-food restaurants that normally paid $6 per hour now paid $9 or $10. Burger King was even offering a $1,500 bonus for entry-level workers. Upscale restaurants that normally paid minimum wage plus tips now paid premium rate plus tips. Restaurants that remained open often had a much younger staff and it was evident that the managers and assistant managers were working overtime to train these new workers. Restaurant patrons had to learn patience because there would be mistakes by these eager, but largely untrained workers.

Questions

1. How were the human resource functions affected by Hurricane Rita?
2. Do you believe that the HR situation described regarding Hurricane Rita would be typical in a disaster? Explain.

HRM INCIDENT **2**

Downsizing

As the largest employer in Ouachita County, Arkansas, International Forest Products Company (IFP) is an important part of the local economy. Ouachita County is a mostly rural area in south central Arkansas. It employs almost 10 percent of the local workforce, and few alternative job opportunities are available in the area.

Scott Wheeler, the human resource director at IFP, tells of a difficult decision he once had to make. According to Scott, everything was going along pretty well despite the economic recession, but he knew that sooner or later the company would be affected. "I got the word at a private meeting with the president, Janet Deason, that we would have to cut the workforce by 30 percent on a crash basis. I was to get back to her within a week with a suggested plan. I knew that my plan would not be the final one, since the move was so major, but I knew that Ms. Deason was depending on me to provide at least a workable approach.

"First, I thought about how the union would react. Certainly, workers would have to be let go in order of seniority. The union would try to protect as many jobs as possible. I also knew that all of management's actions during this period would be intensely scrutinized. We had to make sure that we had our act together.

"Then there was the impact on the surrounding community to consider. The economy of Ouachita County had not been in good shape recently. Aside from the influence on the individual workers who were laid off, I knew that our cutbacks would further depress the area's economy. I knew that there would be a number of government officials and civic leaders who would want to know how we were trying to minimize the harm done to the public in the area.

"We really had no choice but to make the cuts, I believed. First of all, I had no choice because Ms. Deason said we were going to do it. Also, I had recently read a news account that one of our competitors, Johns Manville Corporation in West Monroe, Louisiana, had laid off several hundred workers in a cost-cutting move. To keep our sales from being further depressed, we had to ensure that our costs were just as low as those of our competitors. The wood products market is very competitive and a cost advantage of even 2 or 3 percent would allow competitors to take many of our customers.

"Finally, a major reason for the cutbacks was to protect the interests of our shareholders. A few years ago a shareholder group disrupted our annual meeting to insist that IFP make certain antipollution changes. In general, though, the shareholders seem to be more concerned with the return on their investments than with social responsibility. At our meeting, the president reminded me that, just like every other manager in the company, I should place the shareholders' interests above all else. I really was quite overwhelmed as I began to work up a human resource plan that would balance all of these conflicting interests."

Questions

1. List the elements in the company's environment that will affect Scott's suggested plan. How legitimate is the interest of each of these?

2. Is it true that Scott should be concerned first and foremost with protecting the interests of shareholders? Discuss.

Notes

1. David Smith, "Time to Start Hiring?" *BusinessWeek Online* (November 25, 2009): 4.
2. Soumya Gaddam, "Modeling Employer Branding Communication: The Softer Aspect of HR Marketing Management," *ICFAI Journal of Soft Skills* 2 (2008): 45–55.
3. "Employer Branding Vital," *Finweek* (May 3, 2007): 50–52.
4. Julie Barker, "How to Pick the Best People (And Keep Them)," *Potentials* 38 (November 2005): 33–36.
5. "Employer Branding Vital."
6. "HR Brand-Building in Today's Market," *HR Focus* 82 (February 2005): 1–15.
7. James Blockett, "Employer Branding Still Makes Its Mark," People Management 15 (March 12, 2009): 12–13.
8. Daniel Wain, "The Ronseal Test," *People Management* 15 (September 10, 2009): 17.
9. "Get the Right Mix," *Personnel Today* (January 20, 2009): 4–6.
10. John Sullivan, "Disconnected HR," *Workforce Management* 87 (March 17, 2008): 50.
11. R. Wayne Mondy, Robert M. Noe, and Robert E. Edwards, "What the Staffing Function Entails," *Personnel* 63 (April 1986): 55–58.
12. Robert Rodriguez, "Learning's Impact on Talent Flow," *Chief Learning Officer* 7 (April 2008): 50–64.
13. Mike Brennan and Andrew Gebavi, "Managing Career Paths: The Role of the CLO," *Chief Learning Officer* 7 (March 2008): 48–51.
14. Kenneth E. Goodpaster and John B. Matthews, Jr., "Can a Corporation Have a Conscience?" *Harvard*

Business Review 60 (January–February 1982): 132–141.

15. Steve Bates, "Report: Prepare For Increased Shareholder Activism," *HRMagazine* 54 (June 2009): 32.

16. "E-Learning Tools and Techniques," *Benefits & Compensation Digest* 45 (July 2008): 12.

17. Penelope Trunk, "The New Workforce Will Job-Hop. And That's Good," *HVACR Distribution Business* (March 2010): 20–22.

18. Steve McKee, "Social Media Is Nothing New," *BusinessWeek Online* (February 10, 2010): 15.

19. Majorie Derven, "Social Networking: A Force for Development?" *T+D* 63 (July 2009): 58–63.

20. Mary Oleniczak, Charlie Pike, Jitendra Mishra, and Mishra Bharat, "Employers Use Facebook too, for Hiring," *Advances in Management* 3 (January 2010): 13–17.

21. Todd Henneman, "Firms Making Friends with Social Media," *Workforce Management* 89 (April 2010): 4.

22. "BIMA's Walsh Proves to Be a Prize Twitter," *Revolution* (June 2008): 78.

23. Bill Roberts, "Social Networking at the Office," *HRMagazine* 53 (March 2008): 81–83.

24. Ibid.

25. Majorie Derven, "Social Networking: A Force for Development?" *T+D* 63 (July 2009): 58–63.

26. Ibid.

27. Pat Galagan, "Dude, How'd I Do?" *T+D* 63 (July 2009): 26–28.

28. Ibid.

29. Rick Docksai, "Networked Learning," *Futurist* 44 (January/February 2010): 12.

30. Sharon Gaudin, "Business Use of Twitter, Facebook Exploding," *Macworld* 27 (February 2010): 70.

31. "Employers Need More Social Media Rules," *HR Focus* 86 (December 2009): 2.

32. Rex Stephens, "In a Dither over Twitter? Get a Policy," *HRMagazine* 54 (June 2009): 30.

33. Diann Daniel, "What Keeps Your CEO Up at Night?" *CIO* 21 (June 1, 2008): 16.

34. "How to Select HRIS Software—& Defend Your Planned Purchase," *HR Focus* 86 (September 2009): 3–4.

35. Lin Grensing-Pophal, "Mission: Organized HR!" *Credit Union Management* 31 (October 2008): 36–39.

36. "Outsourced Benefits Administration: Separating Fact from Fiction," *Workforce Management* 88 (March 16, 2009): S3.

37. Clare DeCapua, "Smart Outsourcing," *Smart Business Chicago* 6 (September 2009): 22.

38. "HR Strategies to Cope with the Economy," *HR Focus* 86 (January 2009): 1–9.

39. Fidel Baca, "Considering HR Outsourcing? Consider SaaS," *Financial Executive* 25 (October 2009): 59–60.

40. Rick Wartzman, "Insourcing and Outsourcing: the Right Mix," *BusinessWeek Online* (February 8, 2010): 14.

41. "Should I Embrace or Resist HR Outsourcing," *People Magazine* (February 25, 2010): 56.

42. Lynn Gresham, "Spring Thaw," *Employee Benefit News* 24 (April 2010): 1–18.

43. Joel Berg, "Employers Outsource HR Work in Recession," *Central Penn Business Journal* 25 (November 13, 2009): 17–21.

44. Alan Bellinger, "Outsourcing Needs a Training Element," *ITTraining* (April 2005): 12.

45. "End-to-End Large Market HR Outsourcing Providers," *Workforce Management* 89 (March 2010): 12.

46. Jessica Marquez, "Kraft-IBM Deal Could Signal HRO Rebound," *Workforce Management* 88 (February 16, 2009): 12–13.

47. http://newsroom.accenture.com/fact+sheet/, February 13, 2010.

48. Ian Herbert, "The Role of Shared Services," *Management Services* 53 (Spring 2008): 43–47.

49. "HR Metrics: HR Labor Costs per Employee Average $798 at 1,000-employee Companies," *Controller's Report* 2009 (January 2009): 15.

50. "Employee Leasing Company Owners Liable for 100% Payroll Tax Penalty," *Payroll Manager's Letter* 25 (May 21, 2009): 1.

51. "Professional Employer Organizations," *Monthly Labor Review* 132 (January 2009): 40.

52. Louis Basso and Barry Shorten, "Growing PEO Industry Continues to Raise Its Standards," *CPA Journal* 79 (October 2009): 10–11.

53. Henry Eibirt, "The Development of Personnel Management in the United States," *Business History Review* 33 (August 1969): 348–349.

54. Ed Frauenheim, "Seats at the Table, but Who's Ready?" *Workforce Management* 87 (May 19, 2008): 21.

55. John Freivalds, "Nokia Comes to the US: Cultural Differences" *MultiLingual* 20 (September 2009): 30–31.

56. Norm Kamikow, "Lost in Translation," *Chief Learning Officer* 8 (September 2009): 4.

57. Phillip Stilels, "A World of Difference?" *People Management* 13 (November 15, 2007): 36–41.

58. Richard Miller, "Taste for Risk Varies Across Europe," *Business Insurance* 43 (September 28, 2009): 9–10.

59. Julie Barker, "The Cultural Divide," *Incentive* 182 (March 2008): 2–6.

60. Norman Thorpe, "Employees Take Trips to Understand Other Cultures," *Automotive News* (July 1, 2005): 24I.

61. John Tantillo, "Gaining Global Perspectives," *Profiles in Diversity Journal* 10 (March/April 2008): 24.

62. Kathleen Begley, "Managing Across Cultures at Home," *HRMagazine* 54 (September 2009): 115.

CHAPTER

2 Business Ethics and Corporate Social Responsibility

HRM in Action: Satyam: The Case of the Vanishing Millions

Many of the world's well-known financial scandals have involved companies in the United States and Western Europe. Many cases immediately spring to mind such as Enron, Worldcom, and Anglo Irish Bank. More recently, Goldman Sachs has been accused of fraud by the regulator. The recent case of Satyam, the Indian software company, clearly demonstrated that unethical practices could happen anywhere.

Many previous corporate wrongdoings have been discovered by assiduous investigations, but the scale of this fraud was only discovered after its main perpetrator offered his resignation and a confession in January 2009.

On his departure, Ramalinga Raju revealed that he had falsely reported Satyam's financial position for several years, during which the company had undergone massive growth. The reality was that 50.4 billion rupees ($1.04 billion) of the 53.6 billion of 2009 second quarter assets were fictional. Revenue was also substantially lower than had been reported. It has been suggested that the underlying motivation for the fraud was to stay in the game against other rapidly expanding Indian outsourcing giants.

Raju took sole responsibility for the scam in his resignation letter and stressed that no other board members were involved.

Some indication of Ramalinga's approach to corporate governance was demonstrated shortly before his fraud confession, when he revealed to institutional investors that he intended to purchase infrastructure companies that were the property of his family. Pankaj Gupta of SBI Mutual, the fund management company, scathingly

After completing this chapter, students should be able to:

1. Define ethics and understand the model of ethics.

2. Explain attempts at legislating ethics.

3. Understand the importance of a code of ethics and describe linking pay to ethical behavior.

4. Explain human resource ethics and describe ethics training.

5. Describe the professionalization of human resource management.

6. Describe the concept of corporate social responsibility.

7. Explain what is meant by stakeholder analysis and the social contract.

8. Describe how a corporate social responsibility program is implemented.

suggested that future foreign direct investment in India was being jeopardized by corporate governance activities such as this. They did not however realize at that time that this was the last desperate attempt by Ramalinga to add real assets to the company balance sheet. The deal would have cost $1.6 billion, but was eventually prevented by the rest of the board. It is believed that this was the event that finally drove Ramalinga to confess.

Satyam's clients included many Fortune 500 companies and the news was particularly shocking to corporations such as General Motors, General Electric, Nestle, and Ford, who rushed to disassociate themselves from the firm. Investors in Satyam were also stunned by the scale and duration of the cover-up and the value of company shares slumped by 75 percent. The Indian stock market also immediately dropped by 7 percent. The United States exchange was also affected by the crisis as Satyam earned more than half its profits in that country. Naturally, investors have demanded to know how PricewaterhouseCoopers, the internationally known accountants, could have failed to notice the fraud for up to seven years.

It does seem that the World Bank may have had suspicions about Satyam's activities because the company was barred from installing spy software on World Bank computers. At that point, however, the World Bank did not expand on the reasons for the ban.

News also emerged recently that former Satyam Vice President, G. Ramakrishna, attempted to destroy crucial evidence on a number of occasions by erasing incriminating information from a laptop.

In the fallout from the scandal, questions have been asked about the state of corporate governance in India. Indian investors have been rightly concerned about the impact of the fraud on the willingness of foreign investors to put funds into Indian companies, without at least rigorously checking their accounts.

Fortunately for the 53,000 staff employed at the company, it survived the scandal and company shares rallied when a board appointed by the government took control of the company. The company has since been bought by IT services and telecom giant Tech Mahindra, who recently announced their intention to merge operations between the two companies.[1]

This chapter begins by discussing Ramalinga Raju's unethical and scandalous approach to running an international company followed by a discussion of ethics and the presentation of a model of ethics. Next, attempts that have been made to legislate ethics are presented. Then, the importance of a code of ethics, linking pay to ethical performance, human resource ethics, and ethics training is discussed. The professionalization of human resource management is then described. This is followed by a discussion of the concept of corporate social responsibility and strategic corporate social responsibility. Following that, stakeholder analysis and the social contract are discussed. Next, we examine how a corporate social responsibility program is implemented, and the chapter concludes with a global perspective feature entitled "Can Corporate Social Responsibility Succeed in the Global Environment?"

Ethics

Ethics is the discipline dealing with what is good and bad, or right and wrong, or with moral duty and obligation.

As was seen in the HRM in Action at the beginning of the chapter, today we have many new examples of companies and individuals who behaved unethically. We forgot to guard against the type of abuses that ultimately bankrupted companies like Bear Stearns and Lehman Brothers.[2] CEOs have to be clear that unethical behavior is not acceptable. In one survey, 67 percent of investors said they would move their account if they discovered the company was involved in unethical behavior.[3] Jeff Immelt, GE's CEO, begins and ends each annual meeting of 220 officers and of its 600 senior managers by restating the company's fundamental integrity principles: "GE's business success is built on our reputation with all stakeholders for lawful and ethical behavior. Commercial considerations never justify cutting corners. Upholding this standard is the specific responsibility of the leaders in the room."[4] As one executive said, "just do the right thing." The image of the business world would be in much better shape if this simple advice had been followed. Hopefully ethical standards are improving since a biennial study found that most key measures of ethical behavior actually improved from those reported in 2007.[5]

Most of the 500 largest corporations in the United States now have a code of ethics, which encompasses written conduct standards, internal education, and formal agreements on industry standards, ethics offices, social accounting, and social projects. Even so, business ethics scandals continue to be headline news today. Lying on résumés, obstruction of justice, destruction of records, stock price manipulation, cutting corners to meet Wall Street's expectations, fraud, waste, and abuse, unfortunately, are occurring all too often when those in business go wrong ethically.

However, business is not alone. There is virtually no occupation that has not had its own painful ethical crises in recent years. There was the coach who altered his star pitcher's birth certificate in the Little League World Series and teachers who provided answers on standardized tests to improve their schools' performance. Doctors who make money by falsely billing Medicare do not even make the headlines any more.

But certainly a devastating blow to society was dealt by business, and ethical breaches in business continue today. Stock-options-backdating has involved hundreds of executives and led to the resignations of some high-profile executives.

The Bad and the Ugly; Now Comes the Good

At the beginning of the chapter, you read about the illegal and unethical exploits of Ramalinga Raju and others and how they epitomized what was wrong with business. We are seemingly constantly bombarded with news about the outrageous activities of a few business executives. To the naked eye, it might appear that everyone was on the "take." Although there were a small number of ruthless individuals such as Ramalinga, there are many individuals and organizations that provide a model for what business executives and organizations should be.[6]

Companies that focused on short-term profits seemingly to the exclusion of everything else were the culprits of the 2008/10 financial crisis. Other organizations had a steady moral compass and went safely through it. Charles Schwab & Co. and US Bancorp have largely avoided the financial disaster. Both companies share the qualities of having a keen focus on customer service and being honest and transparent. Behavior such as this comes from having a strong culture.[7]

Charles Schwab & Co. and US Bancorp viewed the subprime mortgage securitization market as risky and simply not the kind of business that served their company's long-term interests. They did not choose to have their employees sell unethical mortgages to customers, a practice other more unethical companies chose to take. This higher purpose sense filtered downward in the organization. Traditionally, Schwab had a policy of providing uncomplicated products and excellent customer service. US Bancorp has been a "straight shooter with a particularly strong practice focused on high-net-worth individuals." Both organizations have successfully come through the crisis and are poised for a productive future.[8]

Organizations outside of banking also had developed "an internal voice and a moral compass." Companies such as Cisco Systems, Southwest Airlines, and Costco Wholesale have come through this current crisis with flying colors. The pre-crisis events at Costco provide an example of the long-term thinking that a company needs to possess. For years, Wall Street analysts "have long chastised Costco's management for paying high wages and keeping employees around for a long time, resulting in higher benefits costs." Jim Sinegal, Costco's CEO, believed that it was strategic for long term growth and success to keep good employees. His decisions obviously were the proper ones because per-employee sales are much higher than those of competitors such as Target and Walmart. Sinegal gets a compensation package that many on Wall Street would laugh at. He receives salary and bonus of less than $800,000, although he gets a much larger amount in options on shares. But, this is still low when compared to companies of equivalent size. Sinegal sets the culture of the company which filters down to employees and customers.[9]

Fortunately the majority of organizations in the U.S. are also directing their efforts through the help of an ethical compass. We hear so much about what is bad in business; it is good to know that there are also those who have developed and followed the ethical path to success.

A Model of Ethics

One CEO once said, "There is a difference between what's legal and what's ethical. But we don't often talk about it, and I've wondered why. Maybe people think it's too soft . . . too hard to define . . . or, in corporate language, not 'actionable.' Maybe it's easier for us to defer to new laws and regulations as the solution. But new laws are only part of the solution. And, in my view, they don't get to the heart of the problem."[10] Compliance with the law sets the minimum standard of ethical behavior; ethics is much more, however. There must be leaders who are able and willing to instill ethics throughout the culture of the organization.

Ethics is about deciding whether an action is good or bad and what to do about it if it is bad. Ethics is a philosophical discipline that describes and directs moral conduct. Those in management make ethical (or unethical) decisions every day. Do you hire the best-qualified person, who is a minority? Do you forget to tell a candidate about the dangerous aspect of a certain job? Some ethical decisions are major and some are minor. But decisions in small matters often set a pattern for the more important decisions a manager makes. Attitudes such as "It's standard practice. It's

Figure 2.1

A Model of Ethics

Source: R. Wayne Mondy and Shane R. Premeaux, *Management: Concepts, Practices, and Skills,* 7th ed. (Upper Saddle River, NJ: Prentice Hall, 1995), p. 91.

not a big deal. It's not my responsibility. I want to be loyal." are simply not acceptable.[11] The great Roman philosopher Cicero echoed this situation when he said, "It is a true saying that one falsehood leads easily to another."[12]

A model of ethics is presented in Figure 2.1. As can be seen, ethics consists mainly of two relationships, indicated by the horizontal arrows. A person or organization is ethical if both relationships are strong and positive. The first element in the model is sources of ethical guidance. One might use a number of sources to determine what is right or wrong, good or bad, moral or immoral. These sources include the Bible and other holy books. They also include the small voice that many refer to as conscience. Many believe that conscience is a gift of God or the voice of God. Others see it as a developed response based on the internalization of societal mores. Another source of ethical guidance is the behavior and advice of the people psychologists call "significant others"—our parents, friends, and role models and members of our churches, clubs, and associations. For most professionals, there are codes of ethics that prescribe certain behavior. Without this conscience that has developed it might be easy to say, "Everyone does it," "Just this once won't hurt," or "No one will ever know."

Laws also offer guidance to ethical behavior, prohibiting acts that can be especially harmful to others. If a certain behavior is illegal, most would consider it to be unethical as well. There are exceptions, of course. For example, through the 1950s, laws in most southern states relegated blacks to the backs of buses and otherwise assigned them inferior status. Martin Luther King Jr. resisted such laws and, in fact, engaged in civil disobedience and other nonviolent forms of resistance to their enforcement. King won the Nobel Peace Prize for his efforts.

Notice in Figure 2.1 that the sources of ethical guidance should lead to our beliefs or a conviction about what is right or wrong. Most would agree that people have a responsibility to avail themselves of these sources of ethical guidance. In short, individuals should care about what is right and wrong and not just be concerned with what is expedient. The strength of the relationship between what an individual or an organization believes to be moral and correct and what available sources of guidance suggest is morally correct is **Type I ethics**.

For example, suppose a manager believes it is acceptable to not hire minorities, despite the fact that almost everyone condemns this practice. This person is unethical in a Type I sense.

Having strong beliefs about what is right and wrong and basing them on the proper sources may have little relationship to what one does. Figure 2.1 illustrates that **Type II ethics** is the strength of the relationship between what one believes and how one behaves. For example, if a manager knows that it is wrong to discriminate, but does so anyway, the manager is being unethical in a Type II sense. If a board of directors considers it wrong to pay excessive salaries to the CEO, yet pays salaries that are shameful, this behavior is unethical also. Generally, a person is not considered ethical unless the person possesses both types of ethics.

As you move through this book, you will find ethical dilemmas to consider in each chapter. Take a moment to determine how you would handle each dilemma. In all instances it should be readily evident what the ethical response should be. Decisions are nice and neat in an academic environment. Then you should ask yourself, are there other factors that some would consider in making a decision? Often there is considerable evidence that might sway a person to make a less-than-ethical decision.

Type I ethics
Strength of the relationship between what an individual or an organization believes to be moral and correct and what available sources of guidance suggest is morally correct.

Type II ethics
Strength of the relationship between what one believes and how one behaves.

ETHICAL DILEMMA

A Selection Quandary

You are being promoted to a new assignment within your company, and your boss has asked you to nominate one of your subordinates as your replacement. The possible candidates are Randy Carlton, who is obviously more qualified, and James Mitchell, who, though not as experienced, is much better liked by the workers. If Randy is given the promotion, you are not certain the workers will accept him as their leader. James, on the other hand, is a hard worker and is well liked and respected by the others, including Randy. As you labor over the decision, you think about how unfair it would be to Randy if the feelings of the other workers kept him from getting a deserved promotion. At the same time, you feel that your primary responsibility should be to maintain the productivity of the work unit. If your former division fell apart after your departure, it would hurt your reputation, not to mention the company.

What would you do?

This is the only place in this text where I will recommend the ethical choice and also identify other factors that might make a person take a less-than-ethical stand. What would you have done if placed in a situation such as this?

Ethical Choice: Recommend Randy, who is the best-qualified employee.

Factors Influencing Another Decision: The department might fall apart if Randy is given the promotion. Other workers might not work for Randy and the workers would more readily accept James. Your reputation may be hurt if the department productivity declines. Besides, Randy can work with James.

OBJECTIVE 2.2
Explain the attempts at legislating ethics.

Legislating Ethics

In 1907, Teddy Roosevelt said, "Men can never escape being governed. If from lawlessness or fickleness, from folly or self-indulgence, they refuse to govern themselves, then in the end they will be governed [by others]."[13] Many contend that ethics cannot be legislated. Although laws cannot mandate ethics, they may be able to identify the baseline separating what is good and what is bad. Much of the current legislation was passed because of business ethics breakdowns. There have been three attempts to legislate business ethics since the late 1980s.

The first, the Procurement Integrity Act of 1988, prohibits the release of source selection and contractor bid or proposal information. Also, a former employee who served in certain positions on a procurement action or contract in excess of $10 million is barred from receiving compensation as an employee or consultant from that contractor for one year. The Act was passed after there were reports of military contracts for $500 toilet seats. There was also a $5,000 hammer.

The second attempt occurred with the passage of the 1992 Federal Sentencing Guidelines for Organizations Act (FSGO), which outlined an effective ethics training program and explained the seven minimum requirements for an effective program to prevent and detect violations.[14] The FSGO promised softer punishments for wayward corporations that already had ethics programs in place. In the law were recommendations regarding standards, ethics training, and a system to report misconduct anonymously. Executives were supposed to be responsible for the misconduct of those lower in the organization. If executives were proactive in their efforts to prevent white-collar crime it would lessen a judgment against them and reduce the liability. Organizations responded by creating ethics officer positions, installing ethics hotlines, and developing codes of ethics. But, it is one thing to have a code of ethics and quite another to have this code instilled in all employees from top to bottom. For example, the Enron debacle was not supposed to happen. The Enron Code of Ethics was 62 pages long and had a foreword by Kenneth L. Lay, who was then the company's chairman, saying "Enron's reputation finally depends on its people, on you and me. Let's keep that reputation high."[15] Even with the ethical code, it is apparent that Enron's top management pursued business as usual. That ethics program obviously served as a smoke screen to deflect attention or culpability resulting from illegal actions.

The third attempt at legislating business ethics was the Corporate and Auditing Accountability, Responsibility, and Transparency Act of 2002, which criminalized many corporate acts that were previously relegated to various regulatory structures. Known as the

Sarbanes–Oxley Act, its primary focus is to redress accounting and financial reporting abuses in light of corporate scandals. The Act contains broad employee whistle-blower protections that subject corporations and their managerial personnel to significant civil and criminal penalties for retaliating, harassing, or discriminating against employees who report suspected corporate wrongdoing. The whistle-blower protections of the Act apply to corporations listed on U.S. stock exchanges; companies otherwise obligated to file reports under the Securities and Exchange Act; and officers, employees, contractors, subcontractors, and agents of those companies.

The Act states that management may not discharge, demote, suspend, threaten, harass, or in any other manner discriminate against an employee protected by the Act. It protects any employee who lawfully provides information to governmental authorities concerning conduct he or she reasonably believes constitutes mail, wire, or securities fraud; violations of any rule or regulation issued by the Securities and Exchange Commission (SEC); or violations of any other federal law relating to fraud against shareholders. The Act evidently has teeth, because in the 2003 *Bechtel v Competitive Technologies Inc.* Supreme Court case involving wrongful termination under Sarbanes–Oxley's whistle-blower-protection rule, the Court ruled that the company violated the Act by firing two employees and ordered them reinstated. They were fired because during a meeting they had raised concerns about the company's decision not to report, on its SEC filing, an act they thought should have been disclosed.[16]

The law prohibits loans to executives and directors. It requires publicly traded companies to disclose whether or not they have adopted a code of ethics for senior officers.[17] The Act does not require SEC reporting banks and bank-holding companies to have a code of ethics, but if an SEC reporting company does not have one, it must explain why.[18] However, as former SEC Chairman Arthur Levitt said, "While the Sarbanes–Oxley Act has brought about significant change, the greatest change is being brought about not by regulation or legislation, but by humiliation and embarrassment and private rights of action."[19]

Code of Ethics

OBJECTIVE 2.3
Understand the importance of a code of ethics, and describe linking pay to ethical behavior.

For organizations to grow and prosper, good people must be employed. Companies are also searching for new employees who have a sound ethical base because they have discovered that an ethical person tends to be more successful. Dov Seidman, a management guru who advocates corporate virtue to many companies believes that companies that "outbehave" their competitors ethically will generally outperform them financially.[20] Further, the ethical—or unethical—behavior of an organization is a critical factor for new college graduates seeking jobs, according to the National Association of Colleges and Employers.[21]

By fostering a strong ethical culture, firms are better able to gain the confidence and loyalty of their employees and other stakeholders, which can result in reduced financial, legal, and reputation risks, as well as improvements in organizational performance. Organizations are redesigning their ethics programs to facilitate a broader and more consistent process that incorporates the analysis of outcomes and continual improvement. To build and sustain an ethical culture, organizations need a comprehensive framework that encompasses communication of behavior expectations, training on ethics and compliance issues, stakeholder input, resolution of reported matters, and analysis of the entire ethics program. To make it really work, involvement by top management is also necessary.

A distinction needs to be made between a code of conduct and a code of ethics; the former should tell employees what the rules of conduct are.[22] The code of ethics helps employees know what to do when there is not a rule for something.[23] A broad-based participation of those subject to the code is important. Michael Coates, CEO of Hill and Knowlton Canada, said, "For a company to behave ethically, it must live and breathe its code of ethics, train its personnel, and communicate its code through its visioning statements. It cannot just print a manual that sits on a corporate shelf."[24] The code is a statement of the values adopted by the company, its employees, and its directors, and sets the official tone of top management regarding expected behavior. Many industry associations adopt such codes, which are then recommended to members. There are many kinds of ethical codes. An excellent example of a code of ethics was developed by the Society for Human Resource Management (SHRM). Major provisions in the SHRM code of ethics include professional responsibility, professional development, ethical leadership, fairness and justice, conflicts of interest, and use of information.

Just what should be included in a code of ethics? Topics typically covered might be business conduct, fair competition, and workplace and HR issues. For example, employees in purchasing or other disciplines would be shown what constitutes a conflict of interest. The same would occur for sales. At Walmart, it is considered unethical to accept gifts from suppliers. Gifts are either destroyed or given to charity. Fidelity International recently fired two Hong Kong-based fund managers over breaches of its internal code of ethics. Fidelity said, "Our routine checks discovered a pattern of behavior that breached our internal policies."[25]

To keep the code on the front burner for employees, larger firms appoint an ethics officer. The ethics officer is the point person in guiding everyone in the company toward ethical actions. This individual should be a person who understands the work environment. To obtain the involvement of others within the organization, an ethics committee is often established.

There are reasons to encourage industry associations to develop and promote codes of ethics. It is difficult for a single firm to pioneer ethical practices if its competitors take advantage of unethical shortcuts. For example, U.S. companies must comply with the Foreign Corrupt Practices Act, which prohibits bribes of foreign government officials or business executives (discussed at length in Chapter 14). Obviously, the law does not prevent foreign competitors from bribing government or business officials to get business and such practices are common in many countries. This sometimes puts U.S. companies at a disadvantage.

Even the criteria for winning the Baldrige National Quality Award have changed, and an increased emphasis on ethics in leadership is now stressed. The criteria say senior leaders should serve as role models for the rest of their organizations. Baldrige applicants are asked questions about how senior leaders create an environment that fosters and requires legal and ethical behavior, and how the leaders address governance matters such as fiscal accountability and independence in audits.

The Adolph Coors Company of Golden, Colorado, has developed one of the nation's most comprehensive ethics programs. The company offers its employees considerable resources, including interactive online courses, ethics leadership training, a decision map, a highly detailed set of policies, and a help line. Warren Malmquist, who developed the program and serves as director of Coors Audit Services, says, "The goal of the program is to step beyond rules and guidelines and teach employees how to think, clarify, and analyze situations." When the program was started in 1990, the company's ethics policy was little more than a basic code of conduct and set of guidelines. Since then, the firm has continually added features that are deliberately focused on a strategy of prevention rather than investigation. "We realized that it was essential to develop a code of ethics that is meaningful rather than a legal-based document that's difficult to understand," said Caroline McMichen, group manager of ethics and audit services.[26]

Linking Pay to Ethical Behavior

I discuss the importance of linking pay to performance in Chapter 9 but it also is appropriate as a topic here. You will learn that "what you reward is what you get." If the statement is correct, then a problem exists with regard to compensation because most companies do not link pay to ethical behavior. A survey of 358 compliance and ethics professionals by the Society of Corporate Compliance and Ethics (SCCE) and the Health Care Compliance Association found that only a few companies have made ethics and compliance a process for determining how employees are compensated, and only about one company in six ties employee bonuses and incentives to ethical performance.[27] When asked how much impact the ethics and compliance function has on the compensation process for the executives, just 34 percent of respondents said it had some or a great deal of impact. The majority indicated that compliance and ethics played very little (27 percent) or no role (29 percent), while the balance was unsure of the role of ethics and compliance.[28] CEO Roy Snell of SCCE said, "The net result is that there is more work to be done in aligning business practices with stated commitment to compliant, ethical behavior."[29] For example, performance expectation could be related to ethics, making it part of the performance review and the results tied to pay raises.[30]

OBJECTIVE 2.4
Explain the human resource ethics and describe ethics training.

human resource ethics
Application of ethical principles to human resource relationships and activities.

Human Resource Ethics

It is vitally important that those who work in human resource management understand those practices that are unacceptable and ensure that organizational members behave ethically in dealing with others. **Human resource ethics** is the application of ethical principles to human resource relationships and activities.

Some believe that those in human resources have a great deal to do with establishing an organization's conscience. Certainly ethics is a quality the HR professionals should possess.[31] It is the duty of HR professionals to help create an ethical climate in their organization.[32]

HR professionals can help foster an ethical culture, but that means more than just hanging the ethics codes posters on walls. Instead, since the HR professionals' primary job is dealing with people, they must help to instill ethical practices into the corporate culture. Those values must be clearly communicated to all employees, early and often, beginning with the interviewing process, reinforced during employee orientation, and regularly recognized during performance reviews, public ceremonies, celebrations, and awards.[33] They need to help establish an environment in which employees throughout the organization work to reduce ethical lapses. The ethical bearing of those in HR goes a long way toward establishing the credibility of the entire organization.

Throughout your text there are many topics through which HR professionals can have a major impact on ethics and, therefore, on corporate culture. Even though these topics are yet to be covered, you should know that there are certain ethical situations that will be touched upon. Some ethical questions you may wish to consider as you study your text include:

- Do you strive to create a diverse workforce (Chapter 3)?
- Do you insist that job descriptions are developed to accurately depict jobs that are dangerous or hazardous (Chapter 4)?
- Do you strive to recruit and select the best-qualified applicant for the job (Chapters 5 and 6)?
- Are your training initiatives geared so that everyone will have an opportunity to receive the best training and development possible (Chapter 7)?
- Is your performance management and appraisal system able to identify those who are indeed the best producers (Chapter 8)?
- Is your compensation and benefit system developed so that employees will view it as fair and impartial (Chapters 9 and 10)?
- Does your organization make a sincere attempt to provide a safe and healthy work environment (Chapter 11)?
- Does your organization attempt to develop a work environment in which employees will not feel compelled to join a union (Chapter 12)?
- Are your internal employee relations consisting of disciplinary action, promotion, transfer, demotion, resignation, discharge, layoff, and retirement fair and impartial (Chapter 13)?
- Does your firm adhere to ethical norms when operating in the global environment (Chapter 14)?

HR should review, develop, and enforce organizational policies to ensure a high level of ethics throughout the organization. All employees should know what is ethical and unethical in their specific area of operations. It is insufficient to say that everyone should be ethical. Dialogue should be developed so that workers in different areas know what is ethical.

Ethics Training

As previously mentioned, the Federal Sentencing Guidelines for Organizations Act outlined an effective ethics training program and explained the seven minimum requirements for an effective program to prevent and detect violations. The fourth requirement stated, "Educate employees in the company's standards and procedures through publications and training."[34] Ann Subervi, president and CEO of Utopia Communications, said, "Companies think to train employees on many things, but they rarely think to train them on ethics, and that's a big mistake."[35] Because of its inclusion within the FSGO, a brief discussion of ethics training will be provided in this chapter rather than in Chapter 7 (Training and Development).

Companies that consistently rank high on the lists of best corporate citizens tend to make ethics training part of a company-wide initiative to promote integrity.[36] Ethics training should begin at the top and be driven down the organization by senior management. Business ethics expert Christopher Bauer believes that everyone in the company should be targeted for ethics training. He said, "Remember that the integrity of your organization is judged on the basis of everyone in it, not just the managers, executives, and board."[37] However, training should take into consideration the differences in these levels. While top management sets the ethical tone, middle managers are the ones who will likely be the first to receive reports of unethical behavior.

KPMG believes that there are three fundamental factors in handing ethics issues: provide multiple channels for raising alarms, eliminate fear of retaliation for those who raise questions, and ensure consistent investigation and resolution of all matters reported. To report an ethics issue, individuals should start with their supervisor and office leadership. If the nature of the issue creates a potential conflict, the individual is encouraged to contact the general counsel's office, the ethics and compliance organization, or human resources. To handle reports anonymously, an ethics hotline and an ombudsman may be used. Individuals who report potential ethics violations could be subject to retaliation, so KPMG monitors performance reviews and other metrics to proactively identify retaliatory behavior. The credibility of the program requires all reports to be consistently investigated and resolved.[38]

If *ethical behavior* is the norm, workers will have no problem in reporting unethical behavior to the manager. One thing is for certain, just reading a handbook that contains a section on ethics and signing off on it is not enough. Trainers must be able to communicate to participants core company values, reinforce best practices, and establish behaviors and standards for all employees. A major point is that the training provided must mesh with the organization's culture. Once these values have been communicated to participants, ethical behavior must be monitored and the code must be enforced.

Ethics training for global organizations is more complicated than preparing the training for U.S. employees. One must also train for the country in which the global company operates. LRN develops ethics training and works with hundreds of companies in 120 countries around the world to help them foster an ethical culture through its courses. A few of their customers include CBS, Dow Chemical, eBay, 3M, and Siemens. LRN has trained 12 million workers and delivered training in over 40 languages. Chris Campbell, creative director at LRN, says, "Localization is as important as the accuracy of the translation process. Learners need to be able to connect in a way that is believable to them. Otherwise, you don't make that strong emotional connection that allows us to facilitate an emotional change."[39]

Ernst & Young (E&Y), who has more than 120,000 people in 140 countries, works to provide employees with an ethical foundation. E&Y implemented a formal ethics curriculum, which has a mandatory two-hour, Web-based ethics course titled, "Living Our Core Values." The first 45 minutes of the course provides the ethical foundation and values for the firm. The remaining portion is experiential, in that it applies the firm's collective wisdom regarding those values to real-life situations. Michael Hamilton, chief learning and development officer for the Americas, said, "We put employees in situations and ask them to take the firm's values and ethics to solve problems at the firm itself. It's the only way you can give them that experience. You can talk at them all day, but when it comes to making tough calls and essentially interpreting between the lines, you have to let people have an emotional connection that says, 'This is what I feel, in my heart, is right, based on the firm's values.' You can't expect people to exercise the right answers unless you give them a chance to apply them to real-life situations."[40]

Cisco created a unique ethics training program that showcased cartoon contestants singing about various ethical workplace situations found in Cisco's Code of Business Conduct. Jeremy Wilson, manager, ethics office for Cisco Systems, Inc., said, "We wanted what was right for our employees, based upon our own risk analysis. We pose questions to employees as to which judge's answer they agree with," says Wilson. "Employees can provide feedback, see how the rest of the company voted, and see the official Cisco answer as to which judge is correct in his or her assessment of the situation." When Cisco created its program, it invited input from more than 120 people from departments across the organization, including legal, human resources, IT security, and records management. "When we rolled it out, 20 different departments helped us," says Wilson.[41]

Saying that a company has an ethical culture and actually having one may be two different things. One way to create and sustain an ethical culture is to audit your ethics, much as you might audit your finances each year.[42] An ethics audit is simply a systematic, independent, and documented process for obtaining evidence regarding the status of an organization's ethical culture. It is taking a closer look at a firm's ethical culture instead of just allowing it to remain unexamined.[43]

Professionalization of Human Resource Management

A **profession** is a vocation characterized by the existence of a common body of knowledge and a procedure for certifying members. Performance standards are established by members of the profession rather than by outsiders; that is, the profession is self-regulated. Most professions also have effective representative organizations that permit members to exchange ideas of mutual concern. These characteristics apply to the field of human resources, and several well-known organizations serve the profession. Among the more prominent are the Society for Human Resource Management, the Human Resource Certification Institute (HRCI), the American Society for Training and Development, and WorldatWork.

Society for Human Resource Management

The largest national professional organization for individuals involved in all areas of human resource management is the Society for Human Resource Management (SHRM). The basic goals of the society include defining, maintaining, and improving standards of excellence in the practice of human resource management. Founded in 1948, SHRM presently represents more than 250,000 individual members in more than 140 countries, and has a network of more than 575 affiliated chapters in the United States, as well as offices in China and India.[44]

SHRM publishes a monthly journal, *HRMagazine,* and a monthly newspaper, *HRNews.* A major subsidiary of SHRM, Staffing Management, offers in-depth information on issues addressing employment and retention issues, whereas SHRM offers a broader coverage of HR issues.[45]

Human Resource Certification Institute

One of the more significant developments in the field of HRM has been the establishment of the Human Resource Certification Institute (HRCI), an affiliate of SHRM. Founded in 1976, HRCI's goal is to recognize human resource professionals through a certification program. HRCI offers three certifications for HR professionals—PHR (Professional in Human Resources), SPHR (Senior Professional in Human Resources), and GPHR (Global Professional in Human Resources). There are more than 100,000 HR professionals with the PHR, SPHR or GPHR designation.[46] Certification encourages human resource professionals to update their knowledge and skills continuously. It provides recognition to professionals who have met a stated level of training and work experience.

American Society for Training and Development

Founded in 1944, the American Society for Training and Development (ASTD) is the world's largest association dedicated to workplace learning and performance professionals. ASTD's members come from more than 100 countries and connect locally in almost 130 U.S. chapters and more than 30 international partners. Members work in thousands of organizations of all sizes, in government, as independent consultants, and suppliers.[47] The ASTD Certification Institute has the Certified Professional in Learning and Performance (CPLP™) credential to provide a way for workplace learning and performance professionals to prove their value to employers and to be confident about their knowledge of the field.[48]

WorldatWork

WorldatWork is a professional association focused on compensation, benefits, work–life effectiveness and integrated total rewards—strategies to attract, motivate, and retain an engaged and productive workforce. WorldatWork was founded in 1955 as the American Compensation Association (ACA) and provides a network of more than 30,000 members and professionals with training, certification, research, conferences, and community. WorldatWork Society of Certified Professionals is an organization that certifies human resource professionals in the disciplines of compensation, benefits, and work–life. WorldatWork Society designations include Certified Compensation Professional (CCP), Certified Benefits Professional (CBP), Global Remuneration Professional (GRP), and Work-Life Certified Professional (WLCP).[49]

OBJECTIVE 2.6
Describe the concept of corporate social responsibility.

Corporate Social Responsibility

What do the following U.S. companies have in common: Advanced Micro Devices, Alcoa Inc., Amazon.com Inc., Baxter International Inc., Coca Cola Company, Dell Inc., Eastman Kodak Company, FPL Group Inc., Genzyme Corp., Goldman Sachs Group Inc., Hewlett-Packard Company, Intel Corp., Nike Inc., PG & E Corp., Pinnacle West Capital Corp., Procter & Gamble Company, Prologis, State Street Corp., and United Technologies Corp.? They have been identified as having a commitment to excellence in the area of corporate social responsibility and are included in the 2009 Global 100 Most Sustainable Corporations in the World. These companies have demonstrated the ability to manage the "triple bottom line" of social responsibility (society, environment, and economy). They represent the top five percent of socially responsible companies.

corporate social responsibility (CSR)
Implied, enforced, or felt obligation of managers, acting in their official capacity, to serve or protect the interests of groups other than themselves.

Corporate social responsibility (CSR) is the implied, enforced, or felt obligation of managers, acting in their official capacity, to serve or protect the interests of groups other than themselves.

When a corporation behaves as if it has a conscience, it is said to be socially responsible. CSR considers the overall influence of corporations on society at large and goes beyond the interests of shareholders. It is how a company as a whole behaves toward society. Social responsibility has moved from nice-to-do to must-do. More and more companies are issuing corporate social responsibility reports that detail their environmental, labor, and corporate-giving practices. Some firms, such as Burger King, have created the position of director of corporate social responsibility.[50]

Apparently, socially responsible behavior pays off on the bottom line. When GE CEO Jeffrey Immelt announced that the company would double its spending on green technology research, it was no grand attempt to save the planet; it was an example of astute business strategy. Immelt said, "We plan to make money doing it."[51] Social responsibility has also impacted the recruiting process. Barry Anderson, CEO for Gifts in Kind, said, "This generation wants to work for a corporation that is socially responsible. When I entered the workforce that never came up."[52]

Numerous companies are also working toward becoming eco-friendly. For example, Target's waste-reduction efforts have cut waste by 70 percent. Home Depot attempts to make sure that wood and lumber sold in its stores come from sustainable forests. McDonald's has eliminated the use of containers made with ozone-depleting chlorofluorocarbons, cut down on the amount and type of packaging it uses, and implemented a program of purchasing goods made from recycled materials. Walmart is working on sustainable initiatives. Solar panels are being installed in all of the retailer's super centers with unused energy being sold back into the energy grid, a cost-saving move for the community.[53]

HR Web Wisdom

Business for Social Responsibility
http://www.bsr.org
This is a global organization that helps member companies achieve success in ways that respect ethical values, people, communities, and the environment.

Procter & Gamble has long believed it has a responsibility for the long-term benefit of society as well as the company. Over the years, P&G has pursued programs to strengthen U.S. education, to encourage employment opportunities for minorities and women, to develop and implement environment-protection technology, and to encourage employee involvement in civic activities and the political process.

Deborah Leipziger, a Ethical Corporation Institute researcher, said, "The more credible efforts tend to be led by key players within a company. Somebody who works directly with the CEO, for example, shows that the company is a lot more serious about sustainable initiatives than an individual in public relations, for instance, which may signal that the company is looking at it more as a communications exercise.[54] An organization's top executives usually determine a corporation's approach to social responsibility. For example, when McDonald's began, it was

TRENDS & INNOVATIONS

Strategic Corporate Social Responsibility

HR professionals must assume a strategic role when it comes to the management of human resources and change the way they work. Some HR professionals have helped their careers by doing work that impacts the bottom line and focusing their efforts on corporate social responsibility. HR professionals who are leaders of CSR activities place themselves in the spotlight for top management to see.[55]

Tareyece Scoggin, employee relations manager at Standard Parking in Chicago, drives CSR at her company and says, "CSR aligns HR with the goals of the company and the C-suite. So much of the CSR sweet spot [where social good overlaps business opportunity] lives in HR. We have a unique position to leverage the human capital that we're charged with recruiting, retaining, and developing. In the end, we are able to be much more of a business partner through CSR."[56]

A survey by the Society for Human Resource Management found that approximately two-thirds of U.S. HR professionals are directly involved in CSR activities; 13 percent of HR professionals were mainly responsible for creating CSR strategy, and 23 percent were charged with implementing the strategy. Lin Blair, HR project leader at Arkansas Blue Cross Blue Shield, said, "A lot of times [the responsibility for] CSR falls to the

public relations and marketing departments, but if you start talking to CEOs about morale, loyalty, and employer-of-choice [through CSR], it becomes very obvious that HR needs to lead it. But HR needs to raise its hands."[57]

The background, experience, and skills of HR professionals fit quite nicely into the profiles of individuals needed to develop and direct the CSR strategy. Scoggin, who serves on the SHRM Corporate Social Responsibility Special Expertise Panel, says, "We are already collaborating with other functions. We are negotiating daily and using our soft skills—all of which are necessary to gain acceptance of CSR."[58]

HR may be leading the social responsibility effort but many organizational disciplines need to be involved, and that requires collaboration. Lew Karabatsos, executive vice president of client relations at CreateHope, a citizenship consulting firm in Washington, D.C., says, "There needs to be collaboration. HR shouldn't drive the environmental agenda, for example, but it needs to work with the environmental folks to embellish on that strategy." HR professionals are trained in people-related skills. Ron Vassallo, managing director, international, at CreateHope, says, "Despite the fact that CEOs or the board might be behind the cause, [they] don't give it legs. Employees are cynical. CSR only gets legs and acceptance when employees embrace it. HR can engage employees in the strategy." Finally, Scoggin said, "If you are working on CSR initiatives, you are being strategic; it's no longer an ephemeral topic. it's a way to align the HR function with business objectives, with our career advancement and [with] the advancement of the profession."[59]

Ray Kroc's philosophy to be a community-based business. His philosophy from the very beginning was to give back to the communities that McDonald's served.[60]

One of the best benchmarks for defining social responsibility in manufacturing is the one-page set of operating principles developed 60 years ago by Robert Wood Johnson, then Johnson & Johnson's chairman of the board. The document is still in use today and addresses supporting good works and charities.[61]

OBJECTIVE 2.7

Explain what is meant by stakeholder analysis and the social contract.

organizational stakeholder

Individual or group whose interests are affected by organizational activities.

Stakeholder Analysis and the Social Contract

Most organizations, whether profit or not-for-profit, have a large number of stakeholders. An **organizational stakeholder** is an individual or group whose interests are affected by organizational activities.

Society is increasingly holding corporate boards of directors and management accountable for putting the interest of stakeholders first.[62] However, managers may not acknowledge responsibility for all of them. Some of the stakeholders for Crown Metal Products, a fictitious manufacturer, are shown in Figure 2.2. But only a few, identified by bold arrows, are viewed as constituencies by Crown management. Each firm will have different stakeholders based on the organization's mission and the focus of social responsibility efforts.

The actions of many corporate executives are designed to serve interests other than those of the common shareholder. For example, a number of managements have placed large amounts of company stock in employee stock ownership trusts for the purpose of avoiding takeover attempts that were clearly in the interests of common shareholders. This benefited the employees, of

Figure 2.2

Stakeholders of Crown Metal Products

Source: R. Wayne Mondy and Shane R. Premeaux, *Management: Concepts, Practices, and Skills,* 7th ed. (Upper Saddle River, NJ: Prentice Hall, 1995), p. 80.

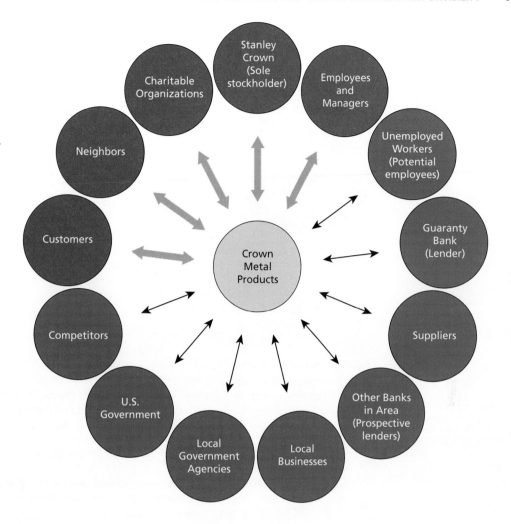

course, but it also helped the managers keep their jobs. Other companies make gifts of company resources, often cash, to universities, churches, clubs, and so forth, knowing that any possible benefit to shareholders is remote. In fact, 94 percent of U.S. companies said they had donated money to community groups or charitable causes.[63] Some authorities favor this trend and suggest that members of the public should be placed on major corporate boards to protect the interests of non-owner stakeholders.

One approach to stakeholder analysis involves consideration of the social contract. The **social contract** is the set of written and unwritten rules and assumptions about acceptable interrelationships among the various elements of society. Much of the social contract is embedded in the customs of society. For example, in integrating minorities into the workforce, society has come to expect companies to do more than the law requires.

Some of the contract provisions result from practices of the parties to the contract. Like a legal contract, the social contract often involves a quid pro quo (something exchanged for something). One party to the contract behaves in a certain way and expects a certain pattern of behavior from the other. For example, a relationship of trust may have developed between a manufacturer and the community in which it operates. Because of this, each will inform the other well in advance of any planned action that might cause harm, such as the phasing down of a plant's operations by the company. The widespread belief that such a relationship was rare prompted Congress to pass the Worker Adjustment and Retraining Notification Act of 1988 (discussed further in Chapter 13).

The social contract concerns relationships with individuals, government, other organizations, and society in general, as Figure 2.3 illustrates. Each of these relationships will be considered individually in the following sections.

social contract
Set of written and unwritten rules and assumptions about acceptable interrelationships among the various elements of society.

Figure 2.3

The Social Contract

Source: R. Wayne Mondy and Shane R. Premeaux, *Management: Concepts, Practices, and Skills,* 7th ed. (Upper Saddle River, NJ: Prentice Hall, 1995), p. 82.

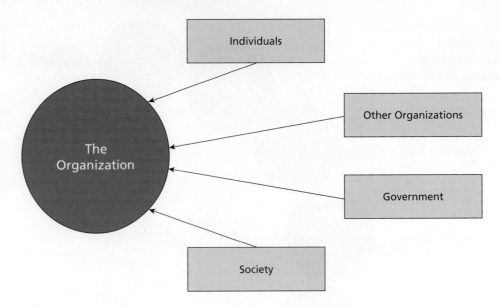

Obligations to Individuals

Organizations have certain obligations to their employees. Individuals often find healthy outlets for their energies through joining organizations. From their employers, they expect a fair day's pay for a fair day's work, and perhaps much more. Many expect to be paid for time off to vote, perform jury service, and so forth. To the extent that individuals' expectations are acknowledged as responsibilities by the organization, they become part of the social contract.

Obligations to Other Organizations

Managers must be concerned with relationships involving other organizations, both organizations that are like their own, such as competitors, and very different ones. Commercial businesses are expected to compete with one another on an honorable basis, without subterfuge or reckless unconcern for their mutual rights. However, some organizations appear to have a certain amount of disdain for competitors, especially when it comes to recruiting. Charities, such as the United Way, expect support from businesses, often including the loan of executives to help with annual fund drives. At the same time, such institutions are expected to come, hat in hand, to business managers, requesting rather than demanding assistance.

In the traditional view of social responsibility, businesses best meet obligations through pursuit of their own interests. Some companies view the social contract mainly in terms of the company's interests. For example, FMC Corporation, a major diversified manufacturer, has firm policies about how it will direct its contributions. The basic criteria FMC applies are that contributions must help areas around company facilities or where its employees live and that their gifts must improve the corporation's business environment. FMC might contribute to a university in an area where it has a plant, but it would not give gifts to distant universities.

Obligations to Government

Government is an important party to the social contract for every kind of organization. Under the auspices of government, companies have a license to do business, along with patent rights, trademarks, and so forth. Churches are often incorporated under state laws and given nonprofit status. Many quasi-governmental agencies, such as the Federal Deposit Insurance Corporation, regional planning commissions, and local school boards, have been given special missions by government.

In addition, organizations are expected to recognize the need for order rather than anarchy and to accept some government intervention in organizational affairs. They are expected to work with the guidelines of governmental organizations such as the Equal Employment Opportunity Commission and the Office of Federal Compliance Programs (discussed in Chapter 3).

Obligations to Society in General

The traditional view of business responsibility has been that businesses should produce and distribute goods and services in return for a profit. Businesses have performed this function effectively, giving the United States one of the highest overall standards of living in the world. A high percentage of the population has its basic needs for food, clothing, shelter, health, and education reasonably well satisfied. And most citizens are afforded some leisure time. Profitable firms are able to pay taxes to the government and make donations to charities. All this should be a matter of some pride for business owners and managers.

Businesses operate by public consent with the basic purpose of satisfying the needs of society. As those needs are more fully met, society demands more of all of its institutions, particularly large business firms. Possible social issues that private companies might be involved with include environmental protection, support of education, and economic development in poor communities. When the competition is very aggressive, as in retail, CSR activities make the company more visible and may help sales and profit. But this is not always the case, as in the manufacture of computer chips where the market is dominated by only a few purchasers.[64]

At the same time, remember that in order to survive, businesses must make a profit over the long run. If they fail, they will not be able to contribute. As responsible corporate citizens, businesses should follow the spirit of the law as well as the letter. There is a major difference in adhering to equal employment laws and being an equal opportunity employer.

In the 16th century, Sir Thomas More said, "If virtue were profitable, common sense would make us good and greed would make us saintly."[65] More knew that virtue is not profitable, so people must make hard choices from time to time. Common sense hardly makes one good. In the United States today, the consensus is clear. Corporate strategists are being held to a higher standard than just pursuing their own interests, or even those of stockholders; they must consider the interests of other groups, too.

OBJECTIVE 2.8
Describe how a corporate social responsibility program is implemented.

social audit
Systematic assessment of a company's activities in terms of its social impact.

Implementing a Corporate Social Responsibility Program

To overcome the negative publicity of corporate misdeeds and to restore trust, businesses are now conducting audits of their social responsibility activities, not just financial audits. A **social audit** is a systematic assessment of a company's activities in terms of its social impact.

Some of the topics included in the audit focus on core values such as social responsibility, open communication, treatment of employees, confidentiality, and leadership. Firms are now acknowledging responsibilities to various stakeholder groups other than corporate owners.[66]

Some even set specific objectives in social areas. They are attempting to formally measure their contributions to various elements of society and to society as a whole. An increasing number of companies, as well as public and voluntary sector organizations, are trying to assess their social performance systematically. Three possible types of social audits are currently being used: (1) simple inventory of activities, (2) compilation of socially relevant expenditures, and (3) determination of social impact. The inventory is generally a good starting place. It consists of a listing of socially oriented activities undertaken by the firm. Here are some examples: minority employment and training, support of minority enterprises, pollution control, corporate giving, involvement in selected community projects by executives, and a hard-core unemployment program. The ideal social audit would go well beyond a simple listing and involve determining the true benefits to society of any socially oriented business activity.

The following steps are recommended for establishing and implementing a CSR program. First, a person should be assigned the responsibility for the program and a structure should be developed. This individual should, at a very minimum, report to senior management or a board member. Second, a review of what the company is currently doing with regard to CSR should be determined. The difference between where the company is at present and where it wants to be should be determined (a gap analysis). Third, shareholders' expectations and perspectives are determined. Fourth, a policy statement is written covering CSR areas such as environmental, social, and community issues. Fifth, a set of corporate objectives and an action

A GLOBAL PERSPECTIVE

Can Corporate Social Responsibility Succeed in the Global Environment?

The global environment often judges management primarily on protecting the firm's bottom line. If this is so, it may be easy to be socially responsible in a prospering economy but more difficult when the economy is bad. The recession of 2008/10 had some global firms questioning the wisdom of being socially responsible. The question asked is, "Can firms competing in the global environment continue the lowest possible production costs while still being in compliance with national laws and also be socially responsible?"[67]

Even before the 2008/2010 recession began, corporations and their contractor manufacturers (often Korean, Taiwanese, and Hong Kong companies operating throughout the world) focused on obtaining the lowest production costs regardless of the accompanying social and environmental impacts. Todd Cheung, the general manager of an export sports shoe factory in China's Pearl River Delta, said, "we will either move inland or out of China altogether. It's not political, it's economic. A lot of Taiwanese companies are moving to inner provinces because the land is cheap, the labor is cheap, and the local governments don't insist on expensive anti-pollution measures as they do here."[68]

Worker protection laws of countries have caused companies to try to undermine government efforts at worker protection and are moving their operations. Adidas CEO Herbert Hainer told the German business magazine *Wirtchaftswoche* that "salaries which are set by the government have become too high in China. Countries like Laos, Cambodia, and Vietnam will be aided. Production will also return to former Soviet republics and eastern European countries."[69]

Since the global economic crisis began, adherence to CSR issues has declined. "There have been reports in China where factory managers fled to Hong Kong even though workers were owed wages and severance pay set by Chinese law. Managers have abandoned their factories, leaving many of the 20 million unemployed workers without even the back wages needed to return home to the countryside." In addition to sudden cancellation and nonpayment of contracts, there have been demands for longer and longer periods to pay their contractors. Payment periods of 30–45 days after delivery have been stretched to 90 and even 120 days. Some have even imposed a 2–3 percent "settlement fee" on contractors who insist on getting paid on time. While some companies, especially in Asia, continue to say that they are fully committed to CSR, their less-than-socially-responsible behavior speaks otherwise.[70]

The United Nation's all-voluntary, anti-sweatshop initiative "Global Compact" de-listed 630 companies worldwide who had agreed to the principles of the compact but were found to be out of compliance. Approximately 30 percent of these companies were from China, India, and Southeast Asia. Many are local contractors for well-known retailers of consumer products in the United States. Governments in the developing world are receiving increased pressure to lower the pressure on foreign investment. China, for instance, "has frozen scheduled increases in minimum wage, reduced or suspended employer payments into the social insurance system, restored export tax credits, and made clear that enforcement of the new 2008 labor laws will be 'relaxed' for the foreseeable future."[71]

There is a growing recognition among leading global CSR organizations that the first 15 years of CSR efforts has not produced the desired results, and that significant changes will have to be made if CSR is to be anything more than an expensive exercise in "reputational management." Dan Rees, director of the UK's Ethical Trading Initiative, said that "CSR in general has become a bit of a victim of its own hype . . . we have to stop pretending that companies in and of themselves can on their own transform industrial relation in foreign lands."[72]

The jury is still out in determining whether or not corporate social responsibility can succeed in the global environment. When managers are judged entirely on their achieving lowest bottom line cost, CSR efforts will be difficult if not impossible to achieve.

---

plan to implement the policies should be developed. Sixth, company-wide quantitative and qualitative targets and key performance indicators over a two- to five-year period, together with the necessary measurement, monitoring, and auditing mechanisms, should be created. These actions and strategies should focus on the core business of the organization. Seventh, communicate to stakeholders and fund managers the direction of CSR for the company. Eighth, the progress of the CSR program should be determined. Finally, the progress of the CSR program should be reported.[73]

The CSR program should not be a one-time-only activity but rather a continuing effort to monitor and report the firm's achievements in the area of social responsibility.

Summary

1. *Define ethics and understand the model of ethics.* Ethics is the discipline dealing with what is good and bad, or right and wrong, or with moral duty and obligation. Ethics consists mainly of two relationships. The first element in the model is sources of ethical guidance. The strength of the relationship between what an individual or an organization believes to be moral and correct and what available sources of guidance suggest is morally correct is Type I ethics. Type II ethics is the strength of the relationship between what one believes and how one behaves. Generally, a person is not considered ethical unless the person possesses both types of ethics.

2. *Explain the attempts at legislating ethics.* There have been three attempts to legislate business ethics since the late 1980s. The Procurement Integrity Act of 1988 prohibits the release of source selection and contractor bid or proposal information. Also, a former employee who served in certain positions on a procurement action or contract in excess of $10 million is barred from receiving compensation as an employee or consultant from that contractor for one year. The second attempt occurred with the passage of the 1992 Federal Sentencing Guidelines for Organizations that outlined an effective ethics program. The third attempt at legislating business ethics was the Corporate and Auditing Accountability, Responsibility, and Transparency Act, which focused on the accounting and financial reporting abuses in light of recent corporate scandals.

3. *Understand the importance of a code of ethics and describe linking pay to ethical behavior.* A code of ethics establishes the rules that the organization lives by. A survey of 358 compliance and ethics professionals by the Society of Corporate Compliance and Ethics (SCCE) and the Health Care Compliance Association found that only a few companies have made ethics and compliance a process for determining how employees are compensated, and only about one company in six ties employee bonuses and incentives to ethical performance.

4. *Explain human resource ethics and describe ethics training.* Human resource ethics is the application of ethical principles to human resource relationships and activities. Ethics training is not merely for top-level managers; it should be for everyone from the bottom to the top.

5. *Describe the professionalization of human resource management.* Several well-known organizations serve the profession. Among the more prominent are the Society for Human Resource Management (SHRM), the Human Resource Certification Institute (HRCI), the American Society for Training and Development (ASTD), and WorldatWork (formerly the American Compensation Association).

6. *Describe the concept of corporate social responsibility.* Corporate social responsibility is the implied, enforced, or felt obligation of managers, acting in their official capacity, to serve or protect the interests of groups other than themselves. It is how a company as a whole behaves toward society.

7. *Explain what is meant by stakeholder analysis and the social contact.* Protecting the diversity of stakeholder interests requires answering questions regarding how you will treat the various stakeholders. Answering such questions is termed stakeholder analysis. The social contract is the set of written and unwritten rules and assumptions about acceptable interrelationships among the various elements of society.

8. *Describe how a corporate social responsibility program is implemented.* First, a person should be assigned the responsibility for the program and a structure should be developed. Second, a review of what the company is presently doing with regard to CSR should be determined. Third, shareholders' expectations and perspectives are determined. Fourth, a policy statement is written covering CSR areas such as environmental, social, and community issues. Fifth, a set of corporate objectives and an action plan to implement the policies should be developed. Sixth, company-wide quantitative and qualitative targets and key performance indicators should be created. Seventh, communicate to stakeholders and fund managers the direction of CSR for the company. Eighth, the progress of the CSR program should be determined. Finally, the progress of the CSR program should be reported.

Key Terms

ethics   50
Type I ethics   52
Type II ethics   52
human resource ethics   56

profession   58
corporate social responsibility
   (CSR)   59
organizational stakeholder   60

social contract   61
social audit   63

Questions for Review

1. Define *ethics*. Describe the model of ethics presented in your text. Distinguish between Type I and Type II ethics.
2. What laws have been passed in an attempt to legislate ethics?
3. What are human resource ethics?
4. Why is it important to have a code of ethics?
5. Why is it important to link pay to ethical behavior?
6. What are the areas in which HR professionals can have a major impact on ethics?
7. Define *profession*. Do you believe that the field of human resource management is a profession? Explain your answer.
8. What is corporate social responsibility?
9. What is meant by the terms *organizational stakeholder* and *social contract?*
10. What are the steps that are involved in implementing a corporate social responsibility program?

HRM INCIDENT 1

An Ethical Flaw

Amber Davis had recently graduated from college with a degree in general business. Amber was quite bright, although her grades did not reflect this. She had thoroughly enjoyed school, dating, playing tennis, and swimming, but found few stimulating academic endeavors. When she graduated, she had not found a job. Her dad was extremely upset when he discovered this, and he took it upon himself to see that Amber became employed.

Amber's father, Allen Davis, was executive vice president of a medium-sized manufacturing firm. One of the people he contacted in seeking employment for Amber was Bill Garbo, the president of another firm in the area. Mr. Davis purchased many of his firm's supplies from Garbo's company. After telling Bill his problem, Allen was told to send Amber to Bill's office for an interview. Amber went, as instructed by her father, and before she left Bill's firm, she was surprised to learn that she had a job in the accounting department. Amber may have been lazy, but she certainly was not stupid. She realized that Bill had hired her because he hoped that his action would lead to future business from her father's company. Although Amber's work was not challenging, it paid better than the other jobs in the accounting department.

It did not take long for the employees in the department to discover the reason she had been hired; Amber told them. When a difficult job was assigned to Amber, she normally got one of the other employees to do it, implying that Mr. Garbo would be pleased with that person if he or she helped her out. She developed a pattern of coming in late, taking long lunch breaks, and leaving early. When the department manager attempted to reprimand her for these unorthodox activities, Amber would bring up the close relationship that her father had with the president of the firm. The department manager was at the end of his rope.

Questions

1. From an ethical standpoint, how would you evaluate the merits of Mr. Garbo's employing Amber? Discuss.
2. Now that she is employed, what course would you follow to address her on-the-job behavior?

HRM INCIDENT 2

"You Can't Fire Me"

Norman Blankenship came in the side door of the office at Consolidation Coal Company's Rowland mine, near Clear Creek, West Virginia. He told the mine dispatcher not to tell anyone he was there. Norman was general superintendent of the Rowland operation. He had been with Consolidation for 23 years, having started out as a mining machine operator.

Norman had heard that one of his section bosses, Tom Serinsky, had been sleeping on the job. Tom had been hired two months earlier and assigned to the Rowland mine by the regional personnel office. He had gone to work as section boss, working the midnight to 8:00 A.M. shift. Because of his age and experience, Serinsky was the senior person in the mine on his shift.

Norman took one of the battery-operated jeeps used to transport personnel and supplies in and out of the mine and went to the area where Tom was assigned. Upon arriving, he saw Tom lying on an emergency stretcher. Norman stopped his jeep a few yards away from where Tom was sleeping and approached him. "Hey, are you asleep?" Norman asked. Tom awakened with a start and said, "No, I wasn't sleeping."

Norman waited for Tom to collect his senses and then said, "I could tell that you were sleeping, but that's beside the point. You weren't at your workstation. You know that I have no choice but to fire you." After Tom had left, Norman called his mine foreman and asked him to come in and complete the remainder of Tom's shift.

The next morning, Norman had the mine HR manager officially terminate Tom. As part of the standard procedure, the mine HR manager notified the regional HR manager that Tom had been fired and gave the reasons for firing him. The regional HR manager asked the mine HR manager to get Norman on the line. The regional HR manager said, "Norm, you know Tom is Eustus Frederick's brother-in-law, don't you?" Frederick was a regional vice president. "No, I didn't know that," replied Norman, "but it doesn't matter. The rules are clear. I wouldn't care if he was Frederick's son."

The next day, the regional human resource manager showed up at the mine just as Norman was getting ready to make a routine tour of the mine. "I guess you know what I'm here for," said the HR manager. "Yeah, you're here to take away my authority," replied Norman. "No, I'm just here to investigate," said the regional HR manager.

By the time Norman returned to the mine office after his tour, the regional HR manager had finished his interviews. He told Norman, "I think we're going to have to put Tom back to work. If we decide to do that, can you let him work for you?" "No, absolutely not," said Norman. "In fact, if he works here, I go." A week later, Norman learned that Tom had gone to work as section boss at another Consolidation coal mine in the region.

Questions

1. What would you do now if you were Norman?
2. Do you believe the regional HR manager handled the matter in an ethical manner? Explain.

Notes

1. "Satyam Episode Highlights India's Corporate Flaws," Financial Times, (Jan 18, 2010); "Satyam Case Will Test the Rights of Foreign Investors in Indian Companies," *Financial Times*, (2010); "Satyam Chief Admits Huge Fraud," *Bloomberg*, (2009).
2. Engle, "Making Compliance Effective."
3. "Investors Are Looking Closely at Corporate Ethics," *Corporate Board* 28 (September 2007): 28.
4. Ben W. Heineman, Jr., "Avoiding Integrity Land Mines," *Harvard Business Review* 85 (April 2007): 100–108.
5. Verschoor, "Are We Experiencing an Ethics Bubble?"
6. Vivek Wadhwa, "Why Be an Ethical Company? They're Stronger and Last Longer," *Business Week Online* (August 18, 2009): 18.
7. Ibid.
8. Ibid.
9. Ibid.
10. Kenneth D. Lewis, "The Responsibility of the CEO: Providing Ethical and Moral Leadership," *Vital Speeches of the Day* 69 (October 15, 2002): 6–9.
11. Mary C. Gentile, "Keeping Your Colleagues Honest," *Harvard Business Review* 88 (March 2010): 114–17.
12. T. L. Stanley, "Ethics in Action," *Supervision* 69 (April 2008): 14–16.
13. Kenneth D. Lewis, "The Responsibility of the CEO: Providing Ethical and Moral Leadership," *Vital Speeches of the Day* 69 (October 15, 2002): 6–9.
14. Joyce A. Ostrosky, Linda M. Leinicke, John Digenan, and W. Max Rexroad, "Assessing Elements of Corporate Governance: A Suggested Approach," *CPA Journal* 79 (February 2009): 70–72.
15. Alec Wilkinson, "The Enron Example," *New Yorker* 81 (July 4, 2005): 30–31.
16. Cathleen Flahardy, "SOX Gives DOL Power to Reinstate Whistleblowers," *Corporate Legal Times* 15 (August 2005): 24–26.
17. Kathryn Tyler, "Do the Right Thing," *HR Magazine* 50 (February 2005): 99–102.
18. Melissa Klein Aguilar, "Questions Arise on Timely Ethics Disclosure," *Compliance Week* 7 (March 2010): 58–59.
19. Howard Stock, "Ethics Trump Rules, Levitt Says," *Investor Relations Business* (April 7, 2003): 1.

20. Richard McGill Murphy, "Why Doing Good Is Good for Business," *Fortune* 161 (February 8, 2010): 90–95.

21. "Ethics as Recruiting Tool," *Journal of Accountancy* 207 (January 2009): 21.

22. Andy Schotz, "Code Not Meant to be Rule or Law," *Quill* 98 (January/February 2010): 30.

23. Christopher Bauer, "Baking Ethics into Company Culture," *Financial Executive* 25 (May 2009): 18–21.

24. Peter R. Kensicki, "Create Your Own Ethical Statement," *National Underwriter* 106 (October 21, 2002): 33–34.

25. "Fidelity Fires Hong Kong Managers," *Fund Action* (February 22, 2010): 76.

26. Samuel Greengard, "Golden Values," *Workforce Management* 84 (March 2005): 52–53.

27. Sven Erik Holmes, "Under Pressure: Maintaining an Effective Ethics and Compliance Program," *Directorship* 35 (October/November 2009): 72.

28. "Few Tie Executive Pay or Bonuses to Compliance," *Compliance Week* 6 (July 2009): 10.

29. S. Steffee, "Weak Link between Business Ethics and Executive Compensation," *Internal Auditor* 66 (August 2009): 16.

30. Patricia J. Harned, "Encourage Ethical Behavior as Economy Recovers," *HR Specialist: Compensation & Benefits* 5 (January 2010): 5.

31. "What Makes a Good HR Leader?" *HR Focus* 86 (May 2009): 8.

32. Ken Sloan and Joanne H. Gavin, "Human Resource Management: Meeting the Ethical Obligations of the Function," *Business & Society Review* 115 (Spring 2010): 57–74.

33. William A. Nelson and John Donnellan, "An Executive-Driven Ethical Culture," *Healthcare Executive* 24 (November/December 2009): 44–46.

34. Curtis C. Verschoor, "How Good Is Your Ethics and Compliance Program?" *Strategic Finance* 88 (April 2007): 19–20.

35. Cynthia Kincaid, "Corporate Ethics Training: The Right Stuff," *Training* 46 (May 2009): 35.

36. Luis Ramos, "Outside-the-Box Ethics," *Leadership Excellence* 26 (April 2009): 19.

37. "Are Enough of Your Employees Getting Ethics Training?" *Broker Magazine* 10 (April 2008): 7.

38. Jerry Maginnis and Joseph P. Charles, "Build a Strong Ethical Culture," *Pennsylvania CPA Journal* 80 (Summer 2009): 1–2.

39. Ron Miller, "It's a Small World After All," *EContent* 31 (January/February 2008): 26–31.

40. Kellye Whitney, "Ernst & Young Ethics Training: Part of the Company Fabric," *Chief Learning Officer* 6 (July 2007): 32.

41. Cynthia Kincaid, "Corporate Ethics Training: The Right Stuff," *Training* 46 (May 2009): 35.

42. Eric Krell, "How to Conduct an Ethics Audit," *HRMagazine* 55 (April 2010): 48–51.

43. Jennifer L. Baker, Janice M. Dahl, "How Are Your Ethics?" *Associations Now* 5 (February 2009): 43–46.

44. About The Society for Human Resource Management, http://www.shrm.org/about, February 13, 2010.

45. SHRM Staffing Management Focus Area, http://www.shrm.org/hrdisciplines/staffingmanagement/, February 13, 2010.

46. http://www.hrci.org/aboutus/history/ History-of-HR-Certification-Institute, February 13, 2010.

47. American Society for Training & Development, http://www.astd.org/ASTD/aboutus, February 13, 2010.

48. Certified Professional in Learning and Performance (CPLP), http://www.astd.org/content/ASTDcertification, February 13, 2010.

49. About WorldatWork, The Total Rewards Association, http://www.worldatwork.org/waw/myprofile/html/profile-join.html, February 13, 2010.

50. "News and Trends," *Nation's Restaurant News* 42 (February 18, 2008): 32.

51. Simon Zadek, "Responsibility Isn't a Blame Game," *Fortune (Europe)* 152 (October 3, 2005): 70–73.

52. Michael Laff, "Triple Bottom Line," *T+D* 63 (February 2009): 34–39.

53. Ibid.

54. Jaclyn Jaeger, "Choosing Among a Vast Array of CSR Initiatives," *Compliance Week* 6 (October 2009): 60–70.

55. Adrienne Fox, "Be an Insider on Social Responsibility," *HRMagazine* 53 (February 2008): 75–77.

56. Ibid.

57. Ibid.

58. Ibid.

59. Ibid.

60. "Social Responsibility: An Ongoing Mission for a Good Corporate Citizen," *Nation's Restaurant News* (April 11, 2005): 60–66.

61. John S. McClenahen, "Defining Social Responsibility," *Industry Week* 254 (March 2005): 64–65.

62. Telis Demos, "Managing Beyond the Bottom Line," *Fortune (Europe)* 152 (October 3, 2005): 68–70.

63. Mike Hofman, "The Best Cause of All," *Inc.* 30 (June 2008): 23–24.

64. "When Does Philanthropy Pay?" *HRMagazine* 53 (May 2008): 12.

65. Quoted in Robert Bolt, *A Man for All Seasons* (New York: Random House, 1962).

66. John Peloza, "Using Corporate Social Responsibility as Insurance for Financial Performance," *California Management Review* 48 (Winter 2006): 52–72.

67. Garrett Brown, "Corporate Social Responsibility: The Moment of Truth Arrives," *Industrial Safety & Hygiene News* 43 (May 2009): 36.
68. Ibid.
69. Ibid.
70. Ibid.
71. Ibid.
72. Ibid.
73. Andreas King, "How to Get Started in Corporate Social Responsibility," *Financial Management* (October 2002): 5.

3 Workforce Diversity, Equal Employment Opportunity, and Affirmative Action

HRM in Action: Do-it-yourself Diversity in Times of Recession

Recruiting older workers has been something many companies may have shied away from in the past. After all, aren't older workers supposed to be resistant to change, work at a slower pace, and have more time off work? Well, these are at least some of the myths surrounding the employment of more mature employees. In the past, older workers have tended to suffer more in recessions and the prospects of many workers over 50 returning to work once they are out of employment has normally been bleak, particularly for men. Attitudes in the United Kingdom have been changing, but, even so, the government has felt it necessary to enact legislation to ensure older workers are fairly treated in the shape of the 2006 Age Discrimination Act.

Fortunately, for some companies, employing and retaining older workers even in times of recession makes great business sense. B & Q, a large do-it-yourself specialist in the UK, found this to be particularly true after branching out into giant warehouse style stores a few years ago. However, their commitment to a diverse workforce goes much further back than that, and since the 1980s they have had an over 50's recruitment policy in place. Consequently, boomers and other older workers now make up 25 percent of the B & Q workforce.

For B & Q there have always been good reasons for the recruitment of older employees. Firstly, older workers make up a large and increasing proportion of the UK workforce and this is set to increase when the retirement age is raised. Secondly, B & Q believe that older workers already possess a sound knowledge of DIY as well as life experiences that can

After completing this chapter, students should be able to:

1. Describe the projected future diverse workforce by the year 2050.

2. Describe diversity and diversity management.

3. Explain the various components of the diverse workforce.

4. Identify the major laws affecting equal employment opportunity.

5. Identify some of the major Supreme Court decisions that have had an impact on equal employment opportunity and affirmative action.

6. Describe the Equal Employment Opportunity Commission.

7. Explain the purpose of the *Uniform Guidelines on Employee Selection Procedures*.

8. Describe disparate treatment and adverse impact.

9. Describe the *Uniform Guidelines* related to sexual harassment, national origin, and religion.

10. Explain caregiver discrimination.

11. Explain affirmative action as required by presidential Executive Orders 11246 and 11375.

12. Describe affirmative action programs.

contribute to good customer service. They believe that the profile of their staff should match more closely the profile of their customer base. Experience from older workers can also be passed on to younger recruits, thus older employees can make excellent mentors.

B & Q were so confident about the value of older employees that in 1989 they opened two stores entirely staffed by workers over 50 in Exmouth and Macclesfield in order to benchmark these against four typical supercenters. Subsequent research in conjunction with Warwick University found that profits in the two stores were 18 percent higher, staff turnover was six times lower, and absenteeism improved by 39 percent. In addition, there was an improvement in how customer service was perceived and the skills base of their employees was also enhanced. These findings more than vindicated B & Q's belief in the value of older workers and, needless to say, they have continued to repudiate ageism and promote a truly diverse workforce.

Research conducted amongst the over 50's at B &Q suggested that they valued the opportunity to interact with customers and share their life skills with them. Like the rest of the workforce, older workers have the opportunity to work flexibly and 62 percent of the workforce now works flexible hours. Unlike some other organizations, B & Q does not insist on its employees retiring at the government statutory retirement age. They believe that age is no barrier, and that employees can make a valuable contribution far beyond that age—the oldest employee is over 90 years of age.

B & Q make every attempt to promote their values in terms of age and diversity and as such they are founder members of the Employers Forum on Age. They actively encourage other businesses to follow their lead by employing a more age-diverse workforce. Marks and Spencer's and Tesco are just two notable examples of this and the continued success of these companies in times of recession is testament to the value of this policy.[1]

In this chapter, we first describe the importance of keeping the boomers in recession times. Then the projected future diverse workforce into the year 2050 is explained, followed by a discussion of diversity and diversity management and the various components of the diverse workforce. The development of this diverse workforce did not just happen; laws, executive orders, and Supreme Court decisions have had a major impact in formulating this new work environment. Therefore, the second part of this chapter provides an overview of the major Equal Employment Opportunity legislation that impacted human resource management and helped to create this diverse workforce. Toward this end, significant equal employment opportunity laws affecting human resource management are discussed; significant Supreme Court decisions affecting equal employment opportunity and affirmative action are presented; and the Equal Employment Opportunity Commission is described. The *Uniform Guidelines on Employee Selection Procedures* are then explained and the issues of disparate treatment and adverse impact are addressed. Additional guidelines on employee selection procedures are also explained in addition to caregiver discrimination. The importance of presidential Executive Orders 11246 and 11375 and affirmative action programs is also discussed. This chapter concludes with a global perspective feature entitled "Multinational Whistle-blowing."

Workforce Projection: 2050[2]

The U.S. labor force was 125.8 million in 1990, 142.6 million in 2000, and 149.3 million in 2005. It is projected to reach 166.4 million in 2020 and 194.8 million in 2050. The 0.6-percent annual growth rate from 2005 to 2050 reflects a projected population of 322.6 million and a labor force participation rate of 60.4 percent by 2050. The period to 2050 will witness the baby-boom generation ascending the age ladder until the group moves out of the labor force. The growth rate of the labor force was significantly affected by the sizable increase in the labor force participation of women during the 1970s and 1980s. However, women's labor force participation rates appear to have peaked at 60 percent.

Of all the age groups, the prime-aged workers (25 to 54 years) have the strongest ties to the labor market. Their labor force numbered 88.3 million in 1990, 101.4 million in 2000, and 102.8 million in 2005. The Bureau projects that, by 2050, the prime-aged workforce will reach 124.4 million. The number of persons 55 years and older who are working is on an upward trend, with an annual growth rate several times the rate of the overall labor force. There were 15 million workers 55 years and older in 1990, accounting for nearly 12 percent of the labor force. In 2020, the 55-years and-older age group will reach 39.6 million and have a 23.8-percent share of the labor force. By 2050, the group will number more than 44.6 million workers and constitute 23.0 percent of the labor force. Within this age group, the 55- to 64-year-olds are projected to be 28.4 million in 2020 and the 65- to 74-year-olds are expected to be nearly 9 million then.

Immigration will further diversify the population and the labor force in the future. The Hispanic labor force was 10.7 million in 1990, but is expected to reach 47.3 million in 2050, 24.3 percent of the total labor force. The Asian labor force also is expected to grow at an annual rate of 2.0 percent and is projected to reach 9.5 million in 2020 and 16.1 million, or 8.3 percent of the total workforce, in 2050. The black labor force is projected to reach 20.7 million in 2020 and 26.8 million in 2050, nearly 14 percent of the total labor force. The white non-Hispanic share of the total labor force is projected to decrease from nearly 70 percent in 2005 to 51.4 percent in 2050. In addition, the retirement of the baby boomers, a group that has a large share of white non-Hispanics—especially white non-Hispanic men—will further lower the white non-Hispanic share of the total labor force.

Immigration accounts for more than 40 percent of the growth of the U.S population. In fact, according to the U.S. Bureau of Labor Statistics, foreign-born workers numbered 24 million in 2008, or 16 percent of the U.S. civilian labor force age 16 and older. According to the Census Bureau's Web site, the United States posts one birth every 8 seconds, one death every 11 seconds, one (net) international migrant every 31 seconds, and a net gain of one person every 14 seconds. Changes in future immigration policies could affect the growth rate of the population, which is the major factor in labor force projections.

The median age is defined as that age in which half the population is older and half is younger. With increases in life expectancies and decreases in fertility, the median age of the U.S. population, as well as that of the labor force, has increased significantly. The overall median age of the labor force is projected to continue to increase and reach 42 years in 2020.

Diversity and Diversity Management

OBJECTIVE 3.2
Describe diversity and diversity management.

diversity
Any perceived difference among people: age, race, religion, functional specialty, profession, sexual orientation, geographic origin, lifestyle, tenure with the organization or position, and any other perceived difference.

Twenty-five years ago, diversity was primarily concerned with race and gender.[3] Today, the definition is quite different. **Diversity** refers to any perceived difference among people: age, race, religion, functional specialty, profession, sexual orientation, geographic origin, lifestyle, tenure with the organization or position, and any other perceived difference.

The challenge for managers in the future will be to recognize that people with characteristics that are common but are different from those in the mainstream, often think, act, learn, and communicate differently. Because every person, culture, and business situation is unique, there are no simple rules for managing diversity, but diversity experts say that employers need to develop patience, open-mindedness, acceptance, and cultural awareness. Diversity is more than equal employment and affirmative action (topics to be discussed later in this chapter); the actual definition is constantly changing and expanding.[4] Diversity aims to create workforces that mirror the populations and customers that organizations serve.[5] R. Roosevelt Thomas Jr., former president of the American Institute for Managing Diversity, clarified some misconceptions about diversity in corporate America when he said, "People vary along an infinite number of possibilities." Thomas also believes, "They vary according to race and gender, but they also vary according to age, sexual orientation, and when they joined the company. Some workers are union members; some are not. Some are exempt; some are nonexempt. The variety is endless. Your definition has to be sufficiently broad to encompass everyone."[6] In a recent study, diversity was among the most important predictors of sales revenue, customer numbers, and profitability.[7]

diversity management
Ensuring that factors are in place to provide for and encourage the continued development of a diverse workforce by melding actual and perceived differences among workers to achieve maximum productivity.

Diversity management is ensuring that factors are in place to provide for and encourage the continued development of a diverse workforce by melding these actual and perceived differences among workers to achieve maximum productivity.

"If organizations want to remain competitive in the marketplace, diversity has to be a part of the strategic goal," said Susan Meisinger, former president and CEO of SHRM.[8] American Honda Motor Co. has opened an office that promotes workplace diversity. Marc Burt, senior manager of Honda's Office of Inclusion and Diversity, said, "he seeks to empower Honda employees of all cultural and ethnic backgrounds to feel comfortable expressing ideas. Diverse ideas will help us create products that are more appealing to people who buy them."[9]

According to a SHRM survey, workforce diversity is becoming a top-level initiative around the world.[10] In a Gallup survey, 61 percent of respondents who placed their company's diversity efforts in the upper third of companies surveyed said they are extremely satisfied with their company. But among employees who rate their company's diversity efforts in the lower third, only 21 percent said they were extremely satisfied with their company.[11]

HR Web Wisdom

Workforce diversity

http://www.doi.gov/ diversity

Current diversity news is provided.

Diversity management is about pursuing an inclusive culture in which newcomers feel welcome, and everyone sees the value of his or her job. It involves creating a supportive culture in which all employees can be effective. In creating this culture it is important that top management strongly support workplace diversity as a company goal and include diversity initiatives in their companies' business strategies. It has grown out of the need for organizations to recognize the changing workforce and other social pressures that often result. Achieving diversity is more than being politically correct; it is about fostering a culture that values individuals and their wide array of needs and contributions. Diversity is therefore viewed as a benefit to the firm.[12] Promoting diversity can be a sound business strategy that leads to increased market share and a reputation as being a place people want to work.

OBJECTIVE 3.3
Explain the various components of the diverse workforce.

Components of the Diverse Workforce

Components that combine to make up the diverse workforce will be discussed next.

Single Parents and Working Mothers

The number of single-parent households in the United States is growing. Although the divorce rate peaked in the early 1980s, the percentage of marriages ending in divorce remains around 50 percent. Often, one or more children are involved. Of course, there are always widows and widowers who have children, and there are some men and women who choose to raise children outside of wedlock. Approximately 72 percent of mothers with children under 18 are in the workforce, a figure up sharply from 47 percent in 1975.[13] A recent study concluded that being a mother does not significantly change young women's career ambitions.[14]

Managers need to be sensitive to the needs of working parents. Many women who formerly remained at home to care for children and the household now need and want to work outside the home. If this valuable segment of the workforce is to be effectively utilized, organizations must fully recognize the importance of addressing work-family issues. Businesses are seeing that providing child-care services and workplace flexibility may influence workers' choice of employers. More and more companies provide paid maternity leave, and some offer paternity leave. Companies that were chosen in the top among *Working Mother* magazine's 100 best companies to work for placed greater emphasis on work-life balance, telecommuting, and flextime.[15] The topic of workplace flexibility will be discussed in greater detail in Chapter 10.

Women in Business

Numerous factors have contributed to the growth and development of the U.S. labor force. However, nothing has been more prominent than the rise in the number of women in the labor force. In fact in 2010, for the first time ever, women made up the majority of the American workforce.[16] More and more women are entering the labor force in high-paying, professional jobs. Therefore, the base of building a diverse workforce rests on an employer's ability to attract and retain women.

Professional women are entering the workforce at the same rates as men.[17] However, many are opting out of the corporate life. But this does not mean that they are opting out of business careers. Instead, they are making their own career paths that allow them to combine work and life on their own terms. As a result, organizations are losing talented employees in whom they have made substantial investments.[18] Numerous companies are working diligently to keep professional women in the workforce although more work needs to be done. Many of the workplace flexibility topics discussed in Chapter 10 such as flextime, telecommuting, and job sharing are having a major impact on retaining women in the workforce.[19]

Many women who quit the corporate world are now starting their own businesses. For example, according to The Guardian Small Business Research Institute, women-owned small businesses will contribute more than 5 million new jobs across the United States within the next 10 years. Women-owned small businesses will generate more than half of the 9.72 million new small business jobs and approximately one-third of the 15.3 million total new jobs anticipated by 2018.[20]

Mothers Returning to the Workforce

Today, more new mothers are leaving the labor force only to return later. To get them to return, companies are going beyond federal law and giving mothers a year or more for maternity leave. Other businesses are specifically trying to recruit them.

While some companies are recruiting these women, other employers have programs that help their own employees leave and later return. IBM offers a program that allows employees to take up to three years off. Typically, working mothers who use the program take a year or more off, and then they use the remainder of their leave to re-enter work on a part-time basis. After the three years are up, they have the option of returning either full- or part-time. IBM surveyed employees who had taken the leave and found 59 percent would have left the company if the program had not been available. "We didn't want a situation where women had to opt out," says Maria Ferris, manager of work-life and women's initiatives at IBM. "We've invested in them, trained them. We want to retain them."[21]

Dual-Career Families

dual-career family
A situation in which both husband and wife have jobs and family responsibilities.

The increasing number of **dual-career families**, families in which both husband and wife have jobs and family responsibilities, presents both challenges and opportunities for organizations. Women in dual career families are contributing more to family income, from 39 percent in 1997 to 44 percent in 2008.[22] The majority of children growing up today have both parents working outside the home.[23] Households consisting of a male breadwinner married to a housewife were a majority in the U.S. in 1950, but in the 21st century the proportion of U.S. households is less than 20 percent.[24]

Today, employees have turned down relocations because of spouses' jobs and concerns about their children. Of the top three reasons employees turn down assignments, family or spouse's career is cited almost twice as often as concern with the employee's career or compensation.[25] As a result, firms are developing polices to assist the spouse of an employee who is transferred. Some are offering assistance in finding a position for the spouse of a transferred employee.

Some dual-career families have established long-distance jobs to ensure that both couples are able to advance in their careers. The shift is coming as job relocations create a mobile workforce, leaving many professional couples grappling with career tracks that diverge. More are choosing to live in separate cities so both partners can get ahead. However, companies may need to learn how to handle dual-career couples as more and more companies go global. If companies make the willingness to locate globally a requirement for promotion, many in this group will reject the offer, thereby reducing the size of the labor pool.

Workers of Color

Workers of color (including Hispanics, African Americans, and Asians) are at times stereotyped. They may encounter misunderstandings and expectations based on ethnic or cultural differences. Members of ethnic or racial groups are socialized within their particular culture. Many are socialized as members of two cultural groups, the dominant culture and their racial or ethnic culture. Ella Bell, professor of organizational behavior at MIT, refers to this dual membership as biculturalism. In her study of African-American women, Bell identifies the stress of coping with membership in two cultures simultaneously as bicultural stress. She indicates that role conflict, competing roles from two cultures; and role overload, too many expectations to comfortably fulfill, are common characteristics of bicultural stress. Although these issues can be applied to other minority groups, they are particularly intense for women of color. This is because this group experiences dynamics affecting both minorities and women.[26]

Socialization in one's culture of origin can lead to misunderstandings in the workplace. This is particularly true when the manager relies solely on the cultural norms of the majority group. According to these norms, within the American culture it is acceptable, even considered positive, to publicly praise an individual for a job well done. However, in cultures that place primary value on group harmony and collective achievement, this method of rewarding an employee may cause emotional discomfort. Some employees feel that, if praised publicly, they will lose face within their group.

Older Workers

As a result of the recession of 2008/10, 60 percent of workers over age 60 say they are putting off their retirement because of the impact of the financial crisis on their long-term savings and some say that they may never retire.[27] Further, some who have retired are re-entering the workforce because of losses to their 401(k) plans.[28] An offshoot of older workers remaining longer is causing problems for the new generation of workers since job vacancies are decreasing.[29]

But ultimately they will retire and businesses are wondering how they are going to be able to replace them. Several challenges are expected to be encountered by employers as boomers begin to retire en masse. First, institutional memory or corporate culture will begin to disappear. Essentially a brain drain will occur once massive retirements occur.[30] Second, rising pension and health care costs will affect labor cost. Finally, experienced and qualified managers will be difficult to replace.[31]

Numerous organizations today are actively courting older employees to entice them to remain on the job longer (remember the HRM in Action at the beginning of the chapter). To do so, a culture needs to be developed that will encourage them to remain.[32] They are doing everything from restructuring jobs to offering phased-retirement plans. As the workforce ages, its needs and interests may change. Some will become bored with their present careers and desire different challenges. According to a recent study by AARP's Public Policy Institute, less stress and more flexibility are two of the top priorities for older workers and retirees who opt to switch jobs or "recareer," even if they will have to take pay cuts and give up benefits and managerial responsibilities.[33]

People with Disabilities

Common disabilities include limited hearing or sight, limited mobility, mental or emotional deficiencies, and various nerve disorders. Such disabilities limit the amount or kind of work a person can do or make its achievement unusually difficult. In jobs for which they are qualified, however, disabled workers do as well as unimpaired workers in terms of productivity, attendance, and average tenure. In fact, in certain high-turnover occupations, disabled workers have lower turnover rates. A recent Department of Labor survey found that a majority of large businesses are hiring people with disabilities and discovering that costs for accommodations differ very little from those for the general employee population. The survey also showed that once an employer hires one person with a disability, it is much more likely that employer will hire other people with disabilities.[34] Walgreens recently opened its second state-of-the-art distribution center in Windsor, Connecticut, designed specifically to employ people with disabilities. Its goal is to fill at least one-third of the available jobs with individuals with disabilities.[35]

Immigrants

Large numbers of immigrants from Asia and Latin America have settled in many parts of the United States. Some are highly skilled and well educated and others are only minimally qualified and have little education. They have one thing in common: an eagerness to work. They have brought with them attitudes, values, and mores particular to their home country cultures. After the end of hostilities in Vietnam, Vietnamese immigrants settled along the Mississippi and Texas Gulf Coast. At about the same time, thousands of Thais fleeing the upheaval in Thailand came to the Boston area to work and live. New York's Puerto Rican community has long been an economic and political force there. Cubans who fled Castro's regime congregated in southern Florida, especially Miami. A flood of Mexicans and other Hispanics continues across the southern border of the United States. The Irish, the Poles, the Italians, and others who came here in past decades have long since assimilated into, and indeed became, the culture. Newer immigrants require time to adapt. Meanwhile, they generally take low-paying and menial jobs, live in substandard housing, and form enclaves where they cling to some semblance of the cultures they left.

Wherever they settle, members of these ethnic groups soon begin to become part of the regular workforce in certain occupations and break out of their isolation. They begin to adopt the English language and American customs. They learn new skills and adapt old skills to their new country. Managers can place these individuals in jobs appropriate to their skills, with excellent results for the organization. As corporations employ more foreign nationals in this country, managers must work to understand the different cultures of their employees.

Foreign Workers

The H-1B employment visa brings in upwards of 115,000 skilled foreign workers annually, including some 30,000 researchers and academicians not subject to the annual visa cap set by Congress. Of those 115,000, 85,000 are distributed to employers through a lottery system each

April held by U.S. Citizenship and Immigration Services (USCIS), an arm of the U.S. Department of Homeland Security (DHS). However, the exact number of H-1B visa holders is difficult to determine. A three-year initial visa can be renewed for another three years, and if a worker is on track for a green card, H-1B status can be renewed annually.[36]

Until the recession of 2008/10 hit the U.S., demand far outpaced supply, and companies constantly encouraged Congress to raise the cap. Many employers say the H-1B visa program provided the only practical avenue for finding high-tech workers with cutting-edge skills.[37] Others do not agree and there continues to be a debate regarding the hiring of foreign workers. Still, U.S. employers at both ends of the skills spectrum say they have no choice.[38]

Young Persons with Limited Education or Skills

The unemployment rate for 16-to-19-year-olds as of November 2009 was 27 percent, the highest recorded since the government began tracking it in the 1940s.[39] Even so, each year, thousands of young, unskilled workers are hired, especially during peak periods, such as holiday buying seasons. These workers generally have limited education, sometimes even less than a high school diploma. Those who have completed high school often find that their education hardly fits the work they are expected to do. Many of these young adults and teenagers have poor work habits; they tend to be tardy or absent more often than experienced or better-educated workers.

Although the negative attributes of these workers at times seem to outweigh the positive ones, they are a permanent part of the workforce. Certainly, when teenagers are hired, an organization is not hiring maturity or experience; but young people possess many qualities, such as energy, enthusiasm, excitement, and eagerness to prove themselves. There are many jobs they can do well. More jobs can be de-skilled, making it possible for lower-skilled workers to do them. A well-known example of de-skilling is McDonald's use of pictures on its cash register keys. Managers should also look for ways to train unskilled workers and to further their formal education.

Equal Employment Opportunity: An Overview

As can be seen from the previous discussion, the workforce of today has become truly diverse. But, this was not the case in the early 1960s; in fact, little of the workforce of those days remotely resembles that of today. Then, few mainstream opportunities were available to women, minorities, and those with disabilities. If this were so today, our economy would certainly grind to a halt. But diversity did not just happen. Legislation (federal, state, and local), Supreme Court decisions, and executive orders have encouraged both public and private organizations to tap the abilities of a workforce that was largely underused before the mid-1960s. The concept of equal employment opportunity has undergone much modification and fine-tuning since the passage of the Equal Pay Act of 1963, the Civil Rights Act of 1964, and the Age Discrimination in Employment Act of 1967.

Numerous amendments to these acts have been passed, as well as other acts in response to oversights in the initial legislation. Major Supreme Court decisions interpreting the provisions of the acts have also been handed down. Presidential executive orders were signed into law that provided for affirmative action. Nearly five decades have passed since the introduction of the first legislation, and equal employment opportunity has become an integral part of the workplace.

Although equal employment opportunity has come a long way since the early 1960s, continuing efforts are required because some problems still exist. While perfection is elusive, the majority of businesses today do attempt to make employment decisions based on who is the best qualified, as opposed to whether an individual is of a certain gender, race, religion, color, national origin, or age or is disabled. Throughout the remainder of this chapter, hiring standards to avoid will be identified based on some of the laws, executive orders, and Supreme Court decisions that have had a major impact in creating this diverse workforce.

OBJECTIVE 3.4
Identify the major laws affecting equal employment opportunity.

Laws Affecting Equal Employment Opportunity

Numerous national laws have been passed that have had an impact on equal employment opportunity. The passage of these laws reflects society's attitude toward the changes that should be made to give everyone an equal opportunity for employment. The most significant of these laws will be described in the following sections.

Civil Rights Act of 1866

The oldest federal legislation affecting staffing is the Civil Rights Act of 1866, which is based on the Thirteenth Amendment to the U.S. Constitution. Specifically, this Act provides that all citizens have the same right "as enjoyed by white citizens . . . to inherit, purchase . . . hold, and convey . . . property, [and that] all persons . . . shall have the same right to make and enforce contracts . . . as enjoyed by white citizens." As interpreted by the courts, employment, as well as membership in a union, is a contractual arrangement. Blacks and Hispanics are covered by this Act if they are discriminated against on the basis of race. Until 1968, it was assumed that the Act was applicable only when action by a state or state agency, and not by private parties, was involved. That year the Supreme Court overruled this assumption and broadened the interpretation of the Act to cover all contractual arrangements. There is no statute of limitations to the Act, as evidenced by the fact that it continues to be used today. For example, in 2008, the Supreme Court ruled 7–2 in the case of *CBOCS West Inc. v Humphries,* that there is an implied right to sue on a retaliation basis under the Civil Rights Act of 1866, even though that law does not explicitly include a cause of action for retaliation. A former African-American Cracker Barrel assistant manager claimed he was fired for complaining to management about race discrimination.[40]

Equal Pay Act of 1963, Amended in 1972

Passed as an amendment to the Fair Labor Standards Act, the Equal Pay Act of 1963 (EPA) prohibits an employer from paying an employee of one gender less money than an employee of the opposite gender, if both employees do work that is substantially the same. The Act was passed largely to overcome the outdated belief that a man should be paid more in society than a woman and covers work within the same physical place of business. For example, an employer could pay a female more in San Francisco than a male working in the same position in Slippery Rock, Pennsylvania, even if the jobs were substantially the same, because of the cost-of-living difference. A key point to remember is that the pay difference must be substantial and that small pay differences might be acceptable. Once a prima facie case of gender discrimination under the EPA has been made, then liability may be avoided by showing one of the following affirmative defenses which allow unequal pay for equal work:

- Seniority system
- Merit system
- System which measures earnings by quantity or quality of production
- Any other factor other than sex

For the first nine years of the EPA, the requirement of equal pay for equal work did not extend to persons employed in an executive, administrative, or professional capacity, or as an outside salesperson. In 1972, Congress enacted the Educational Amendment of 1972, which now covers those individuals. One thing is certain, the Equal Pay Act has teeth and they will get sharper because the U.S. Department of Labor is aggressively enforcing the Act and seeking harsher penalties against companies that violate it.

Lilly Ledbetter Fair Pay Act of 2009

In the 2007 Supreme Court case of *Ledbetter v Goodyear Tire & Rubber Co., Inc.,* the Court said that discrimination charges must be filed within 180 days after the allegedly discriminatory pay decision. Lilly Ledbetter had worked for Goodyear for many years but she did not realize until she was close to retirement that she was being discriminated against because of pay. Since she did not file a discrimination charge within 180 day of her employment, the Supreme Court ruled against her. In order to reverse the Ledbetter decision, the Lilly Ledbetter Fair Pay Act was passed by Congress and signed into law in 2009.[41] The law creates a rolling or open time frame for filing wage discrimination claims.[42] Each paycheck that unfairly pays a worker less than it should is a discriminatory act. The Act gives the worker a fresh 180-day period (300 days in some states) to file a charge of discrimination with the EEOC. The law covers Equal Pay Act claims pending at the EEOC or in federal court as of May 28, 2007.[43] As a result of the law, Dianna Johnston, EEOC assistant legal counsel, said, "employers should keep records longer for "performance appraisals that affect pay and job classification decisions."[44]

Comparable Worth

comparable worth
Determination of the values of dissimilar jobs (such as company nurse and welder) by comparing them under some form of job evaluation, and the assignment of pay rates according to their evaluated worth.

Since the passage of the Equal Pay Act, there has been much discussion to expand its coverage to include the concept comparable worth, or pay equity. **Comparable worth** requires determination of the values of dissimilar jobs (such as company nurse and welder) by comparing them under some form of job evaluation, and the assignment of pay rates according to their evaluated worth. While the Equal Pay Act requires equal pay for equal work, comparable worth advocates prefer a broader interpretation of requiring equal pay for comparable worth, even if market rates vary and job duties are considerably different. Although the Supreme Court has ruled the law does not require comparable worth, a number of state and local governments, along with some jurisdictions in Canada, have passed legislation mandating this version of pay fairness.

Title VII of the Civil Rights Act of 1964, Amended 1972

The statute that has had the greatest impact on equal employment opportunity is Title VII of the Civil Rights Act of 1964, as amended by the Equal Employment Act of 1972. Under Title VII, it is illegal for an employer to discriminate in hiring, firing, promoting, compensating, or in terms, conditions, or privileges of employment on the basis of race, color, sex, religion, or national origin. The Act also forbids retaliation against an employee who has participated in an investigation, proceeding, or hearing. The Supreme Court ruling in *Vicky S. Crawford v Metropolitan Government of Nashville and Davidson County, Tennessee* said that Title VII protection of the Civil Rights Act extends beyond employees who file complaints about discrimination to employees who cooperate in an employer's investigation.[45]

Title VII covers employers engaged in or affecting interstate commerce who have 15 or more employees for each working day in each of 20 calendar weeks in the current or preceding calendar year. Also included in the definition of employers are state and local governments, schools, colleges, unions, and private employment agencies that procure employees for an employer with 15 or more employees. All private employers who are subject to the Civil Rights Act of 1964 as amended with 100 employees or more must annually submit an EEO-1 (see Figure 3.1).

Three notable exceptions to discrimination as covered by Title VII are bona fide occupational qualifications (BFOQs), seniority and merit systems, and testing and educational requirements. According to the Act it is not: an unlawful employment practice for an employer to hire and employ employees . . . on the basis of his religion, sex, or national origin in those certain instances where religion, sex, or national origin is a bona fide occupational qualification reasonably necessary to the normal operation of the particular business or enterprise. For example, religious institutions, such as churches or synagogues, may legally refuse to hire teachers whose religious persuasion is different from that of the hiring institution. Likewise, a maximum-security correctional institution housing only male inmates may decline to hire females as security guards. The concept of bona fide occupational qualification was designed to be narrowly, not broadly, interpreted and has been so construed by the courts in a number of cases. The burden of proving the necessity for a BFOQ rests entirely on the employer.

The second exception to discrimination under Title VII is a bona fide seniority system such as the type normally contained in a union contract. Differences in employment conditions among workers are permitted, provided that such differences are not the result of an intention to discriminate because of race, color, religion, sex, or national origin. Even if a bona fide seniority system has an adverse impact on those individuals protected by Title VII (i.e., it affects a class or group), the system can be invalidated only by evidence that the actual motives of the parties to the agreement were to discriminate.

Finally, in the matter of testing and educational requirements, Title VII states that it is not "an unlawful employment practice for an employer to give, and to act upon, the results of any professionally developed ability test provided that such test, its administration, or action upon the results is not designed, intended, or used to discriminate because of race, color, religion, sex, or national origin." Employment testing and educational requirements must be job-related, and when adverse impact is shown, the burden of proof is on the employer to establish that a demonstrable relationship exists between actual job performance and the test or educational requirement.

Persons not covered by Title VII include aliens not authorized to work in the United States and members of the Communist party. Homosexuals are also not protected under Title VII. The courts have consistently ruled that where the term *sex* is used in any federal statute that term refers to biological gender and not to sexual preference.

Figure 3.1a

Equal Employment Opportunity Employer Information Report

Section D—EMPLOYMENT DATA   SF 100—Page 2

Employment at this establishment—Report all permanent full- and part-time employees including apprentices and on-the-job trainees unless specifically excluded as set forth in the instructions. Enter the appropriate figures on all lines and in all columns. Blank spaces will be considered as zeros.

Job Categories	Number of Employees (Report employees in only one category)														
	Race/Ethnicity														Total Col A - N
	Hispanic or Latino		Not-Hispanic or Latino												
			Male						Female						
	Male	Female	White	Black or African American	Native Hawaiian or Other Pacific Islander	Asian	American Indian or Alaska Native	Two or more races	White	Black or African American	Native Hawaiian or Other Pacific Islander	Asian	American Indian or Alaska Native	Two or more races	
	A	B	C	D	E	F	G	H	I	J	K	L	M	N	O
Executive/Senior Level Officials and Managers 1.1															
First/Mid-Level Officials and Managers 1.2															
Professionals 2															
Technicians 3															
Sales Workers 4															
Administrative Support Workers 5															
Craft Workers 6															
Operatives 7															
Laborers and Helpers 8															
Service Workers 9															
TOTAL 10															
PREVIOUS YEAR TOTAL 11															

1. Date(s) of payroll period used: _____   (Omit on the Consolidated Report.)

Approval

O.M.B. No. 3046-0007
Revised 01/2006
Expires 1/2009

Figure 3.1b (*continued*)

The Civil Rights Act of 1964 also created the Equal Employment Opportunity Commission (EEOC) and assigned enforcement of Title VII to this agency. Consisting of five members appointed by the president, the EEOC is empowered to investigate, conciliate, and litigate charges of discrimination arising under provisions of Title VII. In addition, the commission has the responsibility of issuing procedural regulations and interpretations of Title VII and the other statutes it enforces. The most significant regulation issued by EEOC is the *Uniform Guidelines on Employee Selection Procedures* (discussed later).

The Act continues to be important. Recently Chicago-based Ceisel Masonry settled a race and national-origin discrimination suit with the EEOC for $500,000.[46] Talbert Builders agreed to settle a race discrimination suit with the EEOC for $80,000. The suit claimed that co-workers and supervisors had created a racially hostile work environment and the EEOC additionally required the firm's supervisors and employees to undergo training on race-based harassment.[47]

Pregnancy Discrimination Act of 1978

Passed as an amendment to Title VII of the Civil Rights Act, the Pregnancy Discrimination Act prohibits discrimination in employment based on pregnancy, childbirth, or related medical conditions. Questions regarding a woman's family and childbearing plans should not be asked. Similarly, questions relating to family plans, birth control techniques, and the like may be viewed as discriminatory because they are not asked of men. The basic principle of the Act is that women affected by pregnancy and related conditions must be treated the same as other applicants and employees on the basis of their ability or inability to work.[48] A woman is therefore protected against such practices as being fired or refused a job or promotion merely because

HR Web Wisdom

Office of Contract Compliance Programs

http://www.dol.gov/ofccp/

Home page for the OFCCP, the agency responsible for ensuring that employers doing business with the federal government comply with the laws and regulations requiring nondiscrimination and affirmative action.

she is pregnant or has had an abortion. She usually cannot be forced to take a leave of absence as long as she can work. If other employees on disability leave are entitled to return to their jobs when they are able to work again, so too are women who have been unable to work because of pregnancy. Also, limiting job advancement opportunities while a woman is pregnant may be a violation of the Act.

The same principle applies in the benefits area, including disability benefits, sick leave, and health insurance. A woman unable to work for pregnancy-related reasons is entitled to disability benefits or sick leave on the same basis as employees unable to work for other medical reasons. Also, any health insurance provided must cover expenses for pregnancy-related conditions on the same basis as expenses for other medical conditions. However, health insurance for expenses arising from an abortion is not required except where the life of the mother would be endangered if the fetus were carried to term or when medical complications have arisen from an abortion.

In a class action suit originally filed in 1978, but not settled until July 1991, American Telephone & Telegraph Company (AT&T) agreed to settle a pregnancy discrimination suit with the EEOC for $66 million. This suit was the largest cash recovery in the agency's history and involved more than 13,000 then-present and former female AT&T workers. The 1978 suit charged that Western Electric required pregnant workers to leave their jobs at the end of their sixth month of pregnancy, denied them seniority credit, and refused to guarantee them a job when they returned.

Pregnancy discrimination cases continue and pregnancy-discrimination settlements are at an all-time high. Recently, the Kinston, North Carolina-based Britthaven nursing home and assisted-living chain settled a pregnancy discrimination claim with the EEOC for $300,000. The agreement settles a lawsuit brought by pregnant employees who claimed they were treated differently from other employees because the company required them to obtain full medical clearance as soon as it learned they were pregnant. As a result, even though the women were still capable of performing their jobs, they were forced to take leave—or be terminated.[49]

Civil Rights Act of 1991

During 1988–1989, the Supreme Court rendered six employment discrimination decisions of such magnitude that a congressional response was required to overturn these decisions.[50] The result was passage of the Civil Rights Act of 1991. The Act amended five statutes: (1) the Civil Rights Act of 1866; (2) Title VII of the Civil Rights Act of 1964, as Amended; (3) the Age Discrimination in Employment Act of 1967, as Amended; (4) the Rehabilitation Act of 1973; and (5) the Americans with Disabilities Act of 1990.

The Civil Rights Act of 1991 had the following purposes:

- To provide appropriate remedies for intentional discrimination and unlawful harassment in the workplace.
- To codify the concepts of *business necessity* and *job-related* pronounced by the Supreme Court in *Griggs v Duke Power Co.*
- To confirm statutory authority and provide statutory guidelines for the adjudication of disparate impacts under Title VII of the Civil Rights Act of 1964. Disparate impact occurs when certain actions in the employment process work to the disadvantage of members of protected groups. Disparate impact will be discussed below under the concept of *Adverse Impact*.
- To respond to decisions of the Supreme Court by expanding the scope of relevant civil rights statutes in order to provide adequate protection to victims of discrimination.

Under this Act, a complaining party may recover punitive damages if the complaining party demonstrates that the company engaged in a discriminatory practice with malice or with reckless indifference to the law. However, the following limits, based on the number of people employed by the company, were placed on the amount of the award:

- Between 15 and 100 employees—$50,000
- Between 101 and 200 employees—$100,000
- Between 201 and 500 employees—$200,000
- More than 500 employees—$300,000

In each case, aggrieved employees must be with the firm for 20 or more calendar weeks in the current or preceding calendar year.

With regard to burden of proof, a complaining party must show that a particular employment practice causes a disparate impact on the basis of race, color, religion, sex, or national origin. It must also be shown that the company is unable to demonstrate that the challenged practice is job-related for the position in question and consistent with business necessity. The Act also extends the coverage of the Civil Rights Act of 1964 to extraterritorial employment. However, the Act does not apply to U.S. companies operating in other countries if compliance "would cause such employer, or a corporation controlled by such employer, to violate the laws of the country in which such workplace is located."[51] The Act also extends the nondiscrimination principles to Congress and other government agencies, such as the General Accounting Office and the Government Printing Office.

Also included in the Civil Rights Act of 1991 is the Glass Ceiling Act. The **glass ceiling** is the invisible barrier in organizations that impedes women and minorities from career advancement. This act established a Glass Ceiling Commission to study the manner in which businesses fill management and decision-making positions, the developmental and skill-enhancing practices used to foster the necessary qualifications for advancement to such positions, and the compensation programs and reward structures currently used in the workplace. It was also to study the limited progress made by minorities and women. It established an annual award for excellence in promoting a more diverse skilled workforce at the management and decision-making levels in business.

glass ceiling
Invisible barrier in organizations that impedes women and minorities from career advancement.

Age Discrimination in Employment Act of 1967, Amended in 1978 and 1986

As originally enacted, the Age Discrimination in Employment Act (ADEA) prohibited employers from discriminating against individuals who were 40 to 65 years old. The 1978 amendment provided protection for individuals who were at least 40, but less than 70 years old. In a 1986 amendment, employer discrimination against anyone age 40 or older is illegal. Questions asked about an applicant's age or date of birth may be ill-advised. However, a firm may ask for age information to comply with the child labor law. For example, the question could be asked, "Are you under the age of 18?" Also, questions about the ages of children, if any, could be potentially discriminatory because a close approximation of the applicant's age often is obtained through knowledge of the ages of the applicant's children. The EEOC is responsible for administering this Act. The Act pertains to employers who have 20 or more employees for 20 or more calendar weeks (either in the current or preceding calendar year); unions with 25 or more members; employment agencies; and federal, state, and local government subunits.

Because of the massive number of layoffs caused by the recession of 2008/10, age discrimination suits became the fastest-growing category of EEOC discrimination complaints. Recently, 24,582 age discrimination claims were filed with the agency which was a 28.7 percent increase over the previous year and approximately 9,000 more than in 2005.[52] Automotive rubber parts manufacturer Freudenberg-NOK G.P. settled a discrimination suit filed on behalf of a man claiming he was denied a job with the company because of his age. The settlement brought by the EEOC provides $80,000 to Timothy Poh, an applicant for the controller position at Freudenberg-NOK's Bristol, New Hampshire, site. Poh interviewed for the job and was told that although he was well-qualified, the company was looking for someone "not quite so old with as much experience." The firm eventually offered the position to two younger applicants and hired a younger, less-qualified person.[53]

Enforcement begins when a charge is filed, but the EEOC can review compliance even if no charge is filed. The Age Discrimination in Employment Act differs from Title VII of the Civil Rights Act in providing for a trial by jury and carrying a possible criminal penalty for violation of the Act. The trial-by-jury provision is important because juries are thought to have great sympathy for older people who may have been discriminated against. The criminal penalty provision means that a person may receive more than lost wages if discrimination is proved. The 1978 amendment also makes class action suits possible.

Age Can Actually Be a Bona Fide Occupational Qualification

Age can actually be a bona fide occupational qualification when it is reasonably necessary to the essence of the business, and the employer has a rational or factual basis for believing that all, or substantially all, people within an age class would not be able to perform satisfactorily. Courts have continued to rule that the Federal Aviation Administration adequately explained its long-standing rule that it can force commercial pilots to retire at age 60. The age 60 rule was first imposed in 1959 and was long controversial. However, in 2007, the retirement age for commercial pilots was raised to 65.

This ruling supported the 1974 Seventh Circuit Court decision that Greyhound did not violate the ADEA when it refused to hire persons 35 years of age or older as intercity bus drivers. Again, the likelihood of risk or harm to its passengers was involved. Greyhound presented evidence concerning degenerative physical and sensory changes that humans undergo at about age 35 that have a detrimental effect on driving skills, and that the changes are not detectable by physical tests.[54]

Rehabilitation Act of 1973

The Rehabilitation Act prohibits discrimination against disabled workers who are employed by certain government contractors and subcontractors and organizations that receive federal grants in excess of $2,500. Individuals are considered disabled if they have a physical or mental impairment that substantially limits one or more major life activities or if they have a record of such impairment. Protected under the Act are diseases and conditions such as epilepsy, cancer, cardiovascular disorders, AIDS, blindness, deafness, mental retardation, emotional disorders, and dyslexia.

There are two primary levels of the Act. All federal contractors or subcontractors exceeding the $2,500 base are required to post notices that they agree to take affirmative action to recruit, employ, and promote qualified disabled individuals. If the contract or subcontract exceeds $50,000, or if the contractor has 50 or more employees, the employer must prepare a written affirmative action plan for review by the Office of Federal Contract Compliance Programs (OFCCP), which administers the Act. In it, the contractor must specify that reasonable steps are being taken to hire and promote disabled persons.

In an interpretation of Section 8 of the Rehabilitation Act, federal technology buyers are forced to think about people who are blind, deaf, paralyzed, or have other disabilities before they buy software, computers, printers, copiers, fax machines, kiosks, telecommunications devices, or video and multimedia products. Federal Web-site designers also have to make their sites accessible to disabled users, and anyone in government who develops or maintains technology products has to make sure those technologies are accessible. Recently, the OFCCP announced it would be reviewing contractors' online application systems "to ensure the contractor is providing equal opportunity to qualified individuals with disabilities and disabled veterans."[55]

Americans with Disabilities Act of 1990

The Americans with Disabilities Act (ADA) prohibits discrimination against qualified individuals with disabilities. The ADA prohibits discrimination in all employment practices, including job application procedures, hiring, firing, advancement, compensation, training, and other terms, conditions, and privileges of employment. It applies to recruitment, advertising, tenure, layoffs, leaves, benefits, and all other employment-related activities. The employment provisions apply to private employers, state and local governments, employment agencies, and labor unions. Persons discriminated against because they have a known association or relationship with a disabled individual is also protected. Employers with 15 or more employees are covered. The ADA defines an individual with a disability as a person who has, or is regarded as having, a physical or mental impairment that *substantially limits* one or more major life activities, and has a record of such an impairment, or is regarded as having such an impairment.

The EEOC guidelines on pre-employment inquiries and tests regarding disabilities prohibit inquiries and medical examinations intended to gain information about applicants' disabilities before a conditional job offer. In the Supreme Court case of *Leonel v American Airlines,* the Court ruled that the airline violated the ADA's required sequence for pre-hire medical inquiries/examinations by making medical inquiries and requiring individuals to take medical examinations before completing and making its hiring decisions.

The guiding principle is to ask only about potential employees' ability to do the job, and not about their disabilities. Lawful inquiries include those regarding performance of specific functions or possession of training, while illegal inquiries include those that ask about previous medical conditions or extent of prior drug use. The ADA does not protect people currently using illegal drugs. It does protect those in rehabilitation programs who are not currently using illegal drugs, those who have been rehabilitated, and those erroneously labeled as drug users. Coverage under the ADA continues to evolve.

Americans with Disabilities Act Amendments Act of 2008

The Americans with Disabilities Act Amendments Act (ADAAA) brings millions more people within the ADA's protection. The ADA Amendments Act expands the definition of "disability" and many more applicants and employees are eligible for reasonable accommodations. The ADAAA broadened the ADA's definition of disability by expanding the term "major life activities," doing away with the "substantially limited" requirement (previously mentioned) for those regarded as having a disability, and overturning two U.S. Supreme Court decisions that interpreted the ADA's definition of disability narrowly. The ADA still covers only qualified individuals with disabilities and provides that to be disabled, an individual must have "a physical or mental impairment that substantially limits one or more major life activities," or must have a record of such an impairment, or must be regarded as having such an impairment. The ADAAA also defines and vastly expands the term "major life activities" as including "caring for oneself, performing manual tasks, seeing, hearing, eating, sleeping, walking, standing, lifting, bending, speaking, breathing, learning, reading, concentrating, thinking, communicating, and working." The amendment states that major life activities include the operation of a major bodily function, such as "functions of the immune system, normal cell growth, digestive, bowel, bladder, neurological, brain, respiratory, circulatory, endocrine, and reproductive functions."[56] The only exception to this rule is that if a person's vision can be corrected with eyeglasses or contact lenses, he or she will not be considered disabled.

Immigration Reform and Control Act of 1986

The desire to stem illegal immigration prompted Congress to enact the Immigration Reform and Control Act (IRCA) of 1986.The IRCA granted amnesty to approximately 1.7 million long-term unauthorized workers in an effort to bring them out of the shadows and improve their labor market opportunities. It also established criminal and civil sanctions against employers who knowingly hire unauthorized aliens.[57] The Act also makes unlawful the hiring of anyone unless the person's employment authorization and identity are verified. When dealing with the national origin provision of the Civil Rights Act, IRCA reduces the threshold coverage from 15 employees to 4.

The IRCA toughened criminal sanctions for employers who hire illegal aliens, denied illegal aliens federally funded welfare benefits, and legitimized some aliens through an amnesty program. To comply with the IRCA, candidates for employment are not required to be U. S. citizens, but they must prove they are eligible to work in the United States. Employers must require all new employees to complete and sign a verification form (Form I-9) to certify their eligibility for employment. These individuals can establish their eligibility for employment by presenting a U.S. passport, alien registration card with photograph, or a work permit that establishes their identity and employment eligibility. Employers should recognize that faked documents are not uncommon and should protect themselves by conducting a background investigation. In 2009, the new E-Verify system (discussed in Chapter 6) regulation applies to federal contracts. [58]

The U.S. Immigration & Customs Enforcement Agency is aggressively pursuing violators of the Act. Of recent, investigators concentrate on building cases against businesses suspected of hiring undocumented immigrants before they raid workplaces and round up any illegal workers.[59] For instance, the nation's largest pallet manufacturing company, IFCO Systems North America, recently agreed to a nearly $21 million settlement to avoid criminal prosecution for hiring illegal workers. David Wortman of Cloudburst Lawn and Sprinkler Systems in Grand Island, Nebraska, got 30 months in prison on federal charges of hiring illegal immigrant workers.[60]

Illegal Immigration Reform and Immigrant Responsibility Act of 1996

The Illegal Immigration Reform and Immigrant Responsibility Act was passed partly in response to the fact that at least one of the terrorists who blew up the World Trade Center in 1993, killing six people and wounding 1,000, had legally entered on a student visa. The law places severe limitations on persons who come to the United States and remain in the country longer than permitted by their visas and/or persons who violate their nonimmigrant status. Anyone unlawfully present in the United States for 180 days, but less than one year, is subject to a three-year ban for admission to the United States. Anyone unlawfully present in the United States for one year or more is subject to a 10-year ban from admission to the United States. There are certain exceptions, however, such as extreme hardship. However, since 9/11, the law has been enforced more rigorously.

Uniformed Services Employment and Reemployment Rights Act of 1994

The Uniformed Services Employment and Reemployment Rights Act (USERRA) provide protection to Reservists and National Guard members. Under this Act, those workers are entitled to return to their civilian employment after completing their military service.[61] The Act is intended to eliminate or minimize employment disadvantages to civilian careers that can result from service in the uniformed services.[62] USERRA was enacted to protect the reemployment benefits and nondiscrimination rights of individuals who voluntarily or involuntarily take a leave of absence from employment to serve in the military. As a general rule, a returning employee is entitled to reemployment in the same job position that he or she would have attained with reasonable certainty if not for the absence to serve in the military. Known as the escalator principle, this requirement is designed to ensure that a returning employee is not penalized (by losing a pay raise, promotion, etc.) for the time spent on active duty, not exceeding five years.[63] There are no special rights under USERRA for temporary workers or the new hires taking over reservists' jobs.

Veterans' Benefits Improvement Act of 2004

The Veterans' Benefits Improvement Act (VBIA) amends portions of the USERRA. The VBIA enhances housing, education, and other benefits for veterans. Two provisions are of particular importance to employers: (1) a provision requiring employers to post a notice informing employees of their rights under USERRA; and (2) a provision increasing the health care continuation period for employees on military leave from 18 months to 24 months.

State and Local Laws

Numerous state and local laws also affect equal employment opportunity. A number of states and some cities have passed fair employment practice laws prohibiting discrimination on the basis of race, color, religion, gender, or national origin. Even prior to federal legislation, several states had antidiscrimination legislation relating to age and gender. For instance, New York protected individuals between the ages of 18 and 65 prior to the 1978 and 1986 ADEA amendments, and California had no upper limit on protected age. San Francisco has voted to ban weight discrimination. The Board of Supervisors added body size to city laws that already bar discrimination based on race, color, religion, age, ancestry, sex, sexual orientation, disability, place of birth, or gender identity. The State of California even has a law that requires sexual harassment prevention training. Washington explicitly prohibits bias against transgender people. When EEOC regulations conflict with state or local civil rights regulations, the legislation more favorable to women and minorities applies.

OBJECTIVE 3.5
Identify some of the major Supreme Court decisions that have had an impact on equal employment opportunity and affirmative action.

Significant U.S. Supreme Court Decisions Affecting Equal Employment Opportunity

Knowledge of the law is obviously important for those involved with human resource management; however, the manner in which the courts interpret the law is vital. Also, court interpretations continuously change, even though the law may not have been amended. Discussions of some of the more significant U.S. Supreme Court decisions affecting equal employment opportunity follow.

ETHICAL DILEMMA

What Was the Real Message?

You were recently hired as information technology manager, and one of your first tasks was to prescreen candidates for an IT position with a subsidiary. After interviewing 20 candidates, you recommend to upper management that the individual you consider most qualified be invited for a second interview. A day later, you are taken aside by a friend and told in vague phrases, accompanied by less ambiguous body language that you should not waste management's time by sending certain types (nudge-nudge-wink-wink) for an interview.[64] The intent of the message was clear: if you want to be accepted as a team player with this company, you had better get with the program.

What would you do?

Griggs v Duke Power Company

A major decision affecting the field of human resource management was rendered in 1971. A group of black employees at Duke Power Company had charged job discrimination under Title VII of the Civil Rights Act of 1964. Prior to Title VII, the Duke Power Company had two workforces, separated by race. After passage of the Act, the company required applicants to have a high school diploma and pass a paper-and-pencil test to qualify for certain jobs. The plaintiff was able to demonstrate that, in the relevant labor market, 34 percent of the white males but only 12 percent of the black males had a high school education. The plaintiff was also able to show that people already in those jobs were performing successfully even though they did not have high school diplomas. No business necessity could be shown for this educational requirement. The *Griggs v Duke Power Company* case continues to be a benchmark case in employment law.

In an 8–0 vote, the Supreme Court ruled against Duke Power Company and stated, "If an employment practice which operates to exclude Negroes cannot be shown to be related to job performance, the practice is prohibited." A major implication of the decision is that when human resource management practices eliminate substantial numbers of minority or women applicants (prima facie evidence), the burden of proof is on the employer to show that the practice is job-related. This Court decision significantly affected the human resource practices of many firms. Questions in employment procedures that should be avoided if not job-related include credit record, conviction record, garnishment record, and education. It should be noted that actually asking non-job-related questions is not illegal; it is how a hiring person uses the gained information that makes it illegal.[65] For instance, asking a person his or her age is not in and of itself illegal. Using this information to systematically eliminate older workers from consideration is illegal. Stating that a job requires a college degree when it could be accomplished effectively by a high school graduate can potentially be discriminatory.

Albemarle Paper Company v Moody

In 1966, a class action suit was brought against Albemarle Paper Company and the plant employees' labor union. A permanent injunction was requested against any policy, practice, custom, or usage at the plant that violated Title VII. In 1975, the Supreme Court, in *Albemarle Paper Company v Moody,* reaffirmed the idea that any test used in the selection process or in promotion decisions must be validated if it has an adverse impact on women and minorities. The employer has the burden of proof for showing that the test is valid. Subsequently, the employer must show that any selection or promotion device actually measures what it is supposed to measure.

Phillips v Martin Marietta Corporation

In 1971, the Court ruled that Martin Marietta had discriminated against a woman because she had young children. The company had a rule prohibiting the hiring of women with school-age children. The company argued that it did not preclude all women from job consideration, only those women with school-age children. Martin Marietta contended that this was a business requirement. The argument was obviously based on stereotypes and was rejected. A major implication of this decision is that a firm cannot impose standards for employment only on women. For example, a firm cannot reject women with school-age children if it does not also reject men with school-age children. Neither application forms nor interviews should contain questions for women that do not also apply to men. Examples of questions that should not be asked are: "Do you wish to be addressed as Ms., Miss, or Mrs.?" "Are you married?" "Do you have children?" "Do you plan on having any more children?" "Where does your husband work?"

Espinoza v Farah Manufacturing Company

In 1973, the Supreme Court ruled that Title VII does not prohibit discrimination on the basis of lack of citizenship. The EEOC had previously said that refusing to hire anyone who was a noncitizen was discriminatory, as this selection standard was likely to have an adverse impact on individuals of foreign national origin. Because 92 percent of the employees at the Farah facility in question were Hispanics who had become American citizens, the Court held that the company had not discriminated on the basis of national origin when it refused to hire a Hispanic who was not a U.S. citizen.

Dothard v Rawlingson

At the time Rawlingson applied for a position as correctional counselor trainee, she was a 22-year-old college graduate whose major course of study had been correctional psychology. She was refused employment because she failed to meet the minimum height and weight requirements. In this 1977 case, the Supreme Court upheld the U.S. District Court's decision that Alabama's statutory minimum height requirement of five feet, two inches and minimum weight requirement of 120 pounds for the position of correctional counselor had a discriminatory impact on women applicants. The contention was that minimum height and weight requirements for the position of correctional counselor were job-related. However, the Court stated that this argument does not rebut prima facie evidence showing these requirements have a discriminatory impact on women, whereas no evidence was produced correlating these requirements with a requisite amount of strength thought essential to good performance.

American Tobacco Company v Patterson

This 1982 Supreme Court decision allows seniority and promotion systems established since Title VII to stand, although they unintentionally hurt minority workers. Under *Griggs v Duke Power Co.,* a prima facie violation of Title VII may be established by policies or practices that are neutral on their face and in intent, but that nonetheless discriminate against a particular group. A seniority system would fall under the *Griggs* rationale if it were not for Section 703(h) of the Civil Rights Act, which provides:

> Notwithstanding any other provision of this subchapter, it shall not be an unlawful employment practice for an employer to apply standards of compensation, or different terms, conditions, or privileges of employment pursuant to a bona fide seniority or merit system . . . provided that such differences are not the result of an intention to discriminate because of race, color, religion, sex, or national origin, nor shall it be an unlawful employment practice for an employer to give and to act upon the results of any professionally developed ability test provided that such test, its administration or action upon the results is not designed, intended or used to discriminate because of race, color, religion, sex, or national origin.

Thus, the court ruled that a seniority system adopted after Title VII may stand even though it has an unintended discriminatory impact.

O'Connor v Consolidated Coin Caterers Corp.

The U.S. Supreme Court unanimously ruled that an employee does not have to show that he or she was replaced by someone younger than 40 to bring suit under the ADEA. The Court declared that discrimination is illegal even when all the employees are members of the protected age group. The case began in 1990 when James O'Connor's job as a regional sales manager was eliminated. The company did not select O'Connor, age 56, to manage either of its two remaining sales territories. He later was fired. His replacement was 40 years old. O'Connor was evidently doing so well that he earned a bonus of $37,000 the previous year. Apparently, O'Connor's new boss told him "he was too damn old for the kind of work he was doing and that what the company needed was new blood."

Writing for the Court, Justice Scalia stated, "The ADEA does not ban discrimination against employees because they are aged 40; it bans discrimination against employees because of their age, but limits the protected class to those who are 40 or older." Thus, it is not relevant that one member in the protected class has lost out to another member in that class, so long as the person lost out because of his or her age. The Court also found that being replaced by someone substantially younger was a more reliable indicator of age discrimination than being replaced by someone outside the protected class.

Significant U.S. Supreme Court Decisions Affecting Affirmative Action

Discussed below are some of the more significant U.S. Supreme Court decisions affecting affirmative action.

University of California Regents v Bakke

University of California Regents v Bakke was an affirmative action case and was the first major test involving reverse discrimination. The University of California had reserved 16 places in each beginning medical school class for minorities. Allen Bakke, a white man, was denied admission even though he scored higher on the admission criteria than some minority applicants who were admitted. The Supreme Court ruled 5–4 in Bakke's favor. As a result, Bakke was admitted to the university and later received his degree. But, at the same time, the Court reaffirmed that race may be taken into account in admission decisions.

Adarand Constructors v Pena

In a 5–4 decision, the U.S. Supreme Court in 1995 criticized the moral justification for affirmative action, saying that race-conscious programs can amount to unconstitutional reverse discrimination and even harm those they seek to advance. The *Adarand* case concerned a Department of Transportation policy that gave contractors a bonus if they hired minority subcontractors. A white contractor challenged the policy in court after losing a contract to build guardrails, despite offering the lowest bid. A federal appeals court upheld the program as within the proper bounds of affirmative action. The Supreme Court decision did not uphold or reject that ruling, but instead sent the case back for further review under new, tougher rules. As a result, the ruling seems to invite legal challenges to other federal affirmative action programs. However, since the 2003 rulings in the case of *Grutter v Bollinger* and *Gratz v Bollinger* (discussed next), organizations are unsure how the Supreme Court will address affirmative action in the private sector.

Grutter v Bollinger

The Supreme Court appeared to support the *Bakke* decision. In the case of *Grutter v Bollinger,* the Court ruled in a 5–4 decision that colleges and universities have a compelling interest in achieving diverse campuses. Schools may favor black, Hispanic, and other minority students in admissions as long as administrators take the time to assess each applicant's background and potential. Justice Sandra Day O'Connor, in writing for the majority opinion, said, "Effective participation by members of all racial and ethnic groups in the civic life of our nation is essential if the dream of one nation, indivisible, is to be realized."

Gratz v Bollinger

In the case involving *Gratz v Bollinger,* the Court, in a 6–3 decision, said that in trying to achieve diversity, colleges and universities could not use point systems that blindly give extra credit to minority applicants. The university used a point system to determine admissions criteria in its College of Literature, Science, and the Arts, with minority applicants receiving bonus points.

The court determined that Michigan's 150-point index for screening applicants, which gave an automatic 20 points to minority applicants, was not the proper way to achieve racial diversity. The ruling in this decision was quite similar to the *Bakke* decision previously discussed.

Ricci v DeStefano

The City of New Haven, Connecticut, administered a test to determine which firefighters were qualified for promotion to fill vacant lieutenant and captain positions. The results of the tests showed that white candidates had outperformed minority candidates. Of the 43 whites, 19 blacks, and 15 Hispanics who took the lieutenant test, only 34 candidates passed: 25 whites, 6 blacks, and 3 Hispanics. The hiring authority needed to choose a candidate from among the top three scorers, meaning that only the top ten candidates, all white, were eligible to fill the eight vacant lieutenant positions. Fearing lawsuits, the city threw out the results. The plaintiffs who passed the test but did not get promoted sued. [66] The U.S. Supreme Court in a 5-4 decision reversed a Second Circuit decision and held that the City discriminated against white and Hispanic firefighters who likely would have been promoted to lieutenant or captain but for the city's decision to avoid risking disparate impact liability, by throwing out the results of examinations it otherwise would have used in considering the promotions. The evidence demonstrates that the city rejected the test results because the higher-scoring candidates were white. The majority held that the city had to show a "strong basis in evidence" that the tests were not job-related or that another, less discriminatory test existed.[67]

OBJECTIVE 3.6
Describe the Equal Employment Opportunity Commission.

Equal Employment Opportunity Commission

Title VII of the Civil Rights Act, as amended, created the Equal Employment Opportunity Commission, which is charged with administering the Act. Under Title VII, filing a discrimination charge initiates EEOC action. The EEOC continually receives complaints. Recently U.S. employees filed 93,277 workplace discrimination charges with the Equal Employment Opportunity Commission. The EEOC obtained approximately $376 million in monetary relief for thousands of discrimination victims as well as significant nonmonetary remedies from employers.[68]

Charges may be filed by one of the presidentially appointed EEOC commissioners, by any aggrieved person, or by anyone acting on behalf of an aggrieved person. Charges must be filed within 180 days of the alleged act; however, the time is extended to 300 days if a state or local agency is involved in the case. Because of this time restriction, the Civil Rights Act of 1866 may be called into play because it has no statute of limitations.

Notice in Figure 3.2 that when a charge is filed, the EEOC first attempts a no-fault settlement. Essentially, the organization charged with the violation is invited to settle the case with no admission of guilt. Most charges are settled at this stage. Failing settlement, the EEOC investigates the charges. Once the employer is notified that an investigation will take place, no records relating to the charge may be destroyed. During the investigative process, the employer is permitted to present a position statement. After the investigation has been completed, the district director of the EEOC will issue a probable cause or a no probable cause statement.

In the event of a probable cause statement, the next step involves attempted conciliation. In the event this effort fails, the case will be reviewed for litigation potential. Some of the factors that determine whether the EEOC will pursue litigation are: (1) the number of people affected by the alleged practice; (2) the amount of money involved in the charge; (3) other charges against the employer; and (4) the type of charge. Recommendations for litigation are then passed on to the general counsel of the EEOC. If the recommendation is against litigation, a right-to-sue notice will be issued to the charging party. The EEOC files suit in only about 1 percent of all charges.

HR Web Wisdom

EEOC

www.eeoc.gov

The home page for the Equal Employment Opportunity Commission is presented.

OBJECTIVE 3.7
Explain the purpose of the *Uniform Guidelines on Employee Selection Procedures*.

Uniform Guidelines on Employee Selection Procedures

Prior to 1978, employers were faced with complying with several different selection guidelines. In 1978, the Equal Employment Opportunity Commission, the Civil Service Commission, the Department of Justice, and the Department of Labor adopted the *Uniform Guidelines on*

Figure 3.2

EEOC Procedure Once a Charge is Filed

Source: © 2008 by Prentice Hall

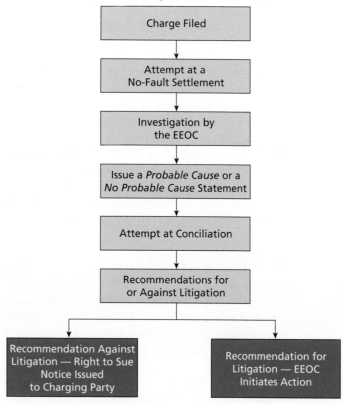

Steps in Handling a Discrimination Case

Employee Selection Procedures. These guidelines cover several federal equal employment opportunity statutes and executive orders, including Title VII of the Civil Rights Act, EO 11246, and the Equal Pay Act.

The *Uniform Guidelines* provide a single set of principles that were designed to assist employers, labor organizations, employment agencies, and licensing and certification boards in complying with federal prohibitions against employment practices that discriminate on the basis of race, color, religion, sex, and national origin. The *Uniform Guidelines* provide a framework for making legal employment decisions about hiring, promotion, demotion, referral, retention, licensing and certification, the proper use of tests, and other selection procedures. Under the *Uniform Guidelines,* recruiting procedures are not considered selection procedures and therefore are not covered.

Regarding selection procedures, the *Uniform Guidelines* state that a test is

> *any measure, combination of measures, or procedures used as a basis for any employment decision. Selection procedures include the full range of assessment techniques from traditional paper-and-pencil tests, performance tests, testing programs or probationary periods, and physical, education, and work experience requirement through informal or casual interviews and unscored application forms.*

OBJECTIVE 3.8
Describe disparate treatment and adverse impact.

disparate treatment
Employer treats some people less favorably than others because of race, religion, color, sex, national origin, or age.

Using this definition, virtually any instrument or procedure used in the selection decision is considered a test.

Concept of Disparate Treatment

Unlawful employment discrimination, as established through various Supreme Court decisions, can be divided into two broad categories: adverse impact and disparate treatment. **Disparate treatment** means that an employer treats some employees less favorably than others because of race, religion, color, sex, national origin, or age. It is the most easily understood form of discrimination.

For example, males are treated differently from females; whites are treated differently from blacks. The crux of disparate treatment is different treatment on the basis of some non-allowable criterion. It may be thought of as direct discrimination. Common forms of disparate treatment include selection rules with a racial, sexual, or other premise; prejudicial action; unequal treatment on an individual basis; and different hiring standards for different groups. *McDonald v Santa Fe Trail Transportation Company* offers an example of disparate treatment. Three of the company's employees, two whites and one black, had allegedly misappropriated 60 gallons of antifreeze. Santa Fe took disciplinary action against the workers by terminating the two whites, but not the black employee. The discharged white workers filed suit against the company, charging that their termination violated both Title VII and the Civil Rights Act of 1866. The Supreme Court, in a 1977 decision, agreed with the plaintiffs that they had been the recipients of unequal treatment on the basis of their race. Central to disparate treatment is the matter of proof. The plaintiff must first be able to establish a prima facie case, and, second, be able to establish that the employer was acting on the basis of a discriminatory motive.

Concept of Adverse Impact

adverse impact
Concept established by the *Uniform Guidelines* occurs if women and minorities are not hired at the rate of at least 80 percent of the best-achieving group.

Prior to the issuance of the *Uniform Guidelines,* the only way to prove job-relatedness was to validate each test. The *Uniform Guidelines* do not require validation in all cases. Essentially, it is required only in instances in which the test or other selection device produces an adverse impact on a minority group. **Adverse impact**, a concept established by the *Uniform Guidelines,* occurs if women and minorities are not hired at the rate of at least 80 percent of the best-achieving group.

Under the *Uniform Guidelines*, adverse impact has been described in terms of selection rates, the selection rate being the number of qualified applicants hired or promoted, divided by the total number of qualified applicants. This has also been called the four-fifths rule, which is actually a guideline subject to interpretation by the EEOC. The groups identified for analysis under the guidelines are: (1) blacks, (2) Native Americans (including Alaskan natives), (3) Asians, (4) Hispanics, (5) women, and (6) men.

The following formula is used to compute adverse impact for hiring:

$$\frac{\text{Success rate for least-achieving group of applicants}}{\text{Success rate for best-achieving group of applicants}} = \text{Determination of adverse impact}$$

The success rate for the least-achieving group (often women and minority applicants) is determined by dividing the number of members of a specific group employed in a period by the number of qualified applicants in a period. The success rate of best-achieving group applicants is determined by dividing the number of people in the best-achieving group employed by the number of the best-achieving group applicants in a period.

Using the formula, let us determine whether there has been adverse impact in the following case. During 2011, 400 people were hired for a particular job. Of the total, 300 were white and 100 were black. There were 1,500 qualified applicants for these jobs, of whom 1,000 were white and 500 were black. Blacks were determined to be the least-achieving group because 100/500 = .2. Whites were determined to be the best-achieving group because 300/100 = .3. Using the adverse formula, you have:

$$\frac{100/500}{300/1000} = \frac{0.2}{0.3} = 66.67\%$$

Thus, adverse impact exists.

Evidence of adverse impact involves more than the total number of minority workers employed. Also considered is the total number of qualified applicants. For instance, assume that 300 blacks and 300 whites were hired. But there were 1,500 qualified black applicants and 1,000 qualified white applicants. Blacks were determined to be the least-achieving group because $300/1500 = .2$. Whites were determined to be the best-achieving group because $300/1000 = .3$. Putting these figures into the adverse impact formula, it can be concluded that adverse impact still exists.

$$\frac{300/1500}{300/1000} = \frac{0.2}{0.3} = 66.67\%$$

Thus, adverse impact exists.

Therefore, it is clear that firms must monitor their recruitment efforts very carefully. Obviously, firms should attempt to recruit qualified individuals because once in the applicant pool, they will be used in computing adverse impact.

Assuming that adverse impact is shown, employers have two avenues available to them if they still desire to use a particular selection standard. First, the employer may validate a selection device by showing that it is indeed a predictor of success. For instance, the employer may be able to show a strong relationship between the selection device and job performance, and that if it did not use this procedure, the firm's training costs would become prohibitive. If the device has proved to be a predictor of job performance, business necessity has been established.

The second avenue available to employers should adverse impact be shown is the bona fide occupational qualification (BFOQ) defense. The BFOQ defense means that only one group is capable of performing the job successfully. Courts have narrowly interpreted this defense because it almost always relates to sex discrimination. For instance, courts have rejected the concept that because most women cannot lift 100 pounds, all women should be eliminated from consideration for a job requiring heavy lifting.

Creators of the *Uniform Guidelines* adopted the bottom-line approach in assessing whether a firm's employment practices are discriminatory. For example, if a number of separate procedures are used in making a selection decision, the enforcement agencies will focus on the end result of these procedures to determine whether adverse impact has occurred. Essentially, the EEOC is more concerned with what is occurring than how it occurs. It admits that discriminatory employment practices that cannot be validated may exist; however, the net effect, or the bottom line, of the selection procedures is the focus of the EEOC attention.

Additional Guidelines on Employment Selection Procedures

OBJECTIVE 3.9
Describe the *Uniform Guidelines* related to sexual harassment, national origin, and religion.

Since the *Uniform Guidelines* were published in 1978, they have been modified several times. Some of these changes reflect Supreme Court decisions; others clarify implementation procedures. The three major changes discussed are the Guidelines on Sexual Harassment, Guidelines on Discrimination because of National Origin, and Guidelines on Discrimination because of Religion.

Guidelines on Sexual Harassment

Recently the U.S. Equal Employment Opportunity Commission fielded more than 13,867 charges of sexual harassment. From 1990 to 2009, the percentage of sexual harassment claims filed by male employees has doubled from 8 to 16 percent.[69] Awards to charging parties amounted to more than $47.4 million, not counting monetary benefits obtained through litigation.

As previously mentioned, Title VII of the Civil Rights Act generally prohibits discrimination in employment on the basis of gender. The EEOC has also issued guidelines that state that employers have a duty to maintain a workplace that is free from sexual harassment. The OFCCP has issued similar guidelines. Managers in both for-profit and not-for-profit organizations must be particularly alert to the issue of sexual harassment. The EEOC issued the guidelines because of the belief that sexual harassment was a widespread problem. Table 3.1 contains the EEOC's definition of sexual harassment. As you see, there are two distinct types of sexual harassment: (1) where a hostile work environment is created, and (2) when there is a quid pro quo, for example, an offer of promotion or pay raise in exchange for sex.

Table 3.1 EEOC Definition of Sexual Harassment

Unwelcome sexual advances, requests for sexual favors, and verbal or physical conduct of a sexual nature that occur under any of the following situations:

1. When submission to such conduct is made either explicitly or implicitly a term or condition of an individual's employment
2. When submission to or rejection of such contact by an individual is used as the basis for employment decisions affecting such individual
3. When such conduct has the purpose or effect of unreasonably interfering with an individual's work performance or creating an intimidating, hostile, or offensive working environment

According to these guidelines, employers are totally liable for the acts of their supervisors, regardless of whether the employer is aware of the sexual harassment act. In *Faragher v City of Boca Raton* and *Burlington Industries, Inc. v Ellerth*, the Supreme Court held that an employer is strictly liable, meaning that it has absolutely no defense, when sexual harassment by a supervisor involves a tangible employment action. Courts expect employers to carefully train supervisors so they do not engage in any type of behavior that could be construed as sexual harassment. As with the Civil Rights Act of 1964, retaliation is forbidden against an employee who has participated in an investigation, proceeding, or hearing. Recently, the U.S. Supreme Court gave a Nashville schools employee the green light to move forward on her sexual harassment retaliation claim; a jury ultimately awarded her $1.5 million in back pay, damages, and future wages.[70]

Where co-workers are concerned, the employer is responsible for such acts if the employer knew, or should have known, about them. This so called "purpose ignorance" is no defense in a sexual harassment case involving co-workers.[71] The employer is not responsible when it can show that it took immediate and appropriate corrective action on learning of the problem. Another important aspect of these guidelines is that employers may be liable for acts committed by nonemployees in the workplace if the employer knew, or should have known, of the conduct and failed to take appropriate action.

Firms are responsible for developing programs and policies to prevent sexual harassment in the workplace. They must also investigate all formal and informal complaints alleging sexual harassment. Failure to do so constitutes a violation of Title VII, as interpreted by the EEOC. To prevail in court, companies must have clear procedures for handling sexual harassment complaints. Typically, employers choose an impartial ombudsperson to hear and investigate charges before lawyers get involved. If the sexual harassment complaint appears legitimate, the company must take immediate and appropriate action. However, this does not mean that everyone who is guilty of sexual harassment must be fired; a measured approach may be sufficient.[72]

There have been numerous sexual harassment court cases and the Supreme Court continues to refine the concept. In *Miller v Bank of America*, a U.S. Circuit Court of Appeals held an employer liable for the sexually harassing acts of its supervisors, even though the company had a policy prohibiting such conduct, and even though the victim did not formally notify the employer of the problem. Another U.S. Circuit Court of Appeals ruled that sexual harassment, in and of itself, is a violation of Title VII. The court ruled that the law does not require the victim to prove that she or he resisted harassment and was penalized for that resistance. If the activity is "unwelcome," it does not matter if the employee agreed to the supervisor's demands.[73]

The first sexual harassment case to reach the U.S. Supreme Court was the case of *Meritor Savings Bank v Vinson* in 1986. In the *Vinson* decision, the Supreme Court recognized for the first time that Title VII could be used for offensive-environment claims. According to the EEOC, specific actions that could create a hostile workplace include a pattern of threatening, intimidating, or hostile acts and remarks, negative sexual stereotyping, or the display of written or graphic materials considered degrading. The 1993 Supreme Court decision in *Harris v Forklift Systems, Inc.*, expanded the hostile-workplace concept and made it easier to win sexual harassment claims. In a unanimous decision, the Supreme Court held that "to be accountable as abusive work environment harassment, conduct need not seriously affect... the psychological well-being or lead the plaintiff to suffer injury." No longer does severe psychological injury have to be proved. Under this ruling, the plaintiff only needs to show that his or her employer allowed a hostile-to-abusive work environment to exist. In a Seventh U.S. Circuit Court of Appeals ruling, a company president's one-time sexual proposition to a subordinate was sufficient to constitute a hostile work environment. The decision was made in light of the president's position of significant authority and the closeness in which the individual worked.[74] In another case involving a company president, the CEO offered a female employee $1 million to sleep with him. After she refused, she was fired; then she sued for sexual harassment and was awarded $5.3 million.[75]

The sexual harassment effort does not have to be directed at the plaintiff. The U.S. Court of Appeals for the Eleventh Circuit wrote in *Reeves v C.H. Robinson Worldwide, Inc.*, "the court gave as examples of 'sex specific' profanity words that are 'more degrading to women than to men,' and thus may form the basis of a sexual harassment claim." The court held that "[D]aily exposure to language and radio programming that are particularly offensive to women but not targeted at the plaintiff are sufficient to satisfy the 'based on' [gender] and 'severe or pervasive' elements of a hostile work environment claim."[76]

Duane Reade, the New York/New Jersey drug store chain, agreed to settle an EEOC lawsuit for $240,000 for allowing the work environment at one of its New York stores to become hostile. The store manager frequently made vulgar remarks about women's anatomy, sexually propositioned female employees, made lewd comments about them during pregnancies, assigned pregnant women the least desirable store tasks, and sometimes grabbed female employees' buttocks while they worked.[77]

For a long time, an unresolved question in employment law has been whether same-sex harassment (for example, males harassing males) is unlawful under Title VII of the Civil Rights Act of 1964. The Supreme Court, in the case of *Oncale v Sundowner Offshore Services*, held that same-sex sexual harassment may be unlawful under Title VII. The Supreme Court decided that a plaintiff could make out a claim for sexual harassment as long as the harassing conduct was because of sex. The Court emphasized that Title VII does not prohibit all verbal or physical harassment in the workplace, only that which constitutes discrimination because of sex.[78]

Guidelines on Discrimination Because of National Origin

Both EEOC and the courts have interpreted national origin protection under Title VII as extending far beyond discrimination against individuals who came from, or whose forebears came from, a particular country. National origin protection also covers: (1) marriage or association with a person of a specific national origin; (2) membership in, or association with, an organization identified with, or seeking to promote the interests of national groups; (3) attendance at, or participation in, schools, churches, temples, or mosques generally used by persons of a national origin group; and (4) use of an individual's or spouse's name that is associated with a national origin group. As Table 3.2 shows, the EEOC has identified certain selection procedures that may be discriminatory.

Harassment on the basis of national origin is a violation of Title VII. Employers have a duty to maintain a working environment free from such harassment. Ethnic slurs and other verbal or physical conduct relating to an individual's national origin constitute harassment when this conduct: (1) has the purpose or effect of creating an intimidating, hostile, or offensive working environment; (2) has the purpose or effect of unreasonably interfering with an individual's work performance; or (3) otherwise adversely affects an individual's employment opportunity.

Table 3.2 Selection Procedures That May Be Discriminatory with Regard to National Origin

1. Fluency in English requirements: One questionable practice involves denying employment opportunities because of an individual's foreign accent or inability to communicate well in English. When this practice is continually followed, the Commission will presume that such a rule violates Title VII and will study it closely. However, a firm may require that employees speak only in English at certain times if business necessity can be shown.
2. Training or education requirements: Denying employment opportunities to an individual because of his or her foreign training or education, or practices that require an individual to be foreign trained or educated may be discriminatory.

OBJECTIVE 3.10
Explain caregiver
discrimination.

Of interest with regard to national origin is the English-only rule. Courts have generally ruled in the employer's favor if the rule would promote safety and product quality and stop harassment. For example, suppose a company has a rule that only English must be spoken except during breaks. That rule must be justified by a compelling business necessity. In *Garcia v Spun Steak*, the Ninth Circuit Court of Appeals (the Supreme Court refused to review) concluded that the rule did not necessarily violate Title VII. Spun Steak's management implemented the policy after some workers complained they were being harassed and insulted in a language they could not understand. The rule allowed workers to speak Spanish during breaks and lunch periods. A recent ruling supported the job-related aspect of the English-only rule. In *Montes v Vail Clinic, Inc.*, the tenth circuit court agreed with the English-only rule prohibiting housekeepers from speaking Spanish while working in the operating room. However, English-only policies that are not job-related have been challenged and eliminated. For instance, recently the U.S. Equal Employment Opportunity Commission (EEOC) settled a Title VII lawsuit against a company that enforced an English-only rule solely against Hispanics. "What was strange was that the rule was only targeted at Hispanics. Tagalog, a Spanish language spoken in the Philippines, was openly spoken," said Anna Park, the EEOC's regional attorney in Los Angeles. "This was very troublesome."[79]

Guidelines on Discrimination Because of Religion

The number of religion-related discrimination complaints filed with the EEOC continues to increase. According to the Supreme Court's decision in *TWA v Hardison*, employers have an obligation to accommodate religious practices as long as the requested accommodation does not create more than a minimum cost to the employer. Courts generally do not require employers to hire additional employees just to cover for another employee who needs a religious accommodation.[80] The most common claims filed under the religious accommodation provisions involve employees objecting to either Sabbath employment or membership in or financial support of labor unions. Consideration is given to identifiable costs in relation to the size and operating costs of the employer and the number of individuals who actually need the accommodation. These guidelines recognize that regular payment of premium wages constitutes undue hardship, whereas these payments on an infrequent or temporary basis do not. Undue hardship would also exist if an accommodation required a firm to vary from its bona fide seniority system.

These guidelines identify several means of accommodating religious practices that prohibit working on certain days. Some of the methods suggested included voluntary substitutes, flexible scheduling, lateral transfer, and change of job assignments. Some collective bargaining agreements include a provision that each employee must join the union or pay the union a sum equivalent to dues. When an employee's religious beliefs prevent compliance, the union should accommodate the employee by permitting that person to make an equivalent donation to a charitable organization.

OBJECTIVE 3.11
Explain affirmative action
as required by presidential
Executive Orders 11246
and 11375.

executive order (EO)
Directive issued by the
president that has the force
and effect of law enacted
by Congress as it applies to
federal agencies and federal
contractors.

**caregiver (family
responsibility)
discrimination**
Discrimination against
employees based on their
obligations to care for
family members.

Affirmative Action: Executive Order 11246, as Amended by Executive Order 11375

An **executive order (EO)** is a directive issued by the president and has the force and effect of a law enacted by Congress as it applies to federal agencies and federal contractors. Many believe that the concept of affirmative action got its beginning in 1948 when President Harry S. Truman officially ended racial segregation in all branches of the military by issuing Executive Order 9981.[81]

However, officially it began in 1965 when President Lyndon B. Johnson signed EO 11246, which establishes the policy of the U.S. government as providing equal opportunity in federal employment for all qualified people. It prohibits discrimination in employment because of race, creed, color, or national origin. The order also requires promoting the full realization of equal employment opportunity through a positive, continuing program in each executive department and agency. The policy of equal opportunity applies to every aspect of federal employment policy and practice.

A major provision of EO 11246 requires adherence to a policy of nondiscrimination in employment as a condition for the approval of a grant, contract, loan, insurance, or guarantee. Every executive department and agency that administers a program involving federal financial assistance must include such language in its contracts. Contractors must agree not to discriminate in employment because of race, creed, color, or national origin during performance of a contract.

TRENDS & INNOVATIONS

Caregiver (Family Responsibility) Discrimination

Caregiver (family responsibility) discrimination is discrimination against employees based on their obligations to care for family members. The EEOC has issued a technical assistance document on how employers of workers with caregiving responsibilities can avoid violations of Title VII of the 1964 Civil Rights Act and other fair employment laws and reduce the likelihood of discrimination complaints. It is titled "Employer Best Practices for Workers with Caregiving Responsibilities."[82] Washington, D.C., employment attorney Leslie Silverman of Proskauer Rose said, "It is a form of discrimination to make an assumption based on what you assume to be true about a group, including people with family responsibilities."[83]

According to the EEOC, the guidance "is not binding on employers but rather offers "best practices" that are "proactive measures that go beyond federal nondiscrimination requirements." Federal law does not prohibit discrimination on the basis of "caregiver status" but rather "is implicated when workers with caregiving responsibilities are treated differently based on a characteristic that is protected by laws—such as gender, race, or association with an individual with a disability." The National Partnership for Women and Families estimates that family caregivers provide 80 percent of all long-term care received by Americans with chronic conditions, an economic benefit whose value is estimated at $350 billion per year. [84]

Caregiver discrimination is the current "hot topic" in labor law and the new battleground in employment claims.[85] The statutory bases for these claims encompass a wide range of causes of action from:

- Title VII of the Civil Rights Act of 1964;
- Pregnancy Discrimination Act;
- Family and Medical Leave Act;
- Americans with Disabilities Act;
- Equal Pay Act;
- Employee Retirement Income Security Act;

- State fair employment practice laws; and
- Common law causes of action, such as wrongful discharge and breach of contract.[86]

Individuals claiming caregiver discrimination use Title VII more often than other statute to support caregiver discrimination claims.

In recent years, employees have begun filing more and more caregiver discrimination lawsuits.[87] Most cases share a common element—the employee alleges that the caregiving responsibilities cause the alleged discriminatory action by the employer. In EEO related suits, plaintiffs win in only about 20 percent of cases alleging race, sex, or other more familiar types of discrimination. However, with caregiver discrimination, the win rate is twice that.[88] The challenge for employers is to develop the right mix of flexibility and fairness in work scheduling, leave policies, dependent-care assistance, and benefits. This will promote positive employee relations, recruit and retain a diverse and well-qualified workforce, address and resolve job-related issues, and defend against claims of unfair or unlawful conduct.

EEOC Assistant Legal Counsel Dianna B. Johnston stated that "The economic downturn has brought renewed interest in the question of flexible workplace options, which are particularly important to caregivers."[89] An increasing number of employees are suing their employers because they lost their jobs, were passed over for promotion, or were treated unfairly based on their responsibilities to care for children or other relatives. A maintenance employee, who was the primary caregiver for his aging parents, requested and received intermittent FMLA leave but ultimately was fired. The evidence presented at trial indicated a clear bias against caregivers on the part of the supervisor and, by implication, the employer. As a result, the employee was awarded $11.65 million.[90]

The ADA has also been used by caregivers to charge employers with discrimination based on "relationship or association" with disabled individuals for whom they provide care. The individual receiving the care must meet the ADA's definition of "disability" for the ADA to extend protection to the caregiver. The EEOC has long held the position that the ADA's "association" provision prohibits discrimination against an individual who takes time off or who is not hired because of his or her caregiving responsibilities.

---

affirmative action

Stipulated by Executive Order 11246, it requires employers to take positive steps to ensure employment of applicants and treatment of employees during employment without regard to race, creed, color, or national origin.

Affirmative action, stipulated by EO 11246, requires covered employers to take positive steps to ensure employment of applicants and treatment of employees during employment without regard to race, creed, color, or national origin. In 1968, EO 11375, which changed the word "creed" to "religion" and added sex discrimination to the other prohibited items, amended EO 11246. These EOs are enforced by the Department of Labor through the Office of Federal Contract Compliance Programs (OFCCP).

Covered human resource practices relate to employment, upgrading, demotion, transfer, recruitment or recruitment advertising, layoffs or termination, rates of pay or other forms of compensation, and selection for training, including apprenticeships. Employers are required to post notices explaining these requirements in conspicuous places in the workplace. In the event of contractor noncompliance, contracts can be canceled, terminated, or suspended in whole or in part, and the contractor may be declared ineligible for future government contracts.

OBJECTIVE 3.12
Describe affirmative action programs.

affirmative action program (AAP)
Approach developed by organizations with government contracts to demonstrate that workers are employed in proportion to their representation in the firm's relevant labor market.

Affirmative Action Programs

An **affirmative action program (AAP)** is an approach developed by organizations with government contracts to demonstrate that workers are employed in proportion to their representation in the firm's relevant labor market.

An affirmative action program may be voluntarily implemented by an organization. In such an event, goals are established and action is taken to hire and move minorities and women up in the organization. In other situations, an AAP may be mandated by the OFCCP.

The degree of control the OFCCP will impose depends on the size of the contract, with contracts of $10,000 or less not covered. The first level of control involves contracts that exceed $10,000 but are less than $50,000. These contractors are governed by the equal opportunity clause, as shown in Table 3.3. The second level of control occurs if the contractor: (1) has 50 or

Table 3.3 Equal Opportunity Clause—Government Contracts

1. The contractor will not discriminate against any employee or applicant for employment because of race, color, religion, sex, or national origin. The contractor will take affirmative action to ensure that applicants are employed, and that employees are treated during employment, without regard to their race, color, religion, sex, or national origin. Such action shall include, but not be limited to the following: employment, upgrading, demotions, or transfer; recruitment or recruitment advertising, layoff or termination; rates of pay or other forms of compensation; and selection for training, including apprenticeship. The contractor agrees to post in conspicuous places, available to employees and applicants for employment, notices to be provided by the contracting officer setting forth the provisions for this nondiscrimination clause.

2. The contractor will in all solicitations or advertisements for employees placed by or on behalf of the contractor, state that all qualified applicants will receive consideration for employment without regard to race, color, religion, sex, or national origin.

3. The contractor will send to each labor union or representative of workers with which he or she has a collective bargaining agreement or other contract or understanding, a notice to be provided by the agency contracting officer, advising the labor union or workers' representative of the contractor's commitments under section 202 of Executive Order 11246 of September 24, 1965, and shall post copies of the notice in conspicuous places available to employees and applicants for employment.

4. The contractor will comply with all provisions of Executive Order 11246 of September 24, 1965, and the rules, regulations, and relevant orders of the Secretary of Labor.

5. The contractor will furnish all information and reports required by Executive Order 11246 of September 24, 1965, and by the rules, regulations, and orders of the Secretary of Labor, or pursuant thereto, and will permit access to his or her books, records, and accounts by the contracting agency and the Secretary of Labor for purposes of investigation to ascertain compliance with such rules, regulations, and orders.

6. In the event of the contractor's noncompliance with the nondiscrimination clauses of this contract or with any of such rules, regulations, or orders, this contract may be canceled, terminated, or suspended in whole or in part and the contractor may be declared ineligible for further Government contracts in accordance with procedures authorized in Executive Order 11246 of September 24, 1965, or by rule, regulation, or order of the Secretary of State, or as otherwise provided by law.

7. The contractor will include the provisions of paragraphs (1) through (7) in every subcontract or purchase order unless exempted by rules, regulations, or orders of the Secretary of Labor issued pursuant to section 204 of Executive Order 11246 of September 24, 1965, so that such provisions will be binding upon each subcontractor or vendor. The contractor will take such action with respect to any subcontract or purchase order as may be directed by the Secretary of Labor as a means of enforcing such provisions including sanctions for noncompliance: Provided, however, that in the event the contractor becomes involved in, or is threatened with litigation with a subcontractor or vendor as a result of such direction, the contractor may request the United States to enter into such litigation to protect the interests of the United States.

Source: Federal Register, 45, no. 251 (Tuesday, December 30, 1980): 86230.

more employees; (2) has a contract of $50,000 or more; (3) has contracts which, in any 12-month period, total $50,000 or more or reasonably may be expected to total $50,000 or more; or (4) is a financial institution that serves as a depository for government funds in any amount, acts as an issuing or redeeming agent for U.S. savings bonds and savings notes in any amount, or subscribes to federal deposit or share insurance. Contractors meeting these criteria must develop a written affirmative action program for each of their establishments and file an annual EEO-1 report. Note that the threshold is 50 employees here, but it was 100 with regard to those covered by the Civil Rights Act of 1964.

The third level of control on contractors is in effect when contracts exceed $1 million. All previously stated requirements must be met, and in addition, the OFCCP is authorized to conduct preaward compliance reviews. In determining whether to conduct a preaward review, the OFCCP may consider, for example, the items presented in Table 3.4.

If an investigation indicates a violation, the OFCCP first tries to secure compliance through persuasion. If persuasion fails to resolve the issue, the OFCCP serves a notice to show cause or a notice of violation. A show cause notice contains a list of the violations, a statement of how the OFCCP proposes that corrections be made, a request for a written response to the findings, and a suggested date for a conciliation conference. The firm usually has 30 days to respond. Successful conciliation results in a written contract between the OFCCP and the contractor. In a conciliation agreement, the contractor agrees to take specific steps to remedy noncompliance with an EO. Firms that do not correct violations can be passed over in the awarding of future contracts. The procedures for developing affirmative action plans were published in the *Federal Register* of December 4, 1974. These regulations are referred to as Revised Order No. 4. The OFCCP guide for compliance officers, outlining what to cover in a compliance review, is known as Order No. 14.

The OFCCP is very specific about what should be included in an affirmative action program. A policy statement has to be developed that reflects the CEO's attitude regarding equal employment opportunity, assigns overall responsibility for preparing and implementing the affirmative action program, and provides for reporting and monitoring procedures. The policy should state that the firm intends to recruit, hire, train, and promote persons in all job titles without regard to race, color, religion, gender, or national origin, except where gender is a bona fide occupational qualification (BFOQ). The policy should guarantee that all human resource actions involving areas such as compensation, benefits, transfers, layoffs, return from layoffs, company-sponsored training, education, tuition assistance, and social and recreational programs will be administered without regard to race, color, religion, gender, or national origin. Revised Order No. 4 is quite specific with regard to dissemination of a firm's EEO policy, both internally and externally. An executive should be appointed to manage the firm's equal employment opportunity program. This person should be given the necessary support by top management to accomplish the assignment. Revised Order No. 4 specifies the minimum level of responsibility associated with the task of EEO manager.

An acceptable AAP must include an analysis of deficiencies in the utilization of minority groups and women. The first step in conducting a utilization analysis is to make a workforce analysis. The second step involves an analysis of all major job groups. An

Table 3.4 **Factors that the OFCCP May Consider in Conducting a Preaward Review**

1. The past EEO performance of the contractor, including its current EEO profile and indications of underutilization.
2. The volume and nature of complaints filed by employees or applicants against the contractor.
3. Whether the contractor is in a growth industry.
4. The level of employment or promotional opportunities resulting from the expansion of, or turnover in, the contractor's workforce.
5. The employment opportunities likely to result from the contract in issue.
6. Whether resources are available to conduct the review.

A GLOBAL PERSPECTIVE

Multinational Whistle-blowing

Multinational companies face significant challenges when they try to encourage whistle-blowing across a wide variety of cultures. There are a number of cultural factors that discourage international employees from reporting misconduct. In parts of East Asia, members of the corporation are a family; if you view them as family members, it is wrong to report them. In Japan, lifetime employment and a strict seniority system can discourage workers from questioning management decisions, dictating, instead, that employees show unbounded loyalty to their co-workers. In Korea, a subordinate's loyalty to a superior is even greater than his or her loyalty to the company. In China, attempts to introduce corporate hotlines can remind employees of the horrors of the Cultural Revolution when citizens were encouraged to report *illegal activities* to authorities, which included children reporting against parents, students against teachers, and neighbors against neighbors. In Germany, encouraging anonymous or confidential reporting can bring to mind Gestapo tactics from

World War II. The aversion to whistle-blowing has been heightened by recent revelations of the far-reaching informant networks of the Stasi in former East Germany.[91]

Numerous time zones and languages also prevent international employees from using corporate whistle-blowing resources. International 800 numbers and international collect calls either do not work or are unknown in many countries. In some locations, even gaining access to a telephone can be difficult. Guy Dehn, Director of the United Kingdom–based Public Concern at Work, confirmed in a recent interview, "If you're in a village in Northern Indonesia, where are you going to get the telephone to call the Alert Line? At a public telephone with others listening?"[92]

Information tends to leak out though an informal network in Hong Kong, Taiwan, and China, and the whistle-blower's future becomes difficult. In addition to the real threat of losing a job, whistle-blowers can also be subject to legal sanctions and loss of personal reputation. Whistle-blowers in Russia subject themselves to possible persecution (legal or criminal) from company managers or owners. Finally, in certain parts of the world, there have been reports that employees have been murdered in countries from Russia to Guatemala for exposing corruption.[93]

explanation of the situation is required if minorities or women are currently being underutilized. A *job group* is defined as one or more jobs having similar content, wage rates, and opportunities.

Underutilization is defined as having fewer minorities or women in a particular job group than would reasonably be expected by their availability. The utilization analysis is important because the calculations determine whether underutilization exists. For example, if the utilization analysis shows that the availability of blacks for a certain job group is 30 percent, the organization should have at least 30 percent black employment in that group. If actual employment is less than 30 percent, underutilization exists, and the firm should set a goal of 30 percent black employment for that job group.

The primary focus of any affirmative action program is on goals and timetables, with the issue being how many and by when. Goals and timetables developed by the firm should cover its entire affirmative action program, including correction of deficiencies. These goals and timetables should be attainable; that is, they should be based on results that the firm, making good-faith efforts, could reasonably expect to achieve. Goals should be significant and measurable, as well as attainable. Two types of goals must be established regarding underutilization: annual and ultimate. The annual goal is to move toward elimination of underutilization, whereas the ultimate goal is to correct all underutilization. Goals should be specific in terms of planned results, with timetables for completion. However, goals should not establish inflexible quotas that must be met. Rather, they should be targets that are reasonably attainable. Some techniques that can be used to improve recruitment and increase the flow of minority and women applicants are shown in Table 3.5.

Table 3.5 **Techniques to Improve Recruitment of Minorities and Women**

- Identify referral organizations for minorities and women.
- Hold formal briefing sessions with representatives of referral organizations.
- Encourage minority and women employees to refer applicants to the firm.
- Include minorities and women on the Personnel Relations staff.
- Permit minorities and women to participate in Career Days, Youth Motivation Programs, and related activities in their community.
- Actively participate in job fairs and give company representatives the authority to make on-the-spot commitments.
- Actively recruit at schools having predominant minority or female enrollments.
- Use special efforts to reach minorities and women during school recruitment drives.
- Undertake special employment programs whenever possible for women and minorities. These might include technical and nontechnical co-op programs, after-school and/or work-study jobs, summer jobs for underprivileged individuals, summer work-study programs, and motivation, training, and employment programs for the hardcore unemployed.
- Pictorially present minorities and women in recruiting brochures.
- Include the minority news media and women's interest media when expending help wanted advertising.

Source: Federal Register, 45, no. 251 (Tuesday December 30, 2008): 86243.

Summary

1. *Describe the projected future diverse workforce by the year 2050.* The U.S. workforce will experience significant change by 2050.
2. *Describe diversity and diversity management.* *Diversity* refers to any perceived difference among people: age, race, religion, functional specialty, profession, sexual orientation, geographic origin, lifestyle, tenure with the organization, or position, and any other perceived difference. *Diversity management* is ensuring that factors are in place to provide for and encourage the continued development of a diverse workforce by melding these actual and perceived differences among workers to achieve maximum productivity.
3. *Explain the various components of the diverse workforce.* The workforce may include the following: single parents and working mothers, women in business, mothers returning to the workforce, dual-career families, workers of color, older workers, people with disabilities, immigrants, foreign workers, and young persons with limited education or skills.
4. *Identify the major laws affecting equal employment opportunity.* Major laws include the Civil Rights Act of 1866; Equal Pay Act of 1963, As Amended in 1972; Lilly Ledbetter Fair Pay Act of 2009; Title VII of the Civil Rights Act of 1964, as Amended in 1972; Pregnancy Discrimination Act of 1978; Civil Rights Act of 1991; Age Discrimination in Employment Act of 1967, as Amended in 1978 and 1986; Rehabilitation Act of 1973; Americans with Disabilities Act of 1990; Americans with Disabilities Act Amendments Act (ADAAA) of 2009; Immigration Reform and Control Act (IRCA) of 1986; Illegal Immigration Reform and Immigrant Responsibility Act of 1996; Uniformed Services Employment and Reemployment Rights Act of 1994; and the Veterans' Benefits Improvement Act of 2004.
5. *Identify some of the major Supreme Court decisions that have had an impact on equal employment opportunity and affirmative action.* Major decisions include *Griggs v Duke Power Company, Albemarle Paper Company v Moody, Phillips v Martin Marietta Corporation, Espinoza v Farah Manufacturing Company, Dothard v Rawlingson, University of California Regents v Bakke, American Tobacco Company v Patterson, O'Connor v Consolidated Coin Caterers Corp., Adarand Constructors v Pena, Grutter v Bollinger, Gratz v Bollinger, and Ricci v DeStefano.*
6. *Describe the Equal Employment Opportunity Commission.* Title VII of the Civil Rights Act, as amended, created the Equal Employment Opportunity Commission. It was initially charged with administering the Act.
7. *Explain the purpose of the Uniform Guidelines on Employee Selection Procedures.* The *Guidelines* adopted a single set of principles that were designed to assist employers, labor organizations, employment agencies, and licensing and certification boards to comply with requirements of federal law prohibiting employment practices that discriminated on the basis of race, color, religion, sex, and national origin. They were

designed to provide a framework for determining the proper use of tests and other selection procedures.

8. *Describe disparate treatment and adverse impact.* With disparate treatment, an employer treats some people less favorably than others because of race, religion, sex, national origin, or age. Adverse impact is a concept established by the *Uniform Guidelines;* it occurs if women and minorities are not hired at the rate of at least 80 percent of the best-achieving group.

9. *Describe the Uniform Guidelines related to sexual harassment, national origin, and religion.* The EEOC has also issued interpretive guidelines that state that employers have an affirmative duty to maintain a workplace free from sexual harassment. The EEOC broadly defined discrimination on the basis of national origin as the denial of equal employment opportunity because of an individual's ancestors or place of birth or because an individual has the physical, cultural, or linguistic characteristics of a national origin group. Employers have an obligation to accommodate religious practices

unless they can demonstrate a resulting hardship.

10. *Explain caregiver discrimination.* Caregiver discrimination is discrimination against employees based on their obligations to care for family member.

11. *Explain affirmative action as required by presidential Executive Orders 11246 and 11375.* Affirmative action, stipulated by EO 11246, requires covered employers to take positive steps to ensure employment of applicants and treatment of employees during employment without regard to race, creed, color, or national origin. The order prohibited discrimination in employment because of race, creed, color, or national origin. EO 11375 changed the word "creed" to "religion" and added sex discrimination to the other prohibited items, amended EO 11246.

12. *Describe affirmative action programs.* An affirmative action program is an approach that an organization with government contracts develops to demonstrate that women or minorities are employed in proportion to their representation in the firm's relevant labor market.

Key Terms

diversity   73
diversity management   73
dual-career family   75
comparable worth   79
glass ceiling   83

disparate treatment   91
adverse impact   92
caregiver (family responsibility)
  discrimination   97

executive order (EO)   96
affirmative action   97
affirmative action program
  (AAP)   98

Questions for Review

1. What is the expected composition of the future diverse workforce by 2050?
2. Define *diversity* and *diversity management.*
3. What are the components that combine to make up the present diverse workforce? Briefly describe each.
4. Briefly describe the following laws:
   a. Civil Rights Act of 1866
   b. Equal Pay Act of 1963
   c. Lilly Ledbetter Fair Pay Act of 2009
   d. Title VII of the Civil Rights Act of 1964, as amended in 1972
   e. Pregnancy Discrimination Act of 1978
   f. Civil Rights Act of 1991
   g. Age Discrimination in Employment Act of 1967, as amended in 1978 and 1986
   h. Rehabilitation Act of 1973
   i. Americans with Disabilities Act of 1990
   j. Americans with Disabilities Act Amendments Act (ADAAA) of 2009
   k. Immigration Reform and Control Act (IRCA) of 1986

   l. Illegal Immigration Reform and Immigrant Responsibility Act of 1996
   m. Uniformed Services Employment and Reemployment Rights Act of 1994
5. What is the purpose of the Office of Federal Contract Compliance Programs?
6. What are the significant U.S. Supreme Court decisions that have had an impact on equal employment opportunity? On affirmative action?
7. What is the purpose of the *Uniform Guidelines on Employee Selection Procedures?*
8. Distinguish between disparate treatment and adverse impact.
9. How does the Equal Employment Opportunity Commission (EEOC) define sexual harassment?
10. What is meant by the term *"caregiver discrimination"?*
11. What is a presidential executive order? Describe the major provisions of EO 11246, as amended by EO 11375.
12. What is an affirmative action program?

HRM INCIDENT 1

I Feel Great

Les Partain, manager of the training and development department for Gazelle Corporation, was 64 years old and had been with the firm for more than 30 years. For the past 12 years he had served as Gazelle's training and development manager and felt that he had been doing a good job. This belief was supported by the fact that during the past five years he had received excellent performance reports from his boss, LaConya Caesar, HR director.

Six months before Les's birthday, he and LaConya were enjoying a cup of coffee together. "Les," said LaConya, "I know that you're pleased with the progress our T&D section has made under your leadership. We're really going to miss you when you retire this year. You'll certainly live the good life because you'll receive the maximum retirement benefits. If I can be of any assistance to you in developing the paperwork for your retirement, please let me know."

"Gee, LaConya," said Les. "I really appreciate the good words, but I've never felt better in my life, and although our retirement plan is excellent, I figure that I have at least five more good years. There are many other things I would like to do for the department before I retire. I have some excellent employees, and we can get many things done within the next five years." After finishing their coffee, both returned to their work. As LaConya left, she was thinking, "My gosh, I had no idea that character intended to hang on. The only reason I gave him those good performance appraisals was to make him feel better before he retired. He was actually only an average worker and I was anxious to move a more aggressive person into that key job. We stand to lose several good people in that department if Les doesn't leave. From what they tell me, he's not doing too much of a job."

Questions

1. From a legal viewpoint, what do you believe LaConya can do regarding this situation? Discuss.
2. What actions should LaConya have taken in the past to avoid her current predicament?

HRM INCIDENT 2

So, What's Affirmative Action?

It would be fair to say that over the years London has had its share of problems involving a build-up of tension between ethnic groups. Clearly it would be unreasonable to expect everything to go smoothly given the existence of some areas of deprivation, high unemployment, and, in some quarters, strong prejudices.

London does in fact have one of the most culturally diverse communities in the world. During the 1950s, many migrants from former colonies came to large cities like London in search of work. Since then, many economic migrants from other parts of the European community have arrived.

The challenging and difficult task of enforcing law and order in this situation falls to the Metropolitan Police. In recent years, Police Chiefs have emphasized the necessity of being responsive and sensitive to the needs of the various communities served by the Met.

It has also sometimes been necessary for the Met to defend itself from criticisms of racism within the force. Nick Timmins, an employment lawyer, suggested that an "old boys network" existed in the Met, comprising of officers who liked to socialize in pubs, and those who needed to abstain because religious beliefs were not part of this culture. More seriously, accusations of institutional racism have often been made against the force in previous years, although this problem is not confined to the Met.

The Association of Police Chief Officers in the UK met in 2007 to discuss what action to take. A recruitment target of 25.9 percent of officers from ethnic minorities was put in place for 2009 for the Met as well as a 7 percent overall target for the UK, although it was acknowledged that previous targets have proved extremely difficult to achieve.[94]

Questions

1. Explain why the Metropolitan Police needed an affirmative action policy?
2. Why might some applicants find this type of recruitment policy difficult to accept?

Notes

1. B & Q Diversity, "Our Greatest Asset," (2010): http://www.diy.com/diy/jsp/corporate/pdfs/diversity.pdf; The Employers Forum on Age, (2010): http://www.efa.org.uk/
2. Mitra Toossi, "A New Look at Long-term Labor Force Projections to 2050," *Monthly Labor Review* 129 (November 2006): 19–39.
3. Marie Y. Philippe, "Corporate Diversity Training: Is Yours Meeting 21st Century Needs?" *Profiles in Diversity Journal* 12 (January/February 2010): 60.
4. Jessica Tremayne, "Debunking Diversity," *Smart Business Cleveland* 20 (April 2009): 84–90.
5. Susan Meisinger, "Diversity: More Than Just Representation," *HRMagazine* 53 (January 2008): 8.
6. Kelley M. Butler, "Workplace Diversity Can Increase Employee Loyalty," *Employee Benefit News* 20 (March 2006): 16–17.
7. "Workplace Diversity Predicts Profitability," *Work-Life Newsbrief & Trend Report* (May 2009: 1.
8. "Diversity Pays Financially As Well As in Other Ways," *HR Focus* 82 (December 2005): 9.
9. Arlena Sawyers, "American Honda Opens Workplace Diversity Office," *Automotive News* 82 (January 21, 2008): 90.
10. "Diversity and Inclusion are Priorities for Top Executives, SHRM Research Finds," *HRMagazine* 54 (August 2009): 18.
11. Bill Leonard, "Gallup: Workplace Bias Still Prevalent," *HRMagazine* 51 (February 2006): 34.
12. "Best Practices for Developing Diversity & Inclusion," *HR Focus* 87 (January 2010): 7.
13. Claudia Wallis, Esther Chapman, Wendy Cole, Lrostom Kloberdanz, Sarah Sturmon Dale, Julie Rawe, Betsy Rubiner, Sonja Steptoe, and Deirdre van Dyk, "The Case for Staying Home," *Time* 163 (March 22, 2004): 50–59.
14. "Attitudes About Work And Family Changing," *Office Pro* 69 (June/July 2009): 6.
15. McLean Robbins, "Flexibility Rules at Working Mother's 100 Best Companies," *Employee Benefit News* 22 (December 2008): 58.
16. "We Did It," *Economist* 394 (January 2, 2010): 7.
17. Elizabeth Cabrera, "Fixing the Leaky Pipeline: Five Ways to Retain Female Talent," *People & Strategy* 32 (2009): 40–45.
18. Ibid.
19. Cathy Leibow, "The Pursuit of Happiness," *Employee Benefit News* 24 (January 2010): 39–49.
20. Ann Pace, "Ready or Not, Guys: Here They Come," *T+D* 64 (March 2010): 18.
21. Kelley M. Butler, "Today's Working Women Seek Mentors, Motherhood Transition," *Employee Benefit News* 20 (April 2006): 17–19.
22. Attitudes About Work And Family Changing."
23. "Work-Family Conflicts Affect Employees at All Income Levels," *HR Focus* 87 (April 2010): 9.
24. Cabrera, "Fixing the Leaky Pipeline: Five Ways to Retain Female Talent."
25. Lorraine Bello and Galen Tinder, "Dual Career Implications on Workforce Mobility: The Evolution of the Relocating Spouse/Partner" *Benefits & Compensation Digest* 46 (September 2009): 36–39.
26. Ella Bell, "The Bicultural Life Experience of Career Oriented Black Women," *Journal of Organizational Behavior* 11 (November 1990): 459–478.
27. "60 Percent of Older Workers Delay Retirement," *HRMagazine* 54 (May 2009): 22.
28. Kelly Evans, "Ranks of Older Workers Swell as Losses Shorten Retirement," *Wall Street Journal - Eastern Edition* 253 (April 9, 2009): A2.
29. "Older Workers Staying Longer," *Office Pro* 69 (October 2009): IS9.
30. Kelly M. Butler, "A Breather from Health Care Can Help Employers Focus on the Brain Drain," *Employee Benefit News* 24 (February 2010): 8.
31. Jean M. Phillips, Mary Pomerantz, and Stanley M. Gully, "Plugging the Boomer Drain," *HRMagazine* 52 (December 2007): 54–58.
32. "As Boomers Gray, Savvy Employers Could See Silver Lining," *HR Specialist: Compensation & Benefits* 5 (January 2010): 4.
33. "What Older Workers Seek in Positions," *Community Banker* 18 (August 2009): 14.
34. "Findings of Most Extensive Employer Survey on People with Disabilities Released," *EHS Today* 2 (February 2009): 19.
35. Susan J. Wells, "Counting on Workers with Disabilities," *HRMagazine* 53 (April 2008): 45–49.
36. Rita Zeidner, "Does the United States Need Foreign Workers?" *HRMagazine* 54 (June 2009): 42–47.
37. Ibid.
38. Ibid.
39. Stephen Gandel, "The Teen Job Chop," *Time* 175 (January 18, 2010): 38–43.
40. "Retaliation Claims OK Under Civil Rights Act," *HR Focus* 85 (July 2008): 2.
41. Michael Brittan and Amy Onder, "Managing the Expanding Definition of 'Discrimination': A Practical Review of the Ledbetter Fair Pay Act and Its Consequences for Employers," *Employee Relations Law Journal* 35 (Fall 2009): 3–29.
42. Bill Leonard, "President Signs Wage Bias Law," *HRMagazine* 54 (March 2009): 13.
43. "Check Your Records! Some Old Pay-bias Cases Get New Life under Ledbetter Law," *HR Specialist: Compensation & Benefits* 5 (February 2010): 3.
44. Allen Smith, "Ledbetter Act Adds Lengthy To-Do List," *HRMagazine* 54 (April 2009): 16.
45. Judy Greenwald, "High Court Expands Bias Protection for Employees," *Business Insurance* 43 (February 9, 2009): 4–17.
46. "Bias Settlement Chips $500,000 out of Ceisel Masonry," *HR Specialist: Illinois Employment Law* 3 (July 2009): 5.
47. "Talbert Builders Settles Race Discrimination Suit," *HR Specialist: North Carolina Employment Law* 3 (July 2009): 5.

48. "How to Legally Manage Pregnancy and Maternity Leaves," *HR Specialist: Florida Employment Law* 4 (July 2009): 4.
49. "Britthaven Nursing Home Settles Pregnancy Discrimination Claim," *HR Specialist: North Carolina Employment Law* 3 (June 2009): 5.
50. The six cases are *Ward Cove Packing Co., Inc., v Antonio, Price Waterhouse v Hopkins, Patterson v McClean Credit Union, Martin v Wilks, West Virginia Hospitals v Casey,* and *Lorence v AT&T.*
51. Tyler M. Paetkau, "When Does a Foreign Law Compel a U.S. Employer to Discriminate Against U.S. Expatriates? A Modest Proposal for Reform," *Labor Law Journal* 60 (Summer 2009): 92–103.
52. Russ Banham, "Age Bias Claims Rise," *Treasury & Risk* (May 2009): 14–15.
53. Brad Dawson, "Freudenberg-NOK Settles EEOC Age Lawsuit," *Rubber & Plastics News* 39 (Septembr 21, 2009): 5.
54. Donald L. Caruth, Robert M. Noe III, and R. Wayne Mondy, *Staffing the Contemporary Organization* (New York: Quorum Books, 1988): 49.
55. "Feds Want a Look at Online Job Sites," *HRMagazine* 53 (November 2008): 12.
56. Victoria Zellers, "Make a Resolution: ADA Training," *HRMagazine* 54 (January 2009): 81–83.
57. Michael G. Sherrard, "Criminal Convictions Upheld," *HRMagazine* 53 (January 2008): 84.
58. Bill Leonard, "Many Federal Contractors Now Must Use E-Verify," *HRMagazine* 54 (January 2009): 17.
59. Bill Leonard, "Immigration Agents Will Target Employers," *HRMagazine* 54 (June 2009): 19.
60. Bill Zalud, "The Illegal Trap When Hiring," *Security: For Buyers of Products, Systems & Services* 46 (March 2009): 66–68.
61. "Treating Returning Veteran as New Employee Violated USERRA," *Fair Employment Practices Guidelines* (April 1, 2010): 1–4.
62. "USERRA Requirements for a Returning Veteran," *401K Advisor* 16 (February 2009): 7–9.
63. "The ABCs of USERRA," *Payroll Manager's Letter* 26 (March 7, 2010): 6.
64. Peter de Jager, "Ethics: Good, Evil, and Moral Duty," *Information Management Journal* (September/October 2002): 82–85.
65. Liz Ryan, "Scuttling Some Job-Hunt Myths," *Business Week Online* (March 23, 2006): 4.
66. "Discrimination-Disparate Treatment-Reverse Discrimination-Civil Service Promotional Examinations," *Benefits Quarterly* 25 (2009 Third Quarter): 50–51.
67. Mark Schoeff, Jr., "Ruling Raises Bar on Testing for Employment," *Workforce Management* 88 (July 20, 2009): 11.
68. "Employees Still Filing Job-discrimination Complaints in Near-record Numbers," *HR Specialist* 8 (February 2010): 8.
69. Men Now Filing One-sixth of All Sexual Harassment Claims," *HR Specialist: North Carolina Employment Law* 4 (April 2010):1.
70. Rita Zeidner, "Retaliation Can Exist Without Formal Complaint," *HRMagazine* 55 (March 2010): 18.
71. "'Purposeful Ignorance' Is No Defense for Sexual Harassment," *HR Focus* 87 (March 2010): 2.
72. "Not All Harassers Need Immediate Firing," *HR Specialist: Florida Employment Law* 5 (February 2010): 1–2.
73. Contrary to Popular Belief, Consent Doesn't Mean It Wasn't Harassment," *HR Specialist* 7 (September 2009): 3.
74. Maria Greco Danaher, "Exec's Isolated Come-On Supports Hostile Environment Claim," *HRMagazine* 48 (February 2003): 105.
75. "Supervisor's Offer to Female Employee: $1 Million to Spend the Night Together," *Legal Alert for Supervisors* 3 (June 2, 2008): 4.
76. "Case of First Impression: "Sex Specific" Language, Not Directed at Plaintiff, May Still Form Basis of Sexual Harassment Claim," *Fair Employment Practices Guidelines* (June 1, 2008): 3–4.
77. "Duane Reade Settles Sex Harassment Lawsuit," *HR Specialist: New York Employment Law* 4 (August 2009): 5.
78. "Know the 3 Criteria for Same-sex Harassment," *HR Specialist: Texas Employment Law* 4 (August 2009): 3.
79. Allen Smith, "EEOC Settlement Reflects Challenges of English-Only Policies," *HRMagazine* 54 (June 2009): 26.
80. Mark D. Downey, "Keeping the Faith," *HRMagazine* 53 (January 2008): 85–88.
81. *http://www.trumanlibrary.org/9981.htm*
82. "Beware Local Laws on Family Care Bias," *HR Focus* 87 (March 2010): 2.
83. Rita Zeidner, "Handle with Care," *HRMagazine* 54 (November 2009): 22–28.
84. "New EEOC Guidance Addresses Caregiver Workers' Issues," *HR Focus* 86 (July 2009): 2.
85. Abigail Crouse, "Be Careful! Caregiver Discrimination Claims Are on the Rise," *HR Specialist: Minnesota Employment Law* 3 (April 2010): 6.
86. Roger S. Kaplan, "Family Responsibilities Discrimination: Examining the Issues, Understanding the Legal Risks, and Exploring Positive Solutions," *Employee Relations Law Journal* 34 (Summer 2008): 3–13.
87. Crouse, "Be Careful! Caregiver Discrimination Claims Are on the Rise."
88. Zeidner, "Handle with Care."
89. Dave Wieczorek, "The Parent Trap," *InsideCounsel* 20 (July 2009): 26–28.
90. Consuela A. Pinto, "Family Responsibilities Discrimination: The Next Frontier in Public Sector Employment Law," *Illinois Public Employee Relations Report* 25 (Winter 2008): 1–9.
91. Lori Tansey Martin and Amber Crowell, "Whistleblowing: A Global Perspective (Part I)," *Ethikos* 15 (May 1, 2002): 6.
92. Ibid.
93. Ibid.
94. BBC News, "Police Heads Debate Ethnic Quotas," (2007): http://news.bbc.co.uk/1/hi/uk/6570545.stm; "HR Director Backs Positive Discrimination for Police," *Personnel Today*, (2007): http://www.personneltoday.com/articles/2007/05/01/40380/hr-director-backs-positive-discrimination-for-police.html.

CHAPTER

4 Job Analysis, Strategic Planning, and Human Resource Planning

HRM In Action: Strategic Talent Management Systems

Talent management is a strategic endeavor to optimize the use of human capital, which enables an organization to drive short- and long-term results by building culture, engagement, capability, and capacity through integrated talent acquisition, development, and deployment processes that are aligned to business goals.[1] It integrates HR topics such as compensation, recruiting, performance management, learning management, career development, and succession planning. All of these topics will be covered in your text. It attempts to ensure that the right person is in the right job at the right time. Brian Wilkerson, global director of talent management at Watson Wyatt, said, "Automating and integrating these talent management processes, including compensation, would enable companies to better manage their workforce, anticipate future needs, and keep employees engaged."[2] A fully integrated talent management system helps answer many questions that a CEO may ask such as, "Do I have the executive talent to lead an initiative?" or "How long before we have enough knowledge and skills within the organization for the initiative to take hold?"[3] They want assurance that they have the workers available to achieve their business goals, both now and in the future.[4]

More and more companies are automating the talent management process into a single information system. At Chevron Corporation, Taryn Shawstad, general manager of global workforce development, works with a database of about 60,000 employees from approximately 180 countries. She says, "In the past, we were siloed by country. Now, instead of looking at the United States or Indonesia or Nigeria, we can look across the globe at job families, capabilities, supply, and demand. If you don't have the data, it's

After completing this chapter, students should be able to:

1. Describe strategic talent management.

2. Explain why job analysis is a basic human resource tool and explain the reasons for conducting job analysis.

3. Describe the types of information required for job analysis and describe the various job analysis methods.

4. Identify who conducts job analysis and describe the components of a job description.

5. Explain O*NET as the Occupational Information Network, Standard Occupational Classification (SOC), job sculpting, timeliness of job analysis, job analysis for team members, and describe how job analysis helps satisfy various legal requirements.

6. Describe the need for the human resource manager to be a strategic partner.

7. Explain the strategic planning process and describe the human resource planning process.

8. Describe forecasting human resource requirements and availability and how databases can assist in matching internal employees to positions.

9. Identify what a firm can do when either a shortage or a surplus of workers exists.

10. Explain succession planning and disaster planning in today's environment.

11. Describe manager and employee self-service.

12. Describe some job design concepts.

difficult to do the analysis." According to Jeff Oberlin, president of Jeff Oberlin, Inc. in Elmhurst, Illinois, "from line employees all the way up to the CEO, companies need to ensure that they have a long-range view of where they are going, what type of talent they will need, the competencies required in particular jobs and across the board, and also the number of employees needed with certain skill sets."[5]

According to research conducted by The Hackett Group, companies with more mature talent management capabilities reap strong bottom-line benefits, including earnings that are 18 percent higher than typical Global 1000 companies.[6] Basically, talent management exists to support company objectives. In today's dynamic international environment, talent management provides HR with a significant and demanding challenge. As Vic Speers, director of talent management at Hudson, a provider of talent management services worldwide, says: "The second war for talent is brewing. Young and talented employees are increasingly rare in an aging population where more people retire every year than join the workforce." Organizations are finding it increasingly difficult to recruit quality talent because competitors want these same individuals.[7]

The successful firms in this dynamic global environment will be the ones that have been successful at talent management.[8] Much has changed in the world today, and firms that move beyond the traditional approach to talent management will have the advantage. Topics relating to talent management will be discussed throughout this text.

This chapter begins by describing strategic talent management systems. Next, the reason why job analysis is a basic human resource management tool is shown and the reasons for conducting job analysis are explained.

talent management
Strategic endeavor to optimize the use of human capital, which enables an organization to drive short- and long-term results by building culture, engagement, capability, and capacity through integrated talent acquisition, development, and deployment processes that are aligned to business goals.

Then, the types of job analysis information required are reviewed and job analysis methods are discussed. Conducting job analysis is then presented, and the components of a job description are explained. O*NET as the Occupational Information Network, Standard Occupational Classification (SOC), and job sculpting are then explained. The timeliness of job analysis, job analysis for team members, and the way job analysis helps to satisfy various legal requirements are then discussed. Next, the need for the human resource manager to be a strategic partner is described. Then, the strategic planning process and the human resource planning process are explained. Next, forecasting of human resource requirements and availability is shown followed by how HR databases can assist matching internal employees to positions. Then, actions that can be taken, should either a shortage or a surplus of workers exist, are presented including a discussion of alternatives to layoffs. Succession planning and disaster planning are then described. Sections devoted to manager and employee self-service and some job design concepts are then described. The chapter concludes with a global perspective entitled "Global Job Rotation as a Unique Fast Track Benefit."

job analysis
Systematic process of determining the skills, duties, and knowledge required for performing jobs in an organization.

job
Group of tasks that must be performed for an organization to achieve its goals.

position
Collection of tasks and responsibilities performed by one person.

Job Analysis: A Basic Human Resource Management Tool

Job analysis is the systematic process of determining the skills, duties, and knowledge required for performing jobs in an organization.[9]

With job analysis, the tasks needed to perform the job are identified. Traditionally, it is an essential and pervasive human resource technique and the starting point for other human resource activities.[10] In today's rapidly changing work environment, the need for a sound job analysis system is critical. New jobs are being created, and old jobs are being redesigned or eliminated. A job analysis that was conducted only a few years ago may now be obsolete. Some have even suggested that changes are occurring too fast to maintain an effective job analysis system.

A **job** consists of a group of tasks that must be performed for an organization to achieve its goals. A job may require the services of one person, such as that of the president, or the services of 75, as might be the case with machine operators in a large firm. A **position** is the collection of tasks and responsibilities performed by *one* person; there is a position for every individual in an organization.

In a work group consisting of a supervisor, two senior analysts, and four analysts, there are three jobs and seven positions. A small company might have 25 jobs for its 75 employees, whereas in a large company 2,000 jobs may exist for 50,000 employees. In some firms, as few as 10 jobs may make up 90 percent of the workforce.

The purpose of job analysis is to obtain answers to six important questions:

1. What physical and mental tasks does the worker accomplish?
2. When is the job to be completed?
3. Where is the job to be accomplished?
4. How does the worker do the job?
5. Why is the job done?
6. What qualifications are needed to perform the job?

Job analysis provides a summary of a job's duties and responsibilities, its relationship to other jobs, the knowledge and skills required, and working conditions under which it is performed. Job facts are gathered, analyzed, and recorded, as the job exists, not as the job should exist. Determining how the job should exist is most often assigned to industrial engineers, methods analysts, or others. Job analysis is conducted after the job has been designed, the worker has been trained, and the job is being performed.

job description
Document that provides information regarding the essential tasks, duties, and responsibilities of a job.

job specification
A document that outlines the minimum acceptable qualifications a person should possess to perform a particular job.

| OBJECTIVE 4.2
Explain why job analysis is a basic human resource tool and explain the reasons for conducting job analysis.

Job analysis is performed on three occasions: (1) when the organization is founded and a job analysis program is initiated for the first time; (2) when new jobs are created; and (3) when jobs are changed significantly as a result of new technologies, methods, procedures, or systems. Jobs also change when there is increased emphasis on teamwork in organizations, empowerment of employees, or other managerial interventions such as quality management systems. Job analysis is most often performed because of changes in the nature of jobs and is used to prepare both job descriptions and job specifications.

The **job description** is a document that provides information regarding the essential tasks, duties, and responsibilities of the job. The minimum acceptable qualifications a person should possess in order to perform a particular job are contained in the **job specification**. Both types of documents will be discussed in greater detail later in this chapter.

Reasons for Conducting Job Analysis

As Figure 4.1 shows, data derived from job analysis in the form of the job description/specification can have an impact on virtually every aspect of human resource management. In practice, both the job description and job specification are combined into one document with the job specification presented after the job description.

Staffing

All areas of staffing would be haphazard if the organization did not know the qualifications needed to perform the various jobs. A major use of job analysis data is found in the area of human resource planning (discussed later in this chapter). Merely knowing that the firm will need 1,000 new employees to produce goods or services to satisfy sales demand is insufficient. Each job requires different knowledge, skills, and ability levels. Obviously, effective human resource planning must take these job requirements into consideration. Also, lacking up-to-date job descriptions and specifications, a firm would have to recruit and select employees for jobs without having clear guidelines; this practice could have disastrous consequences. The desired outcomes need to be specific and measurable, not vague statements.

Training and Development

Job description information often proves beneficial in identifying training and development needs. If it suggests that the job requires a particular knowledge, skill, or ability, and the person filling the position does not possess all the qualifications required, training and/or development are probably in order. Training should be directed at assisting workers in performing duties specified in their present job descriptions or at developing skills for broader responsibilities.

Figure 4.1

Job Analysis: A Basic Human Resource Management Tool

Performance Appraisal

Most workers want to know precisely what they are supposed to accomplish and good job descriptions provide that.[11] Then, employees should be evaluated in terms of how well they accomplish the duties specified in their job descriptions and any other specific goals that may have been established. A manager who evaluates an employee on factors not clearly predetermined is left open to allegations of discrimination.

Compensation

In the area of compensation, it is helpful to know the relative value of a particular job to the company before a dollar value is placed on it. Jobs that require greater knowledge, skills, and abilities should be worth more to the firm. For example, the relative value of a job calling for a master's degree normally would be higher than that of a job that requires a high school diploma. This might not be the case if the market value of the job requiring only a high school diploma was higher, however. Such a situation occurred in a major West Coast city a number of years ago. It came to light that city sanitation engineers (garbage collectors) were paid more than better-educated public schoolteachers.

Safety and Health

Information derived from job analysis is also valuable in identifying safety and health considerations. For example, employers are required to state whether a job is hazardous. The job description/specification should reflect this condition. In addition, in certain hazardous jobs, workers may need specific information about the hazards in order to perform their jobs safely.

Employee and Labor Relations

Job analysis information is also important in employee and labor relations. When employees are considered for promotion, transfer, or demotion, the job description provides a standard for evaluation and comparison of talent.[12] Regardless of whether the firm is unionized, information obtained through job analysis can often lead to more objective human resource decisions.

Legal Considerations

A properly prepared job analysis is particularly important for supporting the legality of employment practices. Prior to the equal employment opportunity movement in the early 1960s and 1970s, few firms had effective job analysis systems.[13] But, the need to validate basic job requirements hastened the growth in the use of job analysis to prepare job descriptions/specifications. The importance of job analysis is well documented in the *Uniform Guidelines on Employee Selection Procedures*.[14] Job analysis data are needed to defend decisions involving termination, promotion, transfers, and demotions. Job analysis provides the basis for tying the HR functions together and the foundation for developing a sound human resource program.

Types of Job Analysis Information

OBJECTIVE 4.3
Describe the types of information required for job analysis and describe the various job analysis methods.

Considerable information is needed for the successful accomplishment of job analysis. The job analyst identifies the job's actual duties and responsibilities and gathers the other types of data such as work activities; worker-oriented activities; machines, tools, equipment, and work aids used; and personal requirements. Essential functions of the job are determined in this process. This information is used later to help determine the job skills needed. In addition, the job analyst looks at job-related tangibles and intangibles, such as the knowledge needed, the materials processed, and the goods made or services performed.

Some job analysis systems identify job standards. Work measurement studies may be needed to determine how long it takes to perform a task. With regard to job content, the analyst studies the work schedule, financial and nonfinancial incentives, and physical working conditions. Specific education, training, and work experience pertinent to the job are identified. Because many jobs are often performed in conjunction with others, organizational and social contexts are also noted. Subjective skills required, such as strong interpersonal skills, should be identified if the job requires the jobholder to be personable.

Job Analysis Methods

Job analysis has traditionally been conducted in a number of different ways because organizational needs and resources for conducting job analysis differ. Selection of a specific method should be based on the purposes for which the information is to be used (job evaluation, pay increases, development, and so on) and the approach that is most feasible for a particular organization. The historically most common methods of job analysis are discussed in the following sections.

Questionnaires

Questionnaires are typically quick and economical to use. The job analyst may administer a structured questionnaire to employees, who identify the tasks they perform. In some cases, employees may lack verbal skills, a condition that makes this method less useful. Also, some employees may tend to exaggerate the significance of their tasks, suggesting more responsibility than actually exists.

Observation

When using the observation method, the job analyst watches the worker perform job tasks and records his or her observations. This method is used primarily to gather information on jobs emphasizing manual skills, such as those of a machine operator. It can also help the analyst identify interrelationships between physical and mental tasks. Observation alone is usually an insufficient means of conducting job analysis, however, particularly when mental skills are dominant in a job. Observing a financial analyst at work would not reveal much about the requirements of the job.

Interviews

An understanding of the job may also be gained through interviewing both the employee and the supervisor. Usually, the analyst interviews the employee first, helping him or her describe the duties performed. Then, the analyst normally contacts the supervisor for additional information, to check the accuracy of the information obtained from the employee, and to clarify certain points.

Employee Recording

In some instances, job analysis information is gathered by having employees describe their daily work activities in a diary or log. With this method, the problem of employees exaggerating job importance may have to be overcome. Even so, valuable understanding of highly specialized jobs, such as, recreational therapist, may be obtained in this way.

Combination of Methods

Usually an analyst does not use one job analysis method exclusively. A combination of methods is often more appropriate. In analyzing clerical and administrative jobs, the analyst might use questionnaires supported by interviews and limited observation. In studying production jobs, interviews supplemented by extensive work observations may provide the necessary data. Basically, the analyst should use the combination of techniques needed for accurate job descriptions/specifications.

Over the years, attempts have been made to provide more systematic methods of conducting job analysis. Several of these approaches are discussed in Table 4.1.

Table 4.1   **Other Methods Available for Conducting Job Analysis**

Department of Labor Job Analysis Schedule

The U.S. Department of Labor established a method of systematically studying jobs and occupations called the job analysis schedule (JAS). When the JAS method is used, a trained analyst gathers information. A major component of the JAS is the Work Performed Ratings section. Here, what workers do in performing a job with regard to data (D), people (P), and things (T) is evaluated. Each is viewed as a hierarchy of functions, with the items higher in the category being more difficult. The codes in the worker functions section represent the highest level of involvement in each of the three categories.

The JAS component "Worker Traits Ratings" relates primarily to job requirement data. The topics general education designation (GED), specific vocational preparation (SVP), aptitudes, temperaments, interests, physical demands, and environmental conditions are included. The Description of Tasks section provides a specific description of the work performed. Both routine tasks and occasionally performed tasks are included.

Functional Job Analysis

Functional job analysis (FJA) is a comprehensive job analysis approach that concentrates on the interactions among the work, the worker, and the organization. This approach is a modification of the job analysis schedule. It assesses specific job outputs and identifies job tasks in terms of task statements.

Position Analysis Questionnaire

The position analysis questionnaire (PAQ) is a structured job analysis questionnaire that uses a checklist approach to identify job elements. It focuses on general worker behaviors instead of tasks. Some 194 job descriptors relate to job-oriented elements. Advocates of the PAQ believe that its ability to identify job elements, behaviors required of job incumbents, and other job characteristics makes this procedure applicable to the analysis of virtually any type of job. Each job descriptor is evaluated on a specified scale such as extent of use, amount of time, importance of job, possibility of occurrence, and applicability.

Each job being studied is scored relative to the 32 job dimensions. The score derived represents a profile of the job; this can be compared with standard profiles to group jobs into known job families, that is, job of a similar nature. In essence, the PAQ identifies significant job behaviors and classifies jobs. Using the PAQ, job descriptions can be based on the relative importance and emphasis placed on various job elements. The PAQ has been called one of the most useful job analysis methods.

Management Position Description Questionnaire

The management position description questionnaire (MPDQ) is a method of job analysis designed for management positions; it uses a checklist to analyze jobs. The MPDQ has been used to determine the training needs of individuals who are slated to move into managerial positions. It has also been used to evaluate and set compensation rates for managerial jobs and to assign the jobs to job families.

Guidelines-Oriented Job Analysis

The guidelines-oriented job analysis (GOJA) responds to the legislation affecting staffing and involves a step-by-step procedure to define the work of a particular job classification. It is also used for developing selection tools, such as application forms, and for documenting compliance with various legal requirements. The GOJA obtains the following types of information: (1) machines, tools, and equipment; (2) supervision; (3) contacts; (4) duties; (5) knowledge, skills, and abilities; (6) physical and other requirements; and (7) differentiating requirements.

OBJECTIVE 4.4
Identify who conducts job analysis and describe the components of a job description.

Conducting Job Analysis

The person who conducts job analysis is interested in gathering data on what is involved in performing a particular job. The people who participate in job analysis should include, at a minimum, the employee and the employee's immediate supervisor. Large organizations may have one or more job analysts, but in small organizations line supervisors may be responsible for job analysis. Organizations that lack the technical expertise may use outside consultants to perform job analysis.

Regardless of the approach taken, before conducting job analysis, the analyst should learn as much as possible about the job by reviewing organizational charts and talking with individuals acquainted with the jobs to be studied. Before beginning, the supervisor should introduce the analyst to the employees and explain the purpose of the job analysis. Although employee attitudes about the job are beyond the job analyst's control, the analyst must attempt to develop mutual trust and confidence with those whose jobs are being analyzed. Failure in this area will detract from an otherwise technically sound job analysis. Upon completion of the job analysis, two basic human resource documents, job descriptions and job specifications, can be prepared. As previously mentioned, in practice, both the job description and job specification are combined into one document with the job specification presented after the job description.

Job Description

Information obtained through job analysis is crucial to the development of job descriptions. Earlier, *job description* was defined as a document that states the tasks, duties, and responsibilities of the job. It is vitally important that job descriptions are both relevant and accurate.[15] They should provide concise statements of what employees are expected to do on the job, how they do it, and the conditions under which the duties are performed. Concise job descriptions put an end to the possibility of hearing "that's not my job." Having accurate job descriptions is the starting point for most HR tasks.[16]

Among the items frequently included in a job description are these:

- Major duties performed
- Percentage of time devoted to each duty
- Performance standards to be achieved
- Working conditions and possible hazards
- Number of employees performing the job, and to whom they report
- The machines and equipment used on the job

The contents of the job description vary somewhat with the purpose for which it will be used. The next sections address the parts of a job description.

Job Identification

The job identification section includes the job title, the department, the reporting relationship, and a job number or code. A good title will closely approximate the nature of the work content and will distinguish that job from others. Unfortunately, job titles are often misleading. An executive assistant in one organization may be little more than a highly paid clerk, whereas a person with the same title in another firm may practically run the company. For instance, one former student's first job after graduation was with a major tire and rubber company as an *assistant district service manager*. Because the primary duties of the job were to unload tires from trucks, check tread wear, and stack tires in boxcars, a more appropriate title would probably have been *tire checker and stacker*.

Date of the Job Analysis

The job analysis date is placed on the job description to aid in identifying job changes that would make the description obsolete. Some firms have found it useful to place an expiration date on the document. This practice ensures periodic review of job content and minimizes the number of obsolete job descriptions.

Job Summary

The job summary provides a concise overview of the job. It is generally a short paragraph that states job content.

Duties Performed

The body of the job description delineates the major duties to be performed. Usually, one sentence beginning with an action verb (such as *receives, performs, establishes,* or *assembles*) adequately explains each duty. Essential functions may be shown in a separate section to aid in complying with the Americans with Disabilities Act. An example of a job description of a records clerk is shown in Figure 4.2.

Job Specification

Recall that *job specification* was defined as a document containing the minimum acceptable qualifications that a person should possess in order to perform a particular job. Job specifications should always reflect the minimum, not the ideal qualifications for a particular job. Several

HR Web Wisdom

*O*NET™ OnLine*

**http://online.
onetcenter.org**

Making occupational information interactive and accessible for all.

Figure 4.2

**Job Description/
Specification
Example**

Administrative Information
Job Title: Records Clerk
Department: Loan Operations
Reports To: Loan Operation Manager
Job Number: 11

Date of Job Analysis
January 21, 2011

Expiration Date
January 2014

Job Summary
Returns all consumer paid loan documents to customers. Supervises the daily activities of two clerks.

Essential Functions Performed
Receives monthly files for accounts that have been paid in full and require the return of contracts, mortgage documents, auto titles, and other documents.
Answers telephone and e-mail inquiries from customers or loan officers concerning documents.
Maintains file on temporary automobile titles until permanent title is received.
Files permanent automobile titles, contracts, mortgage documents, and other documents in customer files on a daily basis.
Supervises two file clerks who maintain correspondence and other general files.
Performs file clerk duties as needed.
Performs other duties, as required, on a temporary basis, to maintain section or departmental operations and services.

Job Specifications

Education
High school diploma preferred, but not required
Experience
Six months or more in a financial institution and familiarity with various loan documents
Skills Required
Working knowledge of Microsoft Word and Excel
Ability to enter data at a rate of 35 words per minute

problems may result if specifications are inflated. First, if specifications are set too high, they might systematically eliminate minorities or women from consideration for jobs. Therefore, the organization runs the risk of being charged with discrimination. Second, compensation costs will increase because ideal candidates will have to be compensated more than candidates with minimum skills. Third, job vacancies will be harder to fill because ideal candidates are more difficult to find than minimally qualified candidates.

Determining the appropriate qualifications for a job is undoubtedly the most difficult part of job analysis. It requires a great deal of probing on the part of the job analyst as well as a broad understanding of the skills needed to perform varieties of work. Items typically included in the job specification are factors that are job-related, such as educational requirements, experience, and job related personality traits and physical abilities. As previously mentioned, in practice, job specifications are often included as a major section of job descriptions.

After jobs have been analyzed and the descriptions written, the results should be reviewed with the supervisor and the worker to ensure that they are accurate, clear, and understandable. The courtesy of reviewing results with employees also helps to gain their acceptance.

O*NET, the Occupational Information Network

O*NET, the Occupational Information Network, is a comprehensive, government-developed database of worker attributes and job characteristics. It is the nation's primary source of occupational information. It is a flexible, easy-to-use database system that provides a common language for defining and describing occupations. Its flexible design also captures rapidly changing job requirements. It provides the essential foundation for facilitating career counseling, education, employment, and training activities by containing information about knowledge, skills, abilities; interests; general work activities; and work context.[17]

Standard Occupational Classification (SOC)

Recently, the federal government released updated job descriptions for all U.S. workers in more than 800 occupations. The 2010 SOC replaces the 2000 system. The SOC's substantive structural changes are based on actual changes in the nature or organization of work activities being performed in the economy. The update also provides an opportunity for professional organizations and labor groups to seek recognition or a higher profile for their members' occupations by gaining a separate listing or reclassification. Most current occupations will be unaffected except perhaps for a change in the description's wording.[18]

Job Sculpting

Job sculpting involves modifying the typical job descriptions to take advantage of the talents, interests, and experiences of each employee. Employers first determine if a person has the qualifications to perform the job as described in the job description. Then an attempt is made to improve the "value" of a person to the organization by sculpting or tailoring it to the strengths of the specific individual.[19]

Job sculpting requires more work on the part of the person who will do it. A job description is first prepared for those who are performing similar tasks. The individual performing the job sculpting must first have an in-depth knowledge of the business and understand how fine-tuning can improve the organization as a whole. Second, the person who is performing the job sculpting must have an in-depth knowledge of the talents, interests, and values of each individual. Third, the job description must be clearly understood. The purpose of job sculpting a job is not to change the job description; you want to make it better for a specific individual.[20]

The final step involves actually matching the strengths of each person to the job description. If a strength is not specifically mentioned in the job description, it should be added, thereby creating a new and improved job description. Because the job description is being customized to the individual, the worker feels more engaged and involved to do the best job possible. Employees do not feel bored, thereby improving job performance.[21] Job sculpting is not easy but the potential benefits are large.

OBJECTIVE 4.5
Explain the timeliness of job analysis and job analysis for team members, and describe how job analysis helps satisfy various legal requirements.

Timeliness of Job Analysis

The rapid pace of technological change makes the need for accurate job analysis even more important. Historically, job analysis could be conducted and then set aside for several years. Today, however, job requirements are changing so rapidly that they must be constantly reviewed to keep them relevant. Recall from Chapter 1 that today's employees will change careers (not merely "jobs") three times in their life. If this projection is correct, the need for accurate and timely job analysis is becoming even more important. Further, because of the fast-paced world we live in today, the amount of time that can be devoted to job analysis has diminished. Streamlined methods of job analysis have had to be developed. Darin E. Hartley has developed what he calls *Job Analysis at the Speed of Reality* which is a speeded-up version of the interview method of job analysis. Through this process, a validated job analysis can be completed in two or three hours as opposed to two or three days.[22]

Job Analysis for Team Members

Historically, companies have established permanent jobs and filled these jobs with people who best fit the job description. The jobs then continued in effect for years to come. In many firms today, people are being hired as team members. Whenever someone asks a team member, "What is your job description?" the reply might well be "Whatever." What this means is that if a project has to be completed, individuals do what has to be done to complete the task.

With team design, there are no narrow jobs. Today, the work that departments do is often bundled into teams. The members of these teams have a far greater depth and breadth of skills than would have been required in traditional jobs. Formerly, there might have been 100 separate job classifications in a facility. With team design, there may be just 10 or fewer broadly defined roles of teams. Another dimension is added to job analysis when teams are considered: Job analysis may determine how important it is for employees to be team players and work well in group situations.

Jobs are changing by getting bigger and more complex. The last duty shown on the job description, "And any other duty that may be assigned," is increasingly becoming *the* job description. This enlarged, flexible, complex job changes the way many tasks are performed. Managers cannot simply look for individuals who possess narrow job skills. They must go deeper and seek competencies, intelligence, ability to adjust, and ability and willingness to work in teams. Today, more than ever, people go from project to project and from team to team. Job definitions become blurred, and titles become almost meaningless as job descriptions have become even more all-encompassing. Basically, what matters is what you know and how well you apply it to the business.

Job descriptions frequently focus heavily, if not exclusively, on minimum objective requirements, such as education and job experience. However, these documents often pay little or no attention to the more subjective behavioral competencies essential to a job, such as flexibility, agility, and strategic insight. When you recruit and hire for one task, it will not be long before the firm asks the employee to do several others as well. With such wide-ranging expectations from the company, the employee will obviously need a broader variety of skills and abilities. Some firms are dealing with this situation by striving to employ individuals who are bright and adaptable and can work effectively in teams. Hiring for organizational *fit* is discussed in Chapter 6.

Job Analysis and the Law

Effective job analysis is essential to sound human resource management as an organization recruits, selects, and promotes employees. Legislation requiring thorough job analysis includes the following acts:

- *Fair Labor Standards Act:* Employees are categorized as exempt or nonexempt, and job analysis is basic to this determination. Nonexempt workers must be paid time and a half when they work more than 40 hours per week. Overtime pay is not required for exempt employees.

- *Equal Pay Act:* If jobs are not substantially different, the employees performing them must receive similar pay. When pay differences exist, job descriptions can be used to show whether jobs are substantially equal in terms of skill, effort, responsibility, and working conditions.

- *Civil Rights Act:* Human resource management has focused on job analysis because selection methods need to be clearly job-related. Job descriptions may provide the basis for an equitable compensation system and an adequate defense against unfair discrimination charges in initial selection, promotion, and all other areas of human resource administration. When job analysis is not performed, defending certain qualifications established for the job is usually difficult. Remember in the *Griggs v Duke Power Company* case in Chapter 3, the company stated that supervisors must have a high school diploma. However, the company could show no business necessity for this standard. Placing a selection standard in the job specification without having determined its necessity through job analysis makes the firm vulnerable in discrimination suits.

- *Occupational Safety and Health Act:* Job descriptions are required to specify elements of the job that endanger health or are considered unsatisfactory or distasteful by the majority of the population. Showing the job description to the employee in advance is a good defense.

- *Americans with Disabilities Act (ADA):* Employers are required to make reasonable accommodations for workers with disabilities who are able to perform the *essential functions* of a job and job analysis is needed to obtain this information. The EEOC defines *reasonable accommodation* as any modification or adjustment to a job, an employment practice, or the work environment that makes it possible for an individual with a disability to enjoy an equal employment opportunity.

OBJECTIVE 4.6
Describe the need for the human resource manager to be a strategic partner.

HR as a Strategic Business Partner

In Chapter 3, you saw the many laws, court cases, and executive orders that impact the HR environment. When these laws were passed, managers often did not know how to operate within this new compliance environment. They were bombarded with questions regarding what to do and what not to do in hiring, promoting, and even firing a person. There were so many myths that surfaced during this time such as "You can't fire that person because he or she is—black, a woman, disabled, etc." Someone was needed to restore calm and inform managers what were facts and what were fiction. Some believe that the growth of HR as a profession grew in number and importance as it moved into this administrative and compliance arena. There were forms to complete such as the EEO-1 and managers to educate as to hiring standards to avoid. Over time, the administrative role of HR has diminished as equal employment opportunity became understood by the general workforce.

Today, HR professions are increasingly expected to take on the role of being a strategic partner with upper management.[23] No longer is an administrative and compliance role acceptable as their primary jobs. HR executives have become a strategic partner in achieving organizational plans and results.[24] HR professions are moving to add greater value through a more strategic focus.[25] In doing so, they understand the operational side of the business and help to determine the strategic capabilities of the company's workforce, both today and in the future.[26] HR professionals are becoming agile in their thinking as they adapt to the ebbs and flows of business. In doing so, HR executives are ensuring that human resources support the firm's mission. The 2008/10 recession gave HR professionals the opportunity to further establish their role as a strategic partner with increased responsibility and accountability for the bottom line.[27]

The most forward-thinking HR professionals have changed the way they work.[28] Working as a strategic business partner requires a much deeper and broader understanding of business issues. What exactly strategically should HR be doing? Richard Pinola, chair and CEO of Right Management Consultants, Inc. (Philadelphia), during a session at a SHRM conference, listed the following tasks that CEOs want from HR:

- Make workforce strategies integral to company strategies and goals.
- Leverage HR's role in major change initiatives, such as strategic planning, mergers, and acquisitions.
- Earn the right to a seat at the corporate table.
- Develop awareness and/or an understanding of the business.
- Understand finance and profits.
- Help line managers achieve their goals.[29]

Human resource professionals can give the CEO and CFO a powerful understanding of the role human capital plays in the organization and the way it combines with business processes to expand or shrink shareholder value. To answer the question of whether the HR executive is involved strategically, William Schiemann, chair and CEO of Metrus Group, suggests that the following questions be answered:

1. Is HR present at mergers and acquisitions planning meetings, strategy reviews, and restructuring discussions?
2. Does HR provide an annual report on its ROI?
3. Does HR lead the people strategy? Has it developed performance indicators for the success of that strategy?
4. Is HR rated by its customers?
5. Does the organization conduct strategic versus entitlement employee surveys?
6. Are employee and other survey initiatives linked to customer and financial metrics?
7. Is there an ROI process to evaluate HR initiatives connected to the business strategy?[30]

Much has changed in recent years as HR professionals moved from an administrative focus to a more strategic one. The following ad for a Senior Human Resources Executive would not have been advertised even a decade ago:

Reporting to the president, the successful candidate will be a member of the executive management team with leadership and management accountability for the entire HR organization. The successful candidate should have 15–20 years of progressive and senior-level HR demonstrated success in developing and implementing HR strategies and programs. An advanced degree and PHR/SPHR designation is highly desirable.[31]

HR professionals are integrating the goals of HR with the goals of the organization and focusing on expanding its strategic and high-level corporate participation with an emphasis on adding value. In doing so, HR is demonstrating that it can produce a return on investment for its programs. It analyzes HR activities to determine whether they are maintaining acceptable profit margins.[32] The CEO needs help in matters that human resource professionals are qualified to handle. As one HR expert said, "They (HR) are the enablers, they are the ones who should know about change and develop strategies to make it work."

As HR managers become strategic partners in their organizations, they are showing how they add value to the company. Mark Fogel, head of the HR function for Leviton Manufacturing, said, "At Leviton, I get to do work that's every HR executive's dream. Things most people only read about in *HRMagazine*." Fogel has been primarily responsible for aligning HR with organization's goals. He said, "I used to call myself an HR executive. Today, I view myself as a business executive, and the entire HR team as businesspeople."[33] As you move through the text, the importance of strategic HR will be emphasized, as was the case of strategic talent management described at the beginning of the chapter.

Strategic Planning Process

OBJECTIVE 4.7
Explain the strategic planning process and the human resource planning process.

strategic planning
Process by which top management determines overall organizational purposes and objectives and how they are achieved.

A noted in the previous discussion, HR executives are now focusing their attention on how human resources can help the organization achieve its strategic objectives. Thus, HR executives are highly involved in the strategic planning process. In the past they often waited until the strategic plan was formulated before beginning human resource planning. **Strategic planning** is the process by which top management determines overall organizational purposes and objectives and how they are achieved.

Strategic planning is an ongoing process that is dynamically changing and seeking a competitive advantage.[34] At times an organization may see the need to diversify and increase the variety of the goods that are made or sold. At other times, downsizing may be required in response to the external environment. Or, the strategic plan may see integration, the unified control of a number of successive or similar operations, as their driving force. Strategic planning attempts to position the organization in terms of the external environment. Remember the many external environmental factors that were described in Chapter 1. For example, the recession of 2008/10 showed weakness in the marketplace for some firms, which led to lower company valuations, increased business failures, and firms spinning out or selling off their non-core business units. Forward thinking companies found opportunities that were not available when business was booming such as expanding their company through acquisition.[35] They are always looking for ways to stay competitive, gain market share, and be the first to innovate a new product or service.[36]

Strategic planning at all levels of the organization can be divided into four steps: (1) determination of the organizational mission, (2) assessment of the organization and its environment, (3) setting of specific objectives or direction, and (4) determination of strategies to accomplish those objectives (see Figure 4.3). The strategic planning process described here is basically a derivative of the SWOT (strengths, weaknesses, opportunities, and threats) framework that affects organizational performance, but it is less structured.

Mission Determination

mission
Unit's continuing purpose or reason for being.

The first step in the strategic planning process is to determine the corporate mission. The **mission** is a unit's continuing purpose, or reason for being. The corporate mission is the sum total of the organization's ongoing purpose. Arriving at a mission statement should involve answering the questions: What are we in management attempting to do for whom? Should we maximize profit so shareholders will receive higher dividends or so share price will increase? Or should we emphasize stability of earnings so employees will remain secure? Certainly, HR can provide valuable assistance in answering these questions.

Figure 4.3

Strategic Planning Process

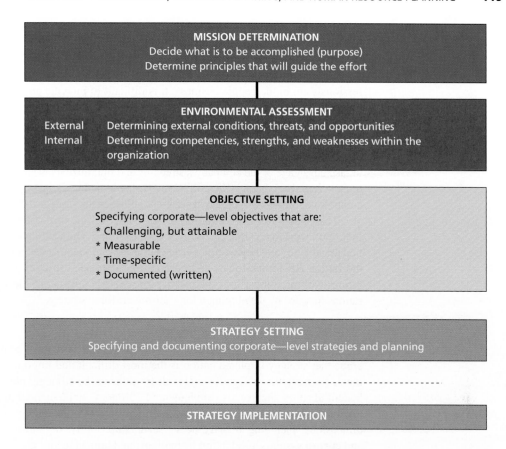

MISSION DETERMINATION
Decide what is to be accomplished (purpose)
Determine principles that will guide the effort

ENVIRONMENTAL ASSESSMENT
External   Determining external conditions, threats, and opportunities
Internal   Determining competencies, strengths, and weaknesses within the organization

OBJECTIVE SETTING
Specifying corporate—level objectives that are:
* Challenging, but attainable
* Measurable
* Time-specific
* Documented (written)

STRATEGY SETTING
Specifying and documenting corporate—level strategies and planning

STRATEGY IMPLEMENTATION

There are many other mission possibilities. Mission determination also requires deciding on the principles on which management decisions will be based. Will the corporation be honorable or dishonorable, ruthless or considerate, devious or forthright, in dealing with its various constituencies? The answers to these questions tend to become embedded in a corporate culture and help determine the organizational mission. Top management expects HR activities to be closely aligned to this mission and add value toward achieving these goals.

Environmental Assessment

Once the mission has been determined, the organization should assess its *strengths* and *weaknesses* in the internal environment and the *threats* and *opportunities* from the external environment (often referred as a SWOT analysis). Making strategic plans involves information flows from both the internal and the external environments. From inside comes information about organizational competencies, strengths, and weaknesses. Scanning the external environment allows organizational strategists to identify threats and opportunities, as well as constraints. In brief, the strategy would be to take advantage of the company's strengths and minimize its weaknesses in order to grasp opportunities and avoid threats.

HR professionals are in the best position to identify workforce strengths and weaknesses. Through the use of human resource information systems, the demographics of the present workforce can be determined. Should the company be considering, for instance, a merger or acquisition, HR would be able to work with top management to determine whether the present workforce can be effectively integrated into the workforce of the merged company. For example, does the workforce of the merged company improve the overall value of the company, or is there only duplication of talent? Any reorganization affects people and HR professionals must be in the forefront of people-related matters.

Objective Setting

Objectives are the desired end results of any activity. Objectives should have four basic characteristics: (1) They should be expressed in writing, (2) they should be measurable, (3) they should be specific as to time, and (4) they should be challenging but attainable. HR metrics are discussed in Chapter 6. Strategic objectives might be directed at factors such as profitability, customer satisfaction, financial returns, technological leadership, and operating efficiency. Objectives should be developed only after a cost–benefit analysis of each alternative is considered. Since HR professionals are in the people business, it is difficult to imagine any strategic objective that would not involve them in some manner.

Strategy Setting

Strategies can now be developed for accomplishing those objectives. Strategies should be developed to take advantage of the company's strengths and minimize its weaknesses in order to grasp opportunities and avoid threats. HR professionals should be highly involved in these activities, since the composition of the workforce will certainly influence the strategies chosen.

There has never been a more pressing time for HR professionals and leaders to develop a long-term workforce strategy for their organizations. The leading organizations will be the ones that are able to look beyond the current situation and identify the competencies they will need in the future. HR professionals and corporate leaders need to work together to define what their future workforce must look like. HR professionals are taking the opportunity to lead corporations forward by developing a long-term workforce strategy.[37]

Strategy Implementation

Once the strategic planning process is complete, the strategy must be implemented. Some people argue that strategy implementation is the most difficult and important part of strategic management. No matter how creative and well formulated the strategic plan, the organization will not benefit if it is incorrectly implemented. Strategy implementation requires changes in the organization's behavior, which can be brought about by changing one or more organizational dimensions, including management's leadership ability, organizational structure, information and control systems, production technology, and human resources.[38]

LEADERSHIP HR must take the leadership role in dealing with human resource matters. In a recent report entitled "Leading Now, Leading the Future: What Senior HR Leaders Need to Know," which was released by the Society for Human Resource Management, the following eight leadership skills essential for HR business leaders were identified: knowledge of business, HR, and organizational operations; strategic thinking and critical/analytical thinking; leading change; effective communication; credibility; results orientation/drive for performance; ethical behavior; and persuasiveness and influencing others. Each of these qualities relates positively to that of HR professionals being a strategic partner.[39]

ORGANIZATIONAL STRUCTURE A company's organizational structure is typically illustrated by its organizational chart. The particular form of structure needed is determined by the needs of the firm. It may be informal and highly changeable in small, uncomplicated businesses. By contrast, large, diverse, and complex organizations usually have a highly formalized structure. But that should not mean the structure is so rigid that it does not change, perhaps even frequently. Newly formed high-technology companies are most likely to restructure or reorganize frequently, but lately some of the largest *Fortune* 500 industrial firms such as General Motors and Chrysler experienced major reorganizations. Many variations of organizational structures are available for use today. HR should be in a good position to recommend the most effective structure needed by the organization.

INFORMATION AND CONTROL SYSTEMS Among the information and control systems are reward systems; incentives; objectives-oriented systems; budgets for allocating resources; information systems; and the organization's rules, policies, and implementations. Certainly, HR should be a valuable asset in developing and working with these systems. A proper mix of information and control systems must be developed to support the implementation of the strategic plan.

TECHNOLOGY The knowledge, tools, and equipment used to accomplish an organization's assignments comprise its technology. The appropriate level of technology must be found for proper implementation of the strategic plan. I mentioned in Chapter 1 how technology is revolutionizing how organizations operate today.

HR Web Wisdom

Bureau of Labor Statistics

http://stats.bls.gov

Vital information related to human resource planning is available on this site.

human resource planning (workforce planning)
Systematic process of matching the internal and external supply of people with job openings anticipated in the organization over a specified period of time.

HUMAN RESOURCES   The human resource functions must be properly aligned to successfully implement the strategic plan. HR will be central to understanding the future of an asset that is increasingly important to the organization—the intellectual and productive capacity of its workforce. In essence, a proper balance of human resources must be developed to support strategy implementation. Once strategic planning has taken place, human resource planning may be developed to help implement the strategic plan.

Human Resource Planning

Human resource planning (workforce planning) is the systematic process of matching the internal and external supply of people with job openings anticipated in the organization over a specific period of time. In a recent SHRM survey, the primary focus of companies now is workforce planning.[40] Through workforce planning, organizations attempt to predict future human resource needs.[41] The recession of 2008/10 caused workforce planning to become even more important to organizations. According to Jamie Hale, national practice leader of workforce planning at Watson Wyatt, "Workforce-planning activities will clearly get more attention as employers look for ways to perform during this weakened economy. Having the right numbers of people performing in the right roles will be crucial for companies to position themselves strongly for when the economy recovers."[42] Companies that plan not just for tomorrow but plan for the long haul will achieve greater success.[43]

The human resource planning process is illustrated in Figure 4.4 Note that strategic planning precedes human resource planning. Human resource planning has two components: *requirements*

Figure 4.4

The Human Resource Planning Process

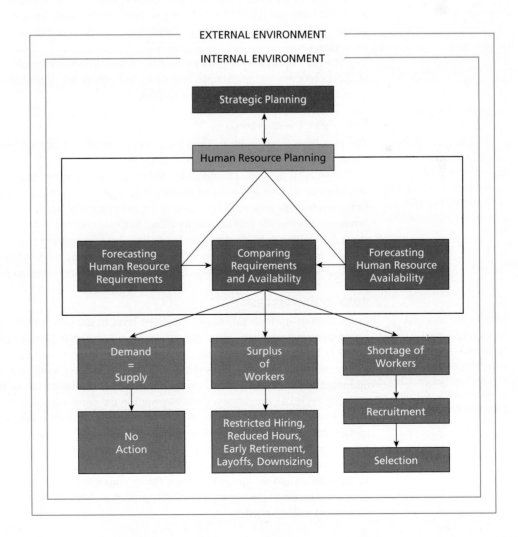

requirements forecast
Determining the number, skill, and location of employees the organization will need at future dates in order to meet its goals.

availability forecast
Determination of whether the firm will be able to secure employees with the necessary skills, and from what sources.

and *availability*. A **requirements forecast** involves determining the number, skill, and location of employees the organization will need at future dates in order to meet its goals.

The determination of whether the firm will be able to secure employees with the necessary skills, and from what sources, is called an **availability forecast.**

When employee requirements and availability have been analyzed, the firm can determine whether it will have a surplus or shortage of employees. Ways must be found to reduce the number of employees if a surplus is projected. If a worker shortage is forecast, the firm must obtain the proper quantity and quality of workers from outside the organization. In this case, external recruitment and selection are required.

Because conditions in the external and internal environments can change quickly, the human resource planning process must be continuous. Changing conditions could affect the entire organization, thereby requiring extensive modification of forecasts. The recession of 2008/10 provided a major challenge as firms raced to develop a downsizing strategy.

OBJECTIVE 4.8
Describe forecasting human resource requirements and availability and how databases can assist in matching internal employees to positions.

Forecasting Human Resource Requirements

As previously defined, a *requirements forecast* involves determining the number, skill, and location of employees the organization will need at future dates in order to meet its goals. Before human resource requirements can be projected, demand for the firm's goods or services must be forecasted. This forecast is then converted into people requirements for the activities necessary to meet this demand. For a firm that manufactures personal computers, activities might be stated in terms of the number of units to be produced, number of sales calls to be made, number of vouchers to be processed, or a variety of other activities. For example, manufacturing 1,000 laptop computers each week might require 10,000 hours of work by assemblers during a 40-hour week. Dividing the 10,000 hours by the 40 hours in the work week gives 250 assembly workers needed. Similar calculations are performed for the other jobs needed to produce and market the computers.

Several techniques for forecasting human resource requirements are currently used. Some of the techniques are qualitative in nature, and others are quantitative. Several of the better-known methods are described in this section.

Zero-Base Forecasting

zero-base forecasting
Forecasting method that uses the organization's current level of employment as the starting point for determining future staffing needs.

The **zero-base forecasting** method uses the organization's current level of employment as the starting point for determining future staffing needs.

Essentially, the same procedure is used for human resource planning as for zero-base budgeting, whereby each budget must be justified each year. If an employee retires, is fired, or leaves the firm for any other reason, the position is not automatically filled. Instead, an analysis is made to determine whether the firm can justify filling it. Equal concern is shown for creating new positions when they appear to be needed. The key to zero-base forecasting is a thorough analysis of human resource needs. Frequently, the position is not filled and the work is spread out among remaining employees. Plans may also involve outsourcing or other approaches as an alternative to hiring.

Bottom-Up Forecast

bottom-up forecast
Forecasting method in which each successive level in the organization, starting with the lowest, forecasts its requirements, ultimately providing an aggregate forecast of employees needed.

In the **bottom-up forecast**, each successive level in the organization, starting with the lowest, forecasts its requirements, ultimately providing an aggregate forecast of employees needed.

It is based on the reasoning that the manager in each unit is most knowledgeable about employment requirements. Beginning with the lowest-level work units in the organization, each unit manager makes an estimate of personnel needs for the period of time encompassed by the planning cycle. As the process moves upward in the company, each successively higher level of management in turn makes its own estimates of needs, incorporating the input from each of the immediately preceding levels. The result, ultimately, is an aggregate forecast of needs for the entire organization. This process is often highly interactive in that estimated requirements from the previous level are discussed, negotiated, and reestimated with the next level of management as the forecast moves upward through the organization. The interactive aspect of managerial estimating is one of the advantages of this procedure because it forces managers to justify their anticipated staffing needs.

Figure 4.5

Relationship of Sales Volume to Number of Employees

Relationship between Volume of Sales and Number of Workers Required

Historically, one of the most useful predictors of employment levels is sales volume. The relationship between demand and the number of employees needed is a positive one. As you can see in Figure 4.5, a firm's sales volume is depicted on the horizontal axis, and the number of employees actually required is shown on the vertical axis. In this illustration, as sales decrease, so does the number of employees. Using such a method, managers can approximate the number of employees required at different demand levels.

Workforce Planning Software

Workforce planning software refers to applications that allow companies to forecast the number and kind of employees they will need at some point in the future. Workforce planning tends to hone in on key job families or skills that will be required. In many cases, the tools let firms experiment with different scenarios, examining what workforce costs or risks may result from taking steps such as entering a new geographical market or eliminating a business unit.[44]

Workforce planning software tends to fall into two categories. The first is short-term or operational workforce planning, meaning preparing for changes within months. This type of planning is used with mergers and restructuring. HumanConcepts, Acquire, and Nakisa provide this type product, which is basically a tool for representing a firm's employees graphically in organization charts. Longer-term, strategic workforce planning software providers design products to help envision the workforce as far out as three to five years. Vendors involved with long-term planning include business software giant SAP, Aruspex, Vemo, and Infohrm.[45]

Forecasting Human Resource Availability

In order to forecast availability, the human resource manager looks to both internal sources (current employees) and external sources (the labor market). The determination of whether the firm will be able to secure employees with the necessary skills, and from what sources, is an *availability forecast*. It helps to show whether the needed employees may be obtained from within the company, from outside the organization, or from a combination of the two sources. Another possibility is that the required skills are not immediately available from any feasible source. Consider the following example.

A large manufacturing firm on the West Coast was preparing to begin operations in a new plant. Analysts had already determined there was a large long-term demand for the new product. Financing was available and equipment was in place. But production did not begin for two years! Management had made a critical mistake: It had studied the demand side of human resources but not the supply side. There were not enough qualified workers in the local labor market to operate the new plant. New workers had to receive extensive training before they could move into the newly created jobs.

This illustration provides one more instance of the importance of HR involvement in strategic planning.

HR Web Wisdom

*HR Planning
Organization*
http://www.hrps.org
This is the Web site for
the Human Resource
Planning Society.

Human Resource Databases

A *human resource database* contains employee information that permits management to make HR decisions. Information that might appear in such databases includes, but is not limited to, the following: work history and experience, specific skills and knowledge, licenses or certifications held, organizational training completed, educational background, previous performance appraisal evaluations, assessment of strengths and weaknesses, developmental needs, promotion potential at present, and with further development, current job performance, field of specialization, job preferences, geographic preferences, career goals and aspirations, anticipated retirement date, and personal history, including psychological assessments. As may be seen from the above list, the employee information that is included in such databases can affect virtually any topic related to the management of human resources.

Many of the workers needed for future positions likely already work for the firm and are included in the database. However, information not only includes present workers but also data regarding former workers and prospective members as they apply for jobs in the company. For example, in Chapter 5, I say that former employees often desire to return to the company. And, as individuals make application with the firm, they too become part of the HR data.

OBJECTIVE 4.9
Identify what a firm can
do when either a
shortage or a surplus of
workers exists.

Shortage of Workers Forecasted

When firms are faced with a shortage of workers, organizations will have to intensify their efforts to recruit the necessary people to meet the needs of the firm. Some possible actions will be discussed next.

Innovative Recruiting

A shortage of personnel often means that new approaches to recruiting must be used. The organization may have to recruit in different geographic areas than in the past, explore new methods, and seek different kinds of candidates. In using innovative recruiting, businesses must attempt to determine who their prospective employees are and what motivates them.

Compensation Incentives

Firms competing for workers in a high-demand situation may have to rely on compensation incentives. Premium pay is one obvious method; however, this approach may trigger a bidding war that the organization cannot sustain for an extended period. To offset the bidding war, some organizations have signing bonuses to entice individuals to join the firm. More subtle forms of rewards may be required to attract employees to a firm, such as four-day workweeks, flexible working hours, telecommuting, part-time employment, and child-care centers. These topics are discussed in Chapter 10.

Training Programs

Special training programs may be needed to prepare previously unemployable individuals for positions with a firm. Remedial education and skills training are two types of programs that may help attract individuals to a particular company. For example, a small firm in Los Angeles expanded its market by hiring people with few, if any, qualifications. The firm was willing to spend the necessary time and money needed to provide even basic training.

Different Selection Standards

Another approach for dealing with shortages of workers is the lowering of employment standards. Selection criteria that screen out certain workers may have to be altered to ensure that enough people are available to fill jobs. Instead of desiring extensive work experience, a firm may be willing to hire an inexperienced worker and train the individual to do the job.

ETHICAL DILEMMA

Which "Thinker" Should Go?

Your company is a leading producer of advanced microchips. You are the chief researcher in your firm's *think tank,* which consists of eight people with various specialties. Your group has generated most of the ideas and product innovations that have kept the company an industry leader for 10 years. In fact, the think tank has been so successful that another one has been organized to support the company's newest manufacturing operation on the West Coast. The individuals included in the new think tank have already been selected, but your boss has just assigned you the task of deciding who from your group of thinkers will head the new organization.

The person best qualified for the job is Tim Matherson. Tim is an MIT graduate, the informal team leader, and the individual who personally spearheaded three of the team's five most successful product advancements. However, if Tim is given the promotion, the void created by his leaving will be difficult to fill. On the other hand, the boss forced his nephew, Robert Jones, into your group. He is a sharp graduate of the local state university, but he is not a team player and he is always trying to push you around. You can either recommend Tim, illustrating that those who produce the most benefit the most, or you can recommend Robert, making the boss happy, getting rid of a problem, and, most important of all, keeping your best performer.

What would you do?

Surplus of Employees Forecasted

When a comparison of requirements and availability indicates that a worker surplus will result, most companies look to alternatives to layoffs (described in the Trends & Innovation below) but downsizing may ultimately be required. A major section in Chapter 13 is devoted to discussing downsizing.

OBJECTIVE 4.10
Explain succession planning and disaster planning in today's environment.

succession planning
Process of ensuring that qualified persons are available to assume key managerial positions once the positions are vacant.

Succession Planning: A Component of Strategic Planning

Succession planning is the process of ensuring that qualified persons are available to assume key managerial positions once the positions are vacant.

Nothing could be as important to the strategic well-being of a company as ensuring that a qualified person is in place to lead the company both now and in the future. This definition includes untimely deaths, resignations, terminations, or the orderly retirements of key managerial personnel. The goal is to help ensure a smooth transition and operational efficiency, but the transition is often difficult. The Institute for Corporate Productivity (i4cp) paper, "Succession Planning Highlight Report," found that 34 percent of organizations with more than 10,000 employees are not prepared to fill their leadership roles. The report also concluded that succession planning will be among the top five challenges executives face in the future.[46] Research, in collaboration with the National Association of Corporate Directors, shows that nearly 8 in 10 directors view the identification and preparation of capable CEOs as one of their most important responsibilities, yet less than 25 percent rate their boards as "excellent" in that area.[47]

Because of the tremendous changes that will confront management this century, succession planning is taking on more importance than ever before.[48] It is not only deaths that have created an increased focus on succession planning. The premature firing of CEOs is no longer a rare event. CEOs are being terminated more quickly than in the past. Estimates are that the tenure for CEOs will continue to grow shorter.

TRENDS & INNOVATIONS

Layoff Alternatives

The headlines in 2008/10 seemed to constantly remind us that the country was in a recession. They daily reported companies laying off workers. At times, layoffs can be a necessary cost-cutting measure. However, there are counterproductive problems associated with layoffs such as increased turnover, especially among the best, most productive workers and creating anxiety among remaining staff, resulting in lower morale, reduced worker engagement, and decreased productivity.[49] Diminished by the downsizing headlines was the fact that many companies were looking for alternatives to layoff and retaining as many workers as possible.[50]

One of the first alternatives to layoffs is to implement a restricted hiring policy which reduces the workforce by not replacing employees who leave. Ellen Raim, principal in the Corragio Group, an HR consulting firm in Portland, Oregon, said, "If hiring can be controlled, the theory is that more drastic actions such as layoffs can be avoided." There are basically three forms of freezes. A *hard freeze* means that no new workers are hired to replace a vacated position. A *soft freeze* means that the company is only hiring to fill critical positions. New workers are hired only when the overall performance of the organization may be affected. A new term, *smart freeze*, entered the HR vocabulary with the recession of 2008/10. HR and managers evaluate every position to determine the ones the company could not survive without and those that are difficult to fill and continue to hire them. Some companies are even laying off some marginal workers in critical positions and seeking more qualified workers to fill these positions.[51]

Early retirement is another way to reduce the number of workers. Some employees will be delighted to retire, but others will be somewhat reluctant. However, the latter may be willing to accept early retirement if the total retirement package is made sufficiently attractive. Other traditional approaches as alternatives to layoffs include encouraging workers to use their vacation time and reducing the use of contingent workers.

A tactic that is popular in the construction market is swapping employees.[52] Some companies loan out staff to partner companies during slow times, while promising to hire back the workers when conditions improve. While the workers were away, they learned new skills and those left behind learned the skills to replace them.

Another alternative to layoffs is permitting an employee to go from full-time to 30 hours a week without losing health benefits.[53] Some companies offered job-sharing arrangements. This arrangement can enable organizations to retain top talent in lieu of layoffs while having minimal impact on the overall labor budget. For example, employee benefits can be fairly managed on a per-employee basis, as two 20-hour-a-week part timers may have comparably pro-rated, scaled back benefits.[54]

Other companies reduced the workweek from five days to four, thereby having a 20 percent reduction in wages. Jason Zickerman, president and CEO of The Alternative Board, said, "You don't lose eight hours of productivity. You gain loyalty. When your team knows you're fighting for them, they will fight for you." Some companies offered an unpaid holiday option where instead of taking two weeks off, employees are being asked to take five, with three unpaid. Zickerman points out that millennials often do not have mortgages and family expenses and they might jump at the chance to take an extended holiday that would be impossible in busier times. Unpaid holiday weeks can be broken up so that employees can budget for them. Zickerman adds, "It shows a good faith effort. If presented properly, it can be seen as doing everything you can to take care of them."[55]

Even sabbaticals to selected employees were used. With a sabbatical comes a reduction in pay. However, the company typically pays for any training they undergo (in new software, for example). Upon returning from the sabbatical they will hopefully be more valuable than before they left. "This by no means is delivered for the purposes of a perk," says Zickerman, "but they may prefer this to losing their jobs."[56]

Approximately one-third of the CEOs of the *Fortune* 1000 companies were recruited externally.[57] However, hiring CEOs from external sources poses problems because boards of directors cannot know them as well as they know their own people. Also, in the search for a new CEO, boards tend to be harder on internal candidates than on external ones. However, the internal candidates are well known. Boards have had the opportunity to see them perform over a long period of time and have witnessed their successes and failures.[58] In contrast, because external candidates may present themselves in the best possible light, they may appear to be a perfect match. But, studies show that on average, outsiders perform no better than insiders. Although at times there are justifications for searching externally for top-level executives, an internal succession process may be best.

In recent years, succession planning is going much deeper into the workforce. One VP of HR of a wholesale/distribution facility said, "We have good succession planning for the top level of the company but have failed to do anything about the levels where all the work is performed."[59] "The biggest thing that is going on is a movement away from traditional succession planning, which was focused on top executives of the company," says James Holincheck, a research vice president at Gartner Inc. in Chicago. Tom McKinnon, a consultant for Novations Group, a global consulting firm based in Boston, said, "Expanding succession management to take in middle managers and to develop them helps assure that key roles below the C-suite have ready replacements."[60] The availability of newer software associated with performance management systems permits organizations to deal with larger numbers of employees at more levels in the firm.

Disaster Planning: A Component of Strategic Planning

Disaster plans should focus on possible catastrophes that range from natural calamities such as hurricanes, earthquakes, and floods, to human-made crises such as 9/11. Certainly the 2010 oil spill disaster on the Gulf coast caused companies to review and update their disaster plan.[61]

I personally witnessed the destruction that resulted when Hurricane Rita struck my hometown of Lake Charles, Louisiana. The town in southwest Louisiana, where I lived, truly looked like a war zone. Businesses were not only damaged by wind but some also faced flood damage and destruction of their products. For a long time there was no electricity, mail service, or newspaper delivery. Employees were scattered across the country. Business owners often had to also contend with the destruction of their own homes. Where a dense forest once stood, one could now see clearly because trees lay broken and twisted on the ground or on top of homes. Houses that had withstood the wind often had the roof covered with a blue tarp, compliments of FEMA. Looking at the massive destruction, one might wonder if businesses in the area could ever recover. It quickly became evident that quite a few organizations had poorly designed disaster plans, or none at all.

Many wished that they had devoted more time to disaster planning. However, some businesses had excellent disaster plans. Although the petroleum refineries were hit hard, they were able to recover quickly because of their detailed disaster recovery plans. In speaking with managers and workers alike, I found that workers knew precisely what their roles were. The plan called for a few critical workers to remain in safe havens within the refineries, to be able to hasten the recovery after the hurricane passed. These individuals were able to tell returning individuals the extent of the damage and what resources were needed to begin repairs. Many predicted recovery would take years; but because of the detailed disaster planning, these companies were up and running in record time.

In the aftermath of Hurricanes Katrina and Rita, companies lost track of their employees because the mandatory evacuation order had sent them in all directions. Organizations that had disaster plans in place to communicate with their employees were back in operation rapidly, even though their headquarters might have been inoperative. When Katrina struck New Orleans, financial planners from Wachovia set up shop in Lake Charles and conducted business there until they had to move to Lafayette, Louisiana, due to Hurricane Rita.

McNeese State University, located in Lake Charles, Louisiana, was severely damaged by the hurricane. Plans were already in place to move the Internet server that connected students and faculty to another location. Plans had also been made for payroll to be processed at another university in the state, and employees could access their money through Western Union anywhere in the country. Even though the buildings at McNeese were inoperative, learning continued. Within a week after the storm, some students and faculty were again at work, and some students who had evacuated to their homes in Mexico were conducting research, writing papers, and communicating with their professors over the Internet. Without a well-developed disaster plan, it is likely that the semester would have had to be cancelled.

When disaster strikes business, there are always significant human resource issues to address. While plans should focus on a wide variety of catastrophes that range from natural calamities to human-made crises, they should also cover day-to-day occurrences such as power failures, server malfunctions, and virus attacks. These plans need to address how the company will respond when employees who play a critical role or possess unique skills and knowledge suddenly become incapacitated or unavailable for some extended period of time. To fill these voids, it is necessary to identify which positions and personnel within the company are critical to the organization's continued ability to accomplish its primary mission. Critical positions are those that cannot be left vacant even briefly without disastrous results and which would be very difficult to fill. HR software is available to assist in this task. For critical positions, the company should identify the name of the person, key responsibilities, required competencies, classification, a pool of candidates for progression, the candidates' existing competencies, and training required for candidates. That information should serve as the basis for the contingency plan, which should document those who could potentially step in to fulfill that role, the person with the authority to invoke that contingency plan, and other information required to ensure a smooth transition.[62]

OBJECTIVE 4.11
Describe manager and employee self-service.

manager self-service (MSS)
The use of software and the corporate network to automate paper-based human resource processes that require a manager's approval, record-keeping, or input, and processes that support the manager's job.

Manager Self-Service

HR software is increasingly available to permit managers to perform tasks that were previously done by HR. **Manager self-service (MSS)** is the use of software and the corporate network to automate paper-based human resource processes that require a manager's approval, record-keeping or input, and processes that support the manager's job.

There are distinct levels of self-service, from basic administrative tasks to strategic MSS. The basis MSS automates paper, workflow, and processes associated with routine transactions, such as awarding pay increases, arranging transfers, and approving vacation time and travel expenses. More advanced processes include recruiting, compensation planning, and performance management. Even before MSS was implemented, many companies had already automated selection processes, using public Web sites and commercial software.

The decision to develop an MSS system may be easy, but implementation has been difficult. At times, the culture of the organization has to change, and that takes time. There is the difficulty of getting people to accept a new way of doing things. Managers have gotten used to telling the HR department to handle the transactions that MSS now requires managers to perform. Some view an MSS as extra work placed on managers. Monica Barron, an analyst at IT consulting firm AMR Research Inc. of Boston, said, "Managers may complain, 'Why am I doing HR's work?' When that happens, MSS has not been properly presented as beneficial to the organization."[63] According to recent research from professional services firm Towers Perrin, 62 percent of HR service-centers staff/administrators reported that MSS reduced their workload. "That's encouraging because otherwise HR might be seen to be dumping more work on managers," says Towers Perrin principal Hugh Shanks.[64]

employee self-service (ESS)
Processes that automate transactions that previously were labor-intensive for both employees and HR professionals.

Employee Self-Service

Employee self-service (ESS) consists of processes that automate transactions that previously were labor-intensive for both employees and HR professionals. ESS applications can free up valuable HR staff time, reducing administrative time and costs.[65] In a recent survey by *CedarCrestone*, 60 percent of respondents have pay-related self-service applications and another 10 percent plan to add them. Benefits-related self-service was in use at 59 percent of responding organizations and will be joined by another 14 percent shortly.[66] In another survey by Towers Perrin, 33 percent of respondents intend to offer employees the ability to plan their careers. A similar percentage will allow workers to update performance goals online, and 52 percent will allow employees to enroll in training courses online.[67] In addition, a growing number of employers provide access to tools and information that can give employees an accurate picture of their financial health.

OBJECTIVE 4.12
Describe some job design concepts.

job design
Process of determining the specific tasks to be performed, the methods used in performing these tasks, and how the job relates to other work in an organization.

job enrichment
Changes in the content and level of responsibility of a job so as to provide greater challenges to the worker.

Job Design Concepts

We previously said that new jobs were being created at a rapid pace. If this is so, jobs have to be designed. **Job design** is the process of determining the specific tasks to be performed, the methods used in performing these tasks, and how the job relates to other work in the organization. Several concepts related to job design will be discussed next.

Job Enrichment

Strongly advocated by Frederick Herzberg, **job enrichment** consists of basic changes in the content and level of responsibility of a job so as to provide greater challenges to the worker. Job enrichment provides a vertical expansion of responsibilities.

The worker has the opportunity to derive a feeling of achievement, recognition, responsibility, and personal growth in performing the job. Although job enrichment programs do not always achieve positive results, they have often brought about improvements in job performance and in the level of worker satisfaction in many organizations.

According to Herzberg, five principles should be followed when implementing job enrichment:

- *Increasing job demands:* The job should be changed in such a way as to increase the level of difficulty and responsibility.
- *Increasing the worker's accountability:* More individual control and authority over the work should be allowed, while the manager retains ultimate accountability.
- *Providing work-scheduling freedom:* Within limits, individual workers should be allowed to schedule their own work.
- *Providing feedback:* Timely periodic reports on performance should be made directly to workers rather than to their supervisors.
- *Providing new learning experiences:* Work situations should encourage opportunities for new experiences and personal growth.[68]

Today, job enrichment is moving toward the team level, as more teams become autonomous, or self-managed.

Job Enlargement

job enlargement
Increasing the number of tasks a worker performs, with all of the tasks at the same level of responsibility.

There is a clear distinction between job enrichment and job enlargement. **Job enlargement** is defined as increasing the number of tasks a worker performs, with all of the tasks at the same level of responsibility.

Job enlargement involves providing greater variety to the worker. For example, instead of knowing how to operate only one machine, a person is taught to operate two or even three, but no higher level of responsibility is required. Both job enrichment and job enlargement can be used with workers who have progressed as far as they can in their present jobs or are victims of burnout.

Job Rotation

job rotation
Moves workers from one job to another to broaden their experience.

Job rotation (cross-training) moves employees from one job to another to broaden their experience. Higher-level tasks often require this breadth of knowledge. Rotational training programs help employees understand a variety of jobs and their interrelationships, thereby improving productivity. Job rotation is often used by organizations to relieve boredom, stimulate better performance, reduce absenteeism, and provide additional flexibility in job assignments.[69] Streamlined firms have to do more with less, so it makes sense to develop employees who can jump in anywhere they are needed. Job rotation is also effective in protecting a company against the loss of key employees.[70]

Reengineering

reengineering
Fundamental rethinking and radical redesign of business processes to achieve dramatic improvements in critical, contemporary measures of performance such as cost, quality, service, and speed.

Reengineering is "the fundamental rethinking and radical redesign of business processes to achieve dramatic improvements in critical contemporary measures of performance, such as cost, quality, service, and speed."[71]

A GLOBAL PERSPECTIVE

Global Job Rotation as a Unique Fast Track Benefit

As previously stated, job *rotation* involves moving employees from one job to another to broaden their experience. Most of us view job rotation as being primarily concentrated on movement from job to job with the same company in the United States. However, job rotation is also being used extensively in the global environment to relieve boredom, stimulate better performance, reduce absenteeism, and provide additional flexibility in job assignments. High achievers are now being sent overseas to broaden their experience. Overseas job rotation is seen as a way to retain and develop star players.[72]

India-based Tata Consultancy Services (TCS), a software services and consulting company, uses job rotation as a key strategy for developing its workforce and delivering added value to customers. They send India-born workers to countries such as China, Hungary, and South America, among others. Tada has offices in 42 countries globally and customers spread throughout the world; having globally experienced workers is a must. It also helps TCS provide better service. Ajoy Mukherjee, vice president, head, global human resources, says, "It gives us the opportunity to offer a value proposition to our customers from the point of view of quality and knowledge."[73]

Typical overseas assignments at TCS last between 18 to 24 months. Upon returning to India, the worker usually will continue working on the same kinds of projects that were worked on abroad, thereby transferring the knowledge gained overseas to the home office. Mukherjee said, "The rotation is essential in building the competency of our people. They are able to go onsite and meet face-to-face with our customers, and see how things work in another country." In addition to enhancing technical skills, the international people skills of those on overseas assignments are boosted. "They gain an understanding of the culture of these countries, and some of them even pick up the language."[74]

New York-based professional services company Deloitte has had success with its overseas job rotation program and is looking to expand it. Deloitte also sees value-added for customers, along with a benefit to itself. Jennifer Gardner, director, talent deployment, Deloitte Services LP, said, "The objectives are twofold: to meet client needs and to develop the skills of our professionals. The experience of working in another culture often can fundamentally change a person—expand his or her perspective, introduce new ideas and ways of working. And the exchange of capabilities, skills, and ideas often goes both ways—both the sending and receiving countries benefit."[75]

Various types of job rotation plans are available at Deloitte. A long-term plan is between 18 months and three years; short-term plans average six months. Gardner said, "Top leaders of the U.S. organization are committed to aggressively expanding our commitment to these global assignments. Our goal is to increase both our inbound and outbound participation to 2,000 participants over the next three years."[76]

Global job rotation is valuable to both workers and customers but there are also some challenges. Gardner said, "The biggest challenge for Deloitte, as it is for most companies, is to look for appropriate and challenging opportunities for our professionals when they repatriate at the end of the international assignment. The key is to consider career planning at the front end of the assignment and stay connected during the duration. Every effort is made to engage in career development and planning discussions throughout the process. As a result, we build the experience of repatriation into the foundation of the assignment."[77]

Scotiabank, based in Canada, also encourages job rotation and recognizes the importance of a smooth transition of workers as they depart and return home. "Candidates accepted into the program participate in four to five six-month rotations (one of which can be a field or overseas rotation) to give them practical experience in the core areas of international banking," says Barb Rosen Schreiber, program director, international associates, mentoring, and metrics. She also said, "As in any training program, or any rotation assignment—whether local or overseas—it is critical to identify clear objectives and expectations at the beginning of a rotation."[78]

Reengineering essentially involves the firm rethinking and redesigning its business system to become more competitive. It emphasizes the radical redesign of work in which companies organize around process instead of by functional departments. Incremental change is not what is desired; instead, radical changes are wanted that will alter entire operations at one time. Essentially, the firm must rethink and redesign its business system from the ground up.

Reengineering focuses on the overall aspects of job designs, organizational structures, and management systems. It stresses that work should be organized around outcomes as opposed to tasks or functions. Reengineering should never be confused with downsizing (discussed in Chapter 13), even though a workforce reduction often results from this strategy. Naturally, job design considerations are of paramount concern because as the process changes, so do essential elements of jobs.

Summary

1. *Describe strategic talent management systems.* Talent management is a strategic endeavor to optimize the use of human capital, which enables an organization to drive short- and long-term results by building culture, engagement, capability, and capacity through integrated talent acquisition, development, and deployment processes that are aligned to business goals.

2. *Explain why job analysis is a basic human resource tool and explain the reasons for conducting job analysis.* Job analysis is the systematic process of determining the skills, duties, and knowledge required for performing jobs in an organization. It is an essential and pervasive human resource technique. In today's rapidly changing work environment, the need for a sound job analysis system is extremely critical. New jobs are being created, and old jobs are being redesigned or eliminated.

   Without a properly conducted job analysis, it would be difficult, if not impossible, to satisfactorily perform the other human resource–related functions.

3. *Describe the types of information required for job analysis and describe the various job analysis methods.* Work activities, worker-oriented activities, and the types of machines, tools, equipment, and work aids used in the job are important. This information is used to help determine the job skills needed. In addition, the job analyst looks at job-related tangibles and intangibles.

   The job analyst may administer a structured questionnaire or witness the work being performed, or he or she may interview both the employee and the supervisor or ask them to describe their daily work activities in a diary or log. A combination of methods is often used.

4. *Identify who conducts job analysis and describe the components of a job description.* The people who participate in job analysis should include, at a minimum, the employee and the employee's immediate supervisor. Large organizations may have one or more job analysts, but in small organizations line supervisors may be responsible for job analysis. Organizations that lack the technical expertise may use outside consultants to perform job analysis.

   Components include the job identification section, which includes the job title, department, reporting relationship, and a job number or code; the job analysis date; the job summary; and the body of the job description that delineates the major duties to be performed.

5. *Explain O*NET as the Occupational Information Network, Standard Occupational Classification (SOC), job sculpting, timeliness of job analysis, job analysis for team members, and describe how job analysis helps satisfy various legal requirements.* O*NET, the Occupational Information Network, is a comprehensive, government-developed database of worker attributes and job characteristics. The 2010 Standard Occupational Classification (SOC) replaces the 2000 system. The SOC's substantive structural changes are based on actual changes in the nature or organization of work activities being performed in the economy. Job sculpting involves modifying the typical job descriptions to take advantage of the talents, interests, and experiences of each employee. The rapid pace of technological change makes the need for accurate job analysis even more important now and in the future. In many firms today, people are being hired as team members. Whenever someone asks a team member, "What is your job description?" the reply might well be "Whatever." What this means is that if a project has to be completed, individuals do what has to be done to complete the task. Legislation requiring thorough job analysis includes the following acts: Fair Labor Standards Act, Equal Pay Act, Civil Rights Act, Occupational Safety and Health Act, and the Americans with Disabilities Act.

6. *Explain the need for the human resource manager to be a strategic partner.* If HR is to be a strategic partner, HR executives must work with top management in achieving concrete plans and results. It is necessary for them to understand the operational side of the business and comprehend the complex organizational design. They must also be able to determine the capabilities of the company's workforce, both today and in the future, and ensure that human resources support the firm's mission.

7. *Explain the strategic planning process and describe the human resource planning process.* Strategic planning is the process by which top management determines overall organizational purposes and objectives and how they will be achieved. It is an ongoing process that is dynamic and ever changing. Strategic planning at all levels of the organization can be divided into four steps: (1) determination of the organizational mission, (2) assessment of the organization and its environment, (3) setting of specific objectives or direction, and (4) determination of strategies to accomplish those objectives.

After strategic plans have been formulated, strategic human resource planning can be undertaken. Human resource planning (sometimes called workforce planning) is the systematic process of matching the internal and external supply of people with job openings anticipated in the organization over a specified period of time. Human resource planning has two components: requirements and availability.

8. ***Describe forecasting human resource requirements and availability and how databases can assist in matching internal employees to positions.*** A requirements forecast is an estimate of the numbers and kinds of employees the organization will need at future dates in order to realize its goals. Determining whether the firm will be able to secure employees with the necessary skills and from what sources these individuals may be obtained is called an "availability forecast."

Databases are being used by organizations to enable human resources to match people with positions.

9. ***Identify what a firm can do when either a shortage or a surplus of workers exists.*** When a shortage of workers exists, creative recruiting, compensation incentives, training programs, and different selection standards are possible. When a comparison of requirements and availability indicates that a worker surplus will result, most companies look to alternatives to layoffs, but downsizing may ultimately be required.

10. ***Explain strategic succession and disaster planning in today's environment.*** Succession planning is the process of ensuring that qualified persons are available to assume key managerial positions once the positions are vacant. This definition includes untimely deaths, resignations, terminations, or the orderly retirements of company officials.

Disaster plans focus on catastrophes that range from natural calamities such as hurricanes, earthquakes, and floods, to man-made crises such as 9/11.

11. ***Describe manager and employee self-service.*** Manager self-service is the use of software and the corporate network to automate paper-based human resource–related processes that require a manager's approval, record-keeping or input, and processes that support the manager's job. Employee self-service consists of processes that automate transactions that used to be labor-intensive for both employees and HR professionals.

12. ***Describe some job design concepts.*** Job design is the process of determining the specific tasks to be performed, the methods used in performing the tasks, and how the job relates to other work in the organization. Job enrichment consists of basic changes in the content and level of responsibility of a job so as to provide greater challenge to the worker. Job enrichment provides a vertical expansion of responsibilities. Job enlargement is defined as increasing the number of tasks a worker performs, with all of the tasks at the same level of responsibility. Job rotation (sometimes called cross-training) moves employees from one job to another to broaden their experience. Reengineering is the fundamental rethinking and radical redesign of business processes to achieve dramatic improvements in critical contemporary measures of performance, such as cost, quality, service, and speed.

Key Terms

talent management   106
job analysis   108
job   108
position   108
job description   109
job specification   109
strategic planning   118
mission   118

human resource planning (workforce planning)   121
requirements forecast   122
availability forecast   122
zero-base forecasting   122
bottom-up forecast   122
succession planning   125
manager self-service (MSS)   128

employee self-service (ESS)   128
job design   129
job enrichment   129
job enlargement   129
job rotation   129
reengineering   129

Questions for Review

1. What is talent management?
2. What is the distinction between a job and a position? Define job analysis.
3. Why is job analysis considered to be a basic human resource tool?
4. When is job analysis performed?
5. What are the types of information required for job analysis?
6. What are the methods used to conduct job analysis? Describe each type.

7. What are the basic components of a job description? Briefly describe each.
8. Describe how effective job analysis can be used to satisfy each of the following statutes: (a) Fair Labor Standards Act, (b) Equal Pay Act, (c) Civil Rights Act, (d) Occupational Safety and Health Act, and (e) Americans with Disabilities Act.
9. Why does the human resource manager need to be a strategic partner with top management?
10. What are the steps involved in the strategic planning process?
11. What are the steps involved in the human resource planning process?
12. What are the human resource forecasting techniques?
13. Distinguish between forecasting human resource requirements and availability.
14. What actions could a firm take if it forecasted a shortage of workers?
15. What are some alternatives to layoffs?
16. Define succession planning. Why is it important?
17. Why is disaster planning important?
18. What are manager and employee self-service?
19. Define each of the following: (a) job design, (b) job enrichment, (c) job enlargement, (d) job rotation, and (e) reengineering.

HRM INCIDENT 1

A Degree for Beauty Therapists

Tony was appointed as the HR manager for Tangerine Center Sdn Bhd, a beauty center that catered solely to ladies in the town of Kuantan. The beauty center was doing well and the number of clientele was rapidly escalating. The growth was expected to continue and plans were being made to expand the center. This expansion concerned Tony. In the previous year itself, Tony had struggled to recruit enough qualified job applicants. He knew that the new expansion would intensify the problem. At that time, the beauty center employed locally certified beauty therapists who only held the Malaysia JPK (SKM) Tahap III Certificate.

Tony was particularly concerned about the beauty therapists. The beauty therapists had to be able to professionally deliver skilled beauty treatments, had to have a pleasant personality and good communication skills. Beauty therapists would not need decision making skills but they would need to possess practical skills in order to apply the hands-on beauty treatments. The center offered beauty treatments such as facials, slimming treatments, massages, and aromatherapy. Customers would come to the center and expect to be treated courteously and to receive high-quality, expert beauty treatments. The pay was $5.00 an hour, low for a skilled worker in the area and the job required employees to work on the weekends. It was also a job that involved long hours and being pleasant to clients at all times. Tony had already had considerable difficulty recruiting and keeping the beauty therapist positions filled.

Tony was thinking about how to attract more job applicants when he received a call from Jenny Seow, the Director of the company. "Tony," Jenny said. "I think we need to upgrade our image. I am not happy that we only employ beauty therapists who hold the local certificate level (Malaysia JPK (SKM)). We need higher-qualified professionals in the company because I am looking to provide different types of services such as a spa, beauty consultants, skin therapists, and medical esthetics. I have decided to change the education requirement for the beauty therapist role from a locally recognized certification level to that of an internationally recognized diploma level such as CIDESCO."

"But Mrs. Seow," protested Tony, "the company is growing rapidly. If we are to have enough people to fill those jobs, we can't just insist on taking in diploma holders to do such tasks and at such a pay scale. I don't see how we will be able to meet our future needs for the job with such an unrealistic job qualification."

Jenny ended the conversation by saying, "I have made up my mind. We need to upgrade the people within our organization. By getting higher-qualified people through the door, we will be able to upgrade our image as well. This can only be done if we have CIDESCO qualified beauty therapists who can bring in new services. This is the final decision and it has been cleared with the other Director."

Questions

1. Should there be a minimum education requirement for the beauty therapist job? Discuss.

2. What is your opinion of Jenny's effort to upgrade the people in the organization?

3. What legal ramifications, if any, should Jenny have considered?

HRM INCIDENT 2

Strategic HR?

Brian Charles, the vice president of marketing for Sharpco Manufacturing, commented at the weekly executive directors' meeting, "I have good news. We can get the large contract with Medord Corporation. All we have to do is complete the project in one year instead of two. I told them we could do it."

Charmagne Powell, vice president of human resources, brought Brian back to reality by reminding him, "Remember the strategic plan we were involved in developing and we all agreed to? Our present workers do not have the expertise required to produce the quality that Medord's particular specifications require. Under the two-year project timetable, we planned to retrain our present workers gradually. With this new time schedule, we will have to go into the job market and recruit workers who are already experienced in this process. We all need to study your proposal further. Human resource costs will rise considerably if we attempt to complete the project in one year instead of two. Sure, Brian, we can do it, but with these constraints, will the project be cost-effective?"

Questions

1. Was Charmagne considering the strategic nature of human resource planning when she challenged Brian's "good news" forecast? Discuss.

2. How did the involvement in developing the corporate strategic plan assist Charmagne in challenging Brian?

Notes

1. Andrew Paradise, "Talent Management Defined," *T+D* 63 (May 2009): 68–69.
2. "Talent Management Continues to Go High Tech," *HR Focus* 86 (October 2009): 8–9.
3. Lois Webster, "Leaving Nothing to Chance," *T+D* 63 (February 2009): 54–60.
4. Larry Israelite, "Talent Management is the New Buzzword," *T+D* 64 (February 2010): 14.
5. Webster, "Leaving Nothing to Chance."
6. "Study Finds Experienced Talent Management Brings Higher Earnings & Other Benefits," *HR Focus* 87 (March 2010): 8–9.
7. Cushing Anderson, "Talent Management as Survival Skill," *Chief Learning Officer* 9 (March 2010): 46–48.
8. Joseph Daniel McCool, "Talent Management Function Gains Momentum," *BusinessWeek Online* (March 8, 2010): 9.
9. R. Wayne Mondy, Robert M. Noe, and Robert E. Edwards, "What the Staffing Function Entails," *Personnel* 63 (April 1986): 55–58.
10. Philip Bobko, Philip L. Roth, and Maury A. Buster, "A Systematic Approach for Assessing the Currency ("Up-to-Dateness") of Job-Analytic Information," *Public Personnel Management* 37 (Fall 2008): 261–277.
11. Hank Dorlington, "Human Resources: A Top Priority in Tough Times," *Kitchen & Bath Design News* 27 (May 2009): 34.
12. "In All Promotion Notices, Include Specifics about Minimum Job Requirements," *HR Specialist: Employment Law* 40 (February 2010): 2.
13. Thomas A. Stetz, Scott B. Button, and W. Benjamin Poor, "New Tricks for an Old Dog: Visualizing Job Analysis Results," *Public Personnel Management* 38 (Spring 2009): 91–100.
14. *Uniform Guidelines on Employee Selection Procedures*, *Federal Register*, Friday, August 25, 1978, Part IV.
15. Laurie Burkhard, "Define Employees' Roles and Responsibilities," *Advisor Today* 104 (January 2009): 59–60.
16. Lee Froschheiser, "Recruitment Fundamentals," *Adhesives & Sealants Industry* 16 (February 2009): 34–35.
17. http://online.onetcenter.org/ February 13, 2010.
18. www.bls.gov/soc, February 13, 2010.
19. Jay Forte, "Job Sculpting," *Sales & Service Excellence* 8 (October 2008): 4.
20. Ibid.
21. Ibid.
22. Darin E. Hartley, "Job Analysis at the Speed of Reality," *T+D* 58 (September 2004): 20–22.
23. Edward Lawler III and John W. Boudreau, "What Makes HR a Strategic Partner?" *People & Strategy* 32 (2009): 14–22.
24. "Staying Strategic in a Changing Economy," *HR Focus* 86 (March 2009): 3–4.

25. Dave Ulrich and Wayne Brockbank, "The *HR* Business-Partner Model: Past Learnings and Future Challenges," *People & Strategy* 32 (2009): 5–7.

26. Dave Ulrich, Wayne Brockbank, and Dani Johnson, "The Role of Strategy Architect in the Strategic *HR* Organization," *People & Strategy* 32 (2009): 24–31.

27. Russell Pomeranz, "The Evolution of Human Resources Directors' Responsibilities," CPA Journal 79 (July 2009): 12–13.

28. Laurence O'Neil, "HR's Time to Lead," *HRMagazine* 54 (April 2009): 8.

29. Richard Pinola, "What CEOs Want from HR," *HR Focus* 79 (September 2002): 1.

30. "Trends to Watch in HR's Future," *HR Focus* 79 (December 2002): 7.

31. Susan Meisinger, "Employers Demanding More from HR," *HRMagazine* 53 (April 2008): 10.

32. Eddie Obeng, "Economic Storm Clouds Have Silver Lining for Strategic HR," *People Management* 14 (May 15, 2008): 20.

33. Ann Pomeroy, "Business Strategy, Not Just HR Strategy," *HRMagazine* 52 (November 2007): 47–48.

34. Mona Pearl, "Going Global: What Is Your Competitive Edge," *Manufacturing Today* 10 (Winter 2010): 12–15.

35. Rory Cooper, "Smart HR Strategies in an Unpredictable Economy," *Maryland Banker* (Third Quarter 2009): 8.

36. Lisa Ann Edwards, "Recruiting Stars: Does It Really Pay Off?" *Journal of Corporate Recruiting Leadership* 4 (September 2009): 10–15.

37. Penn Wells and Stanna Brazeel, "Human Resource's Strategy for the Future," *Power Engineering* 113 (June 2009): 2.

38. J. R. Gallbraith and Robert K. Kazannian, *Strategy Implementation: Structure, Systems, and Process*, 2nd ed. (St. Paul, MN: West Publishing, 1986), p. 115.

39. "What Makes a Good *HR* Leader?" *HR Focus* 86 (May 2009): 8.

40. "Leveraging HR and Knowledge Management in a Challenging Economy," *HRMagazine* 54 (June 2009): Special section 1–9.

41. Peter Cappelli, "A Supply Chain Approach to Workforce Planning," *Organizational Dynamics* 38 (January–March 2009): 8–15.

42. "Down Economy Is Driving More Workforce Planning: Watson Wyatt," *HR Focus* 86 (February 2009): 8.

43. Adrienne Hedger, "3 Staffing Resolutions in a Slow Economy," *Workforce Management* 88 (January 19, 2009): 36–38.

44. Ed Frauenheim, "Talent Planning for the Times," *Workforce Management* 88 (October 19, 2009): 37–43.

45. Ibid.

46. Robert Kleinsorge, "Expanding the Role of Succession Planning," *T+D* 64 (April 2010): 66–69.

47. Mark Nadler, Steve Krupp, and Richard Hossack, "Overcoming the Obstacles to CEO Succession Planning," *Corporate Governance Advisor* 17 (March 2009): 7–13.

48. Eileen McKeown, "Turbulent Times Highlight the Need for Succession Planning," *T+D* 64 (January 2010): 18–19.

49. Laurence O'Neil, "Bucking the Layoff Trend With Creative HR," *HRMagazine* 54 (March 2009): 8.

50. "Maximize Productivity, Minimize Layoffs," *HR Focus* 86 (April 2009): 1/15.

51. Adrienne Fox, "The Big Chill," *HRMagazine* 54 (March 2009): 28–33.

52. "In the Midst of Layoffs, There are Alternatives," *Min's B2B* 11 (December 15, 2008): 2–4.

53. Darryl Demos, "Flexible Staffing Meets Branch Needs," *CU360* 35 (July 7, 2009): 4–5.

54. Jennifer Schramm, "Work Turns Flexible," *HRMagazine* 54 (March 2009): 88.

55. "In the Midst of Layoffs, There are Alternatives."

56. Ibid.

57. Nat Stoddard and Claire Wyckoff, "A Higher Order of Thinking," *Directorship* 34 (October/November 2008): 61–64.

58. Robert C. Muschewske, "Choosing a New CEO: This Board Got It Right," *Directors & Boards* 33 (2008 4th Quarter): 30–33.

59. "HR Works to Transfer Workforce Knowledge and Skills," *HR Focus* 85 (January 2008): S1–S4.

60. "Succession Planning Not Limited to the C-Suite," *HRMagazine* 53 (April 2008): 16.

61. Alan M. Field, "Disaster Planning Grows Contagious," Journal of Commerce 10 (May 11, 2009): 10–13.

62. Margery Weinstein, "Disaster Planning Needs All Hands on Deck," *Training* 46 (March 2009): 14.

63. Bill Roberts, "Empowerment or Imposition?" *HRMagazine* 49 (June 2004): 157–166.

64. "Manager Self-Service Trends," *Human Resources* (March 2009): 32.

65. Janet H. Marler, Sandra L. Fisher, and Weiling Ke, "Employee Self-Service Technology Acceptance: A Comparison of Pre-Implementation and Post-Implementation Relationships," *Personnel Psychology* 62 (Summer 2009): 327–358.

66. "Talent Programs Remain Robust," *HR Focus* 86 (March 2009): 1–15

67. "Self-Service Will Star In Staff & Performance Development," *HR Focus* 82 (April 2005): 8.

68. Frederick Herzberg, "One More Time: How Do You Motivate Employees?" *Harvard Business Review* 65 (September/October 1987): 109–120.

69. "Postural Assessments & Job Rotation," *Professional Safety* 53 (February 2008): 32–36.

70. Margaret Fiester, "Job Rotation," *HRMagazine* 53 (August 2008): 33–34.

71. Michael Hammer and James Champy, *Reengineering the Corporation: A Manifesto for Business Revolution* (New York: Harper Collins Publishers, 1993): 32.

72. Margery Weinstein, "Foreign but Familiar," *Training* 46 (January 2009): 20–23.

73. Ibid.

74. Ibid.

75. Ibid.

76. Ibid.

77. Ibid.

78. Ibid.

5 Recruitment

HRM in Action: Recruiting by Promising an Interview

Many think the sequence of events to get a job involves getting an interview, impressing the interviewer, and going to work shortly thereafter. The U.S. Army, in conjunction with the private workforce, does it a different way. Army recruiters have another means of enticing young men and women to enlist in the Army. Partnership for Youth Success (PaYS) represents one such program. Army PaYS Program Manager Robert A. Qualls says, "PaYS is an enlistment option that enables a young man or woman to select a post-Army partner for an employment interview when joining the Army, Army Reserve, or advanced ROTC. PaYS is designed to connect soldiers with post-Army opportunities before they even join."[1]

PaYS appeals to young people who are interested in obtaining a quality civilian job after military service. The Army recruiter first works with prospective recruits to determine their career interests and needs and helps them determine their specialty. Recruits then looks at PaYS for career opportunities after Army service. There are more than 300 PaYS partners to link up with after completing active duty. Interested employers accepted as PaYS partners sign an agreement promising to provide an interview to qualified soldiers who select the partner company to explore post-military employment. Qualls said, "We simply say, 'Let us have them first, teach them a skill and refine them with the Army values, and then go to work for your company. We want to have the premier employers in the local job markets as PaYS partners.'" Partners may interview soldiers before leaving on active duty but most interviews occur after serving when they obtain basic and job skill training. ROTC cadets interview as college seniors.[2]

After completing this chapter, students should be able to:

1. Define *recruitment* and explain alternatives to recruitment.

2. Explain the external environment of recruitment and describe how promotion policies influence recruitment.

3. Describe the recruitment process.

4. Describe internal recruitment methods.

5. Identify external recruitment sources.

6. Describe online recruitment methods and discuss the possibility of job search scams.

7. Identify traditional external recruitment methods.

8. Describe how recruitment methods and sources are tailored to each other.

Fifteen thousand regular Army soldiers and 5,935 reservists have enlisted with the PaYS option. The Army furnishes companies with contact information for soldiers selecting them as employer partners so that they can establish contact. "We send a postcard to every new soldier who enlists with PaYS to remind the soldier to keep in contact via e-mail with the HR contact in the company," Qualls says. "We also have a reporting and communication tool that our partners can use to contact soldiers individually or by groups."[3]

The program has its opportunities but also its challenges. Turnover affects both the Army and corporate America and it may be difficult to maintain contacts. In addition, the military's Web site applications can be incompatible with some corporate communications networks. Sally Hart, national military recruiting director for Cincinnati-based Cintas Corporation, says, "It's at least four years before anyone can be placed due to their military commitment," Hart says. "Out of every 1,000 recruits, 25 percent drop out of the military, 25 percent re-enlist, 25 percent may no longer be interested in the company or the location they selected when they get out. That leaves 25 percent that might still be interested. But they still need to remember to contact the employer. So, overall, the numbers going into the system are big, but the ones coming out right now are small." Still Sally believes her efforts are worth the investment.[4]

This chapter begins by discussing how soldiers can interview a company, join the Army, and perhaps later on join the company he or she initially selected. Next, recruitment is defined and alternatives to recruitment are explained which includes a discussion of contingent workers of the future.

This is followed by a discussion of the external environment of recruitment and promotion policies. A description of the recruitment process precedes a discussion of internal recruitment methods. Then, external sources of recruitment, online recruitment methods, and job search scams are examined. Traditional external recruiting methods are presented next. Then the importance of tailoring recruitment methods and sources is discussed. The chapter concludes with a global perspective entitled "Our Company Headquarters Has Been Outsourced!"

OBJECTIVE 5.1
Define *recruitment* and explain alternatives to recruitment.

recruitment
Process of attracting individuals on a timely basis, in sufficient numbers, and with appropriate qualifications to apply for jobs with an organization.

Recruitment Defined

Recruitment is the process of attracting individuals on a timely basis, in sufficient numbers, and with appropriate qualifications to apply for jobs with an organization.

The firm may then select those applicants with qualifications most closely related to job descriptions. Finding the appropriate way of encouraging qualified candidates to apply for employment is extremely important; however, recruiting costs can be expensive. Thus, a properly functioning recruiting program can have a major impact on the bottom line of a company.

How many times do we hear CEOs state, "Our employees are our most important asset"? Instead they should be saying, "The right employees are our most important asset." Hiring the best people available has never been more critical than it is today, because of the economy and global competition. Phil Amundsen, vice chairman and national managing partner for Deloitte LLP's technology, media and telecommunications group, said, "A company's ability to recruit and manage talent has become the bellwether for the overall health and longevity of the organization."[5] It is estimated that just the cost of replacing an employee alone when a bad decision is made is two to three times the employee's annual salary.[6] Therefore, it is crucial to have a finely tuned recruitment process if the selection process is to function properly. However, before beginning the recruitment process, alternatives to recruitment need to be considered.

Alternatives to Recruitment

Even when HR planning indicates a need for additional employees, a firm may decide against increasing the size of its workforce. Recruitment and selection costs are significant when you consider all the related expenses. Therefore, a firm should consider alternatives such as outsourcing, contingent workers, professional employer organizations (employee leasing), and overtime carefully before engaging in recruitment.

Outsourcing

Outsourcing is the process of hiring an external provider to do the work that was previously done internally. The topic was discussed in Chapter 1 only as it pertained to the HR outsourcing. Here, the discussion of outsourcing is broadened to include any job within the firm. Outsourcing has become a widespread and increasingly popular alternative involving virtually every business area. Subcontracting of various functions to other firms has been a common practice in industry for decades.

Offshoring refers to the migration of all or a significant part of the development, maintenance and delivery of services to a vendor located in another country, typically in developing countries like India and China. Today many information technology jobs are being offshored. Some are quite concerned about this trend, citing lost wages of $135 billion, 3.3 million lost jobs, and reduced salaries for the jobs that remain.[7] Even so, the trend is not likely to reverse itself in the near future.

TRENDS & INNOVATIONS

Are Contingent Workers the Workforce of the Future?

Contingent workers provide another alternative to recruitment. **Contingent workers**, described as the "disposable American workforce" by a former secretary of labor, have a nontraditional relationship with the worksite employer and work as part-timers, temporaries, or independent contractors.[8] They are the human equivalents of just-in-time inventory. These *disposable workers* permit distinct advantages: maximum flexibility for the employer and lower labor costs. Historically, contingent workers have been called the bookends of recessions. They are the first to go when a recession begins and the last to be recalled when the economy gets better. However, toward the end of the recession of 2008/10, many companies were reversing this trend and following the strategy of holding off on the hiring of regular full-time employees and choosing instead to use contingent workers.[9]

The recession caused companies to rethink the way work gets done. This brought a refocus on the use of contingent workers which can be added or cut as demand requires.[10] A recent survey found that 34 percent of employers find that contingent workers play an important role in their overall workforce strategies.[11] Garry Mathiason, vice chairman of Littler Mendelson in San Francisco, said, "Something really remarkable is happening. The world is starting to change. In the future companies will likely make wider use of staffing methods similar to those practiced by the film industry. There,

entire crews of contingent production workers are assembled for a movie, then disbanded once it is finished." Barry Asin, chief analyst at Staffing Industry Analysts, a research firm that covers the contingent workplace, said, "I think that it is a little bit early to tell if there is a fundamental shift going on. I do think that we have had an unprecedented decline in the use of temporary and contingent workers over the last year or two, which is exactly what it is supposed to be doing."[12] If the use of contingent workers is indeed the trend, the manner that human resource is practiced will experience considerable change.

Contingent workers provide the flexibility that employers desire when cuts need to be made. Joanie Ruge, senior vice president of staffing company Adecco Group North America, says, "We work with many Fortune 500 executives, and what we see in our conversations with them is that they really want flexibility with their workforces. It is starting to become one of the most important initiatives and priorities as they look to future planning and forecasting. They want to be able to ramp up or scale back based on business needs. I think we will see that more."[13]

The challenge facing organizations will be how to integrate contingent workers into their organizations successfully so they are able to work effectively. Ruge said, "Companies are not just looking to use more contingent workers for lower-skilled jobs; they want to expand into higher-level positions as well. More and more we are seeing requests for professional skills: engineers, information technicians, health care workers, specialists in accounting and finance."[14] Because of the rise in the use of contingent workers, software is available that helps manage this growing workforce.[15]

---

contingent workers
Described as the "disposable American workforce" by a former secretary of labor, have a nontraditional relationship with the worksite employer and work as part-timers, temporaries, or independent contractors.

Professional Employer Organizations (Employee Leasing)

As discussed in Chapter 1, a *professional employer organization* (PEO) is a company that leases employees to other businesses. When a decision is made to use a PEO, the company releases its employees, who are then hired by the PEO. The PEO manages the administrative needs associated with those employees. The PEO pays the employees; it also pays workers' compensation premiums, payroll-related taxes, and employee benefits. The PEO is the employees' legal employer. Therefore, the leasing company is responsible for recruiting activities.

Overtime

Perhaps the most commonly used alternative to recruitment, especially in meeting short-term fluctuations in work volume, is overtime. Overtime may help both employer and employee. The employer benefits by avoiding recruitment, selection, and training costs. The employees gain from increased income during the overtime period.

There are potential problems with overtime, however. Some managers believe that when employees work for unusually long periods, the company pays more and receives less in return. Employees may become fatigued and lack the energy to perform at a normal rate. Two additional possible problems relate to the use of prolonged overtime. Consciously or not, employees may pace themselves to ensure overtime. They may also become accustomed to the added income resulting from overtime pay. Employees may even elevate their standard of living to the level permitted by this additional income. Then, when a firm tightens its belt and overtime is limited, employee morale may deteriorate along with the pay.

External Environment of Recruitment

Like other human resource functions, the recruitment process does not occur in a vacuum. Factors external to the organization can significantly affect the firm's recruitment efforts.

Labor Market Conditions

Of particular importance is the demand for and supply of specific skills in the labor market. A firm's recruitment process may be simplified when the unemployment rate in an organization's labor market is high as was the case in the recession when it jumped to over 10 percent in 2009. However, even in a depressed economy, top quality workers are in demand and forward thinking organizations are looking to entice these individuals to join their firms.[16] The number of unsolicited applicants is usually greater, and the increased size of the labor pool provides a better opportunity for attracting qualified applicants. If demand for a particular skill is high relative to supply, an extraordinary recruiting effort may be required. Further, the area of country may impact the labor market conditions. In 2009, the U.S. job market was strongest in the South and weakest in the West.[17] Today, the labor market for many professional and technical positions is much broader and truly global.

Active or Passive Job Seekers

The recruitment method that proves to be most successful will depend to an extent on whether the recruited individual is an active or passive job seeker. *Active job seekers*, whether presently employed or not, are committed to finding another job. These individuals are usually easier to identify because their names have been placed in the job market. Their résumés are on job boards and friends, associates, or companies have been contacted directly to learn about job opportunities. *Passive candidates*, on the other hand, are typically employed, satisfied with their employer, and content in their current role. However, if the right opportunity came along, they might like to learn more. These individuals want to move slower and will ask a lot of questions before making a job change. They are more hesitant to risk leaving a good job for a new challenge and increased risk.[18] As you read through this chapter, numerous recruitment methods will be identified. Some are more useful in identifying active job seekers and others are better used in recruiting passive job seekers. Naturally, some will be directed at both groups.

Legal Considerations

Legal matters also play a significant role in recruitment practices in the United States. This is not surprising, since the candidate and the employer first make contact during the recruitment process. A poorly conceived recruiting process can do much to create problems in the selection process. Therefore, it is essential for organizations to emphasize nondiscriminatory practices at this stage.

The Labor Department has issued guidelines concerning the online recruiting policies of federal contractors and subcontractors. Companies must keep detailed records of each online job search. They must also identify what selection criteria were used and be able to explain why a person with protected status was not hired. Equal Employment Opportunity Commission (EEOC) guidelines suggest that companies with more than 100 employees keep staffing records for a minimum of two years. The threshold coverage is 50 employees if dealing with the Office of Federal Contract Compliance Programs (OFCCP). This information enables a compilation of demographic data, including age, race, and gender, based on that applicant pool. The EEOC uses these data to determine whether a company's hiring practices are discriminatory.

A dramatic increase in firms using the Internet for recruiting has added to management's challenge to comply with the OFCCP.[19] Under the rule, there are four criteria to determine whether an individual is an Internet applicant:

- The job seeker has expressed interest through the Internet. Applicants have gone to the corporate career Web site and applied for a particular job that is listed.
- The employer considers the job seeker for employment in a particular open position. If the applicant does not meet specific qualifications spelled out in the job-specification section of the job description, the résumé does not have to be considered.
- The job seeker has indicated he or she meets the position's basic qualifications. If the position description calls for three years of experience, and the individual has three years of experience in previous jobs, he or she would believe that meets the basic qualifications.
- The applicant has not indicated he or she is no longer interested in the position.[20]

Employers must keep records of any and all expressions of interest through the Internet, including online résumés and internal databases. Employer are also expected to obtain the gender, race, and ethnicity of each applicant, when possible.

Promotion Policies

An organization's promotion policy can have a significant impact on recruitment. A firm can stress a policy of promotion from within its own ranks or one in which positions are generally filled from outside the organization. Depending on specific circumstances, either approach may have merit, but usually a combination of the two approaches proves best.

promotion from within (PFW)
Policy of filling vacancies above entry-level positions with current employees.

Promotion from within (PFW) is the policy of filling vacancies above entry-level positions with current employees.

When an organization emphasizes promotion from within, its workers have an incentive to strive for advancement. When employees see co-workers promoted, they become more aware of their own opportunities. Motivation provided by this practice often improves employee morale. For this reason, managers appear to be using internal promotions more and more. You know an internal hire understands your culture. It also communicates to the workers that it wants them to succeed.

Another advantage of internal recruitment is that the organization is usually well aware of its employees' capabilities. An employee's job performance, by itself, may not be a reliable criterion for promotion. Nevertheless, management will know many of the employee's personal and job-related qualities. The employee has a track record, as opposed to being an *unknown entity*. Also, the company's investment in the individual may yield a higher return. Still another positive factor is the employee's knowledge of the firm, its policies, and its people.

It is unlikely, however, that a firm can (or would even desire to) adhere rigidly to a practice of promotion from within. A strictly applied "PFW" policy eventually leads to inbreeding, a lack of cross-fertilization, and a lack of creativity.[21] Although seldom achieved, a good goal would be to fill 80 percent of openings above entry-level positions from within. Frequently, new blood provides new ideas and innovation that must take place for firms to remain competitive. In such cases, even organizations with PFW policies may opt to look outside the organization for new talent. In any event, a promotion policy that first considers insiders is great for employee morale and motivation, which is beneficial to the organization.

OBJECTIVE 5.3
Describe the recruitment process.

Recruitment Process

employee requisition
Document that specifies job title, department, the date the employee is needed for work, and other details.

As previously defined, *recruitment* is the process of attracting individuals on a timely basis, in sufficient numbers, and with appropriate qualifications, to apply for jobs with an organization. Figure 5.1 shows that when human resource planning indicates a need for employees, the firm may evaluate alternatives to hiring. If these alternatives prove to be inappropriate, the recruitment process starts. Frequently, recruitment begins when a manager initiates an **employee requisition,** a document that specifies job title, department, the date the employee is needed for work, and other details. With this information, managers can refer to the appropriate job description to determine the qualifications the recruited person needs.

Figure 5.1
The Recruitment Process

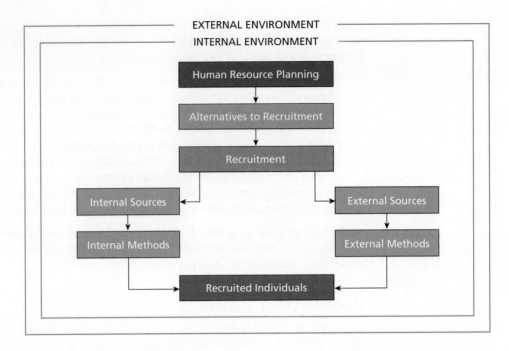

The next step in the recruitment process is to determine whether qualified employees are available within the firm (the internal source) or if it is necessary to look to external sources, such as colleges, universities, and other organizations. Because of the high cost of recruitment, organizations need to use the most productive recruitment sources and methods available.

recruitment sources
Where qualified candidates are located.

Recruitment sources are where qualified candidates are located, such as colleges or competitors. **Recruitment methods** are the specific means used to attract potential employees to the firm, such as online recruiting.

recruitment methods
Specific means used to attract potential employees to the firm.

Tapping productive sources of applicants and using suitable recruitment methods are essential to maximizing recruiting efficiency and effectiveness. When a firm identifies the sources of candidates, it uses appropriate methods for either internal or external recruitment to accomplish recruitment objectives. A candidate responds to the firm's recruitment efforts by submitting professional and personal data on either an application for employment or a résumé, depending on the company's policy. These two instruments are discussed in the next chapter.

Companies may discover that some recruitment sources and methods are superior to others for locating and attracting potential talent. For instance, one large, heavy-equipment manufacturer determined that medium-sized, state-supported colleges and universities located in rural areas were good sources of potential managers. To maximize recruiting effectiveness, using recruitment sources and methods tailored to specific needs is vitally important (a topic discussed later in this chapter).

OBJECTIVE 5.4
Describe internal recruitment methods.

Internal Recruitment Methods

Management should be able to identify current employees who are capable of filling positions as they become available. Helpful tools used for internal recruitment include employee databases, job postings, and job bidding procedures. As mentioned in Chapter 4, human resource databases permit organizations to determine whether current employees possess the qualifications for filling open positions. As a recruitment device, these databases have proven to be extremely valuable to organizations. Databases can be valuable in locating talent internally and supporting the concept of promotion from within.

job posting
Procedure for informing employees that job openings exist.

Job Posting and Job Bidding

Job posting is a procedure for informing employees that job openings exist. **Job bidding** is a procedure that permits employees who believe that they possess the required qualifications to apply for a posted job.

job bidding
Procedure that permits employees who believe that they possess the required qualifications to apply for a posted position.

Hiring managers usually want to give internal candidates priority. The job posting and bidding procedures can help minimize the commonly heard complaint that insiders never hear of a job opening until it is filled. Typically, vacant jobs are posted before external recruiting takes place. A number of forums are available today to advise employees that a vacancy exists. In years past, jobs were literally posted on a bulletin board. Today, companies use the intranet, the Internet, or the company's online newsletter to post jobs. Some companies send out e-mails and voice mail to selected managers and employees advising them that a vacancy exists.

Many organizations, including Whirlpool, BMW Manufacturing Co., Kellogg, Hyatt, and Hewlett-Packard, manage internal candidates with Web-based applications. Employees create profiles that detail their skills and interests for their next ideal position and are notified when such a position exists. FedEx's philosophy is that employees should be doing the kind of work they want to do. Its Web site helps candidates identify their ideal job. Using drop-down lists, it prompts them to enter data about desires; location, type of work, and so forth; and to describe their skills. When jobs open, managers have instant access to these electronic résumés in which the candidates have specified what they can and want to do.

Today, if a worker does not know about a vacancy, it is because he or she did not check the internal posting system regularly. Yet, even with an online system, a job posting and bidding system has some negative features. For one thing, an effective system requires the expenditure of time, effort, and money. Organizations need to be sure to treat internal candidates properly so they will not be discouraged or prompted to leave if they do not get the job. When bidders are unsuccessful, someone must explain to them why they were not selected. Management must choose the most qualified applicant or else the system will lack credibility. Still, complaints may occur, even in a well-designed and well-implemented system.

Employee Referrals

Employee referrals continue to be the way that top performers are identified.[22] Organizations like Southwest Airlines, Microsoft, Disney, and Ritz Carlton reportedly get from 50 to 70 percent of their new hires exclusively through employee referrals.[23] It is just human nature that people do not want to recommend a person unless they believe they are going to fit in and be productive. Thus, it is a powerful recruiting tool. Because of this, many companies are strengthening their employee referral program. These organizations have found that their employees can serve an important role in the recruitment process by actively soliciting applications from among their friends and associates.

Some firms give incentives to their employees for successful referrals. A WorldatWork, Bonus Program Practices survey found that 66 percent of companies offer referral bonuses, and 18 percent more are considering one. Typically, the types of positions that a company would pay referral bonuses for include professionals, technical, IT staff, and sales.[24] However, the trucking firm of CRST Malone offers its drivers a $1,000 bonus for recruiting other drivers.[25] Often those who are referred by a present employee are more productive. Jody Ordioni, president of New York City employee communications brand consulting firm Brandemix, said, "Costs can be 75 percent lower than using advertising or agencies. Using referrals also reduces turnover among both new and existing employees because applicants come pre-screened for culture fit."[26] Small companies especially prefer to find candidates through *referrals* and networks of people they trust.[27]

A note of caution should be observed with regard to the extensive use of employee referral. The EEOC Compliance Manual, issued in 2006, updates guidance on the prohibition of discrimination under Title VII of the Civil Rights Act of 1964. The manual explicitly warns that recruiting only at select colleges or relying on word-of-mouth recruiting, which includes employee referral programs, may generate applicant pools that do not reflect diversity in the labor market.

Employee enlistment is a unique form of employee referral in which every employee becomes a company recruiter. This is not the same as merely asking employees to refer friends to the company. The firm supplies employees with simple business cards that do not contain names or positions. Instead, these cards have a message similar to: "We are always looking for

HR Web Wisdom

Social Network Recruiting

https://www.linkedin. com

LinkedIn is an online social network Web site.

great _____. For additional information, log on to our Web site." Employees then distribute the cards wherever they go, at parties, sports events, family gatherings, picnics, or the park. The purpose is to let people know that the company really does want people to apply. An interesting way of using e-mail in the recruitment process is to ask employees to put a footer in their e-mails reminding people that their company is hiring. It might say something like the following: "Note: We're hiring amazing engineers, BD people, and a star Ops person. Refer a friend and get a fully paid trip to Hawaii for two."[28]

<table>
<tr><td>**OBJECTIVE 5.5**
Explain external recruitment sources.</td></tr>
</table>

External Recruitment Sources

At times, a firm must look beyond its own borders to find employees, particularly when expanding its workforce. External recruitment is needed to: (1) fill entry-level jobs; (2) acquire skills not possessed by current employees; and (3) obtain employees with different backgrounds to provide a diversity of ideas. As Figure 5.2 shows, even with internal promotions, firms still have to fill entry-level jobs from the outside. Thus, after the president of a firm retires, a series of internal promotions follows. Ultimately, however, the firm has to recruit externally for the entry-level position of salary analyst. If an outside candidate was selected for the president's position, the chain reaction of promotions from within would not have occurred. If no current employee has the desired qualifications, candidates may be attracted from a number of outside sources.

High Schools and Vocational Schools

Organizations concerned with recruiting clerical and other entry-level employees often depend on high schools and vocational schools. Many of these institutions have outstanding training programs for specific occupational skills, such as home appliance repair and small engine mechanics. Some companies work with schools to ensure a constant supply of trained individuals with specific job skills. In some areas, companies even loan employees to schools to assist in the training programs.

Community Colleges

Many community colleges are sensitive to the specific employment needs in their local labor markets and graduate highly-sought-after students with marketable skills. Typically, community colleges have two-year programs designed for both a terminal education and preparation for a four-year

Figure 5.2

Internal Promotion and External Recruitment

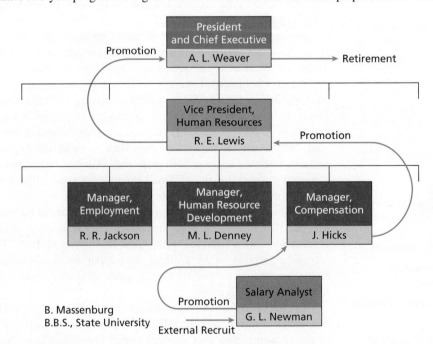

university degree program. Many community colleges also have excellent mid-management programs combined with training for specific trades. Sowela Technical Community College located in Lake Charles, Louisiana, has a well-respected culinary program that is known nationwide. Career centers often provide a place for employers to contact students, thereby facilitating the recruitment process.

Colleges and Universities

Colleges and universities represent a major recruitment source for many organizations. Organizations typically find potential professional, technical, and management employees in these institutions. Placement directors, faculty, and administrators can be helpful to organizations in their search for recruits. Establishing a relationship with faculty members is important because most professors are well aware of their students' academic performance and abilities.[29] Because on-campus recruitment is mutually beneficial, both employers and universities should take steps to develop and maintain close relationships. It is important that the firm knows the school and the school knows the firm.

Competitors in the Labor Market

When recent experience is required, competitors and other firms in the same industry or geographic area may be the most important source of recruits. Another name for actively recruiting employees from competitors is called *poaching*.[30] In fact, the most highly qualified applicants often come directly from competitors in the same labor market, as people typically do not enter the workforce loaded with experience and job skills. Competitors and other firms serve as external sources of recruitment for high-quality talent. Even organizations that have policies of promotion from within occasionally look elsewhere to fill positions.

Smaller firms in particular look for employees trained by larger organizations that have greater developmental resources. For instance, one optical firm believes that its own operation is not large enough to provide extensive training and development programs. Therefore, a person recruited by this firm for a significant management role is likely to have held at least two previous positions with a competitor.

Former Employees

At one time, when employees quit, their managers and peers tended to view them as being disloyal, ungrateful, and they were "punished" with no-return policies. A common attitude was that if you left your firm, you did not appreciate what the company had done for you. These days are gone and often "goodbye" may not be forever.[31] Today's young workers are more likely to change jobs and later return to a former employer than their counterparts who entered the workforce 20 or 30 years ago and smart employers try to get their best ex-employees to come back. The boomerang effect might happen because there was a stronger bond with previous coworkers or the new job was not what the employee envisioned.[32]

The advantage of tracking former employees is that the firm knows their strengths and weaknesses and the ex-employees know the company. Tracking, recruiting, and hiring a former employee can be a tremendous benefit and can encourage others to stay with the firm. It sends the message that things are not always greener on the other side of the fence. Paul Austermuehle, senior vice president of Bernard Hodes Group and an employer branding expert, said, "Our study proves the old truism that 'People don't quit companies, they quit supervisors.' It's great news to know that one in five of those people find a way to return to the company."[33]

The recession of 2008/10 created a situation where many well-qualified employees were laid off. Instead of viewing these terminations as a permanent situation, some companies are attempting to stay in touch with their former employees, called alumni, in the hope that with improved economic conditions they can be enticed to return. Companies are encouraging former employees to go to alumni social networks. They offer former employees and retirees a place to establish profiles and friend lists, share news and ideas with ex-colleagues, and participate on blogs and message boards.[34] Some organizations are looking to rehire past employees to

ETHICAL DILEMMA

Unfair Advantage?

You are the vice president of human resources for a high-tech company that is competing for a major government project. You believe that one of your key competitors is ahead of you in project development and you would like to recruit some of its engineers who are knowledgeable about the project. You receive an anonymous e-mail that includes the names and phone numbers of key people involved in your competitor's project. If you use the information and are able to hire some of the competitor's key people, your company has a chance to beat the competitor and you will become a hero. If you do not use the information, your company may lose a great deal of money.

What would you do?

respond to market opportunities as the economy rebounds. Melvin Scales, senior vice president at Right Management, said, "Some employers are currently hiring back past employees because they realize they may have cut too deep with the last round of layoffs."[35]

Unemployed

The unemployed often provide a valuable source of recruits. Qualified applicants join the unemployment rolls every day for various reasons. Companies may downsize their operations, go out of business, or merge with other firms, leaving qualified workers without jobs, which was certainly the case in the recession of 2008/10. Employees are also fired sometimes merely because of personality differences with their bosses. Not infrequently, employees become frustrated with their jobs and quit. Even individuals who have been out of work for extended periods should not be overlooked. In 2010, over six million people had been out of work for six months or more.[36]

Military Personnel

Operation Transition is a program that offers employers two vehicles for tapping into the military labor pool at no cost: the Defense Outplacement Referral System (DORS) and the Transition Bulletin Board (TBB). DORS is an automated résumé and referral system that allows employers to request résumés for open positions. The TBB is a bulletin board on which companies can post jobs online. Job seekers at military bases around the world see these listings.

Hiring of former service members may make sense to a lot of employers because many of these individuals typically have a proven work history and are flexible, motivated, and drug-free. Another valuable characteristic of veterans is their goal and team orientation. General Electric found an endless supply of talent in junior military officers. Many were graduates of U.S. military academies who had spent four to five years in the service. They were found to be hardworking, smart, and intense; they had leadership experience and were flexible. Walmart, along with many other companies, have discovered (or rediscovered) the benefits of recruiting military talent. It has even hired a retired Army brigadier general, Gary Profit, to expand military recruiting to all levels and divisions of the business.[37]

Service members nationwide looking for jobs can also go to HirePatriots.com. "We help citizens and businesses to thank our current military, veterans, and their spouses by posting their job opportunities on our free military job posting and search Web site," said Mark Baird, president of Patriotic Hearts.[38]

Self-Employed Workers

The self-employed worker may also be a good potential recruit. These individuals may be true entrepreneurs who are ingenious and creative. For many firms, these qualities are essential for continued competitiveness. Such individuals may constitute a source of applicants for any number of jobs requiring technical, professional, administrative, or entrepreneurial expertise within a firm.

Ex-Offenders

Some organizations have discovered it beneficial to hire ex-offenders. There are approximately 2.3 million criminals behind bars in the United States, the most of any country, according to the

International Center for Prison Studies at Kings College in London. Many are nonviolent substance abusers locked up because of federal and state drug laws. According to Multicultural Foodservice & Hospitality Alliance President Gerry Fernandez, "ex-offenders are a viable labor pool for restaurants, if a controversial one. I'm aware of several [chains] that have programs to hire ex-offenders, though they do not want publicity. Who do you think works third shift, where they don't come in contact with customers?"[39] Some organizations actively support the hiring of ex-cons. For example, Philadelphia has a program, being headed by an ex-offender, that gives $10,000 a year in municipal tax credits to companies that hire former prisoners and provide them tuition support or vocational training. In another example, supermarket retail consultant and restaurateur Howard Solganik has launched a program that puts ex-offenders to work helping area farmers increase the supply of local, seasonal produce accessible to consumers. Sloganik said, "My experience in the restaurant business exposed me to ex-offenders. I saw that most were hard workers and also were grateful for the jobs they were given. I realized small farms have a difficult time finding workers, and then, I thought about ex-offenders trying, so often in vain, to find jobs."[40]

Online Recruitment Methods

OBJECTIVE 5.6
Describe online
recruitment methods.

Online recruiting has revolutionized the way companies recruit employees and job seekers search and apply for jobs.[41] Discussed are various components of online recruiting.

Internet Recruiter

Internet recruiter
Person whose primary
responsibility is to use the
Internet in the recruitment
process (also called "cyber
recruiter").

The **Internet recruiter,** also called a "cyber recruiter," is a person whose primary responsibility is to use the Internet in the recruitment process.

Most companies currently post jobs on their corporate career Web site. Individuals must be in place to monitor and coordinate these activities. The more companies recruit on the Internet, the greater the need for Internet recruiters. Currently, high-tech firms have the greatest needs, and Internet recruiters can sometimes be quite aggressive.

Virtual Job Fair

virtual job fair
Online recruiting method
engaged in by a single
employer or group of
employers to attract a large
number of applicants.

A **virtual job fair** is an online recruiting method engaged in by a single employer or group of employers to attract a large number of applicants.

KPMG's recent virtual job fair attracted nearly 11,000 people from 167 countries. The participants had the opportunity to chat online with KPMG recruiters and other firm professionals. There was lots of interaction and the average participant was logged onto the job fair for 71 minutes. In addition to the number of résumés and good contacts made by the firm's people, the online job fair was very cost-effective.[42]

Corporate Career Web Sites

**corporate career
Web sites**
Job sites accessible from a
company homepage that
list available company
positions and provide a way
for applicants to apply for
specific jobs.

Corporate career Web sites are job sites accessible from a company homepage that list the company positions available and provide a way for applicants to apply for specific jobs. They have become a major resource for both job seekers and companies seeking new employees.

A career Web site should be upbeat and informative. It should be used as a selling device that promotes the company to prospective job candidates.[43] Writing effective recruitment ads on the Internet is different from the short, one-inch-column ads in the Sunday newspaper. The Internet provides enough space to fully describe the job, location, and company. A good Web site should provide a feeling of the kind of corporate culture that exists within the company.

Of late, another dimension has entered the equation with regard to making the corporate career Web site acessible to job seekers. Now it is important that job boards and recruitment sites are easy to use on handheld mobile devices. According to a recent survey, about 85 percent of Americans have cell phones and 32 percent have accessed the Internet with mobile devices. Some recommendations to assist mobile device use include: "make a 'light' version of your site; don't skimp on content; take it easy with ads; don't use Java; make redirection to the mobile site automatic; and allow access to the full site."[44]

HR Web Wisdom

HR Internet Guides
www.hr-guide.com

This Web site contains
links to other Internet-
based resources for
topics such as
recruitment, selection,
and EEO.

Weblogs (Blogs for Short)

Weblogs, or *blogs,* have changed the ways in which individuals access information. Google or a blog search engine such as Technorati.com can be used. All a person has to do is type in a key phrase like *marketing jobs.* The blogs themselves make it pretty easy to find, with names like AttorneyJobs.com and SalesJobs.com. Some employers and employment agencies have discovered that blogging is a way to do detailed and stealthy background checks. Cynthia Shapiro, author of *What Does Somebody Have to Do to Get a Job Around Here?,* is quoted as saying, "If what pops up is a ranting blog about the evils of corporate America or a picture of you topless in Cancun with a beer in your hand, you're in trouble."[45] Since you personally put the information on the Internet, no disclosure is required.

General-Purpose Job Boards

Firms use general-purpose job boards by typing in key job criteria, skills, and experience, and indicating their geographic location. Job seekers can search for jobs by category, experience, education, location, or any combination of categories. General-purpose job boards continue to attract large number of applicants. Many believe that the general-purpose big job boards are best for job seekers in professions that experience high turnover like sales but often are less effective for highly qualified applicants or those looking for work in smaller industries.[46] Therefore, only the two most widely recognized general employment Web sites, Monster.com and CareerBuilder.com, will be briefly discussed.

MONSTER.COM   Monster Worldwide, Inc. is the parent company of Monster. It has $1 billion in sales and 80 million resumes on file.[47] Information helpful to job seekers such as résumé tips, interview tips, salary information, and networking information is available on the site. The company acquired rival HotJobs for $225 million from Yahoo! In 2010.

CAREERBUILDER.COM   Owned by Gannett Co, Inc., Tribune Company, The McClatchy Company, and Microsoft Corp., CareerBuilder offers a vast online and print network to help job seekers connect with employers. CareerBuilder.com powers the career sites for more than 9,000 Web sites, including 140 newspapers and broadband portals such as MSN and AOL.[48]

NACElink Network

The **NACElink Network**, the result of an alliance among the National Association of Colleges and Employers, DirectEmployers Association, and Symplicity Corporation, is a national recruiting network and suite of Web-based recruiting and career services automation tools serving the needs of colleges, employers, and job candidates. Currently there are more than 900 colleges using the NACElink system.[49] The system includes three components: job posting, résumé database, and interview scheduling. It is available to employers to post jobs and search for students and new graduates.

AllianceQ

In a potential blow to headhunters and a boost to managers seeking to slash recruiting costs, certain large companies have begun pooling job candidates through a consortium known as AllianceQ.[50] Those passed over by one company are invited to submit their résumés to the AllianceQ database. "It's a no-brainer," says Phil Hendrickson, a recruiting manager at member company Starbucks. Alliance Q has 300,000 resumes and is adding 27,000 a month. For large member companies, which Alliance Q hopes will top out at 100 (currently at 45 members), access to the database will remain free.[51]

Niche Sites

Sites that specialize by industry and level of employment are becoming much more common.[52]
      Niche sites are Web sites that cater to highly specialized job markets such as a particular profession, industry, education, location, or any combination of these specialties; a few of these sites will be identified next.

There seems to be a site for virtually everyone. A few catchy ones include:

- cfo.com (a comprehensive online resource center for senior finance executives).
- accountantsworld.com (an online recruiting service that provides CPA firms with assistance in locating qualified employees).
- dice.com (a leading provider of online recruiting services for technology professionals).
- internshipprograms.com (employers who are exclusively looking for interns).
- hospitalsoup.com (global hospital careers).
- joyjobs.com (international employment for teachers).
- techjobbank.com (focuses on the recruiting needs of the technology companies).
- coolworks.com (find seasonal job or career in places such as Yellowstone, Yosemite, or other national parks).
- sixfigurejobs.com (provides executives and experienced professionals with access to some of the most exclusive executive jobs, executive recruiters, and career-management tools available).
- TVjobs.com (jobs in broadcasting).
- layover.com (jobs in trucking).
- college.monster.com (job listings and résumé service that targets college students and alumni).
- JobsInLogistics.com (dedicated to logistics jobs and logistics careers).
- Job.com (maintains sites specialized by geography (such as Californiajobnet.com), industry (medicalcareernet.com), and field (HRjobnet.com)[53]

A niche site is even available for professors who desire to change jobs. Formerly, college and university professors had to go to their library and thumb through the many pages of *The Chronicle of Higher Education* to hunt for a job. Now, sitting in the comfort of their own homes they can enter www.chronicle.com, *The Chronicle of Higher Education* Web site. All the jobs listed with the *Chronicle* are available to view free. Each position announcement has a hotlink to a university home page where additional information can be obtained. The universities pay the fees.

Contract Workers' Sites

Earlier, contract workers were mentioned as part of the contingent workforce as an alternative to recruitment. Sites are also available to assist these workers. Specialized Web sites let workers advertise their skills, set their price, and pick an employer. Three such sites are listed below:

- Freelance.com is a company that offers to clients the services of talented freelancers.
- AllFreelanceWork.com is a central information base for freelancers to find everything that they could need all in one place.
- Guru.com is an online marketplace for freelance talent.

Hourly Workers' Job Sites

After years of focusing primarily on professionals and their prospective employers, job sites are now available to attract blue-collar and service workers. Traditionally, there have been major differences between the ways hourly and salaried workers look for jobs. Most hourly workers pursue jobs by filling out applications rather than creating and sending out résumés. So sites allow job seekers to build an application that can be viewed by employers. Recognizing that some hourly workers do not have computer access, they have set up phone-based services to accept applications. Some job boards have bilingual call center operators who can help job applicants through the process. Many of the large boards such as Monster.com and CareerBuilder.com have moved into this large market.[54]

Social Network Recruiting

Some organizations are leaving general-purpose job boards and turning instead to such avenues as social networking recruiting. "Social networking" is the business buzzword in recruiting these days. As previously mentioned, it is well known that networking is one of the best recruiting tools and numerous Web sites have been developed to utilize social network recruiting. Sites such as Twitter, Facebook, and LinkedIn are used.[55] The chief operating officer of an information technology company said, "We have integrated Twitter, Linked-In, a Facebook fan page, and our web site to not only drive our brand into the market for customers/prospects, but to also attract top talent for our myriad client opportunities for which we need new hires."[56]

BreakingPoint Systems, a company that provides tools for testing computer networks, lets the ideal employee find it through the use of Twitter. Pam O'Neal, BreakingPoint's vice president of marketing, received tweets from Boston marketing professional Kyle Flaherty expressing his interest in a position. He had heard about the job from a former colleague who does business with BreakingPoint. Impressed with Flaherty's experience, communication skills and blog, O'Neal began a Twitter exchange with him. Within weeks of first contacting O'Neal, Flaherty received an interview. After several more weeks of Twitter exchanges, Flaherty accepted BreakingPoint's job offer. O'Neal says social media tools are especially attractive for small businesses eager to cut hiring costs. Contracting a recruiter to find an executive who earns $150,000 annually can cost $15,000 in fees or more. Posting ads on job search sites like Monster.com could mean spending hundreds of dollars—and precious hours poring over résumés. In contrast, social media tools are mostly free and offer added value as candidates bring their own online networks, blog content, and references, which speeds up the interview process.[57]

Sites such as LinkedIn, XING, and other professional social networks are excellent for searching for passive candidates. These sites house millions of passive candidates and include tools that let would-be employers search for candidates by geography, skills, interests, and numerous other criteria.[58] Giant consulting firm Accenture planed to hire 50,000 in 2010 and plans to make as many as 40 percent of hires in the next few years through social media. John Campagnino, Accenture's head of global recruiting, said, "This is the future of recruiting for our company."[59] New York-based accounting and consulting firm Deloitte LLP has launched its recruiting campaign through social media, which allow potential recruits to have a glimpse on the working environment of the company. A Deloitte Facebook page features photos, videos, and interactive message boards so potential recruits can chat with HR and employees. "Our goal is to offer recruits the most in-depth look at our organization to help them decide if Deloitte is truly the place for them," said Diane Borhani, Deloitte's U.S. campus recruiting leader.[60]

Corporate recruiter Elisa Bannon of US Cellular in Chicago used to spend up to $4 million a year to post jobs and screen resumes through Monster and CareerBuilder. Then her 2009 budget got cut to $1 million and she had 2,500 openings to fill. The big boards had to go and Bannon signed a deal with social networking site LinkedIn. For an annual fee of $60,000, she now has access to the network's 42 million members, many of whom are employed. These passive candidates are often the best individual to recruit since they already have jobs. Using LinkedIn, Bannon made a hire in 30 days for a position that typically takes six months to fill. "It's a great product at an attractive price," she says. "Finding passive candidates—that's our sweet spot," says David Hahn, LinkedIn's director of product management. Scott Morrison, director of global recruiting programs at software giant salesforce.com, said, "We could not believe the candidates we got from LinkedIn. This is a gold mine for us."[61]

Talent Revolution founder and president Amanda Hite says that "entire demographic groups now live out large portions of their lives online. Too many employers do not take that into account when it comes to recruiting. It makes me weep when I see the talent that you all are turning down because of old hiring paradigms." For example, restaurant chain Raising Cane's has a jobs section on its Facebook page where it lists current openings and uses extensive photos and video to convey messages about the company culture. YouTube can essentially do the same thing as well as provide career opportunities on job fairs. Giuseppe Rosati, founder of the restaurant jobs portal www.restogigs.com, said, "When passive job seekers stumble upon your job postings on social media sites, it opens up a whole new group of potential candidates, candidates that would not see the job on a traditional job site because they're not actively looking."[62]

A word of caution is evolving with regard to using social network sites for recruiting. Depending heavily on these sites for recruiting could lead to age and race discrimination suits because the sites contain few minority and older people.[63] Also, candidates have sued companies because they believe they were rejected for a job based on content posted on their profile on a social networking site.[64]

Job Search Scams

The high unemployment economy brought out job scammers en masse. In searching for a job online, one should be alert to the fact that there are those out there who will attempt to steal personal information from you and set up fraudulent credit-card accounts. Often crooks search for potential victims through posting a high paying job on a popular job-search Web sites. Once you apply for a job, naturally in order to conduct a thorough background check, they will need personal information such as your bank-account or credit-card number to check you out. Do not do it! True, firms use bank information, but that happens after you are hired. Countless crooks are out there waiting for you to make a mistake. "When the economy is down, scammers take advantage of people who are anxious about their financial position," says Karen Hobbs, an attorney with the Federal Trade Commission (FTC).[65]

Scammers do not just target high paying jobs. The FTC has been cracking down on job scammer firms like Job Safety USA, a front company that targeted people seeking maintenance and cleaning work. The company's ads claimed that for $98, Job Safety would send a credential called a "certificate registration number" and then help the registrant find a job. Naturally, the credential was bogus, and the job placement never occurred. Here is another situation that should send out an alert for a possible scam. If a posted job includes an e-mail address with a domain like Gmail, Hotmail, or Yahoo!, you should be concerned. Most legitimate companies have a company e-mail address.[66]

Susan Joyce, publisher of employment portal Job-Hunt.org, tries to identify fake jobs, first by Googling the hiring firm. "If all you find are other job postings on other job boards, that's a red flag," she says. To verify whether a company is legitimate, corporate phone numbers can be obtained by using sites such as Hoovers.com. Call the company to determine if the position is legitimate. Joyce finds out that about one-third of the posting are not legitimate.[67]

Your social security number and date of birth are also valuable in the hands of the scammer. True, it may be needed to conduct a background check, but you should hesitate to provide them until after an in-person meeting.

OBJECTIVE 5.7
Identify traditional external recruitment methods.

Traditional External Recruitment Methods

Although online recruiting has greatly impacted how recruiting is accomplished, traditional methods are not dead.

Media Advertising

Advertising communicates the firm's employment needs to the public through media such as newspapers, trade journals, radio, television, and billboards. The firm's previous experience with various media should suggest the most effective approach for specific types of jobs. Although few individuals base their decision to change jobs on advertising, ads create awareness, generate interest, and encourage a prospect to seek more information about the firm and the job opportunities that it provides. A traditional common form of advertising that provides broad coverage at a relatively low cost is the newspaper ad. Firms using the newspaper ad attempt to appeal to the self-interest of prospective employees, emphasizing the job's unique qualities. The use of newspaper advertising has declined because of online recruiting. Newspapers are literally bleeding readers; only two of the top 25 dailies, the *Wall Street Journal* and *USA Today*, gained readers. Between 2005 and 2012, eMarketer projects that newspaper ad revenue will decline from $49.4 billion to $28.4 billion, a drop of 42.5 percent.[68] In 2008, newspapers made just under $10 billion in revenues from classifieds, down from $19.6 billion in 2000.[69]

Certain media attract audiences that are more homogeneous in terms of employment skills, education, and orientation. Advertisements placed in publications such as the *Wall Street Journal* relate primarily to managerial, professional, and technical positions. The readers of these publications are generally individuals qualified for many of the positions advertised. Focusing on a specific labor market minimizes the likelihood of receiving marginally qualified or even totally unqualified applicants. Like most professional publications, jobs that are advertised in the paper copy of the *Journal* are also available on the publication's Web site. Trade journals are also widely used.

Qualified prospects who read job ads in newspapers and professional and trade journals may not be so dissatisfied with their present jobs that they will pursue opportunities advertised. Therefore, in high-demand situations, a firm needs to consider all available media resources. Such resources include radio, billboards, and television. These methods are likely to be more expensive than newspapers or journals, but, in specific situations, they may prove successful. For instance, a regional medical center used billboards effectively to attract registered nurses. One large manufacturing firm had considerable success in advertising for production trainees by means of spot advertisements on the radio. A large electronics firm used television to attract experienced engineers when it opened a new facility and needed more engineers immediately. Thus, in situations in which hiring needs are urgent, television and radio may provide good results. Broadcast messages can let people know that an organization is seeking recruits. A primary limitation is the amount of information they can transmit.

Private Employment Agencies

Private employment agencies, often called "head hunters," are best known for recruiting white-collar employees and offer an important service in bringing qualified applicants and open positions together. Firms and job hunters use private employment agencies for virtually every type of position. Job seekers should carefully select the employment agency to use because there are both good and bad recruiters. Today, private employment agencies often specialize in filling a particular niche in the job market.[70] Select one that has knowledge of the industry and the specific position that you are seeking.

Private employment agencies fees can range up to 35 percent of a person's first year salary.[71] The one-time fees that some agencies charge often turn off candidates, although many private employment agencies deal primarily with firms that pay the fees. Either way, the head hunter does not get paid until a person is placed. The recession of 2008/10 has significantly impacted the use of private employment agencies resulting in a general retrenchment of the industry.

Public Employment Agencies

Public employment agencies are operated by each state but receive overall policy direction from the U.S. Employment Service. Public employment agencies have become increasingly involved in matching people with technical, professional, and managerial positions. Some use computerized job-matching systems to aid in the recruitment process, and they provide their services without charge to either the employer or the prospective employee.

Recruiters

Recruiters most commonly focus on technical and vocational schools, community colleges, colleges, and universities. The key contact for recruiters on college and university campuses is often the student placement director. This administrator is in an excellent position to arrange interviews with students possessing the qualifications desired by the firm. Placement services help organizations use their recruiters efficiently. They identify qualified candidates, schedule interviews, and provide suitable rooms for interviews.

The company recruiter plays a vital role in attracting applicants. The interviewee often perceives the recruiter's actions as a reflection of the character of the firm. If the recruiter is dull, the interviewee may think the company is dull; if the recruiter is apathetic, discourteous, or vulgar, the interviewee may well attribute these negative characteristics to the firm. Recruiters must always be aware of the image they present at the screening interview, because it makes a lasting impression. Recruitment success comes down to good personal selling, appealing to the candidate's priorities, and addressing his or her concerns. The recruiter should underscore the job's opportunities and keep the lines of communication open.

Some firms are using videoconferencing with equipment at both corporate headquarters and on college campuses. Recruiters can communicate with college career counselors and interview students through a videoconferencing system without leaving the office.

Job Fairs

A **job fair** is a recruiting method engaged in by a single employer or group of employers to attract a large number of applicants to one location for interviews.

From an employer's viewpoint, a primary advantage of job fairs is the opportunity to meet a large number of candidates in a short time. Conversely, applicants may have convenient access to a number of employers. As a recruitment method, job fairs offer the potential for a much lower cost per hire than traditional approaches. Job fairs are often organized by universities to assist their students in obtaining jobs. Here, employers from many organizations meet at a single point on the campus. Students from disciplines from across the university are represented. Students and employers can meet to ask and answer questions and students can drop off résumés.

At times job fairs are tailored to specific types of individuals. At a Tucson, Arizona, job fair, the event was designed to bring together senior citizens and companies looking to hire them, as well as offer assistance to those seeking to improve their job skills as a first step toward employment. The job fair attracted two dozen companies seeking to fill positions for everything from teachers' aides to bank tellers to tour bus drivers and call-center staff.[72] Job fairs are also held to bring together service members and companies with openings to fill.

Internships

An **internship** is a special form of recruitment that involves placing a student in a temporary job with no obligation either by the company to hire the student permanently or by the student to accept a permanent position with the firm following graduation.

An internship typically involves a temporary job for the summer months or a part-time job during the school year. It may also take the form of working full-time one semester and going to school full-time the next. In the job market today, just having a degree is often not enough; internships are often the deciding factor in getting a good job or not.[73] Employers are able to *try out* future employees prior to making a job offer If the trial period proves unsuccessful, there is no obligation on either side. Google has long been known for using the internship as a recruiting method. Even in the slowed economy of 2010, Google offered competitive pay and on-site perks that include free gourmet food, a gym, fitness classes, massage therapy, bike repair, dry cleaning, a hair stylist, oil changes, and car washes.[74]

During the internship, the student gets to view business practices firsthand. At the same time, the intern contributes to the firm by performing needed tasks. In addition to other benefits, internships provide opportunities for students to bridge the gap from business theory to practice. Through this relationship, a student can determine whether a company would be a desirable employer. Similarly, having a relatively lengthy time to observe the student's job performance, the firm can make a better judgment regarding the person's qualifications. Students with internship and co-op experience are often able to find jobs more easily and they progress much further and faster in the business world than those without. Numerous job sites focus on assisting students in obtaining internships

Executive Search Firms

Executive search firms are organizations used by some firms to locate experienced professionals and executives when other sources prove inadequate. The key benefit of executive search firms is the targeting of ideal candidates. In addition, the search firm can find those not actively looking for a job.

An executive search firm's representatives often visit the client's offices and interview the company's management. This enables them to gain a clear understanding of the company's goals and the job qualifications required. After obtaining this information, they contact and interview potential candidates, check references, and refer the best-qualified person to the client for the selection decision. Search firms maintain databases of résumés for this process. Other sources used include networking contacts, files from previous searches, specialized directories, personal calls, previous clients, colleagues, and unsolicited résumés. The search firm's task is to present candidates who are eminently qualified to do the job; it is the company's decision whom to hire.

Professional Associations

Virtually every professional group publishes a journal and has a Web site that is widely used by its members. Many professional associations in business areas including finance, marketing, accounting, and human resources provide recruitment and placement services for their members. Jobs advertised are placed in the journal in hard copy and also advertised on the professional group's Web site. The Society for Human Resource Management (SHRM), for example, operates a job referral service for members seeking new positions and employers with positions to fill. SHRM has a first-rate Web site for human resource professionals and most national professional associations operate their career sites in much the same manner.

Unsolicited Applicants

In Chapter 1, the importance of a company having a positive image was stressed (employer branding). If an organization has the reputation of being a good place to work, it may be able to attract qualified prospects even without extensive recruitment efforts. Acting on their own initiative, well-qualified workers may seek out a specific company to apply for a job. Unsolicited applicants who apply because they are favorably impressed with the firm's reputation often prove to be valuable employees. In the Internet age, applicants can go to the firm's corporate career Web site and *walk in* by making an application online.

Open Houses

Open houses are a valuable recruiting tool, especially during days of low unemployment. Here, firms pair potential hires and recruiters in a warm, casual environment that encourages on-the-spot job offers. Open houses are cheaper and faster than hiring through recruitment agencies, and they are also more popular than job fairs. There are pros and cons to holding a truly *open* house. If the event is open, it may draw a large turnout, but it also may attract a number of unqualified candidates. Some companies prefer to control the types of candidates they host, and so they conduct invitation-only sessions. In this scenario, someone screens résumés in response to ads, then invites only preselected candidates. Advertising of open houses may be through both conventional media and the Internet, where a firm might feature its open house on its homepage.

Event Recruiting

event recruiting
Recruiters going to events being attended by individuals the company is seeking.

Event recruiting involves having recruiters go to events being attended by individuals the company is seeking. Cisco Systems pioneered event recruiting as a recruitment approach. In the case of programmers in the Silicon Valley, the choice spots have been marathons and bike races. Companies that participate in these events become involved in some way that promotes their name and cause. For example, they might sponsor or cosponsor an event, pass out refreshments, and give away prizes. Individuals should know that the company is recruiting and the types of workers it is seeking. Event recruiting gives a company the opportunity to reflect its image.

Sign-on Bonuses

Employers use sign-on bonuses to attract top talent, particularly within high-demand fields such as health care, sales, marketing, accounting, and finance. Steve Gross, senior consultant for Mercer Human Resource Consulting in Philadelphia, said, "Bonuses allow you to pay a premium to attract individuals without dramatically upsetting your salary scale."[75] Typical signing bonuses for middle managers and professionals ranges from 5 to 10 percent of the base salary. Nearly all companies allow executives, middle and upper management, and professional personnel to be eligible for sign-on bonuses.[76]

Competitive Games

Google has a unique way to get individuals interested in applying for technical positions. It sponsors an annual computer programming competition in which students from around the world enter and the winners of the competition are sure to be noticed. "We've hired some people through the Google Code Jam, and we're continually exploring opportunities to find brighter, talented engineers to join our team," a Google spokeswoman stated.[77]

Google is not the only company that uses games as a recruiting tool. TopCoder is a Glastonbury, Connecticut, company that creates software coding competitions. Internet advertising firm DoubleClick hired TopCoder to run a software coding competition contest between students from Columbia University and New York University. TopCoder identified about 100 programmers to participate in this software competition, and 10 made it to the final round. DoubleClick Chief Information Officer Mok Choe says the company has already hired a few of the winners. "We can filter out the cream of the crop," says Choe.[78]

L'Oréal makes use of recruiting games to uncover the best and brightest future employees. L'Oréal stages a series of intensely challenging business games at universities around the world. Martial Lalancette, senior vice-president of human resources, said, "These games immerse students from high-end universities in the reality of today's professional business world. It's an incredible learning opportunity." The games challenge teams to undertake complex case studies and market analyses to find business solutions. The students must make critical decisions that have a direct impact and major consequences on their simulated businesses.[79]

Tailoring Recruitment Methods to Sources

OBJECTIVE 5.8
Describe how recruitment methods and sources are tailored to each other.

Because each organization is unique, so are the needed types and qualifications of workers to fill positions.[80] Thus, to be successful, a firm must tailor its recruitment sources and methods to its specific needs.

Figure 5.3 shows a matrix that depicts sources and methods of recruitment for an information systems manager. Managers must first identify the *source* (where prospective employees are located) before choosing the *methods* (how to attract them). Suppose, for example, that a large firm has an immediate need for an experienced information technology (IT) manager

Figure 5.3

Methods and Sources of Recruitment for an Information Technology Manager

External Sources \ External Methods	Online recruiting	Advertising	Employment agencies	Recruiters	Job fairs	Internships	Executive search firms	Professional associations	Walk-in applicants	Open houses	Event recruiting	Sign-on bonuses	High Tech Competition
High/Vocational schools													
Community colleges													
Colleges and universities													
Competitors in the labor market	X	X	X				X	X					
Unemployed													
Self-employed													
Former employees													
Military personnel													
Ex-offenders													

A GLOBAL PERSPECTIVE

Our Company Headquarters Has Been Outsourced!

In recent years there has been considerable discussion regarding outsourcing and offshoring. By and large, the discussion has centered on sending jobs that can be done more economically to other countries with headquarters remaining in the United States. But, another trend is also occurring. What would your reaction be if a company from another country with culture quite different than yours purchased your company? How would you react if your corporate headquarters was moved to that country? Certainly, the job of the HR professional when the company headquarters has been offshored is challenging.[81]

There are numerous examples of offshoring headquarters. Doosan, based in Seoul, South Korea, bought the Bobcat unit from Ingersoll Rand Co. in 2007. Doosan immediately began a familiarization program for employees on both sides of the Pacific. "They even sent U.S. employees to Seoul to immerse themselves in Korean culture," says Bonnie Guttormson, director of compensation and benefits at Doosan. Guttormson notes that Korean culture is "very hierarchical, so where here in the United States we're very free to talk with higher officials about differences, there the process is to go through the hierarchy."[82] This cultural difference at times creates adaptability problems.

If the purchaser of the U.S. company is a first-time buyer, there may initially be difficulties. According to Donald Dowling Jr., an attorney with White & Case LLP in New York, "There will be a huge difference among foreign buyers that have U.S. operations and foreign buyers purchasing their first U.S. ventures." Dowling also says, "When the foreign-based buyer has other existing U.S. operations, it will likely aim toward integrating this new operation with its other U.S. business lines. When the foreign-based buyer is taking its first acquisition steps into the U.S., that is where the cultural and HR problems are likely to be most acute."[83]

Foreign executives may need to be familiarized with U.S. laws. HR professionals must be prepared to inform their new leaders not just what they want to hear but how a procedure that may be quite acceptable in their country would lead to legal challenges in the United States.[84] They may be unfamiliar with laws such as the Americans with Disabilities Act and the Family and Medical Leave Act. As Dowling stated, "they don't understand the role documentation procedures and policies have in reducing risks." Dowling also said, "European executives hear horror stories about U.S. court judgments—multi-million dollar verdicts, runaway juries, class actions, and unpredictable results." HR must steer them through these potential land mines.[85]

The code of conduct in a foreign company may be quite different from that permissible in the U.S. At times they are just not practical in the U.S. For example, the foreign country may have provisions prohibiting mandatory overtime, even though mandatory overtime may be an industry norm in the United States. Laurence Stuart, an attorney with Stuart & Associates PC in Houston, recommends that U.S. HR professionals and attorneys conduct due diligence and look into overseas policies that would be unlawful if applied in the United States. For example, mandatory retirement is common overseas. Also, foreign executives may not understand the exempt/nonexempt distinctions under federal and state wage and hour laws. They also may not know that employee benefits are provided at the employer's discretion in most circumstances, or that the amount and quality of benefits a company provides affects its ability to attract and retain employees.[86]

and no one within the firm has these qualifications. It is likely that other firms, possibly competitors, employ such individuals. After considering the recruitment source, the recruiter must then choose the method (or methods) of recruitment that offers the best prospects for attracting qualified candidates. Perhaps it would be appropriate to advertise the job in the classified section of the *Wall Street Journal* and use online recruiting. Alternatively, an executive search firm may serve as viable options. In addition, the recruiter may attend meetings of professional information technology associations. One or more of these methods will likely yield a pool of qualified applicants.

In another scenario, consider a firm's need for 20 entry-level machine operators, whom the firm is willing to train. High schools and vocational schools would probably be good recruitment sources. Methods of recruitment might include newspaper ads, public employment agencies, recruiters, visiting vocational schools, and employee referrals.

Summary

1. *Define recruitment and explain alternatives to recruitment. Recruitment* is the process of attracting individuals on a timely basis, in sufficient numbers, and with appropriate qualifications, to apply for jobs with an organization. Alternatives include outsourcing, contingent workers, employee leasing, and overtime.

2. *Explain the external environment of recruitment and describe how promotion policies influence recruitment.* Factors external to the organization can significantly affect the firm's recruitment efforts. Of particular importance is the demand for and supply of specific skills in the labor market, legal considerations, whether an applicant is active or passive.

   An organization's promotion policy can have a significant impact on recruitment. A firm can stress a policy of promotion from within its own ranks or one in which positions are generally filled from outside the organization. Depending on specific circumstances, either approach may have merit. Promotion from within is the policy of filling vacancies above entry-level positions with current employees.

3. *Describe the recruitment process.* Recruitment frequently begins when a manager initiates an employee requisition. Next, the firm determines whether qualified employees are available from within (the internal source) or must be recruited externally from sources such as colleges, universities, and other firms. Sources and methods are then identified.

4. *Describe internal recruitment methods.* Job posting is a method of internal recruitment that is used to communicate the fact that job openings exist. Job bidding is a system that permits individuals in an organization to apply for a specific job within the organization.

5. *Identify external recruitment sources.* External sources of recruitment include high schools and vocational schools, community colleges, colleges and universities, competitors and other firms, the unemployed, older individuals, military personnel, self-employed workers, and ex-offenders.

6. *Describe online recruitment methods and discuss the possibility of job search scams.* Perhaps the biggest change in the way that organizations recruit has been the rise in the use of online recruiting. Some online methods include: Internet recruiter, virtual job fairs, corporate career Web sites, Weblogs, general purpose job boards, head hunter, the NACElink Network, AllianceQ, niche sites, contract workers' sites, hourly workers' job sites, and social network recruiting.

   In searching for a job online, one should be alert to the fact that there are those out there who will attempt to steal personal information from you and set up fraudulent credit-card accounts.

7. *Identify traditional external recruitment methods.* Traditional external recruitment methods include media advertising, private employment agencies, public employment agencies, recruiters, job fairs, internships, executive search firms, professional associations, unsolicited applicants, open houses, event recruiting, sign-on bonuses, and high-tech competition.

8. *Describe how recruitment methods and sources are tailored to each other.* Recruitment must be tailored to the needs of each firm. In addition, recruitment sources and methods often vary according to the type of position being filled.

Key Terms

recruitment   138
contingent workers   139
promotion from within (PFW)   141
employee requisition   141
recruitment sources   142
recruitment methods   142

job posting   142
job bidding   142
internet recruiter   147
virtual job fair   147
corporate career
    Web sites   147

NACElink Network   148
niche sites   148
job fair   153
internship   153
event recruiting   154

Questions for Review

1. Define *recruitment*.
2. What are the typical alternatives to recruitment that a firm may use?
3. What are factors external to the organization that can significantly affect the firm's recruitment efforts?
4. What is meant by the policy of *promotion from within*?
5. What are the steps involved in the recruitment process?
6. What are some internal recruitment methods?
7. Why is employee referral so important in the recruitment process?
8. Define *sources* and *methods* of recruitment.
9. What external sources of recruitment are available?
10. What is an *Internet recruiter*?
11. Define the following:
    a. Virtual job fair
    b. Corporate career Web site
    c. NACElink Network
    d. Niche sites
12. What is the difference between contract workers' sites and hourly workers' job sites?
13. How can social networking be used in the recruiting process?
14. What traditional external methods of recruitment are available?
15. What are the sources and methods of recruitment that might be used for the following jobs:
    a. college professor who just received his or her Ph.D.
    b. senior accountant with a CPA
    c. entry-level accountant
    d. skilled automobile mechanic
    e. entry-level machine operator

HRM INCIDENT 1

A Problem Ad?

Dorothy Bryant was the new recruiting supervisor for International Manufacturing Company in Salt Lake City, Utah. One of Dorothy's first assignments was to recruit two software design engineers for International. Design engineers are hard to recruit because of the difficulty of their training and the high demand for them. After considering various recruitment alternatives, Dorothy placed the following ad in a local newspaper with a circulation in excess of 1,000,000:

Employment Opportunity for Software Design Engineers

2 positions available for engineers desiring career in growth industry.
Prefer recent college graduates with good appearance.
Good credit rating
Apply Today! Send your résumé,
in confidence, to: D. A. Bryant
International Manufacturing Co., P.O. Box 1515
Salt Lake City, UT 84115

More than 300 applications arrived in the first week, and Dorothy was elated. When she reviewed the applicants, however, it appeared that few people possessed the desired qualifications for the job.

Questions

1. Dorothy overlooked some of the proper recruiting practices, which resulted in an excessive number of unqualified people applying. What are they?
2. Are there any hiring standards that should be avoided? Identify them and explain why they should be avoided.

HRM INCIDENT **2**

"The Grass is Greener on the Other Side" or Is It?

Hani Hayek is the recruitment officer at Retail Us, a luxury retail company in Beirut, Lebanon. Most employees have been with the company since its inception in 1982. In 2010, the Human Resources Manager, Mr. Ghazi Haddad, retired; thus, a replacement needed to be found.

Hani called for a staff meeting, acknowledged the contributions of all employees, and explained the situation at hand. He continued to say that a recruitment advertisement would be run and encouraged anyone who felt qualified to apply. As Hani spoke, Bushra, the assistant HR manager had a big smile on her face. She felt confident that she was next in line. After all, isn't that how these things were supposed to work?

Hani read through the main job requirements for the Human Resources Manager position. These were to:

- Enhance morale and productivity, limit job turnover, increase performance, and improve business results;
- Diagnose organizational effectiveness and implement solutions;
- Create a strategic recruitment and selection plan;
- Evaluate company culture and provide recommendations on activities, events, and changes to accomplish company goals and objectives.

Candidates had to be enthusiastic, diplomatic, attentive to detail, a team player and had to have a university degree and at least 3 years experience.

The pool of candidates included external candidates and people from within the company but Bushra felt confident that she would get the position. After the process was completed, the new HR manager was going to be announced in a separate meeting.

Once again, Hani called a staff meeting. This time, Mr. Haddad was sitting to one side of Hani and to the other side was a new face. Bushra's heart skipped a beat and a hundred thoughts ran through her head.

At this point, all eyes were focused on Bushra. They all knew how much she wanted this position after ten years at the company.

With the adjournment of the meeting, staff members welcomed Aziz Kamal, the newly appointed HR Manager. Hani called Bushra over, introduced her to Aziz Kamal, and asked her to wait in his office; he needed to speak with her.[87]

Questions

1. Do you think that the promotion from within (PFW) policy was abused in this case?
2. Why do you think Bushra was not chosen? How could Hani have decreased the disappointment Bushra experienced?
3. What advice would you give Aziz Kamal as someone who is new to Retail Us?

Notes

1. Theresa Minton-Eversole, "Mission: Recruitment," *HRMagazine* 54 (January 2009): 42–45.
2. Ibid.
3. Ibid.
4. Ibid.
5. "Despite Talent Shortage, Tech and Telecom Companies Rely on Traditional Recruitment Methods," *CMA Management* 82 (April 2008): 9.
6. Marc Savage, "Eight Lessons from a Master Recruiter," *U.S. Business Review* 9 (April/May 2009): 16–17.
7. Rudy Hirschheim, "Offshoring and the New World Order," *Communications of the ACM* 52 (November 2009): 132–135.
8. "Contingent Workers and Contingent Health," *Safety Compliance Letter* (June 1, 2008): 12.

9. Anne Kates Smith, "You're Hired, At Least for Now," *Kiplinger's Personal Finance* 64 (March 2010): 13–14.

10. Peter Coy, Michelle Conlin, Moira Herbst, and Carol Matlack, "The Disposable Worker," *BusinessWeek* (January 18, 2010): 32–39.

11. "Use More Contingent Workers, Study Advises," *Report on Salary Surveys* 9 (December 2009): 8.

12. Irwin Speizer, "An On-Demand Workforce," *Workforce Management* 88 (October 19, 2009: 45–49.

13. Ibid.

14. Ibid.

15. Ed Frauenheim, "Tracking the Contingents," *Workforce Management* 89 (April 2010): 27–33.

16. Laurence O'Neil, "HR Resolutions for a Happier New Year," *HRMagazine* 54 (January 2009): 8.

17. Dennis Jacobe, "U.S. Job Market Best in the South; Worst in the West," *Gallup Poll Briefing* (July 9, 2009): 2.

18. Evan Cohen, "Innovative Recruiting—Targeting Passive Professionals," *Power Engineering* 113 (October 2009): 8–10.

19. Allen Smith, "Definition of 'Applicant' Will Not Change," *HRMagazine* 53 (May 2008): 23.

20. Judy Greenwald, "Employers Face Bias Rule for Internet Job Applications," *Business Insurance* 40 (January 2, 2006): 4–19.

21. Meredith McKenzie, "Hire or Promote?" *Smart Business Atlanta* 7 (January 2010): 26.

22. "The High Stakes of First Jobs," *U.S. News & World Report* 147 (May 2010): 36–37.

23. Leslie Hamel, "Recruiting Top Employees," *Convenience Store Decisions* 19 (September 2008): 32–35.

24. "Study Finds Bonus Pay Geared to Attract, Not Retain, Talent," *Report on Salary Surveys* 9 (March 2009): 1–7.

25. William B. Cassidy, "Flatbed Carrier Doubles Driver Referral Bonus," *JOC Online* (March 19, 2010): 5.

26. Mark Henricks, "You Know Who?" *Entrepreneur* 35 (May 2007): 89–90.

27. John Tozzi, "Where to Find Top Talent," *BusinessWeek Online* (December 17, 2008): 25.

28. Auren Hoffman, "Seeking Great Candidates Online," *BusinessWeek Online* (December 10, 2009): 1.

29. Joseph M. Larkin, "Extend Your Reach to Bring in New Recruits," *Pennsylvania CPA Journal* 78 (Winter 2008): 22.

30. Patrick J. Kiger, "A Case for Poaching," *Workforce Management* 89 (April 2010): 3.

31. Cathy Clonts, "Keep Your Foot in the Door," *E&P* 81 (September 2008): 128.

32. Leah Carlson Shepherd, "Boomerang Them Back," *Employee Benefit News* 22 (September 2008): 17–18.

33. "Talent Management: Now It's the Top Priority for CEOs & Their Organizations," *HR Focus* 85 (February 2008): 8–9.

34. Stephen Baker, "You're Fired—But Stay in Touch," *BusinessWeek* (May 4, 2009): 54–55.

35. "Will Your Organization Rehire Laid-Off Workers?" *HR Focus* 87 (February 2010): 8–9.

36. Donna Rosato, "Weathering a Long Job Search," *Money* 39 (April 2010): 53–55.

37. Brian O'Keefe, Jon Birger, and Doris Burke, "Battle-Tested," *Fortune* 161 (March 22, 2010): 108–118.

38. Agency Group 09, "America Supports You: Group Helps Troops, Families Find Jobs," FDCH Regulatory Intelligence Database (January 30, 2008): Department of Defense, 703-695-0192.

39. David Farkas, "Employee Search," *Chain Leader* 13 (June 2008): 44–45.

40. Roseanne Harper, "CSA Offers Second Chance," *Supermarket News* 57 (September 14, 2009): 30.

41. Lakhwinder Singh, and Leenu Narang, "Behavioral Revelation Concerning E-Recruitments," *ICFAI Journal of Organizational Behavior* 7 (October 2008): 45–53.

42. "KPMG Virtual Job Fair a 'Hit'," *Public Accounting Report* 32 (November 15, 2008): 2.

43. "Career Sites Missing Their Mark," *eWeek* 25 (April 21, 2008): 53.

44. Aliah D. Wright, "Job Search Goes Mobile," *HRMagazine* 55 (January 2010): 10.

45. Barry Shulman and Gordon Chiang, "How to Jump-start Your Search for Communications Talent and Other Secrets for Getting the Most Out of Your Executive Recruiting Firm," *Public Relations Tactics*; 15 (April 2008): 23.

46. "Is Your Next Job a Click Away?" *U.S. News & World Report* 147 (May 2010): 31.

47. Matthew Boyle, "Enough to Make Monster Tremble," *BusinessWeek* (July 6, 2009): 43–45.

48. http://www.careerbuilder.com/share/AboutUs/, February 13, 2010.

49. http://www.nacelink.com/nl_central_school.php January 11, 2010.

50. http://www.allianceq.com/ April 7, 2010.

51. "This Résumé Pool Is Deepening Fast," *BusinessWeek* (July 13, 2009): 72.

52. Ed Frauenheim, "Logging Off of Job Boards," *Workforce Management* 88 (June 22, 2009): 25–29.

53. Sharon Kahn, "The Virtual Talent Search," *Fortune* 160 (December 21, 2009): 122.

54. http://itmanagement.earthweb.com/career/article.php/ 1559531 December 8, 2010.

55. Charles Bretz, "How to Use Social Media to Acquire Staff," *Baseline* (January 2010): 14.

56. "Recruiting and Marketing Are Top Benefits of Social Media," *HR Focus* 87 (January 2010): S1–S4.

57. David Koeppel, "HR by Twitter," *Fortune Small Business* 19 (September 2009): 57.

58. Auren Hoffman, "Seeking Great Candidates Online," *BusinessWeek Online* (December 10, 2009): 1.

59. Jessi Hempel, "How Linked In Will Fire Up Your Career," *Fortune* 161 (April 1, 2010): 74–82.

60. "Deloitte Recruits Grads Through Social Media," *HR Specialist: Compensation & Benefits* 5 (May 2010): 7.

61. Boyle, "Enough to Make Monster Tremble."
62. Dana Tanyeri, "How to Hire Now," *Restaurant Business* 109 (January 2010): 18.
63. "Heed New Legal Risk of Recruiting via Facebook, LinkedIn," *HR Specialist* 8 (January 2010): 8.
64. Connie Stamper, "Common Mistakes Companies Make Using Social Media Tools in Recruiting Efforts," *CMA Management* 84 (April 2010): 12–14.
65. Barbara Kiviat, "Job Search Scams," *Time* 174 (October 26, 2009): 53.
66. Ibid.
67. Ibid.
68. Sean Callahan, "Can Newspapers Still Deliver?" *B to B* 94 (January 19, 2009): 1/27.
69. Douglas MacMillan, "Craigslist Fuels Online Classified-Ad Surge," *BusinessWeek Online* (May 25, 2009): 6.
70. Betsy Goldberg, "Getting a Leg Up on a Job Search," *Money* 39 (March 2010): 36.
71. "Reducing Recruiting Costs," *Compensation & Benefits for Law Offices* 9 (June 2009): 2–3.
72. Philip S. Moore, "Seniors Flood Older Worker Fair," *Inside Tucson Business* 14 (March 3, 2005): 15–17.
73. "When a Degree Isn't Enough," *U.S. News & World Report* 147 (May 2010): 52.
74. "Employers Are Being Creative With Perks & Pay for Internships," *HR Focus* 87 (March 2010): 9.
75. Drew Robb, "The Price of Admission," *HRMagazine* 52 (April 2007): 91–94.
76. "Study Finds Bonus Pay Geared to Attract, Not Retain, Talent."
77. Thomas Claburn, "One Way to Land a Job at Google," *InformationWeek* (October 10, 2005): 77.
78. Spence Ante, "Hiring Techies Is as Tricky as Ever," *BusinessWeek Online* (April 4, 2004).
79. "Got Game," *Marketing Magazine* 113 (December 22, 2008): 14.
80. R. Wayne Mondy, Robert M. Noe, and Robert Edwards, "Successful Recruitment: Matching Sources and Methods," *Personnel* 64 (September 1987): 42–46.
81. Allen Smith, "Offshored Headquarters," *HRMagazine* 54 (November 2009): 49–52.
82. Ibid.
83. Ibid.
84. Ibid.
85. Ibid.
86. Ibid.
87. "Executive Vacancies. PrimeJob S.A.L." *Executive Magazine*. Issue No. 134. (September, 2010): 112.

6 Selection

HRM in Action: From E-Verify to Biometrics

Employers are now required to use E-Verify to check out new hires and present employees at federal contractors and subcontractors with contracts of $100,000 or more. The Federal Acquisition Regulation requires government contractors and subcontractors to use E-Verify to determine that all of their new hires and all existing employees directly performing work on a federal contract are authorized to work in the United States.[1] E-Verify is a web-based system that lets employers check Social Security and visa numbers submitted by workers against government databases.[2] The program verifies information in the worker's *Employment Eligibility Verification Form* (I-9).[3] The system is not checking for citizenship, but for eligibility to be lawfully employed in the United States.[4] The E-Verify system is not flawless since a recent report found that 6 percent passed the E-Verify checks because they had used fraudulent or stolen identities.[5]

Because of this problem, some want to pursue a biometric verification tool that would replace or enhance E-Verify. Senator Charles Schumer, D-N.Y., chairman of the Senate Judiciary Committee's Subcommittee on Immigration, suspects that E-Verify does not work and plans to address a biometric component to verification within an immigration reform package. He said E-Verify "is an example of a halfhearted and flawed system. Simply put, it is not difficult for illegal workers to scam the system by providing the personal information of a legal worker." He further believes that E-Verify is unable to stop identity theft and that companies using E-Verify have been subject to worksite raids because employees have stolen information from legal citizens. Schumer's proposal would create a system to "authenticate the employee's identity by using a specific and unique

After completing this chapter, students should be able to:

1. Explain the significance of employee selection.

2. Identify environmental factors that affect the selection process.

3. Describe the selection process and explain applicant tracking systems.

4. Explain the importance of preliminary screening.

5. Describe reviewing applications and résumés.

6. Describe sending résumés via the Internet.

7. Explain the advantages and potential problems of using selection tests.

8. Describe the characteristics of properly designed selection tests.

9. Explain test validation approaches; describe types of employment tests, online assessment, the use of an assessment center, and unique forms of testing.

10. Explain the importance of the employment interview and describe the general types of interviewing.

11. Describe the various methods of interviewing, potential interviewing problems, and concluding the interview.

12. Explain the use of pre-employment screening, including background investigations and reference checks, automated reference checking, and negligent hiring.

13. Describe the selection decision, the medical examination, notification of candidates, and candidate relationship management.

14. Explain the metrics for evaluating recruitment/selection effectiveness.

biometric identifier," such as a fingerprint. He said, "The only way to stop illegal immigration is to stop employers from hiring illegal immigrants. We must adopt a system that relies upon objective, rather than subjective, criteria to prove identity and legal status. The system must be nonforgeable and airtight."[6]

So what is this system that might replace E-Verify? Biometrics deal with a variety of traits that are not subject to change, including fingerprints, facial patterns, eye retinas and irises, venous patterns of the hands, and hand and palm geometry. Even behavioral identifiers, such as handwriting that measure the pressure, speed, and rhythm of a person's writing and gait analysis technologies that recognize you by the way you walk, fall into the realm of biometrics.[7] A biometric system designed for identification purposes attempts to determine who a particular person is. It gathers biometric information from the subject and compares it with the corresponding information from the total number of templates stored in its database.

A biometric identification card is the primary focus of immigration reform legislation being debated in Congress. It would be the primary tool in a national system for identifying people. To accomplish this, every U.S. worker would have to present a birth certificate and other identification documents, then have his or her biometric, such as a fingerprint, captured. Some say such databases would create privacy and security risk.[8] Others say that the government already has considerable information on each of us. Lawrence P. Lataif, senior immigration counsel at the Florida law firm of Shutts & Bowen LLP, said, "Consider the databases federal government agencies already have on each of us: Social Security, Department of Defense, FBI, IRS, immigration and border patrol, passport office.... Can anyone imagine any data on an ID card that is not already in a computer database? If we're honest, we must admit that we have lost much of our privacy as a result of computer saturation."[9] Ultimately HR would likely be responsible for collecting and storing this vast amount of data as it is already doing with E-Verify.

This chapter begins with a discussion of E-Verify and biometrics, followed by a discussion of the significance of employee selection and identification of environmental factors that affect the selection process. Next, the general selection process and applicant tracking systems are described. The next two sections involve preliminary screening and review of applications and résumés. A section on sending résumés via the Internet follows, and the advantages and potential problems and characteristics of properly designed selection tests are then explained. Test validation approaches, and types of employment tests are next discussed, and topics related to genetic testing, graphoanalysis, and polygraph tests are described. Aspects of online assessment and the use of assessment centers are then presented, and the importance of the employment interview and the general types of interviewing is discussed. Then we examine the various methods of interviewing, interviewing through crowd sourcing, potential interviewing problems, and concluding the interview. Next, the use of pre-employment screening, including background investigations and reference checks, is presented, followed by a discussion of negligent hiring. Topics related to the selection decision, the medical examination, notification of candidates, candidate relationship management, and automated reference checking is discussed. Metrics for evaluating recruitment/selection effectiveness are then explained. The chapter concludes with a global perspective entitled "Leadership Effectiveness in the Global Environment."

OBJECTIVE 6.1
Explain the significance of employee selection.

selection
Process of choosing from a group of applicants the individual best suited for a particular position and the organization.

Significance of Employee Selection

Selection is the process of choosing from a group of applicants the individual best suited for a particular position and the organization. Properly matching people with jobs and the organization is the goal of the selection process. If individuals are overqualified, underqualified, or for any reason do not fit either the job or the organization's culture, they will be ineffective and probably leave the firm, voluntarily or otherwise. There are many ways to improve productivity, but none is more powerful than making the right hiring decision.[10] A firm that selects high-quality employees reaps substantial benefits, which recur every year the employee is on the payroll. On the other hand, poor selection decisions can cause irreparable damage. A bad hire can negatively affect the morale of the entire staff, especially in a position where teamwork is critical.

Many companies would rather go short and work overtime than hire one bad apple. If a firm hires many bad apples, it cannot be successful for long even if it has perfect plans, a sound organizational structure, and finely tuned control systems. Competent people must be available to ensure the attainment of organizational goals. Today, with many firms having access to the same technology, *people* make the real difference.

Environmental Factors Affecting the Selection Process

OBJECTIVE 6.2
Identify environmental factors that affect the selection process.

A standardized selection process followed consistently would greatly simplify the selection process. However, circumstances may require making exceptions. The following sections describe environmental factors that affect the selection process.

HR Web Wisdom

Business Owner's Toolkit

http://www.toolkit.cch.com

Offers detailed instructions for the small business owner to hire, manage, and retain employees.

Other HR Functions

The selection process affects, and is affected by, virtually every other HR function. If the compensation package is inferior to those provided by competitors, hiring the best-qualified applicants will be difficult or impossible. The same situation applies if the firm's safety and health record is substandard or if the firm has a reputation of providing minimal training.

Legal Considerations

Remember from Chapter 3 that legal matters play a significant role in HR management because of legislation, executive orders, and court decisions. Although the basic purpose of selection is to determine candidates' eligibility for employment, it is also essential for organizations to maintain nondiscriminatory practices. The guiding principles in determining what information to get from an applicant are: why am I asking this question and why do I want to know this information? If the information is job-related, usually asking for the information is appropriate.

Speed of Decision Making

The time available to make the selection decision can also have a major effect on the selection process. Conditions also can impact the needed speed of decision making. Suppose, for instance, that the only two quality-control inspectors on a production line just had a fight and both resigned, and the firm cannot operate until the positions are filled. In this situation, speed is crucial, and a few phone calls, two brief interviews, and a prayer may constitute the entire selection procedure. On the other hand, conducting a national search to select a chief executive officer may take months or even a year. In bureaucracies, it is not uncommon for the selection process to take a considerable amount of time.

Organizational Hierarchy

Organizations usually take different approaches to filling positions at varying levels. For instance, consider the differences in hiring a chief executive officer versus filling a clerical position. Extensive background checks and multiple interviews would most likely apply for the executive position. On the other hand, an applicant for a clerical position would probably take a word-processing test and perhaps have a short employment interview.

Applicant Pool

applicant pool
Number of qualified applicants recruited for a particular job.

The number of qualified applicants recruited for a particular job makes up the **applicant pool**. The process can be truly selective only if there are several qualified applicants. Yet, only one or two applicants with the required skills may be available. The selection process then becomes a matter of choosing from whoever is at hand. The expansion and contraction of the labor market also affects the size of the applicant pool. A low unemployment rate often means that the applicant pool is smaller, whereas a high unemployment rate may expand the pool, which is what happened in the recession of 2008/10.

The number of people hired for a particular job compared to the number of individuals in the applicant pool is often expressed as a **selection ratio**, or

selection ratio
Number of people hired for a particular job compared to the number of individuals in the applicant pool.

$$\text{Selection Ratio} = \frac{\text{Number of people hired}}{\text{Number of qualified applicants (applicant pool)}}$$

A selection ratio of 1.00 indicates that there was only one qualified applicant for an open position. The lower the ratio falls below 1.00, the more alternatives the manager has in making a selection decision. For example, a selection ratio of 0.10 indicates that there were 10 qualified applicants for an open position.

Note in the above selection ratio formula that "qualified" applicants are sought, not just a warm body to fill a vacant position. One might think that during the 2008/10 recession that it was easy to find "qualified" applicants for vacant positions. True, in a recession there are often many candidates for almost every job, but after screening for qualified applicants, the realistic selection pool may be greatly reduced.[11] Despite the abundance of job seekers and nearly 10 percent unemployment, a recent study by Robert Half International found 37 percent of executives reporting that it's challenging to find skilled professionals today.[12]

Type of Organization

The type of organization employing individuals, such as private, governmental, or not-for-profit, can also affect the selection process. A private-sector business is heavily profit oriented. Prospective employees who can help achieve profit goals are the preferred candidates. Consideration of the total individual, including job-related personality factors, is involved in the selection of employees for this sector.

Government civil service systems typically identify qualified applicants through competitive examinations. Often a manager may select only from among the top three applicants for a position. A manager in this sector may not have the prerogative of interviewing other applicants.

Individuals considered for positions in not-for-profit organizations (such as the Boy Scouts and Girl Scouts, YMCA, or YWCA) confront still a different situation. The salary level in these organizations may not be competitive with those of private and governmental organizations. Therefore, a person who fills one of these positions must be not only qualified but also dedicated to this type of work.

Probationary Period

Many firms use a probationary period that permits them to evaluate an employee's ability based on established performance. The purpose of a probationary period is to establish the suitability of a new employee for the role that has been offered to them and to resolve any issues there might be in the new employee's performance over the first three months or so.[13] This practice may be either a substitute for certain phases of the selection process or a check on the validity of the process. The rationale is that if an individual can successfully perform the job during the probationary period, the process does not require other selection tools. From a legal viewpoint, the use of a probationary period in the selection process is certainly job-related. In any event, newly hired employees need monitoring to determine whether the hiring decision was a good one.

Even in unionized firms, the labor/management agreement typically does not protect a new employee until after a certain probationary period. This period is typically from 60 to 90 days. During that time, an employee can be terminated with little or no justification. On the other hand, firing a marginal employee in a union environment may prove to be quite difficult after the probationary period.

OBJECTIVE 6.3
Describe the selection process and describe applicant tracking systems.

Selection Process

Figure 6.1 illustrates a generalized selection process that may vary by organization. It typically begins with preliminary screening. Next, applicants complete the firm's application for employment or provide a résumé. Then they progress through a series of selection tests, one or more employment interviews, and pre-employment screening, including background and reference checks. The hiring manager then offers the successful applicant a job, subject to successful completion of a medical examination. Notice that an applicant may be rejected at any time during the selection process. To a point, the more screening tools used to assess a good fit, the greater the chance of making a good selection decision.

Applicant Tracking Systems

applicant tracking systems (ATS)
Software application designed to help an enterprise select employees more efficiently.

An **applicant tracking system (ATS)** is a software application designed to help an enterprise select employees more efficiently. Current ATSs permit human resource and line managers to oversee the entire selection process. They often involve screening résumés and spotting qualified candidates, conducting personality and skills tests, and handling background checks. They allow companies to compile job applications electronically, to more quickly amass candidates, set up interviews, and get new hires on board. An ATS can be used to post job openings on a corporate Web site or job board and generate interview requests to potential candidates by e-mail. Other features may include individual applicant tracking, requisition tracking, automated résumé ranking, customized input forms, prescreening questions and response tracking, and multilingual

Figure 6.1

Selection Process

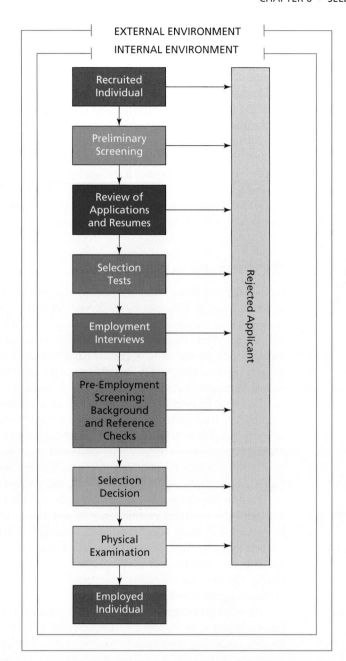

capabilities. ATSs are used extensively to help ease the labor-intensive process of sorting résumés from online job boards.[14] In most cases, the goal is not merely to reduce costs but also to speed up the hiring process and find people who fit an organization's success profile. ATSs continue to be enhanced to make recruiters more efficient and extend sourcing into the global market. Developers of applicant tracking systems are now focusing efforts on developing quality-of-hire metrics.

Helene Richter, director of talent operations for Liz Claiborne, New York City, said, "People choose an applicant-tracking tool to streamline process. But you have EEO and compliance issues that you need to streamline as well." The applicant-tracking function does both.[15]

OBJECTIVE 6.4

Explain the importance of preliminary screening.

Preliminary Screening

The selection process often begins with preliminary screening. The basic purpose of the preliminary screening is to eliminate those who obviously do not meet the position's requirements. The preliminary screening may take the form of reviewing for obviously unqualified applicants with a brief interview, test, or only a review of the application or résumé for obvious mismatches. In addition to eliminating clearly unqualified job applicants quickly, preliminary screening may produce other positive benefits for the firm. It is possible that the position for which the applicant applied is not the only one available. The person doing the assessment will know about other vacancies in the firm and may be able to steer the prospective employee to another position. For instance, the assessor may decide that although an applicant is not a good fit for the applications-engineering job, she is an excellent candidate for an internal R&D position. This type of assessment not only builds goodwill for the firm but also can maximize recruitment and selection effectiveness.

At times, a short test may be used to determine if a person should proceed in the selection process. For example, in the recruitment of sales representatives, a brief sales aptitude test may be administered to determine if the applicant has a talent or interest in sales. Then the company knows that the people they interview are already more likely to succeed in the role. By conducting a quick assessment before scheduling interviews, the company would be more likely to hire people who will add value to the organization.[16]

OBJECTIVE 6.5
Describe reviewing applications and résumés.

Review of Applications

Having the candidate complete an application for employment is another early step in the selection process. This may either precede or follow preliminary screening. The employer then evaluates it to see whether there is an apparent match between the individual and the position. A well-designed and properly used application form can be helpful, since essential information is included and presented in a standardized format. Completion of an application may not be initially required for many management and professional positions. In these cases, a résumé may suffice. A complete application usually is obtained at a later time.

The specific information requested on an application form may vary from firm to firm, and even by job type within an organization. An application typically contains sections for name, address, telephone number, e-mail address, military service, education, and work history. Managers compare the information contained in a completed application to the job description to determine whether a potential match exists between the firm's requirements and the applicant's qualifications. As you might expect, this judgment is often difficult.

Several preprinted statements are usually included on the application form. First, by signing the form, the applicant certifies that information provided on the form is accurate and true. Employers will likely reject candidates who make false claims for major issues. Second, when not prohibited by state law, the form should also state that the position is *employment at will* and that either the employer or the employee can terminate employment at any time for any reason. Finally, the form should contain a statement whereby the candidate gives permission to have his or her background and references checked.

An employment application form must reflect not only the firm's informational needs but also Equal Employment Opportunity Commission (EEOC) requirements. Potentially discriminatory questions inquiring about such factors as gender, race, age, convictions, national origin, citizenship, birthplace, dependents, disabilities, religion, color, and marital status should not be used.

Applicants sometimes deliberately leave out information on the application that may present them in a negative light. To combat this, many employers are requiring all applicants to use online applications that force a person to complete a required field before the application is successfully submitted.[17] In fact, corporations have increasingly declined to accept a printed résumé and applicants are directed to company Web sites for employment application and résumé submission.[18] For the first time since it started building cars in the United States, Honda accepted only online job applications at its southeastern Indiana plant. Honda hired 2,000 workers for the factory and 300 for other jobs at the plant. During just a two-week period, Honda received 31,000 online applications.[19]

résumé
Goal-directed summary of a person's experience, education, and training developed for use in the selection process.

Review of Résumés

A **résumé** is a goal-directed summary of a person's experience, education, and training developed for use in the selection process.

Professional and managerial applicants often begin the selection process by submitting a résumé. Figure 6.2 illustrates a traditional résumé. Note that the résumé includes the career

Figure 6.2

**Example of a
Traditional Résumé**

Marianne Sanders

Current Address:
4289 Tiger Bend Road
Baton Rouge, LA 71220
Phone: 555.555.5151
E-mail: MSanders@internet.com

Objective:	To obtain an entry level position in accounting.
Education:	University of Phoenix **Master of Business Administration, June 2010** **GPA: 3.61/4.0** McNeese State University Bachelor of Science, Accounting, May 2008 GPA: 3.5/4.0
Experience:	January 2007 - Present McElroy, Quirk, & Burch APC (Accounting firm) Lake Charles, LA Accountant • Prepare individual tax returns. • Amend tax returns (Safe Harbor). • Investigate/Respond to tax notices. January 2005 – December 2006 McNeese State University (Financial Aid) Lake Charles, LA Student Worker • Assist full-time worker with office work. • Help students with financial aid questions/forms.
Honors:	Beta Gamma Sigma Honor Fraternity Beta Alpha Psi Honor Fraternity Pi Beta Lambda – Business Professionals President Honor Role (Six times) McElroy, Quirk, & Burch Scholarship
Personal:	Hard-working, goal-oriented, conscientious, positive thinker, work well in teams, excellent people skills
Interests:	Accounting, physical fitness, traveling, tennis
Software Proficiency:	Microsoft Office 2003/2007 – Excel, Word, PowerPoint

objective for the specific position the applicant is seeking (a vita does not contain a career objective). Some HR professionals suggest that a professional summary at the beginning of the résumé is more useful to the recruiter.[20] However, young job seekers with little work experience may be best served by using a career objective statement. The remainder of the résumé should be directed toward showing how a person has the necessary skills and competencies necessary to accomplish the position identified in the career objective statement.[21] Using the firm's job description should assist an applicant in preparing the résumé.[22] Only information necessary to show a relationship to the objective should be included. The all-important concept of relevancy is crucial in selling the applicant to the company.

In developing a résumé, the sender should be careful not to misrepresent the truth. An applicant who is three hours away from graduation has not graduated. Certainly, the résumé should be designed to present the applicant in a positive light but care should be taken to not exaggerate excessively.[23] With regard to job history, make sure dates of employment are accurate. It goes without saying that résumés should not contain grammar and spelling errors. The résumé should show that the applicant has an understanding of the job and how his or her job history can assist in accomplishing the job.

Sending Résumés via the Internet

When sending a résumé via the Internet, applicants should realize that most large companies now use applicant-tracking systems. These systems assume a certain résumé style. Résumés that deviate from the assumed style are ignored or deleted. These systems scan résumés into databases, search the databases on command, and rank the résumés according to the number of resulting "hits" they receive. At times such searches use multiple (10–20) criteria. Some systems flag résumés that appear to misrepresent the truth, present misleading information, or are in other ways suspicious.

The use of applicant-tracking systems coupled with the downsizing of human resource departments, has resulted in a situation where many résumés are never seen by human eyes once they enter the system. Therefore, a job applicant should make his or her résumé as computer/scanner friendly as possible so that its life in a database will be extended. Debra Feldman of JobWhiz, an executive job search consultant said, "Even if you are a perfect match for the job, your résumé may never get to someone who could decipher your potential value."[24] To make the process work, a keyword résumé style should be used. **Keywords** refer to those words or phrases that are used to search databases for résumés that match. A **keyword résumé** contains an adequate description of the job seeker's characteristics and industry-specific experience presented in keyword terms in order to accommodate the computer search process. The keywords are often job titles, skills, or areas of expertise related to the position.[25] Keywords tend to be more of the noun or noun-phrase type (Word 2007, UNIX, Biochemist) as opposed to power action verbs often found in traditional résumés (developed, coordinated, empowered, organized). Another way to look at keyword phrases is to think in terms of job duties. According to CareerBuilder.com, the terms employers search for most often are: problem solving and decision making, oral and written communication, customer service or retention, performance and productivity improvement, leadership, technology, team-building, project management, and bilingual.[26]

Applicants should study the job posting and industry ads to get an overview of the phrases that keep reappearing. Detailing an individual's job duties may require a change in mindset away from traditional résumé writing. Recruiters should be mindful that applicants have gotten smarter in résumé preparation and at times "stuff" the résumé with words that hardly resemble the past accomplishment of the individual.[27]

Selection Tests: Advantages and Potential Problems

Recognizing the shortcomings of other selection tools, many firms have added selection tests to their hiring process. These tests rate factors such as aptitude, personality, abilities, and motivation of potential employees, allowing managers to choose candidates according to how they will fit into the open positions and corporate culture. Tests alone are not enough to make a sufficient evaluation of a candidate because they are not foolproof. Firms need to use them in conjunction with other selection tools.

Advantages of Selection Tests

Research indicates that customized tests can be a reliable and accurate means to predict on-the-job performance. Organizations use tests to identify attitudes and job-related skills that interviews cannot recognize. Also, the cost of employment testing is small in comparison to ultimate hiring costs. They are a more efficient way to get at that type of information and may result in better-qualified people being hired.

Potential Problems of Selection Tests

Job performance depends on an individual's ability and motivation to do the work. Selection tests may accurately predict an applicant's ability to perform the job, the "can do," but they are less successful in indicating the extent to which the individual will be motivated to perform it, the "will do." The most successful employees have two things in common: they identify with their firm's goals, and they are highly motivated. For one reason or another, many employees

ETHICAL DILEMMA

Employee Selection Criteria?

You are the newly appointed sales manager for a large manufacturing organization that has been struggling of late, even though your region is the firm's most successful one. Your office is located in a very close-knit community where people place a high value on local basketball. In fact, it didn't take you long to realize that to most people, local basketball is even more important than the Super Bowl. While you were watching a game the other night with your biggest customer, who purchases almost 40 percent of your yearly volume, he told you that the star on the team may soon be leaving the community because his father was laid off. He has heard that your region has an opening for a sales representative, and he asks you to hire the boy's father. You tell him that you will be glad to review the man's résumé, but you think that you have already found an extremely qualified person.

As you are reviewing the résumé of your customer's recommended candidate the next day, the person you are replacing comes by the office to say good-bye. In the conversation he mentions that in this town, people do each other favors, and that is how they build trust. He also tells you that if the boy's father is not hired, the firm may lose most, if not all, of the buyer's business. That is quite a shock because you realize that the customer's candidate lacks some qualifications for the position.

What would you do?

---

with high potential never seem to reach it. The factors related to success on the job are so numerous and complex that selection may always be more of an art than a science.

Employers should be aware that tests might be unintentionally discriminatory. Office of Federal Contract Compliance Programs (OFCCP) former director Charles E. James Sr. said, "Testing is a 'necessary business tool' to help employers select qualified candidates. Hiring the wrong person puts your company at risk. The key is to make the test fit the job you're using it for."[28] When a test excludes a protected class at a significant rate, the test should be avoided unless the employer can show the test is job-related for the position in question and consistent with business necessity. Using selection tests carries with it legal liabilities of two types. One is a lawsuit from rejected applicants who claim a test was not job-related or that it unfairly discriminated against a protected group, violating federal employment laws. Organizations must ensure that their selection tests do not discriminate against members of protected classes. The second potential legal problem relates to *negligence hiring* lawsuits filed by victims of employee misbehavior or incompetence (a topic discussed later in this chapter).

Test anxiety can also be a problem. Applicants often become quite anxious when confronting yet another hurdle that might eliminate them from consideration. The test administrator's reassuring manner and a well-organized testing operation should serve to reduce this threat. Actually, although a great deal of anxiety is detrimental to test performance, a slight degree is helpful.

The problems of hiring unqualified or less-qualified candidates and rejecting qualified candidates will continue regardless of the procedures followed. Well-developed tests administered by competent professionals help organizations minimize such consequences.

OBJECTIVE 6.8
Describe the characteristics of properly designed selection tests.

Characteristics of Properly Designed Selection Tests

Properly designed selection tests are standardized, objective, based on sound norms, reliable, and, of utmost importance, valid. The application of these concepts is discussed next.

Standardization

standardization
Uniformity of the procedures and conditions related to administering tests.

Standardization is the uniformity of the procedures and conditions related to administering tests. In order to compare the performance of several applicants on the same test, it is necessary for all to take the test under conditions that are as identical as possible. For example, the content of instructions provided and the time allowed must be the same, and the physical environment must be similar. If one person takes a test in a room with jackhammers operating just outside and another takes it in a more tranquil environment, differences in test results are likely.

Objectivity

objectivity
Condition that is achieved when everyone scoring a given test obtains the same results.

Objectivity in testing occurs when everyone scoring a test obtains the same results. Multiple-choice and true–false tests are objective. The person taking the test either chooses the correct answer or does not.

Norms

norm
Frame of reference for comparing an applicant's performance with that of others.

A **norm** is a frame of reference for comparing an applicant's performance with that of others. Specifically, a norm reflects the distribution of many scores obtained by people similar to the applicant being tested. A score by itself is insignificant. It becomes meaningful only when compared with other applicants' scores.

When a sufficient number of employees are performing the same or similar work, employers can standardize their own tests. Typically, this is not the case, and a national norm for a particular test is used. A prospective employee takes the test, the score obtained is compared to the norm, and the significance of the test score is then determined.

Reliability

reliability
Extent to which a selection test provides consistent results.

Reliability is the extent to which a selection test provides consistent results. Reliability data reveal the degree of confidence placed in a test. If a person scores 130 on a certain intelligence test this week and retakes the test next week and scores 80, the test reliability would likely be low. If a test has low reliability, its validity as a predictor will also be low. However, the existence of reliability alone does not guarantee the test's validity.

Validity

validity
Extent to which a test measures what it claims to measure.

The basic requirement for a selection test is that it be valid. **Validity** is the extent to which a test measures what it claims to measure. If a test cannot indicate ability to perform the job, it has no value. And, if used, it will result in poor hiring decisions and a potential legal liability for the employer.

Here is an example describing the difference between reliability and validity. If a person weighs 200 pounds but the scale show a wide difference such as 455, 150, 295, and 240, the scale is not reliable. If the scale consistently reads "100" and you weigh 200 pounds, then it is reliable, but not valid. If it reads "200" each time, then the measurement is both reliable and valid.

Validity, commonly reported as a correlation coefficient, summarizes the relationship between two variables. For example, these variables may be the score on a selection test and some measure of employee performance. A coefficient of 0 shows no relationship, whereas coefficients of either +1.0 or −1.0 indicate a perfect relationship, one positive and the other negative. Naturally, no test will be 100 percent accurate, yet organizations strive for the highest feasible coefficient. If a job performance test has a high positive correlation coefficient, most prospective employees who score high on the test will probably later prove to be high performers.

Title VII requires the test to work without having an adverse impact on minorities, females, and individuals with backgrounds or characteristics protected under the law. If using the test results in an adverse impact on certain members of protected groups, the firm must have a compelling reason why it is used; that is, it must validate the test. Employers are not required to validate their selection tests automatically. Remember from Chapter 3 that validation is required only when the selection process as a whole results in an adverse impact on women or minorities.

criterion-related validity
Test validation method that compares the scores on selection tests to some aspect of job performance determined, for example, by performance appraisal.

OBJECTIVE 6.9
Explain test validation approaches, describe types of employment tests, unique forms of testing, online assessment, and the use of an assessment center.

Test Validation Approaches

The *Uniform Guidelines on Employee Selection Procedures* established three approaches to validating selection tests: criterion-related validity, content validity, and construct validity.

Criterion-Related Validity

Criterion-related validity is a test validation method that compares the scores on selection tests to some aspect of job performance determined, for example, by performance appraisal.

Performance measures might include quantity and quality of work, turnover, and absenteeism. A close relationship between the score on the test and job performance suggests that the test is valid. The two basic forms of criterion-related validity are concurrent and predictive validity.

CONCURRENT VALIDITY *Concurrent validity* is determined when the firm obtains test scores and the criterion data at essentially the same time. For instance, it administers the test to all currently employed telemarketers and compares the results with company records that contain current information about each employee's job performance. If the test is able to identify productive and less productive workers, one could say that it is valid. A potential problem in using this validation procedure results from changes that may have occurred within the work group. For example, firms may have fired the less productive workers, and promoted the more productive employees out of the group.

PREDICTIVE VALIDITY *Predictive validity* involves administering a test and later obtaining the criterion information. For instance, all applicants take the test but the firm uses other selection criteria, not the test results, to make the selection decision. After observing employee performance over time, the company analyzes test results to determine whether they differentiate the successful and less successful employees. Predictive validity is a technically sound procedure. Because of the time and cost involved, however, its use is often not feasible.

Content Validity

content validity
Test validation method whereby a person performs certain tasks that are actually required by the job or completes a paper-and-pencil test that measures relevant job knowledge.

Content validity is a test validation method whereby a person performs certain tasks that are actually required by the job or completes a paper-and-pencil test that measures relevant job knowledge. Although statistical concepts are not involved, many practitioners believe that content validity provides a sensible approach to validating a selection test. This form of validation requires thorough job analysis and carefully prepared job descriptions. An example of the use of content validity is giving a word processing test to an applicant whose primary job would be word processing. Court decisions have supported the concept of content validity.

Construct Validity

construct validity
Test validation method that determines whether a test measures certain constructs, or traits, that job analysis finds to be important in performing a job.

Construct validity is a test validation method that determines whether a test measures certain constructs, or traits, that job analysis finds to be important in performing a job. For instance, a job may require a high degree of creativity or reasoning ability. Or, a sales representative position may require the applicant to be extroverted and aggressive. Construct validity in and of itself is not a primary method for validating selection tests.

Types of Employment Tests

Individuals differ in characteristics related to job performance. These differences, which are measurable, relate to cognitive abilities, psychomotor abilities, job-knowledge, work-sample, vocational interests, and personality.

Cognitive Aptitude Tests

cognitive aptitude tests
Tests that determine general reasoning ability, memory, vocabulary, verbal fluency, and numerical ability.

Cognitive aptitude tests are tests that determine general reasoning ability, memory, vocabulary, verbal fluency, and numerical ability.

Cognitive aptitude tests are a form of IQ tests. They may be helpful in identifying job candidates who have extensive knowledge bases. As the content of jobs becomes broader and more fluid, employees must be able to adapt quickly to job changes and rapid technological advances. It is likely that testing for more general traits will be necessary to match the broader range of characteristics required for successful performance of these flexible jobs. The National Football League uses the Wonderlic Personnel Test which is designed as a way to measure cognitive ability, the applicant's natural aptitude for learning new information.[29]

Psychomotor Abilities Tests

psychomotor abilities tests
Tests that measure strength, coordination, and dexterity.

Psychomotor abilities tests are tests that measure strength, coordination, and dexterity. Miniaturization in assembly operations has accelerated the development of tests to determine these abilities. Much of this work is so delicate that magnifying lenses are necessary, and the psychomotor abilities required to perform the tasks are critical.

Job-Knowledge Tests

job-knowledge tests
Tests designed to measure a candidate's knowledge of the duties of the job for which he or she is applying.

Job-knowledge tests are tests that measure a candidate's knowledge of the duties of the job for which he or she is applying. Such tests are commercially available but individual firms may also design them specifically for any job, based on data derived from job analysis.

Work-Sample Tests

work-sample tests
Tests that require an applicant to perform a task or set of tasks representative of the job.

Work-sample tests are tests that require an applicant to perform a task or set of tasks representative of the job. For positions that require heavy use of spreadsheets, having the applicant sit at a computer and construct a sample spreadsheet, with data the firm provides, will be useful in assessing a required ability. Such tests, by their nature, are job-related. Not surprisingly, the evidence concerning this type of test is that it is valid, reduces adverse impact, and is more acceptable to applicants. A real test of validity, in the opinion of some experts, should be a performance assessment: take individuals to a job and give them the opportunity to perform it.

Vocational Interest Tests

vocational interest tests
Tests that indicate the occupation a person is most interested in and the one likely to provide satisfaction.

Vocational interest tests are tests that indicate the occupation a person is most interested in and the one likely to provide satisfaction. These tests compare the individual's interests with those of successful employees in a specific job. The assumption here is that if a person shows a definite interest in a certain vocation they will be more productive on the job. But, having interest in a job and being able to effectively perform it may not be the same. A person may have an interest in being a brain surgeon but not the aptitude for it. Although interest tests have application in employee selection, their primary use has been in counseling and vocational guidance.

Personality Tests

personality tests
Self-reported measures of traits, temperaments, or dispositions.

Personality tests are self-reported measures of traits, temperaments, or dispositions. Personality tests, unlike ability tests, are not time constrained and do not measure specific problem-solving skills. These questionnaires tap into softer areas, such as leadership, teamwork, and personal assertiveness. It has been estimated that 30–40 percent of large firms use some form of psychological testing in their employment selection. Many large firms and even the NFL use personality tests.[30] A properly designed personality profile can measure and match the appropriate personality dimensions to the requirements of the job.

In sales jobs, personality tests are more typically reliable than interviews and résumé.[31] More and more companies are using specially designed *personality tests* such as Myers-Briggs to identify top sales recruits.[32] Research indicates that two important predictors for successful salespeople are extroversion and conscientiousness. The ability to test for these traits can mean a significant increase in selection effectiveness.

Most large companies now use psychometric testing to identify future managers. These individuals are being assessed for their ability to bring about long-term change and their ability to handle day-to-day management tasks, and personality tests can help identify both skills. Generally, fire departments and law enforcement agencies use the Minnesota Multiphasic Personality Inventory (MMPI) test, which consists of 567 statements that help to determine a subject's degree of paranoia, depression, mania, or anxiety. In police departments the MMPI is used to detect the inclination toward substance abuse and psychopathology. These types of tests are typically used in the early stage of the selection process.

Some firms use these tests to classify personality types. With this information, organizations can create diverse teams for creativity or homogeneous teams for compatibility. Hewlett-Packard offers a personality test so workers can determine whether they are suited to telecommute.[33]

Honesty and integrity are important personality traits to consider in the selection process. Since the polygraph test (discussed later) has been effectively banned in the private sector as a hiring tool, psychological tests have often been used to detect dishonesty in candidates.

Online Assessment

Organizations are increasingly using the Internet to assess various skills required by applicants. Firms may design and have their own tests available online or use an external source. Companies are using online assessment to make it faster and easier to process applications. More companies want assessments that can be given directly on their Web-based career centers with the results funneled to an applicant tracking system or talent management systems. Online personality tests are created to change depending on examinee's answers and were built on years of research in computer adaptive tests for cognitive skills. The tests include conscientiousness and openness, which are used to help predict performance in many jobs.[34]

Simulation-type assessments that use Web-based interactive media, role-playing, and even video games to make tests more fun and interesting for job applicants have been used. Dollar Store used skills-based assessments to screen job candidates for certain administrative positions and turnover dropped significantly. As a result, it added online assessments to screenings for open positions among the company's 700 corporate and branch-level managers. Job seekers can go to the career center on Dollar Tree's Web site to see what management positions are open, apply online, and, if they pass initial screenings, complete any necessary assessments. Those assessments include questions to obtain information on such things as a prospect's leadership and communications style.[35]

Church's Chicken and Strategic Restaurants Inc. uses a pre-interview service, called JobApp Network, which screens and ranks applicants. It saves unit managers time and effort, and ultimately improves the quality of new hires. Church's reported that during its initial six-month test with 46 restaurants, turnover decreased by 63 percent.[36]

Tests are available that check job applicants on their alleged technical abilities. Know It All, Inc. offers job-skills testing as a service to firms that lack the resources to evaluate candidates on their own. For a small fee, a company can confirm job candidates' skills online without ever seeing them. The tests are not merely pass-fail, but measure applicants' skill levels as well.

Assessment Centers

assessment center
Selection technique that requires individuals to perform activities similar to those they might encounter in an actual job.

An **assessment center** is a selection approach that requires individuals to perform activities similar to those they might encounter in an actual job. The assessment center is one of the most powerful tools for assessing managerial talent because it is designed to determine if they will be effective in performing a specific job.[37] Research has established the validity of the assessment center approach to predicting performance.[38] Many of America's top companies have set up assessment centers where they can first interview potential employees, then evaluate them in real work situations. It provides an excellent way to evaluate an individual's capabilities to perform an entry-level management job.

In an assessment center, candidates perform a number of exercises that simulate the tasks they will carry out in the job they seek. Among the typical assessment center tests, the applicants may complete *in-basket exercises* and perform in *management games, leaderless discussion groups, mock interviews,* and other simulations. The traditional in-basket exercise may receive a technological boost by replacing the paper memos with e-mail messages, faxes, tweets, or voice mail. Assessment centers measure candidates' skills in prioritizing, delegating, and decision making. The professional assessors who evaluate the candidates' performances usually observe them away from the workplace over a certain period of time, perhaps a single day. The assessors selected are typically experienced managers who may not only evaluate performances, but also participate in the exercises.

An advantage of the assessment center approach is the increased reliability and validity of the information provided. Research has shown that the in-basket exercise, a typical component of assessment centers, is a good predictor of management performance. Its validity provides an alternative to paper-and-pencil tests.

Unique Forms of Testing

Three unique forms of testing—genetic testing, graphoanalysis (handwriting analysis), and polygraph testing—will next be discussed.

HR Web Wisdom

Genetic Testing

http://ghr.nlm.nih.gov/

Your guide to understanding genetic conditions.

genetic testing
Tests given to identify predisposition to inherited diseases, including cancer, heart disease, neurological disorders, and congenital diseases.

Genetic Testing

Genetic testing is performed to identify predisposition to inherited diseases, including cancer, heart disease, neurological disorders, and congenital diseases. DNA-testing companies can tell us our potential risk for breast cancer, cystic fibrosis, and Alzheimer's disease and other common chronic conditions.[39] Scientists have assembled the entire set of genetic instructions for building a human body, and world leaders likened this achievement to putting a human being on the moon. This brings both hope and concerns to the forefront in employment testing.

Genetic tests may predict a predisposition to having a disease. However, such tests cannot tell whether a person is certain to get the disease or whether he or she would become ill at age 30 or 90. In addition, everyone has some disposition to genetic disease and a genetic predisposition is not the same as a preexisting condition.

The major concerns with genetic testing relate to the possible misuse of information. Some perceive the process as being highly invasive and believe it communicates to employees that the firm really does not care about them. Also, once the results of a genetic test are in a medical record, they may be made available to employers and insurers without an individual's knowledge or consent.

The EEOC has issued guidelines stating that healthy individuals with a genetic predisposition to a disease, and thus perceived as disabled, are protected by the Americans with Disabilities Act. The Genetic Information Nondiscrimination Act of 2008 is designed to prohibit the improper use of genetic information in health insurance and employment. The Act prohibits group health plans and health insurers from denying coverage to a healthy individual or charging that person higher premiums based solely on a genetic predisposition to developing a disease in the future. The legislation also bars employers from using individuals' genetic information when making hiring, firing, job placement, or promotion decisions.[40]

Graphoanalysis (Handwriting Analysis)

graphoanalysis
Use of handwriting analysis as a selection factor.

The use of handwriting analysis as a selection factor is **graphoanalysis**. Many in the United States view handwriting analysis in the same context as psychic readings or astrology. In Europe, however, many employers use graphoanalysis to help screen and place job applicants. One study estimated that 85 percent of European companies use handwriting analysis.[41] It is not unusual for European companies to have full-time handwriting analysts on staff. With graphoanalysis, every stroke of handwriting has a meaning which can be understood only within the context of the other strokes present in the handwriting.

Although no definitive study exists on the extent of its use in the United States, according to some handwriting experts, graphoanalysis is becoming more common. A basic reason for the reluctance of U.S. employers to use this approach appears to be a concern over the ability to validate such tests. And, there is little research demonstrating the effectiveness of graphology in employee selection. This and the worry about possible legal action seem to make many American employers wary of the process.

Polygraph Tests

For many years, another means used to verify background information was the polygraph, or lie-detector test. One purpose of the polygraph was to confirm or refute the information contained in a candidate's application. However, the Employee Polygraph Protection Act of 1988 severely limited the use of polygraph tests in the private sector. It made unlawful the use of a polygraph test by any employer engaged in interstate commerce. However, the Act does not apply to governmental employers, and there are other limited exceptions. Even here, the technology has been found to be flawed. Effective techniques for beating lie detectors, which only measure stress and anxiety have been developed and are available for use.[42]

The Act permits use of polygraph tests in the private sector to certain prospective employees of security service firms and pharmaceutical manufacturers, distributors, and dispensers. The Act also permits, with certain restrictions, polygraph testing of certain employees reasonably suspected of involvement in a workplace incident, such as theft or embezzlement. Persons who take polygraph tests have a number of specific rights. For example, they have the right to a written notice before testing, the right to refuse or discontinue a test, and the right not to have test results disclosed to unauthorized persons.

OBJECTIVE 6.10
Explain the importance of the employment interview and describe the general types of interviewing.

employment interview
Goal-oriented conversation in which an interviewer and an applicant exchange information.

Employment Interview

The **employment interview** is a goal-oriented conversation in which the interviewer and applicant exchange information. Traditionally, interviews have not been valid predictors of success on the job.[43] In fact, courts are often suspicious of hiring decisions based primarily on interview results because of their inherently subjective nature.[44] For 500 years, Leonardo da Vinci's *Mona Lisa* has confounded viewers who try to read her expression. Like the *Mona Lisa*, every job applicant presents a mysterious façade. Nevertheless, interviews continue to be the primary method companies use to evaluate applicants. The employment interview is especially important because the applicants who reach this stage are the survivors. They have endured preliminary screening, had their applications reviewed, and scored satisfactorily on selection tests. At this point, the candidates appear to be qualified, at least on paper. Every seasoned manager knows, however, that appearances can be quite misleading. Additional information is needed to indicate whether the individual is willing to work and can adapt to that particular organization.

Interview Planning

Interview planning is essential to effective employment interviews. A primary consideration should be the speed in which the process occurs. Many studies have demonstrated that the top candidates for nearly any job are hired and off the job market within anywhere from 1 to 10 days.

The physical location of the interview should be both pleasant and private, providing for a minimum of interruptions. The interviewer should possess a pleasant personality, empathy, and the ability to listen and communicate effectively. He or she should become familiar with the applicant's qualifications by reviewing the data collected from other selection tools. As preparation for the interview, the interviewer should develop a job profile based on the job description/specification. After listing job requirements, it is helpful to have an interview checklist that includes:

- Compare an applicant's application and résumé with job description.
- Develop questions related to the qualities sought.
- Prepare a step-by-step plan to present the position, company, division, and department.
- Determine how to ask for examples of past job-related applicant behavior.[45]

Content of the Interview

Both the interviewer and the candidate have agendas for the interview. After establishing rapport with the applicant, the interviewer seeks additional job-related information to complement data provided by other selection tools. The interview permits clarification of certain points, the uncovering of additional information, and the elaboration of data needed to make a sound selection decision. The interviewer should provide information about the company, the job, and expectations of the candidate. Other areas typically included in the interview are discussed next.

OCCUPATIONAL EXPERIENCE The interviewer will explore the candidate's knowledge, skills, abilities, and willingness to handle responsibility. Although successful performance in one job does not guarantee success in another, it does provide an indication of the person's ability and willingness to work.

ACADEMIC ACHIEVEMENT In the absence of significant work experience, a person's academic record takes on greater importance. Managers should, however, consider grade point average in light of other factors. For example, involvement in work, extracurricular activities, or other responsibilities may have affected an applicant's academic performance.

INTERPERSONAL SKILLS An individual may possess important technical skills significant to accomplishing a job. However, if the person cannot work well with others, chances for success are slim. This is especially true in today's world, with the increasing use of teams. The biggest mistake an interviewee can make is thinking that firms hire people only for their technical skills.[46]

PERSONAL QUALITIES Personal qualities normally observed during the interview include physical appearance, speaking ability, vocabulary, poise, adaptability, assertiveness, leadership ability, and cooperative spirit.[47] As with all selection criteria, employers should consider these attributes only if they are relevant to job performance.

organizational fit
Management's perception of the degree to which the prospective employee will fit in with the firm's culture or value system.

ORGANIZATIONAL FIT A hiring criterion that historically is not prominently mentioned in the literature is organizational fit. **Organizational fit** refers to management's perception of the degree to which the prospective employee will fit in with the firm's culture or value system. There are numerous reasons that a hire does not work out but none is as important as cultural fit. Statements such as "the chemistry was just not right" may describe a poor fit situation. A poor fit harms organizational effectively, hurts morale, and drains creativity.[48]

Using *fit* as a criterion may raise legal and diversity questions, and perhaps this explains the low profile of its use. Nevertheless, there is evidence that managers use it in making selection decisions and that it is not a minor consideration. In a recent survey, 30 percent of CEOs said that up to half of their employees are a poor fit for the job.[49] Fit is important for each hire but it is even more critical when considering individuals for upper-level positions. Complicating the situation further is the fact that the same employee may be a poor fit with one firm and a perfect fit with another.[50] Applicants also should consider organizational fit when debating whether to accept a job offer. A variety of factors can lead to a bad job fit, ranging from holding opposing views on etiquette or ethics to possessing conflicting views on the direction of the department.

Russell Yaquinto, who coaches managerial job seekers for the outplacement firm Right Management Consultants in Dallas, states that "There's very widespread agreement…that you can have the credentials, but if you aren't going to fit [the culture], it doesn't matter. Before long, you'll be out of there." An employee who fits not only the skill requirements but also the culture, values, and belief systems of the organization is typically three times more productive and two times less likely to leave the firm.[51] A lot more attention is being given to selecting employees for that "good fit."

Candidate's Role and Expectations

While the interviewer will provide information about the company, it is still important for candidates to do their homework, including checking the Internet (including the firm's Web site) prior to the interview. Most company sites include information tailored to job seekers.[52] These sites often provide a history of the company and a description of its products and customers. WetFeet.com provides insightful profiles of companies, careers, and industries to guide job seekers toward finding the right career, the right industry, the right company, and the right job for them. A person applying for a management position, especially, should have a thorough understanding of the firm's business priorities, its strengths and weaknesses, and its major competitors. Applicants should consider how they would address some of the issues facing the company. They need to be able to show how their experiences can help in addressing these issues.

Recruiters need to remember that interviewees also have objectives for the interview. One might be to determine what the firm is willing to pay as a starting salary. Job seekers have other goals that may include the following:

- To be listened to and understood
- To have ample opportunity to present their qualifications
- To be treated fairly and with respect
- To gather information about the job and the company
- To make an informed decision concerning the desirability of the job

Candidates can learn what interviewing skills they need to improve by undergoing a mock interview or two. Having a colleague or friend interview them, then critically reviewing their own responses can be beneficial. This mock interview allows candidates to analyze the strengths and interests that they would bring to a job. The process would also help them prioritize the points they want to make in the real interview.

General Types of Interviews

Types of interviews are often broadly classified as structured, unstructured, and behavioral. A discussion of the differences follows.

Unstructured Interview

unstructured interview
Interview in which the job applicant is asked probing, open-ended questions.

An **unstructured interview** is one in which the interviewer asks probing, open-ended questions. This type of interview is comprehensive, and the interviewer encourages the applicant to do much of the talking. Questions such as "What professional accomplishments are you most proud of and why?" "What is your greatest professional strength, and how have you used it to overcome a challenge in your career?" and "What specifically attracted you to our organization?" might be asked.[53] The unstructured interview is often more time consuming than the structured interview and results in obtaining different information from different candidates. This adds to the potential legal woes of organizations using this approach. Compounding the problem is the likelihood of discussing ill-advised, potentially discriminatory information. The applicant who is being encouraged to pour his heart out may volunteer facts that the interviewer does not need or want to know. Unsuccessful applicants subjected to this interviewing approach may later claim in court that the reason for their failure to get the job was the employer's use of this information.

Structured Interview

structured interview
Interview in which the interviewer asks each applicant for a particular job the same series of job-related questions.

In the **structured interview**, the interviewer asks each applicant for a particular job the same series of job-related questions. Although interviews have historically been very poor predictors of job success, use of structured interviews increases reliability and accuracy by reducing the subjectivity and inconsistency of unstructured interviews.

A structured job interview typically contains four types of questions:

- *Situational questions* are those that pose a typical job situation to determine what the applicant did in a similar situation.
- *Job-knowledge questions* are those that probe the applicant's job-related knowledge; these questions may relate to basic educational skills or complex scientific or managerial skills.
- *Job-sample simulation questions* involve situations in which an applicant may be required to answer questions related to performance of a task.
- *Worker requirements questions* are those that seek to determine the applicant's willingness to conform to the requirements of the job. For example, the interviewer may ask whether the applicant is willing to perform repetitive work or move to another city.

Behavioral Interview

behavioral interview
Structured interview in which applicants are asked to relate actual incidents from their past relevant to the target job.

Traditional interviewing has a reputation of being a poor predictor of job success. In fact, the traditional interview is only 7 percent accurate in predicting on-the-job performance, whereas behavioral interviews were found to be 54 percent accurate.[54] Because of the low success rate of traditional interviews, the behavioral interview is being increasingly used. The **behavioral interview** is a structured interview in which applicants are asked to relate actual incidents from their past relevant to the target job. Once used exclusively for senior executive positions, behavioral interviewing is now a popular technique for lower-level positions also. The assumption is that past behavior is the best predictor of future behavior. It avoids having to make judgments about applicants' personalities and precludes hypothetical and self-evaluative questions. Behavioral interviews ask applicants about specific events as opposed to just having them tell about themselves. They are designed to test applicants' abilities to work under pressure and to work with others and to determine whether they can resolve conflicts. The behavioral interview assist in determining if a person is functionally sound and if the applicant will be a good fit in the organization.[55]

Behavioral interviewers look for three main things: a description of a challenging situation, what the candidate did about it, and measurable results. In the behavioral interview, the situational behaviors are selected for their relevance to job success. Questions are formed from the behaviors by asking applicants how they performed in the described situation. For example, when probing for professional or technical knowledge, the candidate might be requested to, "Describe a situation in which your expertise made a significant difference." Or, if seeking to determine the applicant's enthusiasm, the request might be, "Relate a scenario during which you were responsible for motivating others." Behavioral interviewers ask each candidate the same open-ended questions, then score responses on a scale. Interviewing is based on the principle that what you did previously in your life is a good predictor of what you will do in the future. Interviewees are asked to give an example of a situation when they faced a dilemma, a problem, or a situation.[56]

In behavioral interviews, candidates may unwittingly reveal information about their attitudes, intelligence, and truthfulness. Arrogance, lack of cooperation with team members, and anger can all spill out during such an interview. Although some candidates may think the interview is all about technical skills, it is as much about them as a person as anything. In one study of hiring managers, lack of the necessary technical skills was given as the reason for failure only 11 percent of the time. However, 26 percent failed because they could not accept feedback, 23 percent because they could not understand and manage emotions, 17 percent because they lacked motivation, and 15 percent because they had the wrong temperament for the job.[57]

Questions asked in behavior interviewing are legally safe since they are job-related. Equally important, since both questions and answers are related to successful job performance, they are more accurate in predicting whether applicants will be successful in the job they are hired to perform. It answers the one question both the hiring manager and the candidate want to know most: Is this a good fit?

One difficulty with behavioral interviewing is that some job seekers have gotten wise to the process. A growing number of candidates, especially those coming from business and law schools, deliberately misrepresent themselves during the interview. The stories some tell about who they are and what they did in real-life situations are pure fiction.

Methods of Interviewing

OBJECTIVE 6.11
Describe the various methods of interviewing, potential interviewing problems, and concluding the interview.

Organizations conduct interviews in several ways. The level of the open position and the appropriate labor market determine the most fitting approach. A discussion of these methods follows.

One-on-One Interview

In a typical employment interview, the applicant meets one-on-one with an interviewer. As the interview may be a highly emotional occasion for the applicant, meeting alone with the interviewer is often less threatening. This method provides a better opportunity for an effective exchange of information to take place.

Group Interview

group interview
Meeting in which several job applicants interact in the presence of one or more company representatives.

In a **group interview**, several applicants interact in the presence of one or more company representatives. This approach, although not mutually exclusive of other interview types, may provide useful insights into the candidates' interpersonal competence as they engage in a group discussion. Another advantage of this technique is that it saves time for busy professionals and executives.

Board (or Panel) Interview

board interview
An interview approach in which several of the firm's representatives interview a candidate at the same time.

In a **board interview**, several of the firm's representatives interview a candidate at the same time. Companies use the board interview to gain multiple viewpoints because there are many cross-functional workplace relationships in business these days.[58] Once the interview is complete, the board members pool their evaluation of the candidate. Most professors who have received a Ph.D. are quite familiar with the board interview, as they were required to defend their dissertation as their professors asked questions. At times some candidates claimed that professors having opposing views were deliberately placed on the board and the candidate had to tiptoe through the session, hoping not to offend members.

Multiple Interviews

At times applicants are interviewed by peers, subordinates, and potential superiors. This approach permits the firm to get a more encompassing view of the candidate. It also gives the candidate a chance to learn more about the company from a variety of perspectives. The result of this type of interview is a stronger, more cohesive team that shares the company's culture and helps ensure organizational fit as was the case with Google in the use of crowd sourcing.

Stress Interview

stress interview
Form of interview in which the interviewer intentionally creates anxiety.

What would you do if you were in an interview that was going quite well and all at once the interviewer said, "I think your answer is totally inadequate: it doesn't deal with my concerns at all, can't you do better than that?" You may not realize it but you have just been exposed to a stress interview. In the **stress interview**, the interviewer intentionally creates anxiety.

TRENDS & INNOVATIONS

Interviewing Through Crowd Sourcing

Google is a multibillion dollar company with more than 20,000 employees. If you want to work for Google, you will find out that the hiring process is quite different from other companies. In making hiring decisions, they use "crowd sourcing" in making employment decisions. Crowd sourcing is based on the premise that any given group of people is always smarter than any given expert.[59] Google's hiring premise is based on James Surowiecki's *The Wisdom of Crowds: Why the Many Are Smarter Than the Few and How Collective Wisdom Shapes Business, Economies, Societies and Nations*. Google's employer brand (discussed in Chapter 1) is unique and the company has an excellent image among college students. According to the company's manager of HR technology and operations, Melissa Karp, "Virtually every person who interviews at Google talks to at least four interviewers, drawn from both management and potential colleagues. Everyone's opinion counts, ensuring our hiring process is fair while maintaining high standards as we grow."

Crowd sourcing is based on the management concept of *synergism*, the cooperative action of two or more persons working together to accomplish more than they could working separately. This management concept recognizes that greater effect may be achieved when two workers are placed together. From a mathematical standpoint, you might say that one plus one has the potential to be greater than two.[60] A concept useful in the management world is also beneficial in the hiring process.

Here is what happens in the hiring process with crowd sourcing. Once a prospective employee applies for a job, the company uses its applicant tracking system and asks workers to check out the individual online. It matches current employees with information provided by the applicant. For example, a University of Texas graduate might be matched with a University of Texas applicant. Basically, it becomes an internal reference. Employees respond via e-mail to update the system. Present employees understand the culture that the applicant will be entering and can assess them for potential hires. "Google people love this stuff," Karp said. "It goes back to our culture, and, culturally, people like the fact that we're asking their opinions."[61]

Most interviewers strive to minimize stress for the candidate. However, in the stress interview, the interviewer deliberately makes the candidate uncomfortable by asking blunt and often discourteous questions. The purpose is to determine the applicant's tolerance for stress that may accompany the job. Knowledge of this factor may be important if the job requires the ability to deal with a high level of stress.

Amazon.com interviewers have been known to ask job candidates to guess how many gas stations there are in the United States or to ballpark a bill for washing all of Seattle's windows. Google had a billboard built along Highway 101 in the Silicon Valley that contained a intricate math problems. Those who saw the billboard were asked to submit their solution to a Web site. If you got to the site, you were asked a second, harder question. If you passed that hurdle, Google asks you to submit your résumé. Once you got to the Googleplex for an interview, a favorite question was: "You are shrunk to the height of a nickel and your mass is proportionally reduced so as to maintain your original density. You are then thrown into an empty glass blender. The blades will start moving in 60 seconds. What do you do?"[62] The answer is not as important as your logic in approaching an answer.

Stress interviews are not new. The late Admiral Hyman G. Rickover, father of the U.S. Navy's nuclear submarine program, was known to offer interviewees a chair that had one or two legs shorter than the other. The candidates' problems were compounded by the chair's polished seat. The admiral once stated that "they had to maintain their wits about them as they answered questions while sliding off the chair."[63]

Realistic Job Preview

Many applicants have unrealistic expectations about the prospective job and employer. They may have been told the exciting part of the job but the less glamorous areas are not mentioned.[64] This inaccurate perception may have negative consequences, yet it is often encouraged when interviewers paint false, rosy pictures of the job and the company. This practice leads to

realistic job preview (RJP)
Method of conveying both positive and negative job information to an applicant in an unbiased manner.

mismatches of people and positions. What compounds the problem is when candidates exaggerate their own qualifications. To correct this situation from the employer's side, firms should provide a **realistic job preview (RJP)**, conveying both positive and negative job information to the applicant in an unbiased manner. This should typically be done early in the selection process and, definitely, before a job offer is made.

An RJP conveys information about tasks the person would perform and the behavior required to fit into the culture of the organization. This approach helps applicants develop a more accurate perception of the job and the firm. Research shows employers who give detailed RJPs get two results: fewer employees accept the job offer, and applicants who do accept the offer are less likely to leave the firm. Given an RJP, some candidates will take themselves out of the selection process, minimizing the number of unqualified candidates. Another reason to use RJPs is the benefit a firm receives from being an up-front, ethical employer.

Potential Interviewing Problems

Potential interviewing problems that can threaten the success of employment interviews are discussed next. After studying this information, it becomes clear that being a good interviewer requires careful attention to the task.

Inappropriate Questions

Although no questions are illegal, many are clearly hiring standards to avoid. When they are asked, the responses generated create a legal liability for the employer. The most basic interviewing rule is this: "Ask only job-related questions." Recall from Chapter 3 that the definition of a test in the *Uniform Guidelines* includes "physical, education, and work experience requirement through *informal or casual interviews*." Because the interview is a test, if adverse impact is shown, it is subject to the same validity requirements as any other step in the selection process.

Simon Mitchell, director at DDI, a consultancy company, says: "Clearly some managers and HR professionals responsible for recruitment have not got the message that probing candidates about their private lives or personal views is not only wildly inappropriate, but can even put them at risk of getting into legal hot water. They are also wasting valuable time gathering irrelevant and unhelpful information."[65] For unstructured interviews, this constraint presents special difficulties. Historically, the interview has been more vulnerable to charges of discrimination than any other tool used in the selection process. One simple rule governs interviewing: *all questions must be job-related.*

The Americans with Disabilities Act also provides a warning for interviewers. Interviewers should inquire about the need for reasonable accommodations in only a few situations. For example, the topic is appropriate if the applicant is in a wheelchair or has an obvious disability that will require accommodation. Also, the applicant may voluntarily disclose a disability or even ask for some reasonable accommodation. Otherwise, employers should refrain from broaching the subject. Instead, interviewers should frame questions in terms of whether applicants can perform the essential functions of the jobs for which they are applying.

Permitting Non-Job-Related Information

If a candidate begins volunteering personal information that is not job-related, the interviewer should steer the conversation back on course. The interviewer might do well to begin the interview by tactfully stating something like, "This selection decision will be based strictly on qualifications. Let's not discuss topics such as religion, social activities, national origin, gender, or family situations. We are definitely interested in you, personally. However, these factors are not job-related and will not be considered in our decision." This enables better decisions to be made while decreasing the likelihood of discrimination charges.[66]

To elicit needed information in any type of interview, the interviewer must create a climate that encourages the applicant to speak freely. However, the conversation should not become too casual. Whereas engaging in friendly chitchat with candidates might be pleasant, in our litigious society, it may be the most dangerous thing an interviewer can do. Asking a woman a question about her children that has nothing to do with the job would not be appropriate.

Premature Judgment

Research suggests that interviewers often make judgments about candidates in the first few minutes of the interview.[67] Apparently, these interviewers believe that they have the ability to determine immediately whether a candidate will be successful or not. When this occurs, a great deal of potentially valuable information is not considered. Even if an interviewer spent a week with an applicant, the sample of behavior might be too small to judge the candidate's qualifications properly. In addition, the candidate's behavior during an interview is seldom typical or natural, thereby making a quick judgment difficult.

Interview Illusion

Closely related to premature judgment but not the same is *interview illusion*. I have heard numerous managers say something to the effect of "Give me just five minutes with an applicant and I can tell if they will be successful with our company." Their belief in their interview ability was likely exaggerated. Psychologist Richard Nisbett calls this the "'interview illusion'—our certainty that we're learning more in an interview than we really are."[68] One has to be careful about placing excessive weight on interviews and thinking "I just feel good about this applicant" when making the hiring decision.[69]

Interviewer Domination

In successful interviews, relevant information must flow both ways. Sometimes, interviewers begin the interview by telling candidates what they are looking for, and then are excited to hear candidates parrot back their own words. Other interviewers are delighted to talk through virtually the entire interview, either to take pride in their organization's accomplishments or to express frustrations over their own difficulties. After dominating the meeting for an hour or so, these interviewers feel good about the candidate. Therefore, interviewers must learn to be good listeners as well as suppliers of information.

Contrast Effect

An error in judgment may occur when, for example, an interviewer meets with several poorly qualified applicants and then confronts a mediocre candidate. By comparison, the last applicant may appear to be better qualified than he or she actually is. The opposite can also occur. Suppose that a clearly outstanding candidate is followed by a very good candidate. The second candidate may not be considered even if the first candidate turns down the job offer.

Lack of Training

Anyone who has ever conducted an interview realizes that it is much more than carrying on a conversation with another person. The interviewer is attempting to gain insight into how the applicant answers job-related questions. There should be a reason for asking each question. For instance, suppose the applicant is told, "Tell me about yourself." A trained interviewer asks this question to determine whether the applicant's life experiences qualify the applicant for the job, not the fact that he or she had a little dog named Moe as a child. Interviewers should be trained to have a job-related purpose for asking each question. When the cost of making poor selection decisions is considered, the expense of training employees in interviewing skills can be easily justified.

Nonverbal Communication

Body language is the nonverbal communication method in which physical actions such as motions, gestures, and facial expressions convey thoughts and emotions. The interviewer is attempting to view the nonverbal signals from the applicant. Applicants are also reading the nonverbal signals of the interviewer. Therefore, interviewers should make a conscious effort to view themselves as applicants do to avoid sending inappropriate or unintended nonverbal signals. Research has shown that 90 percent of first impressions are based on nonverbal communication and only 10 percent on verbal communications.[70] It is important for the interviewer to be aware of how he or she is communicating nonverbally.

Concluding the Interview

When the interviewer has obtained the necessary information and answered the applicant's questions, he or she should conclude the interview. Management must then determine whether the candidate is suitable for the open position and organization. If the conclusion is positive, the process continues; if there appears to be no match, the candidate is no longer considered. Also, in concluding the interview, the interviewer should tell the applicant that he or she will be notified of the selection decision shortly. Keeping this promise helps maintain a positive relationship with the applicant. In Chapter 1, employer branding was discussed. One aspect of employer branding is for the interviewee to leave the interview with a positive feeling about the company. The interview experience should have the interviewee feeling valued and respected regardless of whether or not a job offer is made.[71]

OBJECTIVE 6.12

Explain the use of pre-employment screening, including background investigations, reference checks, automated reference checking, and negligent hiring.

Pre-Employment Screening: Background Investigations

Pre-employment screening has experienced tremendous growth since the terrorist attack of 9/11. It went from a possible step in the selection process to that of a necessary step. Estimates are that between 85 and 90 percent of companies conduct background investigations today. Diligent background investigation is more important than ever due to the rise in negligent hiring (to be discussed later in this chapter) lawsuits, recent corporate scandals, and national security concerns. The principal reason for conducting background investigations is to hire better workers.[72] At this stage of the selection process, an applicant has normally completed an application form or submitted a résumé, taken the required selection tests, and undergone an employment interview. On the surface they look qualified. It is now time to determine the accuracy of the information submitted or to determine whether vital information was not submitted.

Background investigations involve obtaining data from various sources, including previous employers, business associates, credit bureaus, government agencies, and academic institutions, and have become increasingly more important. Fingerprinting is becoming a more common part of checks, especially for companies that employ workers in charge of securing a worksite—for example, airports, the financial services industry, hospitals, schools, the gaming industry, and hazardous materials services. Reasons for leaving jobs or gaps in employment may be cleverly disguised to present a work history that does not provide an accurate or complete picture. Letters of recommendation from companies that are no longer in existence and differences between their résumé and completed job application may raise a red flag. In addition to a candidate's previous job history, a background investigation can involve checking citizenship status, educational background, driving history, and criminal records. Other checks may include if a candidate has declared bankruptcy in the past 10 years or is on the list of registered sex offenders.[73] Checking for criminal records is important because most applicants with criminal records tend to lie about it on their applications.[74] Nick Fishman, chief marketing officer and executive vice president of employeescreenIQ, said his company finds a criminal record of some sort on about 14 percent of the job applicants it screens.[75]

The number of companies that run credit checks has risen to 35 percent, up from 19 percent in 1996.[76] In addition, some companies are also gathering information regarding an applicant's mode of living and his or her character. However, there are other critical reasons as well. For example, in a Security Management Survey, when security directors were asked what the best way to stop insider theft was, background screening was identified as the top preventive measure.[77] The intensity of background investigations depends on the nature of the open position's tasks and its relationship to customers or clients. To be legally safe, employers should ask applicants to sign a liability waiver permitting a background investigation. The waiver is typically a statement on the application form that releases former employers, business references, and others from liability. It also authorizes checks of court records and the verification of the applicant's educational history and other credentials.

The cost of a background check has come down from what it used to be because the computer has made background checking much easier.[78] Databases are standardized and the background check companies know where to look. Investigations that once cost hundreds of dollars now cost a little over $100. They can range from verifying résumés and college degrees to verifying prior employment periods and, importantly, looking for convictions.

Continuous Background Investigation

Background investigations are not just for pre-employment any more. Some employers are screening their employees on an ongoing basis.[79] In certain industries, such as banking and health care, employers are required by regulation to routinely research the criminal records of employees. People and events are ever-changing. For example, financial devastation, marital collapse, or a medical crisis can send a person with the cleanest record over the edge. It has been estimated that every year one or two of every 1,000 existing employees acquire a new criminal record. Since only 5 percent of convictions lead to jail time, the employer may never know of a conviction unless there is an ongoing background check.

Background Investigation with Social Networking

An increasing number of employers are using social networking Web sites to conduct background investigations on potential employees.[80] Employers use an applicant's personal Web site, LinkedIn profile, and postings made on an industry blog to find out about individuals they are considering hiring.[81] There is usually no difficulty in searching such sites as MySpace and Facebook because personal information is put into the public domain. In a recent Careerbuilder.com survey, 45 percent of employers said that they use social networking sites to research job candidates, which is up from 22 percent only a year earlier and another 11 percent plan to start using social networking sites for screening. Of those who conduct online searches/background checks of job candidates, 29 percent use Facebook, 26 percent use LinkedIn, 21 percent use MySpace, 11 percent search blogs, and 7 percent follow job candidates on Twitter. Industries most likely to conduct background checks on applicants are those that specialize in technology and sensitive information.[82]

Employers reported that they have found content on social networking sites that caused them not to hire the candidate. Some examples include posting provocative or inappropriate photographs or information, posting content about alcohol or drug use, and posting negative comments about their previous employer, co-workers, or clients. Other information found on these sites supported their decision to hire the candidate. For example, the profile provided a good feel for the candidate's personality and fit within the organization, the profile supported candidate's professional qualifications, and other people posted good references about the candidate.[83]

Remembering Hiring Standards to Avoid

Some of the standards used in the background investigation have the potential to violate a hiring standard to avoid that was discussed in Chapter 3. A word of caution is advised in situations where an applicant acknowledges that he or she has been convicted of a crime. Remember that a major implication of the *Griggs v Duke Power Company* Supreme Court case in Chapter 3 was that when human resource management practices eliminate substantial numbers of minority or women applicants (prima facie evidence), the burden of proof is on the employer to show that the practice is job related. Thus, if having a criminal conviction cannot be shown to be job related, caution should be used in having the conviction used as a hiring criteria.[84]

The same rationale can be said for conducting credit checks.[85] If a disproportionate number of members of a protected group are rejected through the use of the credit check, the company would need to validate the use of credit check. Certainly, if a company does a credit check on all applicants, it is difficult to say that the credit check was job related.

Some do not support using social networking sites in the hiring process because its use might discriminate against members of protected group.[86] They say that seeing a person's picture on Facebook lets the recruiter know the race, sex, age, and other potentially hiring standards to avoid.[87] There may ultimately be a court case test to determine this claim.

Congress created somewhat of an obstacle for employers when it amended the federal Fair Credit Reporting Act (FCRA). This 1997 amendment places obligations on employers who use certain information brought to light through background investigations. Failure to comply can result in substantial legal risks, including damages, penalties, fines, punitive damages, and attorneys' fees awards.[88] Employers' obligations are triggered under the Act when they use consumer reports that contain information about an individual's personal and credit characteristics, character, general reputation, and lifestyle. To avoid legal problems, employers need to allow sufficient time between notifying an applicant or employee of a less than favorable consumer report and taking an adverse action as a result of the report.[89] The FCRA covers only reports that are prepared by a consumer reporting agency such as a credit bureau.

Pre-Employment Screening: Reference Checks

reference checks
Validations from individuals who know the applicant that provide additional insight into the information furnished by the applicant and verification of its accuracy.

Reference checks are validations from those who know the applicant that provide additional insight into the information furnished by the applicant and allow verification of its accuracy. They are a valuable source of information to supplement the background investigation. Applicants are often required to submit the names of several references that can provide additional information about them. A possible flaw with reference checking is that virtually everyone can name three or four individuals willing to make favorable statements about him or her. Even so, there is anecdotal evidence that personal references do not always provide favorable information. They may not necessarily be committed to shading the truth for the applicant.

A related problem in obtaining information from previous employers is their general reluctance to reveal such data. Employers and employees in the private sector have become very sensitive to the privacy issue. There are two schools of thought with regard to supplying information about former employees. One is, "Don't tell them anything." The other is, "Honesty is the best policy." In the more conservative approach, the employer typically provides only basic data such as name, job title, and dates of employment. The honesty approach is based on the reality that facts honestly given or opinions honestly held constitute a solid legal defense. When former employers are unwilling to give any information about a job applicant, both the potential employer and the applicant are at a disadvantage.[90] A red flag is quickly raised when a former employer refuses to talk about a one-time employee. For firms that freely give out information about previous employees, questions about the applicant's integrity and character are appropriate. It is helpful to know why the person left that job. If the response differs from that given by the applicant, it is definitely a red flag.

The amount of protection given to those who provide references varies greatly. Laws on the books in many states and jurisdictions shield employers from liability for harm to an ex-employee based on the contents of a job reference. The intent of this legislation is to make it easier for employers to give and receive meaningful information. A Texas employer can tell a recruiter about the job performance, attendance, attitudes, effort, knowledge, behaviors, and skills of a former employee. Even so, there continues to be some hesitancy on the part of firms to take advantage of it. Although protective laws do exist, apparently there is a wait-and-see attitude among some employers. It will likely take litigation and court rulings before employers fully understand, and have confidence in, the statutes.

Automated Reference Checking

Traditional reference checking has been heavily labor intense. Automated reference checking (ARC) has been a boom in this area. With ARC, references are anonymous, more efficient, and a more comprehensive report can be provided. Yves Lermusi, chief executive officer of Checkster in Mill Valley, California, whose company offers a product called Reference Checkup, said, "It's simply automating one of the last elements of recruiting that used to be heavily manual. Because it is confidential, people are more forthcoming. And because it's online, the process goes faster." Reference checking requires an e-mail link to the job candidate. It is the candidate, not the recruiter, who contacts references to fill out the questionnaire. The system collects the surveys and prepares a report for the recruiter. Referencing is much faster going from an average of four to an average of 1.2 days. ARC can help reduce the legal risks for the company seeking the reference because the request comes from the candidate, not the organization. The company does not run the risk of a recruiter asking an inappropriate question since the questions have been preapproved.[91]

Negligent Hiring

negligent hiring
Liability a company incurs when it fails to conduct a reasonable investigation of an applicant's background, and then assigns a potentially dangerous person to a position in which he or she can inflict harm.

Negligent hiring is the liability an employer incurs when it fails to conduct a reasonable investigation of an applicant's background, and then assigns a potentially dangerous person to a position in which he or she can inflict harm. The typical negligent hiring case involves a deliberate inflicting of harm committed by an employee including fraud, assault, battery, or interference with contractual relations. Reasonable investigation varies according to the nature of the job. The risk of harm to third parties, for example, requires a higher standard of care when hiring a taxi driver as opposed to a machinist. The taxi cab driver is alone and has control of his or her customer during the time the customer is in the car. This would not be the case for the machinist. Employers who operate home-service businesses, day-care centers, and home health care operations are particularly at risk, as are those with employees who drive company vehicles, visit customer locations, handle money, or work with children, the elderly, or the impaired. The primary consideration in negligent hiring is whether the risk of harm from a dangerous employee was reasonably foreseeable. In one negligent hiring case a hospital nursing assistant was hired without a background check and the medical center did not ask former employers why the worker had left. If it had, the medical center would have discovered that the worker had previously sexually harassed, assaulted, and inappropriately touched female patients. Once hired, the worker was left alone in rooms with vulnerable female patients and sexually abused them.[92]

OBJECTIVE 6.13
Describe the selection decision, the medical examination, notification of candidates, and candidate relationship management.

Selection Decision

At this point, the focus is on the manager who must take the most critical step of all: the actual hiring decision. If a firm is going to invest thousands of dollars to recruit, select, and train an employee, it is important for the manager to hire the most qualified available candidate, according to the firm's criteria. The final choice is made from among those still in the running after reference checks, selection tests, background investigations, and interview information have been evaluated. Usually, the person selected has qualifications that most closely conform to the requirements of the open position and the organization.

The person who normally makes the final selection is the manager who will be responsible for the new employee's performance, especially for higher-level positions. In making this decision, the manager will review results of the selection methods used. All will not likely be weighted the same. The question then becomes, "Which data are most predictive of job success?" For each firm or group of jobs, the optimal selection method may be different.

Medical Examination

The Americans with Disabilities Act (ADA) does not prohibit pre-employment medical examinations. However, it does determine the point at which they may be administered during the selection process. The ADA explicitly states that all exams must be directly relevant to the job requirements and that a firm cannot order a medical exam until the applicant is offered employment. Typically, a job offer is contingent on the applicant's passing this examination. The basic purpose of the medical examination is to determine whether an applicant is physically capable of performing the work. Managers must be aware of the legal liabilities related to medical examinations. The *Uniform Guidelines* state that these examinations can be used to reject applicants only when the results show that job performance would be adversely affected.

Notification of Candidates

Management should notify both successful and unsuccessful candidates of selection decisions as soon as possible. This action is a matter of courtesy and good public relations. Any delay may also result in the firm losing a prime candidate, as top prospects often have other employment options.

Employers may reject applicants at any time during the selection process. Research has indicated that most people can accept losing if they lose fairly. Problems occur when the selection process appears to be less than objective. It is therefore important for firms to develop and use rational selection tools. Time constraints prevent firms from spending much time explaining a decision to an unsuccessful candidate. If the person rejected was an internal candidate, managers may visit or make a personal phone call to the rejected applicant. A rejection letter is a more likely method. However, a letter with a personal touch may reduce the stigma of rejection and avoid the applicant's having a negative feeling about the company. An impersonal letter is likely to have the opposite effect. The best an organization can do is to make selection decisions objectively. Hopefully, most unsuccessful individuals can, with time, accept the fact that they were not chosen.

Candidate Relationship Management

The Internet has created a situation where a large number of résumés are received, and this is compounded when the economy is depressed. Often, candidates send an application and never get a reply. Whether as a result of arrogance, ignorance, or incompetence, companies often fail to inform applicants after they have been rejected. To overcome this situation, some organizations are adopting candidate relationship management (CRM) software to ensure that job seekers have good experiences on the companies' Web sites and to bolster efforts to build talent pools that can be tapped when companies are able to hire again. Besides, companies truly dedicated to CRM do not stop after sending an auto reply; they also let them know when the position has been filled. Sean Rehder, principal at CRM consultancy, said, "CRM is about keeping relationships warm. When you have an immediate opportunity to hire someone, a recruiter wants to e-mail that person and have them e-mail right back, or call and get a call back." Gerry Crispin, a principal at the consulting firm CareerXroads in Kendall Park, New Jersey, said, "Candidate relationship management systems can provide information that helps a candidate recognize himself as an employee of the company, creating an 'I'd fit there' attitude."[93]

Human Capital Metrics

human capital metrics
Measures of HR performance.

Human capital metrics are measures of HR performance. Even though employees account for as much as 80 percent of the worth of a corporation, the task of measuring and understanding how they contribute to the bottom line is often difficult. Therefore, human capital metrics must be closely tied to whether company strategic goals are being achieved.[94] HR metrics are needed to drive strategic change.[95] Management has for years been able to measure the success or failure of a production process. They focused on return on investment, the bottom line, and profit. Today, HR is under the same scrutiny and management wants to know how HR activities contribute to the organization's bottom line.

Bob Proctor, managing director of CLC Metrics, a measurement firm, said, "Measurement is critical when resources are finite, because HR cannot be all things to all people." One survey revealed that companies with best-in-class talent acquisition programs were most successful at measuring the following four performance criteria: time to hire, quality of hire, new-hire retention, and hiring managers' overall satisfaction with the program.[96]

There is, however, no one-size-fits-all approach that employers can adopt to achieve greater hiring efficiency. The metrics that will best suit each company depends on a variety of factors, including its business goals.

The recession of 2008/10 heightened the need to have metrics regarding the productivity of employees. When employee cost-cutting decisions must be made, it is important that the most productive employees are retained.[97]

OBJECTIVE 6.14

Explain the metrics for evaluating recruitment/ selection effectiveness.

Metrics for Evaluating the Effectiveness of Recruitment/Selection

Possible metrics for evaluating the effectiveness of recruitment/selection are described next. Metrics for evaluating other functions are discussed at the appropriate time.

Quality of Hire

The question of how to measure quality of hire and set standards for new-hire performance is difficult to determine, but it is an important decision that HR professionals are constantly striving to determine. Realistically, it depends on the system, the company, and the implementation. For quality of hire to be usable, one needs to have performance assessment for two or three years before the real capabilities of a new hire will be understood.

Time Required to Hire

As previously stated, the top candidates for nearly any job are hired and off the job market within anywhere from 1 to 10 days. It then becomes crucial for the time required to hire be as low as possible. Research by the Aberdeen Group found that best-in-class organizations have shortened time to hire by an average of 22 percent.[98]

New Hire Retention

It is important to measure new hire retention because costs go up dramatically if a position has to be filled again in a short period. New hire retention is determined by determining the percent of the new hires that remain with the company at selected intervals, typically one or two years. If this situation is happening excessively, HR should analyze the selection process to determine if there are flaws in the system that causes new hires to terminate prematurely. Perhaps, as was mentioned earlier in the chapter, a realistic job preview needs to be instituted.

Hiring Manager Overall Satisfaction

The manager is largely responsible for the success of his of her department. It is the quality of his or her employees in the workgroup that have a major impact on success of the department. A manager's belief that employees being hired through the system do not perform as well as expected casts doubt on the entire selection process. Some firms provide a rating scale for the manager to evaluate how a new hire is performing after the employee's first 90 days.

Turnover Rate

Turnover rate is the number of times on average that employees have to be replaced during a year. For example, if a company has 200 employees and 200 workers had been hired during the year, a 100 percent turnover rate would be experienced. As one might expect, a 100 percent rate is quite costly to the organization, and ways need to be found to reduce the rate. Employees who are hired and then quit within 120 days are called "False Starts" and considered to be especially expensive, since the company spends money on their hire but then quickly must spend even more to replace them.[99]

Recruiting Costs

In determining the recruiting cost per hire, the total recruiting expense must first be calculated. Then, the cost per hire may be determined by dividing the recruiting expenses by the number of recruits hired. Naturally, the difficulty associated with this measure is in determining the exact costs to include as recruiting expenses. It may be beneficial for a firm to use a benchmark cost per hire to compare to the specific cost for the company.

A GLOBAL PERSPECTIVE

Leadership Effectiveness in the Global Environment

More often than not, trying to make different styles of leadership work in foreign lands is an exercise in frustration. Regardless of how far-flung their markets and operations, multinationals retain and reflect the cultural mores of their home countries. D. Quinn Mills, a professor emeritus of business administration at Harvard Business School, said, "They are very much shaped by national culture. That's why it's very hard to lead an organization that's of a different national culture." Think of global business styles as a continuum with U.S. executives at one end and their Asian counterparts at the other. American executives, and the companies they lead, are generally more comfortable with risk and uncertainty than those in Europe and, particularly, Asia. That is partly an outgrowth of the individualism and entrepreneurialism so ingrained in U.S. society.[100]

Craig Crossland at the University of Texas-Austin said, "It's also why there is no global market for CEOs. Only a few outsider CEOs are leading multinationals." Of course, there are exceptions. Carlos Ghosn is the very model of the modern major corporate leader in a globalized world. He was born in Brazil to Lebanese parents, educated in France, and speaks four languages fluently. He is chief executive officer of both French automaker Renault and its alliance partner Nissan, the Japanese car company. Simon Collinson, professor of international business and innovation at Britain's Warwick Business School, said, "There is a huge variety of styles, partly produced by historical, cultural, and regulatory differences." Two additional examples are Howard Stringer, a naturalized U.S. citizen who was born in Wales and runs Japan's Sony, and Indian-born Indra Nooyi, chief of PepsiCo. Of the 140 Fortune Global 500 American companies listed, only 17 were headed by CEOs not born in the United States. What then is the American style of corporate leadership, and how does it differ from those of Asia and Europe? Certainly American CEOs differ in styles, but there appears to be one common denominator. Crossland said, "They have more discretion to stamp their idiosyncratic style on a firm, for good or bad. They have more latitude to make large, strategic decisions themselves." Jaideep Prabhu, an expert on Indian business at the University of Cambridge, said, "The U.S. style is more presidential. It's a 'the buck stops here' attitude." If things go wrong or right, the CEO gets the credit. On the other hand, blaming a good or bad decision on an Asian CEO would be difficult because the style is consensus-driven and collaborative. Only after considerable consultation has taken place and all involved have agreed, will a decision be made. The style reflects the Asian culture of risk aversion that is inherent and the valued concept of collectivism. Donald Hambrick, professor of management at Pennsylvania State University, said, "Culturally, it is hard to make big, bold decisions if you don't have everyone on board." A CEO in Asia may need consensus to operate, but there is no doubt as to who is in charge. The American system is tied to pay, bonuses, and promotions if a task is done well. That's not always the case at large companies in Asia. At times, this attitude can result in the wrong people being rewarded. Prabhu says, "people were promoted just by being around for a long time." Under an American philosophy, if the CEO does a good job, large pay packages follow; a bad job gets them fired.[101]

Neal Hartman, a managerial communications expert at MIT's Sloan School of Management, said, "One trademark of the American style is a focus on achieving results, short-term and long-term." Therefore, decisions are made rather rapidly which is typically not the case in Asia where decision making is often slow and plodding. Mills says, "Asian companies are not as sophisticated as Americans in dealing with equity and bond markets. And a lot are wondering if they want to be." Americans are good at controlling costs. In Europe "they're nowhere near as good at it"—in part because culture and politics make it harder to lay off workers.[102]

Some wonder if the various styles of executives will come together. Hambrick said, "It's too early to tell." The evidence is thin. However, there appears to be a shift away from emulating American leaders, especially since the financial crisis of 2008/10. Linda A. Hill, a Harvard business administration professor, said, "I don't think the American style of leadership is the one that will be adopted by all. And if it was, I don't think that would be a good thing." Sometimes the high-risk, more flexible style of the American CEOs will be superior and at other times the consensus-driven styles of Asian execs will prove superior. Hambrick says, "there's no best way to run a company. It's all a matter of it being a cultural fit."[103]

Selection Rate

The number of applicants hired from a group of candidates expressed as a percentage is the *selection rate*. Certainly, the selection rate is affected by the condition of the economy. Also, the validity of the selection process (previously discussed) will impact the selection rate.

Acceptance Rate

Once an offer has been extended, the firm has said that this applicant meets the requirements for the position. The *acceptance rate* is the number of applicants who accepted the job divided by the number who were offered the job. If this rate is unusually low, it would be wise to determine the reason that jobs are being turned down. A low acceptance rate increases recruiting cost.

Yield Rate

It has been suggested that the selection process can be viewed somewhat as a funnel, with the number of applicants available at each stage of the selection process getting smaller. A *yield rate* is the percentage of applicants from a particular source and method that make it to the next stage of the selection process. For example, if 100 applicants submitted their résumés through the firm's corporate career Web site and 25 were asked in for an interview, the yield rate for the corporate career Web site would be 25 percent. Each recruitment method would be analyzed in a similar manner.

Cost/Benefit of Recruitment Sources and Methods

Each organization should maintain employment records and conduct its own research in order to determine which recruitment sources and methods are most suitable under various circumstances. For each method, there is a cost attached to it. Likewise, for each method, there should be a benefit attached. Over time the effectiveness of each recruitment source and method can be determined.

Summary

1. *Explain the significance of employee selection.* Selection is the process of choosing from a group of applicants the individual best suited for a particular position. There are many ways to improve productivity, but none is more powerful than making the right hiring decision.

2. *Identify environmental factors that affect the selection process.* The environmental factors that affect the selection process include legal considerations, speed of decision making, organizational hierarchy, applicant pool, type of organization, and probationary period.

3. *Describe the selection process and explain applicant tracking systems.* The selection process typically begins with preliminary screening, during which obviously unqualified candidates are rejected. Next, applicants complete the firm's application form, and this is followed by the administration of selection tests and a series of employment interviews with reference and background checks. Once the selection decision has been made, the prospective employee may be given a company medical examination. An applicant tracking system (ATS) is a software application designed to help an enterprise select employees more efficiently. Current ATSs permit human resource and line managers to oversee the entire selection process.

4. *Explain the importance of preliminary screening.* The selection process begins with an initial screening of applicants to remove individuals who obviously do not fulfill the position requirements.

5. *Describe reviewing applications and résumés.* Having the applicant complete an application for employment is another early step in the selection process. The employer evaluates this application to see whether there is an apparent match between the individual and the position. Historically, managers and HR representatives reviewed résumés manually, a time-consuming process. However, this practice has evolved into a more advanced procedure, with résumés automatically evaluated in terms of typos, spelling errors, and job-hopping.

6. *Describe sending résumés via the Internet.* When writing their résumés, applicants should realize that most companies now use automated résumé systems. These systems assume a certain résumé style. Résumés that deviate from the assumed style are ignored or deleted.

7. *Explain the advantages and potential problems of using selection tests.* Recognizing the shortcomings of other selection tools, many firms have added pre-employment tests to their hiring process. Research indicates that customized tests can be a reliable and accurate means to predict on-the-job performance. And, the cost of employment testing is small in comparison to ultimate hiring costs; a successful program will bolster a firm's bottom line. The reason organizations use tests is to identify attitudes and job-related skills that interviews cannot recognize.

   Job performance depends on an individual's ability and motivation to do the work. Selection tests may accurately predict an applicant's ability to perform the job, the "can do," but they are less successful in indicating the extent to which the individual will be motivated to perform it, the "will do." Employers should also be aware that tests might be unintentionally discriminatory. Test anxiety can also be a problem. The problems of hiring unqualified or less-qualified candidates and rejecting qualified candidates, along with other potential legal problems, will continue regardless of the procedures followed.

8. *Describe the characteristics of properly designed selection tests.* Standardization is the uniformity of procedures and conditions related to administering tests. Objectivity is the condition that is achieved when everyone scoring a given test obtains the same results. Norm is the frame of reference for comparing an applicant's performance with that of others. Reliability is the extent to which a selection test provides consistent results. Validity is the extent to which a test measures what it claims to measure.

9. *Explain test validation approaches; describe types of employment tests, online assessment, the use of an assessment center, and unique forms of testing.* Criterion-related validity is determined by comparing the scores on selection tests to some aspect of job performance as determined, for example, by performance appraisal. Content validity is a test validation method whereby a person performs certain tasks that are actually required by the job or completes a paper-and-pencil test that measures relevant job knowledge. Construct validity is a test validation method that determines whether a test measures certain constructs, or traits, that job analysis finds to be important in performing a job.

   Types of employment tests include cognitive aptitude, psychomotor abilities, job-knowledge, work-sample, and vocational interest tests. Genetic

testing, graphoanalysis, and polygraph testing are three unique forms of testing.

   The Internet is increasingly being used to assess various skills required by applicants. An assessment center is a selection approach that requires individuals to perform activities similar to those they might encounter in an actual job.

10. *Explain the importance of the employment interview and describe the general types of interviewing.* The interview permits clarification of certain points, the uncovering of additional information, and the elaboration of data needed to make a sound selection decision. The interviewer should provide information about the company, the job, and expectations of the candidate.

    The general types of interviews are the unstructured interview and the structured interview, including the behavioral interview. The interviewer should provide information about the company, the job, and expectations of the candidate.

11. *Describe the various methods of interviewing and potential interviewing problems.* The methods of interviewing include meeting one-on-one with an interviewer, a group interview, the board interview, multiple interviews, and realistic job preview.

    Potential interviewing problems include inappropriate questions, premature judgments, interview domination, permitting non-job-related information, contrast effect, lack of training, and nonverbal communication.

12. *Explain the use of pre-employment screening, including background investigations, reference checks, automated reference checking, and negligent hiring.* Background investigations primarily seek data from various sources, including professional references. Reference checks are validations from those who know the applicant that provide additional insight into the information furnished by the applicant and allow verification of its accuracy. With automated reference checking, references are anonymous, more efficient, and a more comprehensive report can be provided.

    Negligent hiring is the liability an employer incurs when it fails to conduct a reasonable investigation of an applicant's background, and then assigns a potentially dangerous person to a position in which he or she can inflict harm.

13. *Describe the selection decision, the medical examination, notification of candidates, and candidate relationship management.* The selection decision is when the final choice is made from among those still in the running after reference checks, selection tests, background

investigations, and interview information are evaluated. The medical examination is used to screen out individuals who have a contagious disease and to determine whether an applicant is physically capable of performing the work. The medical examination information may be used to determine whether there are certain physical capabilities that differentiate between successful and less successful employees.

The selection process results should be made known to both successful and unsuccessful candidates as soon as possible. Some organizations are adopting candidate relationship management software to ensure that job seekers have good experiences on the companies' Web sites and to bolster efforts to build talent pools that can be tapped when the companies are able to hire again.

14. ***Explain metrics for evaluating recruitment/selection effectiveness.*** Metrics available to assess HR efficiency are numerous, and a comprehensive set of metrics can be produced to evaluate recruitment and selection. Possible metrics include: quality of hire, time required to hire, new hire retention, hiring manager overall satisfaction, turnover rate, recruiting costs, selection rate, acceptance rate, yield rate, cost/benefit of recruitment sources and methods, and time required to hire.

Key Terms

selection 164	criterion-related validity 172	employment interview 177
applicant pool 165	content validity 173	organizational fit 178
selection ratio 165	construct validity 173	unstructured interview 178
applicant-tracking system (ATS) 166	cognitive aptitude tests 173	structured interview 179
résumé 168	psychomotor abilities tests 173	behavioral interview 179
keywords 170	job-knowledge tests 174	group interview 180
keyword résumé 170	work-sample tests 174	board interview 180
standardization 171	vocational interest tests 174	stress interview 180
objectivity 172	personality tests 174	realistic job preview (RJP) 182
norm 172	assessment center 175	reference checks 186
reliability 172	genetic testing 176	negligent hiring 187
validity 172	graphoanalysis 176	human capital metrics 188

Questions for Review

1. What is the significance of employee selection?
2. What environmental factors could affect the selection process? Discuss each.
3. What would be the selection ratio if there were 15 applicants to choose from and only 1 position to fill? Interpret the meaning of this selection ratio.
4. What are the typical steps in the selection process?
5. What is an applicant-tracking system?
6. What is the general purpose of preliminary screening?
7. What is the purpose of the application form?
8. What types of questions should be asked on an application form?
9. Define a *résumé, keyword,* and *keyword résumé.*
10. What are the advantages and potential problems in the use of selection tests?
11. What are the basic characteristics of a properly designed selection test?
12. What are the test validation approaches? Define each.
13. Identify and describe the various types of employment tests.
14. Describe genetic testing, graphoanalysis, and polygraph tests.
15. Explain the use of online assessment.
16. What is the purpose of an assessment center?
17. With regard to the selection process, what is meant by the term *organizational fit*?
18. What are the general types of interviews? Explain each.
19. What is a behavioral interview? What types of questions would make up a behavioral interview?
20. What are the various methods of interviewing? Define each.

21. What are some potential interview problems?
22. Why is background investigation important to the selection process?
23. Why is automated reference checking important?
24. Why should an employer be concerned about negligent hiring?

25. Why should the selection decision be made before conducting a medical examination?
26. What is candidate relationship management?
27. What are human capital metrics? What are some metrics for evaluating recruitment and selection?

HRM INCIDENT 1

A Matter of Priorities

As production manager for Thompson Manufacturing, Sheila Stephens has the final authority to approve the hiring of any new supervisors who work for her. The human resource manager performs the initial screening of all prospective supervisors and then sends the most likely candidates to Sheila for interviews.

One day recently, Sheila received a call from Pete Peterson, the human resource manager: "Sheila, I've just spoken to a young man who may be just who you're looking for to fill the final line supervisor position. He has some good work experience and appears to have his head screwed on straight. He's here right now and available if you could possibly see him."

Sheila hesitated a moment before answering. "Gee, Pete," she said, "I'm certainly busy today, but I'll try to squeeze him in. Send him on down."

A moment later Allen Guthrie, the applicant, arrived at Sheila's office and she introduced herself. "Come on in, Allen," said Sheila. "I'll be right with you after I make a few phone calls." Fifteen minutes later Sheila finished the calls and began talking with Allen. Sheila was quite impressed. After a few minutes, Sheila's door opened and a supervisor yelled, "We have a small problem on line one and need your help." Sheila stood up and said, "Excuse me a minute, Allen." Ten minutes later Sheila returned, and the conversation continued for ten more minutes before a series of phone calls again interrupted the pair.

The same pattern of interruptions continued for the next hour. Finally, Allen looked at his watch and said, "I'm sorry, Mrs. Stephens, but I have to pick up my wife."

"Sure thing, Allen," Sheila said as the phone rang again. "Call me later today."

Questions

1. What should Sheila have done to avoid interviews like this one?
2. Explain why Sheila, not Pete, should make the selection decision.

HRM INCIDENT 2

The Best Person for the Job?: A Matter of Fit!

As junior project manager for Avengis Construction, Johan Kruger had very tight deadlines to meet. He urgently needed a good construction site manager to replace Thabo Mnyandu. Since he was new to interviewing, Johan was somewhat apprehensive when the first candidate arrived. "Welcome, Ms Mandini. Have a seat. Let's get started right away." Shirley Mandini, an ethnic *Zulu*, felt somewhat uneasy with proceeding into the interview so abruptly. Johan was not sure what questions to ask. He was also acutely aware of an inspection team due to arrive soon. "So, tell me a little bit about yourself, Shirley," Johan enquired. During the next thirty minutes Johan had difficulty directing the flow of the interview.

After the inspection team departed, Johan welcomed the second candidate, Phil Görgens, a German expat. Johan tried a new approach with his interview questions. "Phil, I see you have a Masters degree in Engineering. What was the topic of your dissertation?"

After the interview, Johan had a good feeling about Phil, but thought to himself, "I'm not sure I have a good idea which candidate to appoint for the role. Did I ask the right questions?" He looked at both applicants' résumés again, picked up the phone and called his HR administrator. "Hannes, I've decided I want Phil for the job as site manager. Can you prepare the paperwork and put together an offer?"

Questions

1. How could Johan have prepared better for the job interviews?

2. Explain the potential benefits of improving the quality of the interviewing process Johan used, as well as his skills as an interviewer.

Notes

1. "Final Rule Requires Federal Contractors to Use E-Verify," *HR Focus* 86 (January 2009): 8.

2. Roy Maurer, "Biometric Verification Proposal Under Way," *HRMagazine* 54 (October 2009): 14.

3. "E-Verify for Federal Contractors Gets Final Go-Ahead," *Payroll Manager's Letter* 25 (August 7, 2009): 4–6.

4. Renea I. Saade, "E-Verify or Face Consequences: Checking Out Eligibility of Employees Fast and Easy," *Alaska Business Monthly* 26 (February 2010): 98–99.

5. Bill Leonard, "Researchers: Stolen Identities Often Slip Through E-Verify," *HRMagazine* 55 (April 2010): 11.

6. Mauer, "Biometric Verification Proposal Under Way."

7. John K. Waters, "Reading Between the Lines," *T H E Journal* 36 (October 2009): 23–27.

8. Roy Maurer, "Opponents of National ID Card Cite Myriad Concerns, Dangers," *HRMagazine* 55 (June 2010): 20.

9. Aliah D. Wright, "Can HR Professionals Adapt As Biometric Data Become Reality?" *HRMagazine* 55 (June 2010): 20.

10. Claudio Fernández-Aráoz, Boris Groysberg, and Nitin Nohria, "The Definitive Guide to Recruiting in Good Times and Bad," *Harvard Business Review* 87 (May 2009): 74–84

11. Liz Ryan, "Yes, There's Still a Talent War," *BusinessWeek Online* (April 6, 2009): 19.

12. "How to Stand Out From the Crowd and Kick-Start Your Own Recovery," *U.S. News & World Report* 147 (May 2010): 14–16.

13. Emma Burrows, "Rights at the Start of Employment: Probationary Periods," *Third Sector* (February 3, 2009): 21.

14. "Feds Want a Look at Online Job Sites," *HRMagazine* 53 (November 2008): 12.

15. "Automate Recruiting and Onboarding," *Chain Store Age* 85 (April 2009): 19.

16. Adrienne Hedger, "Three Ways to Improve Your Employee Screening," *Workforce Management* 88 (March 16, 2009): 26–30.

17. Kathryn Benezine, "Applying for Jobs," *Caterer & Hotelkeeper* (2009 Careers Guide): 4–5.

18. Nancy M. Schullery, Linda Ickes, and Stephen E. Schullery, "Employer Preferences for Résumés and Cover Letters," *Business Communication Quarterly* 72 (June 2009): 163–176.

19. Ralph Kisiel, "Honda Taps Web for Workers," *Automotive News* 82 (February 21, 2008): 102.

20. "2010 Résumé: What's In, What's Out," *Administrative Professional Today* 36 (March 2010): 1–2.

21. Greg Schaffer, "Six Ways to Ruin Your Résumé," *Computerworld* 43 (April 13, 2009): 26–28.

22. Kyle Potvin, "Landing the Interview: How to Get to the Top of the Résumé Pile," *Public Relations Tactics* 16 (May 2009): 20.

23. "Look Beyond Clichés and Puffery to Find Résumé Truths," *HR Specialist* 8 (April 2010): 6.

24. Liz Wolgemuth, Kimberly Palmer, Katy Marquardt, Matthew Bandy, Rick Newman, Marty Nemko, "Career Guide 2008," *U.S. News & World Report* 144 (March 24, 2008): 45–61.

25. "Getting Your Résumé Noticed," *Administrative Professional Today* 36 (May 2010): 6.

26. "Make Your Résumé Pop," *Journal of Accountancy* 206 (November 2008): 28.

27. Nicole Amare and Alan Manning, "Writing for the Robot: How Employer Search Tools Have Influenced Résumé Rhetoric and Ethics," *Business Communication Quarterly* 72 (March 2009): 35–60.

28. "Validate Hiring Tests to Withstand EEO Scrutiny: DOL & EEOC Officials," *HR Focus* 85 (May 2008): 8–9.

29. Jason Van Steenwyk, "Using Tests to Screen Employees," *Journal of Financial Planning* (November/December 2008): 5–10.

30. Alan M. Goldstein and Shoshanah D. Epstein, "Personality Testing in Employment: Useful Business Tool or Civil Rights Violation?" *Labor Lawyer* 24 (Fall 2008): 243–252.

31. Jack Kwicien, "Improving Sales Management Effectiveness: Selection," Employee Benefit Advisor 8 (April 2010): 54–56.

32. Susan Greco, "He Can Close, but How Is His Interpersonal Sensitivity?" *Inc.* 31 (March 2009): 96–98.

33. "Out of Sight, Yes. Out of Mind, No," *Business Week* (February 18, 2008): 60.

34. Ed Frauenheim, "Personality Tests Adapt to the Times," *Workforce Management* 89 (February 1, 2010): 4.

35. Michelle V. Rafter, "Assessment Providers Scoring Well," *Workforce Management* 88 (January 19, 2009): 24–25.

36. Dana Tanyeri, "How to Hire Now," *Restaurant Business* 109 (January 2010): 18.

37. Justin Spray, "How to Run an Assessment Centre," *People Management* (January 28, 2010): 31.

38. George C. Thornton III and Michael J. Potemra, "Utility of Assessment Center for Promotion of Police Sergeants," *Public Personnel Management* 39 (Spring 2010): 59–69.

39. Brendan L. Smith, "The EEOC's Brave New World," *ABA Journal* 95 (June 2009): 22–23.

40. Carmen McCormick and John E. Steiner Jr., "Thoughts on the Genetic Information Nondiscrimination Act of 2008," *Managed Care Outlook* 23 (January 15, 2010): 1–8.

41. Michael Alter, "Handwriting Analysis," *Landscape Management* 44 (October 2005): 86.

42. "Lie Detection Science Improves but Remains a Legal Minefield," *Security Director's Report* 9 (March 2009): 4–6.

43. Gary C. Oliphant, Katharine Hansen, and Becky J. Oliphant, "A Review of a Telephone-Administered Behavior-Based Interview Technique," *Business Communication Quarterly* 71 (September 2008): 383–386.

44. "In Hiring, Don't Overvalue Interview Skills; Courts Question Subjective Decision-making," *HR Specialist* 8 (March 2010): 4.

45. Paul Falcone, "Career Counselor Interviewing," *HRMagazine* 51 (January 2006): 97–101.

46. "How to Spot Star Job Candidates," *Managing People at Work* (June 2009): 6.

47. Kimberly Thompson, "Remember Intangibles When Applying for Work," *Phi Kappa Phi Forum* 90 (Spring 2010): 23.

48. Robert J. Grossman, "Hiring to Fit the Culture," *HRMagazine* 54 (February 2009): 41.

49. Lee Froschheiser, "Recruitment Fundamentals," *Adhesives & Sealants Industry* 16 (February 2009): 34–35.

50. "What Is Culture?" *HRMagazine* 54 (February 2009): 42–44.

51. Bill Carpitella, "Interviewing 101: Listen for Organizational Fit," *Professional Builder* 66 (December 2001): 30.

52. Mary Civiello, "Communication Counts in Landing a Job," *T+D* 63 (February 2009): 82–83.

53. "The 5 Worst Interview Questions & What to Ask Instead," *HR Specialist* 8 (January 2010): 6.

54. Agatha Gilmore, "How to Rock the Situational Interview," *Certification Magazine* 10 (November 2008): 36.

55. "Behavioral Interviews Are Focused on Retention," *Work-Life Newsbrief & Trend Report* (September 2008): 4.

56. "How to Screen for Cultural Fit?" *HRMagazine* 54 (February 2009): 46–50.

57. Mark Murphy, "Hiring IQ," *Leadership Excellence* 23 (January 2006): 11.

58. Joel Koppelman, "Building the Team," *Smart Business Philadelphia*," 5 (December 2008): 11.

59. Aliah D. Wright, "At Google, It Takes A Village To Hire an Employee," *HRMagazine* 53 (December 2008): 56–57.

60. R. Wayne Mondy and Shane R. Premeaux, *Management: Concepts, Practices, and Skills* (Englewood Cliffs, N.J., Prentice-Hall, 7th Edition, 1995): 420.

61. Wright, "At Google, It Takes A Village To Hire an Employee."

62. Michael Kaplan, "Job Interview Brainteasers," *Business 2.0* 8 (September 2007): 35–37.

63. Martha Frase-Blunt, "Games Interviewers Play," *HRMagazine* 46 (January 2001): 107–108.

64. "Hire Better with Targeted Descriptions," *Communication Briefings* 29 (April 2010): 5.

65. "Firing Off . . . When Interviews Go from Formal to Farce," *Personnel Today* (January 15, 2008): 28.

66. "Job Interviews: How to Pose Risky Questions the Legal Way," *HR Specialist: New Jersey Employment Law* 5 (April 2010): 6.

67. "Why Should We Pick You?" *Director* 63 (April 2010): 31–33.

68. Dan Heath and Chip Heath, "Hold the Interview," *Fast Company* (June 2009): 51–52.

69. "The Hidden Risks of Hiring Based on 'Chemistry'," *HR Specialist* 8 (February 2010): 1–2.

70. R. Wayne Mondy and Shane R. Premeaux, *Management: Concepts, Practices, and Skills* (Orlando, FL: Harcourt, Inc., 2000): 291.

71. Kristen Weirick, "The Perfect Interview," *HRMagazine* 53 (April 2008): 85–88.

72. "How and Why Employers Are Doing Background Screenings," *Security Director's Report* 9 (February 2009): 8.

73. "Conducting Thorough Background Checks on Job Candidates," *Teller Vision* (October 2008): 5.

74. Meredyth McKenzie, "Evaluating Potential Hires," *Smart Business Atlanta* 6 (July 2009): 22.

75. Judy Stringer, "Background Checks," *Tire Business* 26 (January 5, 2009): 5.

76. Whitney Ward, "Use and Misuse of Screening Devices for Hiring and Promotion," *Labor & Employment Law* 37 (Fall 2008): 7.

77. "Favorite Strategies to Stop Employee Thieves," *Security Director's Report* 6 (March 2006): 8.

78. "ABA Offers Fast Background Checks," *Teller Vision* (January 2009): 4–5.

79. "Continuous Screening May Create Issues for Employers," *Workforce Management* 89 (February 1, 2010): 30.

80. Mary Oleniczak, Charlie Pike, Jitendra Mishra, and Mishra Bharat, "Employers Use Facebook too, for

Hiring," *Advances in Management* 3 (January 2010):13–17.

81. Dave Willmer, "Managing Your Digital Footprint," *T+D* 63 (June 2009): 84–85.

82. "Nearly Half of Employers Use Social Media to Research Candidates," *HR Focus* 86 (December 2009): 8.

83. Ibid.

84. Adam Klein, "Making a Case for Hiring Bars," *Workforce Management* 89 (February 1, 2010): 28.

85. "Feds Turning Up Heat on HR Background Checks," *HR Specialist: Employment Law* 40 (May 2010): 1–2.

86. Oleniczak, Pike, Mishra, and Bharat, "Employers Use Facebook Too, for Hiring."

87. Connie Stamper, "Common Mistakes Companies Make Using Social Media Tools in Recruiting Efforts," *CMA Management* 84 (April 2010): 12–14.

88. "Conducting Background Checks that Comply with the FCRA," *HR Specialist: Florida Employment Law* 4 (May 2009): 6.

89. "'Sufficient Time' to Dispute the Accuracy of Background Checks Under the Fair Credit Reporting Act," *Venulex Legal Summaries* (2008 Q4, Special section): 1–2.

90. Shey Zeemer Hable, "The Trouble with Online References," *Tire Business* 27 (March 1, 2010): 5.

91. Adrienne Fox, "Automated Reference Checking Puts Onus on Candidates," *HRMagazine* 53 (December 2008): 66–69.

92. "Stakes Rise for Preventing Sexual Harassment and Age Discrimination," *Security Director's Report* 9 (March 2009): 8.

93. Bill Roberts, "Manage Candidates Right from the Start," *HRMagazine* 53 (October 2008): 73–76.

94. J. M., "Open to Misinterpretation," *CFO* 25 (July/August 2009): 34.

95. Becca Baird, "Using Human Capital Metrics To Develop Strategic Objectives: Putting The Cart Before The Horse," *PA Times* 32 (January 2009): 10–11.

96. Theresa Minton-Eversole, "Quality Measurement: Key to Best-in-Class Talent Acquisition," *HRMagazine* 53 (December 2008): 64–66.

97. Bill Roberts, "How to Put Analytics 'On Your Side,'" *HRMagazine* 54 (October 2009): 43–46.

98. Minton-Eversole, "Quality Measurement: Key to Best-in-Class Talent Acquisition."

99. "Track Turnover to Save Money," *Report on Salary Surveys* 9 (March 2009): 9.

100. Thomas K. Grose, "When in Rome, Do as Roman CEOs Do," *U.S. News & World Report* 146 (November 2009): 38–41.

101. Ibid.

102. Ibid.

103. Ibid.

7 Training and Development

HRM in Action: Executive Integration, the Sink or Swim Approach Does Not Work

Research has shown that up to 40 percent of externally hired executives fail within the first 18 months. What is causing this problem? Could it be that they are not getting the type of information that is needed to succeed? Research indicates that what new executives need to know in order to be effective differs significantly from the focus of most general employee orientation programs. For example, new executives must understand the unwritten rules, processes, and networks that influence how things really get done in their organization in order to be successful in their role. Too often executives are just given the key to their executive suite and are expected to sink or swim. That approach will not work if an organization is searching for ways to help them succeed. Thus a new approach is needed to integrate executives into the firm.

The Corporate Leadership Council identifies six common reasons new executives fail: failure to establish key connections and partnerships; lack of political savvy or support to effectively navigate the organization; failure to establish a cultural fit; confusion about role expectations; lack of feedback and coaching; and ineffective people management team building skills.[1] Obtaining this information cannot occur with the customary employment orientation intended to familiarize an executive with his or her new colleagues and working environment in the early days of the job.

There is a major difference between executive orientation and executive *integration* or *assimilation*. Orientation enables an executive to perform in a new role, whereas integration offers the first feedback on how you are doing in that role. Integration occurs

After completing this chapter, students should be able to:

1. Define *training* and *development*.

2. Explain factors influencing T&D.

3. Describe the T&D process.

4. Describe the various T&D methods.

5. Describe training and development delivery systems.

6. Describe management development, mentoring, and coaching.

7. Define *orientation* and explain implementing training and development programs.

8. Explain the metrics for evaluating training and development.

9. Describe the Workforce Investment Act.

10. Define *organization development (OD)* and describe various OD techniques.

long after the typical executive orientation is provided in the early days of the job. Integration wants to reduce the high turnover statistic caused by a sink-or-swim attitude that often exists in executive succession. This emerging practice of evaluating individual performance early in their tenure is critical because it provides the kind of intelligence an executive can use to set things right before it is too late. Giving a new executive a first impression view of his or her progression perhaps some 90, 100, or perhaps 120 days into a new management role helps correct a course of action if needed and prevents them from failing.[2]

When Bristol-Myers Squibb, the global pharmaceutical manufacturer, studied the retention rates of its recently hired executives, it discovered that the company was losing promising new executives because it was not taking steps to ensure their success. It then made new executives the object of keen focus during the first 100 days of their employment, providing guidelines, clarifying roles, setting up meetings with influential colleagues, and fostering each newcomer's understanding of the company's cultural norms.[3] Follow-up meetings also need to be held during the executive's first year to check progress and resolve problems. A.G. Lambert, vice president of product marketing at Saba, a talent management firm based in Redwood Shores, California, said, "When you think of the lifecycle of an employee, the first step is getting them engaged. It's much more important than getting them enrolled in the 401(k) plan. A company does not want to mess up the integration process."[4]

Executive search firms, leadership coaches, and consultants are building specialized "executive integration" to their services. "It's like an insurance policy for your placement," says Rich Rosen, a partner in Heidrick's leadership consulting practice.[5] Companies want executives who "fit in" to the environment they face. Integration gives them the tools for making that possible. Integration amounts to an organizational poll about how a new leader is fulfilling the objectives of his or her role and executing the company's strategic mandate.[6]

The first portion of this chapter is devoted to executive integration. Next, strategic training and development (T&D) and the factors influencing T&D will be explained. Following this, we examine the T&D process and how T&D needs are determined and objectives established. Then, the numerous T&D methods are discussed and T&D delivery systems are described followed by a discussion of telepresence as a delivery system. Management development and orientation are then discussed. The means by which T&D programs are implemented are then explained, followed by a discussion of the metrics for evaluating training and development. After that, the Workforce Investment Act is explained, organization development is described, and the chapter concludes with a global perspective entitled "Buddies Across the Globe."

OBJECTIVE 7.1
Define *training* and *development*.

training and development (T&D)
Heart of a continuous effort designed to improve employee competency and organizational performance.

training
Activities designed to provide learners with the knowledge and skills needed for their present jobs.

development
Learning that goes beyond today's job and has a more long-term focus.

learning organization
Firm that recognizes the critical importance of continuous performance-related T&D and takes appropriate action.

Strategic Training and Development

Training and development (T&D) is the heart of a continuous effort designed to improve employee competency and organizational performance. **Training** provides learners with the knowledge and skills needed for their present jobs. Showing a worker how to operate a lathe or a supervisor how to schedule daily production are examples of training. On the other hand, **development** involves learning that goes beyond today's job and has a more long-term focus. It prepares employees to keep pace with the organization as it changes and grows. T&D activities have the potential to align a firm's employees with its corporate strategies. Some possible strategic benefits of T&D include employee satisfaction, improved morale, higher retention, lower turnover, improved hiring, a better bottom line, and the fact that satisfied employees produce satisfied customers.

Learning Organization

Improved performance, the bottom-line purpose of T&D, is a strategic goal for organizations. Toward this end, many firms have become or are striving to become learning organizations. A **learning organization** is a firm that recognizes the critical importance of continuous performance-related T&D and takes appropriate action. A learning organization has three basic characteristics: 1) it provides a supportive learning environment, 2) it provides specific learning processes and practices, and 3) the leadership behavior in the organization supports and reinforces learning.[7]

A learning management system moves beyond delivering tactical training projects to initiating learning programs aligned with strategic corporate goals. Once undervalued in the corporate world, training programs are now credited with strengthening customer satisfaction, contributing to partnership development, enhancing research and development activities, and, finally, reinforcing the bottom line. Being recognized as a company that encourages its employees to continue to grow and learn can be a major asset in recruiting. Learning organizations view learning and development opportunities in all facets of their business and try to constantly look ahead and ensure that all employees are taking full advantage of the learning tools important to their careers.[8] This is especially important in recruiting Generation Y workers. In a learning organization, employees are rewarded for learning and are provided enriched jobs, promotions, and compensation. Organizations with a reputation for having a culture of being a learning leader tend to attract more and better-qualified employees.

In the competition to become listed in the "100 Best Companies to Work for in America," learning and growth opportunities were a high priority. On nearly every survey, training and development ranks in the top three benefits that employees want from their employers, and they search for firms that will give them the tools to advance in their profession. It is clear that T&D is not merely a nice thing to provide. It is a strategic resource; one that firms must tap to energize their organizations in the 21st century.

OBJECTIVE 7.2

Explain factors influencing T&D.

HR Web Wisdom

American Society for Training and Development

http://www.astd.org

The homepage for the American Society for Training and Development is presented.

Factors Influencing Training and Development

There are numerous factors that both impact and are impacted by T&D.

Top Management Support

For T&D programs to be successful, top management support is required; without it, a T&D program will not succeed. The most effective way to achieve success is for executives to provide the needed resources to support the T&D effort.[9]

The recession of 2008/10 saw many training budgets suffer as executives looked for ways to reduce costs. In a Business Industrial Network survey, 40 percent say they cut training budgets because of the economic climate.[10] However, as Pat Galagan, executive editor for the American Society for Training & Development, said, "Often in tough times, companies will change direction. They will change their business model or decide to put more emphasis on a particular function, such as sales. Those things require more training rather than less."[11] Training resources that remain are being allocated to high-impact initiatives. The open enrollment policies of the past "are being replaced with a more prescriptive approach that seeks to match high-potential employees with development initiatives that tackle strategic business issues," said Karen O'Leonard, a principal analyst with Bersin.[12]

Technological Advances

Change is occurring at an amazing speed, with knowledge doubling every year.[13] Perhaps no factor has influenced T&D more than technology. The computer, Internet, BlackBerrys, cell phones, text messaging, and e-mail are dramatically affecting how training is conducted. As emphasized throughout this chapter, technology has played a huge role in changing the way knowledge is delivered to employees, and this change is constantly being extended.

World Complexity

The world is simply getting more complex, and this has had an impact on how an organization operates. No longer does a firm just compete against other firms in the United States. The entire world provides opportunities and threats that must be confronted. Organizations have to think of the entire workforce and how it will be staffed and trained in this global environment.

Lifetime Learning

Largely due to the work environment workers confront today, learning can never stop; it is a continuous process. The psychological value of lifelong learning cannot be overstated. Employees who participate in ongoing education will feel as if their careers are advancing and they are better able to provide for their families. Things will change faster tomorrow than they did today, and even faster the day after that. Employees who are not staying ahead of the curve are going to be left behind and their value to the firm diminishes.[14]

Learning Styles

Although much remains unknown about the learning process, some generalizations stemming from the behavioral sciences have affected the way firms conduct training. For example, learners progress in an area of learning only as far as they need to in order to achieve their purposes. Professors have long known that telling students the important concepts that they should know elicits studying that material, especially if the information is really on the test. Research indicates that unless there is relevance, meaning, and emotion attached to the material taught, learners will not learn.

ETHICAL DILEMMA

Tough Side of Technology

You are the human resource director for a large manufacturing firm that is undergoing major changes. Your firm is in the process of building two technologically advanced plants. When these are completed, the company will close four of its five old plants. It is your job to determine who will stay with the old plant and who will be retrained for the newer plants.

One old-plant employee is a 56-year-old production worker who has been with your firm for 10 years. He seems to be a close personal friend of your boss, as they are often seen together socially. However, in your opinion, he is not capable of handling the high-tech work required at the new plants, even with additional training. He is not old enough to receive any retirement benefits and there are other qualified workers with more seniority who want to remain at the old plant.

What would you do?

The best time to learn is when the learning can be useful. One way this impacts T&D is the need for training on a timely basis. **Just-in-time training (on-demand training)** is training provided anytime, anywhere in the world when it is needed. Computer technology, the Internet, and intranets have made these approaches economically feasible to a degree never before possible. The ability to deliver knowledge to employees on an as-needed basis, anywhere on the globe, and at a pace consistent with their learning styles, greatly enhances the value of T&D.

Research on student learning styles indicates that most college students have a practical orientation to learning, with a preference for concrete learning activities, rather than a theoretical, abstract orientation. Active modes of teaching and learning appear to be more effective; it is learning based on the assumption that students learn best by doing because it provides students with the opportunity not only to apply and practice what they have learned, but also to see the results of their practice, determine whether they really understood what they did, and gain insight for subsequent application.

just-in-time training (on-demand training)
Training provided anytime, anywhere in the world when it is needed.

Other Human Resource Functions

Successful accomplishment of other human resource functions can also have a crucial impact on T&D. For instance, if recruitment-and-selection efforts or its compensation package attract only marginally qualified workers, a firm will need extensive T&D programs.

OBJECTIVE 7.3
Describe the T&D process.

Training and Development Process

Major adjustments in the external and internal environments necessitate corporate change. The general T&D process that anticipates or responds to change may be seen in Figure 7.1. First, an organization must determine its specific training needs. Then specific objectives need to be established. The objectives might be quite narrow if limited to the supervisory ability of a manager, or they might be broad enough to include improving the management skills of all first-line supervisors. In exemplary organizations, there is a close link between the firm's strategic mission and the objectives of the T&D program. Review and periodic updating of these objectives is necessary to ensure that they support the changing strategic needs of the organization. After setting the T&D objectives, management can determine the appropriate methods and the delivery system to be used. Naturally, management must continuously evaluate T&D to ensure its value in achieving organizational objectives.

Determine Specific Training and Development Needs

The first step in the T&D process is to determine specific T&D needs. In today's highly competitive business environment, undertaking a program because other firms are doing it is asking for trouble. A systematic approach to addressing bona fide needs must be undertaken.

Figure 7.1

**Training and
Development
Process**

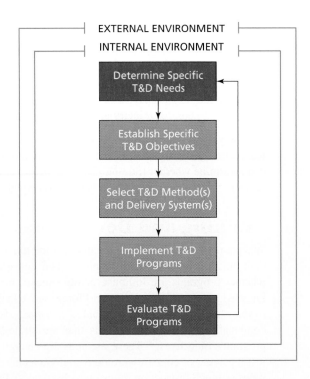

Training and development needs may be determined by conducting analyses on several levels:

- *Organizational analysis:* From an *overall organizational* perspective, the firm's strategic mission, goals, and corporate plans are studied, along with the results of strategic human resource planning.
- *Task analysis:* The next level of analysis focuses on the *tasks* required to achieve the firm's purposes. Job descriptions are important data sources for this analysis level.
- *Person analysis:* Determining *individual training needs* is the final level. The relevant questions are, "Who needs to be trained?" and "What kind of knowledge, skills, and abilities (KSAs) do employees need?" Performance appraisals and interviews or surveys of supervisors and job incumbents are helpful at this level.

Companies now train for specific needs and trainers are asking, "What knowledge do you want your people to have? What skills do they need? What do they need to do differently from what they're doing today? Trainers want to find out what job knowledge and skills the person needs to have to get the job done.

Establish Specific Training and Development Objectives

T&D must have clear and concise objectives and be developed to achieve organizational goals. Without them, designing meaningful T&D programs would not be possible.[15] Worthwhile evaluation of a program's effectiveness would also be difficult, at best. Consider these purposes and objectives for a training program involving employment compliance:

Training Area: Employment Compliance

PURPOSE To provide the supervisor with

1. Knowledge and value of consistent human resource practices
2. The intent of Equal Employment Opportunity Commission (EEOC) legal requirements
3. The skills to apply them

OBJECTIVES To be able to

1. Cite the supervisory areas affected by employment laws on discrimination
2. Identify acceptable and unacceptable actions
3. State how to get help on EEOC matters
4. Describe why we have disciplinary action and grievance procedures
5. Describe our disciplinary action and grievance procedures, including who is covered

As you see, the *purpose* is established first. The specific *learning objectives* that follow leave little doubt about what the training should accomplish. With these objectives, managers can determine whether training has been effective. For instance, in the example above, a trainee either can or cannot state how to get help on equal employment opportunity matters.

Training and Development Methods

OBJECTIVE 7.4
Describe the various T&D methods.

When a person is working in a garden, some tools are more helpful in performing certain tasks than others. The same logic applies when considering various T&D methods. Regardless of whether programs are in-house or outsourced, firms use a number of methods for imparting knowledge and skills to the workforce and usually more than one method, called *blended training* (also referred to as *blended learning*), is used to deliver T&D. It involves using a combination of training methods that are strategically combined to best achieve a training program's objectives.[16] These methods are changing continuously. For instance, ten years ago, just 9 percent of courses were delivered via technology-based methods. Today, more than three times as much instruction relies on technology.[17] Each training method is evaluated and chosen for what it does best. T&D methods are discussed next.

Instructor-Led

The instructor-led method, where the instructor physically stands in front of students, continues to be effective for many types of T&D. One advantage of instructor-led T&D is that the instructor may convey a great deal of information in a relatively short time. The effectiveness of instructor-led programs improves when groups are small enough to permit discussion, and when the instructor is able to capture the imagination of the class and use multimedia in an appropriate manner. Also, the charisma or personality that the instructor brings to class may excite the students to want to learn.

E-Learning

e-learning
T&D method for online instruction.

The tradition of instructors physically lecturing in front of live corporate students has diminished somewhat in recent years.[18] Today, instructors can deliver their lectures virtually. **E-learning** is the T&D method for online instruction. It takes advantage of the speed, memory, and data-manipulation capabilities of the computer for greater flexibility of instruction. It is often the most convenient delivery method for adult learners. It can be self-paced, can often be individualized, and can be done while at work or off-shift.[19] A concept can be viewed as often as needed. Help screens can also be included in the program to give additional explanation for those who need it. Individuals using e-learning can be working on different parts of a program, at varying speeds, and in different languages.

The instructor is still in charge of the class, but is not physically standing in front of students. Students can still do practically anything they could do in a traditional classroom. They can share a whiteboard, communicate as individuals and groups, view video material, and so forth. Students do not have to wait for a professor's office hours to communicate with the teacher, since an e-mail may be sent anytime.

I appreciated firsthand the power of e-learning when my university took a direct hit from Hurricane Rita in 2005. Under the mandatory evacuation order, students and faculty scattered in every direction, going to different states and countries. A few days after the hurricane struck, it was evident that the brick-and-mortar university would be out of service for some time. Soon after I evacuated, I went to Blackboard and e-mailed my students, asking them to reply if they received the e-mail. Blackboard is a software application for education online and has powerful capabilities for managing courses and tailoring instruction to enhance student outcomes.[20] Luckily, the server had been transferred to another school in the state and Blackboard could still be used by students. Surprisingly, most students responded, some from as far away as New York, Mexico, Asia, and the Philippines.

Prior to the hurricane, students had been assigned a term paper, requiring use of EBSCOhost, a research database. I encouraged them to continue their research and to communicate with me. We began a steady stream of two-way communication. Rough drafts of research papers passed between us; students read lectures on Blackboard. Other instructors were also using Blackboard to keep in touch with their students. The semester was ultimately completed, and only 8 percent of the student population failed to complete the semester.

E-learning systems may also be enlivened by using multimedia to enhance learning with audio, animation, graphics, and interactive video. Amy Hackett, director of training for Maryville, Tennessee–based Ruby Tuesday, uses an online training product to teach hourly employees. She said, "Until a year ago we used to train by traditional methods: in-person and seminars. But, before e-learning, there were shortcuts being made to the (five-day) training program." Hackett continued, "One of the biggest measures of e-learning's success has been a rise in tip percentages. I think this reflects [greater] menu knowledge." says Hackett.[21]

The advantages of using e-learning are numerous; however, the biggest advantage is cost savings. According to Gordon Johnson, vice president of marketing for infrastructure provider Expertus, "Online meetings are one-third the cost of face-to-face meetings, so the question becomes not which is best, but whether face-to-face training is three times better. Usually not."[22]

For Union Pacific, the largest railroad company in North America, both distance and time have been hurdles to learning. About 19,000 of its 48,000 widely disbursed employees work on the railroad's locomotives and freight cars, many on different schedules. So the company uses a blend of traditional learning and e-learning that provides the kind of training far-flung employees require, at a time when they can use it.

Firms that consistently have a high turnover rate have turned to e-learning because classroom learning is not cost-effective. Nike faced a challenge that a number of retailers today are confronting. Nike designed an online training program that the company could offer to employees in its own stores as well as at other retailers that sell Nike products. The program conveys a lot of information quickly, but it is also easy to learn. This is important because the training is directed at 16- to 22-year-olds. The concept of Sports Knowledge Underground (SKU) was developed. The layout for SKU resembles a subway map, with different stations representing different training themes. For example, Apparel Union Station branches off into the apparel technologies line, the running products line, and the Nike Pro products line. The Cleated Footwear Station offers paths to football, whereas the Central Station offers such broad lines as customer skills. Each segment is three to seven minutes long and gives associates the basic knowledge they need about various products. The program reaches approximately 20,000 associates.[23]

Virtual reality (also called *3D learning*) is an extension of e-learning that permits trainees to view objects from a perspective that is otherwise impractical or impossible. For example, it is not feasible to turn a drill press on its side so a trainee can inspect it from the bottom. 3D learning permits the learner to see parts from all sides, turn them upside down, and thoroughly investigate them. Computer technology easily permits this type of manipulation.

Case Study

The **case study** is a T&D method in which trainees study the information provided in the case and make decisions based on it.

If an actual company is involved, the student would be expected to research the firm to gain a better appreciation of its financial condition and environment. Research on companies has been significantly enhanced through the availability of library databases such as EBSCOhost. Often, the case study method occurs with an instructor who serves as a facilitator.

Behavior Modeling and Twittering

Behavior modeling is a T&D method that permits a person to learn by copying or replicating behaviors of others. Behavior modeling has been used to train supervisors in such tasks as

---

virtual reality
Extension of e-learning that permits trainees to view objects from a perspective that is otherwise impractical or impossible.

case study
T&D method in which trainees are expected to study the information provided in the case and make decisions based on it.

behavior modeling
T&D method that permits a person to learn by copying or replicating behaviors of others to show managers how to handle various situations.

conducting performance reviews, correcting unacceptable performance, delegating work, improving safety habits, handling discrimination complaints, overcoming resistance to change, orienting new employees, and mediating individuals or groups in conflict.

Social networking has been used as a learning tool involving behavior modeling. "In a corporation, micro-blogging can be a way to augment behavior modeling," says Sarah Millstein, author of the *O'Reilly Radar Report*. This is how it works. A person who excels at a task would send out frequent updates about what he or she is doing. The company might formalize the process to the extent that it would select exemplary performers to post regularly, and pick those who should follow their posts. "This is an easy way to prompt conversation and questions with role models," says Millstein.[24]

Role-Playing

role-playing
T&D method in which participants are required to respond to specific problems they may encounter in their jobs by acting out real-world situations.

Role-playing is a T&D method in which participants are required to respond to specific problems they may encounter in their jobs by acting out real-world situations. Rather than hearing an instructor talk about how to handle a problem or discussing it, they learn by doing. Role-playing is often used to teach such skills as disciplinary action, interviewing, grievance handling, conducting performance-appraisal reviews, team problem solving, effective communication, and leadership-style analysis. It has also been used successfully to teach workers how to deal with individuals who are angry, irate, or out of control. Some restaurant chains use role-playing to train servers how to deal with difficult situations such as a couple having an argument at the dinner table.

Business Games

business games
T&D method that permits participants to assume roles such as president, controller, or marketing vice president of two or more similar hypothetical organizations and compete against each other by manipulating selected factors in a particular business situation.

Business games is a T&D method that permits participants to assume roles such as president, controller, or marketing vice president of two or more similar hypothetical organizations and compete against each other by manipulating selected factors in a particular business situation. Participants make decisions affecting such factors as price levels, production volumes, and inventory levels. Typically, a computer program manipulates their decisions, with the results simulating those of an actual business situation. Participants are able to see how their decisions affect other groups and vice versa. The best thing about this type of learning is that if a poor decision costs the company $1 million, no one gets fired, yet the business lesson is learned.

In-Basket Training

in-basket training
T&D method in which the participant is asked to establish priorities for and then handle a number of business papers, e-mail messages, memoranda, reports, and telephone messages that would typically cross a manager's desk.

In-basket training is a T&D method in which the participant is asked to establish priorities for and then handle a number of business papers, e-mails, texts, memoranda, reports, and telephone messages that would typically cross a manager's desk. The messages, presented in no particular order, call for anything from urgent action to routine handling. The participant is required to act on the information contained in these messages. In this method, the trainee assigns a priority to each particular situation before making any decisions. This form of training has been quite beneficial to help predict performance success in management jobs. Assessment centers, discussed in Chapter 6, commonly make use of this training method in the selection process.

On-the-Job Training

on-the-job training (OJT)
An informal T&D method that permits an employee to learn job tasks by actually performing them.

The next three T&D methods involve learning by actually doing work-related tasks. **On-the-job-training (OJT)** is an informal T&D method that permits an employee to learn job tasks by actually performing them. Often OJT will also have a significant impact on personal development.[25] The key to this training is to transfer knowledge from a highly skilled and experienced worker to a new employee, while maintaining the productivity of both workers. OJT is used to pass on critical "how to" information to the trainee. Individuals may also be more highly motivated to learn because it is clear to them that they are acquiring the knowledge needed to perform the job. At times, however, the trainee may feel so much pressure to produce that learning is negatively affected. Firms should be selective about who provides on-the-job training. Sometimes two workers are paired as buddies and experienced workers show less-experienced workers how to do a task. Regardless of who does the training, that person must have a good work ethic and correctly model the desired behavior.

Internships

In Chapter 5, internship programs were described as a recruitment method typically involving students in higher education who divide their time between attending classes and working for an organization. Internships as a T&D method allow participants to integrate theory learned in the classroom with business practices. Internships are not just valuable in getting a job. Claudia Tattanelli, chief executive officer of Philadelphia-based research firm Universum Communications, said, "Not too long ago, many employers were still unsure whether to even have a formal internship program. Now it's a necessity for large prestigious companies and firms if they want to appeal to a Gen Y crowd that craves engaging work. You can't just have [an internship program]. You have to have one and give them meaningful work."[26]

Apprenticeship Training

apprenticeship training
Training method that combines classroom instruction with on-the-job training.

Apprenticeship training is a training method that combines classroom instruction with on-the-job training. The National Association of Manufacturers projects that by 2020 some 10 million skilled workers will be needed[27] and apprenticeships remain one of the most vital sources for new talent in manufacturing.[28] Such training is common with craft jobs, such as those of plumber, carpenter, machinist, welder, fabricator, laser operator, electrician, and press brake operator.[29] While in training, the employee earns less than the master craftsperson who is the instructor. Many organizations are partnering with high schools, vocational schools, and universities as they search for new skilled workers. Organizations are donating look-alike equipment to the schools so students can be trained on the system.

Recently, the U.S. Department of Labor implemented new regulations governing apprenticeships. Historically, apprenticeships were defined by the amount of instruction time—typically 10,000 hours over four years. The new regulations offer provisions for competency-based apprenticeships, electronic and distance training, and the issuance of interim credentials. These credentials can be used toward college credits. "It's nice because a person isn't waiting until the end of the program to get some kind of reward," says Steve Mandes, executive director at National Institute for Metalworking Skills (NIMS).[30]

Training and Development Delivery Systems

OBJECTIVE 7.5
Describe training and development delivery systems.

The section above focused on the various T&D methods available to organizations, and the list is constantly changing. In this section, our attention is devoted to how training may be delivered to participants.

Corporate Universities

corporate university
T&D delivery system provided under the umbrella of the organization.

A T&D delivery system provided under the umbrella of the organization is referred to as a **corporate university**. The corporate T&D institution's focus is on creating organizational change that involves areas such as company training, employee development, and adult learning. It aims to achieve its goals by conducting activities that foster individual and organizational learning and knowledge. It is proactive and strategic rather than reactive and tactical and can be closely aligned to corporate goals. Even though called universities, they are not so in the straightest sense since they do not grant degrees in specific subjects. GE has its Crotonville campus and McDonald's has its Hamburger University.[31] Intel University in Arizona administers programs developed by 73 training groups located worldwide. The university also teaches nontechnical skills such as dealing with conflict and harassment avoidance.

Growth in the number of corporate universities may be attributed to their flexibility, which permits students to learn on their own time. Also, firms are better able to control the quality of training and to ensure all employees receive the same messages.

Colleges and Universities

For decades, colleges and universities have been the primary delivery system for training professional, technical, and management employees. Many public and private colleges and universities are taking similar approaches to training and education as have the corporate universities. Corporate T&D programs often partner with colleges and universities or other organizations, such as the American Management Association, to deliver both training and development.

Community Colleges

Community colleges are publicly funded higher education establishments that deliver vocational training and associate-degree programs. Some employers have discovered that community colleges can provide certain types of training better and more cost effectively than the company can. Rapid technological changes and corporate restructuring have created a new demand by industry for community college training resources.

Online Higher Education

online higher education
Educational opportunities including degree and training programs that are delivered, either entirely or partially, via the Internet.

A form of online e-learning that has increased substantially in recent years, is the use of online higher education. **Online higher education** is defined as formal educational opportunities including degree and training programs that are delivered, either entirely or partially, via the Internet. One reason for the growth of online higher education is that it allows employees to attend class at lunchtime, during the day, or in the evening. It also saves employees time because it reduces their need to commute to school. It increases the range of learning opportunities for employees and increases employee satisfaction. Another point that needs to be made is that skepticism regarding the quality of online degrees appears to be fading.[32] Many say that online courses are even more difficult than traditional lecture courses.[33]

Enrollment in online universities continues to grow. The University of Phoenix has the largest student body in North America with an enrollment of 420,700 undergraduate students and 78,000 graduate students. The university has more than 200 campuses worldwide and confers degrees in over 100 degree programs at the associate's, bachelor's, master's and doctoral levels. The University of Florida has a 275-student distance MBA program that's been online since 1999; the MBA Online program at Arizona State University has 420 students.[34] The recession of 2008/10 hastened even more the growth of online higher education. Enrollment in online degree programs increased amid high unemployment, when people were afraid they will might lose their jobs or miss out on promotions because they did not have degrees.[35]

In recent years, programs have been introduced that provide students with more and more autonomy and control of their programs of study. There are basically three categories of online higher education programs available: hybrid, synchronous, and asynchronous. *Hybrid programs* permit students to take some classes online and some in a traditional university setting. *Online synchronized study* offers students the choice of studying through an online portal system; however, the student is expected to appear for most classes on a real-time schedule. With this approach, students interact with a real professor and obtain real-time support for the learning material. With *asynchronous learning,* students have a series of assignments that need to be completed in a certain time frame. A system is available that allows students to communicate with the professor and classmates.[36] Marianne Mondy, a legislative auditor for Louisiana, received her MBA with the University of Phoenix. She was given the option to totally complete her MBA online or to do a portion of her work on campus. She chose the online option because of her work schedule. All courses are six weeks in length and each assignment must be completed in a fixed time frame. Key to succeeding in an asynchronous learning environment is that the student must be motivated to learn.[37]

Vestibule System

vestibule system
T&D delivery system that takes place away from the production area on equipment that closely resembles equipment actually used on the job.

Vestibule system is a T&D delivery system that takes place away from the production area on equipment that closely resembles equipment actually used on the job. For example, a group of lathes may be located in a training center where the trainees receive instruction in their use. A primary advantage of the vestibule system is that it removes the employee from the pressure of having to produce while learning. The emphasis is focused on learning the skills required by the job.

Video Media

The use of video media such as DVDs, videotapes, and film clips continues to be a popular T&D delivery system. These media are especially appealing to small businesses that cannot afford more expensive training methods and are often incorporated in e-learning and instructor-led instruction. In addition, they provide the flexibility desired by any firm. Behavior modeling, previously mentioned, has long been a successful training method that uses video media.

TRENDS & INNOVATIONS

Telepresence—High-Tech Videoconferencing

Although videoconferencing has been around for decades, it has been greatly improved over time with the ultimate form of videoconferencing being telepresence.[38] Telepresence systems provide the illusion of sitting across a conference table from the individuals you are "meeting" with. You have the perception of being able to "look them in the eye."[39] Telepresence systems have been called "the Cadillac[s] of Videoconferencing" by Claire Schooley, senior industry analyst.[40] Until recently, the status of business travelers was measured by frequent-flier miles, their admission to VIP lounges, and names of famous people they met at conferences. For years, Irv Rothman, CEO of Hewlett-Packard's Financial Services division, flew at least once a quarter with his top three lieutenants from his New Jersey base to HP's Silicon Valley headquarters. After a six-and-a-half hour flight, he would meet with their boss, then do it all over again. With telepresence, the flight time is eliminated. Nortel's Rick Dipper says, "When you say you were able to have a meeting in London and then go home and have dinner with your children, that's what people are jealous of now."[41]

Telepresence systems are made by such firms as Polycom, Cisco Systems, Tandberg, and LifeSize Communications.[42] Here is how a telepresence videoconferencing system works. A telepresence facility typically includes half a conference room table with chairs behind it. In place of the missing half of the conference room table is a bank of multiple, 65-inch monitors that contain video feed images. The system creates the impression of participants being in the same room with each other even if participants are thousands of miles apart.

The global economy that organizations confront has created pressure to keep training costs low while increasing performance outcomes. Owens-Illinois, a manufacturer of glass products with 140 locations worldwide and 34,000 employees, saves $500,000 per year on travel costs alone by delivering annual government mandated awareness training through telepresence.[43] Telepresence systems cost range from $60,000 to $350,000, in addition to monthly service fees but are said to usually pay for themselves in as little as nine months. Eliminating travel costs including airfare, parking, meals, hotels, and lost employee productivity can offset the cost of videoconferencing equipment in a matter of months. Hewlett-Packard estimates its own internal travel has been reduced 40 percent by increased reliance on telepresence.[44]

According to Schooley, "It's not cheap. But if we are talking about conducting high stakes meetings where reading the subtleties of body language is a requirement, then these systems are ideal." Howard Lichtman, president of the Human Productivity Lab, a consultancy specializing in visual collaboration and videoconferencing, said, "Moreover, it's what the technology isn't—an intrusion on a person-to-person meeting experience—that's key to these systems' appeal. Previous systems didn't support a true experience of meeting a person. This shows off fluid image presentation, natural flesh tones and colors, and has sound coming from the direction of the person doing the talking. These systems can help cement relationships without the wear and tear of travel."[45]

Simulators

simulators
T&D delivery system comprised of devices or programs that replicate actual job demands.

Simulators are a T&D delivery system comprised of devices or programs that replicate actual job demands. The devices range from simple paper mock-ups of mechanical devices to computerized simulations of total environments. Training-and-development specialists may use simulated sales counters, automobiles, and airplanes. A prime example is the use of simulators to train airline pilots; simulated crashes do not cost lives or deplete the firm's fleet of jets.

OBJECTIVE 7.6
Describe management development, mentoring, and coaching.

Management Development

Management development consists of all learning experiences provided by an organization resulting in upgrading skills and knowledge required in current and future managers. Although leadership is often depicted as an exciting and glamorous endeavor, there is another side; failure can quickly result in losing one's position. The risks are especially high because of today's rapid changes. This situation magnifies the importance of providing development opportunities for a firm's management group. Even in the depression of 2008/10, the demand for management development continued to be strong. Even as budgets were being slashed, managers and executives were asking for more help. A recent study found that almost 70 percent of companies believe that senior executives need to improve their leadership skills. More than half of companies reported

management development
Consists of all learning experiences provided by an organization resulting in upgrading skills and knowledge required in current and future managerial positions.

their top leaders needed to also improve their strategic planning skills. Several other skills that leaders need are encouraging teamwork, motivating people, and creativity.[46]

A firm's future lies largely in the hands of its managers. This group performs certain functions essential to the organization's survival and prosperity. Managers must make the right choices in most of their decisions; otherwise, the firm will not grow, and may even fail. Therefore, it is imperative that managers keep up with the latest developments in their respective fields and, at the same time, manage an ever-changing workforce operating in a dynamic environment. Also note that as managers reach higher levels in the organization, it is not so much their technical skills that they need, but their interpersonal skills and their business knowledge.[47]

First-line supervisors, middle managers, and executives may all participate in management development programs. These programs are available in-house, by professional organizations, and at colleges and universities. T&D specialists often plan and present in-house programs, at times using line managers. Organizations such as the Society for Human Resource Management and the American Management Association conduct conferences and seminars in a number of specialties. Numerous colleges and universities also provide management T&D programs. Colleges and universities may possess expertise not available within business organizations. In these cases, academicians and management practitioners can advantageously present T&D programs jointly.

Mentoring and Coaching

Mentoring and coaching have become important means of management development. Because the purposes of mentoring and coaching are similar in concept and the terms are often used interchangeably in the literature, they are discussed together. Coaching and mentoring activities, which may occur either formally or informally, are primarily development approaches emphasizing one-on-one learning. The concept of a mentor is believed to have its origins in Greek mythology when Odysseus set out for the Trojan War and placed the running of his palace in the hands of his trusted friend, Mentor.[48] **Mentoring** is an approach to advising, coaching, and nurturing, for creating a practical relationship to enhance individual career, personal, and professional growth and development. Mentors may be anywhere in the organization or even in another firm. For years, mentoring has repeatedly been shown to be the most important factor influencing careers.[49]

mentoring
Approach to advising, coaching, and nurturing, for creating a practical relationship to enhance individual career, personal, and professional growth and development.

Most *Fortune* 500 companies have a mentoring program. Mentors equip protégés to learn for themselves by sharing experiences, asking demanding questions, challenging decision making and expanding problem-solving skills.[50] It focuses on skills to develop protégés to perform to their highest potential, leading to career advancement. Mentors have the potential to help mentees discover their strengths and weaknesses, formulate a career path, set goals, manage stress, and balance work and personal obligations.[51] Organizations are using mentoring to prepare a successor and also to transition knowledge and skills within the organization.[52] Technology can be used to match up mentors and mentees. These relationships may be quite fluid and form and dissolve around specific issues, such as helping younger people to build their professional networks.[53]

SHRM established a mentoring program and has 3,000 members consisting of approximately 1,500 mentors and 1,561 mentees. Experienced HR professionals fill out profiles, as do potential protégés, who list the characteristics that they want in a mentor. Michael Salokas, a consultant with Anticipatory Employment in Issaquah, Washington, and an active mentor with nearly 30 years of human resource experience said, "Most of his mentees seemed to be, 'I'm in a bad situation. How can I get out of that situation?'"[54] E-mentoring is being used more often as opposed to face-to-face interaction and is yielding positive outcomes.[55]

Most believe that women can truly benefit from a female mentor who has knowledge and experience and can show them "the ropes."[56] For various reasons, mentors tend to seek out their mirror images. Since women and minorities are not equally represented at the firm's top levels, they may be left without a mentor. Studies show that women who are mentored, particularly by other women, are more likely to enhance and expand career skills, advance in their careers, receive higher salaries, and enjoy their work more.[57] Women want and need to have advantages provided by mentors to effectively use their talents and realize their potential, not only for their personal benefit but to assist their firms.[58] Joan Gosier, a business executive, said, "Having a mentor is imperative. Some people think you can just work hard. But without a sponsor, you don't know the unwritten rules that can take you to the next level."[59]

coaching
Often considered a
responsibility of the
immediate boss, who
provides assistance, much
like a mentor.

Coaching is often considered a responsibility of the immediate boss, who provides assistance, much like a mentor, but the primary focus is about performance. Coaching involves helping workers see why they have been selected to perform the task or why they have been selected for the team.[60] The coach has greater experience or expertise than the protégé and is in the position to offer wise advice. It is employee development that is customized to each individual and is therefore immediately applicable and does not require stepping away from work for extended periods of time.[61] Karen O'Boyle, president of Drake Beam Morin Inc. of North America said, "Businesses that invest in human capital by effectively leveraging executive coaching to groom talent throughout the enterprise are witnessing a significant impact on both operational excellence and the bottom line."[62] Only fifty percent of employees believe they get coaching. Of those who do get coaching, 87 percent appreciate the attention and believe their performance has improved.[63]

Reverse Mentoring

reverse mentoring
A process in which older
employees learn from
younger ones.

Reverse mentoring is a process in which older employees learn from younger ones. There are people in organizations who are approaching retirement who do not want to retire, and who have tremendous knowledge that should not go to waste. There are young people who know things others do not know and who are anxious to expand their horizons. The existence of these two diverse, but potentially mutually helpful, populations has led to reverse mentoring. At Procter & Gamble, the reverse mentoring program allows senior management to be mentored in an area such as biotechnology. It pairs scientists and top managers in order to explore the potential impact of biotechnology on P&G's customers, suppliers, and overall business.[64] Time Warner has launched a Digital Reverse Mentoring Program between their executives and technology savvy college students seeking help in social networking, iTunes, and text messaging from Generation Y people.[65] Phil McKinney, a VP at Hewlett-Packard, uses reverse mentoring by spending time with his company's college interns to understand what motivates them and how they work.[66]

Bharti Airtel, India's largest cellular services company, has begun using reverse mentoring. Bharti wants to expand the market to the country's 60 million youth who are 25 years old or younger. Sanjay Kapoor, the deputy CEO of Bharti said, "India's young people will be transforming every business. Do we understand them? Do we know what they eat, drink and wear, and how they socialize?" Bharti has assigned young guides to help its high-level managers understand the demands of a growing segment of cell phone users. At the beginning of the program, nine top executives in their 40s and 50s were teamed up with nine managers in their 20s to help them understand the shifting needs of a generation. "Through mentoring we wanted to stay contemporary in our vision and strategy for our young and modern customers," says Kapoor.[67]

OBJECTIVE 7.7
Define *orientation* and
explain implementing
training and development
programs.

orientation
Initial T&D effort for new
employees that informs
them about the company,
the job, and the work
group.

Orientation

Orientation is the initial T&D effort for new employees that inform them about the company, the job, and the work group. A good orientation program is quite important because first impressions are often the most lasting.[68] In fact, new employees usually decide whether or not to stay at a company within their first six months of employment.[69] Orientation programs give organizations an opportunity to get the relationship off to a good start. After all, considerable time, money, and effort often have gone into the selection process.

Orientation formats are unique to each firm. However, some basic purposes are listed below.

- *The Employment Situation.* At an early point in time, it is helpful for the new employee to know how his or her job fits into the firm's organizational structure and goals.
- *Company Policies and Rules.* Every job within an organization must be performed within the guidelines and constraints provided by policies and rules. Employees must understand these to ensure a smooth transition into the workplace.
- *Compensation.* Employees have a special interest in obtaining information about the reward system. Management normally provides this information during the recruitment-and-selection process and often reviews it during orientation.
- *Corporate Culture.* The firm's culture reflects, in effect, "How we do things around here." This relates to everything from the way employees dress to the way they talk. Remember our earlier discussion in Chapter 6 of the importance of *organizational fit* to an employee's success.

- *Team Membership.* A new employee's ability and willingness to work in teams was likely determined before he or she was hired. In orientation, the program may again emphasize the importance of becoming a valued member of the company team.
- *Employee Development.* An individual's employment security is increasingly becoming dependent on his or her ability to acquire needed knowledge and skills that are constantly changing. Thus, firms should keep employees aware not only of company-sponsored developmental programs, but also those available externally.
- *Socialization.* To reduce the anxiety that new employees may experience, the firm should take steps to integrate them into the informal organization. Some organizations have found that employees subjected to socialization programs, including the topics of politics and career management, perform better than those who have not undergone such training.

Although orientation is often the joint responsibility of the training staff and the line supervisor, peers often serve as excellent information agents. There are several reasons for using peers in performing this function. For one thing, they are accessible to newcomers, often more so than the boss. Peers also tend to have a high degree of empathy for new people. In addition, they have the organizational experience and technical expertise to which new employees need access. Some organizations assign a mentor or "buddy" to each new hire to work with them until they are settled in.

While orientation can occupy a new employee's first few days on the job, some firms believe that learning is more effective if spread out over time. For example, a company may deliver a program in a system of 20 one-hour sessions over a period of several weeks. Some firms are sensitive to information overload and make information available to employees on an as-needed basis. For example, a new supervisor may eventually have the responsibility for evaluating his or her subordinates. But, knowledge of how to do this may not be needed for six months. A training segment on performance evaluation may be placed on the Internet or a firm's intranet and be available when the need arises. This approach is consistent with *just-in-time training*, mentioned earlier.

Implementing Training and Development Programs

A perfectly conceived training program will fail if management cannot convince the participants of its merits. Participants must believe that the program has value and will help them achieve their personal and professional goals. A long string of successful programs certainly enhances the credibility of T&D.

Implementing T&D programs is often difficult. One reason is that managers are typically action-oriented and feel that they are too busy for T&D. According to one management development executive, "Most busy executives are too involved chopping down the proverbial tree to stop for the purpose of sharpening their axes." Another difficulty in program implementation is that qualified trainers must be available. In addition to possessing communication skills, the trainers must know the company's philosophy, its objectives, its formal and informal organization, and the goals of the training program. Training and development requires more creativity than perhaps any other human resource function.

Implementing training programs presents unique problems. Training implies change, which employees may vigorously resist. It may also be difficult to schedule the training around present work requirements. Unless the employee is new to the firm, he or she undoubtedly has specific full-time duties to perform. Another difficulty in implementing T&D programs is record keeping. It is important to maintain training records, including how well employees perform during training and later on the job. This information is important in terms of measuring program effectiveness and charting the employees' progress in the company. The problems mentioned have solutions, and the more effectively and efficiently they are resolved, the better the chances for success.

Metrics for Evaluating Training and Development

Managers should strive to develop and use T&D metrics because such information can smooth the way to budget approval and executive buy-in. Most managers agree that training does not cost, it pays, and that training is an investment, not an expense. The five-level Kirkpatrick/Phillips model for training evaluation is widely used in learning environments. The levels in this model are: (1) participant reaction, (2) level of learning achieved, (3) changes in learner behavior, (4) business results derived from training, and (5) the return-on-investment from training.[70] Benchmarking is also discussed here as a means of evaluating training and development.

Participant Reaction

Evaluating a T&D program by asking the participants' opinions of it is an approach that provides a response and suggestions for improvements, essentially a level of customer satisfaction. You cannot always rely on such responses, however. The training may have taken place in an exotic location with time for golfing and other fun activities, and the overall experience may bias some reports. Nevertheless, this approach is a good way to obtain feedback and to get it quickly and inexpensively.

Level of Learning Achieved

Some organizations administer tests to determine what the participants in a T&D program have learned. The pretest–posttest control group design is one evaluation procedure that may be used. In this procedure, both groups receive the same test before and after training. The experimental group receives the training but the control group does not. Each group receives randomly assigned trainees. Differences in pretest and posttest results between the groups are attributed to the training provided. A potential problem with this approach is controlling for variables other than training that might affect the outcome.

Changes in Learner Behavior

Tests may accurately indicate what trainees learn, but they give little insight into whether the training leads participants to change their behavior. For example, it is one thing for a manager to learn about motivational techniques but quite another matter for this person to apply the new knowledge. A manager may sit in the front row of a training session dealing with empowerment of subordinates, absorb every bit of the message, understand it totally, make a grade of 100 on a test on the material, and then return the next week to the workplace and continue behaving in the same old autocratic way. The best demonstration of value occurs when learning translates into lasting behavioral change.

Business Results Derived from Training

Still another approach to evaluating T&D programs involves determining the extent to which business results derived from training. Have training programs actually impacted performance? For instance, if the objective of an accident-prevention program is to reduce the number and severity of accidents by 15 percent, comparing accident rates before and after training provides a useful metric of success.

Return-on-Investment from Training

With the Kirkpatrick/Phillips model, the highest level of training effectiveness is return-on-investment (ROI) from training.[71] CEOs want to see value in terms that they can appreciate such as business impact, business alignment, and return-on-investment.[72] However, in some circumstances, the actual ROI number may be hard to establish because of the difficulty in isolating the effects of training. Nevertheless, in today's global competitive environment, training will not be rewarded with continued investment unless training results in improved performance which impacts the bottom line. Today, organizations can only justify investing in training that is clearly essential to business success and that actually delivers results that enable the company to compete effectively.[73]

Benchmarking

Benchmarking is the process of monitoring and measuring a firm's internal processes, such as operations, and then comparing the data with information from companies that excel in those areas. Because training programs for different firms are unique, the training measures are necessarily broad. Common benchmarking questions focus on metrics such as training costs, the ratio of training staff to employees, and whether new or more traditional delivery systems are used. Information derived from these questions probably lacks the detail to permit specific improvements of the training curricula. However, a firm may recognize, for example, that another organization is able to deliver a lot of training for relatively little cost. This information could then trigger the firm to follow up with interviews or site visits to determine whether that phenomenon represents a "best practice."

ISO 9001 Quality Assurance Training Standards

One ISO 9001 quality assurance standard states: "Employees should receive the training and have the knowledge necessary to do their jobs." In order to comply with the standard, companies must maintain written records of their employee training to show that employees have been properly trained. Think of possible questions that a compliance auditor might ask when auditing a firm. Some might be "How does your firm assess the need for the types and amounts of training and education received by all categories of employees? What percent of employees receives training annually? What is the average number of hours of training and education per employee?" Under ISO 9001, monitoring the quality of training is important.

Workforce Investment Act

The Workforce Investment Act (WIA) replaced the problem-riddled Job Training Partnership Act (JTPA) and consolidated more than 70 federal job-training programs. It provides states with the flexibility to develop streamlined systems in partnership with local governments. It provides employment and training services designed to benefit employers, dislocated workers, and low-income youth. A primary focus of WIA is to meet the needs of business for skilled workers and to satisfy the training, education, and employment needs of individuals.

One-stop service centers are at the heart of the system. These centers provide job seekers with a range of services, including career counseling, skill assessments, training, job search assistance, and referrals to programs and services, depending on need. Each year, one stops provide about 15 million workers with information about the characteristics of available jobs, strategies to land the best possible new jobs, and the benefits and costs of enrolling in training programs.[74]

Organization Development: A Strategic HR Tool

Individuals and groups receive the bulk of T&D effort. However, some firms believe that to achieve needed change, they must move the entire organization in a different direction. Efforts to achieve this are the focus of **organization development** (OD)—planned and systematic attempts to change the organization, typically to a more behavioral environment. OD education and training strategies are designed to develop a more open, productive, and compatible workplace despite differences in personalities, culture, or technologies. The organization development movement has been strongly advocated by researchers such as Chris Argyris and Warren Bennis.[75] Organization development applies to an entire system, such as a company or a plant. Organization development is a major means of achieving change in the corporate culture.[76] Remember from Chapter 1 that employer branding was discussed as a corporate culture means of affecting the image of a firm. Various factors in the firm's corporate culture affect employees' behavior on the job. To bring about desired changes in these factors and behavior, organizations must be transformed into market-driven, innovative, and adaptive systems if they are to survive and prosper in today's highly competitive global environment. This type of development is increasingly important as both work and the workforce diversify and change.

Numerous OD interventions are available to the practitioner. Interventions covered in the following section include survey feedback, a technique often combined with other interventions; quality circles; team building; and sensitivity training.

Survey Feedback

survey feedback
Process of collecting data from an organizational unit through the use of questionnaires, interviews, and objective data from other sources, such as records of productivity, turnover, and absenteeism.

The organization development method of basing change efforts on the systematic collection and measurement of subordinate's attitudes through anonymous questionnaires is **survey feedback**. It enables management teams to help organizations create working environments that lead to better working relationships, greater productivity, and increased profitability. Survey feedback generally involves the following steps:

1. Members of the organization, including top management, are involved in planning the survey.
2. All members of the organizational unit participate in the survey.
3. The OD consultant usually analyzes the data, tabulates results, suggests approaches to diagnosis, and trains participants in the feedback process.
4. Data feedback usually begins at the top level of the organization and flows downward to groups reporting at successively lower levels.
5. Feedback meetings provide an opportunity to discuss and interpret data, diagnose problem areas, and develop action plans.

Quality Circles

quality circles
Groups of employees, who voluntarily meet regularly with their supervisors to discuss problems, investigate causes, recommend solutions, and take corrective action when authorized to do so.

America received the concept of quality circles from Japan several decades ago. This version of employee involvement is still in use today, improving quality, increasing motivation, boosting productivity, and adding to the bottom line. **Quality circles** are groups of employees who voluntarily meet regularly with their supervisors to discuss their problems, investigate causes, recommend solutions, and take corrective action when authorized to do so. The team's recommendations are presented to higher-level management for review, and the approved actions are implemented with employee participation.

Toyota North America Inc. uses quality circles to develop a competitive workforce spirit. Approximately 37 percent of the auto maker's assemblers participate in Toyota's global "Quality Circles" competition that pits worker against worker in a friendly competition to develop more efficient manufacturing methods. The ultimate target is 100 percent. Quality circles are one way that Toyota sees as providing an edge over the competition. Pat D'Eramo, Toyota North America Vice President-manufacturing says "Technology is necessary to continue to improve quality and consistency. But the proliferation of technology is accelerating, so that the technology advantage diminishes with time. The real advantage is developing a workforce that can learn, execute, and most importantly, improve on the investment you've made." Toyota holds competitions twice a year to identify the best ideas.[77]

Team Building

team building
Conscious effort to develop effective work groups and cooperative skills throughout the organization.

Team building is a conscious effort to develop effective work groups and cooperative skills throughout the organization. It helps members diagnose group processes and devise solutions to problems. Effective team building can be the most efficient way to boost morale, employee retention, and company profitability. Whether it's a lieutenant leading troops into battle or executives working with their managers, the same principles apply. An important by-product of team building is that it is one of the most effective interventions for improving employee satisfaction and work-related attitudes. Individualism has deep roots in American culture. This trait has been a virtue and will continue to be an asset in our society. Now, however, there are work situations that make it imperative to subordinate individual autonomy in favor of cooperation with a group. It seems apparent that teams are clearly superior in performing many of the tasks required by organizations. The building of effective teams, therefore, has become a business necessity.

Team building uses *self-directed teams,* each composed of a small group of employees responsible for an entire work process or segment. Team members work together to improve their operation or product, to plan and control their work, and to handle day-to-day problems. They may even become involved in broader, company-wide issues, such as vendor quality, safety, and business planning. There are basically two types of team building exercises. In the first, there is an attempt to break down barriers to understanding that workers have built. In the second, participants "place their lives" in the hand of others such as falling backwards believing that the team will catch you.[78] Team building exercises run the spectrum from a paint-ball battle[79] to the raw egg exercise that Southwest Airlines creates. At Southwest Airlines, the firm divides new employees into teams and gives them a raw egg in the shell, a handful of straws, and some masking tape. Their task is, in a limited amount of time, to protect that delicate cargo from an eight-foot drop. The exercise prepares teams of employees for creative problem solving in a fast-paced environment.

In one team building exercise, participants were instructed to untangle a 60-foot yellow rope. At first participants tried to untangle the rope on an individual basis which resulted in failure. Ultimately, they began to share their ideas on how to untangle the rope, and within minutes it was untangling.[80]

Pump It Up company sells inflatable playgrounds throughout the U.S. and uses the playgrounds and childlike activities to create team building exercises. The head office worked with team-building experts for a year to devise a handbook of business related team-building activities include: "Leading the Crowd Playfully" (to break the ice) and "Tag Team Climbing" (to improve cooperation). However just bouncing around—in socks, in full view of the boss may improve team morale.[81]

The Lake Forest Graduate School of Management has developed an approach it calls "Team Banquets." An internationally recognized executive chef helped develop this program, which brought together people with different knowledge, skills, and experience to accomplish a single goal: create a banquet. The exercise is based on the discovery that some of the most effective, efficient teams in the world are in the kitchens of fine restaurants. These settings serve as models of organization, communication, and results-oriented processes. The Team Banquet brings together 25–30 employees and challenges them to prepare a gourmet banquet within two hours. Only the raw ingredients and equipment are provided. The assigned roles may put a mail clerk in charge while a group manager serves as an assistant. Each team is assigned a specific portion of the banquet preparation, from entrée to decorations and food presentation. Participants receive safety instructions but not recipes. Teams must rely on their own knowledge and creativity in devising the dishes they serve. The initial response to this approach was skepticism. However, management and participants soon discovered that the exercise provided an excellent analogy to the workplace and provided an outstanding means for developing teamwork.[82]

Sensitivity Training

sensitivity training
Organization development technique that is designed to help individuals learn how others perceive their behavior (also known as T-group training).

Sensitivity training, is a procedure designed to help individuals learn how others perceive their behavior. It is based on the assumption that a number of individuals meeting in an unstructured situation will develop working relations with each other. From this experience, they will learn much about themselves as perceived by the other group members. It differs from many traditional forms of training, which stress the learning of a predetermined set of concepts. When sensitivity training begins, there is no agenda, no leaders, no authority, and no power positions. Essentially, a vacuum exists until participants begin to talk. Through dialogue, people begin to learn about themselves and others. The trainer's purpose is to serve as a facilitator in this unstructured environment. Participants are encouraged to learn about themselves and others in the group. Some objectives of sensitivity training are to increase the participants' self-awareness and sensitivity to the behavior of others. The training also strives to develop an awareness of the processes that facilitate or inhibit group and intergroup functioning, and to increase the participants' ability to achieve effective interpersonal relationships. T-group training was once a prominent OD intervention. A central problem with sensitivity training, according to some, is that its purpose is to change individuals, not necessarily the environment in which they work. When participants attempt to use what they have learned, they often find their co-workers unwilling to accept it, or worse, what they have learned may not be appropriate for their own work situation.

A GLOBAL PERSPECTIVE

Buddies Across the Globe

Gone are the days where a new hire is given an employment handbook and other written materials about the organization and told to read it. In this fast paced global world, companies cannot slowly move a new hire into a productive mode. To pave the way for immediate success, orientation programs are changing. Organizations are supporting their new hires by pairing them with an experienced "buddy," to do the orientation (they still give them the written material).[83]

There are many advantages to using a buddy, most importantly accelerating the productivity of the new hire and lowering the fears associated with the new job. The buddy system makes the new employee feel welcomed; and since it is not the boss that is talking, the new worker feels free to ask pointed questions, even about the boss. It helps build an immediate personal connection between the new employee and the organization. Buddies should be a seasoned employee who understands the organization's practices, culture, processes and systems. It is obviously important that the buddy have a positive attitude about the organization and be a good communicator.[84]

The use of the buddy system is not confined to the United States. The Japanese have found considerable success with it. Steve Roesler, president of Roesler Consulting Group in Medford, New Jersey says, "The Japanese assign one or two people to take a new employee to lunch. The veterans tell stories about former employees at the company who have succeeded—and who haven't. It's their way of letting the new employee know what can get them promoted and what can get them zapped in the end."[85]

Many companies are using a buddy system when sending expatriates on overseas assignment. Buddies at Balfour Beatty often inform expatriates of host-office norms and politics, invite them into their homes, introduce them to friends and networks, and help bolster their credibility in the office. They show expatriates where to receive emergency medical assistance, school their children, buy groceries, and eat out. Balfour Beatty, KPMG International, and some other global companies invest in buddy systems to alleviate the stress new expatriates and their families normally endure, to reduce the time it takes for expatriates to operate at peak productivity, and to help lessen the cost of expatriate programs.[86]

"When you go to a cocktail party for the first time in a new country, you can post yourself in a corner and observe how people behave. You can watch how they greet each other, whether they eat a lot or not at all, and other facets of their behavior," notes Dominique J. Herrmann, executive director of global mobility at KPMG International in Woodcliff Lake, New Jersey. "You don't have that same opportunity when you attend a business meeting for the first time in a new country."[87]

In moving to Colombia, Noel Kreicker, founder of IOR Global Services in Chicago, personally experienced the difficulties expatriates face. When Kreicker, her husband, and their three children arrived in the country, her husband's new colleagues said they were too busy to help the newly relocated family get settled. So the Kreickers had to find, on their own, a school for their son. Fortunately, a parent at the school helped them find housing. That was not the only difficulty to overcome. Their luggage sat on a rain-soaked airport tarmac for three weeks because no one in the host office had informed them that it was customary to give local customs officials a *gift* to have the luggage located and delivered to their hotel. "People can lose it when they're waiting in long lines for their taxpayer ID number or trying to get their car registered in assignment locations" warns Timothy Dwyer, national director for international HR advisory services at KPMG LLP in New York. "That downtime takes them away from being productive in the office."[88]

Summary

1. *Define training and development.* Training is designed to permit learners to acquire knowledge and skills needed for their present jobs. Development involves learning that goes beyond today's job.

2. *Explain factors influencing T&D.* There are numerous factors that both impact and are impacted by T&D including top management support, technological advances, world complexity, lifetime learning, learning styles, and other human resource functions.

3. *Describe the T&D process.* First, an organization must determine its specific training needs. Then specific objectives need to be established. After setting the T&D objectives, management can determine the appropriate methods and the delivery system to be used. Naturally, management must continuously evaluate T&D

to ensure its value in achieving organizational objectives.

4. *Describe the various T&D methods.* Training and development methods include instructor-led, e-learning, case study, behavior modeling, role-playing, business games, in-basket training, on-the-job training, internships, and apprenticeship training.

5. *Describe training and development delivery systems.* Delivery systems include corporate universities, colleges and universities, community colleges, online higher education, vestibule system, video media, and simulators.

6. *Describe management development, mentoring, and coaching.* Management development consists of all learning experiences provided by an organization for the purpose of providing and upgrading skills and knowledge required in current and future managerial positions. Mentoring is an approach to advising, coaching, and nurturing, for creating a practical relationship to enhance individual career, personal, and professional growth and development. Coaching, often considered a responsibility of the immediate boss, provides assistance much like a mentor.

7. *Define orientation and explain implementing training and development programs.* Orientation is the guided adjustment of new employees to the company, the job, and the work group.

Implementing T&D programs is often difficult. One reason is that managers are typically action-oriented and feel that they are too busy for T&D. Another difficulty in program implementation is that qualified trainers must be available. Training and development requires more creativity than perhaps any other human resource function.

8. *Explain the metrics for evaluating training and development.* The five-level Kirkpatrick/Phillips model for training evaluation is widely used in learning environments. The levels in this model are: (1) participant reaction, (2) level of learning achieved, (3) changes in learner behavior, (4) business results derived from training, and (5) the return-on-investment from training. Benchmarking is also discussed here as a means of evaluating training and development.

9. *Describe the Workforce Investment Act.* The Workforce Investment Act (WIA) consolidated more than 70 federal job-training programs. It provides states with the flexibility to develop streamlined systems in partnership with local governments.

10. *Define organization development (OD) and describe various OD techniques.* Organization development is planned and systematic attempts to change the organization, typically to a more behavioral environment. OD techniques include survey feedback, a technique often combined with other interventions, quality circles, team building, and sensitivity training.

Key Terms

training and development (T&D) 200
training 200
development 200
learning organization 200
just-in-time training (on-demand training) 202
virtual reality 205
case study 205
behavior modeling 205
role-playing 206

business games 206
in-basket training 206
on-the-job training (OJT) 206
apprenticeship training 207
corporate university 207
online higher education 208
vestibule system 208
e-learning 204
simulators 209
management development 209

mentoring 210
coaching 211
reverse mentoring 211
orientation 211
benchmarking 214
organization development (OD) 214
survey feedback 215
quality circles 215
team building 215
sensitivity training 216

Questions for Review

1. Define *training* and *development.*
2. What is a learning organization?
3. What are some factors that influence T&D?
4. What are the steps in the T&D process?
5. What are the various training and development methods? Briefly describe each.
6. What are the various training and development delivery systems? Briefly describe each.

7. Define *management development.* Why is it important?
8. Distinguish between mentoring and coaching. What is reverse mentoring?
9. Define *orientation,* and explain the purposes of orientation.
10. What are some metrics for evaluating training and development?

11. What is the Workforce Investment Act?

12. Define each of the following:
   a. organization development
   b. survey feedback
   c. quality circles
   d. sensitivity training
   e. team building

HRM INCIDENT **1**

Training at Keller-Globe

Lou McGowen was worried as she approached the training director's office. She supervises six punch press operators at Keller-Globe, a maker of sheet metal parts for the industrial refrigeration industry. She had just learned that her punch presses would soon be replaced with a continuous-feed system that would double the speed of operations. She was thinking about how the workers might feel about the new system when the training director, Bill Taylor, opened the door and said, "Come on in, Lou. I've been looking forward to seeing you."

After a few pleasantries, Lou told Bill of her concerns. "The operators really know their jobs now. But this continuous-feed system is a whole new ball game. I'm concerned, too, about how the workers will feel about it. The new presses are going to run faster. They may think that their job is going to be harder."

Bill replied, "After talking with the plant engineer and the production manager, I made a tentative training schedule that might make you feel a little better. I think we first have to let the workers know why this change is necessary. You know that both of our competitors changed to this new system last year. After that, we will teach your people to operate the new presses."

"Who's going to do the teaching?" Lou asked. "I haven't even seen the new system."

"Well, Lou," said Bill, "the manufacturer has arranged for you to visit a plant with a similar system. They'll also ship one of the punch presses in early so you and your workers can learn to operate it."

"Will the factory give us any other training help?" Lou asked.

"Yes, I have asked them to send a trainer down as soon as the first press is set up. He will conduct some classroom sessions and then work with your people on the new machine."

After further discussion about details, Lou thanked Bill and headed back to the production department. She was confident that the new presses would be a real benefit to her section and that her workers could easily learn the skills required.

Questions

1. Evaluate Keller-Globe's approach to training.

HRM INCIDENT **2**

Career versus Job Security?

J. D. Wallace, III, is an Area Project Engineer with Bechtel Engineering, headquartered in Houston, Texas. He possesses a Six Sigma Black Belt earned after an intensive selection and training program at Bechtel. In the section below he describes his assessment of career development.

"The Petroleum and Chemical industrial is a very volatile industry. Companies in this industry cycle from having 5 or 6 projects in-house to as few as 1 or 2. Therefore, it is important that an individual maintains a competitive edge in order to stay employed and advance your career. New technologies are a consistent part of our work life. When I started my career all design drawings were done by hand. In today's work place all design drawing are created on computers. Computers are more efficient and provide multiple means of defect detection. The result is less staff and short project schedule. It is important to continually learn your industries new technology. When the industry shifted to computers, many of the 20 years plus employees chose not to embrace the change. In a relatively short time span of five years, they were no longer in the industry. Individuals that keep up with the new technologies increase their market valve."

"Most companies will provide limited training for new software. It has been my experience that 70 percent of the people enrolled in the first training class are the same people that were in the last training. It is not surprising that they are also ranked in the top 10 percent. Community colleges and local universities also provide training. These classes are often given at night and on weekends. They are often taught by people that work in the industry. I once took micro-station training at the office and received the basic training. Although I had the basics I was not able to fully utilize the software. I enrolled in an advanced micro-station class at the local university. After the training I had more knowledge of the software than any other person at my company. I was also offered a position in the instructors company. It is common for competitive firms to recruit individuals that are known to have good work ethics and strong technical abilities within the industry. It is also common for them to receive increases in salary of 15–20 percent. Your knowledge is your portfolio within your current work place or within the industry."

Questions

1. Is J. D. concerned more with job security or career security? Discuss.

2. Do you agree with J. D.'s statement that "Your knowledge is your portfolio within your current work place or within the industry?" Discuss.

Notes

1. Maggie Moore, "Spotlight on Executive Onboarding," *PA Times* 31 (October 2008): 5.
2. Joseph Daniel McCool, "'On boarding:' Crucial Feedback for *Executive* Hires," *BusinessWeek Online* (December 3, 2008): 14.
3. Rita L. Fritz, "The First 100 Days: How to Accelerate the Learning Curve for Executives," *Healthcare Executive* 22 (November/December 2007): 8–14.
4. Kelley M. Butler, "Getting Employees to Stay on Board Instead of Jumping Ship," *Employee Benefit News* 22 (January 2008): 13–14.
5. "How to Take The Reins at Top Speed," *BusinessWeek Online* (September 14, 2007): 9.
6. McCool, "'On boarding:' Crucial Feedback for Executive Hires."
7. David A. Garvin, Amy C. Edmondson, and Gino Francesca, "Is Yours a Learning Organization?" *Harvard Business Review* 86 (March 2008): 109–116.
8. Rich Cordivari, "From Training Company to Learning Organization," *T+D* 64 (January 2010): 60–63.
9. Mark Simon, "E-learning Know How," *T+D* 63 (January 2009): 34–39.
10. Katz Jonathan, "Training Doesn't Have to Be a Budget Buster," *Industry Week* 258 (February 2009): 17.
11. Charlotte Huff, "Training Adapts to the Downturn," *Workforce Management* 88 (March 16, 2009): 20–23.
12. Garry Kranz, "Study: Training More Targeted During Downturn," *Workforce Management* 88 (November 16, 2009): 6.
13. Ted Hoff, "Learning in the 21st Century: A Brave New World," *Chief Learning Officer* 87 (April 2008): 46–49.
14. Tom Camarda, "Lifetime Learning: A Necessity, Not an Option," *Manufacturing Today* 10 (Winter 2010): 26–27.

15. Natalia Muller, "Seven Cures to Skipping the Needs Assessment," *T+D* 64 (March 2010): 32–34.
16. Nanette Miner and Jennifer Hofmann, "More Than a Merger," *T+D* 63 January 2009): 30–33.
17. Alyson Rossette, "Metrics Matter," *T+D* 64 (March 2010): 64–69.
18. Pat Galagan, "Disappearing Act: The Vanishing Corporate Classroom," *T+D* 64 (March 2010): 29–31.
19. "Online Courses Offer More Flexible Training Options," *Instrumentation Newsletter* 20 (2008 4th Quarter): 23.
20. http://www.blackboard.com/Company/What-We-Do.aspx , January 12, 2010.
21. Marcia Passos Duffy, "One-on-One or One-Online?" *Restaurants & Institutions* 118 (May 2008): 48–50.
22. Gail Dutton, "Tech Check," *Training* 46 (January 2009): 24–26.
23. Jessica Marquez, "Faced with High Turnover, Retailers Boot Up e-Learning Programs for Quick Training," *Workforce Management* 84 (August 2005): 74–75.
24. Pat Galagan, "Twitter As a Learning Tool. Really," *T+D* 63 (March 2009): 28–31.
25. Jim Olsztynskin, "A Good Time To Invest In Training," *Supply House Times* 51 (January 2009): 144.
26. Lindsey Gerdes, "Internships: The Best Places to Start," *BusinessWeek Online* (November 30, 2007): 8.
27. James Warren, "Develop a Strategy for Recruiting Future Employees," *Quality* 48 (October 2009): 40–43.
28. Peter B. Alpern, "Need Skilled Workers? Try Growing Your Own," *American Machinist* 153 (May 2009): 40–43.
29. "Internships, Apprenticeships Are Win-Win," *Welding Magazine* 81 (August 2008): 11–12.
30. Alpern, "Need Skilled Workers? Try Growing Your Own."
31. Holly Dolezalek, "University 2.0," *Training* 44 (September 2007): 22–24.

32. Kathryn Tyler, "The Online Universe of Human Resource Studies," *HRMagazine* 55 (May 2010): 64–72.

33. Anne Cumming Rice, "Online Changes to Higher Education," *Northern Colorado Business Report* 15 (November 20, 2009): 9/20.

34. Alysa Teichman, "MBA Learning Go the Distance," *BusinessWeek Online* (December 12, 2008): 7.

35. Rice, "Online Changes to Higher Education."

36. Wayne Anderson, "Online Degrees: Are They Right for You?" *Certification Magazine* 10 (June 2008): 18–23.

37. Ethan Edwards, "Designing Asynchronous E-Learning," *T+D* 63 (February 2009): 84–85.

38. Marci Powell. "Live and Direct," *T+D* 63 (February 2009): 27–29.

39. Scot Case, "Look Them in the Eye," *Government Procurement* 17 (August/September 2009): 26–28.

40. Lauren Bielski, "Telepresence: Costly, but Very Cool," *ABA Banking Journal* 100 (April 2008): 50–52.

41. Michelle Conlin, "The Waning Days of the Road Warrior," *BusinessWeek* (June 2, 2008): 65–66.

42. "Room With a View," *Entrepreneur* 37 (November 2009): 40.

43. Powell, "Live and Direct."

44. Case, "Look Them in the Eye."

45. Bielski, "Telepresence: Costly, but Very Cool."

46. Aparna Nancherla, "C-Level Boot Camp," *T+D* 64 (January 2010): 24.

47. "Tim" Preston Brown, "Having Their Backs: Improving Managers' Skills in Developing Others," *T+D* 64 (April 2010): 60–64.

48. Kristy Allen, "Mentoring Builds a Stronger Profession," *Charter* 81 (February 2010): 54.

49. Louis J. *Zachary and Lory A. Fischler*, "Those Who Lead, Mentor," *T+D* 64 (March 2010): 52–57.

50. David P. Pease, "Making Mentoring Memorable," *HRMagazine* (May 2009): 63–65.

51. Beth N. Carvin, "The Great Mentor Match," *T+D* 63 (January 2009): 46–50.

52. Share Baby Boomers' Knowledge With Inter-generational Mentoring," *HR Focus* 87 (February 2010): 7–13.

53. Majorie Derven, "Social Networking: A Force for Development?" *T+D* 63 (July 2009): 58–63.

54. Aleita Johnson, "Find a Mentor—or Protégé" *HRMagazine* 54 (May 2009): 56.

55. "Mentoring Goes Online," *CU360* 35 (October 19, 2009): 6–8.

56. Nancy O'Reilly, "Women Helping Women: How Mentoring Can Help Your Business," *Business Credit* 110 (March 2008): 56–57.

57. Ibid.

58. Michael Laff, "The Guiding Hand: Mentoring Women," *T+D* 63 (September 2009): 32–35.

59. Donna N. Owens, "Virtual Mentoring," *HRMagazine* 51 (March 2006): 105–107.

60. Kevin J. Sensenig "Human Potential Untangled," *T+D* 63 (April 2009): 54–57.

61. Sophie Oberstein, "Capitalizing on Coaching Challenges," *T+D* 64 (February 2010): 54–57.

62. Pete Wolfinger, "Executive Coaching: On the Rise," *HRMagazine* 53 (December 2008): 39.

63. Les Wallace and Jim Trinka, "Leadership and Employee Engagement," Public Management 91 (June 2009): 10–13.

64. Trish Rintels, "Career Stalled? Get it in Gear with Reverse Mentoring," *Selling* (March 2005): 6.

65. Christian Hamaker, "An Example in Their Youth," *Rural Telecom* 28 (September/October 2009): 9.

66. Richard R. *Reilly* and Karen Sobel Lojeski, "Leading the Dispersed Workforce," *Mechanical Engineering* 131 (November 2009): 30–34.

67. Saritha Rai, "Young at Heart," *Forbes Asia* 5 (June, 8 2009): 22–25.

68. Donald L. *Caruth*, Gail D. Caruth, and Stephanie S. Pane Haden, "Getting Off to a Good Start," *Industrial Management* 52 (March 2010): 12–15.

69. Katharine Giacalone, "Making Employees Successful in Any Economy," *T+D* 63 (Jun2009): 37–39.

70. Laleh Patel, "Overcoming Barriers and Valuing Evaluation," *T+D* 64 (February 2010): 62–63.

71. "You Must Measure With a Purpose," *Training & Coaching Today* (January 2009): 16.

72. Jack J. Phillips and Patti P. Phillips, "Confronting CEO Expectations about the Value of Learning," *T+D* 64 (January 2010): 52–57.

73. Cal *Wick*, Roy *Pollock*, and Andy*Jefferson*, "The New Finish Line for Learning," *T+D* 63 (July 2009): 64–69.

74. Louis S. Jacobson, "Strengthening One-Stop Career Centers: Helping More Unemployed Workers Find Jobs and Build Skills," *Hamilton Project: Discussion Papers* (2009): 2/35.

75. R. Wayne Mondy and Shane R. Premeaux *Management: Concepts, Practices, and Skills,* 7th ed. (Englewood Cliffs, NJ, Prentice Hall, 1995): 497.

76. "Organization Development: A Strategic HR Tool," *HRMagazine* 52 (September 2007): Special section, 1–9.

77. Byron Pope, "Toyota Says Quality Circles Still Paying Dividends," *Ward's Auto World* 44 (June 2008): 20.

78. Mike Donlin, "Take One for the Team," *Corporate Meetings & Incentives* 28 (August 2009): 26.

79. "Team Building Treachery," *Accountancy* 143 (March 2009): 20.

80. René Street, "We Move Forward as a Team*," Women in Business* 61 (December 2009/January 2010): 6.

81. Belinda Luscombe, "Getting Jumpy at Work," 173 (May 25, 2009): 30.

82. Howard Prager, "Cooking up Effective Team Building," *Training & Development* 53 (December 1999): 14–15.

83. "Give a New Hire a Fast Start," *Managing People at Work* (October 2009): 1.

84. Shari Lau, Vicki Neal, and Amy Maingault, "Economic Trends, Buddy Systems, Receiving Criticism," *HRMagazine* 54 (March 2009): 26–27.

85. "Give a New Hire a Fast Start."

86. Eric Krell, "Budding Relationships," *HRMagazine* 50 (June 2005): 114–118.

87. Ibid.

88. Ibid.

7

Career Planning and Development

Job Security versus Career Security

Not too long ago students went to the library, pulled journals and books from the shelves, copied pertinent pages, and wrote term papers. Today, you can sit anywhere with your notebook computer and access libraries through the Internet. Automation has affected what jobs are in demand. Grocery stores do not need as many cashiers, because checkout stands are being automated. FedEx and UPS do not need as many workers, because machines will do more sorting. Not as many loaders will be needed because machines determine which packages belong on which trucks. Wireless and mobile devices impact some of the hottest jobs today.

Jobs now identified for extinction were historically very secure careers. In the past, most people remained with one company and career for the majority of their adult years. The term **job security** implies security in one job, often with one company. Historically, this type of security depended on an employee doing a good job and keeping out of trouble. But, for most workers today, this assumption is not valid. There is no such thing as job security these days even if you have been devoted to your job for many years.[1] Remember from Chapter 1, I said that today's employees will work for approximately nine companies during their careers and that on average, individuals will change careers (not merely "jobs") three times in their life. In fact, the Department of Labor estimates that individuals will remain with a firm an average of 3.6 years before changing jobs.[2] The old social contract between employers and employees no longer exists. The country has largely become a free-agent nation, in which employees are no more loyal to companies than companies are to employees. The decision to leave or stay is based not only on an employee's career prospects in the present company, but also on how it might prepare him or her to move on elsewhere. Therefore, the way people approached their careers in the past is history.

Career security is distinctly different from job security; it requires developing marketable skills and expertise that help ensure employment within a range of careers. Career security results from the ability to perform within a broad range of careers well enough to be marketable in more than one job and to more than one organization. Career security is different from job security in that job security implies security in one job, often with one company. With career security, workers are offered opportunities to improve their skills, and thus their employability in an ever-changing work environment. Under this so-called **employability doctrine**, employees owe the company their commitment while employed and the company owes its workers the opportunity to learn new skills, but that is as far as the commitment goes. Under the employability doctrine, loyalty in either direction is not expected.

The distinction among job and career security often gets confusing when the economy declines as with the recession of 2008/10. Anxiety about keeping your job or obtaining a job may significantly impact the attitudes and motives of post-recession employees. During a recession, workers may become cautious and less likely to leave their current organizations. The stress experienced during the downturn may continue to influence employee behaviors for many years. Or, it may have the opposite effect since job seekers become acclimated to constant change and few guarantees. They may be more open to a variety of opportunities. For example, many young U.S. college graduates have begun to look to emerging economies such as India and China as good places to start their careers.[3] Others are accepting jobs they had not envisioned for themselves.

job security
Implies security in one job, often with one company.

career security
Requires developing marketable skills and expertise that help ensure employment within a range of careers.

employability doctrine
Employees owe the company their commitment while employed and the company owes its workers the opportunity to learn new skills, but that is as far as the commitment goes.

Career and Career Planning Defined

career
General course that a person chooses to pursue throughout his or her working life.

A **career** is a general course that a person chooses to pursue throughout his or her working life. Historically, a *career* was a sequence of work-related positions an individual occupied during a lifetime, although not always with the same company. However, today there are few relatively static jobs. **Career planning** is an ongoing process whereby *an individual* sets career goals and identifies the means to achieve them. Individuals in today's job market must truly manage their careers.[4] Career planning should not concentrate only on advancement opportunities, since the present work environment has reduced many of these opportunities.[5] At some point, career planning should focus on achieving successes that do not necessarily entail promotions.

career planning
Ongoing process whereby an individual sets career goals and identifies the means to achieve them.

Career Planning

As Alice said in *Through the Looking Glass,* "If you don't know where you're going, any road will get you there." Such is the case with career planning. Career planning must now accommodate a number of objectives and enable us to prepare for each on a contingency basis. It will need updating to accommodate changes in our own interests as well as in the work environment. Historically, it was thought that career planning was logical, linear, and indeed, planned. Penda Aiken, founder and owner of the Brooklyn, New York–based human resources firm that bears her name said, "Think of your new job as an assignment during which you're being paid to learn a new task and increase your experience level in case you must leave your job."[6] Because of the many changes that are occurring, career planning is essential for survival for individuals and organizations. Individuals should have a strategy or plan for unexpected career events that begins while they are still employed.[7]

Career Planning: Self-Assessment

Through career planning, a person continuously evaluates his or her abilities and interests, considers alternative career opportunities, establishes career goals, and plans practical developmental activities. A career plan lets you know where you are and where you are going. At times career planning occurs not at the beginning of a person's career but may be planning for a second career or even third career.[8] In any event, career planning must begin with self-understanding or self-assessment. Paul Armstrong, client partner at HR consultancy Penna, advises, "thinking about yourself as a product and listing your selling points, what you like doing and what you want to do less of. It is also important to be aware of your weaknesses but don't underestimate your skills and talents."[9] Then, the person is in a position to establish realistic goals and determine what to do to achieve these goals. This action also lets the person know whether his or her goals are realistic.

self-assessment
Process of learning about oneself.

Self-assessment is the process of learning about oneself.[10] Anything that could affect one's performance in a future job should be considered. It is one of the first things that a person should do in planning a career. A self-assessment can help a person target career choices and goals.[11] Realistic self-assessment may help a person avoid mistakes that could affect his or her entire career progression. Take time to study your past successes and think why they occurred.[12] A thorough self-assessment will go a long way toward helping match an individual's specific qualities and goals with the right job or profession. Remember, you cannot get what you want until you know what you want. Deborah Warner, founder of Career Development Partners, said, "Applicants should pay attention to the skills they want to use and the ones they no longer want to use. When an individual has to frequently use skills [he doesn't] enjoy using, that can lead to job dissatisfaction and burnout."[13] For many people, being fired causes them to take stock of themselves for the first time and to analyze their strengths and weaknesses.[14]

The self-assessment is not something that is done once and forgotten. It is something that spans a career and into retirement. The self-assessment may show that you do not want to retire at 65. Some enjoy working well past what traditionally has been thought of as the retirement age. As a 95 year old former mentor said, "work is what keeps her alive and going, and that everyone she knows who retired died young, and certainly much younger than her."[15]

Some useful tools include a strength/weakness balance sheet and a likes and dislikes survey. However, any reasonable approach that assists self-understanding is helpful.

strength/weakness balance sheet
A self-evaluation procedure, developed originally by Benjamin Franklin, that assists people in becoming aware of their strengths and weaknesses.

STRENGTH/WEAKNESS BALANCE SHEET   A self-evaluation procedure, developed originally by Benjamin Franklin that assists people in becoming aware of their strengths and weaknesses is the **strength/weakness balance sheet**. Employees who understand their strengths can use them to maximum advantage. By recognizing their weaknesses, they are in a better position to overcome them. This statement sums up that attitude; "If you have a weakness, understand it and make it work for you as a strength; if you have a strength, do not abuse it to the point at which it becomes a weakness."

To use a strength/weakness balance sheet, the individual lists strengths and weaknesses as he or she perceives them. This is quite important, because believing, for example, that a weakness exists even when it does not can equate to a real weakness. Thus, if you believe that you make a poor first impression when meeting someone, you will probably make a poor impression. The perception of a weakness often becomes a self-fulfilling prophecy.

The mechanics for preparing the balance sheet are quite simple. To begin, draw a line down the middle of a sheet of paper. Label the left side *Strengths* and the right side *Weaknesses*. Record all perceived strengths and weaknesses. You may find it difficult to write about yourself. Remember, however, that no one else need see the results. The primary consideration is complete honesty.

Table A7.1 shows an example of a strength/weakness balance sheet. Obviously, Wayne (the person who wrote the sheet) did a lot of soul-searching in making these evaluations. Typically, a person's weaknesses will outnumber strengths after the first few attempts. However, as the individual repeats the process, some items that first appeared to be weaknesses may eventually be seen as strengths and should then be moved from one column to the other. A person should devote sufficient time to the project to obtain a fairly clear understanding of his or her strengths and weaknesses. Typically, the process should take a minimum of one week. The balance sheet will not provide all the answers regarding a person's strengths and weaknesses, but many people have gained a better understanding of themselves by completing it. Analyzing oneself should not

Table A7.1   Strength/Weakness Balance Sheet

Strengths	Weaknesses
Work well with people.	Get very close to few people.
Like to be given a task and get it done in my own way.	Do not like constant supervision.
Good manager of people.	Am extremely high-strung.
Hard worker.	Often say things without realizing consequences.
Lead by example.	Cannot stand to look busy when there is no work to be done.
People respect me as being fair and impartial.	Cannot stand to be inactive. Must be on the go constantly.
Tremendous amount of energy.	
Function well in an active environment.	Cannot stand to sit at a desk all the time.
Relatively open-minded.	Basically a rebel at heart but have portrayed myself as just the opposite. My conservatism has gotten me jobs that I emotionally did not want.
Feel comfortable in dealing with high-level businesspersons.	
Like to play politics. (This may be a weakness.)	
Get the job done when it is defined.	Am sometimes nervous in an unfamiliar environment.
Excellent at organizing other people's time.	
Can get the most out of people who are working for me.	Make very few true friends.
Have an outgoing personality—not shy.	Not a conformist but appear to be.
Take care of those who take care of me. (This could be a weakness).	Interest level hits peaks and valleys.
	Many people look on me as being unstable. Perhaps I am. Believe not.
Have a great amount of empathy.	Divorced.
Work extremely well through other people.	Not a tremendous planner for short range.
	Long-range planning is better.
	Impatient—want to have things happen fast.
	Do not like details.
	Do not work well in an environment where I am the only party involved.

Source: Wayne Sanders

be just a one-time event. People change, and every few years the process should again be undertaken. You can determine means to react to your findings and, perhaps, overcome a weakness after you have conducted the self-assessment.

likes and dislikes survey
Procedure that helps individuals recognize restrictions they place on themselves.

LIKES AND DISLIKES SURVEY An individual should also consider likes and dislikes as part of a self-assessment. A **likes and dislikes survey** assists individuals in recognizing restrictions they place on themselves. Connecticut-based career counselor Julie Jansen said, "It's important in identifying what you want to do, what your skills are, and what you don't—and do—like about your current occupation."[16] You are looking for qualities you want in a job and attributes of a job you do not want. For instance, some people are not willing to live in certain parts of the country, and such feelings should be noted as a constraint. Some positions require a person to spend a considerable amount of time traveling. Thus, an estimate of the amount of time a person is willing to travel would also be helpful. Recognition of such self-imposed restrictions may reduce future career problems. Another limitation is the type of firm an individual will consider working for.

The size of the firm might also be important. Some like a major organization whose products or services are well known; others prefer a smaller organization, believing that the opportunities for advancement may be greater or that the environment is better suited to their tastes. All factors that could affect an individual's work performance should be listed in the likes and dislikes survey. An example of this type of survey is shown in Table A7.2

A self-assessment such as this helps a person understand his or her basic motives, and sets the stage for pursuing a career or seeking further technical competence. People who know themselves can more easily make the decisions necessary for successful career planning. Many people get sidetracked because they choose careers based on haphazard plans or the wishes of others, rather than on what they believe to be best for them.

Getting to know yourself is not a singular event. As individuals progress through life, priorities change. Individuals may think that they know themselves quite well at one stage of life and later begin to see themselves quite differently. Therefore, the self-assessment should be viewed as a continuous process. Career-minded individuals must heed the Red Queen's admonition to Alice: "It takes all the running you can do, to keep in the same place."[17] This admonition is very true in today's work environment.

Using the Web for Self-Assessment Assistance

The Internet has valuable information to assist in developing a self-assessment. Some sites are free and others charge a modest fee. Some Web sites that might be valuable as you conduct your self-assessment include:

- *CareerMaze:* An assessment of vocational interests and weaknesses, interests, and capabilities for every job seeker at every level is provided. There is a charge of $19.95 for the Career Maze report.[18]
- *Career-intelligence:* A by-women, for-women career resource with a philosophy of Stretch, Grow, Achieve. Its mission is to help women achieve personal and professional satisfaction by providing the information, support, and tools you need to succeed in today's competitive economy.[19]

Table A7.2   Likes and Dislikes Survey

Likes	Dislikes
Like to travel.	Do not want to work for a large firm.
Would like to live in the East.	Will not work in a large city.
Enjoy being my own boss.	Do not like to work behind a desk all day.
Would like to live in a medium-sized city.	Do not like to wear suits all the time.
	Enjoy watching football and baseball.
	Enjoy playing racquetball.

Source: Wayne Sanders.

- *Holland's Theory of Career Choice:* The Career Key is based on the theory that people like to be around others who have similar personalities. In choosing a career, it means that people choose jobs where they can be around other people who are like them. The test takes about 15 minutes to complete and costs $9.95.[20]
- *Princeton Review Career:* For a free career assessment go to "Learn more about your personal interest and style" to identify potential careers.[21]

Using the Web for Career-Planning Assistance

The Web can often be an excellent tool for assisting you in planning your career. Listed below is some advice on how the Web can assist you.

- There is a large amount of free information available on the Web that should prove helpful. Virtually all of the major job boards provide tips for securing the position you desire.
- The Web can be used to develop and maintain a professional network. It is much easier and more convenient to keep in touch with other professionals through e-mail, texting, LinkedIn, Twitter, and Facebook. This is important, since the number-one way people find a job is through some kind of networking or referral. Individuals whom you have met at conferences or business meetings may provide useful assistance in a job search. A network should be maintained with these individuals even though you are satisfied with your present job.
- The Web should be used to investigate specific companies before seeking employment or going for an interview. For instance, with WetFeet.com, a job seeker can research companies, careers, and industries.

Career Paths and Career Development

career path
A flexible line of movement through which a person may travel during their work life.

A **career path** is a flexible line of movement through which a person may travel during their work life. Following an established career path, the employee can undertake career development with the firm's assistance. From a worker's perspective, following a career path may involve weaving from company to company and from position to position as he or she obtains greater knowledge and experience.

career development
Formal approach used by the organization to ensure that people with the proper qualifications and experiences are available when needed.

Career development is a formal approach used by the organization to ensure that people with the proper qualifications and experiences are available when needed. Beverly Kaye, coauthor of *Love 'Em or Lose 'Em: Getting Good People to Stay,* studied the top 20 reasons employees remain with their company and discovered that career-development opportunities was number one on the list. It was even more important than receiving greater pay.[22] With career development, the organization identifies paths and activities for individual employees as they develop.[23]

Career planning rests with the employee. However, career development must closely parallel individual career planning if a firm is to retain its best and brightest workers. Employees must see that the firm's career development effort is directed toward furthering their specific career objectives. Companies must therefore help their employees obtain their career objectives and, most notably, career security. They must provide them with opportunities to learn and do different things. Performing the same or a similar task over and over provides little development. Through effective career development, a pool of men and women can be developed who can thrive in any number of organizational structures in the future.

Properly designed and implemented career development programs can aid in recruiting and hiring and ensure that the best employees are in the pipeline for future leadership positions.[24] Formal career development is important to maintain a motivated and committed workforce. In fact, Generation Y workers tend to favor personalized career guidance as opposed to big salaries and retirement packages.[25] Further, high-potential employees are more likely to remain with organizations that are willing to invest in their development.[26]

Career development should begin with a person's job placement and initial orientation. Management then observes the employee's job performance and compares it to job standards. At this stage, strengths and weaknesses will be noted, enabling management to assist the employee in making a tentative career decision. Naturally, this decision can be altered later as the process continues. This tentative career decision is based on a number of factors, including personal needs, abilities, and aspirations, and the organization's needs. Management can then schedule development programs that relate to the employee's specific needs.

Career development programs are expected to achieve one or more of the following objectives:

- *Effective development of available talent.* Individuals are more likely to be committed to career development that is part of a specific career plan. This way, they can better understand the purpose of development. Career development consistently ranks high on employees' *want lists,* and they can often be a less expensive option than pay raises and bonuses.
- *Self-appraisal opportunities for employees considering new or nontraditional career paths.* Some excellent workers do not view traditional upward mobility as a career option, since firms today have fewer promotion options available. Other workers see themselves in dead-end jobs and seek relief. Rather than lose these workers, a firm can offer career planning to help them identify new and different career paths.
- *Development of career paths that cut across divisions and geographic locations.* The development should not be limited to a narrow spectrum of one part of a company.
- *A demonstration of a tangible commitment to developing a diverse work environment.* Individuals who recognize a company as desiring a diverse environment often have greater recruiting and retention opportunities.
- *Satisfaction of employees' specific development needs.* Individuals who see their personal development needs being met tend to be more satisfied with their jobs and the organization. They tend to remain with the organization.
- *Improvement of performance.* The job itself is the most important influence on career development. Each job can provide different challenges and experiences.
- *Increased employee loyalty and motivation, leading to decreased turnover.* Individuals who believe that the firm is interested in their career planning are more likely to remain with the organization.
- *A method of determining training and development needs.* If a person desires a certain career path and does not currently have the proper qualifications, this identifies a training and development need.

Career Development Methods

There are numerous methods for career development. Some currently used methods, most of which are used in various combinations, are discussed next.

Manager/Employee Self-Service

We discussed manager and employee self-service in Chapter 4. Many companies are providing managers with the online ability to assist employees in planning their career paths and developing required competencies. Through online employee self-service, employees are provided with the ability to update performance goals online and to enroll in training courses.

Discussions with Knowledgeable Individuals

In a formal discussion, the superior and subordinate employees may jointly agree on what career development activities are best. The resources made available to achieve these objectives may also include developmental programs. In some organizations, human resource professionals are the focal point for providing assistance on the topic. In other instances, psychologists and guidance counselors provide this service. In an academic setting, colleges and universities often provide career planning and development information to students. Students often go to their professors for career advice.

Company Material

Some firms provide material specifically developed to assist in career development. Such material is tailored to the firm's special needs. In addition, job descriptions provide valuable insight for individuals to personally determine whether a match exists between their strengths and weaknesses and specific positions.

Performance-Appraisal System

The firm's performance appraisal system can also be a valuable tool in career development. Discussing an employee's strengths and weaknesses with his or her supervisor can uncover developmental needs. If overcoming a particular weakness seems difficult or even impossible, an alternative career path may be the solution.

Workshops

Some organizations conduct workshops lasting two or three days for the purpose of helping workers develop careers within the company. Employees define and match their specific career objectives with the needs of the company. At other times, the company may send workers to workshops available in the community or workers may initiate the visit themselves. Consider just two of the developmental activities available for HR professionals:

- *Society for Human Resource Management Seminar Series.* Many HR seminars are available to SHRM members.
- *American Management Association, Human Resource Seminars.* There are numerous human resources seminars offered through the AMA.

Possible career paths will next be discussed.

Career Paths

Career paths have historically focused on upward mobility within a particular occupation, a choice not nearly as available as in the past. The days of the cradle to the grave have largely disappeared.[27] Other career paths include the network, lateral skill, dual-career paths, adding value to your career, and even demotion. Cathy Benko in her book, *Mass Career Customization* stated, "No longer a straight climb up the corporate ladder, careers are more commonly an undulating journey of climbs and lateral moves."[28] By selecting an alternative career path, a person may transfer current skills into a new career, one that was only dreamed about in the past. Typically, these career paths are used in combination and may be more popular at various stages of a person's career.[29]

Traditional Career Path

The following is a quote from a *Fortune* magazine article:

> *Close your eyes and picture an object that embodies the word* career. *If you joined the workforce, say, 15 or 20 or 25 years ago, you're probably hard-wired, as the techies say to visualize your working life as a predictable series of narrow and distinctly separate rungs that lead straight up (or down), in other words, a ladder. Ha! Ha, ha, ha! My friend, the ladder has been chopped up into little pieces and dumped in the garbage pile. A team of sanitation engineers disposed of it at dawn, while you were dreaming.*[30]

Although the traditional career path is not as viable a career path option as it previously was, understanding it furthers one's comprehension of the various career path alternatives.

traditional career path
Employee progresses vertically upward in the organization from one specific job to the next.

The **traditional career path** is one in which an employee progresses vertically upward in the organization from one specific job to the next. The assumption is that each preceding job is essential preparation for the next-higher-level job. Therefore, an employee must move, step-by-step, from one job to the next to gain needed experience and preparation. One of the biggest advantages of the traditional career path is that it was straightforward. The path was clearly laid out, and the employee knew the specific sequence of jobs through which he or she must progress.

Today, the old model of a career in which an employee worked his way up the ladder in a single company is becoming somewhat rare. The up-or-out approach, in which employees have to keep getting promoted quickly or get lost, is becoming outmoded.[31] The certainties of yesterday's business methods and growth have disappeared in most industries, and neither organizations nor individuals can be assured of ever regaining them. However, the one certainty that still remains is that there will always be top-level managers and individuals who strive to achieve these positions. Unfortunately, today promotions are just more difficult to obtain.

Network Career Path

network career path
Method of career
progression that contains
both a vertical sequence of
jobs and a series of
horizontal opportunities.

The **network career path** contains both a vertical sequence of jobs and a series of horizontal opportunities. The network career path recognizes the interchangeability of experience at certain levels and the need to broaden experience at one level before promotion to a higher level. Often, this approach more realistically represents opportunities for employee development in an organization than does the traditional career path. For instance, a person may work as an inventory manager for a few years and then move to a lateral position of shift manager before being considered for a promotion. The vertical and horizontal options lessen the probability of blockage in one job. One major disadvantage of this type of career path is that it is more difficult to explain to employees the specific route their careers may take for a given line of work.

Lateral Skill Path

lateral skill path
Career path that allows for
lateral moves within the
firm, taken to permit an
employee to become
revitalized and find new
challenges.

The **lateral skill path** allows for lateral moves within the firm, taken to permit an employee to become revitalized and find new challenges. Neither pay nor promotion may be involved, but by learning a different job, an employee can increase his or her value to the organization and also become revitalized and reenergized.[32] Firms that want to encourage lateral movement may choose to use a skill-based pay system that rewards individuals for the type and number of skills they possess (a topic of Chapter 9). Another approach, which was discussed in Chapter 4, is job enrichment. This approach rewards (without promotion) an employee by increasing the challenge of the job, giving the job more meaning, and giving the employee a greater sense of accomplishment.

Dual-Career Path

dual-career path
Career path that recognizes
that technical specialists can
and should be allowed to
contribute their expertise to
a company without having
to become managers.

The dual career path was originally developed to deal with the problem of technically trained employees who had no desire to move into management through the normal upward mobility procedure. The **dual-career path** recognizes that technical specialists can and should be allowed to contribute their expertise to a company without having to become managers. Some companies are also providing distinct career tracks for those who excel in innovation.[33] A dual-career approach is often established to encourage and motivate professionals in fields such as engineering, sales, marketing, finance, and human resources. Individuals in these fields can increase their specialized knowledge, make contributions to their firms, and be rewarded without entering management. Whether on the management or technical path, compensation would be comparable at each level. The dual system has been a trademark in higher education, where individuals can move through the ranks of instructor, assistant professor, associate professor, and professor without having to go into administration.

Adding Value to Your Career

Adding value to your career may appear to be totally self-serving, but nevertheless, it is a logical and realistic career path. In the rapidly changing world today, professional obsolescence can creep up on a person. John Humphrey, CEO of executive-training powerhouse Forum Corporation, talks about adding personal value as if it could be stored in a toolbox that workers carry with them each day. According to Humphrey, "The old [career] ladder was a rigid thing. Now the question is 'what skills have you got in your toolbox so that you can carry them anywhere and ply your craft?'"[34] An individual's toolbox must be ever expanding, and continual personal development is a necessity. The better an employee's qualifications, the greater the opportunities he or she has in the job market. A person must discover what companies need, then develop the skills necessary to meet these needs as defined by the marketplace. Individuals should always be doing something that contributes significant, positive change to the organization. If any vestige of job security exists, this is it. Basically, the primary tie that binds a worker to the company, and vice versa, is mutual success resulting in performance that adds value to the organization.

Demotion

demotion
Process of moving a worker
to a lower level of duties
and responsibilities, which
typically involves a
reduction in pay.

Demotion is the process of moving a worker to a lower level of duties and responsibilities, which typically involves a reduction in pay. Demotions have long been associated with failure, but limited promotional opportunities in the future and the fast pace of technological change may make demotion a legitimate career option. If the stigma of demotion can be removed, more employees, especially older workers, might choose to make such a move. Joan Lloyd, Milwaukee-based career counselor and author said, "Some people get into a position only to find their skills were better suited to their old job. Sometimes they decide they do not want to have as much responsibility because of things going on in their personal lives."[35] Working long hours for a limited promotional opportunity loses its appeal to some after a while, especially if the worker can financially afford the demotion. In certain instances, this approach might open up a clogged promotional path and at the same time permit a senior employee to escape unwanted stress without being viewed as a failure.

Free Agents (Being Your Own Boss)

free agents
People who take charge of all or part of their careers, by being their own bosses or by working for others in ways that fit their particular needs or wants.

Free agents are people who take charge of all or part of their careers by being their own bosses or by working for others in ways that fit their particular needs or wants. Many have become free agents because of company downsizing and have no desire or have difficulty reentering the corporate environment.[36] Some free agents work full-time; others work part-time. Others work full-time and run a small business in the hope of converting it into their primary work. Free agents come in many shapes and sizes, but what distinguishes them is a commitment to controlling part or all of their careers. They have a variety of talents and are used to dealing with a wide range of audiences and changing their approach on the spot in response to new information or reactions. They also tend to love challenges and spontaneity.

Developing Unique Segments of the Workforce

Career planning and development is essential for the continual evolution of the labor force and the success of organizations, as well as individuals. Never in American history has so many different generations with such different worldviews and attitudes been asked to work together.[37] Certain groups of employees are unique because of the specific characteristics of the work they do or who they are.[38] In previous editions of this text, our discussion began with Generation X and then to Generation Y and Generation I. But, a strange event occurred on the way to Generation I. Up popped the baby boomers again as valued members of the workforce though many had written them off into retirement. Because of certain differences between these groups, each group must be developed in unique ways. Although generalizations about a group are risky, the following are offered to provide additional insight into what some members of each group may require developmentally.

Baby Boomers

baby boomers
People born just after World War II through the mid-1960s.

Baby boomers were born just after World War II through the mid-1960s. The 77 million boomers, the oldest of whom were 60 in 2005, do not appear to be ready for retirement. In an American Association for Retired Persons survey, 80 percent of them stated that they intend to work past age 65.

Corporate downsizing in the 1980s and 1990s cast aside millions of baby boomers. Companies are now again recruiting these retirees. They realize that many older workers have skills and experience that are critically needed. Companies today place high value on skill, experience, and a strong work ethic, characteristics that many boomers possess. Training replacement workers for an organization is very expensive. Bringing back Boomers reduces training costs. Retirees and laid-off former employees can quickly move into production with little or no training. Many companies are recruiting knowledgeable Boomers as an alternative to adding additional staff or hiring unknown outside contractors.

Generation X Employees

Generation X
Label affixed to the 40 million American workers born between the mid-1960s and late 1970s.

Generation X is the label affixed to the 41 million American workers born between the mid-1960s and late 1970s. Many organizations have a growing cadre of Generation X employees who possess lots of energy and promise. They are one of the most widely misunderstood phenomena facing management today. Generation Xers differ from previous generations in some significant ways, including their natural affinity for technology and their entrepreneurial spirit. In fact, four out of five new enterprises are the work of Xers.[39] Job instability and the breakdown of traditional employer–employee relationships brought a new realization to Generation Xers that it is necessary to approach the world of work differently from past generations.[40]

Managers who understand how circumstances have shaped Generation Xers' outlook on career issues can begin to develop a positive relationship with these workers and harness their unique abilities. Developing Generation X employees requires support for their quest to acquire skills and expertise. Generation Xers recognize that their careers cannot be founded securely on a relationship with any one employer. Today, they are very skeptical, particularly when it comes to the business world and job security. They worry about their jobs being outsourced and how they are going to pay for their children's education when wages are rising so slowly. They think of themselves more as free agents in a mobile workforce and expect to build career security, not job security, by acquiring marketable skills and expertise. They are not afraid of changing jobs quite often. The surest way to gain Xers' loyalty is to help them develop career security. When a company helps them expand their knowledge and skills, in essence, preparing them for the job market, Xers will often want to stay on board to learn those very skills.

Generation Y Employees

Generation Y comprises people born between the late 1970s and late 1990s. They have never wound a watch, dialed a rotary phone, or plunked the keys of a manual typewriter. But, without a thought, they download music from the Internet and program a DVD player. They cannot imagine how the world ever got along without computers.[41] These individuals are the leading edge of a generation that promises to be the richest, smartest, and savviest ever. They are well educated, technologically savvy, and brimming with confidence.[42] These Generation Yers, often referred to as the "echo boomers," "Millenials," and "nexters," are the coddled, confident offspring of post–World War II baby boomers. Generation Y individuals are a most privileged generation, who came of age during the hottest domestic economy in memory.

Organizations are attempting to determine how to best attract, develop, and retain Generation Yers as they enter the workforce.[43] Gen Yers tend to have a strong sense of morality and civic-mindedness. They are more ethnically diverse than previous generations, and nearly one-third of them have been raised in single-parent households. They want a workplace that is both fun and rewarding. They want jobs where there is a balance between work and family.[44] They are the only generation of workers that were taught teamwork in school.[45] They want jobs that conform to their interests and do not accept the way things have been done in the past. Generation Y employees want flexible working hours, and this is a benefit that they are very enthusiastic about.[46] They also tend to have more a sense of entitlement not found in other generation of workers.[47]

Because they are technologically savvy and have grown up using personal computers, Gen Yers are referred to as "digital natives"[48] and spend an average of 3 1/2 hours each day online.[49] They are the first generation to grow up in the digital world and they know how to use technology to create a life and work environment that supports their lifestyle. They are increasingly choosing companies that accommodate their personal technology preferences.[50] Their enthusiasm and experience is seemingly of people much older and they are willing to tackle major challenges and have the technology to back it up. Jennie Carlson, executive vice president and director of HR for U.S. Bancorp in Minneapolis said, "the younger generation already does just about everything on cell phones, computers and networks, and will expect to use these tools when they enter the workforce. For this reason, companies are finding ways to deliver soft skills such as management and language training, and mentoring, through e-learning."[51]

Yers' childhoods have been short-lived, as they have been exposed to some of the worst things in life: schoolyard shootings, drug use, terrorism, sex scandal, and war. This new wave of young Americans has given early notice of its potential, especially when it comes to leadership and success.

As companies hire more Gen Y employees, organizations may find that some need additional training in professional behavior, or in basic writing, confidentiality issues, critical thinking, or how to give and receive constructive criticism. Arlene Arnsparger, coauthor of *Succeeding with Colleagues, Cohorts and Customers,* said "Millennials are good at multi-tasking. It doesn't occur to them that it could be offensive. If you're wearing your ear buds hooked to your iPod while talking to me, as a customer, I assume you're ignoring me."[52]

Generation Y
Comprises people born between the late 1970s and early 1990s.

Generation I (Google Generation) as Future Employees

Generation I
Internet-assimilated children
born after the mid-1990s.

First it was Generation X, and then came Generation Y. Next came **Generation I**, the Internet-assimilated children born after the late 1990s. According to Bill Gates, "These kids will be the first generation to grow up with the Internet. The Web will change Generation I's world as much as television transformed our world after World War II. That is why it is so critical to ensure that new teachers understand how to incorporate technology into their instruction and that teachers have the technological training they want and need. We cannot afford to have any teacher locked out of the greatest library on earth, the Internet."[53] Gen Iers are comfortable in working off a keyboard, reading from a computer screen, and keeping in touch with friends and family at all times. Companies are still trying to come up with a selection strategy to attract these young people to the workforce.

Multigenerational Diversity

The concept of generational differences as a legitimate workplace diversity issue has gained increasing recognition.[54] The Baby Boomers are remaining on the job longer because of the economy and often find themselves working with Generation Y employees.[55] Traditionally, discussions of workplace diversity tend to focus on topics of race, ethnicity, gender, sexual orientation and disability.[56] Shirley A. Davis, SHRM's director of diversity and inclusion initiatives, said, "in all parts of the world, there is another category of diversity that cannot be overlooked: multigenerational diversity." Today, there are greater numbers of workers from each age group that bring both new opportunities and challenges. If organizations want to thrive in this competitive environment of global talent management, they need employees and managers who are aware of and skilled in dealing with the four generations that make up the workforce. In recruiting and retaining a multigenerational work force, attention needs to focus not only on the difference but also the similarities.[57] Training this multigenerational workforce, delivering the right training in the right way to each group of learners may be thought of as "performing on the high wire without a net."[58]

Key Terms

job security   222
career security   222
employability doctrine   222
career   223
career planning   223
self-assessment   223
strength/weakness balance sheet   224

likes and dislikes survey   225
career path   226
career development   226
traditional career path   228
network career path   229
lateral skill path   229
dual-career path   229

demotion   229
free agents   230
baby boomers   230
Generation X   230
Generation Y   231
Generation I   232

Notes

1. Lou Ann Lathrop, "9 Ways to Keep Your Career Resolution," *Material Handling Management* 65 (January 2010): 29–30.
2. Robert Rodriguez, "Learning's Impact on Talent Flow,"*Chief Learning Officer* 7 (April 2008): 50–64.
3. Jennifer Schramn, "Meet Your New Employee," *HRMagazine* 54 (October 2009): 96.
4. Mary K. Pratt, "8 Ways to Boost Your Career in '08," *Computerworld* 42 (January 7, 2008): 26–28.
5. Stanna Brazeel, "Career Focus in Economic Uncertainty," Electric Light & Power 87 (March/April 2009): Special section 4.
6. Angeli R. Rasbury, "New Kid on the Job," *Black Enterprise* 38 (May 2008): 60.
7. "New Career Rules Redefines Today's Workforce," *T+D* 64 (February 2010): 22–23.
8. John Mullins, "Career Planning the Second Time Around," *Occupational Outlook Quarterly* 53 (Summer 2009): 12–15.
9. Scott Beagrie, "How to Jump-Start Your Job Search," *Personnel Today* (January 8, 2008): 5.
10. The following section is adapted from James R. Young and Robert W. Mondy, *Personal Selling: Function, Theory and Practice* (Hinsdale, IL: The Dryden Press, 1978): 50–55.
11. Kuldeep Singh, "Career Management and Work-Life Integration: Using Self-Assessment to Navigate Contemporary Careers," *IIMB Management Review*, 20 (September 2008): 342–343.

12. Guerline Jasmin, "Six Small Steps to Breaking Out of a Big Rut," *Receivables Report for American's Health Care Financial Managers 23* (January 2008): 9–10.

13. Emily Walls Ray, "Tap-Tap-Tap into Internet Job Research: Good Tool, but Remember Basic Steps in Any Search," *Richmond Times Dispatch* (February 10, 2002): S-5.

14. Kimberly Palmer, "Re-Energizing Your Career," *U.S. News & World Report* 144 (March 24, 2008): 59.

15. Rebecca Weingarten, "Thinking of Retiring? Not So Fast,"*BusinessWeek Online* (March 26, 2009): 20.

16. John Mullins, "Career Planning the Second Time Around," *Occupational Outlook Quarterly* 53 (Summer 2009): 12–15.

17. Lewis Carroll, *Through the Looking Glass* (New York: Norton, 1971): 127.

18. http://www.careermaze.com/home.asp?licensee= CareerMaze January 9, 2010.

19. http://www.career-intelligence.com/about/about_ career-intelligence.asp January 9, 2010.

20. http://www.careerkey.org/asp/your_personality/ take_test.html January 9, 2010.

21. http://www.workworries.com/i3685-c113 January 9, 2010.

22. Ann Field, "Do Your Stars See a Reason to Stay?" *Harvard Management Update* 13 (June 2008: 3–5.

23. Judith A. Ross, "Five Ways to Boost Retention," *Harvard Management Update* 13 (April 2008): 3–4.

24. Josh Bersin, "Today's High-Impact Learning Organization," *Chief Learning Officer* 7 (August 2008): 54–57.

25. "Tech Companies Shift Talent Investments," *Journal of Accountancy* 205 (June 2008): 22.

26. Annie Stevens and Greg Gostanian, "Retaining Hi-Pos," *Sales & Service Excellence* 8 (March 2008): 15.

27. Daniel J. Blake, "Keys to Employee Recruiting & Retention in Tough Economic Times," *Sum News* 20 (Spring 2009): 8–9.

28. Nick van Dam, "Developing Scalable Business Coaching," *Chief Learning Officer* 7 (February 2008): 14.

29. Janet Wagner, "Personalize Your Career Development Plan," *Strategic Finance* 91 (March 2010): 17–18.

30. Anne Fisher, "Six Ways to Supercharge Your Career," *Fortune* 135 (January 13, 1997): 46+.

31. Laura Fitzpatrick, "We're Getting Off the Ladder," *Time* 173 (May 25, 2009): 45.

32. "The Changing Organizational Chart: Up Isn't the Only Way to Success," *Health Care Collector* 21 (January 2008): 8.

33. Gina Colarelli, Andrew Corbett, and Ron Pierantozzi, "Create Three Distinct Career Paths for Innovators," *Harvard Business Review* 87 (December 2009): 78–79.

34. Fisher, "Six Ways to Supercharge Your Career."

35. "The Changing Organizational Chart: Up Isn't the Only Way to Success," *Health Care Collector* 21 (January 2008): 8.

36. John Hollon, "The Freelance Flood," *Workforce Management* 88 (March 16, 2009): 34.

37. "The Multigenerational Workforce: Opportunity for Competitive Success," *HRMagazine* 54 (March 2009): Special section 1–9.

38. Maggie Leyes, "Talkin' 'Bout My Generation," *Advisor Today* 105 (April 2010): 34–38.

39. Jean Chatzky, "Gen Xers Aren't Slackers After All," *Time* 159 (April 8, 2002): 87.

40. Neil Simmons, "Leveraging Generational Work Styles to Meet Business Objectives," Information Management 44 (January/February 2010): 28–33.

41. Mary Aichlmayr, "The Human Touch," *Material Handling Management* 63 (April 2008): 8.

42. "How 'Recession-Proof' Will Millennial Workers Be?" *HR Focus* 86 (March 2009): 6–7.

43. Jeanne C. Meister, "Learning for the Google Generation," *Chief Learning Officer* 7 (April 2008): 66.

44. "Leading Productivity Killers in Today's Market: Overwork, Stress," *HR Focus* 85 (April 2008): 8.

45. Penelope Trunk, "The New Workforce Will Job-Hop. And That's Good," *HVACR Distribution Business* (March 2010): 20–22.

46. Stephen Moir, "Segmenting Benefits to Suit Staff Is Beneficial," *Employee Benefits* (February 2008): 24.

47. Gary Herbison and Glenn Boseman, "Here They Come-Generation Y, Are You Ready?" *Journal of Financial Service Professionals* 63 (May 2009): 33–34.

48. Kathryn Yeaton, "Recruiting and Managing the 'Why?' Generation: Gen Y," *CPA Journal* 78 (April 2008): 68–72.

49. Maggie Leyes, "Talkin' 'Bout My Generation," *Advisor Today* 105 (April 2010): 34–38.

50. Ann Pace, "Tech Masters," *T+D* 63 (January 2009): 22.

51. Bill Roberts, "Hard Facts about Soft-Skills E-Learning," *HRMagazine* 53 (January 2008): 76–78.

52. Kathryn Tyler, "Generation Gaps," *HRMagazine* 53 (January 2008): 69–72.

53. Bill Leonard, "After Generations X and Y Comes I," *HRMagazine* 45 (January 2000): 21.

54. Rohini Anand, "Embracing Multiple Generations in the Work Force," *Profiles in Diversity Journal* 11 (March/April 2009): 46.

55. "Leveraging HR and Knowledge Management in a Challenging Economy," *HRMagazine* 54 (June 2009): 1–9.

56. "Multigenerational Workforce," *Smart Business Atlanta* 7 (April 2010): 20.

57. "The Multigenerational Workforce: Opportunity for Competitive Success," *HRMagazine* 54 (March 2009): Special section 1–9.

58. Matt Bloch, "Taming Tech Training," *Training* 45 (September 2008): 60–61.

8 Performance Management and Appraisal

HRM in Action: Employee Engagement as a Strategic HR Tool

Employee engagement refers to the level of commitment workers make to their employer, seen in their willingness to stay at the firm and to go beyond the call of duty.[1] Firms want employees that are highly motivated and feel they have a real stake in the company's success. Such employees are willing to finish tasks in their own time and see a strong link between the firm's success and their own career prospects. In short, motivated, empowered employees work hand in hand with employers in an atmosphere of mutual trust. Companies with engaged workforces have also reported less absenteeism, more engagement with customers, greater employee satisfaction, less mistakes, fewer employees leaving, and naturally higher profits. Such is the power of this concept that former Secretary of State for Business, Peter Mandelson, commissioned David McLeod and Nita Clarke to investigate how much UK competitiveness could be enhanced by wider use of employee engagement. David and Nita concluded that in a world where work tasks have become increasingly similar, engaged employees could give some companies the edge over their rivals. They also identified significant barriers to engagement such as a lack of appreciation for the concept of employee engagement by some companies and managers. Full participation by line managers is particularly crucial.

From the employee point of view, it is easy to view engagement as a management fad, particularly if the company fails to demonstrate the necessary commitment. Some also feel that in a recession, employee engagement becomes less of a priority when in

After completing this chapter, students should be able to:

1. Define *performance management* and describe the importance of performance management.

2. Define *performance appraisal* and identify the uses of performance appraisal.

3. Discuss the performance appraisal environmental factors.

4. Describe the performance appraisal process.

5. Identify the various performance criteria (standards) that can be established.

6. Identify who may be responsible for performance appraisal and the performance period.

7. Identify the various performance appraisal methods.

8. List the problems that have been associated with performance appraisal.

9. Explain the characteristics of an effective appraisal system.

10. Describe the legal implications of performance appraisal.

11. Explain how the appraisal interview should be conducted.

fact it could be the factor that enables a business in trouble to stay afloat. Others feel that in an environment where recruitment is easier due to increasing unemployment, firms tend to slacken their commitment to engagement.

A company that has demonstrated the value of employee engagement is John Lewis, who sell a range of household goods, clothes, and electronics. The John Lewis business model has been hailed as a good way to run public services and 70,000 store employees recently received a slice of a £151.3 million bonus.

The engagement strategy of John Lewis is facilitated by its unusual employee-owned structure. Employees are known as partners and the company is run by a Partnership Council, a Partnership Board, and a Chairman. At least 80 percent of the Partnership Council is elected and this is one of the ways employees feel that they can influence the working of the company. At the core of the John Lewis philosophy is a belief that employees are critical to success. Employees benefit from an environment that positively encourages a healthy work–life balance and engagement in community projects and charity work. Tangible benefits include a noncontributory final salary pension scheme, store discounts, subsidized holidays, and even a contribution towards concert tickets.

Tesco is another retailing company that has embraced employee engagement. Chief Executive, Terry Leahy, remarked recently that he knew more about Tesco customers than his employees and set out to improve that situation. One of the most significant factors in this process has been an improved understanding with USDAW, the shop workers union. Tesco also launched two notable engagement projects in 2008, one of which encouraged employees to take part in a talent contest. Vouchers for in-store shopping were also distributed to employees at Christmas.

Tesco is already receiving encouraging results for its investment in employee engagement. Stores with the most committed employees are the most successful in terms of turnover. However, suprisingly, many companies still conclude that employee engagement is not for them.[2]

This chapter begins by discussing employee engagement. Then performance management is defined and the importance of integrating learning and performance management discussed. The relationship of performance management to performance appraisal is then studied. Next, we look at the uses made of appraisal data and the environmental factors affecting the performance appraisal process. The performance appraisal process is then described and the possible criteria used in evaluating performance are discussed. Then the person(s) responsible for appraisal and the appraisal period are described, and the various performance appraisal methods are explained. Problems associated with performance appraisal and characteristics of an effective appraisal system are described next, followed by a discussion of the legal aspects of performance appraisal and the appraisal interview. This chapter concludes with a global perspective entitled "Two Cultures' Views of Performance Appraisal."

OBJECTIVE 8.1
Define *performance management* and describe the importance of performance management.

Performance Management

Performance management (PM) is a goal-oriented process directed toward ensuring that organizational processes are in place to maximize the productivity of employees, teams, and ultimately, the organization. It is a major player in accomplishing organizational strategy in that it involves measuring and improving the value of the workforce. PM includes incentive goals and the corresponding incentive values so that the relationship can be clearly understood and communicated. There is a close relationship between incentives and performance.[3]

performance management (PM)
Goal-oriented process directed toward ensuring that organizational processes are in place to maximize the productivity of employees, teams, and ultimately, the organization.

Performance management systems are one of the major focuses in business today. Although every HR function contributes to performance management, training and performance appraisal play a more significant role. Whereas performance appraisal occurs at a specific time, performance management is a dynamic, ongoing, continuous process. Every person in the organization is a part of the PM system. Each part of the system, such as training, appraisal, and rewards, is integrated and linked for the purpose of continuous organizational effectiveness. With PM, the effort of each and every worker should be directed toward achieving strategic goals. If a worker's skills need to be improved, training is needed. With PM systems, training has a direct tie-in to achieving organizational effectiveness. In addition, pay and performance are directly related to achieving organizational goals.

Robert J. Greene, CEO of Reward Systems Inc., said, "Performance management is the single largest contributor to organizational effectiveness. If you ignore performance management, you fail."[4] Organizations must take a more strategic approach to performance appraisal. Instead of using the familiar "check the box, write a comment" ritual, organizations need to integrate the company's mission, vision, and values into their performance management systems.

performance appraisal (PA)
Formal system of review and evaluation of individual or team task performance.

OBJECTIVE 8.2
Define *performance appraisal* and identify the uses of performance appraisal.

Performance Appraisal

Performance appraisal (PA) is a formal system of review and evaluation of individual or team task performance. A critical point in the definition is the word *formal*, because in actuality, managers should be reviewing an individual's performance on a continuing basis.[5]

PA is especially critical to the success of performance management. Although performance appraisal is but one component of performance management, it is vital, in that it directly reflects

HR Web Wisdom

*Performance
Management*

**http://www.opm.gov/
perform/overview.asp**

Office of Personnel
Management Web site
on performance
management.

the organization's strategic plan. Although evaluation of team performance is critical when teams exist in an organization, the focus of PA in most firms remains on the individual employee. Regardless of the emphasis, an effective appraisal system evaluates accomplishments and initiates plans for development, goals, and objectives.

Performance appraisal is often a negative, disliked activity and one that seems to elude mastery.[6] Managers do not like giving them and employees do not like receiving them.[7] In fact, in one survey, almost 80 percent of workers stated dissatisfaction with their PA process.[8] If this is so, why not just eliminate it? Actually, some managers might do just that *if* they did not need to provide feedback, encourage performance improvement, make valid decisions, justify terminations, identify training and development needs, and defend personnel decisions.[9] Performance appraisal serves many purposes, and improved results and efficiency are increasingly critical in today's globally competitive marketplace. Therefore, abandoning the only program with *performance* in its name and *employees* as its focus would seem to be an ill-advised overreaction. On top of these considerations, managers must be concerned about legal ramifications. Developing an effective performance appraisal system has been and will continue to be a high priority for management.

Uses of Performance Appraisal

For many organizations, the primary goal of an appraisal system is to improve individual and organizational performance. There may be other goals, however. A potential problem with PA, and a possible cause of much dissatisfaction, is expecting too much from one appraisal plan. For example, a plan that is effective for developing employees may not be the best for determining pay increases. Yet, a properly designed system can help achieve organizational objectives and enhance employee performance. In fact, PA data are potentially valuable for virtually every human resource functional area.

Human Resource Planning

In assessing a firm's human resources, data must be available to identify those who have the potential to be promoted or for any area of internal employee relations. Through performance appraisal it may be discovered that there is an insufficient number of workers who are prepared to enter management. Plans can then be made for greater emphasis on management development. Succession planning (discussed previously in Chapter 4) is a key concern for all firms. A well-designed appraisal system provides a profile of the organization's human resource strengths and weaknesses to support this effort.

Recruitment and Selection

Performance evaluation ratings may be helpful in predicting the performance of job applicants. For example, it may be determined that a firm's successful employees (identified through performance evaluations) exhibit certain behaviors when performing key tasks. These data may then provide benchmarks for evaluating applicant responses obtained through behavioral interviews, discussed in Chapter 6. Also, in validating selection tests, employee ratings may be used as the variable against which test scores are compared. In this instance, determination of the selection test's validity would depend on the accuracy of appraisal results.

Training and Development

Performance appraisal should point out an employee's specific needs for training and development. For instance, if Pat Compton's job requires skill in technical writing and her evaluation reveals a deficiency in this factor, she may need additional training in written communication. If a firm finds that a number of first-line supervisors are having difficulty in administering disciplinary action, training sessions addressing this problem may be appropriate. By identifying deficiencies that adversely affect performance, T&D programs can be developed that permit individuals to build on their strengths and minimize their deficiencies. An appraisal system does not guarantee properly trained and developed employees. However, determining T&D needs is more precise when appraisal data are available.

Career Planning and Development

As discussed in the appendix to Chapter 7, *career planning* is an ongoing process whereby *an individual* sets career goals and identifies the means to achieve them. On the other hand, *career development* is a formal approach used by the organization to ensure that people with the proper qualifications and experiences are available when needed. Performance appraisal data is essential in assessing an employee's strengths and weaknesses and in determining the person's potential. Managers may use such information to counsel subordinates and assist them in developing and implementing their career plans.

Compensation Programs

Performance appraisal results provide a basis for rational decisions regarding pay adjustments. Most managers believe that you should reward outstanding job performance tangibly with pay increases. They believe that *the behaviors you reward are the behaviors you get*. Rewarding behaviors necessary for accomplishing organizational objectives is at the heart of a firm's strategic plan. To encourage good performance, a firm should design and implement a reliable performance appraisal system and then reward the most productive workers and teams accordingly.

Internal Employee Relations

Performance appraisal data are also used for decisions in several areas of internal employee relations, including promotion, demotion, termination, layoff, and transfer. For example, an employee's performance in one job may be useful in determining his or her ability to perform another job on the same level, as is required in the consideration of transfers. When the performance level is unacceptable, demotion or even termination may be appropriate.

Assessment of Employee Potential

Some organizations attempt to assess an employee's potential as they appraise his or her job performance. Although past behaviors may be a good predictor of future behaviors in some jobs, an employee's past performance may not accurately indicate future performance in other jobs. The best salesperson in the company may not have what it takes to become a successful district sales manager, where the tasks are distinctly different. Similarly, the best systems analyst may, if promoted, be a disaster as an information technology manager. Overemphasizing technical skills and ignoring other equally important skills is a common error in promoting employees into management jobs. Recognition of this problem has led some firms to separate the appraisal of performance, which focuses on past behavior, from the assessment of potential, which is future-oriented.

OBJECTIVE 8.3
Discuss the performance appraisal environmental factors.

Performance Appraisal Environmental Factors

External and internal environmental factors can influence the appraisal process. For example, legislation requires that appraisal systems be nondiscriminatory. In the case of *Mistretta v Sandia Corporation* (a subsidiary of Western Electric Company, Inc.), a federal district court judge ruled against the company, stating, "There is sufficient circumstantial evidence to indicate that age bias and age based policies appear throughout the performance rating process to the detriment of the protected age group." The *Albemarle Paper v Moody* case also supported validation requirements for performance appraisals, as well as for selection tests. Organizations should avoid using any appraisal method that results in a disproportionately negative impact on a protected group.

The labor union is another external factor that might affect a firm's appraisal process. Unions have traditionally stressed seniority as the basis for promotions and pay increases. They may vigorously oppose the use of a management-designed performance appraisal system used for these purposes.

Factors within the internal environment can also affect the performance appraisal process. For instance, a firm's corporate culture can assist or hinder the process. Today's dynamic organizations, which increasingly use teams to perform jobs, recognize overall team results as

TRENDS & INNOVATIONS

Integrating Learning and Performance Management

Companies are now integrating learning and performance management into a total system. Mike DeVries, vice president of human resources at Cummins Mid-South LLC, said, "We didn't have a good system on goals [and] development plans, tracking progress throughout the year. More time was spent administering [appraisals] than looking at effectiveness. In addition, the company did not have defined learning offerings for all employees."[10]

The company looked for automated solutions to accommodate its 550 employees. Today, DeVries' world is much different. He says, "Now, individual goals are aligned with corporate goals. We can calculate the effectiveness of [employees'] reviews and goals, and the system identifies training needs." More companies are integrating their learning and performance functions as technology makes it easier and more affordable.[11]

There has been a need for integrating learning and performance for years but technology had not caught up to the need. There were learning management systems and performance management systems but they did not work together as a total system. Now they have converged. Most integrated systems use a competency model where competencies or skills are first identified for each job and the competencies provide the basis for performance appraisal. Managers rate the performance of each employee and look for differences between individual ratings and desired ratings. An employee development plan is formulated based on the gaps. Employees can go to the system to review the plan and assess how they are doing. When the next appraisal date arrives, the manager and the employee have a clear record of the employee's development activities.[12]

Historically, HR has struggled with describing to upper management the value of training. David Karel, vice president of product marketing for SuccessFactors, a learning and performance management systems provider in San Mateo, California, said, "In the old world, the learning organization was tracking the number of people trained. Now, learning can tie what they are doing to productivity. They can show much more directly how they are impacting the company." Jon Ciampi, vice president of product management for SumTotal, said, "Employees will leave if they don't see a career path. By identifying skills gaps and a path to get there, you can let employees actively manage their own careers." In addition, time spent on the appraisal has been significantly reduces. DeVries said, "Appraisals are more consistent, there's more content, and employees know what they are being assessed on."[13]

These systems can also assist in staffing. With an integrated system, managers can easily view up-to-date information on employees' skills. Tamar Elkeles, Qualcomm's vice president of learning and organizational development, said, "Without a lot of hiring, you need to find ways to utilize talent differently." For example, if 30 new multimedia engineers are needed, and the system can identify 15 current employees with the necessary skill sets, then only 15 have to be hired.[14]

Those who have lived with the new systems have no desire to go back to the old way. DeVries said, "Without a system like this, it's hard for a manager to understand how to do a development plan and follow through on it, to identify skills gaps and track those. If you're trying to keep up with improving performance without a system like this, I don't see how you can get there."[15]

well as individual contributions. A nontrusting culture does not provide the environment needed to encourage high performance by either individuals or teams. In such an atmosphere, the credibility of an appraisal system will suffer regardless of its merits.

OBJECTIVE 8.4

Describe the performance appraisal process.

Performance Appraisal Process

As shown in Figure 8.1, the starting point for the PA process is identifying specific performance goals. An appraisal system probably cannot effectively serve every desired purpose, so management should select the specific goals it believes to be most important and realistically achievable. For example, some firms may want to stress employee development, whereas other organizations may want to focus on pay adjustments. Too many PA systems fail because management expects too much from one method and does not determine specifically what it wants the system to accomplish.

Figure 8.1

Performance Appraisal Process

The next step in this ongoing cycle continues with establishing performance criteria (standards) and communicating these performance expectations to those concerned. Then the work is performed and the supervisor appraises the performance. At the end of the appraisal period, the appraiser and the employee together review work performance and evaluate it against established performance standards. This review helps determine how well employees have met these standards, determines reasons for deficiencies, and develops a plan to correct the problems. At this meeting, goals are set for the next evaluation period, and the cycle repeats.

OBJECTIVE 8.5
Identify the various performance criteria (standards) that can be established.

Establish Performance Criteria (Standards)

There is an old adage that says "What gets watched gets done." Therefore, management must carefully select performance criteria as it pertains to achieving corporate goals.[16] The most common appraisal criteria are traits, behaviors, competencies, goal achievement, and improvement potential.

Traits

Certain employee traits such as attitude, appearance, and initiative are the basis for some evaluations. However, many of these commonly used qualities are subjective and may be either unrelated to job performance or difficult to define. In such cases, inaccurate evaluations may occur and create legal problems for the organization as well. This was the case in *Wade v Mississippi Cooperative Extension Service* where the circuit court ruled:

> In a performance appraisal system, general characteristics such as leadership, public acceptance, attitude toward people, appearance and grooming, personal conduct, outlook on life, ethical habits, resourcefulness, capacity for growth, mental alertness, and loyalty to organization are susceptible to partiality and to the personal taste, whim, or fancy of the evaluator as well as patently subjective in form and obviously susceptible to completely subjective treatment by those conducting the appraisals.

At the same time, certain traits may relate to job performance and, if this connection is established, using them may be appropriate. Traits such as adaptability, judgment, appearance, and attitude may be used when shown to be job-related.

Behaviors

When an individual's task outcome is difficult to determine, organizations may evaluate the person's task-related behavior or competencies. For example, an appropriate behavior to evaluate for a manager might be leadership style. For individuals working in teams, developing others, teamwork and cooperation, or customer service orientation might be appropriate. Desired behaviors may be appropriate as evaluation criteria because if they are recognized and rewarded, employees tend to repeat them. If certain behaviors result in desired outcomes, there is merit in using them in the evaluation process.

Competencies

competencies
Broad range of knowledge, skills, traits, and behaviors that may be technical in nature, relate to interpersonal skills, or are business-oriented.

Competencies include a broad range of knowledge, skills, traits, and behaviors that may be technical in nature, relate to interpersonal skills, or are business-oriented.

Some managers recommend that cultural competencies such as ethics and integrity be used for all jobs. There are also competencies that are job-specific. For example, analytical thinking and achievement orientation might be essential in professional jobs. In leadership jobs, relevant competencies might include developing talent, delegating authority, and people management skills. The competencies selected for evaluation purposes should be those that are closely associated with job success.

Research conducted by the University of Michigan Business School and sponsored by the Society for Human Resource Management (SHRM) and the Global Consulting Alliance determined that success in HR is dependent on competency and specific skills in the following five key areas:

* *Strategic contribution:* Connecting firms to their markets and quickly aligning employee behaviors with organizational needs.
* *Business knowledge:* Knowing how businesses are run and translating this into action.
* *Personal credibility:* Demonstrating measurable value; being part of an executive team.
* *HR delivery:* Providing efficient and effective service to customers in the areas of staffing, performance management, development, and evaluation.
* *HR technology:* Using technology and Web-based means to deliver value to customers.[17]

Goal Achievement

If organizations consider *ends* more important than *means,* goal achievement outcomes become an appropriate factor to evaluate. The outcomes established should be within the control of the individual or team and should be those results that lead to the firm's success. At upper levels, the goals might deal with financial aspects of the firm such as profit or cash flow, and market considerations such as market share or position in the market. At lower organizational levels, the outcomes might be meeting the customer's quality requirements and delivering according to the promised schedule.

To assist the process, the manager needs to provide specific examples of how the employee can further his or her development and achieve specific goals. Both parties should reach an agreement as to the employee's goals for the next evaluation period and the assistance and resources the manager needs to provide. This aspect of employee appraisal should be the most positive element in the entire process and help the employee focus on behavior that will produce positive results for all concerned.

Improvement Potential

When organizations evaluate their employees' performance, many of the criteria used focus on the past. From a performance management viewpoint, the problem is that you cannot change the past. Unless a firm takes further steps, the evaluation data become merely historical documents. Therefore, firms should emphasize the future, including the behaviors and outcomes needed to develop the employee, and, in the process, achieve the firm's goals. This involves an assessment of the employee's potential. Including *potential* in the evaluation process helps to ensure more effective career planning and development.

You should remember that the evaluation criteria presented here are not mutually exclusive. In fact, many appraisal systems are hybrids of these approaches.

OBJECTIVE 8.6

Identify who may be responsible for performance appraisal and the performance period.

Responsibility for Appraisal

Often the human resource department is responsible for coordinating the design and implementation of performance appraisal programs. However, it is essential that line managers play a key role from beginning to end. These individuals usually conduct the appraisals, and they must directly participate in the program if it is to succeed. Several possibilities exist with regard to the person who will actually rate the employee.

Immediate Supervisor

An employee's immediate supervisor has traditionally been the most logical choice for evaluating performance and this continues to be the case. The supervisor is usually in an excellent position to observe the employee's job performance and the supervisor has the responsibility for managing a particular unit. When someone else has the task of evaluating subordinates, the supervisor's authority may be undermined. Also, subordinate training and development is an important element in every manager's job and, as previously mentioned, appraisal programs and employee development are usually closely related.

On the negative side, the immediate supervisor may emphasize certain aspects of employee performance and neglect others. Also, managers have been known to manipulate evaluations to justify pay increases and promotions and vice versa.

When geography separates subordinates from their supervisors, evaluation becomes increasingly difficult. In other cases, the appraised employee may be more technically knowledgeable than the boss, and this presents another potential problem. One suggestion for overcoming these disadvantages is to bring subordinates into the process more closely. Have them suggest ways to fairly evaluate their performance and then use their suggestions as part of the appraisal criteria.

In most instances, the immediate supervisor will probably continue to be involved in evaluating performance. Organizations will seek alternatives, however, because of technological advances and a desire to broaden the perspective of the appraisal.

Subordinates

Historically, our culture has viewed evaluation by subordinates negatively. However, this thinking has changed somewhat. Some firms conclude that evaluation of managers by subordinates is both feasible and needed. They reason that subordinates are in an excellent position to view their superiors' managerial effectiveness. Advocates believe that this approach leads supervisors to become especially conscious of the work group's needs and to do a better job of managing. In the higher education environment, it is a common practice for instructors to be evaluated by students. Critics are concerned that the manager (and instructors) will be caught up in a popularity contest or that employees will be fearful of reprisal. If this approach has a chance for success, one thing is clear: the evaluators must be guaranteed anonymity. Ensuring this might be particularly difficult in a small department and especially if demographic data on the appraisal form could identify raters.

Peers and Team Members

A major strength of using peers to appraise performance is that they work closely with the evaluated employee and probably have an undistorted perspective on typical performance, especially in team assignments. Organizations are increasingly using teams, including those that are self-directed. The rationale for evaluations conducted by team members includes the following:

- Team members know each others' performance better than anyone and can, therefore, evaluate performance more accurately.
- Peer pressure is a powerful motivator for team members.
- Members who recognize that peers within the team will be evaluating their work show increased commitment and productivity.
- Peer review involves numerous opinions and is not dependent on one individual.

Problems with peer evaluations include the reluctance of some people who work closely together, especially on teams, to criticize each other. On the other hand, if an employee has been at odds with another worker he or she might really "unload on the enemy," resulting in an unfair evaluation. Another problem concerns peers who interact infrequently and lack the information needed to make an accurate assessment.

When employees work in teams, and their appraisal system focuses entirely on individual results, it is not surprising that they show little interest in their teams. But, this problem can be corrected. If teamwork is essential, make it a criterion for evaluating employees; rewarding collaboration will encourage teamwork.

Self-Appraisal

If employees understand their objectives and the criteria used for evaluation, they are in a good position to appraise their own performance. Many people know what they do well on the job and what they need to improve. If they have the opportunity, they will criticize their own performance objectively and take action to improve it. Paul Falcone, vice-president of HR at Nickelodeon, said, "The fascinating thing is that employees are usually tougher on themselves than you will ever be."[18] Also, because employee development is self-development, employees who appraise their own performance may become more highly motivated. Self-appraisal provides employees with a means of keeping the supervisor informed about everything the worker has done during the appraisal period.[19] Even if a self-appraisal is not a part of the system, the employee should at least provide the manager a list of his or her most important accomplishments and contributions over the appraisal period. This will prevent the manager from being blindsided when the employee complains, perhaps justifiably, "You didn't even mention the Bandy contract I landed last December!"

As a complement to other approaches, self-appraisal has great appeal to managers who are primarily concerned with employee participation and development. For compensation purposes, however, its value is considerably less. Some individuals are masters at attributing good performance to their own efforts and poor performance to someone else's.

Customer Appraisal

Customer behavior determines a firm's degree of success. Therefore, some organizations believe it is important to obtain performance input from this critical source. Organizations use this approach because it demonstrates a commitment to the customer, holds employees accountable, and fosters change. Customer-related goals for executives generally are of a broad, strategic nature, whereas targets for lower-level employees tend to be more specific. For example, an objective might be to improve the rating for accurate delivery or reduce the number of dissatisfied customers by half. It is important to have employees participate in setting their goals and to include only factors that are within the employees' control.

Appraisal Period

Formal performance evaluations are usually prepared at specific intervals. Although there is nothing magical about the period for formal appraisal reviews, in most organizations they occur either annually or semiannually. Even more significant, however, is the continuous interaction (primarily informal), including coaching and other developmental activities, that continues throughout the appraisal period. Managers should be conditioned to understand that managing performance is a continuous process that is built into their job every day.

In the current business climate, it may be well for all firms to consider monitoring performance more often. Southwest Airlines has asked its managers to have monthly check-ins with staff rather than semi-annual ones.[20] One study found that 63 percent of high-growth companies review performance more than once a year; in comparison, just 22 percent of low-growth companies review performance more than once a year.[21] Changes occur so fast that employees need to look at objectives and their own roles throughout the year to see whether changes are in order. In high-tech organizations, the speed of change mandates that a performance period be shorter, perhaps every three or four months.

Some organizations use the employee's date of hire to determine the rating period. At times a subordinate's first appraisal may occur at the end of a probationary period, anywhere from

30 to 90 days after his or her start date. However, in the interest of consistency, it may be advisable to perform evaluations on a calendar basis rather than on anniversaries. If firms do not conduct all appraisals at the same time, it may be impossible to make needed comparisons between employees.

Performance Appraisal Methods

OBJECTIVE 8.7
Identify the various performance appraisal methods.

Managers may choose from among a number of appraisal methods. The type of performance appraisal system used depends on its purpose. If the major emphasis is on selecting people for promotion, training, and merit pay increases, a traditional method, such as rating scales, may be appropriate. Collaborative methods, including input from the employees themselves, may prove to be more suitable for developing employees.

360-Degree Feedback Evaluation Method

360-degree feedback evaluation method
Popular performance appraisal method that involves evaluation input from multiple levels within the firm as well as external sources.

HR Web Wisdom

360 Degree Evaluation
http://www. custominsight.com/ 360-degree-feedback/ 360-delivering- feedback.asp

Delivering feedback.

The **360-degree feedback evaluation method** is a popular performance appraisal method that involves evaluation input from multiple levels within the firm as well as external sources.

The 360-degree method is unlike traditional performance reviews, which provide employees with feedback only from supervisors.[22] In this method, people all around the rated employee may provide ratings, including senior managers, the employee himself or herself, supervisors, subordinates, peers, team members, and internal or external customers.[23] As many as 90 percent of *Fortune* 500 companies use some form of 360-degree feedback for either employee evaluation or development.[24] Many companies use results from 360-degree programs not only for conventional applications but also for succession planning, training, and professional development.

Unlike traditional approaches, 360-degree feedback focuses on skills needed across organizational boundaries. Also, by shifting the responsibility for evaluation to more than one person, many of the common appraisal errors can be reduced or eliminated. Software is available to permit managers to give the ratings quickly and conveniently. The 360-degree feedback method may provide a more objective measure of a person's performance. Including the perspective of multiple sources results in a broader view of the employee's performance and may minimize biases that result from limited views of behavior.

Having multiple raters also makes the process more legally defensible. However, it is important for all parties to know the evaluation criteria, the methods for gathering and summarizing the feedback, and the use to which the feedback will be put. An appraisal system involving numerous evaluators will naturally take more time and, therefore, be more costly. Nevertheless, the way firms are being organized and managed may require innovative alternatives to traditional top-down appraisals.

According to some managers, the 360-degree feedback method has problems. Ilene Gochman, director of Watson Wyatt's organization effectiveness practice, says, "We've found that use of the 360 is actually negatively correlated with financial results."[25] GE's former CEO Jack Welch maintains that the 360-degree system in his firm had been "gamed" and that people were saying nice things about one another, resulting in all good ratings.[26] Another critical view with an opposite twist is that input from peers, who may be competitors for raises and promotions, might intentionally distort the data and sabotage the colleague. Yet, since so many firms use 360-degree feedback evaluation, it seems that many firms have found ways to avoid the pitfalls.

Google has a different approach to 360-degree feedback as it provides managers and employees to nominate 'peer reviewers' from anywhere across the organization. According to the company's manager of HR technology and operations, Melissa Karp, "People are fairly candid in their feedback."[27] One might ask, what happens at Google when people write unconstructive comments? Karp said, "managers are encouraged to use that as a 'coachable moment' to talk to the person who wrote something unconstructive. However, at Google this hasn't been too much of a problem."[28]

The biggest risk with 360-degree feedback is confidentiality. Many firms outsource the process to make participants feel comfortable that the information they share and receive is completely anonymous, but the information is very sensitive and, in the wrong hands, could impact careers.

Rating Scales Method

rating scales method
Performance appraisal method that rates employees according to defined factors.

The **rating scales method** is a performance appraisal method that rates employees according to defined factors.

Using this approach, evaluators record their judgments about performance on a scale. The scale includes several categories, normally 5–7 in number, defined by adjectives such as *outstanding, meets expectations,* or *needs improvement.* Although systems often provide an overall rating, the method generally allows for the use of more than one performance criterion. One reason for the popularity of the rating scales method is its simplicity, which permits quick evaluations of many employees. When you quantify the ratings, the method facilitates comparison of employees' performances.

The factors chosen for evaluation are typically of two types: job-related and personal characteristics. Note that in Figure 8.2, job-related factors include quality and quantity of work,

Figure 8.2

Rating Scales Method of Performance Appraisal

Name	Job Title
Supervisor/Manager	Department
Appraisal Period: From	To

Evaluate the performance in each of the following factors on a scale of 1 to 5:
5 = Outstanding, consistently exceeds expectations for this factor.
4 = Above Expectations, consistently meets and occasionally exceeds expectations.
3 = Meets Expectations, consistently meets expectations.
2 = Below Expectations, occasionally fails to meet expectations.
1 = Needs Improvement, consistently fails to meet expectations.

Part 1—Task Outcomes (Weighted 80% of total score)
List mutually agreed-to performance factors from the job description   **Points**
and goals established from the preview performance review.

- _____ ____
- _____ ____
- _____ ____
- _____ ____
- Quality of work   ____
- Quantity of work   ____
                              Total Points   ____
Average Score (Divide total points by number of factors used)   ____ Multiplied by **16** = ____
Comments _____
_____
_____

Part 2—Personal Behaviors (10% of total score)
- Leadership   ____
- Interpersonal skills   ____
- Developing others   ____
- Customer service   ____
- Teamwork   ____
                              Total Points   ____
Average Score (Divide total points by number of applicable factors)   ____ Multiplied by **2** = ____
Comments _____
_____
_____

Figure 8.2

Continued

Part 3—Personal Traits (10% of total score)
- Adaptability _____
- Judgment _____
- Appearance _____
- Attitude _____
- Initiative _____

Total Points _____

Average Score (Divide total points by 5) _____ Multiplied by **2** = _____

Comments _____

_____

_____

Points from Part 1 _____ + Part 2 _____ + Part 3 _____ = Total Points _____

Performance goals for next appraisal period:
- _____
- _____
- _____
- _____
- _____

Self-development activities for this employee

_____

_____

_____

Employee comments

_____

_____

_____

Evaluated By:	Title	Date
Approved	Title	Date
Employee's Signature (Does not necessarily indicate agreement)	Title	Date

whereas personal factors include such behaviors as interpersonal skills and traits, like *adaptability*. The rater (evaluator) completes the form by indicating the degree of each factor that is most descriptive of the employee and his or her performance. In this illustration, evaluators total and then average the points in each part. They then multiply this average by a factor representing the weight given to each section. The final score (total points) for the employee is the total of each section's points.

Some firms provide space for the rater to comment on the evaluation given for each factor. This practice may be especially encouraged, or even required, when the rater gives an extreme rating, either the highest or lowest. For instance, if an employee is rated *needs improvement* (a 1 on the sample form) on *teamwork,* the rater provides written justification for this low evaluation. The purpose of this requirement is to focus on correcting deficiencies and to discourage arbitrary and hastily made judgments.

The more precise the definition of factors and degrees, the more accurately the rater can evaluate worker performance. For instance, in order to receive an *outstanding* rating for a factor such as *quality of work,* a person must consistently go beyond the prescribed work requirements. When the various performance levels are described merely as *above expectations* or *below expectations* without further elaboration, what has the employee really learned? These generalities do not provide the guidance needed for improving performance. It is important that each rater interpret the factors and degrees in the same way. Raters acquire this ability through performance appraisal training. Many rating scale forms also provide for consideration of future behavior. Notice that the form shown as Figure 8.2 has space for performance goals for the next period and self-development activities for the next appraisal period.

Critical Incident Method

critical incident method
Performance appraisal method that requires keeping written records of highly favorable and unfavorable employee work actions.

The **critical incident method** is a performance appraisal method that requires keeping written records of highly favorable and unfavorable employee work actions.

When such an action, a "critical incident," affects the department's effectiveness significantly, either positively or negatively, the manager writes it down. At the end of the appraisal period, the rater uses these records along with other data to evaluate employee performance. With this method, the appraisal is more likely to cover the entire evaluation period and not focus on the past few weeks or months.

Essay Method

essay method
Performance appraisal method in which the rater writes a brief narrative describing the employee's performance.

The **essay method** is a performance appraisal method in which the rater writes a brief narrative describing the employee's performance.

This method tends to focus on extreme behavior in the employee's work rather than on routine day-to-day performance. Ratings of this type depend heavily on the evaluator's writing ability. Supervisors with excellent writing skills, if so inclined, can make a marginal worker sound like a top performer. Comparing essay evaluations might be difficult because no common criteria exist. However, some managers believe that the essay method is not only the most simple but also an acceptable approach to employee evaluation.

Work Standards Method

work standards method
Performance appraisal method that compares each employee's performance to a predetermined standard or expected level of output.

The **work standards method** is a performance appraisal method that compares each employee's performance to a predetermined standard or expected level of output.

Standards reflect the normal output of an average worker operating at a normal pace. Firms may apply work standards to virtually all types of jobs, but production jobs generally receive the most attention. An obvious advantage of using standards as appraisal criteria is objectivity. However, in order for employees to perceive that the standards are objective, they should understand clearly how the standards were set. Management must also explain the rationale for any changes to the standards.

Ranking Method

ranking method
Performance appraisal method in which the rater ranks all employees from a group in order of overall performance.

The **ranking method** is a performance appraisal method in which the rater ranks all employees from a group in order of overall performance.

For example, the best employee in the group is ranked highest, and the poorest is ranked lowest. You follow this procedure until you rank all employees. A difficulty occurs when all individuals have performed at comparable levels (as perceived by the evaluator).

Paired comparison is a variation of the ranking method in which the performance of each employee is compared with that of every other employee in the group. A single criterion, such as overall performance, is often the basis for this comparison. The employee who receives the greatest number of favorable comparisons receives the highest ranking.

Some professionals in the field argue for using a comparative approach, such as ranking, whenever management must make human resource decisions. They believe that employees are promoted or receive the highest pay increases not because they achieve their objectives, but rather because they achieve them better than others in their work group.

Forced Distribution Method

The **forced distribution method** of performance appraisal requires the rater to assign individuals in a work group to a limited number of categories, similar to a normal frequency distribution. The purpose of forced distribution is to keep managers from being excessively lenient and having a disproportionate number of employees in the "superior" category.[29]

Forced distribution systems have been around for decades and firms such as General Electric, Cisco Systems, EDS, Hewlett-Packard, Microsoft, Pepsi, Caterpillar, Sun Microsystems, Goodyear, Ford Motor, and Capital One use them today.[30] Proponents of forced distribution believe they facilitate budgeting and guard against weak managers who are too timid to get rid of poor performers. They think that forced rankings require managers to be honest with workers about how they are doing.

The forced distribution systems tend to be based on three levels. In GE's system, the best performers are placed in the top 20 percent, the next group in the middle 70 percent, and the poorest performing group winds up in the bottom 10 percent. The underperformers are, after being given a time to improve their performance, generally let go.[31] If any of the underperformers are able to improve their performance, you might wonder if any in the 70 percent group would get nervous!

Although used by some prestigious firms, the forced distribution system appears to be unpopular with many managers. In a survey of HR professionals, 44 percent of respondents thought their firm's forced ranking system damages morale and generates mistrust of leadership.[32] Some believe it fosters cutthroat competition, paranoia, and general ill will, and destroys employee loyalty. A Midwestern banker states that his company "began a rank-and-yank system that flies directly in the face of the 'teamwork' that senior management says it wants to encourage. Don't tell me I'm supposed to put the good of the team first and then tell me the bottom 10 percent of us are going to lose our jobs because, team be damned, I'm going to make sure I'm not in that bottom 10 percent."[33] Critics of forced distribution contend that they compel managers to penalize a good, although not a great, employee who is part of a superstar team. One reason employees are opposed to forced ranking is that they suspect that the rankings are a way for companies to rationalize firings more easily.

Behaviorally Anchored Rating Scale Method

The **behaviorally anchored rating scale (BARS) method** is a performance appraisal method that combines elements of the traditional rating scales and critical incident methods; various performance levels are shown along a scale with each described in terms of an employee's specific job behavior.

Table 8.1 illustrates a portion of a BARS system that was developed to evaluate college recruiters. Suppose the factor chosen for evaluation is *Ability to Present Positive Company Image*. On the *very positive* end of this factor would be "Makes excellent impression on college recruits. Carefully explains positive aspects of the company. Listens to applicant and answers questions in a very positive manner." On the *very negative* end of this factor would be "Even with repeated instructions continues to make a poor impression. This interviewer could be expected to turn off college applicants from wanting to join the firm." As may be noted, there are several levels in between the very negative and the very positive. The rater is able to determine more objectively how frequently the employee performs in each defined level.

A BARS system differs from rating scales because, instead of using terms such as *high, medium,* and *low* at each scale point, it uses behavioral anchors related to the criterion being measured. This modification clarifies the meaning of each point on the scale and reduces rater bias and error by anchoring the rating with specific behavioral examples based on job analysis information. Instead of providing a space for entering a rating figure for a category such as *Above Expectations,* the BARS method provides examples of such behavior. This approach

Table 8.1   BARS for Factor: Ability to Present Positive Company Image

Clearly Outstanding Performance	Makes excellent impression on college recruits. Carefully explains positive aspects of the company. Listens to applicant and answers questions in a very positive manner.
Excellent Performance	Makes good impression on college recruits. Answers all questions and explains positive aspects of the company. Answers questions in a positive manner.
Good Performance	Makes a reasonable impression on college recruits. Listens to applicant and answers questions in knowledgeable manner.
Average Performance	Makes a fair impression on college recruits. Listens to applicant and answers most questions in a knowledgeable manner.
Slightly Below Average Performance	Attempts to make a good impression on college recruits. Listens to applicants but at times could be expected to have to go to other sources to get answers to questions.
Poor Performance	At times makes poor impression on college recruits. Sometimes provides incorrect information to applicant or goes down blind avenues before realizing mistake.
Very Poor Performance	Even with repeated instructions continues to make a poor impression. This interviewer could be expected to turn off college applicant from wanting to join the firm.

facilitates discussion of the rating because it addresses specific behaviors, thus overcoming weaknesses in other evaluation methods. Regardless of apparent advantages of the BARS method, reports on its effectiveness are mixed. A specific deficiency is that the behaviors used are activity oriented rather than results oriented. Also, the method may not be economically feasible since each job category requires its own BARS. Yet, among the various appraisal techniques, the BARS method is perhaps the most highly defensible in court because it is based on actual observable job behaviors.

Results-Based System

The manager and subordinate jointly agree on objectives for the next appraisal period in a **results-based system**, in the past a form of *management by objectives*.

In such a system, one objective might be, for example, to cut waste by 10 percent. At the end of the appraisal period, an evaluation focuses on how well the employee achieved this objective.

Problems in Performance Appraisal

As indicated at the beginning of this chapter, performance appraisal is constantly under a barrage of criticism. The rating scales method seems to be the most vulnerable target. Yet, in all fairness, many of the problems commonly mentioned are not inherent in this method but, rather, reflect improper implementation. For example, firms may fail to provide adequate rater training or they may use appraisal criteria that are too subjective and lack job-relatedness. The following section highlights some of the more common problem areas.

Appraiser Discomfort

Conducting performance appraisals is often a frustrating human resource management task. One management guru, Edward Lawler, noted the considerable documentation showing that performance appraisal systems neither motivate individuals nor effectively guide their

results-based system
Performance appraisal method in which the manager and subordinate jointly agree on objectives for the next appraisal period; in the past a form of *management by objectives*.

OBJECTIVE 8.8
List the problems that have been associated with performance appraisal.

development. Instead, he maintains, they create conflict between supervisors and sub-ordinates and lead to dysfunctional behaviors.[34] This caveat is important. If a performance appraisal system has a faulty design, or improper administration, employees will dread receiving appraisals and the managers will despise giving them. In fact, some managers have always loathed the time, paperwork, difficult choices, and discomfort that often accompanies the appraisal process. Going through the procedure cuts into a manager's high-priority work-load and the experience can be especially unpleasant when the employee in question has not performed well.

Lack of Objectivity

A potential weakness of traditional performance appraisal methods is that they lack objec-tivity. In the rating scales method, for example, commonly used factors such as attitude, appearance, and personality are difficult to measure. In addition, these factors may have little to do with an employee's job performance. Although subjectivity will always exist in appraisal methods, employee appraisal based primarily on personal characteristics may place the evaluator and the company in untenable positions with the employee and equal emp-loyment opportunity guidelines. The firm may be hard-pressed to show that these factors are job-related.

Halo/Horn

A **halo error** occurs when a manager generalizes one positive performance feature or incident to all aspects of employee performance, resulting in a higher rating.[35]

For example, Rodney Pirkle, accounting supervisor, placed a high value on neatness, a factor used in the company's performance appraisal system. As Rodney was evaluating the performance of his senior accounting clerk, Jack Hicks, he noted that Jack was a very neat individual and gave him a high ranking on this factor. Also, consciously or unconsciously, Rodney permitted the high ranking on neatness to carry over to other factors, giving Jack unde-served high ratings on all factors. Of course, if Jack had not been neat, the opposite could have occurred. This phenomenon is known as the **horn error**, an evaluation error that occurs when a manager generalizes one negative performance feature or incident to all aspects of employee performance, resulting in a lower rating.

Leniency/Strictness

Some managers are too generous with praise or too hard on a person. Dick Grote, a perform-ance management expert and president of Grote Consulting Corporation, a management con-sulting firm in Dallas, said, "It is not OK to have performance rated differently from manager to manager because these decisions impact compensation, development and succession planning."[36]

Giving undeserved high ratings to an employee is referred to as **leniency**. This behavior is often motivated by a desire to avoid controversy over the appraisal. It is most prevalent when highly subjective (and difficult to defend) performance criteria are used, and the rater is required to discuss evaluation results with employees. When managers know they are evaluat-ing employees for administrative purposes, such as pay increases, they are likely to be more lenient than when evaluating performance to achieve employee development. Leniency, how-ever, may result in failure to recognize correctable deficiencies. The practice may also deplete the merit budget and reduce the rewards available for superior employees. In addition, an organization will find it difficult to terminate poor-performing employees who continuously receive positive evaluations.

Being unduly critical of an employee's work performance is referred to as **strictness**. Although leniency is usually more prevalent than strictness, some managers, on their own initi-ative, apply an evaluation more rigorously than the company standard. This behavior may be due to a lack of understanding of various evaluation factors. The worst situation is when a firm has both lenient and strict managers and does nothing to level the inequities. Here, the weak performers get relatively high pay increases and promotions from a lenient boss, whereas the strict manager shortchanges the stronger employees. This can have a demoralizing effect on the morale and motivation of the top-performing people.

Central Tendency

Central tendency error is an evaluation appraisal error that occurs when employees are incorrectly rated near the average or middle of a scale. This practice may be encouraged by some rating scale systems that require the evaluator to justify in writing extremely high or extremely low ratings. With such a system, the rater may avoid possible controversy or criticism by giving only average ratings. However, since these ratings tend to cluster in the *fully satisfactory* range, employees do not often complain. Nevertheless, this error does exist and it influences the accuracy of evaluations. Typically, when pay raises are given, they will be based on an employee's performance. When a manager gives an underachiever or overachiever, an average rating, it undermines the compensation system.[37]

Recent Behavior Bias

Anyone who has observed the behavior of young children several weeks before Christmas can readily identify with the problem of recent behavior bias. Suddenly, the wildest kids in the neighborhood develop angelic personalities in anticipation of the rewards they hope to receive from Old Saint Nick. Individuals in the workforce are not children, but they are human. Virtually every employee knows precisely when a performance review is scheduled. Although his or her actions may not be conscious, an employee's behavior often improves and productivity tends to rise several days or weeks before the scheduled evaluation. It is only natural for a rater to remember recent behavior more clearly than actions from the more distant past. However, formal performance appraisals generally cover a specified time, and an individual's performance over the entire period should be considered. Maintaining records of performance throughout the appraisal period helps avoid this problem.

Personal Bias (Stereotyping)

This pitfall occurs when managers allow individual differences to affect the ratings they give. If these are factors to avoid such as gender, race, or age, not only is this problem detrimental to employee morale, but it is blatantly illegal and can result in costly litigation. The effects of cultural bias, or stereotyping, can definitely influence appraisals.[38] Managers establish mental pictures of what are considered ideal typical workers, and employees who do not match this picture may be unfairly judged.

Discrimination in appraisal can be based on other factors as well. For example, mild-mannered employees may be appraised more harshly because they do not seriously object to the results. This type of behavior is in sharp contrast to the more outspoken employee, who often confirms the adage: *the squeaky wheel gets the grease.*

Manipulating the Evaluation

In some instances, managers control virtually every aspect of the appraisal process and are therefore in a position to manipulate the system. For example, a supervisor may want to give a pay raise to a certain employee or the supervisor may just "favor" one worker more than another.[39] In order to justify this action, the supervisor may give the employee an undeserved high performance evaluation and perhaps a less favored, but productive, employee a lower rating.[40] Or, the supervisor may want to get rid of an employee and so may give the individual an undeserved low rating. In either instance, the system is distorted and the goals of performance appraisal cannot be achieved. In addition, in the latter example, if the employee is a member of a protected group, the firm may wind up in court. If the organization cannot adequately support the evaluation, it may suffer significant financial loss.

ETHICAL DILEMMA

Abdication of Responsibility

You are the new vice president for human resources of a company that has not been performing well, and everyone, including yourself, has a mandate to deliver results. The pressure has never been greater. Shareholders are angry after 31 months of a tough market that has left their stock underwater. Many shareholders desperately need stock performance to pay for their retirement. Working for you is a 52-year-old manager with two kids in college. In previous evaluations, spineless executives told him he was doing fine, when he clearly was not, and his performance is still far below par.

If you are to show others in the company that you are willing to make tough decisions, you feel you must fire this individual. The question is who's going to suffer: the firm and ultimately shareholders whose retirements are in jeopardy, or a nice guy who's been lied to for 20 years.

What would you do?[43]

One study revealed that more than 70 percent of responding managers believe that inflated and lowered ratings are given intentionally. Table 8.2 shows these managers' explanations for their rationale. The results suggest that the validity of many performance appraisal systems is flawed, although another study indicated that appraisal data are valid 75 percent of the time.[41] Yet, having invalid appraisal data 25 percent of the time would be nothing to brag about. It seems obvious that evaluator training emphasizing the negative consequences of rater errors would pay for itself many times over.

Employee Anxiety

The evaluation process may also create anxiety for the appraised employee. This may take the form of discontent, apathy, and turnover. In a worst-case scenario, a lawsuit is filed based on real or perceived unfairness.[42] Opportunities for promotion, better work assignments, and increased compensation may hinge on the results. This could cause not only apprehension, but also outright resistance. One opinion is that if you surveyed typical employees, they would tell you performance appraisal is management's way of highlighting all the bad things they did all year.

Table 8.2   Reasons for Intentionally Inflating or Lowering Ratings

Inflated Ratings

- The belief that accurate ratings would have a damaging effect on the subordinate's motivation and performance
- The desire to improve an employee's eligibility for merit
- The desire to avoid airing the department's dirty laundry
- The wish to avoid creating a negative permanent record of poor performance that might hound the employee in the future
- The need to protect good performers whose performance was suffering because of personal problems
- The wish to reward employees displaying great effort even though results are relatively low
- The need to avoid confrontation with certain hard-to-manage employees
- The desire to promote a poor or disliked employee up and out of the department

Lowered Ratings

- To scare better performance out of an employee
- To punish a difficult or rebellious employee
- To encourage a problem employee to quit
- To create a strong record to justify a planned firing
- To minimize the amount of the merit increase a subordinate receives
- To comply with an organization edict that discourages managers from giving high ratings

Source: Clinton Longenecker and Dean Ludwig, "Ethical Dilemmas in Performance Appraisal Revisited," *Journal of Business Ethics* 9 (December 1990): 963. Reprinted by permission of Kluwer Academic Publishers.

OBJECTIVE 8.9

Explain the characteristics of an effective appraisal system.

Characteristics of an Effective Appraisal System

The basic purpose of a performance appraisal system is to improve performance of individuals, teams, and the entire organization. The system may also serve to assist in making administrative decisions concerning pay increases, promotions, transfers, or terminations. In addition, the appraisal system must be legally defensible. Although a perfect system does not exist, every system should possess certain characteristics. Organizations should seek an accurate assessment of performance that permits the development of a plan to improve individual and group performance. The system must honestly inform people of how they stand with the organization. The following factors assist in accomplishing these purposes.

Job-Related Criteria

Job-relatedness is perhaps the most basic criterion needed in employee performance appraisals. The *Uniform Guidelines on Employee Selection Procedures* and court decisions are quite clear on this point. More specifically, evaluation criteria should be determined through job analysis. Subjective factors, such as initiative, enthusiasm, loyalty, and cooperation may be important; however, unless clearly shown to be job-related, they should not be used.

Performance Expectations

Managers and subordinates must agree on performance expectations in advance of the appraisal period.[44] How can employees function effectively if they do not know what they are being measured against? On the other hand, if employees clearly understand the expectations, they can evaluate their own performance and make timely adjustments as they perform their jobs, without having to wait for the formal evaluation review. The establishment of highly objective work standards is relatively simple in many areas, such as manufacturing, assembly, and sales. For numerous other types of jobs, however, this task is more difficult. Still, evaluation must take place based on clearly understood performance expectations.

Standardization

Firms should use the same evaluation instrument for all employees in the same job category who work for the same supervisor. Supervisors should also conduct appraisals covering similar periods for these employees. Regularly scheduled feedback sessions and appraisal interviews for all employees are essential.

Formal documentation of appraisal data serves several purposes, including protection against possible legal action. Employees should sign their evaluations. If the employee refuses to sign, the manager should document this behavior. Records should also include a description of employee responsibilities, expected performance results, and the role these data play in making appraisal decisions. Although performance appraisal is important for small firms, they are not expected to maintain performance appraisal systems that are as formal as those used by large organizations. Courts have reasoned that objective criteria are not as important in firms with only a few employees because in smaller firms top managers are more intimately acquainted with their employees' work.

Trained Appraisers

A common deficiency in appraisal systems is that the evaluators seldom receive training on how to conduct effective evaluations. Unless everyone evaluating performance receives training in the art of giving and receiving feedback, the process can lead to uncertainty and conflict. The training should be an ongoing process in order to ensure accuracy and consistency. The training should cover how to rate employees and how to conduct appraisal interviews. Instructions should be rather detailed and the importance of making objective and unbiased ratings should be emphasized. An e-learning training module may serve to provide information for managers as needed.

Continuous Open Communication

Most employees have a strong need to know how well they are performing. A good appraisal system provides highly desired feedback on a continuing basis. There should be few surprises in the performance review. Managers should handle daily performance problems as they occur and not allow them to pile up for six months or a year and then address them during the performance appraisal interview. Continuous feedback is vitally important to help direct, coach, and teach employees to grow and improve performance.[45] When something new surfaces during the appraisal interview, the manager probably did not do a good enough job communicating with the employee throughout the appraisal period. Even though the interview presents an excellent opportunity for both parties to exchange ideas, it should never serve as a substitute for the day-to-day communication and coaching required by performance management.

Conduct Performance Reviews

In addition to the need for continuous communication between managers and their employees, a special time should be set for a formal discussion of an employee's performance. Since improved performance is a common goal of appraisal systems, withholding appraisal results is absurd. Employees are severely handicapped in their developmental efforts if denied access to this information. A performance review allows them to detect any errors or omissions in the appraisal, or an employee may disagree with the evaluation and want to challenge it.

Constant employee performance documentation is vitally important for accurate performance appraisals. Although the task can be tedious and boring for managers, maintaining a continuous record of observed and reported incidents is essential in building a useful appraisal. The appraisal interview will be discussed in a later section.

Due Process

Ensuring due process is vital. If the company does not have a formal grievance procedure, it should develop one to provide employees an opportunity to appeal appraisal results that they consider inaccurate or unfair. They must have a procedure for pursuing their grievances and having them addressed objectively.

OBJECTIVE 8.10
Describe the legal implications of performance appraisal.

Legal Implications

Employee lawsuits may result from negative evaluations. Employees often win these cases, thanks in part to the employer's own performance appraisal procedures. A review of court cases makes it clear that legally defensible performance appraisal systems should be in place. Perfect systems are not expected, and the law does not preclude supervisory discretion in the process. However, the courts normally require these conditions:

- Either the absence of adverse impact on members of protected classes or validation of the process.
- A system that prevents one manager from directing or controlling a subordinate's career.
- The appraisal should be reviewed and approved by someone or some group in the organization.
- The rater, or raters, must have personal knowledge of the employee's job performance.
- The appraisal systems must use predetermined criteria that limit the manager's discretion.

Mistakes in appraising performance and decisions based on invalid results can have serious repercussions. For example, discriminatory allocation of money for merit pay increases can result in costly legal action. In settling cases, courts have held employers liable for back pay, court costs, and other costs related to training and promoting certain employees in protected classes.

An employer may also be vulnerable to a *negligent retention* claim if an employee who continually receives unsatisfactory ratings in safety practices, for example, is kept on the payroll and he or she causes injury to a third party. In these instances, firms might reduce their liability if they provide substandard performers with training designed to overcome the deficiencies.

It is unlikely that any appraisal system will be immune to legal challenge. However, systems that possess the characteristics discussed above are more legally defensible. At the same time, they can provide a more effective means for achieving performance management goals.

OBJECTIVE 8.11

Explain how the appraisal interview should be conducted.

Appraisal Interview

The appraisal interview is the Achilles' heel of the entire evaluation process. In fact, appraisal review sessions often create hostility and can do more harm than good to the employee–manager relationship. To minimize the possibility of hard feelings, the face-to-face meeting and the written review must have performance improvement, not criticism, as their goal. The reviewing manager must use all the tact he or she can muster in discussing areas needing improvement. Managers should help employees understand that they are not the only ones under the gun. Rating managers should emphasize their own responsibility for the employee's development and commitment for support.

The appraisal interview definitely has the potential for confrontation and undermining the goal of motivating employees. The situation improves considerably when several sources provide input, including perhaps the employee's own self-appraisal. Regardless of the system used, employees will not trust a system they do not understand.

Scheduling the Interview

Supervisors usually conduct a formal appraisal interview at the end of an employee's appraisal period. It should be made clear to the employee as to what the meeting is about.[46] Employees typically know when their interview should take place, and their anxiety tends to increase if their supervisor delays the meeting. Interviews with top performers are often pleasant experiences for all concerned. However, supervisors may be reluctant to meet face-to-face with poor performers. They tend to postpone these anxiety-provoking interviews.

Interview Structure

A successful appraisal interview should be structured in a way that allows both the supervisor and the subordinate to view it as a problem-solving rather than a fault-finding session. The manager should consider three basic purposes when planning an appraisal interview:

1. Discuss the employee's performance. Focus on specific accomplishments.[47]
2. Assist the employee in setting goals and personal-development plans for the next appraisal period.
3. Suggest means for achieving established goals, including support from the manager and firm.

For instance, a worker may receive an average rating on a factor such as *quality of production*. In the interview, both parties should agree to the specific improvement needed during the next appraisal period and specific actions that each should take.[48]

During performance reviews, managers might ask employees whether their current duties and roles are effective in achieving their goals. In addition to reviewing job-related performance, they might also discuss subjective topics, such as career ambitions. For example, in working on a project, perhaps an employee discovered an unrealized aptitude. This awareness could result in a new goal or serve as a springboard to an expanded role in the organization.

The amount of time devoted to an appraisal interview varies considerably with company policy and the position of the evaluated employee. Although costs are a consideration, there is merit in conducting separate interviews for discussing: (1) employee performance and development and (2) pay. Many managers have learned that as soon as the topic of pay emerges in an interview, it tends to dominate the conversation, with performance improvement taking a back seat. For this reason, if pay increases or bonuses are involved in the appraisal, it might be advisable to defer those discussions for one to several weeks after the appraisal interview.

Use of Praise and Criticism

As suggested at the beginning of this section, conducting an appraisal interview requires tact and patience on the part of the evaluator. Praise is appropriate when warranted, but it can have limited value if not clearly deserved. If an employee must eventually be terminated because of poor performance, a manager's false praise could bring into question the "real" reason for being fired.[49] Criticism, even if warranted, is especially difficult to give. The employee may not

A GLOBAL PERSPECTIVE

Two Cultures' Views of Performance Appraisal

Performance appraisal is an area of human resource management that has special problems when translated into different cultural environments. Chinese managers often have a different idea about what performance is than do Western managers, as Chinese companies tend to focus appraisals on different criteria. Chinese managers appear to define performance in terms of personal characteristics, such as loyalty and obedience, rather than outcome measurement. Chinese performance appraisals place great emphasis on moral characteristics. Western performance appraisal seeks to help achieve organizational objectives, and this is best obtained by concentrating on individual outcomes and behaviors that are related to the attainment of those objectives.[51]

Chinese organizational objectives often differ widely from the objectives of Western firms. Chinese firms have had to fulfill state political objectives such as maximizing employment, and internal HR management practices are oriented to serve these objectives. Many overseas Chinese business practices are grounded in the traditions of Chinese family business, in which a primary objective is to maintain family control of the business. Even when the business is incorporated and publicly traded, the family often maintains majority control, and this is a major organizational objective even to the extent of tolerating less-than-optimal performance. One implication of this is that performance appraisals would tend to favor workers who supported the family over workers who challenged family authority. These differing objectives will influence the way in which appraisal judgments are made.[52]

There are other well-known characteristics of the Chinese that also have a direct bearing on the practice of performance appraisal. Three such characteristics are face (*mianzi*), fatalism, and the somewhat broad term *Confucianism*. *Mianzi* is the social status that one has, and a person's *mianzi* will have an effect on that person's ability to influence others. It is particularly important that performance reviews be held in private, since a poor review in public will cause a subordinate to lose *mianzi*. It is for this reason that the Chinese tend to avoid the possibility of confrontation and loss of face that could result from a formal appraisal process. This concern with *mianzi* also makes it difficult to publicly act on performance problems.[53]

Fatalism also has a direct impact on performance appraisal. Research has indicated that Chinese individuals are more likely to blame their own problems on external factors, and since the outcome is due to things outside the individual's control, poor achievement will not lead to a loss of face. Such a defensive reaction is natural and occurs in all cultures, but appears to be stronger and more formally ritualized in mainland China.[54]

One legacy of Confucianism is an emphasis on morality as a basis for evaluation. Under the Confucian view, the most important characteristic of an individual was the moral basis of his or her character. A quotation from the Confucian classic *Da Xue* (Great Wisdom) says, "Cultivate oneself, bring order to the family, rule the country, and bring peace to the world." Thus, peace, harmony, and success all start with cultivating oneself, including the cultivation of one's moral character. In the view of the Chinese, a moral worker will also be an effective worker. Therefore, evaluation of performance and achievement carries strong elements of judgments of the employee's moral character.[55]

perceive it as being constructive. It is important that discussions of these sensitive issues focus on the deficiency, not the person. Effective managers minimize threats to the employee's self-esteem whenever possible. When giving criticism, managers should emphasize the positive aspects of performance; criticize actions, not the person; and ask the employee how he or she would change things to improve the situation. Also, the manager should avoid supplying all the answers and try to turn the interview into a win–win situation so that all concerned gain.

Employees' Role

From the employees' side, two weeks or so before the review, they should go through their diaries or files and make a note of all projects worked on, regardless of whether or not they were successful.[50] The best recourse for employees in preparing for an appraisal review is to prepare a list of creative ways they have solved problems with limited resources. They will look especially good if they can show how their work contributes to the value of the company. This information should be on the appraising manager's desk well before the review. Reminding managers of information they may have missed should help in developing a more objective and accurate appraisal.

Concluding the Interview

Ideally, employees will leave the interview with positive feelings about management, the company, the job, and themselves. If the meeting results in a deflated ego, the prospects for improved performance will be bleak. Although you cannot change past behavior, future performance is another matter. The interview should end with specific and mutually agreed-upon plans for the employee's development. Managers should assure employees who require additional training that it will be forthcoming and that they will have the full support of their supervisor. When management does its part in employee development, it is up to the individual to perform in an acceptable manner.

Summary

1. *Define* performance management *and describe the importance of performance management.* Performance management is a goal-oriented process that is directed toward ensuring that organizational processes are in place to maximize productivity of employees, teams, and ultimately, the organization. Whereas performance appraisal is a one-time event each year, performance management is a dynamic, ongoing, continuous process.

2. *Define* performance appraisal *and identify the uses of performance appraisal.* Performance appraisal is a system of review and evaluation of an individual's or team's job performance.

   Performance appraisal data are potentially valuable for use in numerous human resource functional areas, including human resource planning, recruitment and selection, training and development, career planning and development, compensation programs, internal employee relations, and assessment of employee potential.

3. *Discuss the performance appraisal environmental factors.* Legislation requires that appraisal systems be nondiscriminatory. Unions have traditionally stressed seniority as the basis for promotions and pay increases. A firm's corporate culture can assist or hinder the process.

4. *Describe the performance appraisal process.* The identification of specific goals is the starting point for the PA process and the beginning of a continuous cycle. Then job expectations are established with the help of job analysis. The next step involves examining the actual work performed. Performance is then appraised. The final step involves discussing the appraisal with the employee.

5. *Identify the various performance criteria (standards) that can be established.* The most common appraisal criteria include traits, behaviors, task outcomes, goal achievement, and improvement potential.

6. *Identify who may be responsible for performance appraisal and the performance period.* People who are usually responsible for performance appraisal include immediate supervisors, subordinates, peers, groups, the employee, customers; and for the 360-degree feedback evaluation method, perhaps all of the above.

7. *Identify the various performance appraisal methods.* Performance appraisal methods include 360-degree feedback evaluation, rating scales, critical incidents, essay, work standards, ranking, forced ranking, forced distribution, behaviorally anchored rating scales, and results-oriented approaches.

8. *List the problems that have been associated with performance appraisal.* The problems associated with performance appraisals include appraiser discomfort, lack of objectivity, halo/horn error, leniency/strictness, central tendency error, recent behavior bias, personal bias (stereotyping), manipulating the evaluation, and employee anxiety.

9. *Explain the characteristics of an effective appraisal system.* Characteristics include job-related criteria, performance expectations, standardization, trained appraisers, continuous open communication, performance reviews, and due process.

10. *Describe the legal implications of performance appraisal.* It is unlikely that any appraisal system will be totally immune to legal challenge. However, systems that possess certain characteristics are more legally defensible.

11. *Explain how the appraisal interview should be conducted.* A successful appraisal interview should be structured in a way that allows both the supervisor and the subordinate to view it as a problem-solving rather than a fault-finding session.

Key Terms

employee engagement   234
performance management (PM)   236
performance appraisal (PA)   236
competencies   241
360-degree feedback evaluation
   method   244
rating scales method   245

critical incident method   247
essay method   247
work standards method   247
ranking method   247
forced distribution method   248
behaviorally anchored rating scale
   (BARS) method   248

results-based system   249
halo error   250
horn error   250
leniency   250
strictness   250
central tendency error   251

Questions for Review

1. Define *performance management* and *performance appraisal*.
2. What are the uses of performance appraisal?
3. What are the steps in the performance appraisal process?
4. What aspects of a person's performance might an organization evaluate?
5. Many different people can conduct performance appraisals. What are the various alternatives?
6. Briefly describe each of the following methods of performance appraisal:
   a. 360-degree feedback evaluation
   b. Rating scales
   c. Critical incidents
   d. Essay
   e. Work standards
   f. Ranking
   g. Forced distribution
   h. Behaviorally anchored rating scales
   i. Results-based systems
7. What are the various problems associated with performance appraisal? Briefly describe each.
8. What are the characteristics of an effective appraisal system?
9. What are the legal implications of performance appraisal?
10. Explain why the following statement is often true: "The *Achilles' heel* of the entire evaluation process is the appraisal interview itself."

HRM INCIDENT 1

These Things Are a Pain

"The dreaded end of year appraisal is upon us!" Linda exclaimed. Like all employees in her organization, Linda was asked to fill out an appraisal form and submit it to the HR department. Linda's immediate supervisor was heard saying, "Here we go again, the paper pushing session!" All employees were required to look back and reflect on the tasks they did during the year, making sure that all value-added activities were documented and accounted for in the appraisal forms.

Linda's boss, Irene, had hinted that it seemed like a hassle to appraise her subordinates. The appraisal assessed employees on different criteria, including whether their goals are in line with the company's core values. Other criteria included efforts to improve teaching performance, participation in student and college activities, research, and personal attributes.

As Linda was a new lecturer in a private university in Malaysia, she felt nervous. She had undergone the mid-year appraisal and had a negative experience from it. As she filled in the appraisal form she wondered whether she had met all the targets set out for her. "Have I improved in the areas I was told I was weak in?" she thought. Indeed, thinking back to the mid-year performance review Irene had mentioned a few areas of weaknesses. Among them was the need to remain alert about her students' performance and to improve her teaching performance and classroom management. Linda felt that each of these criteria required a different measurement tool.

Linda put down that during the semester she had frequent discussions with her peers as an effort to improve her teaching performance. Linda thought about how would this could be measured in the appraisal session. Most of the discussions with her peers seemed to be about problematic students and an activity that was done to improve the performance of students. Classroom management seemed more quantifiable. In her mind, the mix of students differs from semester to semester and it so happened that during her mid-year review, she had a class of rowdy students who presented some problems to her. These problems ranged from poor attendance to nonsubmission of work.

Being new, Linda felt that there were some instances where she had underperformed. As she was filling in the appraisal form, she realised that she hadn't participated in many college activities and had not undertaken much research.

Linda turned to her colleague, Paul, who had just finished his appraisal session. "How did it go?" she asked. Paul replied, "Thank god that's over. Irene's not in the best of moods. I hope that it doesn't affect my appraisal." Linda said, "Mine's tomorrow." Paul replied, "Well, good luck with it."

Questions

1. Why does Linda have a negative impression about the appraisal session?

2. What would have made the appraisal session a more impressive session for Linda so that she could improve on her performance?

HRM INCIDENT 2

Performance Appraisal?

As the production supervisor for Sweeny Electronics, Nakeisha Joseph was generally well regarded by most of her subordinates. Nakeisha was an easygoing individual who tried to help her employees in any way she could. If a worker needed a small loan until payday, she would dig into her pocket with no questions asked. Should an employee need some time off to attend to a personal problem, Nakeisha would not dock the individual's pay; rather, she would take up the slack herself until the worker returned.

Everything had been going smoothly, at least until the last performance appraisal period. One of Nakeisha's workers, Bill Overstreet, had been experiencing a large number of personal problems for the past year. Bill's wife had been sick much of the time, and her medical expenses were high. Bill's son had a speech impediment, and the doctors had recommended a special clinic. Bill, who had already borrowed the limit the bank would loan, had become upset and despondent over his circumstances.

When it was time for Bill's annual performance appraisal, Nakeisha decided she was going to do as much as possible to help him. Although Bill could not be considered more than an average worker, Nakeisha rated him outstanding in virtually every category. Because the firm's compensation system was heavily tied to performance appraisal, Bill would be eligible for a merit increase of 10 percent in addition to a regular cost-of-living raise.

Nakeisha explained to Bill why she was giving him such high ratings, and Bill acknowledged that his performance had really been no better than average. Bill was very grateful and expressed this to Nakeisha. As Bill left the office, he was excitedly looking forward to telling his work buddies about what a wonderful boss he had. Seeing Bill smile as he left gave Nakeisha a warm feeling.

Questions

1. From Sweeny Electronics' standpoint, what difficulties might Nakeisha's performance appraisal practices create?

2. What can Nakeisha do now to diminish the negative impact of her evaluation of Bill?

Notes

1. Ed Frauenheim, "Downturn Puts New Emphasis on Engagement," *Workforce Management* 88 (July 20, 2009): 8–10.

2. "In Football as in Business, Engagement Leads to Success," *Financial Times*, (March 23, 2010); "Managing Success," *Financial Times*, (Jan 20, 2010); "How to Engage a Workforce that Is Fearing the Worst," *Financial Times*, (Feb 10, 2009); John Lewis, (2010): http://www.johnlewispartnership.co.uk/Display.aspx?&MasterId=768e29e8-41aa-4716-bce2-df302fa1c3d8&NavigationId=543; Tesco PLC, (2010): http://www.tescoplc.com/.

3. David F. Giannetto, "Get Your Money's Worth from Incentives," *Business Performance Management* 7 (June 2009): 12.

4. Kathryn Tyler, "Performance Art," *HRMagazine* 50 (August 2005): 58–63.

5. "Make Staff Reviews Count," *Credit Union Magazine* 74 (January 2009): 12.

6. Jeffrey Russell and Linda Russell, "Talk Me Through It: The Next Level of Performance Management," *T+D* 64 (April 2010): 42–48.

7. Andy Houghton, "Performance Reviews: It's about 'How,' Not 'Why'," *BusinessWeek Online* (January 11, 2010): 11.

8. "Employees Care a Lot More About Performance Reviews Than You May Think," *HR Focus* 86 (July 2009): 9.

9. Adrienne Fox, "Curing What Ails Performance Reviews," *HRMagazine* 54 (January 2009): 52–56.

10. Jennifer Taylor Arnold, "Two Needs, One Solution," *HRMagazine* 54 (May 2009): 75–77.

11. Ibid.

12. Ibid.

13. Ibid.

14. Ibid.

15. Ibid.

16. Hugh J. Watson and Jim Hill, "What Gets Watched Gets Done: How Metrics Can Motivate," *Business Intelligence Journal* 14 (2009): 4–7.

17. Susan Meisinger, "Adding Competencies, Adding Value," *HRMagazine* 48 (July 2003): 8.

18. "Self-Evaluation Key to Effective Staff Appraisals," *People Management* 13 (July 12, 2007): 14.

19. Joan Lloyd, "Performance Reviews Never Easy," *Receivables Report for America's Health Care Financial Managers* 24 (March 2009): 8–10.

20. Jena McGregor, "The Midyear Review's Sudden Impact," *BusinessWeek* (July 6, 2009): 50–52.

21. "More Evidence That Performance Management Yields Higher Profits," *HR Focus* 84 (February 2007): 8–9.

22. Tracy Gallagher, "360-Degree Performance Reviews Offer Valuable Perspectives," *Financial Executive* 24 (December 2008): 61.

23. Sean Drakes, "Everybody Counts" *Black Enterprise* 38 (May 2008): 58–59.

24. Tracy Maylette and Juan Riboldi, "Using 360° Feedback to Predict Performance," *T&D* 61 (September 2007): 48–52.

25. Patrick J. Kiger, "When People Practices Damage Market Value," *Workforce Management* (June 26, 2006): 42.

26. John F. Welch Jr., *Jack: Straight from the Gut* (New York: Warner Business Books, 2001): 157–158.

27. Aliah D. Wright, "At Google, It Takes A Village To Hire an Employee," *HRMagazine* 53 (December 2008): 56–57.

28. Ibid.

29. D.G., "Driving the Truth Into Performance Management," *Conference Board Review* 45 (September/October 2008): 42.

30. Stephen Garcia, "Forced Rankings of Employees Bad for Business," *Machine Design* 79 (September 13, 2007): 4–5.

31. Welch, *Jack: Straight from the Gut.*

32. "Why HR Professionals Are Worried about Forced Rankings," *HR Focus* 81 (October 2004): 8–9.

33. Anne Fisher, "I'm Not Shedding Tears for Dot-Commers Facing Reality," *Fortune* 146 (December 9, 2002): 244.

34. Edward E. Lawler III, "Performance Management: The Next Generation," *Compensation & Benefits Review* 26 (May/June 1994): 16.

35. "Writing and Giving Job Reviews: 8 Do's and Don'ts," *HR Specialist* 8 (February 2010): 6.

36. Joanne Sammer, "Calibrating Consistency," *HRMagazine* 53 (January 2008): 73–75.

37. Tom Krattenmaker, "Appraising Employee Performance in a Downsized Organization," *Harvard Management Update* 14 (May 2009): 3–5.

38. Jeffrey Pfeffer, "Low Grades for Performance Reviews," *BusinessWeek* (August 8, 2009): 68.

39. "Playing Favorites: How to Avoid Unintended Partiality in Decisions, Reviews," *HR Specialist* 7 (October 2009): 6.

40. Adrienne Fox, "Curing What Ails Performance Reviews," *HRMagazine* 54 (January 2009): 52–56.

41. Iris Randall, "Performance Appraisal Anxiety," *Black Enterprise* 25 (January 1995): 60.

42. Thomas S. Clausen, Keith T. Jones, and Jay S. Rich, "Appraising Employee Performance Evaluation Systems," *CPA Journal* 78 (February 2008): 64–67.

43. Skip Waugh, "Delivering Solid Performance Reviews," *Supervision* (August 2002): 16.

44. Kevin J. Sensenig, "Human Potential Untangled," *T+D* 63 (April 2009): 54–57.

45. Jay Forte, "Give Feedback, Get Performance," *Supervision* 70 (February 2009): 3–4.

46. "Addressing Performance Problems: 7 Steps to Success," *HR Specialist* 7 (October 2009): 6.

47. "Cite Specifics," *Communication Briefings* 29 (April 2010): 6.

48. "Performance Prep," *Communication Briefings* 29 (March 2010): 9.

49. "Addressing Performance Problems: 7 Steps to Success."

50. Charlene Kesee, "Toot Your Horn...Loudly," *OfficePro* 70 (March/April 2010): 14–17.

51. Paul S. Hempel, "Differences between Chinese and Western Managerial Views of Performance," *Personnel Review* 30 (2001): 203–226.

52. Ibid.

53. Ibid.

54. Ibid.

55. Ibid.

CHAPTER

9 Direct Financial Compensation

HRM in Action: Are Top Executives Paid Too Much?

Over the past decade, many believe that the rise of executive compensation has gotten out of control. Peter Drucker, the famous management author, once said, "I am for the free market. Even though it doesn't work too well, nothing else works at all. But I have serious reservations about *capitalism* as a system because it idolizes economics as the be-all and end-all of life. It is one-dimensional. For example, I have often advised managers that a 20-to-1 salary ratio between senior executives and rank-and-file white-collar workers is the limit *beyond* which they cannot go if they don't want resentment and falling morale to hit their companies. Today, I believe it is socially and morally unforgivable when managers reap huge profits for themselves but fire workers."[1] Evidently Drucker's advice has not been followed since recent estimates were that CEO pay was about 344 times the average worker's pay.[2]

The outrage over excesses has focused heavily on Wall Street. Occidental Petroleum chief Ray Irani received five-year total compensation of $127,447,000. In 2006, thanks to a rise in oil prices and the company's payment scheme, Irani took home a total of $460 million. In 2010 he took home nearly $59 million in salary, perks, bonuses, and other stock awards.[3] J.P. Morgan Chase CEO James Dimon collected $30 million in cash, stock, and options. When former CEO John Thain joined Merrill Lynch, he received a $15 million signing bonus and a multiyear pay package valued from about $50 million to $120 million.[4] Some CEOs, like Michael Jefferies of Abercrombie & Fitch, took home more pay, despite the fact that their businesses did so badly that their stocks tanked and they laid off many employees.[5] The question of what is excessive compensation has emerged as the number one concern of shareholders.[6] There may be a glimmer of hope since the

After completing this chapter, students should be able to:

1. Define *compensation* and describe the various forms of compensation.

2. Define *financial equity* and explain the concept of equity in direct financial compensation.

3. Identify the determinants of direct financial compensation.

4. Describe the organization as a determinant of direct financial compensation.

5. Describe the labor market as a determinant of direct financial compensation.

6. Explain how the job is a determinant of direct financial compensation.

7. Define *job evaluation* and describe the four traditional job evaluation methods.

8. Describe job pricing.

9. Identify factors related to the employee that are essential in determining direct financial compensation.

10. Describe team-based pay, company-wide pay plans, professional employee compensation, sales representative compensation, and contingent worker compensation.

11. Explain the various elements of executive compensation.

12. Explain a golden parachute contract and the clawback contract provision.

inflation-adjusted average is lower than in 1998, at just over $11 million.[7] A survey of 81 big companies shows that CEO pay dropped by 8.6 percent in 2009.[8]

There continues to be attempts to hold down executive salaries. However, sometimes it appears like once a compensation loophole is filled, another one surfaces to bypass the system. IRS rules, for instance, stated that performance-based compensation does not count toward the $1 million maximum deduction that companies can take on compensation paid to top executives. Thus, there was an explosion in bonuses and deferred compensation. Once that loophole was defused, another one was found. IRS restrictions are relaxed once an executive has left the firm so there was an increase in generous postretirement perks.[9] Jack Welch, once a business school and GE corporate icon, presented an example for corporate excess postretirement perks. His former wife revealed his $9 million annual pension plan payout, plus outrageous perks such as lifetime use of GE's $80,000-per-month Manhattan apartment with free food and free maid service; lifetime use of the GE fleet of corporate jets, including a Boeing 737 business jet; a new Mercedes plus a limousine and driver; and assorted free sports and opera box tickets.[10]

The business and regulatory environment has changed and many organizations are rethinking executive compensation practices, including pay, bonuses, and severance pay. Performance assessment and accountability are the leading trends.[11] The compensation of CEO Paul Stebbins of World Fuel Services provides an excellent example of tying compensation to performance results. Under its *executive* pay plan, almost all of Stebbins' equity grants are tied to the financial performance of the company and do not vest for a number of years. Restricted stock that were granted in 2006 are tied to annual net income growth and do not vest until 2011; stock appreciation rights (similar to stock options), also granted in 2006, are linked to three-year earnings-per-share growth and vested in 2009. He also has $23 million, two-thirds of his net worth, tied up in World Fuel stock.[12] Now if World Fuel Services does well in the long run, both Stebbins and World Fuel benefit. "The days of an individual producer making a $20 million bonus in a year are going to decline," says David Swinford, president and CEO of Pearl Meyer Partners, a New York-based executive compensation consultant.[13]

This chapter begins by considering the question of whether executives are paid too much; various forms of compensation are described and the concept of equity in financial compensation is explained. Then the determinants of direct financial compensation are explained and how the organization influences direct financial compensation is examined. This is followed by discussions of how both the labor market and the job are factors in determining direct financial compensation. Then, topics related to job evaluation and job pricing, factors related to the employee in determining direct financial compensation, and salary compression are described. Team-based pay and company-wide plans are then discussed, and compensation for professionals, sales employees, contingent workers, and executives is studied. The chapter concludes with a global perspective entitled "Global Executive Compensation."

Compensation: An Overview

OBJECTIVE 9.1
Define compensation and describe the various forms of compensation.

compensation
Total of all rewards provided to employees in return for their services.

Compensation administration is one of management's most difficult and challenging human resource functions because it contains many elements and has a far-reaching impact on an organization's strategic goals.[14] **Compensation** is the total of all rewards provided employees in return for their services. The overall purposes of providing compensation are to attract, retain, and motivate employees. The components of a total compensation program are shown in Figure 9.1 **Direct financial compensation** consists of the pay that a person receives in the form of wages, salaries, commissions, and bonuses.

Figure 9.1

Components of a Total Compensation Program

```
┌─────────────────────── EXTERNAL ENVIRONMENT ───────────────────────┐
│ ┌─────────────────── INTERNAL ENVIRONMENT ──────────────────────┐ │
│ │                        Compensation                            │ │
│ │         Financial                      Nonfinancial            │ │
│ │                                                                │ │
│ │  Direct      Indirect (Benefits)    The Job      Job Environment│ │
│ │  Wages       Legally Required       Meaningful and  Sound Policies│
│ │  Salaries    Benefits               Satisfying Job  Capable Managers│
│ │  Commissions  Social Security       Recognition for Competent Employees│
│ │  Bonuses     Unemployment Compensation Accomplishment Congenial Co-workers│
│ │              Workers' Compensation  Feeling of     Appropriate Status Symbols│
│ │              Family & Medical Leave Achievement    Working Conditions│
│ │                                     Possibility of            │ │
│ │              Discretionary Benefits Increased     Workplace Flexibility│
│ │                Payment for Time Not Worked Responsibility Flextime│
│ │                Health Care          Opportunity for Compressed Workweek│
│ │                Life Insurance       Growth and    Job Sharing │ │
│ │                Retirement Plans     Advancement   Telecommuting│ │
│ │                Disability Protection Enjoy Doing the Part-Time Work│
│ │                Employee Stock Option Plans Job               │ │
│ │                Employee Services                             │ │
│ │                Premium Pay                                   │ │
│ │                                                             │ │
│ │              Voluntary Benefits                             │ │
│ └─────────────────────────────────────────────────────────────┘ │
└───────────────────────────────────────────────────────────────────┘
```

direct financial compensation
Pay that a person receives in the form of wages, salary, commissions, and bonuses.

indirect financial compensation (benefits)
All financial rewards that are not included in direct financial compensation.

nonfinancial compensation
Satisfaction that a person receives from the job itself or from the psychological and/or physical environment in which the person works.

OBJECTIVE 9.2
Define financial equity and explain the concept of equity in direct financial compensation.

equity theory
Motivation theory that people assess their performance and attitudes by comparing both their contribution to work and the benefits they derive from it to the contributions and benefits of comparison others whom they select—and who in reality may or may not be like them.

financial equity
Perception of fair pay treatment for employees.

external equity
Equity that exists when a firm's employees receive pay comparable to workers who perform similar jobs in other firms.

internal equity
Equity that exists when employees receive pay according to the relative value of their jobs within the same organization.

employee equity
Equity that exists when individuals performing similar jobs for the same firm receive pay according to factors unique to the employee, such as performance level or seniority.

Indirect financial compensation (benefits) consists of all financial rewards that are not included in direct financial compensation. This form of compensation includes a wide variety of rewards normally received indirectly by the employee. **Nonfinancial compensation** consists of the satisfaction that a person receives from the job itself or from the psychological and/or physical environment in which the person works. This aspect of nonfinancial compensation involves both psychological and physical factors within the firm's working environment.

Equity in Financial Compensation

Equity theory is the motivation theory that people assess their performance and attitudes by comparing both their contribution to work and the benefits they derive from it to the contributions and benefits of *comparison others* whom they select—and who in reality may or may not be like them. It evolved from social comparison theory—the theory that individuals must assess and know their degree of performance and the *correctness* of their attitudes in a situation. Lacking objective measures of performance or correct attitudes, they compare their performance and attitudes to those of others.[15] Equity theory further states that a person is motivated in proportion to the *perceived* fairness of the rewards received for a certain amount of effort as compared with what others receive. Someone might say, "I'm going to stop working so hard. I work harder than Susan and she gets all the raises." This individual has compared his effort and the rewards he received to the effort exerted and the rewards received by Susan. In fact, no actual inequity may exist, but the perception of inequity influences subsequent actions. According to equity theory, individuals are motivated to reduce any perceived inequity. They strive to make the ratios of outcomes to inputs equal. When inequity exists, the person making the comparison strives to make the ratios equal by changing either the outcomes or the inputs.

Understanding equity theory is very important as it pertains to compensation. Organizations must attract, motivate, and retain competent employees. Because a firm's financial compensation system plays a huge role in achieving these goals, organizations ought to strive for equity. **Financial equity** means a perception of fair pay treatment for employees. As will be seen, firms and individuals view fairness from several perspectives. Ideally, compensation will be even-handed to all parties concerned and employees will perceive it as such. However, this is a very elusive goal. As you read this section, remember also that nonfinancial factors can alter one's perception of equity.

External equity exists when a firm's employees receive pay comparable to workers who perform similar jobs in other firms. Compensation surveys help organizations determine the extent to which external equity is present. **Internal equity** exists when employees receive pay according to the relative value of their jobs within the same organization. It was with regard to internal equity that Peter Drucker said at the beginning of the chapter, "I have often advised managers that a 20-to-1 salary ratio between senior executives and rank-and-file white-collar workers is the limit *beyond* which they cannot go if they don't want resentment and falling morale to hit their companies." Certainly internal equity does not exist when CEO pay is about 344 times the average worker's pay. Because of the often wide gap between the leaders and the led, some believe that employee morale is suffering, loyalty is being lowered, and companies are suffering.[16]

Job evaluation (discussed later in the chapter) is a primary means for determining internal equity. Most workers are concerned with both internal and external pay equity. From an employee relations perspective, internal pay equity may be more important because employees have more information about pay matters within their own organizations, and they use this information to form perceptions of equity. On the other hand, an organization must be competitive in the labor market, which is external equity. In a competitive environment, and especially for high-demand employees, it becomes clear that the market is of primary importance (external equity).

Employee equity exists when individuals performing similar jobs for the same firm receive pay according to factors unique to the employee, such as performance level or seniority. Suppose

Figure 9.2

Primary Determinants of Direct Financial Compensation

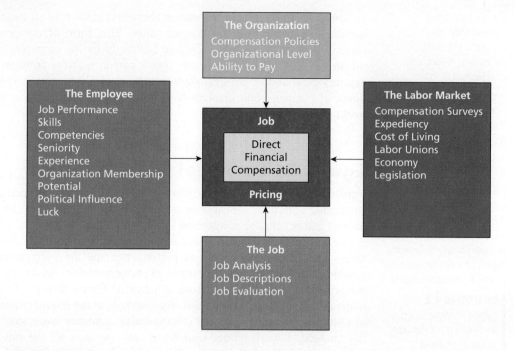

that two accountants in the same firm are performing similar jobs, and one is clearly the better performer. If both workers receive equal pay increases, employee equity does not exist, and the more productive employee is likely to be unhappy. **Team equity** is achieved when teams are rewarded based on their group's productivity. However, achieving equity may be a problem when it comes to team incentives. If all team members contributed equally, there would not likely be a problem. But, that is usually not the case, as more enthusiastic team members may cover for less productive ones.

Inequity in any category can result in morale problems. If employees feel that their compensation is unfair, they may leave the firm. Even greater damage may result for the firm if the employees choose not to leave but stay and restrict their efforts. In either event, the organization's overall performance is damaged.

team equity
Equity that is achieved when teams are rewarded based on their group's productivity.

OBJECTIVE 9.3
Identify the determinants of direct financial compensation.

Determinants of Direct Financial Compensation

Compensation theory has never been able to provide a completely satisfactory answer to what an individual's service for performing a job is worth. Although no scientific approach is available, organizations typically use a number of relevant factors to determine individual pay. These determinants appear in Figure 9.2 Historically, the *organization*, the *labor market*, the *job*, and the *employee* all have influenced job pricing and the ultimate determination of an individual's financial compensation. These factors continue to play an important role.

OBJECTIVE 9.4
Describe the organization as a determinant of direct financial compensation.

Organization as a Determinant of Direct Financial Compensation

Managers tend to view financial compensation as both an expense and an asset. It is an expense in the sense that it reflects the cost of labor. However, financial compensation is clearly an asset when it is instrumental in recruiting and hiring good people and in encouraging them to put forth their best efforts and remain in their jobs. A firm that pays well attracts many applicants, enabling management to pick and choose the skills and traits it values. It holds on to these quality hires by equitably sharing the fruits of its financial success, not only among the management team but also with the rank-and-file. Compensation programs have top management's attention because they have the potential to influence employee work attitudes and behavior that lead to improved organizational performance and implementation of the firm's strategic plan.

Compensation Policies

compensation policy
Policy that provides general guidelines for making compensation decisions.

A **compensation policy** provides general guidelines for making compensation decisions. Some employees may perceive their firm's compensation policies as being fair and unbiased and others may have different opinions. The result of these perceptions may have an effect on employees' perceptions of fairness and result in lower productivity or they may choose to leave the firm. An organization often, formally or informally, establishes compensation policies that determine whether it will be a pay leader, a pay follower, or strive for an average position in the labor market.

pay leaders
Organizations that pay higher wages and salaries than competing firms

PAY LEADERS **Pay leaders** are organizations that pay higher wages and salaries than competing firms. Using this strategy, they feel that they will be able to attract high-quality, productive employees and thus achieve lower per-unit labor costs. Higher-paying firms usually attract more highly qualified applicants than lower-paying companies in the same labor market.

market (going) rate
Average pay that most employers provide for a similar job in a particular area or industry.

MARKET RATE The **market (going) rate** is the average pay that most employers provide for a similar job in a particular area or industry. Many organizations have a policy that calls for paying the market rate. In such firms, management believes that it can employ qualified people and yet remain competitive.

pay followers
Companies that choose to pay below the going rate because of a poor financial condition or a belief that they do not require highly capable employees.

PAY FOLLOWERS Companies that choose to pay below the market rate because of poor financial conditions or a belief that they do not require highly capable employees are **pay followers**. When organizations follow this policy, difficulties often occur. Consider the case of Trig Ekeland.

> Trig managed a large, but financially strapped farming operation in South Dakota. Although no formal policies were established, Trig had a practice of paying the lowest wage possible. One of his farmhands, Charlie Roberts, was paid minimum wage. During a period of three weeks, Charlie wrecked a tractor, severely damaged a combine, and tore out the transmission in a new pickup truck. Charlie's actions prompted Trig to remark, "Charlie is the most expensive darned employee I've ever had."

As Trig discovered, paying the lowest wage possible did not save money; actually, the practice was quite expensive. In addition to hiring unproductive workers, organizations that are pay followers may have a high turnover rate, as their most qualified employees leave to join higher-paying organizations. Equally important, in situations in which incompetent or disgruntled employees make contact with customers, they may not provide the kind of customer service management desires.

Organizational Level

The organizational level in which compensation decisions are made can also have an impact on pay. Upper management often makes these decisions to ensure consistency. However, in some cases, there may be advantages to making pay decisions at lower levels, where better information may exist regarding employee performance. Extreme pressure to retain top performers may override the desire to maintain consistency in the pay structure. Organizations increasingly make exceptions for just this reason.

Ability to Pay

An organization's assessment of its ability to pay is also an important factor in determining pay levels. Financially successful firms tend to provide higher-than-average compensation. However, an organization's financial strength establishes only the upper limit of what it will pay. To arrive at a specific pay level, management must consider other factors.

labor market
Potential employees located within the geographic area from which employees are recruited.

OBJECTIVE 9.5
Describe the labor market as a determinant of direct financial compensation.

Labor Market as a Determinant of Direct Financial Compensation

Potential employees located within the geographic area from which employees are recruited comprise the **labor market**. Labor markets for some jobs extend far beyond the location of a firm's operations. An aerospace firm in St. Louis, for example, may be concerned about the labor market for engineers in Fort Worth or Orlando, where competitive firms are located. Managerial and professional employees are often recruited from a wide geographic area. As global economics increasingly sets the cost of labor, the global labor market grows in importance as a determinant of financial compensation for individuals.

Pay for the same jobs in different labor markets may vary considerably. Administrative assistant jobs, for example, may carry an average salary of over $50,000 per year in a large, urban community but only $25,000 or less in a smaller town. Compensation managers must be aware of these differences in order to compete successfully for employees. The market rate is an important guide in determining pay. Many employees view it as the standard for judging the fairness of their firm's compensation practices.

Compensation Surveys

compensation survey
A means of obtaining data regarding what other firms are paying for specific jobs or job classes within a given labor market.

A **compensation survey** is a means of obtaining data regarding what other firms are paying for specific jobs or job classes within a given labor market. Virtually all compensation professionals use compensation surveys either directly or indirectly. The surveys may be purchased, outsourced to a consulting firm, or conducted by the organization itself. Organizations use surveys for two basic reasons: to identify their relative position with respect to the chosen competition in the labor market, and to provide input in developing a budget and compensation structure. Of all the wage criteria, market rates remain the most important standard for determining pay. In a competitive environment, the marketplace determines economic worth, and this is *the* critical factor.

Expediency

Although standard compensation surveys are generally useful, managers in highly technical and specialized areas occasionally need to use nontraditional means to determine what constitutes competitive compensation for scarce talent and niche positions. They need real-time information and must rely on recruiters and hiring managers on the front lines to let them know what is happening in the job market.

Cost of Living

Although not a problem in recent years, the logic for using cost of living as a pay determinant is both simple and sound: when prices rise over time and pay does not, *real pay* is actually lowered. A pay increase must be roughly equivalent to the increased cost of living if a person is to maintain his or her previous level of real wages. For instance, if someone earns $42,000 during a year in which the average rate of inflation is 4 percent, a $140-per-month pay increase will be necessary merely to maintain the purchasing ability of that employee.

People living on fixed incomes (primarily the elderly and the poor) are hit hard by inflation, but they are not alone, as most employees also suffer financially. In recognition of this problem some firms index pay increases to the inflation rate. In fact, in a questionable practice, some organizations sacrifice *merit pay* (discussed later in the chapter) to provide across-the-board increases designed to offset the results of inflation.

Inflation is not the only factor affecting cost of living; location also comes into play. You can calculate comparative salaries in one city to another by going to www.homefair.com.

Official measures of inflation such as the *Consumer Price Index* (CPI) are market-oriented, measuring only the decrease in our money's power to purchase products currently available for sale. An interesting alternative way to view cost of living includes nonmarket elements of our existence, such as the rising costs from crime, lawsuits, pollution, and family breakdown.

HR Web Wisdom

Calculates Salary Differences from City to City

http://www.homefair. com

Web site to determine numerous costs of a move to another city.

Labor Unions

The National Labor Relations Act (Wagner Act) declared legislative support, on a broad scale, for the right of employees to organize and engage in collective bargaining. Unions normally prefer to determine compensation through the process of collective bargaining, a topic covered in Chapter 12. An excerpt from the Wagner Act prescribes the areas of mandatory collective bargaining between management and unions as "wages, hours, and other terms and conditions of employment." These broad bargaining areas obviously have great potential to impact compensation decisions. When a union uses comparable pay as a standard in making compensation

cost-of-living allowance (COLA)
Escalator clause in a labor agreement that automatically increases wages as the U.S. Bureau of Labor Statistics' cost-of-living index rises.

demands, the employer needs accurate labor market data. When a union emphasizes cost of living, it may pressure management into including a cost-of-living allowance. A **cost-of-living allowance (COLA)** is an escalator clause in the labor agreement that automatically increases wages as the U.S. Bureau of Labor Statistics' cost-of-living index rises. Recently, cost-of-living allowances in union contracts have been disappearing.

Economy

The economy definitely affects financial compensation decisions. For example, a depressed economy generally increases the labor supply, and this serves to lower the market rate. A booming economy, on the other hand, results in greater competition for workers and the price of labor is driven upward. In addition, the cost of living typically rises as the economy expands.

Legislation

Federal and state laws can also affect the amount of compensation a person receives. Remember from Chapter 3 that the Equal Pay Act prohibits an employer from paying an employee of one gender less money than an employee of the opposite gender, if both employees do work that is substantially the same. Equal employment legislation, including the Civil Rights Act, the Age Discrimination in Employment Act, and the Americans with Disabilities Act, prohibits discrimination against specified groups in employment matters, including compensation. The same is true for federal government contractors or subcontractors covered by Executive Order 11246 and the Rehabilitation Act. States and municipal governments also have laws that affect compensation practices. Our focus in the next section, however, is on the federal legislation that provides broad coverage and specifically deals with compensation issues.

DAVIS-BACON ACT OF 1931 The Davis-Bacon Act of 1931 was the first national law to deal with minimum wages. It mandates a *prevailing wage* for all federally financed or assisted construction projects exceeding $2,000. The Secretary of Labor sets the prevailing wage at the union wage, regardless of what the average wage is in the affected locality.

WALSH–HEALY ACT OF 1936 The Walsh–Healy Act of 1936 requires companies with federal supply contracts exceeding $10,000 to pay prevailing wages. This legislation also requires one-and-a-half times the regular pay rate for hours over eight per day or 40 per week.

FAIR LABOR STANDARDS ACT OF 1938, AS AMENDED (FLSA) The most significant law affecting compensation is the Fair Labor Standards Act of 1938. The purpose of the FLSA is to establish minimum labor standards on a national basis and to eliminate low wages and long working hours. The FLSA attempts to eliminate low wages by setting a minimum wage, and to make long hours expensive by requiring a higher pay rate, overtime, for excessive hours. It also requires record keeping, and provides standards for child labor. The Wage and Hour Division of the U.S. Department of Labor (DOL) administers this Act. The amount of the minimum wage has changed several times since it was first introduced in 1938 and continues to do so; it rose from $6.55 to $7.25 per hour in 2009. Tipped workers, on the other hand, will get the same $2.13 minimum wage they have received for the last 18 years. However, if hourly wage plus tips do not add up to the minimum wage, the company must make up the difference. It is here that minimum wage violations often occur.[17]

Labor Secretary Hilda Solis recently said she was "especially pleased that the change will benefit working women," who account for two out of three minimum wage earners.[18] It also requires overtime payment at the rate of one-and-one-half times the employee's regular rate after 40 hours of work in a 168-hour period. In 2010, aggressive action was being taken against companies that failed to pay the overtime requirement.[19] Although the Act covers most organizations and employees, certain classes of employees are specifically exempt from overtime provisions. **Exempt employees** are categorized as executive, administrative, professional, or outside salespersons.

exempt employees
Employees categorized as executive, administrative, professional, or outside salespersons.

An *executive employee* is essentially a manager (such as a production manager) with broad authority over subordinates. An *administrative employee,* although not a manager, occupies an important staff position in an organization and might have a title such as account executive or market researcher. A *professional employee* performs work requiring advanced knowledge in a field of learning, normally acquired through a prolonged course of specialized instruction.[20] This type of employee might have a title such as company physician, legal counsel, or senior statistician. *Outside salespeople* sell tangible or intangible items away from the employer's place of business.

TROUBLED ASSETS RELIEF PROGRAM (TARP) OF 2009   The Emergency Economic Stabilization Act (EESA) was signed into law in 2008. EESA created the Troubled Assets Relief Program (TARP) and included certain executive compensation provisions that were to apply to any financial institution that received financial assistance under TARP. In February of 2009, the American Recovery and Reinvestment Act (ARRA) was signed into law. Among other provisions, ARRA amended the executive compensation provisions that apply to institutions that would receive or had already received TARP funds, so-called "covered institutions."[21] In general, these provisions applied to financial institutions only during the period in which an obligation arising from the receipt of TARP funds remained outstanding, which was known as the "TARP obligation period." Any publicly-traded covered institution (not just companies that received money from TARP) had to permit, in any proxy or consent for any shareholder meeting, a nonbinding shareholder vote to approve the compensation of the institution's executives, disclosed pursuant to the Securities and Exchange Commission's compensation disclosure rules.[22] The Department of the Treasury estimates that the eventual cost of TARP will be $117 billion, as two-thirds of the $550 billion lent to banks and other institutions was repaid by 2010.[23]

Job as a Determinant of Direct Financial Compensation

OBJECTIVE 9.6
Explain how the job is a determinant of direct financial compensation.

The individual employee and market forces are most prominent as wage criteria. However, the job itself continues to be a factor, especially in firms that have internal pay equity as an important consideration. These organizations pay for the value they attach to certain duties, responsibilities, and other job-related factors such as working conditions. Management techniques used for determining a job's relative worth include job analysis, job descriptions, and job evaluation.

Before an organization can determine the relative difficulty or value of its jobs, it must first define their content. Normally, it does so by analyzing jobs. Recall from Chapter 4 that job analysis is the systematic process of determining the skills and knowledge required for performing jobs. Remember also that the primary by-product of job analysis is the job description, a written document that describes job duties or functions and responsibilities.

Job descriptions serve many different purposes, including data for evaluating jobs. They are essential to all *job evaluation* methods that depend heavily on their accuracy and clarity for success.

Job Evaluation

OBJECTIVE 9.7
Define job evaluation and describe the four traditional job evaluation methods

job evaluation
Process that determines the relative value of one job in relation to another.

Job evaluation is a process that determines the relative value of one job in relation to another. Basically, it determines the value of the job to the company. The primary purpose of job evaluation is to eliminate internal pay inequities that exist because of illogical pay structures. For example, pay inequity probably exists if the mailroom supervisor earns more money than the chief accountant. For obvious reasons, organizations prefer internal pay equity. However, when a job's pay rate is ultimately determined to conflict with the market rate, the latter is almost sure to take precedence. Job evaluation measures job worth in an administrative rather than an economic sense. The latter can be determined only by the marketplace and revealed through compensation surveys. Nevertheless, many firms continue to use job evaluation for the following purposes:

- To identify the organization's job structure.
- To eliminate pay inequities and bring order to the relationships among jobs.
- To develop a hierarchy of job value for creating a pay structure.

The human resource department may be responsible for administering job evaluation programs. However, committees made up of individuals familiar with the specific jobs to be evaluated often perform the actual evaluations. A typical committee might include the human resource executive and representatives from other functional areas such as finance, production, information technology, and marketing. The composition of the committee usually depends on the type and level of the jobs being evaluated. In all instances, it is important for the committee to keep personalities out of the evaluation process and to remember it is evaluating the *job,* not the person(s) performing the job. Some people have a difficult time making this distinction. This is understandable, since some job evaluation systems are very similar to some performance-appraisal methods. In addition, the duties of a job may, on an informal basis, expand, contract, or change depending on the person holding the job.

Small and medium-sized organizations often lack job evaluation expertise and may elect to use an outside consultant. When employing a consultant, management should require that the consultant not only develop the job evaluation system, but also train company employees to administer it properly.

The four traditional job evaluation methods are the *ranking, classification, factor comparison,* and *point.* There are innumerable versions of these methods, and a firm may choose one and modify it to fit its particular purposes. Another option is to purchase a proprietary method such as the Hay Plan. The ranking and classification methods are nonquantitative, whereas the factor comparison and point methods are quantitative approaches.

Ranking Method

job evaluation ranking method
Job evaluation method in which the raters examine the description of each job being evaluated and arrange the jobs in order according to their value to the company.

The ranking method is the simplest of the four job evaluation methods. In the **job evaluation ranking method**, the raters examine the description of each job being evaluated and arrange the jobs in order according to their value to the company. The procedure is essentially the same as that discussed in Chapter 8 regarding the ranking method for evaluating employee performance. The only difference is that you evaluate jobs, not people. The first step in this method, as with all the methods, is conducting job analyses and writing job descriptions.

Classification Method

classification method
Job evaluation method in which classes or grades are defined to describe a group of jobs.

The **classification method** involves defining a number of classes or grades to describe a group of jobs. In evaluating jobs by this method, the raters compare the job description with the class description. Class descriptions reflect the differences between groups of jobs at various difficulty levels. The class description that most closely agrees with the job description determines the classification for that job. For example, in evaluating the job of receptionist, the description might include these duties:

1. Greet and announce visitors.
2. Answer phone and route calls.
3. Receive and route mail.

Assuming that the remainder of the job description includes similar routine work, this job would probably be placed in the lowest job class.

Each class is described in such a way that it captures sufficient work detail, yet is general enough to cause little difficulty in slotting a job description into its appropriate class. Probably the best-known illustration of the classification method is the federal government's 18-class evaluation system.

Factor Comparison Method

factor comparison method
Job evaluation method that assumes there are five universal factors consisting of mental requirements, skills, physical requirements, responsibilities, and working conditions; the evaluator makes decisions on these factors independently.

The factor comparison method is somewhat more involved than the two previously discussed qualitative methods. The **factor comparison method** of job evaluation assumes that there are five universal factors consisting of mental requirements, skills, physical requirements, responsibilities, and working conditions; the evaluator makes decisions on these factors independently.

The five universal job factors are:

- Mental requirements, which reflect mental traits such as intelligence, reasoning, and imagination.
- Skills, which pertain to facility in muscular coordination and training in the interpretation of sensory impressions.

point method
Job evaluation method in which the raters assign numerical values to specific job factors, such as knowledge required, and the sum of these values provides a quantitative assessment of a job's relative worth.

hay guide chart-profile method (Hay Plan)
Refined version of the point method used by approximately 8,000 public and private sector organizations worldwide to evaluate clerical, trade, technical, professional, managerial, and/or executive-level jobs.

HR Web Wisdom

The Hay Guide Chart-Profile Method
http://www.haygroup.com

Homepage of the Hay Method, the most widely used job measurement system in the world, is provided.

OBJECTIVE 9.8
Describe job pricing.

job pricing
Placing a dollar value on a job's worth.

pay grade
Grouping of similar jobs to simplify pricing jobs

- Physical requirements, which involve sitting, standing, walking, lifting, and so on.
- Responsibilities, which cover areas such as raw materials, money, records, and supervision.
- Working conditions, which reflect the environmental influences of noise, illumination, ventilation, hazards, and hours.

In this method, the evaluation committee creates a monetary scale, containing each of the five universal factors, and ranks jobs according to their value for each factor. Unlike most other job evaluation methods, which produce relative job worth only, the factor comparison method determines the absolute value as well.

Point Method

In the **point method**, raters assign numerical values to specific job factors, such as knowledge required, and the sum of these values provides a quantitative assessment of a job's relative worth. Historically, some variation of the point plan has been the most popular option.

Point plans require time and effort to design. Historically, a redeeming feature of the method has been that, once developed, the plan was useful over a long time. In today's environment, the shelf life may be considerably less. In any event, as new jobs are created and old jobs substantially changed, job analysis must be conducted and job descriptions rewritten on an ongoing basis. The job evaluation committee then evaluates the jobs. Only when job factors change, or for some reason the weights assigned become inappropriate, does the plan become obsolete.

Hay Guide Chart-Profile Method (Hay Plan)

The **Hay guide chart-profile method (Hay plan)** is a widely used refined version of the point method used by approximately 8,000 public and private-sector organizations worldwide to evaluate clerical, trade, technical, professional, managerial, and/or executive-level jobs.[24] It uses the compensable factors of know-how, problem solving, accountability, and additional compensable elements. Point values are assigned to these factors to determine the final point profile for any job.

Job pricing, and the details involved, is the topic of the next section.

Job Pricing

The process of job evaluation results in a job hierarchy. It might reveal, for example, that the job of senior accountant is more valuable than the job of machinist, which, in turn, is more valuable than the job of receptionist. At this point, you know the *relative* value of these jobs to the company, but not their *absolute* value. **Job pricing** results in placing a dollar value on a job's worth. It takes place after evaluation of a job and the relative value of each job in the organization has been determined. Firms often use pay grades and pay ranges in the job-pricing process.

Pay Grades

A **pay grade** is the grouping of similar jobs to simplify pricing jobs. For example, it is much more convenient for organizations to price 15 pay grades than 200 separate jobs. The simplicity of this approach is similar to a college or university's practice of grouping grades of 90–100 into an *A* category, grades of 80–89 into a *B,* and so on. In following this approach, you also avoid a false suggestion of preciseness. Although job evaluation plans may be systematic, none are scientific.

Plotting jobs on a scatter diagram is often useful to managers in determining the appropriate number of pay grades for a company. Looking at Figure 9.3, notice that each dot on the scatter diagram represents one job. The location of the dot reflects the job's relationship to pay and evaluated points, which reflect its worth. When this procedure is used, a certain point spread determines the width of the pay grade (100 points in this illustration). Although each dot represents one job, it may involve dozens of individuals who have *positions* in that one job. The large dot at the lower left represents the job of receptionist, evaluated at 75 points. The receptionist's

Figure 9.3

Scatter Diagram of Evaluated Jobs Illustrating the Wage Curve, Pay Grades, and Rating Ranges

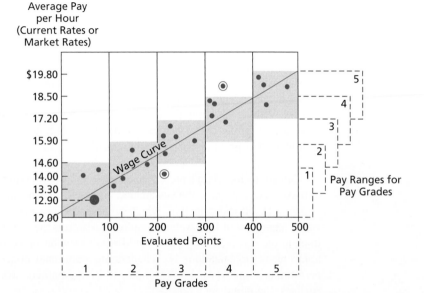

Summary Evaluated Points	Pay Grade	Minimum	Pay Range Midpoint	Maximum
0–99	1	$12.00	$13.30	$14.60
100–199	2	13.30	14.60	15.90
200–299	3	14.60	15.90	17.20
300–399	4	15.90	17.20	18.50
400–500	5	17.20	18.50	19.80

hourly rate of $12.90 represents either the average wage currently paid for the job or its market rate. This decision depends on how management wants to price its jobs.

A **wage curve** (or *pay curve*) is the fitting of plotted points to create a smooth progression between pay grades. The line drawn minimizes the distance between all dots and the line; a line of best fit may be straight or curved. However, when the point system is used, a straight line is often the result, as in Figure 9.3. You can draw this wage line either freehand or by using a statistical method.

wage curve

Fitting of plotted points to create a smooth progression between pay grades (also known as the *pay curve*)

Pay Ranges

After pay grades have been determined, the next decision is whether all individuals performing the same job will receive equal pay or whether you should use pay ranges. A **pay range** includes a minimum and maximum pay rate with enough variance between the two to allow for a significant pay difference. Pay ranges are generally preferred over single pay rates because they allow a firm to compensate employees according to performance and length of service. Pay then serves as a positive incentive. When pay ranges are used, a firm must develop a method to advance individuals through the range. Companies typically use different range spreads for jobs that are more valuable to the company.

pay range

Minimum and maximum pay rate with enough variance between the two to allow for a significant pay difference.

POINTS ALONG THE RANGE Referring again to Figure 9.3, note that anyone can readily determine the minimum, midpoint, and maximum pay rates per hour for each of the five pay grades. For example, for pay grade 5, the minimum rate is $17.20, the midpoint is $18.50, and the maximum is $19.80. The minimum rate may be the *hiring in* rate that a person receives when joining the firm, although in practice, new employees often receive pay that starts above this level. The maximum pay rate represents the maximum that an employee can receive for that job regardless of how well he or she performs the job.

PROBLEM OF TOPPING OUT A person at the top of a pay grade will have to be promoted to a job in a higher pay grade in order to receive a pay increase unless: (1) an across-the-board adjustment is made or (2) the job is reevaluated and placed in a higher pay grade. This situation has caused numerous managers some anguish as they attempt to explain the pay system to an employee who is doing a tremendous job but is at the top of a pay grade. Consider this situation:

> Everyone in the department realized that Beth Smithers was the best administrative assistant in the company. At times, she appeared to do the job of three people. Bob Marshall, Beth's supervisor, was especially impressed. Recently, he had a discussion with the human resource manager to see what he could do to get a raise for Beth. After Bob described the situation, the human resource manager's only reply was, "Sorry, Bob. Beth is already at the top of her pay grade. There is nothing you can do except have her job upgraded or promote her to another position."

Situations like Beth's present managers with a perplexing problem. Many would be inclined to make an exception to the system and give Beth a salary increase. However, this action would violate a traditional principle, which holds that every job in the organization has a maximum value, regardless of how well an employee performs the job. The rationale is that making exceptions to the compensation plan would result in widespread pay inequities. Having stated this, today many organizations are challenging traditional concepts as they strive to retain top-performing employees. For example, if Beth Smithers worked for Microsoft or Southwest Airlines, she might get a raise.

RATE RANGES AT HIGHER LEVELS The rate ranges established should be large enough to provide an incentive to do a better job. At higher levels, pay differentials may need to be greater to be meaningful. There may be logic in having the rate range become increasingly wide at each consecutive level. Consider, for example, what a $200-per-month salary increase would mean to a file clerk earning $2,000 per month (a 10 percent increase) and to a senior cost accountant earning $5,000 per month (a 4 percent increase). Assuming an inflation rate of 4 percent, the accountant's *real pay* would remain unchanged.

Broadbanding

broadbanding
Compensation technique that collapses many pay grades (salary grades) into a few wide bands in order to improve organizational effectiveness.

Broadbanding is a technique that collapses many pay grades (salary grades) into a few wide bands to improve organizational effectiveness.

Organizational downsizing and restructuring of jobs have created broader job descriptions, with the result that employees perform more diverse tasks than they previously did. Broadbanding creates the basis for a simpler compensation system that de-emphasizes structure and control and places greater importance on judgment and flexible decision making. Broadbanding may add flexibility to the compensation system and require less time having to make fine distinctions among jobs. Bands may also promote lateral development of employees and direct attention away from vertical promotional opportunities. The decreased emphasis on job levels should encourage employees to make cross-functional moves to jobs that are on the same or an even lower level because their pay rate would remain unchanged.

The use of broadbanding has declined in recent years. Although broadbanding is successful in some organizations, the practice is not without pitfalls. Since each band consists of a broad range of jobs, the market value of these jobs may also vary considerably. Unless carefully monitored, employees in jobs at the lower end of the band could progress to the top of the range and become overpaid.[25]

Single-Rate System

Pay ranges are not appropriate for some workplace conditions, such as assembly-line operations. For instance, when all jobs within a unit are routine, with little opportunity for employees to vary their productivity, a single-rate (or fixed-rate) system may be more appropriate. When single rates are used, everyone in the same job receives the same base pay, regardless of productivity. This rate may correspond to the midpoint of a range determined by a compensation survey.

Adjusting Pay Rates

When pay ranges have been determined and jobs assigned to pay grades, it may become obvious that some jobs are overpaid and others underpaid. You normally bring underpaid jobs up to the minimum of the pay range as soon as possible. Referring again to Figure 9.3, you can see that a job evaluated at about 225 points and having a rate of $14.00 per hour is represented by a circled dot immediately below pay grade 3. The job was determined to be difficult enough to fall in pay grade 3 (200–299 points). However, employees working in the job are being paid 60 cents per hour less than the minimum for the pay grade ($14.60 per hour). If one or more female employees should be in this circled job, the employer might soon learn more than desired about the Equal Pay Act and the Fair Pay Act. Good management practice would be to correct this inequity as rapidly as possible by placing the job in the proper pay grade and increasing the pay of those in that job.

Overpaid jobs present a different problem. Figure 9.3 illustrates an overpaid job for pay grade 4 (note the circled dot above pay grade 4). Employees in this job earn $19.00 per hour, or 50 cents more than the maximum for the pay grade. This type of overpayment, as well as the kind of underpayment discussed earlier, is called a *red circle rate.*

An ideal solution to the problem of an overpaid job is to promote the employee to a job in a higher pay grade. This is a great idea if the employee is qualified for a higher-rated job and a job opening is available. Another possibility would be to bring the job rate and employee pay into line through a pay cut. Although this decision may appear logical, it is generally not a good management practice, as this action would punish employees for a situation they did not create. Somewhere in between these two possible solutions is a third: to freeze the rate until across-the-board pay increases bring the job into line.

Pricing jobs is not an easy task. It requires effort that never ends. It is one of those tasks that managers may dislike but must do anyway.

Employee as a Determinant of Direct Financial Compensation

OBJECTIVE 9.9
Identify factors related to the employee that are essential in determining direct financial compensation.

In addition to the organization, the labor market, and the job, factors related to the employee are also essential in determining an individual's compensation. These factors include job performance, skills/competencies, seniority, experience, organization membership, potential, political influence, and luck.

Job Performance—Performance-Based Pay

Here the task is to link pay and performance. It recognizes that some workers are just better than another worker performing the same job. In recent years there has been a definite move in the United States toward pay for performance. While executive pay matters in the financial sector when firms such as AIG and Goldman Sachs make the news, most companies outside this sector use pay for performance for their top-level people.[26] The objective of performance-based pay is to improve productivity. Given the proper incentives, most employees will work harder and smarter.[27] An effective performance appraisal program is a prerequisite for any pay system tied to performance. Appraisal data provide input for such approaches as merit pay, bonuses, and piecework. Each of these approaches to compensation management will be discussed in the following sections.

merit pay
Pay increase added to employees' base pay based on their level of performance.

MERIT PAY **Merit pay** is a pay increase added to employees' base pay based on their level of performance. In practice, however, it historically has been merely a cost-of-living increase in disguise.[28] Past studies by compensation professionals have determined that merit pay is *marginally successful* in influencing pay satisfaction and performance.[29] From the employer's viewpoint, a distinct disadvantage to the typical merit pay increase is that it increases the employee's base pay. Therefore, employees receive the added amount each year they are on the payroll regardless of later performance levels. Some firms find it difficult to justify merit pay increases based on a previous employment period but added perpetually to base pay.

The recession of 2008/10 may have created a compensation revolution with regard to merit pay. Pay increases where everyone is treated essentially the same with only small differences between the best performer and mediocre ones are a thing of the past for firms such as Sony and metal manufacturer Precision Castparts. These pay plans are "dedicated to the care and feeding of the people whose positions and performance are making their companies the most money."[30]

Craig E. Schneier, the HR boss at biotechnology giant Biogen Idec., has fine-tuned its employee measurement and performance appraisal systems. He does not believe that all employees and positions are equal. He says, "A lot of companies talk about this. But if you look at their outcomes in regard to pay, you will see they don't necessarily differentiate at the end of the day. Sure, there's a percentage or two difference in the raise or bonus. But most employees in similar positions languish in the same pay bands and are shuttled off to the same conferences as the slackers and sub-stellar." At Biogen, one vice-president might get double what the person in the next office will get. "Twice as big a merit increase, twice as big a bonus, and twice as big an equity grant," says Schneier.[31]

Although many companies continue with traditional merit pay plans, some companies are starting to quietly freeze or cut pay for some so as to be able to reward others. As one researcher said, "They are robbing Peter to pay Paul. Look, there are an awful lot of long-term employees who are poor performers who have locked-in high salaries through cost-of-living increases."[32] With this compensation philosophy, a true merit pay plan can be developed.

bonus
One-time annual financial award, based on productivity, that is not added to base pay.

VARIABLE PAY (BONUS) Companies are increasingly placing a higher percentage of their compensation budget in variable pay as more and more companies embrace the concept of *pay for performance*. The most common type of variable pay for performance is the **bonus**, a one-time annual financial award, based on productivity that is not added to base pay.

In 2009, when the economy was slowing down and employers were holding down across the board pay raises, companies still put 12 percent of salary budgets toward bonuses.[33] The use of bonuses helped employers manage their cash outlay in a tough business environment while laying the foundation to share success with top producers.[34] Managers commonly contend that the use of bonuses is a win–win situation because it boosts production and efficiency and gives employees some control over their earning power. A positive side effect of using bonuses to reward high performance is that it may encourage co-workers to increase their productivity so that they can also receive the bonuses.

spot bonus
Relatively small monetary gifts provided to employees for outstanding work or effort during a reasonably short period of time.

Many organizations today are providing *spot bonuses* for critical areas and talents. **Spot bonuses** are relatively small monetary gifts provided to employees for outstanding work or effort during a reasonably short period of time. If an employee's performance has been exceptional, the employer may reward the worker with a one-time bonus of as low as $50 and $100 or $500 and perhaps $5,000 shortly after the noteworthy actions. According to a WorldatWork, *Salary Budget Survey,* 45 percent of companies use spot bonuses.[35]

piecework
Incentive pay plan in which employees are paid for each unit they produce.

PIECEWORK **Piecework** is an incentive pay plan in which employees are paid for each unit they produce. For example, if a worker is paid $8 a unit and produces 10 units a day, the worker earns $80. Sometimes a guaranteed base is included in a piece-rate plan, meaning that a worker would receive this base amount no matter what the output. Piecework is especially prevalent in the production/operations area. Requirements for the plan include developing output standards for the job and being able to measure the output of a single employee. Obviously, a piecework plan would not be feasible for many jobs.

Skills—Skill-Based Pay

Although quite similar in nature, skill- and competency-based pay will be discussed separately. A compensation planning survey of 950 U.S. firms showed that 15 percent have skill-based plans and 21 percent have competency-based plans.[36] **Skill-based pay** is a system that compensates employees for their job-related *skills* and *knowledge,* rather than his or her present job. Essentially, job descriptions, job evaluation plans, and job-based salary surveys are replaced by skill profiles, skill evaluation plans, and *skill-based* salary surveys. The system assumes that employees who know more are more valuable to the firm and, therefore, they deserve a reward for their efforts in acquiring new skills. When employees obtain additional job-relevant skills, both individuals and the departments they serve benefit. For example, in a department there may be six different types of machines, each requiring different skills to operate. Under a skill-based pay system, for example, the worker would increase his or her pay as additional machines are learned.

skill-based pay
System that compensates employees for their job-related skills and knowledge, not for their job titles.

Although skill-based pay appears to have advantages for both employer and employee, there are some challenges for management. The firm must provide adequate training opportunities or else the system can become a demotivator. Also, since it takes an average of only three years for a worker to reach a maximum level in a skill-based pay system, what will keep employees motivated?

Competencies—Competency-Based Pay

competency-based pay
Compensation plan that rewards employees for the capabilities they attain.

Competency-based pay is a compensation plan that rewards employees for the capabilities they attain. It is a type of skill-based pay plan for professional and managerial employees. Today, there are many alternatives to choose from—core, organizational, behavioral, and technical competencies. The disappearance of the traditional job provides the primary rationale for this change. Today, employees are said to have variable and unstable work assignments, with roles that cannot be assigned a valid pay rate in traditional job evaluation plans.[37] Often, considerable time must be spent determining the specific competencies needed for the different jobs. Blocks of competencies are then priced and management must invest considerable time in developing, implementing, and continuing such a system.

Seniority

seniority
Length of time an employee has been associated with the company, division, department, or job.

Seniority is the length of time an employee has been associated with the company, division, department, or job. Although management generally prefers performance as the primary basis for compensation changes, unions tend to favor seniority. They believe the use of seniority provides an objective and fair basis for pay increases. Many union leaders consider performance evaluation systems to be too subjective, permitting management to reward favorite employees arbitrarily.

Experience

Regardless of the nature of the task, experience has the potential for enhancing a person's ability to perform. However, this possibility materializes only if the experience acquired is positive. Knowledge of the basics is usually a prerequisite for effective use of a person's experience. This is true for a person starting to play golf, learn a foreign language, or manage people in organizations. People who express pride in their many years of managerial experience may be justified in their sentiments, but only if their experience has been beneficial. Those who have been autocratic managers for a number of years would likely not find their experience highly valued by a *Fortune* 100 firm today. Nevertheless, experience is often indispensable for gaining the insights necessary for performing many tasks.

Today, it is possible that *experience* is becoming somewhat irrelevant. In fact, technology may have rendered experience useless unless the person with the experience has kept up with the technology available. Managing in the dot-com world is certainly different from the old economy. Still, employees receive compensation for their experience and the practice is justified if the experience is positive and relevant to the work.

Organization Membership

Employees receive some compensation components without regard to the particular job they perform or their level of productivity. They receive them because they are members of the organization. For example, an average performer occupying a job in pay grade 1 may receive the same number of vacation days, the same amount of group life insurance, and the same reimbursement for educational expenses as a superior employee working in a job classified in pay grade 10. In fact, the worker in pay grade 1 may get more vacation time if he or she has been with the firm longer. The purpose of rewards based on organizational membership is to maintain a high degree of stability in the workforce and to recognize loyalty.

Potential

Potential is useless if it is never realized. However, organizations do pay some individuals based on their potential. In order to attract talented young people to the firm, for example, the overall compensation program must appeal to those with no experience or any immediate ability to perform difficult tasks. Many young employees are paid well, perhaps not because of their ability to make an immediate contribution, but because they have the *potential* to add value to the firm as a professional, first-line supervisor, manager of compensation, vice president of marketing, or possibly even chief executive officer.

Political Influence

Firms should obviously not permit political influence to be a factor in determining financial compensation. However, to deny its existence would be unrealistic. There is an unfortunate element of truth in the statement, "It's not *what* you know, it's *who* you know." To varying degrees in business, government, and not-for-profit organizations, a person's *pull* or political influence may sway pay and promotion decisions. It may be natural for a manager to favor a friend or relative in granting a pay increase or promotion. Nevertheless, if the person receiving the reward is not deserving of it, the work group will soon know about it. The result will probably be devastating to employee morale.

Luck

You have undoubtedly heard the expression, "It helps to be in the right place at the right time." There is more than a little truth in this statement as it relates to compensation. Opportunities are continually presenting themselves in firms. Realistically, there is no way for managers to foresee many of the changes that occur. For instance, who could have known that the purchasing agent, Joe Flynn, a seemingly healthy middle-aged man, would suddenly die of a heart attack? Although the company may have been grooming several managers for Joe's position, none were capable of immediately assuming the increased responsibility. The most experienced person, Tommy Loy, has been with the company only six months. Tommy had been an assistant buyer for a competitor for four years. Because of his experience, Tommy received the promotion and the increased financial compensation. Tommy Loy was lucky; he was in the right place at the right time.

When asked to explain their most important reasons for success and effectiveness as managers, two chief executives responded candidly. One said, "Success is being at the right place at the right time and being recognized as having the ability to make timely decisions. It also depends on having good rapport with people, a good operating background, and the knowledge of how to develop people." The other replied, "My present position was attained by being in the right place at the right time with a history of getting the job done." Both executives recognize the significance of luck combined with the ability to perform. Their experiences lend support to the idea that luck works primarily for the efficient.

<table>
<tr><td>

OBJECTIVE 9.10
Describe team-based pay, company-wide pay plans, professional employee compensation, sales representative compensation, and contingency worker compensation.

</td><td>

Team-Based Pay

Since team performance consists of individual efforts, individual employees should be recognized and rewarded for their contributions. However, if a team is to function effectively, firms should also provide a reward based on the overall team performance as well. Changing a firm's compensation structure from an individual-based system to one that involves team-based pay can have powerful results. By so doing, a firm can improve efficiency, productivity, and profitability.

</td></tr>
</table>

Team incentives have both advantages and disadvantages. On the positive side, firms find it easier to develop performance standards for groups than for individuals. For one thing, there are fewer standards to determine. Also, the output of a team is more likely to reflect a complete product or service. Another advantage is that employees may be more inclined to assist others and work collaboratively if the organization bases rewards on the team's output. Christopher Avery, a Texas-based speaker and consultant who specializes in issues concerning individual and shared responsibility in the workplace and the author of *Teamwork Is an Individual Skill: Getting Your Work Done When Sharing Responsibility,* said, "When teams perform highly, it is the interaction [among] team members, not the members themselves, that creates the high performance. If you ask such members who was singly responsible for the high performance of the team, they'll say 'Huh?' or 'We were' and mean it."[46] A potential disadvantage for team incentives relates to exemplary performers. If individuals in this category perceive that they contribute more than other employees in the group, they may become disgruntled and leave. However, Avery also adds, "If management wants to reward a high-performing team member, give that person a raise."[47]

salary compression
Situation that occurs when less experienced employees are paid as much as or more than employees who have been with the organization a long time due to a gradual increase in starting salaries and limited salary adjustment for long-term employees.

TRENDS & INNOVATIONS

Salary Compression, Why Is the New Guy Making What I Am Making?

Salary compression occurs when less experienced employees are paid as much as or more than employees who have been with the organization a long time due to a gradual increase in starting salaries and limited salary adjustment for long-term employees. Salary compression continued to be a major challenge for compensation managers even in a recession when pay cuts and freezes were the focus of the daily news.[38] As workers discover inequities in their pay, resentment and lower productivity may follow with the employees ultimately leaving the company when the economy improves.[39] Further, from a risk management perspective, companies need to make sure that salary compression is not causing problems with such laws as the Equal Pay Act. Unfortunately, no easy solution is available and it is projected that the gap between current and new employees is getting wider, and will continue to do so.[40]

Salary compression typically occurs when there is only a minimum pay differential with various skills and responsibility levels. Salary compression can cause people in jobs of less responsibility to make more than workers in jobs that have more responsible. For example, salary compression occurs when a worker earns as much or more than their supervisor. Reasons for this imbalance may be caused by the employee being paid overtime or a premium for the job while the supervisor cannot earn these benefits.[41]

Salary compression can also be quite emotional and can cause resentment and disengagement. It is difficult to focus on doing the best job possible when you believe you are not being paid according to your value. Old-timers may resent and refuse to help newcomers who are paid more, taking the attitude that if you pay them more, "let them earn their money." Another problem that can occur is when the employee is being paid more than their supervisor, causing a loss of respect for the supervisor.[42]

The solution to salary compression is simple; unfortunately, the solution usually requires money which is limited for most organizations. A company may build in compression funding to any annual budget increases. Still yet another way to remedy salary compression is to focus a primary portion of raises to your best employees and not waste compensation on across the board adjustments.[43]

There are instances where salary compression is not widespread, but instead limited to certain employees. Here, nonfinancial options may be able to solve the problem. Giving a worker a choice assignment may let them see that the company views their contribution as valuable.

Having a clear career path may also help reduce the tension caused by salary compression. Linda Ulrich of Buck Consultants said, "If people accept they have the opportunity to advance, they may accept that they are being paid a little bit less for the time being but with the knowledge that they're establishing a career and moving up."[44]

Historically, salary compression has become synonymous with the academic environment when new hire salaries are equal to or greater than the salaries of senior faculty. Budgets of most states are often quite limited but new faculty have to be hired to replace retiring or faculty who are leaving for greener pastures. It is not an unusual situation to have a professor retire and the retirement salary is not enough to cover the salary of his/her new replacement.[45]

Company-Wide Pay Plans

In baseball, as with other team sports, you do not judge the team based on its ace pitcher or great outfielder. The criterion for success is overall team performance, its win–loss record. In business, company-wide plans offer a possible alternative to the incentive plans previously discussed. Organizations normally base company-wide plans on the firm's productivity, cost savings, or profitability. Company-wide plans include profit sharing and gainsharing.

profit sharing
Compensation plans that result in the distribution of a predetermined percentage of the firm's profits to employees.

Profit Sharing

Profit sharing is a compensation plan that results in the distribution of a predetermined percentage of the firm's profits to employees. Many firms use this type of plan to integrate the employees' interests with those of the company. Profit-sharing plans can aid in recruiting, motivating, and retaining employees, which usually enhances productivity.

There are several variations of profit-sharing plans, but three basic kinds of plans used today are: current profit sharing, deferred profit sharing, and combination plans.

- *Current plans* provide payment to employees in cash or stock as soon as profits have been determined.
- *Deferred plans* involve placing company contributions in an irrevocable trust, credited to individual employees' accounts. The funds are normally invested in securities and become available to the employee (or his or her survivors) at retirement, termination, or death.
- *Combination plans* permit employees to receive payment of part of their share of profits on a current basis, while deferring payment of part of their share.

Normally, most full-time employees are included in a company's profit-sharing plan after a specified waiting period. *Vesting* determines the amount of *profit* an employee owns in his or her account. Firms often determine this sum on a graduated basis. For example, an employee may become 25 percent vested after being in the plan for two years; 50 percent vested after three years; 75 percent vested after four years; and 100 percent vested after five years. This gradual approach to vesting encourages employees to remain with the firm, thereby reducing turnover.

The results of profit sharing include increased efficiency and lower costs. However, variations in profits may present a special problem. When employees have become accustomed to receiving added compensation from profit sharing, and then there is no profit to share, they may become disgruntled.

A basic problem with a profit-sharing plan stems from the recipients' seldom knowing precisely how they helped generate the profits, beyond just doing their jobs. And, if employees continue to receive a payment, they will come to expect it and depend on it. If they do not know what they have done to deserve it, they may view it as an entitlement program and the intended *ownership* attitude may not materialize.

gainsharing

Plans designed to bind employees to the firm's productivity and provide an incentive payment based on improved company performance.

Scanlon plan

Gainsharing plan that provides a financial reward to employees for savings in labor costs resulting from their suggestions.

Web Wisdom

Scanlon Leadership Network

http://www. scanlonleader.org/ index.php/

A promoter of the Scanlon principles to advance their applications among organizations.

Gainsharing

Gainsharing plans are designed to bind employees to the firm's productivity and provide an incentive payment based on improved company performance. Gainsharing programs, such as the Scanlon, Multicost Scanlon, Rucker, and Improshare plans, are the most popular company-wide plans, and they have been adopted by American corporations.[48] The goal of gainsharing is to focus on improving cost-efficiency, reducing costs, improving throughput, and improving profitability.[49] Gainsharing helps align an organization's people strategy with its business strategy. More than 4,000 American companies now have some form of a gainsharing plans.[50] Gainsharing plans (also known as *productivity incentives, team incentives,* and *performance sharing incentives*) generally refer to incentive plans that involve many or all employees in a common effort to achieve a firm's performance objectives.

Joseph Scanlon, after whom the Scanlon plan was named, developed the first gainsharing plan during the Great Depression, and it continues to be a successful approach to group incentive. The **Scanlon plan** provides a financial reward to employees for savings in labor costs resulting from their suggestions. Employee-management committees evaluate these suggestions. Participants in these plans calculate savings as a ratio of payroll costs to the sales value of what that payroll produces. If the company is able to reduce payroll costs through increased operating efficiency, it shares the savings with its employees. Scanlon plans are not only financial incentive systems, but also systems for participative management. The Scanlon plan embodies management/labor cooperation, collaborative problem solving, teamwork, trust, gainsharing, open-book management, and servant leadership.

Professional Employee Compensation

As previously mentioned, a *professional employee* performs work requiring advanced knowledge in a field of learning, normally acquired through a prolonged course of specialized instruction. Examples of exempt professionals often employed in industry include scientists, engineers, and accountants. Their pay, initially, is for the knowledge they bring to the organization. Gradually,

ETHICAL DILEMMA

Creative Accounting?

You and your best friend Sam work for the same company. You are vice president for human resources and Sam is an accountant. Sam said, "I don't know if I should tell you this, but there's something going on at work you should know about." Sam then told you, in strict confidence, that the company's chief financial officer was planning to take an aggressive stance on sales revenue reporting that, in Sam's view, would stretch the boundaries of acceptable accounting practices. Sam's accounting expertise and responsibilities center on the company's real estate holdings and he does not deal with sales revenue. But he has a pretty good understanding of what's happening in other areas of the company's financial activities, and he was clearly concerned about what the CFO wanted to do.

The CFO's accounting method would increase your firm's earnings outlook and probably help its stock price. "But it could be risky," Sam said. It could "raise questions" about the firm's methods and even its integrity. What's more, Sam said, he wasn't sure the CEO clearly understands the CFO's approach. He might just go along with the CFO since they were college buddies and the CEO personally hired him four years ago. The CEO is 48 and has been with the company for five years. He has boosted sales to double-digit rates every year, but his streak may end soon. Sales gains so far this year have been the lowest in more than six years, and there is no help in the immediate horizon. Your chairman, the son of the founder, is 64 and has been with the company for 35 years. He has spent his career keeping his company on a steady growth path, and he considers the company's reputation and integrity to be a reflection of his own.[51]

What would you do?

however, some of this knowledge becomes obsolete, and their salaries reflect this. At times, this encourages professionals to enter management to make more money. A problem with this move is that they may not be suited for management.

The unstable nature of professional jobs and their salaries results in a heavy emphasis on market data for job pricing. This has resulted in the use of *maturity curves* that reflect the relationship between professional compensation and years of experience. These curves are used primarily to establish rates of pay for scientists and engineers involved in technical work at the professional level. Such maturity curves reveal a rapid increase in pay for roughly five to seven years, and then a more gradual rise as technical obsolescence erodes the value of these jobs.[52]

Sales Representative Compensation

Designing compensation programs for sales employees involves unique considerations.[53] For this reason, this task may belong to the sales staff rather than to human resources. Nevertheless, many general compensation practices apply to sales jobs. For example, job content, relative job worth, and job market value are all relevant factors.

The *straight salary* approach is one extreme in sales compensation. In this method, salespersons receive a fixed salary regardless of their sales levels. Organizations use straight salary primarily to emphasize continued product service after the sale. For instance, sales representatives who deal largely with the federal government often receive this form of compensation.

At the other extreme is *straight commission,* in which the person's pay is totally determined as a percentage of sales. If the salesperson makes no sales, the individual working on straight commission receives no pay. On the other hand, highly productive sales representatives can earn a great deal of money under this plan.

Between these extremes are the endless varieties of *part-salary, part-commission* combinations. The possibilities increase when a firm adds various types of *bonuses* to the basic compensation package. The emphasis given to either commission or salary depends on several factors, including the organization's philosophy toward service, the nature of the product, and the amount of time required to close a sale.

Contingent Worker Compensation

Contingent workers are employed through an employment agency or on an on-call basis and often earn less than traditional employees. As discussed in Chapter 5, flexibility and lower costs for the employer are key reasons for the growth in the use of contingent workers. An inherent compensation problem relates to internal equity. You may have two employees working side by side, one a contingent worker and the other a regular employee, performing the same or near identical tasks, and one makes more money than the other. In most cases, contingents earn less pay and are far less likely to receive health or retirement benefits than their permanent counterparts.

OBJECTIVE 9.11
Explain the various elements of executive compensation.

Executive Compensation

As the recession of 2008/2010 worked its way onward with rank-and-file workers losing income, security, and jobs, executive pay became the focal point of public anger. The pay gap between the most affluent executives and the average worker has become enormous. It is difficult for workers who make $12 to $18 an hour to appreciate why these executives are making such outrageous salaries.[54] Steve Wagner, managing partner at Deloitte & Touche's Center for Corporate Governance, said, "Executive compensation is the lightning rod for the crisis in confidence in corporate America."[55]

With that being said, we must remember that the skills possessed by company executives largely determine whether a firm will prosper, survive, or fail. A company's program for compensating executives is a critical factor in attracting and retaining the best available talent. Designing an executive compensation package begins with determining the organization's goals, its objectives, and the anticipated time for achieving them. The executive package depends on the magnitude of the responsibility, risk, and effort shouldered by the chief executive. Organizations typically prefer to relate salary growth for the highest-level managers to market rates and overall corporate performance, including the firm's market value. But, at times this has not occurred.

Corporate boards of directors are now taking a more active role since the financial services meltdown in the recession of 2008/10 when the question was often asked "Where were the boards?"[56] One of the results of the recent financial crisis is a sharpened focus on ensuring genuine alignment between executive compensation and performance.[57] They are under the proverbial gun to devise compensation plans that reward performance rather than greed. It is one thing for a chief executive to receive lavish compensation when the company is doing well. It is another thing to pay them millions when their company is failing. It is very important to make a commitment to bring compensation in line with performance if shareholders are to be satisfied.[58]

Base Salary

Although it may not represent the largest portion of the executive's compensation package, the base salary provided is obviously important. It is a factor in determining the executive's standard of living. Salary also provides the basis for other forms of compensation; for example, it may determine the amount of bonuses and certain benefits. The U.S. tax law does not allow companies to deduct more than $1 million of an executive's salary; therefore, most firms keep it below that amount. It is because of the million dollar deduction maximum that bonuses and performance-based pay have become popular.

Bonuses and Performance-Based Pay

There is a trend toward more performance-based executive compensation packages. If pay for performance is appropriate for lower-level employees, should top executives be exempt from the same practice? The true superstars can still have huge earnings if their targets are met. As shareholders become increasingly disenchanted with high levels of executive compensation for less-than-stellar accomplishments, performance-based pay is gaining in popularity.

Public companies that rely on the performance-based compensation exception to the $1 million annual deduction limit under section 162(m) of the Internal Revenue Code must adopt annual and long-term incentive plans, set performance goals, certify attainment of performance goals from prior-year plans, disclose performance targets, and address the deductibility of executive compensation in their annual Compensation Discussion and Analysis disclosures. Performance goals must be established in writing no later than 90 days after the beginning of the performance period.[59] If these conditions are not met, compensation over $ 1 million dollars cannot be a tax deduction.

Payment of bonuses reflects a managerial belief in their incentive value. Cash bonuses, paid periodically based on performance goals, often provide real incentives.[60] In the past, bonuses could be quite large and often were not tied to "real" performance goals. Today, there is virtually no such thing as a guaranteed bonus in the vast majority of companies and bonuses in the tens of millions of dollars are unheard of.

Companies receiving TARP assistance are required to ensure that incentive compensation for senior executives does not "encourage unnecessary and excessive risks that threaten the value of the financial institution." Although the requirements are not currently applicable to non-TARP entities, some companies are evaluating whether their incentive compensation arrangements encourage excessive risk-taking. Boards of directors are becoming even more proactive and adept in their exercise of good corporate governance of executive compensation practices.[61]

Stock Option Plans

stock option plan
Incentive plan in which executives can buy a specified amount of stock in their company in the future at or below the current market price.

Stock option plans give the executive the option to buy a specified amount of stock in the future at or below the current market price. The stock option is a long-term incentive designed to integrate the interests of management with those of the organization. To ensure this integration, some boards of directors require their top executives to hold some of the firm's stock. Stock options have lost some of their appeal because of accounting rule changes that require companies to value and book an appropriate expense for options as they are granted. Nevertheless, there are several bona fide reasons for including stock ownership in executive compensation plans. In addition to potentially aligning employees' interests with those of shareholders, retaining top executives is also a factor.

Perquisites

perquisites (perks)
Special benefits provided by a firm to a small group of key executives and designed to give the executives something extra.

Perquisites (perks) are any special benefits provided by a firm to a small group of key executives and designed to give the executives "something extra." Possible executive's perks might include a company-provided car, limousine service, and use of company plane and yacht. In 2007, the Securities and Exchange Commission lowered the threshold for disclosure of executive perks from $50,000 to $10,000.[62] Once-hidden information regarding perks must now be disclosed. Compensation committees are "protecting the core incentives: salaries, bonuses and long-term incentives, and cutting perks and severance," says Andrew Goldstein, North American co-leader of Executive Compensation Consulting at Watson Wyatt in Chicago. "The core categories are what really drive performance. For a CEO package that could go up to millions, [the public and legislators] focus on emotional things. It's the club membership or the car that upsets them."[63] These kind of perks just aren't worth it," says David E. Gordon of Frederic W. Cook & Co., a compensation consultancy. "They are a small fraction of overall compensation but have the ability to get 50% of the attention."[64]

OBJECTIVE 9.12
Explain a golden parachute contract and the clawback contract provision.

golden parachute contract
Perquisite that protects executives in the event that another company acquires their firm or the executive is forced to leave the firm for other reasons.

Golden Parachute Contract

A **golden parachute contract** is a perquisite that protects executives in the event that another company acquires their firm or if the executive is forced to leave the firm for other reasons. At times, golden parachute contracts have been abused. Outrageous golden parachute contracts appear to be lessening but one must wonder if it is enough. In a recent study, the average value of golden parachute payments for CEOs was $22.9 million in 2009, compared to $38.3 million in 2007.[65] Don Delves, president of Chicago-based compensation consultant Delves Group, said, "I think we are going to see a lot more scrutiny on how much and under what circumstances people get this big severance and *golden parachutes*. Now the shareholders can see it right there, and ask the question, 'Do we feel right about giving it to them?'"[66] Under the American Recovery and Reinvestment Act of 2009, TARP recipients generally are prohibited from making any "golden parachute payment," which can be any payment for departure from a company for any reason, except those made for services performed or benefits accrued, to its ten most highly compensated employees.[67]

A GLOBAL PERSPECTIVE

Executive Compensation in the Global Environment

The pay gap between the most affluent executives and the average worker in the U.S. remains wide. In 2009, Standard & Poor's (S&P) 500 chief executive officers averaged $10.5 million a year, 344 times the annual pay of typical U.S. workers. By contrast, the ratio is 22 in Britain, 20 in Canada, and 11 in Japan.[73] In Sweden, the spread is likely to be closer to eight to one. Whereas people in the United States derive great status from high pay, nations in large parts of Europe and Asia shun conspicuous wealth.

Governance of executive pay varies from country to country but there is a definite increase in shareholder influence on executive pay issues from Europe to North America to Asia Pacific and beyond. This trend will likely continue. Shareholders in Europe have been the leaders of the charge. Executives at French firms face binding shareholder votes on certain aspects of their pay packages, including share options and retirement packages.[74] Starting in 2003, public companies in the United Kingdom were required to give shareholders an advisory up-or-down vote on executive pay packages. Although the "say on pay" vote is nonbinding,

advocates believe that it has increased the discussion between companies and large investors which resulted in an improved alignment between pay and performance. As an example, share option plans, which were criticized for rewarding short-term share price volatility over long-term value creation, have been largely replaced with performance-contingent stock.[75]

Investors in the Netherlands, Sweden, and Norway cast a binding vote on executive pay. Some firms in Spain and Switzerland have voluntarily introduced advisory votes. Across Europe, companies are making efforts to improve the disclosure of their executive pay. European governments are trying to exert more direct influence over executive pay as well. A proposal in France requires that severance payments be conditional on performance—a practice essentially unheard of in the past. Legislators in the Netherlands want to limit nonperformance-based compensation by imposing an additional tax on salary and severance payments. It is quite likely these trends will continue in the wake of the recession of 2008/10. The U.S. has been slow to react to compensation governance but there is evidence that this may be changing.[76] Remember from the HRM in Action at the beginning of the chapter, as part of the Restoring American Financial Stability Act of 2010, shareholders get a non-binding vote on executive pay and generous packages set up for executives who part ways with the company.

What most people may not understand is that golden parachute plans and severance payments are not set up by a board of directors after a CEO has quit or been fired. These payments were negotiated prior to being hired. Not only should CEO pay be considered but the total CEO pay contracts should also be examined. Hopefully the environment is changing.[68]

Clawback Contract Provision

Whether right or wrong, compensation programs received much of the blame for the global economic crisis of 2008/10. Many say that the financial services industry compensation programs may have encouraged excessive risk taking by executives and other key employees. As a result, clawback policies have been created in many companies.[69] A clawback policy allows the company to recover compensation if subsequent review indicates that payments were not calculated accurately or performance goals were not met.[70] Of the 100 largest U.S. companies by revenue, 70 say they have so-called clawback provisions that allow them to recoup pay which is up from only 17.6 percent in 2006.[71] TARP-covered institutions are required to implement "clawback" provisions that operate to recover any bonus, retention, or other incentive compensation that was paid to any senior executive officer or any of the next twenty most highly compensated employees of the institution as a result of financial information that is later found to be materially inaccurate.[72]

Summary

1. *Define* compensation *and describe the various forms of compensation.* Compensation is the total of all rewards provided employees in return for their services. Forms of compensation include direct financial compensation, indirect financial compensation (benefits), and nonfinancial compensation.

2. *Define* financial equity *and explain the concept of equity in direct financial compensation.* Financial equity is workers' perceptions that they are being treated fairly. Forms of compensation equity include external equity, internal equity, employee equity, and team equity.

3. *Identify the determinants of direct financial compensation.* The organization, the labor market, the job, and the employee all have an impact on job pricing and the ultimate determination of an individual's financial compensation.

4. *Describe the organization as a determinant of direct financial compensation.* Compensation policies and ability to pay are organizational factors to be considered.

5. *Describe the labor market as a determinant of direct financial compensation.* Factors that should be considered include compensation surveys, expediency, cost-of-living increases, labor unions, the economy, and certain federal and state legislation.

6. *Explain how the job is a determinant of direct financial compensation.* Management techniques used for determining a job's relative worth include job analysis, job descriptions, and job evaluation.

7. *Define* job evaluation *and describe the four traditional job evaluation methods.* Job evaluation is a process that determines the relative value of one job in relation to another. In the job evaluation ranking method, the raters examine the description of each job being evaluated and arrange the jobs in order according to their value to the company. The classification method involves defining a number of classes or grades to describe a group of jobs. In the factor comparison method, raters need not keep the entire job in mind as they evaluate; instead, they make decisions on separate aspects or factors of the job. In the point method, raters assign numerical values to specific job factors, such as knowledge required, and the sum of these values provides a quantitative assessment of a job's relative worth.

8. *Describe job pricing.* Placing a dollar value on the worth of a job is job pricing.

9. *Identify factors related to the employee that are essential in determining direct financial compensation.* The factors include pay for performance, seniority, experience, membership in the organization, potential, political influence, and luck.

10. *Describe team-based pay, company-wide pay plans, professional employee compensation, sales representative compensation, and contingency worker compensation.* If a team is to function effectively, firms should provide a reward based on the overall team performance.

    Organizations normally base company-wide plans on the firm's productivity, cost savings, or profitability.

    Compensation for professionals is for the knowledge they bring to the organization. The unstable nature of professional jobs and their salaries results in a heavy emphasis on market data for job pricing.

    Designing compensation programs for sales employees involves unique considerations.

    Contingent workers are employed through an employment agency or on an on-call basis and often earn less than traditional employees. Flexibility and lower costs for the employer are key reasons for the growth in the use of contingent workers.

11. *Explain the various elements of executive compensation.* In determining executive compensation, firms typically prefer to relate salary growth for the highest-level managers to overall corporate performance. Executive compensation often has five basic elements: (1) base salary, (2) bonuses and performance-based pay, (3) stock option plans, (4) executive performance-based pay, and (5) perquisites.

12. *Explain a golden parachute contract, executive severance pay, and the clawback contract provision.* A golden parachute contract is a perquisite that protects executives in the event that another company acquires their firm or if the executive is forced to leave the firm for other reasons.

    A clawback policy allows the company to recover compensation if subsequent review indicates that payments were not calculated accurately or performance goals were not met.

Key Terms

compensation 264
direct financial compensation 264
indirect financial compensation
   (benefits) 265
nonfinancial compensation 265
equity theory 265
financial equity 265
external equity 265
internal equity 265
employee equity 265
team equity 266
compensation policy 267
pay leaders 267
market (going) rate 267
pay followers 267
labor market 267

compensation survey 268
cost-of-living allowance
   (COLA) 269
exempt employees 269
job evaluation 270
job evaluation ranking
   method 271
classification method 271
factor comparison method 271
point method 272
hay guide chart-profile
   method (Hay plan) 272
job pricing 272
pay grade 272
wage curve 273
pay range 273

broadbanding 274
merit pay 275
bonus 276
spot bonus 276
piecework 276
skill-based pay 276
competency-based pay 277
seniority 277
salary compression 279
profit sharing 279
gainsharing 280
Scanlon plan 280
stock option plan 283
perquisites (perks) 283
golden parachute
   contract 283

Questions for Review

1. Define each of the following terms:
   a. compensation
   b. direct financial compensation
   c. indirect financial compensation
   d. nonfinancial compensation
2. What are the differences among external equity, internal equity, employee equity, and team equity?
3. Why might a firm want to be a pay leader as opposed to paying market rate?
4. What are the primary determinants of direct financial compensation? Briefly describe each.
5. What organizational factors should be considered as determinants of direct financial compensation?
6. What factors should be considered when the labor market is a determinant of direct financial compensation?
7. How has government legislation affected compensation?
8. What is the difference between an exempt and a nonexempt employee?
9. What factors should be considered when the job is a determinant of direct financial compensation?
10. Give the primary purpose of job evaluation.
11. Distinguish between the following job evaluation methods:

   a. ranking
   b. classification
   c. factor comparison
   d. point method
12. Describe the Hay guide chart-profile method of job evaluation.
13. What is the purpose of job pricing? Discuss briefly.
14. State the basic procedure for determining pay grades.
15. What is the purpose of establishing pay ranges?
16. Define *broadbanding*.
17. Distinguish between merit pay, bonus, and piecework.
18. Describe factors related to the employee as a determinant of direct financial compensation.
19. What are some company-wide, team-based pay plans?
20. How is the compensation for professionals determined?
21. How is the compensation for sales representatives determined?
22. What are the various types of executive compensation?
23. Describe each of the following:
   a. Golden parachute contract
   b. Clawback contract provision

HRM INCIDENT 1

A Motivated Worker!

Bob Rosen could hardly wait to get back to work Monday morning. He was excited about his chance of getting a large bonus. Bob is a machine operator with Ram Manufacturing Company, a Wichita, Kansas, producer of electric motors. He operates an armature-winding machine. The machine winds copper wire onto metal cores to make the rotating elements for electric motors.

Ram pays machine operators on a graduated piece-rate basis. Operators are paid a certain amount for each part made, plus a bonus. A worker who produces 10 percent above standard for a certain month receives a 10 percent additional bonus. For 20 percent above standard, the bonus is 20 percent. Bob realized that he had a good chance of earning a 20 percent bonus that month. That would be $1,787.

Bob had a special use for the extra money. His wife's birthday was just three weeks away. He was hoping to get her a car. He had already saved $4,000, but the down payment on the car was $5,500. The bonus would enable him to buy the car.

Bob arrived at work at seven o'clock that morning, although his shift did not begin until eight. He went to his workstation and checked the supply of blank cores and copper wire. Finding that only one spool of wire was on hand, he asked the forklift truck driver to bring another. Then, he asked the operator who was working the graveyard shift, "Sam, do you mind if I grease the machine while you work?"

"No," Sam said, "that won't bother me a bit."

After greasing the machine, Bob stood and watched Sam work. He thought of ways to simplify the motions involved in loading, winding, and unloading the armatures. As Bob took over the machine after the eight o'clock whistle, he thought, "I hope I can pull this off. I know the car will make Kathy happy. She won't be stuck at home while I'm at work."

Questions

1. Explain the advantages and disadvantages of a piecework pay system such as that at Ram.

HRM INCIDENT 2

The Controversial Job

David Rhine, compensation manager for Farrington Lingerie Company, was generally relaxed and good-natured. Although he was a no-nonsense, competent executive, David was one of the most popular managers in the company. This Friday morning, however, David was not his usual self. As chairperson of the company's job evaluation committee, he had called a late-morning meeting at which several jobs were to be considered for reevaluation. The jobs had already been rated and assigned to pay grade 3. But the office manager, Ben Butler, was upset that one was not rated higher. To press the issue, Ben had taken his case to two executives who were also members of the job evaluation committee. The two executives (production manager Bill Nelson and general marketing manager Betty Anderson) then requested that the job ratings be reviewed. Bill and Betty supported Ben's side of the dispute, and David was not looking forward to the confrontation that was almost certain to occur.

The controversial job was that of receptionist. Only one receptionist position existed in the company, and Marianne Sanders held it. Marianne had been with the firm 12 years, longer than any of the committee members. She was extremely efficient, and virtually all the executives in the company, including the president, had noticed and commented on her outstanding work. Bill Nelson and Betty Anderson were particularly pleased with Marianne because of the cordial manner in which she greeted and accommodated Farrington's customers and vendors, who frequently visited the plant. They felt that Marianne projected a positive image of the company.

When the meeting began, David said, "Good morning. I know that you're busy, so let's get the show on the road. We have several jobs to evaluate this morning and I suggest we begin …" Before he could finish his sentence, Bill interrupted, "I suggest we start with Marianne." Betty nodded in agreement. When David regained his composure, he quietly but firmly asserted, "Bill, we are not here today to evaluate Marianne. Her supervisor does that at performance-appraisal time. We're meeting to evaluate jobs based on job content. In order to do this fairly, with regard to other jobs in the company, we must leave personalities out of our evaluation." David then proceeded to pass out copies of the receptionist job description to Bill and Betty, who were obviously very irritated.

Questions

1. Do you feel that David was justified in insisting that the job, not the person, be evaluated? Discuss.

2. Do you believe that there is a maximum rate of pay for every job in an organization, regardless of how well the job is being performed? Justify your position.

3. Assume that Marianne is earning the maximum of the range for her pay grade. In what ways could she obtain a salary increase?

Notes

1. Peter Drucker, "Beyond Capitalism," *Across the Board* 42 (November/December 2005): 14.
2. Jennifer Schramm, "Executive Pay: On Your Radar," *HRMagazine* 54 (April 2009): 108.
3. Geoff Colvin, "As Executive Compensation Becomes Topics A (Again), the Real Outrage Is How CEOs Are Paid, Not How Much," *Fortune* 161 (May 3, 2010): 86.
4. Robert J. Grossman, "Executive Pay: Perception and Reality," *HRMagazine* 54 (April 2009): 26–32.
5. Ibid.
6. Paul Sweeney, "Whose Job Is Corporate Governance?" *Financial Executive* 25 (May 2009): 34–39.
7. Colvin, "As Executive Compensation Becomes Topics A (Again), the Real Outrage Is How CEOs Are Paid, Not How Much."
8. Jessica Silver-Greenberg, Tara Kalwarski, and Alexis Leondis, "CEO Pay Drops…But Cash Is King," *BusinessWeek* (April 5, 2010): 50–56.
9. Karen Dillon, "The Coming Battle over Executive Pay," *Harvard Business Review* 87 (September 2009): 96–103.
10. Robert C. Hazard, Jr., "Corporate Ethics, Corporate Pay and the Lodging Industry," *Lodging Hospitality* 58 (November 2002): 65.
11. James Kristie, "Let's Have No 'Outrageous Failure of Policy.'" *Boardroom Briefing* 7 (Spring 2010): 35/55.
12. Emily Lambert, "The Right Way to Pay," *Forbes* 183 (May 11, 2009): 78–80.
13. Ibid.
14. "How to Go Strategic With Benefits and Pay—and Meet Company Goals," *HR Focus* 85 (June 2008): 3–5.
15. R. Wayne Mondy and Shane R. Premeaux, *Management: Concept, Practices, and Skills* (Englewood Cliffs, NJ: Prentice Hall, 7th Edition, 1995): 23.
16. John Mackey, "Lavish Pay Is Bad Business," *Harvard Business Review* 87 (September 2009): 113.
17. Fay Hansen, "Study Finds Widespread Wage Theft," *Workforce Management* 88 (November 16, 2009): 29.
18. "How the New Federal Minimum Wage May Affect Your Company," *HR Focus* 86 (September 2009): 7–10.
19. Judy Greenwald, "Top Wage-hour Class Action Settlements Soared in 2009," *Business Insurance* 44 (January 25, 2010): 4–19.
20. Roger S. Achille, "FLSA Requires Education for Professional Exemption," *HRMagazine* 55 (February 2010): 70.
21. Linda Lemel Hoseman, "Recent Economic Recovery Legislation Contains Significant New Executive Compensation Requirements," *Employee Benefit Plan Review* 63 (May 2009): 32–34.
22. Ibid.
23. Jai Lynn Yang, "The State of the Bailout," *Fortune* 161 (March 22, 2010): 16.
24. http://www.haygroup.com/ww/about/index.aspx?ID=68. February 11, 2010.
25. Frank L. Giancola, "A Framework for Understanding New Concepts in Compensation Management," *Benefits & Compensation Digest* 46 (September 2009): 1–16.
26. "Caution with Executive Pay Increases," *Report on Salary Surveys* 10 (January 2010): 8–9.
27. Randall Bolten, "Delivering Incentive Compensation Plans That Work," *Financial Executive* 25 (September 2009): 52–54.
28. "Pay for Performance," *Controller's Report 2010* (January 2010): 6–8.
29. "Merit Pay Strategies: Median Targets for 2008 Merit Increases Ranges from 3.3% to 4%," *Controller's Report 2008* (January 2008): 12–13.
30. Michelle Conlin, "The Case for Unequal Perks," *BusinessWeek* (March 23, 2009): 54–55.
31. Ibid.
32. Ibid.
33. "Raises Cut in '09, But Bonus Budgets Inch Up," *Treasury & Risk* (September 2009): 8.
34. Angie Herbers, "Bonus Babies," *Investment Advisor* 30 (February 2010): 47–48.
35. "How to Reward Top Performers on a Tight Budget," *Report on Salary Surveys* 7 (June 2007): 1–14.
36. Frank Giancola, "Skill-Based Pay—Issues for Consideration," *Benefits & Compensation Digest* 44 (May 2007): 1/15.
37. Ibid.

38. "Salary Compression Still Concerns; Experts Provide Solutions," *Report on Salary Surveys* 9 (June 2009): 1–7.
39. Fredrik Heyman, "How Wage Compression Affects Job Turnover," *Journal of Labor Research* 29 (Winter 2008): 11–26.
40. Susan Doughty, "Internal Relativity—Are We Living in Denial?" *Human Resources Magazine* 13 (April/May 2008): 22–23.
41. "Salary Compression."
42. Ibid.
43. Ibid.
44. Ibid.
45. J. Howard Finch, Richard S. Allen, and H. Shelton Weeks, "Salary Premium Required for Replacing Management Faculty: Evidence From a National Survey," *Journal of Education for Business* 85 (May/June 2010): 264-267.
46. Matt Bloch, "Rewarding the *Team,*" *HRMagazine* 52 (February 2007): 91–93.
47. Ibid.
48. Dong-One Kim, "The Choice of Gainsharing Plans in North America: A Congruence Perspective," *Journal of Labor Research* 26 (Summer 2005): 465–483.
49. Woodruff Imberman, "Can You Motivate Your Workers?" *Official Board Markets* 84 (January 15, 2008): 6–8.
50. "Gild Your Bottom Line," *Paint & Coatings Industry* 23 (March 2007): 32–40.
51. Brenda Franklin, David Gebler, Barry Mason, and Jeff Ewing, "Spinning the Numbers," *HRMagazine* 47 (November 2002): 64–69.
52. Richard I. Henderson, *Compensation Management in a Knowledge-Based World* (Upper Saddle River, NJ: Prentice Hall, 2006): 181.
53. Liz Cobb, "Sales Compensation Plans," *Sales & Service Excellence* 8 (December 2008): 9.
54. Grossman, "Executive Pay: Perception and Reality."
55. Sweeney, "Whose Job Is Corporate Governance?"
56. Richard M. Steinberg, "On the Hot Seat with Today's Challenges," *Financial Executive* 25 (October 2009): 28–31.
57. Robin A. Ferracone and Todd M. Gershkowitz, "Performance and Pay Alignment: A Top Priority for Compensation Committees," *Directorship* 36 (April/May 2010): 38–39.
58. Douglas Quenqua, "Public Ire Demands Account for Excessive CEO Payments," *PRWeek (U.S.)* 13 June 2010): 14.
59. "Section 162(m) Pitfalls," *Venulex Legal Summaries* (2009 Q1, Special section): 1–4.
60. Doug Raymond, "Repricing Challenges," *Directors & Boards* 33 (3rd Quarter 2009): 12.
61. "Executive Compensation: Fundamental Change Is Here, Are You Prepared?" *Venulex Legal Summaries* (2009 Q2, Special section): 1–3.
62. Richard Stolz, "Inventive Incentives," *SMB Finance* (July/August 2007): 16–18.
63. Grossman, "Executive Pay: Perception and Reality."
64. Silver-Greenberg, Kalwarski, and Leondis, "CEO Pay Drops…But Cash Is King."
65. Melissa Klein Aguilar, "Golden Parachutes Feeling Pressure, Seeing Change," *Compliance Week* (April 2010): 36–60.
66. Meghan Streit, "Zander's Exit Take Could Top $56M," *RCR Wireless News* 26 (March 12, 2007): 7.
67. "Executive Compensation: Fundamental Change Is Here, Are You Prepared?"
68. Julie Hembrock Daum, "Spencer Stuart Board Index: How Boards Are Changing," *BusinessWeek Online* (March 17, 2010): 12.
69. James E. Earle, "The Emerging Role of Clawback Policies for Managing Risk in Compensation Programs," *Benefits Law Journal* 23 (Spring 2010): 72–79.
70. "Section 162(m) Pitfalls."
71. Alexis Leondis and Margaret Collins, "Empty Clawbacks," *BusinessWeek* (January 25, 2010): 20.
72. Linda Lemel Hoseman, "Recent Economic Recovery Legislation Contains Significant New Executive Compensation Requirements," *Employee Benefit Plan Review* 63 (May 2009): 32–34.
73. Grossman, "Executive Pay: Perception and Reality."
74. "Lack of Global Pay Rules Creates Challenges," *Compliance Reporter* (January 29, 2010): 17.
75. Diane Doubleday and Jennifer Wagner, "New Era for Boards and Executive 'Pay For Performance,'" *Corporate Board* 30 (September/October 2009): 5–12.
76. Ibid.

10 Indirect Financial Compensation (Benefits) and Nonfinancial Compensation

HRM in Action: Two in a Box

Some companies are giving two executives the same responsibilities and the same title and letting them decide how the work is to be divided (Two in a Box). Unlike job sharing, it is a full-time job for both executives. It certainly has some risk, as in the case of the 1998 DaimlerChrysler Corporation disaster of an attempt at two in a box when one executive was unwilling to share authority, resulting in the resignation of the other executive. Problems certainly can occur as the egos of two executives meet, but it has proven successful in certain instances. A major advantage of this approach is that it can ease transition, permitting a manager to learn from a more experienced manager. It is also useful as managers confront the requirement of global traveling. One manager could be at the home office taking care of regular business while the other is traveling. For two-and-a-half years, two executives shared a job as heads of Cisco's routing group. The two had complementary skills and each gained experience from the other. Cisco typically combines a technically oriented manager with a business-oriented one. The Two in a Box approach requires work and constant communication, but for the right two executives, the benefits derived are worth it.

Another Two in a Box example occurred when Peter Chernin, the president of NewsCorp. and head of its Fox subsidiary, appointed Gary Newman and Dana Walden as presidents of 20th Century Fox Television. Both are responsible for the performance of the entire company. "What I was really thinking was where to find the skill set to manage these businesses," Chernin says. "I came to believe that, because of the complexity, if I could find two people with complementary skills, it would probably be better."

After completing this chapter, students should be able to:

1. Define indirect financial compensation (benefits).

2. Describe mandated (legally required) benefits.

3. Explain the various discretionary benefits.

4. Explain premium pay.

5. Explain voluntary benefits.

6. Describe customized benefit plans.

7. Explain health care legislation.

8. Describe the importance of communicating information about the benefits package.

9. Describe the components of nonfinancial compensation.

10. Describe the job itself and the job environment as a non-financial compensation factor.

11. Describe workplace flexibility (work–life balance) factors.

Gary Newman said, "Because there are two of us, we're capable of getting involved in many more things. There's more productivity here than at any other company like this where there's only one person in charge," The arrangement has been great for their family lives. "There's no meeting that I can't cover or that Gary can't cover," Walden says.[1]

In another example of Two in a Box, Aon Consulting is chaired by co-CEOs, Kathryn Hayley and Baljit Dail. Hayley said, "We always have the kid stories and how we spent the weekend, and how we're managing the work/life balance, which is a challenge for every professional these days that's working long hours." It might seem immaterial to the bottom-line for them to chat on family matters as part of the job. But close communication and a healthy relationship are among the keys to success when executive power is shared.[2] In 2010, German business software provider SAP AG appointed Bill McDermott and Jim Hagemann Snabe as co-CEOs, returning the company to the co-CEO structure.[3]

Research by consulting firm Mercer found that as of the end of 2008, just 34 of 6,487 public firms, or 0.5 percent, had co-CEOs. But the number may grow. George Houston, faculty member at the Center for Creative Leadership, said, "Co-CEO setups will get more attention, given the way the business world is assessing leadership challenges and failures. It's an experiment. People are going to be testing it." Other companies that utilize co-CEOs include BlackBerry-device maker Research in Motion, restaurant chain P.F. Chang's China Bistro, and business software provider SAP.[4]

This chapter begins by describing the process of giving two executives the same responsibilities and the same title and letting them decide how the work is to be divided (Two in a Box) and then defining indirect financial compensation (benefits). A discussion of total rewards and mandated benefits is next presented. Discretionary benefits, including topics related to payment for time not worked, health care, life insurance, retirement plans, disability protection, employee stock option plans, and employee services, are discussed next. Then, voluntary benefits and customized benefit plans are presented. Premium pay, health care legislation, and communicating information about the benefit package are presented next. Factors involved in nonfinancial compensation, including the job itself and the job environment, are then presented. Workplace flexibility (work–life balance) is then described. This chapter concludes with a global perspective entitled "Global Job Rotation as a Unique Fast Track Benefit."

OBJECTIVE 10.1
Define indirect financial compensation (benefits).

indirect financial compensations (benefits)
All financial rewards that are not included in direct financial compensation.

Indirect Financial Compensation (Benefits)

Most organizations recognize that they have a responsibility to their employees to provide insurance and other programs for their health, safety, security, and general welfare (see Figure 10.1). **Indirect financial compensations (benefits)** include all financial rewards not included in direct financial compensation. According to a recent SHRM survey, benefits are the second most important driver of job satisfaction, coming in just behind job security.[5] Benefits generally cost the firm money, but employees usually receive them indirectly. For example, an organization may spend thousands of dollars a year contributing to health insurance premiums for each employee. The employee does not receive the money but does obtain the benefit of health insurance coverage. This type of compensation has two distinct advantages: (1) it is generally nontaxable to the employee and (2) the cost of some benefits may be much less for large groups of employees than for individuals.

As a rule, employees receive benefits because of their membership in the organization. Benefits are typically unrelated to employee productivity; therefore, although they may be valuable in recruiting and retaining employees, they do not generally serve as motivation for improved performance. Legislation mandates some benefits, and employers provide other discretionary benefits. *Discretionary benefits* are benefit payments made as a result of unilateral management decisions in nonunion firms and from labor–management negotiations in unionized firms. *Voluntary benefits*, on the other hand, are usually 100 percent paid by the employee but

Figure 10.1

Indirect Financial Compensation (Benefits) in a Total Compensation Program

EXTERNAL ENVIRONMENT
INTERNAL ENVIRONMENT
Compensation

Financial		Nonfinancial	
<u>Direct</u>	<u>Indirect (Benefits)</u>	<u>The Job</u>	<u>Job Environment</u>

Legally Required Benefits
Social Security
Unemployment Compensation
Workers' Compensation

Discretionary Benefits
Payment for Time Not Worked
Health Care
Life Insurance
Retirement Plans
Disability Protection
Employee Stock Option Plans
Employee Services
Premium Pay

Voluntary Benefits

TRENDS & INNOVATIONS

Total Rewards Are Much More Than the Money that Jingles in Your Pocket

Historically, compensation practitioners focused primarily on direct financial compensation and indirect financial compensation (benefits). However, this approach has expanded into the concept of "Total Rewards" and the emphasis is now more encompassing as reflected in the name change of compensation's professional organization. The American Compensation Association is now WorldatWork, the Professional Association for Compensation, Benefits, and *Total Rewards*. HR consultant and co-author of *Reward Management* and *Strategic Reward* Michael Armstrong said, "There are lots of models around, but essentially total reward is about all the ways in which people are rewarded when they come to work—pay, benefits and the other non-financial rewards—put together to make a coherent and integrated whole."[6] According to Duncan Brown of the Institute for Employment Studies, managers should consider a broad rewarding work environment and not just focus on pay and benefits schemes.[7] The definition that has emerged around total rewards goes beyond money and looks at career opportunity and personal and career development as well. Total Rewards also include work–life balance factors to be discussed later in the chapter.

Many compensation packages were developed piecemeal over time, leaving them without a comprehensive and coherent approach to rewarding employees. But they now need to take a fresh tack and develop a total reward strategy that deals with compensation rewards as a whole, taking into account every aspect of working life. "This means looking at the big picture and not simply cash reward," says Dave Lawrence, vice president, compensation and benefits Europe, Middle East, and Africa at Intercontinental Hotels Group (IHG).[8] Everything included in the total reward package is directed toward maximum attainment of corporate goals. Anything that the company provides an employee is included, from base pay and benefits to the organization's culture and environment.[9] With Total Rewards, the idea of a three-legged stool provides an example of how the three forms of compensation are tied together. If one leg of the compensation stool breaks or is weaker than the others, the total compensation package will be less effective. Such would be the case with a person attempting to sit on a stool on which one leg (or two) was shorter than the others.

Some companies are using a total reward statement to show employees the total value of everything they enjoy as a member of the organization. All items that add value to an employee should be included. If it cost $3,000 for training provided an employee, this also should be included. However, there may be a problem in determining the actual value of an item to a specific employee. For instance, it may be easy to compute the training cost for an employee as $3,000 but what value does the employee actually place on the training. It could be zero or it could be much more than $3,000.[10]

Going global has its challenges with regards to total rewards. Not only does an employer have to ensure its strategy fits with the benefits available in each country as well as its culture, it also has to consider issues of communication including language, media, and currency. Elliott Webster, flexible benefits director at consultants PIFC, says, "Different cultures can also be a challenge. For example, in the UK life insurance is seen as a benefit provided by a company but in Norway it is seen as a right."[11]

the employer typically pays the administrative cost. Often a hybrid situation exists in which employers pay a portion of the benefit and the employee pays for additional services.

According to the U.S. Bureau of Labor Statistics, benefits account for nearly 30 percent of employers' total compensation costs, but over the past decade, the change in benefits costs has outpaced the change in the cost of wages and salaries. The magnitude of this expenditure no doubt accounts for the less frequent use of the term *fringe benefits*. In fact, the benefits that employees receive today are significantly different from those of a few decades ago. Also, as benefit dollars compete with financial compensation, some employers are moving away from paternalistic benefits programs and are shifting more responsibilities to employees, as with 401(k) retirement plans (discussed later). However, in a competitive labor market, firms are careful to provide desired benefits to attract and retain employees with critical skills.

OBJECTIVE 10.2
Describe mandated (legally required) benefits.

Mandated (Legally Required) Benefits

Employers provide most benefits, but the law requires others. These legally required benefits currently account for about 10 percent of total compensation costs. They include Social Security, unemployment insurance, and workers' compensation.

ETHICAL DILEMMA

A Poor Bid

You are vice president of human resources for a large construction company, and your company is bidding on an estimated $2.5 million public housing project. A local electrical subcontractor submitted a bid that you realize is 20 percent too low because labor costs have been incorrectly calculated. It is obvious to you that benefits amounting to more than 30 percent of labor costs have not been included. In fact, the bid was some $30,000 below those of the other four subcontractors. But, accepting it will improve your chance of winning the contract for the big housing project.

What would you do?

Social Security

The Social Security Act of 1935 created a system of retirement benefits. It also established the Social Security Administration. Subsequent amendments to the Act added other forms of protection, such as disability insurance, survivors' benefits, and Medicare.

Disability insurance protects employees against loss of earnings resulting from total incapacity. *Survivors' benefits* are provided to certain members of an employee's family when the employee dies. These benefits are paid to the widow or widower and unmarried children. Unmarried children may be eligible for survivors' benefits until they are 18 years old. In some cases, students retain eligibility until they are 19. *Medicare* provides hospital and medical insurance protection for individuals 65 years of age and older and for those who have become disabled.

Although employees must pay a portion of the cost of Social Security coverage, the employer makes an equal contribution and considers this cost to be a benefit. The present tax rate is 6.2 percent for the Social Security portion and 1.45 percent for Medicare. The Social Security rate is applied to a maximum taxable wage of $106,000. The rate for Medicare applies to all earnings. Approximately 95 percent of the workers in this country pay into and may draw Social Security benefits. The Social Security program currently is running a surplus, but the retirement of the 77-million-member baby-boom generation is looming. Unless Congress makes changes by 2041, the program will have used up its surplus and will no longer be able to pay full benefits.

The retirement age today is 66. It will increase in 2027, until it reaches age 67. These changes will not affect Medicare, with full eligibility under this program holding at age 65.

Unemployment Compensation

Unemployment insurance provides workers whose jobs have been terminated through no fault of their own monetary payments for up to 26 weeks or until they find a new job. The intent of unemployment payments is to provide an unemployed worker time to find a new job equivalent to the one lost without suffering financial distress. Without this benefit, workers might have to take jobs for which they are overqualified or end up on welfare. Unemployment compensation also serves to sustain consumer spending during periods of economic adjustment. In the United States, unemployment insurance is based on both federal and state statutes and, although the federal government provides guidelines, the programs are administered by the states and therefore benefits vary by state. A payroll tax paid solely by employers funds the unemployment compensation program.

Workers' Compensation

Workers' compensation benefits provide a degree of financial protection for employees who incur expenses resulting from job-related accidents or illnesses. As with unemployment compensation, the various states administer individual programs, which are subject to federal regulations. Employers pay the entire cost of workers' compensation insurance, and their past experience with job-related accidents and illnesses largely determines their premium expense. These circumstances should provide further encouragement to employers to be proactive with health and safety programs, topics discussed in Chapter 11.

Discretionary Benefits

Although the law requires some benefits, organizations provide numerous other benefits which assist in accomplishing the objectives of both the company and employee.[12] **Discretionary benefits** are benefit payments made as a result of unilateral management decisions in nonunion firms and from labor–management negotiations in unionized firms. An employee's desire for a specific benefit may change, requiring organizations to continuously check the pulse of its workforce to determine the most sought after benefits.[13]

Major categories of discretionary benefits include payment for time not worked, health care, life insurance, retirement plans, employee stock option plans, and employee services. The recession of 2008/10 caused some employers to re-evaluate their benefits program, adding some and reducing some.[14] Some benefits that have been added include public transportation discounts and increased mileage reimbursement rates.

Payment for Time Not Worked

In providing payment for time not worked, employers recognize that employees need time away from the job for many purposes. Discussed in the following are paid vacations, sick pay and paid time off, sabbaticals, and other forms of payment for time not worked.

Paid Vacations

Vacation time serves important compensation goals. For instance, paid vacations provide workers with an opportunity to rest, become rejuvenated, and thus more productive. They may also encourage employees to remain with the firm. Paid vacation time typically increases with seniority. For example, employees with one year of service receive two weeks; ten years' service, three weeks; and fifteen years' service, four weeks.

In a climate of increased outsourcing and job insecurity, it is not surprising that many Americans do not take full advantage of their vacation benefits. Almost one in five workers indicate that they are either afraid of losing their jobs if they go on vacation or feel guilty being away from the office.[15] As compared with other countries, the average of 13 days Americans take annually is small. According to the World Tourism Organization, Italians take 42 days, French take 37 days, and Brazilians take 34 days. Canadians double the number of vacation days per year that are taken in the United States.[16]

Vacation time may vary with organizational rank. For instance, an executive, regardless of time with the firm, may be given a month of vacation. With an annual salary of $1,440,000, this manager would receive a benefit worth approximately $120,000 each year while not working. A junior accountant earning $39,000 a year might receive two weeks of vacation time worth about $1,500.

Sick Pay and Paid Time Off

Each year many firms allocate to each employee a certain number of days of sick pay they may use when ill. Employees who are too sick to report to work continue to receive their pay up to the maximum number of days accumulated. As with vacation pay, the number of sick pay days often depends on seniority.

Some managers are very critical of sick pay programs. At times, individuals have abused the system by calling in sick when all they really wanted was additional paid vacation. One approach in dealing with the problem of unscheduled absences is paid time off. In lieu of sick leave, vacation time, and a personal day or two, a growing number of companies are providing **paid time off (PTO)**, a certain number of days off provided each year that employees can use for any purpose. With a PTO plan, all the reasons for time off—sick, vacation, and personal days—are grouped together and no one has to lie. There are numerous possible benefits for PTO, including simpler administration, fewer carry-over issues, high employee satisfaction, fewer creative excuses for time off, earlier advance notice of time-off needs, fewer last-minute absences, and fewer conflicts about time-off usage.[17] "We had four different time-off programs," said Paula Mutch, manager of compensation and benefits with Mount Clemens General Hospital in Michigan. "The PTO bank folded them together, and it's not only much easier for us to administer, it's easier for employees to understand."[18]

Sabbaticals

sabbaticals
Temporary leaves of absence from an organization, usually at reduced pay.

Sabbaticals are temporary leaves of absence from an organization, usually at reduced pay. Although sabbaticals have been used for years in the academic community, they have only recently entered the private sector. Often sabbaticals help to reduce turnover and keep workers from burning out, hopefully returning revitalized and more committed to their work. UPS and Xerox are among the growing number of companies who pay employees' expenses to participate in extended volunteer sabbaticals. Since 1971, Xerox has maintained its Social Service Leave program, which allows employees to take fully paid leaves from their jobs, ranging from three months to a year, to work full-time on volunteer projects of their own design and choosing. Their jobs are waiting for them upon their return.[19]

Sabbaticals are not without its challenges. Overachievers may experience difficulty in letting go of their work and worry about their job if they are gone for extended periods. Then there is the problem of scheduling who will take up the slack while the person on sabbatical is gone. But, most organizations using sabbaticals have discovered that the benefits outweigh the challenges.[20]

Other Types of Payment for Time Not Worked

Although paid vacations, sick pay, and paid time off comprise the largest portion of payment for time not worked, there are numerous other types that companies use. It is common for organizations to provide payments to assist employees in performing civic duties. For example, companies often give workers time off to work with the United Way. At times, an executive may be on loan to work virtually full-time on such an endeavor.

Some companies routinely permit employees to take off during work hours to handle personal affairs without taking vacation time. When a worker is called for jury duty, some organizations continue to pay their salary; others pay the difference between jury pay and their salary. When the National Guard or military reserve are called to duty, as has been the case with the situations in Afghanistan and Iraq, some companies pay their employees a portion of their salary while on active duty. Further, during an election, many companies permit employees voting time. Still other firms permit bereavement time for the death of a close relative. Finally, there is the payment for time not worked while at the company such as rest periods, coffee breaks, lunch periods, cleanup time, and travel time. It should be noted that the Fair Labor Standards Act discussed in Chapter 9 does not require employers to give workers a rest break, and only 10 states require it to be given. Usually the break mandated is 10 minutes for every four hours worked.[21]

Health Care

Health care represents the most expensive item in the area of indirect financial compensation. Management consultant Towers Perrin found that the cost of insuring employees rose by 7 percent in 2010, making the average spent per employee to be $10,212. The survey also found that the employee share of health premiums would rise 10 percent on average, to $2,292.[22]

A number of factors have combined to create the high cost of health care:

● An aging population
● A growing demand for medical care
● Increasingly expensive medical technology
● Inefficient administrative processes

There appears to be a light at the end of the tunnel. Employers are using programs to better manage costs, such as consumer-driven plans, to give employees financial incentives to use health care services efficiently. Also, the health care bill passed in 2010 (discussed later) will likely have a significant impact on health care.

Managed-Care Health Organizations

health maintenance organization (HMO)

Managed-care health organization that covers all services for a fixed fee but exercises control over which doctors and health facilities a member may use.

Historically, managed-care systems have been the general response to increased medical costs. These networks are comprised of doctors and hospitals that agree to accept negotiated prices for treating patients. Employees receive financial incentives to use the facilities within the network. The following are various forms of managed-care health organizations:

- **Health maintenance organizations (HMOs)** cover all services for a fixed fee but exercise control over which doctors and health facilities a member may use.
- **Preferred provider organizations (PPOs)** are managed-care health organizations in which incentives are provided to members to use services within the system; out-of-network providers may be used at greater cost.
- **Point-of-service (POS)** requires a primary care physician and referrals to see specialists, as with HMOs, but permits out-of-network health care access.
- **Exclusive provider organizations (EPOs)** offer a smaller PPO provider network and usually provides little, if any, benefits when an out-of-network provider is used.

preferred provider organization (PPO)

Managed-care health organization in which incentives are provided to members to use services within the system; out-of-network providers may be used at greater cost.

Managed-care health organizations are losing their luster for some in favor of consumer-driven health care plans.

point-of-service (POS)

Managed-care health organization that requires a primary care physician and referrals to see specialists, as with HMOs, but permits out-of-network health care access.

Consumer-Driven Health Care Plans

Companies are increasingly placing the responsibility for health care responsibility on employees. *Consumer-driven plans* give each employee a set amount of money annually with which to purchase health care coverage which involves high-deductible insurance coverage combined with a tax-advantaged account like a flexible saving account (FSA) or health saving account (HRA). They are a good way for employers to provide the same caliber of benefits to their employees while also reducing premiums and involving employees in the cost of coverage.[23] If patients pay for health care services in "cash" (using pre-tax funds in a HSA or a FSA, for instance), providers will not be subject to the same lengthy, burdensome payments cycle. General Electric is forcing its 75,000 salaried U.S. employees and 8,000 retirees under the age of 65 to choose a consumer-driven health plan, which includes deductibles that run as high as $4,000 a year. GE's former plan, where employees pay higher premiums in exchange for predictable co-pays up front, are no longer available for salaried workers.[24] More than half of large companies offer workers consumer-driven plans, according to a Watson Wyatt Worldwide and National Business Group on Health survey. Another 8 percent said they expect to adopt a consumer-directed plan.[25]

exclusive provider organization (EPO)

Managed-care health organization that offers a smaller preferred provider network and usually provides few, if any, benefits when an out-of-network provider is used.

HEALTH SAVINGS ACCOUNT **Health savings accounts** (HSA) are tax-free health spending and savings accounts available to individuals and families who have qualified high-deductible health insurance policies as determined by IRS regulations. HSAs are an important tool in the search to change consumers' health care spending behaviors and better manage health costs.[26] Individuals deposit money on a pretax basis to pay for doctor visits, prescriptions, and other expenses, as well as to save for future medical expenses and build savings long-term. HSAs let workers put up to $6,150 a year in a pretax account that they can tap for medical expenses.[27] HSA-eligible health plans typically have lower premiums than other plans because of their higher deductibles. Premiums decline an average of $3,836 when an employee switches from a PPO plan to an HSA plan, according to the Kaiser Family Foundation and Health Research & Educational Trust. Unlike flexible spending accounts, employees with HSAs can decide whether to spend their money on medical expenses now or build savings for expenses later. Any amount left over at the end of the year may be used to pay medical expenses in future years. Another advantage is that even if a worker takes another job, the HSA stays with that individual.[28]

health savings account (HSA)

Tax-free health spending and savings accounts available to individuals and families who have qualified high-deductible health insurance policies as determined by IRS regulation.

flexible spending account (FSA)

Benefit plan established by employers that allows employees to deposit a certain portion of their salary into an account (before paying income taxes) to be used for eligible expenses.

FLEXIBLE SPENDING ACCOUNT A **flexible spending account (FSA)** is a health benefit plan established by employers that allows employees to deposit a certain portion of their salary into an account (before paying income taxes) to be used for eligible expenses. The employee consents to a reduced salary by allowing the employer to contribute a salary portion to an FSA. Usually, account holders are issued a Visa or MasterCard Flexible Spending Account card. This keeps an employee from having to reach into his or her pocket whenever expenses arise. There is also no requirement to submit receipts for reimbursement. Instead, your purchase is deducted from the balance in the account. [29] A disadvantage of an FSA is that generally, employees forfeit any amounts left unspent in the accounts at year-end.[30] Under *The Patient Protection and Affordable Care Act* of 2010 there is a limit of $2,500 on a flexible spending account. Also, employees will no longer be able to use FSA funds to pay for over-the-counter medications.[31]

On-Site Health Care (Work-Site Clinics)

What do Toyota, Nissan, Harrah's Entertainment, and Walt Disney Parks and Resorts group have in common? They all provide on-site health care for their employees.[32] On-site health care is one way of curbing health care costs and also providing an employee benefit. Today's trend of providing on-site medical care is growing because it permits employers to better manage and at times reduce the growth of health care costs. On-site health care assists in treating minor illnesses and injuries, vaccinations, physical therapy, and providing follow-up care.[33] Employers can reduce the number of visits employees make to more costly facilities, such as physicians' offices and hospital emergency rooms.[34] The approach reduces time spent on doctors' visits and recovery, and encourages employees to adopt healthier lifestyles. Raymond Fabius, president and chief medical officer of I-trax Inc., a workplace health and productivity consulting company, said, "Controllers generally respect the cost-saving potential of on-site medical clinics because after two years, the return on investment is 2-to-1 or 2.5-to-1."[35]

Walgreens has aggressively tapped into the growing market for worksite medical clinics as part of its effort to rebrand itself as a health and wellness company. In 2007, Walgreens bought Take Care Health Systems, then a retail-based clinic, and the next year acquired two of the largest work-site clinic companies in the country, CHD Meridian Healthcare and Whole Health Management. Today, Walgreens is the largest provider of work-site medical care, with more than 375 Take Care Health clinics.[36]

Major Medical Benefits

Some plans provide for major medical benefits to cover extraordinary expenses that result from long-term or serious health problems. The use of *deductibles* is a common feature of medical benefits. For example, the employee may have to pay the first $500 of medical bills before the insurance takes over payment.

Dental and Vision Care

Dental and vision care are popular benefits in the health care area. Employers typically pay the entire costs for both types of plans except for a deductible, which may amount to $50 or more per year. Dental plans may cover, for example, 70–100 percent of the cost of preventive procedures and 50–80 percent of restorative procedures. Most health care plans offer dental coverage. Some plans also include orthodontic care.

Americans spend more than $50 billion a year on vision problems and more and more companies are providing vision care as a benefit. Vision care plans may cover all or part of the cost of eye examinations and eyeware.

HR Web Wisdom

Types of Retirement Plans

http://www.dol.gov/ dol/topic/retirement/ typesofplans.htm

Retirement information from the U.S. Department of Labor.

Life Insurance

Group life insurance is a benefit provided to protect the employee's family in the event of his or her death. Although the cost of group life insurance is relatively low, some plans call for the employee to pay part of the premium. Coverage may be a flat amount (for instance, $50,000) or based on the employee's annual earnings. For example, workers earning $40,000 per year may have $80,000, twice their annual earnings, worth of group life coverage.

Retirement Plans

Retirement is currently a hot topic because of the aging baby-boomer generation. Employers are in the middle of this challenge since they are one of our society's primary providers of retirement income. Various types of employer retirement plans will be discussed next.

Defined Benefit Plans

defined benefit plan
Retirement plan that provides the participant with a fixed benefit upon retirement.

Retirement plans are generally either *defined benefit* or *defined contribution*. A **defined benefit plan** is a formal retirement plan that provides the participant with a *fixed* benefit upon retirement. Although defined benefit formulas vary, they are typically based on the participant's final years' average salary and years of service. Plans that are considered generous provide pensions equivalent to 50–80 percent of an employee's final earnings. Use of defined benefit plans has declined in recent years. However, many workers lost considerable money in their 401(k)s during the recession of 2008/10, causing them to have more faith in defined benefit plans.[37] Apparently employees want the guarantee of a defined benefit plan but would like a contributory role in the growth of their retirement assets.[38]

Defined Contribution Plans

defined contribution plan
Retirement plan that requires specific contributions by an employer to a retirement or savings fund established for the employee.

A **defined contribution plan** is a retirement plan that requires specific contributions by an employer to a retirement or savings fund established for the employee. One of the most significant changes in the composition of individual household retirement savings over the past 10 years has been the shift from defined *benefits* to defined *contribution* pension plans such as 401(k). For the first time, the majority of Fortune 100 companies now offer new salaried employees only a defined contribution plan.[39] Only as far back as 1996, most companies with retirement plans had defined benefit plans. Employees know in advance how much their retirement income will be under a defined benefit plan; the amount of retirement income from a defined contribution plan will depend on the investment success of the pension fund.

401(k) plan
Defined contribution plan in which employees may defer income up to a maximum amount allowed.

A **401(k) plan** is a defined contribution plan in which employees may defer income up to a maximum amount allowed. Some employers match employee contributions 50 cents for each dollar deferred. Although employers typically pay the expenses for their defined benefit pension plans, there is a wide variety of payment arrangements for 401(k) plans. Some plan sponsors pay for everything, including investment fees and costs. Others pay for virtually nothing, with the result that nearly all fees are paid out of the plan's assets. In the middle are those plans in which the sponsor and participants share the expenses.

The recession of 2008/10 has not been kind to 401(k) accounts. Assets in IRAs and defined-contribution plans such as 401(k)s fell more than $2 trillion in 2008.[40] From the end of 2007 to the end of March 2009, the average 401(k) balance fell 31 percent, according to Fidelity.[41] As a result of the recession, some firms have reduced or eliminated their matches to the account. Mark Dzierzak, specialist leader with Deloitte Consulting and director of the survey, said, "401(k) plans are bent, not broken. Plan sponsors continue to support their plans and will maintain a close watch on their (plans) role as a strategic tool in their overall benefits program."[42]

There are those who believe that the present system is broke beyond repair. "There's a big sense of futility and hopelessness," says Liz Davidson, founder and chief executive of Financial Finesse, a Manhattan Beach, California, educational firm.[43] One author wrote, "The ugly truth, though, is that the 401(k) is a lousy idea, a financial flop, a rotten repository for our retirement reserves. In the past two years, that has become all too clear." The Government Accountability Office recently concluded, "If no action is taken, a considerable number of Americans face the prospect of a reduced standard of living in retirement."[44]

Cash Balance Plans

cash balance plan
Retirement plan with elements of both defined benefit and defined contribution plans.

For some organizations, a hybrid fund may be the desired approach to retirement plans. A **cash balance plan** is a plan with elements of both defined benefit and defined contribution plans. When used as a stand-alone plan, a cash balance plan provides all of the benefits that would otherwise be available under a standard defined benefit plan, plus the additional benefit of allowing for different targeted benefit amounts for different participants in the plan. Cash balance plans help employers who are looking for ways to maximize retirement contributions for their workers beyond a 401(k) plan, such as professionals seeking to contribute more than $49,000 (maximum annual contribution per participant in 2009) to their retirement plan.[45] It resembles a defined contribution plan because it uses an account balance to communicate the benefit amount. However, it is closer to being a defined benefit plan because the employer normally bears the responsibility for and the risks of managing the assets.[46]

Coca-Cola has adopted a cash balance plan for all present and future employees. Kevin Wagner, a senior retirement consultant in the Atlanta office of Watson Wyatt Worldwide, which worked with Coca-Cola in designing the cash balance plan, said, "It is refreshing to see a company understand the value of its defined benefit plan, which, at least in Coca-Cola's situation, brings great value to both the company and its employees." Other companies that have converted to cash balance plans include FedEx, MeadWestvaco, SunTrust Banks, and Dow Chemical. Under the cash balance plan design, employees will receive annual age-weighted credits equal to a percentage of pay, starting at 3 percent. [47]

Disability Protection

Workers' compensation protects employees from job-related accidents and illnesses. Some firms, however, provide additional protection that is more comprehensive. When the short-term plan runs out, a firm's long-term plan may become active; such a plan may provide 50–70 percent of an employee's pretax pay. Long-term disability provides a monthly benefit to employees who, due to illness or injury, are unable to work for an extended period.

Employee Stock Option Plans

employee stock option plan (ESOP)
Defined contribution plan in which a firm contributes stock shares to a trust.

An **employee stock option plan (ESOP)** is a plan in which a firm contributes stock shares to a trust. The trust then allocates the stock to participating employee accounts according to employee earnings. ESOP advocates have promoted employee ownership plans as a means to align the interests of workers and their companies to stimulate productivity. This practice, long reserved for executives, now often includes employees working at lower levels in the firm. The difficulty some see in the plan is that you have to wait until retirement to receive the benefits, and that is a long time for Gen Y employees to see into the future. Robert J. Larison, president of Atlantic Coast Bank in Waycross, Georgia, said, "We lose people to non-ESOP banks all the time. They go across the street for $5,000 a year more in salary when they might have been awarded a $15,000 or $20,000 vesting in their ESOP that year. It seems like it's a 'right now' kind of world."[48]

Although the potential benefits of ESOPs are attractive, some employees want the ability to sell their shares prior to retirement, which ESOPs do not allow. Many people do not want to take the chance that the stock is going to be less valuable when they retire. Periods of wild rides in the stock market, such as with the recession of 2008/10, also dampen worker enthusiasm for ESOPs. Although the potential advantages of ESOPs are impressive, the other side of the coin is the danger of having all your eggs in one basket. The Enron experience makes this point only too well.

Employee Services

Organizations offer a variety of benefits that can be termed "employee services." These benefits encompass a number of areas, including child care, educational assistance, food services/subsidized cafeterias, scholarships for dependents, and relocation benefits.

Child Care

Another benefit offered by some firms is subsidized child care. According to the National Conference of State Legislatures, an estimated 80 percent of employees miss work due to unexpected child-care coverage issues. It is estimated that every $1 invested in backup child care yields $3 to $4 in returned productivity and benefit. At the Abbott Laboratories headquarters campus 30 miles north of Chicago, the company has built a $10 million state-of-the-art child-care center for more than 400 preschool children of Abbott workers. For parents who prefer a different arrangement, if their babysitter is sick, Abbott provides emergency backup service. Company child-care arrangements tend to reduce absenteeism, protect employee productivity, enhance retention and recruiting, promote the advancement of women, and make the firm an employer of choice.

Educational Assistance

Educational assistance plans can go a long way in improving employee retention.[49] Some companies reimburse employees after they have completed a course with a grade of "C" or above, whereas others provide for advance payment of these expenses. Other employers provide half the reimbursement up front and the rest upon satisfactory completion of the course. United Technologies Corporation pays for an employee's entire tuition and books up front. It also offers paid time off—as much as three hours a week, depending on the course load—to study. IBM has a unique form of tuition-reimbursement; employees could contribute up to $1,000 a year to an interest-bearing education account supplemented by company-paid matches. The funds do not have to be used for education related to the employees' present job. Internal Revenue Service regulations allow for educational assistance benefits to be nontaxable up to $5,250 per year, although the average educational reimbursement by employers is $1,600 per year.

Food Services/Subsidized Cafeterias

There is generally no such thing as a free lunch. However, firms that supply food services or subsidized cafeterias provide an exception to this rule. What they hope to gain in return is increased productivity, less wasted time, enhanced employee morale, and, in some instances, a healthier workforce. Most firms that offer free or subsidized lunches feel that they get a high payback in terms of employee relations. Northwestern Mutual is one such company. Free lunches are available in its cafeterias, where the menus list calories instead of prices. Keeping the lunch hour to a minimum is an obvious advantage, but employees also appreciate the opportunity to meet and mix with people they work with. Making one entree a heart-healthy choice and listing the calories, fat, cholesterol, and sodium content in food is also appealing to a large number of employees.

Scholarships for Dependents

According to a Benefits Survey Report by the Society for Human Resource Management, about 27 percent of companies provide scholarships for dependents. Scholarship programs can help boost employee recruitment and retention. Franciscan Health Systems, a nonprofit health care provider in Tacoma, Washington, targets its awards primarily to employees' children who are interested in entering the health care field, although it also awards scholarships for study in other areas.

Relocation Benefits

relocation benefits
Company-paid shipments of household goods and temporary living expenses, covering all or a portion of the real estate costs associated with buying a new home and selling the previously occupied home.

Relocation benefits are company-paid shipments of household goods and temporary living expenses, covering all or a portion of the real estate costs associated with buying a new home and selling the previously occupied home. Relocation packages vary but most companies will pay for household moving and packing expenses and temporary living expenses for up to six months until the home sells. Companies may also pay for weekly or bi-monthly trips back home over the weekends.

While relocating can be a hassle, it can also produce many benefits. "Employees typically feel an investment has been made by their new employer if they are asked to relocate, and are more focused on their new job and performance," says M.J. Helms, director of operations for The Ashton Group.[50] However, employees who once viewed a transfer as a step up are now taking a closer look at not only the economic impact of the move, but also what it does to quality of life.[51] This concern has broadened the scope of relocation services to include providing information about crime statistics, children's sports teams, tutors, churches, and doctors.

Unique Employee Services Benefits

Some companies are experimenting with what some might call unique benefits as they attempt to brand their organization as a good place to work. They want to stand out from the pack. Steve Williams, director of research for the SHRM, said, "You stand out by doing something different." Some of the ideas that Williams suggest might work include: "Paying for child care for a parent who is on company travel, pet care for an employee on travel, paid travel for an employee's spouse, phasing in the return to work of women who had been on maternity leave, concierge services that tackle personal chores, free grocery delivery, on-site dry cleaning pickup and delivery, reimbursement for courses unrelated to work, on-site yoga classes, even a catered dinner for those who must work late."[52] Some small to midsize organizations in the U.S. allow parents to bring their babies to work as a benefit although most firms accept babies only until they can crawl.[53] If any of the mentioned items are important in the workforce, it may be worthwhile to incorporate into the benefit package.

Fortune 500 No. 2 ranked company in 2010, Colgate-Palmolive, has what some would call unique benefits. The company offers emergency home child care, with complete coverage for the first 10 days and then 50 percent for days 11 through 30. Colgate also has backup child care at some locations, and parents get time off on the morning of the first day of school. Colgate's mortgage assistance program helps employees refinance an existing loan or obtain a discounted mortgage to buy a new home. U.S. employees can buy additional vacation days at the beginning of each year or sell unused days and keep the cash. The "You Can Make a Difference" program gives 400 high-performing employees stock worth $250, with nine global winners getting $2,500 each. At some U.S. locations, award winners receive a reserved parking space for a month.[54]

Premium Pay

OBJECTIVE 10.4
Explain premium pay.

premium pay
Compensation paid to employees for working long periods of time or working under dangerous or undesirable conditions.

hazard pay
Additional pay provided to employees who work under extremely dangerous conditions.

shift differential
Additional money paid to employees for the inconvenience of working less-desirable hours.

Premium pay is compensation paid to employees for working long periods of time or working under dangerous or undesirable conditions. As mentioned in Chapter 9, payment for overtime is legally required for nonexempt employees who work more than 40 hours in a given week. However, some firms voluntarily pay overtime for hours worked beyond eight in a given day and pay double time, or even more, for work on Sundays and holidays.

Additional pay provided to employees who work under extremely dangerous conditions is called **hazard pay**. A window washer for skyscrapers in New York City might receive extra compensation because of the precarious working conditions. Military pilots collect extra money in the form of *flight pay* and *combat pay* because of the risks involved in the job. When the U.S. State Department was having difficulty enticing members of the Foreign Service to be assigned to the U.S. Embassy in Baghdad, Iraq, it offered a form of hazard pay. They enticed workers to take jobs in unstable regions with a 70 percent boost in base salary, premium pay for overtime, and 10 weeks off.[55]

Some employees receive **shift differential** pay for the inconvenience of working less-desirable hours. This type of pay may be provided as additional compensation per hour and is used extensively in the health care practitioners and technical occupations.[56] For example, employees who work the second shift (swing shift), from 4:00 P.M. until midnight, might receive $2.00 per hour above the base rate for that job. The third shift (graveyard shift) often warrants an even greater differential; for example, an extra $3.00 per hour may be paid for the same job. Shift differentials are sometimes based on a percentage of the employee's base rate.

Voluntary Benefits

OBJECTIVE 10.5
Explain voluntary benefits.

voluntary benefits
Benefits which are 100 percent paid by the employee but the employer typically pays the administrative cost.

In discretionary benefits, the cost is shouldered totally or partially by the company. As firms search for ways to reduce costs, many organizations are moving to **voluntary benefits** which are 100 percent paid by the employee but the employer typically pays the administrative cost.[57] Employees gain because their premiums typically reflect group discounts and thus are lower than the employees could obtain on their own.[58] Jack Kwicien, managing partner with Daymark Advisors in Baltimore, said, "Voluntary is the only sector in insurance that is enjoying double-digit growth, and has for the last 10 years." Gil Lowerre, president of Eastbridge Consulting, says, "The more voluntary benefits employers offer, the more pressure it takes off them to add employer-paid benefits."[59] Many of the voluntary benefits could not be offered because the company is not able to fund it themselves.[60] Some of the discretionary benefits in this chapter have been converted either partially or full, to voluntary benefits. The most common voluntary products provided include term life insurance, vision insurance, long-term care insurance, long-term disability insurance, accident insurance, and dental insurance. Newer niche voluntary benefits include automobile insurance, homeowners' or renters' insurance, debt counseling and financial planning, identity theft coverage, college savings plans, and pet insurance.[61]

Customized Benefit Plans

Customized benefit plans permit employees to make yearly selections to largely determine their benefit package by choosing between taxable cash and numerous benefits.

Not long ago, firms offered a uniform package that generally reflected a typical employee based on tradition, budgets, and management choices. Today, the workforce has become considerably more heterogeneous, and this prototype is no longer representative. With four generations of workers now in a workplace, customization and flexibility become very important in developing a benefits package that meets the needs of everyone.[62] Workers have considerable latitude in determining how much they will take in the form of salary, life insurance, pension contributions, and other benefits. Customized plans permit flexibility in allowing each employee to determine the compensation components that best satisfy his or her particular needs. Leigh Branham, author of *The 7 Hidden Reasons Employees Leave: How to Recognize the Subtle Signs and Act Before It's Too Late*, said, "I see more and more companies going to a sort of cafeteria approach where people pick and choose what's important to them and I think that is the wave of the future."[63]

Obviously, organizations cannot permit employees to select all their benefits. For one thing, firms must provide the benefits required by law. In addition, it is probably wise to require that each employee have core benefits, especially in areas such as retirement and medical insurance. Some guidelines would likely be helpful for most employees in the long run. However, the freedom to select highly desired benefits would seem to maximize the value of an individual's compensation. Employees' involvement in designing their own benefit plans would also effectively communicate to them the cost of their benefits.

The downside to customized benefit plans is that they are costly. Development and administrative costs for these plans exceed those for traditional plans. Even though customized benefit plans add to the organization's administrative burden, some firms apparently find that the advantages outweigh shortcomings.

Health Care Legislation

Seven pieces of federal legislation related to health care are discussed in the next sections.

Consolidated Omnibus Budget Reconciliation Act

With the high cost of medical care, an individual without health care insurance is vulnerable. The Consolidated Omnibus Budget Reconciliation Act (COBRA) of 1985 was enacted to give employees the opportunity to temporarily continue their coverage, which they would otherwise lose because of termination, layoff, or other changes in employment status. The Act applies to employers with 20 or more employees. Under COBRA, individuals may keep their coverage, as well as coverage for their spouses and dependents, for up to 18 months after their employment ceases. Certain qualifying events can extend this coverage for up to 36 months. The individual, however, must pay for this health insurance, and it is expensive.

Health Insurance Portability and Accountability Act

The Health Insurance Portability and Accountability Act (HIPAA) of 1996 provide protection for Americans who move from one job to another, who are self-employed, or who have preexisting medical conditions. The prime objective of this legislation is to make health insurance portable and continuous for employees, and to eliminate the ability of insurance companies to reject coverage for individuals because of a preexisting condition. As an element of HIPAA, there is now a regulation designed to protect the privacy of personal health information.

Employee Retirement Income Security Act

The Employee Retirement Income Security Act (ERISA) of 1974 strengthens existing and future retirement programs. Mismanagement of retirement funds was the primary spur for this legislation.

Many employees were entering retirement only to find that the retirement income they had counted on was not available. The Act's intent was to ensure that when employees retire, they receive deserved pensions. The purpose of the Act is described here:

It is hereby declared to be the policy of this Act to protect ... the interests of participants in employee benefit plans and their beneficiaries ... by establishing standards of conduct, responsibility and obligations for fiduciaries of employee benefit plans, and by providing for appropriate remedies, sanctions, and ready access to the federal courts.[64]

Note that the word *protect* is used here because the Act does not force employers to create employee retirement plans. It does set standards in the areas of participation, vesting of benefits, and funding for existing and new plans. Numerous existing retirement plans have been altered in order to conform to this legislation.

Older Workers Benefit Protection Act

The Older Workers Benefit Protection Act of 1990 (OWBPA), an amendment to the Age Discrimination in Employment Act, prohibits discrimination in the administration of benefits on the basis of age, but also permits early retirement incentive plans as long as they are voluntary. Employers must offer benefits to older workers that are equal to or greater than the benefits given to younger workers, with one exception. The Act does not require employers to provide equal or greater benefits to older workers when the cost to do so is greater than for younger workers. The Act establishes wrongful termination waiver requirements as a means of protecting older employees by ensuring that workers are fully informed before signing a waiver.

Family and Medical Leave Act

The Family and Medical Leave Act (FMLA) of 1993 applies to private employers with 50 or more employees and to all governmental employers regardless of number. The FMLA provides employees up to 12 weeks a year of unpaid leave in specified situations. The overall intent of the Act is to help employees balance work demands without hindering their ability to attend to personal and family needs. FMLA rights apply only to employees who have worked for the employer for at least 12 months and who have at least 1,250 hours of service during the 12 months immediately preceding the start of the leave. The FMLA guarantees that health insurance coverage is maintained during the leave and also that the employee has the right to return to the same or an equivalent position after a leave.

Pension Protection Act

Some say that the Pension Protection Act (PPA) of 2006 was the most sweeping reform of America's pension laws in more than 30 years.[65] The bill contains a variety of provisions designed to strengthen the funding rules for defined benefit pension plans. The bill seeks to ensure that employers make greater contributions to their pension funds, ensuring their solvency, and avoiding a potential multibillion-dollar taxpayer bailout of the Pension Benefit Guaranty Corporation (PBGC).

Patient Protection and Affordable Care Act

The Patient Protection and Affordable Care Act of 2010, often called the "Health Care Reform Bill," created considerable political debate because it effectively reshaped major portions of the health care industry in the United States. The Act is based on the idea that when more people have health insurance—young, healthy people in addition to older, sicker people—risk will be spread out and costs will come down. All individuals will be required to have health insurance coverage by 2014. Those who choose not to have insurance would pay a penalty.[66] Some of the major features of the bill are: 1) individuals must purchase health insurance or risk being fined; 2) children can stay on their parents' policy until they are 26 years old; 3) insurance companies cannot cancel a policy if the insured gets sick; 4) a person cannot be denied insurance simply because they have a pre-existing health condition; 5) there is no maximum limit on insurance coverage; and 6) there is no waiting time with regard to coverage if a person has a pre-existing condition. The law does not require an individual to drop the health coverage he or she had on the date of enactment. Existing employer plans are "grandfathered" under the new law and can continue to renew current employees and enroll new employees.[67]

OBJECTIVE 10.8

Describe the importance of communicating information about the benefits package.

Communicating Information about the Benefits Package

Employee benefits can help a firm recruit and retain a top-quality workforce. In keeping the program current, management depends on an upward flow of information from employees to determine when benefit changes are needed. In addition, because employee awareness of benefits is often limited, the program information must be communicated downward. Organizations spend millions of dollars for benefits, salaries, bonuses, and other programs. Yet, many do not do a good job of communicating the value of this investment to the employees.[68] Often organizations do not have to improve benefits to keep their best employees; rather, workers need to fully understand the benefits that are provided. For example, a survey of 22,000 MedStar employees found that only 30 percent were satisfied with the firm's compensation and benefits program and did not believe them to be competitive. However, research indicated otherwise. Marjory Zylich, assistant vice president of operational communications and special projects, said, "That's discouraging when half our expenses are on pay and benefits. For a health system our size, that's more than a billion dollars on total compensation." Based on the survey, MedStar began a campaign to educate the workforce regarding their compensation and benefits, resulting in much greater satisfaction in the firm's total compensation program.[69]

The Employee Retirement Income Security Act (previously discussed) provides still another reason for communicating information about a firm's benefits program. This Act requires organizations with a pension or profit-sharing plan to provide employees with specific data at specified times. The Act further mandates that the information be presented in an understandable manner. To improve the employee experience and cut costs, more HR departments rely on one or more technologies to get benefits information to employees. Bruce Finley, Mercer's global leader for workforce communication in New York City, said, "There is an increasing ability to personalize communication, and it is going to continue to evolve. With web applications, we are seeing a whole revolution of interactive material so people can get up-to-date information at the time they have questions."[70]

OBJECTIVE 10.9

Describe the components of nonfinancial compensation.

Nonfinancial Compensation

Historically, compensation departments in organizations have not dealt with nonfinancial factors. However, as indicated in Chapter 9, the new compensation model suggests that this is changing. The components of nonfinancial compensation consist of the job itself and the job environment (see Figure 10.2). A number of work arrangements are included in this environment. These arrangements provide for greater work–life balance resulting in a more desirable life for employees.

Job Itself as a Nonfinancial Compensation Factor

The job itself can be a very powerful factor in the compensation equation. Answering the following questions can provide considerable insight into the value of the job itself:

1. Is the job meaningful and challenging?
2. Is there recognition for accomplishment?
3. Do I get a feeling of achievement from doing the job?
4. Is there a possibility for increased responsibility?
5. Is there an opportunity for growth and advancement?
6. Do I enjoy doing the job itself?[71]

Figure 10.2

Nonfinancial Compensation in a Total Compensation Program

```
┌──────────────────────── EXTERNAL ENVIRONMENT ────────────────────────┐
│  ┌────────────────────── INTERNAL ENVIRONMENT ──────────────────────┐ │
│  │                         Compensation                              │ │
│  │    Financial                              Nonfinancial            │ │
│  │  Direct    Indirect (Benefits)      The Job        Job Environment│ │
│  │                                  Meaningful and   Sound Policies  │ │
│  │                                  Satisfying Job   Capable Managers│ │
│  │                                  Recognition for  Competent Employees │
│  │                                  Accomplishment   Congenial Co-workers │
│  │                                  Feeling of       Appropriate Status Symbols │
│  │                                  Achievement      Working Conditions │
│  │                                  Possibility of                   │ │
│  │                                  Increased        Workplace Flexibility │
│  │                                  Responsibility     Flextime      │ │
│  │                                  Opportunity for    Compressed Workweek │
│  │                                  Growth and         Job Sharing   │ │
│  │                                  Advancement        Telecommuting │ │
│  │                                  Enjoy Doing the    Part-Time Work│ │
│  │                                  Job                              │ │
│  └───────────────────────────────────────────────────────────────────┘ │
└─────────────────────────────────────────────────────────────────────────┘
```

Consider this situation:

> *The workplace atmosphere is highly invigorating. Roy, Ann, Jack, Sandra, Britt, and Patsy are excited as they try to keep up with double-digit growth in sales orders. They do whatever it takes to get the job done, wearing multiple hats that would be difficult to cover in a job description. Their jobs have no salary grades, and no one ever formally reviews their performance. This doesn't worry them, however, because they enjoy the camaraderie and teamwork at their firm. They have complete trust in the firm's highly visible management, and they have total confidence their leaders will do what's right for them and the company. Believe it or not, it is a real-life scene from a real-life company.[72]*

As the situation suggests, some jobs can be so stimulating that the incumbent is anxious to get to work each day. At the evening meal, details of what happened on the job may be shared with family or friends. Given the prospect of getting a generous raise by leaving this job, this worker may quickly say "No" to the opportunity. Unwillingness to change jobs for additional financial compensation suggests that the job itself is indeed an important reward. Such jobs are often meaningful and challenging, workers are recognized for their accomplishments, there is a feeling of achievement, and there is the opportunity for growth and development. Individuals who are engaged in their work find great satisfaction in their job and feel that they are contributing to the success of the organization tend to remain with the organization.[73]

On the other hand, a job may be so boring or distasteful that an individual dreads going to work. A report from The Conference Board based on a survey of 5,000 workers found that only 45 percent are satisfied with their jobs—down from 61.1 percent in 1987.[74] This condition is sad considering the time a person devotes to his or her job. When work is a drag, life may not be very pleasant and, as discussed in Chapter 11, if a boring job creates excessive and prolonged stress, the person involved may eventually become emotionally or physically ill. The job itself is a central issue in many theories of motivation. It is also a vital component in a total compensation program.

OBJECTIVE 10.10

Describe the job itself and the job environment as a nonfinancial compensation factor.

Job Environment as a Nonfinancial Compensation Factor

Performing a challenging, responsible job in a pigsty would not be rewarding to most people. The physical environment of the job must also be satisfactory. Employees can draw satisfaction from their work through several nonfinancial factors, discussed next.

Sound Policies

A *policy* is a predetermined guide established to provide direction in decision making. Human resource policies and practices reflecting management's concern for its employees can serve as positive rewards. Consider how the following policies would contribute to the satisfaction of a worker:

- To provide realistic and practical incentives as a means of encouraging the highest standard of individual performance and to ensure increased quality and quantity of performance.
- To create and maintain good working conditions, to provide the best possible equipment and facilities, and plants and offices that are clean, orderly, and safe.
- To employ people without regard to race, sex, color, national origin, or age.
- To encourage employees to improve their skills by participating in available educational or training programs.
- To provide every possible opportunity for advancement so that each individual may reach his or her highest potential.

If a firm's policies show consideration rather than disrespect, fear, doubt, or lack of confidence, the result can be rewarding to both the employees and the organization. Policies that are arbitrary and too restrictive alienate people.

Capable Managers

Anyone who has worked under a manager who does not possess the skills needed to successfully lead the unit understands the importance of having a capable individual in charge. Many workers quit their jobs because of the way the unit is being managed. Just being around an incompetent boss every day may provide the motivation to call in sick when you are not ill. There may be the autocratic manager who only wants it done his or her way. Then, there is the manager who can seemingly never make a decision. There are endless examples of supervisors who are incapable of performing their jobs, thus making the job environment of their employees less than desirable.

Competent Employees

Working with individuals who are capable and knowledgeable can often create a synergistic environment. *Synergism* is the cooperative action of two or more persons working together to accomplish more than they could working separately. Synergy implies the possibility of accomplishing tasks that could not even be done by people working separately. Solving problems together is often exhilarating when a co-worker is also competent. Successful organizations emphasize continuous development and ensure employment of competent managers and nonmanagers. Competitive environments and the requirement for teamwork will not permit otherwise.

Congenial Co-workers

Although a few individuals in this world may be quite self-sufficient and prefer to be left alone, they will likely be unsuccessful in the team-oriented organizations that exist today. The American culture has historically embraced individualism, yet most people possess, in varying degrees, a desire for acceptance by their work group. It is very important that management develop and maintain congenial work groups. A work group's need for creativity may require individuals with diverse backgrounds. However, to be effective, they must be compatible in terms of sharing common values and goals.

Appropriate Status Symbols

Status symbols are organizational rewards that take many forms such as office size and location, desk size and quality, how close one's private parking space is to the office, floor covering, and job title. Status symbols vary from company to company and sometimes are understood only by persons within the company. Some firms make liberal use of these types of rewards; others tend to minimize them. This latter approach reflects a concern about the adverse effect they may have on creating and maintaining a team spirit among members at various levels in the firm. This is true within many workplaces, where the corner office and private washroom have given way to more democratic arrangements.

Working Conditions

The definition of *working conditions* has broadened considerably over the years. Today, an air-conditioned and reasonably safe and healthy workplace is considered necessary. Another factor of increasing importance is the flexibility or work–life balance employees have in their work situations. These factors will be discussed in the following sections.

OBJECTIVE 10.11
Describe workplace flexibility (work–life balance) factors.

Workplace Flexibility (Work–Life Balance)

Effective work–life programs focus on solving any personal issues that can detract from an employee's work. For employers, creating a balanced work–life environment can be a key strategic factor in attracting and retaining the most talented employees.[75] According to a recent study from the Family and Work Institute as well as ongoing research of the Sloan Center on Aging & Work at Boston College, workplace flexibility is high on employers' lists of company benefits offered and continues to grow.[76] By providing such an environment, employees are better able to fit family, community, and social commitments into their schedule. The homogeneous workforce that the United States once had is quite different now. Consider the following statistics and envision how the workplace profile has changed: 27 percent of single parents are men, 40 percent of the workforce is unmarried, one in five workers is 50 or older, and four million households are multigenerational. Also, nearly 25 percent of Americans are caring for elders.[77]

For men and women seeking to balance work and personal lives, time is nearly as important as money; more important for some. More employees, especially women, are requesting workplace flexible benefits to achieve a better work and life balance.[78] Diane Domeyer, executive director of OfficeTeam, said, "Programs that support work–life balance are attractive to professionals, especially members of the 'sandwich generation'—those caring for both children and elderly parents."[79] Tyler Wigton, project manager of When Work Works at the New York-based Families and Work Institute, said, "Employees are feeling stretched and stressed, with reduced job satisfaction, productivity and health outcomes. We found that flexibility is a critical but overlooked factor in making work work. It can be a strategic business decision."[80] What do most of the top 100 best companies to work for have in common? They offer flextime, a compressed workweek, job sharing, and telecommuting, some of the topics to be discussed next.

Flextime

flextime
Practice of permitting employees to choose their own working hours, within certain limitations.

Flextime is the practice of permitting employees to choose their own working hours, within certain limitations. Even in a depressed economy, flexible work hours remained high on the priority list of what companies could offer them in lieu of a salary increase, although guaranteed job security ranked number one.[81] For many old-economy managers who think they must see their employees every minute to make sure they are working, this may be difficult. However, in a recent survey, 79 percent of employers now allow at least some employees to change their arrival and departure times periodically, up from 68 percent in 1998.[82] Another benefit of flextime is that it can bring better health to employees by reducing employee stress levels.[83]

In a flextime system, employees typically work the same number of hours per day as they would on a standard schedule. However, they work these hours within what is called a bandwidth, which is the maximum length of the workday (see Figure 10.3). Core time is that part of the day

Figure 10.3

Illustration of Flextime

when all employees must be present. *Flexible time* is the period within which employees may vary their schedules. A typical schedule permits employees to begin work between 6:00 A.M. and 9:00 A.M. and to complete their workday between 3:00 P.M. and 6:00 P.M. Marianne Mondy, a staff auditor for the State of Louisiana, goes to work at 6:30 and is off at 3:00, a schedule she very much enjoys. This permits her to miss much of Baton Rouge's horrible traffic congestion.

Because flexible hours are highly valued in today's society, a flexible work schedule gives employers an edge in recruiting new employees and retaining highly qualified ones. Also, flextime allows employees to expand their opportunities. For example, it may be easier for them to continue their education than if they were on a traditional work schedule. The public also seems to reap benefits from flextime. Transportation services, recreational facilities, medical clinics, and other services can be better used by reducing competition for service at conventional peak times. Yet, flextime is not suitable for all types of organizations. For example, its use may be severely limited in assembly-line operations and companies using multiple shifts.

Compressed Work Week

compressed work week
Any arrangement of work hours that permits employees to fulfill their work obligation in fewer days than the typical five-day work week.

The **compressed work week** is an arrangement of work hours that permits employees to fulfill their work obligation in fewer days than the typical five-day, eight-hour-a-day, work week. A common compressed work week is four 10-hour days. Another form of the compressed work week is four nine-hour days and a half day on Friday. Some hospitals permit their registered nurses to work three 12-hour days. There are endless different combinations of compressed work weeks.

Working under this arrangement, employees have reported greater job satisfaction. In addition, the compressed work week offers the potential for better use of leisure time for family life, personal business, and recreation. Employers in some instances have cited advantages such as increased productivity and reduced turnover and absenteeism. Other firms, however, have encountered difficulty in scheduling worker's hours and at times employees become fatigued from working longer hours. In some cases, these problems have resulted in lower product quality and reduced customer service.

Job Sharing

job sharing
Two part-time people split the duties of one job in some agreed-on manner and are paid according to their contributions.

Job sharing is an approach to work that is attractive to people who want to work fewer than 40 hours per week. In **job sharing**, two part-time people split the duties of one job in some agreed-on manner and are paid according to their contributions.

Some have equated the benefits job sharing provides to running a marathon. Given an equal athletic ability, two runners running half a marathon back to back will invariably outrun one runner going the entire distance alone. Although the arrangements vary, the outcome is the same: Job sharing provides the flexibility to enjoy life. It provides an option to retain workers, particularly women who are opting out of the workforce to raise families. Often job sharers work as hard in, say, three days, as those working full time and are "grateful" for the opportunity to be able to combine work and motherhood or other interests.

Job sharing also provides a means of encouraging older workers to remain on the job past retirement age. Sharing jobs has potential benefits that include the broader range of skills the partners bring to the job. For job sharing to work, however, the partners must be compatible, have good communication skills, and have a bond of trust with their manager. Job sharing also can pose challenges, including the need for additional oversight—such as conducting administrative tasks and performance reviews for two employees rather than one.

Examples of Executive Job Sharing

Job sharing normally occurs below executive ranks. However, this is not always the case. If job sharing were a category in the collection of *Guinness World Records,* top honors might go to Charlotte Schutzman and Sue Manix. The two women shared many jobs, surviving two corporate mergers and a relocation while earning two promotions in the process. Schutzman and Manix shared the post of vice president of public affairs and communications at New York–based Verizon Communications Inc. Each worked two days a week and on alternate Wednesdays. They talked by phone at least twice a week, and their close partnership enabled them to stay on track professionally while raising their children—Manix has three, Schutzman has two. "It's been good for us, it's been good for the company," says Schutzman. "If we didn't job-share," she says, "we might have left."[84]

As another example, Sue Osborn and Susan Williams share the chief executive role at the National Patient Safety Agency (NPSA). They have been there since 2001, but they have been job-share partners since 1986. Before joining the NPSA, they were joint chief executives at Barking and Havering Authority. Each of them works three days a week, including Wednesdays, when they overlap. They talk to each other on the phone quite a lot and also leave detailed notes for each other.[85]

Telecommuting

telecommuting
Work arrangement whereby employees, called "teleworkers" or "telecommuters," are able to remain at home (or otherwise away from the office) and perform their work using computers and other electronic devices that connect them with their offices.

Telecommuting is a work arrangement whereby employees, called "teleworkers" or "telecommuters," are able to remain at home (or otherwise away from the office) and perform their work using computers and other electronic devices that connect them with their offices.

For self-motivated workers, telecommuting can increase worker productivity and improve job satisfaction and loyalty. Modern communications and information technologies permit people to work just about anywhere. Telecommuting has become more popular in recent years, thanks to traffic congestion and frustration with commuting, and, of course, the high gas prices. Linda Barrington, research director and labor economist, said, "The issue of whether or not to allow employees to work at a distance is no longer a cost-benefit issue—it is simply the reality of doing business."[86]

Telecommuters generally are information workers. They accomplish jobs that require, for example, analysis, research, writing, budgeting, data entry, or computer programming. Teleworkers also include illustrators, loan executives, architects, attorneys, and publishers. Employees can accomplish both training and job duties without losing either efficiency or quality by using the Internet. Thanks largely to telecommuting, when the New York City transit union went on strike, knowledge workers were able to work from home, which greatly lessened the effect of the strike.[87]

Another advantage of telecommuting is that it eliminates the need for office space. The expense of an employee is not just the person, it's also the cost each year for the office that person sits in. Also, commuting distances are not a factor for teleworkers. The average time it takes to get to work continues to increase, which often contributes to tardiness and lost work hours. With telecommuting, firms may hire the best available employees located virtually anywhere in the world for many jobs. The ability to employ disabled workers and workers with small children further broadens the labor market. Finally, telecommuting is being used as an alternative for executives who are unwilling to relocate. If the company is willing to permit the executive to not work out of headquarters, telecommuting may be the answer.

Although telecommuting has many advantages, it also has some potential pitfalls. For example, it may weaken the ties between employees and their firms. IBM research determined that productivity and happiness was lowered if teams went more than three days without getting together. Telecommuters are now required to get together either physically or virtually every three days for reasons that have nothing to do with completing an assignment.[88]

Telecommuters may also feel a time crunch and believe that the best assignments go to regular employees who were able to collaborate with colleagues face-to-face. In addition, managers have to learn how to manage remotely, which is at times resisted. In a recent survey, almost 80 percent said they believe that the extra costs of telecommuting do pay off, although more than 60 percent said managing same-site employees is easier than managing telecommuters.[89] Also, some workers may be taking advantage of being out of sight to the boss.

A concern that has crept into using telecommuting is how does a company handle the mandates of overtime, minimum wage, and recordkeeping provisions for all employees not

HR Web Wisdom

Telecommuting

http://www.telework. gov/

Governmental Web site for employees who think they might like to telecommute (or are already doing so), for managers and supervisors who supervise teleworkers, and for agency telework coordinators.

A GLOBAL PERSPECTIVE

Global Customized Benefits

I mentioned earlier in the chapter the trend in the United States was to customize benefit plans and not offer a uniform package that generally reflected a typical employee. That approach also applies to the global environment. When dealing with benefits on the global stage, employers must recognize that a "standardized" benefits program for all employees across the globe may be impractical and unsuccessful in achieving key benefits objectives. A one-size-fits-all approach does not meet the needs of a highly diverse global workforce because of the many cultural and legal differences. For example, a company operating in India will likely offer an assortment of child incentives, home incentives, and health plans that include grandparents.[93] They also expect a "dearness allowance" which helps to offset inflation as part of the compensation plan. For India's Informa employees, private health insurance, flexible benefits, and dependent coverage are top commodities. But in the United Kingdom, the wellness programs such as gym memberships and health screenings are highly valued benefits.[94]

U.S. multinationals have also discovered that U.S. insurance plan design was not universally acceptable in other countries. This is caused by labor and tax regulations, which strongly influence employee expectations. For instance, U.S. group life insurance plans deliver lump-sum death benefits, but such benefits are not tax-favored in the Netherlands, where employees expect survivorship annuities to spouses and children in the event of death in service. U.S. firms also place a high priority on health care benefits, whereas many European countries have government-sponsored health care arrangements that differ in design in each country. Additionally, in some countries, employer-paid private medical plans are considered taxable income to the employee.[95]

U.S. multinationals have also learned that U.S.-based insurers were not prepared, or even permitted, to insure employee benefit plans covering workers in Europe. Therefore, group insurance had to be negotiated with local vendors, including terms, conditions, and costs reflecting only coverage for foreign locals. That meant discounts on premium rates would only reflect the group's size in each location, if the group met the minimum number eligible for a group contract at all. Minimum group sizes vary by country and/or provider, which range from 1 in the Netherlands to 25 in Italy.

Some Japanese companies have benefits that might appear quite odd in the United States. Because of a high demand for qualified workers, employers are constantly making an effort to keep workers satisfied. They range from pet allowances to half-days off for bargain-hunting. Nihon Shoken, a major food manufacturer will give each employee a bonus of 1,000 yen a month if a Japanese employee marries a co-worker. Nihon Shoken stresses the importance of a family atmosphere and also hopes that the new family will use their product.[96]

Japan's employment agency Recruit Agent gives its workers a yearly bonus of 100,000 yen (about $973) if they go on a holiday with at least four coworkers; they are seeking to improve communication among employees. Marketing firm Hime & Co. gives its employees a day off to recover from a relationship breakup. The president said, "We're a company that only employs women. When a relationship ends, work is the last thing on their mind. And if someone quits over a breakup it can be expensive for the company."[97]

considered exempt under FLSA? With their notebook computer in hand, employees can handle duties that are normally required at the office. An employer who permits a new mother to remain at home, taking care of the baby, certainly does not work a straight eight-hour shift. The question then arises as to how long she has worked, assuming that she is a nonexempt employee. Overstating or understating time worked is certainly a possibility, which violates the FLSA's record keeping provision.[90]

Part-Time Work

Part-time employment adds many highly qualified individuals to the labor market by permitting employees to address both job and personal needs. Also, having a part-time job helps workers to make the transition from full-time employment. For some organizations, the availability of part-time work provides a plus. Many mothers who work full-time would prefer part-time employment, and some of the at-home mothers would prefer to be working part-time rather than staying out of the workforce. Both parties benefit when part-time employment does work out. Companies that offer part-time employment show increased rates of productivity and less employee turnover than other companies.

At Deloitte, each employee's performance is discussed during twice-a-year evaluations focused not just on career targets but also on larger life goals. Employees can request to do more or less travel or client service. The employee can also request to move laterally into a new role— changes that may or may not come with a pay cut. Current data suggest that about 10 percent of employees choose to "dial up" or "dial down" at any given time. Both women and men are permitted access to the program after it became clear that women are not the only ones seeking flexibility. The program is in response to millennials demanding better work–life balance and boomers looking to ease into retirement.[91]

Just described were the positive aspects of part-time. The recession of 2008/10 caused many workers to take part-time jobs because they could not find full-time ones. In March 2010, the underemployed rate was 20.3 percent.[92]

Summary

1. *Define indirect financial compensation (benefits).* Benefits include all financial rewards that generally are not paid directly to the employee.
2. *Describe mandated (legally required) benefits.* Legally required benefits include Social Security retirement benefits, disability insurance, and survivors' benefits; Medicare; workers' compensation benefits; and unpaid leave, mandated by the Family and Medical Leave Act.
3. *Explain the various discretionary benefits.* Categories of discretionary benefits include: payment for time not worked, health care, life insurance, retirement plans, disability protection, employee stock option plans (ESOPs), and employee services.
4. *Explain premium pay.* Premium pay is compensation paid to employees for working long periods of time or working under dangerous or undesirable conditions.
5. *Explain voluntary benefits.* Many organizations are moving to voluntary benefits which are essentially 100 percent paid by the employee. However, the employer typically pays the administrative cost. Employees gain because their premiums typically reflect group discounting and thus are lower than the employees could obtain on their own.
6. *Describe customized benefit plans.* Customized benefit plans permit employees to make yearly elections to largely determine their benefit package by choosing between taxable cash and numerous benefits.
7. *Explain health care legislation.* The Consolidated Omnibus Budget Reconciliation Act was enacted

to give employees the opportunity to temporarily continue their coverage, which they would otherwise lose because of termination, layoff, or other change in employment status. The Health Insurance Portability and Accountability Act provides protection for Americans who move from one job to another, who are self-employed, or who have preexisting medical conditions. The Employee Retirement Income Security Act was passed to strengthen existing and future retirement programs. The Older Workers Benefit Protection Act is an amendment to the Age Discrimination in Employment Act and extends its coverage to all employee benefits. The Pension Protection Act (PPA) of 2006 is the most sweeping reform of America's pension laws in more than 30 years. The Patient Protection and Affordable Care Act of 2010, often called the "Health Care Reform Bill," created considerable political debate because it effectively reshaped major portions of the health care industry in the United States.

8. *Describe the importance of communicating information about the benefits package.* Many times organizations do not have to improve benefits to keep their best employees; rather, workers need to fully understand the benefits that are provided.
9. *Describe the components of nonfinancial compensation.* The components of nonfinancial compensation consist of the job itself and the job environment.
10. *Describe the job itself and the job environment as a nonfinancial compensation factor.* The job itself can be a very powerful factor in the compensation equation. Some jobs can be so stimulating

that the incumbent is anxious to get to work each day. On the other hand, a job may be so boring or distasteful that an individual dreads going to work.

The physical environment and the psychological climate are important factors. Employees can draw satisfaction from their work through several nonfinancial factors.

Sound policies, capable managers, competent employees, congenial co-workers, appropriate status symbols, and working conditions are all important features.

11. ***Describe workplace flexibility (work–life balance) factors.*** Workplace flexibility factors include flextime, the compressed work week, job sharing, telecommuting, and part-time work.

Key Terms

indirect financial compensations (benefits) 292
discretionary benefits 295
paid time off (PTO) 295
sabbaticals 296
health maintenance organization (HMO) 297
preferred provider organization (PPO) 297
point-of-service (POS) 297

exclusive provider organization (EPO) 297
health savings account (HSA) 297
flexible spending account (FSA) 297
defined benefit plan 299
defined contribution plan 299
401(k) plan 299
cash balance plan 299
employee stock option plan (ESOP) 300

relocation benefits 301
premium pay 302
hazard pay 302
shift differential 302
voluntary benefits 302
customized benefit plan 303
flextime 308
compressed work week 309
job sharing 309
telecommuting 310

Questions for Review

1. Define *indirect financial compensations (benefits).*
2. In compensation terminology, what does "total rewards" mean?
3. What are the mandated or legally required benefits? Briefly describe each.
4. What are the basic categories of discretionary benefits? Describe each.
5. What items are included in the discretionary benefit of payment for time not worked?
6. Define each of the following:
   a. Health maintenance organization (HMO)
   b. Preferred provider organization (PPO)
   c. Point-of-service (POS)
   d. Exclusive provider organization (EPO)
   e. Health savings account (HSA)
   f. Flexible spending account (FSA)
7. There are numerous forms of retirement plans. Describe each of the following:
   a. Defined benefit plan
   b. Defined contribution plan
   c. 401(k) plan
   d. Cash balance plan
8. What is an employee stock option plan?
9. What are topics included within employee services?
10. Why have some firms gone to voluntary benefits as opposed to discretionary benefits?
11. What is a customized benefit plan?
12. Distinguish among premium pay, hazard pay, and shift differential pay.
13. Define each of the following benefit laws:
    a. Consolidated Omnibus Budget Reconciliation Act
    b. Health Insurance Portability and Accountability Act
    c. Employee Retirement Income Security Act
    d. Older Workers Benefit Protection Act
    e. Pension Protection Act
    f. Patient Protection and Affordable Care Act
14. Why is it important to communicate information about the benefits package?
15. What are the components of nonfinancial compensation?
16. Explain the difference between the job itself as a nonfinancial compensation factor and the job environment as a nonfinancial compensation factor.
17. Define each the following workplace flexibility factors:
    a. Flextime
    b. Compressed work week
    c. Job sharing
    d. Telecommuting

HRM INCIDENT 1

Flextime

Kathy Collier is a supervisor of a government office in Washington, D.C. Morale in her office has been quite low recently. The workers have gone back to an 8:00 A.M. to 4:30 P.M. work schedule after having been on flextime for nearly two years.

When the directive came down allowing Kathy to place her office on flextime, she spelled out the rules carefully to her people. Each person was to work during the core period from 10:00 A.M. to 2:30 P.M.; however, they could work the rest of the eight-hour day at any time between 6:00 A.M. and 6:00 P.M. Kathy felt her workers were honest and well motivated, so she did not bother to set up any system of control.

Everything went along well for a long time. Morale improved, and all the work seemed to get done. In November, however, an auditor from the General Accounting Office investigated and found that Kathy's workers were averaging seven hours a day. Two employees had been working only during the core period for more than two months. When Kathy's department manager reviewed the auditor's report, Kathy was told to return the office to regular working hours. Kathy was upset and disappointed with her people. She had trusted them and felt they had let her down.

Questions

1. What are the advantages and disadvantages of flextime?
2. What could Kathy have done to keep the above situation from occurring?

HRM INCIDENT 2

A Benefits Package Designed for Whom?

Wayne McGraw greeted Robert Peters, his next interviewee, warmly. Robert had an excellent academic record and appeared to be just the kind of person Wayne's company, Beco Electric, was seeking. Wayne is the university recruiter for Beco and had already interviewed six graduating seniors at Centenary College.

Based on the application form, Robert appeared to be the most promising candidate to be interviewed that day. He was 22 years old and had a 3.6 grade point average with a 4.0 in his major field, industrial management. Not only was Robert the vice president of the Student Government Association, but he was also activities chairman for Kappa Alpha Psi, a social fraternity. The reference letters in Robert's file reveal that he was both very active socially and a rather intense and serious student. One of the letters from Robert's employer during the previous summer expressed satisfaction with Robert's work habits.

Wayne knew that discussion of benefits could be an important part of the recruiting interview. But he did not know which aspects of Beco's benefits program would appeal most to Robert. The company has an excellent profit-sharing plan, although 80 percent of profit distributions are deferred and included in each employee's retirement account. Health benefits are also good. It also has long-term care insurance. The company's medical and dental plan pays a significant portion of costs. A company lunchroom provides meals at about 70 percent of outside prices, although few managers take advantage of this. Employees get one week of paid vacation after the first year and two weeks after two years with the company. Two weeks are provided each year for sick leave. In addition, there are 12 paid holidays each year. Finally, the company encourages advanced education, paying for tuition and books in full, and, under certain circumstances, allowing time off to attend classes during the day. It also provides scholarships for dependents.

Questions

1. What aspects of Beco's benefits program are likely to appeal to Robert? Explain.
2. In today's work environment, what additional benefits might be more attractive to Robert? Explain.

Notes

1. Jody Miller and Matt Miller, "Get a Life," *Fortune* 152 (November 28, 2005): 109–124.
2. Ed Frauenheim, "CO-CEOs: Two at the Top," *Workforce Management* 88 (May 18, 2009): 40–42.
3. "SAP AG Reports Departure of CEO and Appointment of Co-CEOs," *Telecomworldwire (M2)* (February 8, 2010).
4. Frauenheim, "CO-CEOs: Two at the Top."
5. Mike Simonds, "Better ROI From Benefits," *BusinessWeek Online* (February 11, 2010): 14.
6. Amanda Wilkinson, "Defining a New Era of Benefits," *Employee Benefits* (July 2007): 3–4.
7. "Spotlight on Total Rewards," *Employee Benefits* (July 2009): 11.
8. Jenny Keefe, "Total Rethink," *Employee Benefits* (November 2008): 56–59.
9. "The Power of Total Rewards in Any Economy," *Workforce Management* 88 (April 6, 2009): S7.
10. "How Do Total Reward Statements Differ from Benefit Statements?" *Employee Benefits* (November 2008): 56–57.
11. Keefe, "Total Rethink."
12. Anthony Nugent, "Using Voluntary Benefits Strategically Can Help Employers Address Goals of Retaining Employees and Controlling Costs," *Benefits Quarterly* 25 (2009 Second Quarter): 7–10.
13. "Energy Company Goes Beyond The Norm To Attract, Retain Top-Notch Employees," *Pipeline & Gas Journal* 235 (November 2008): 93.
14. "What to Cut and What to Keep in Your Organization's Benefits," *HR Focus* 86 (June 2009): 11–13.
15. "More Than One-Third of Workers Won't Vacation in 2009," *HR Focus* 86 (July 2009): 12.
16. "Getaway," *New Republic* 237 (August 6, 2007): 3–4.
17. Martha Frase, "Taking Time Off to the Bank," *HRMagazine* 55 (March 2010): 41–46.
18. Diane Cadrain, "Employers Find Smooth Sailing in PTO Waters," *HRMagazine* 50 (September 2005): 29–41.
19. Kelly M. Butler, "Faced with Burnout Employers Pay Employees to Get Away," *Employee Benefit News* 19 (June 1, 2005): 55–56.
20. Elizabeth Pagano and Barbara Pagano, "The Virtues and Challenges of a Long Break," *Journal of Accountancy* 207 (February 2009): 46–51.
21. "Employee Rest Periods: Are They Required by Law?" *Payroll Practitioner's Monthly* 2008 (February 2008): 1–9.
22. Catherine Arnst, "Health Costs: Steeper Still," *BusinessWeek* (October 19, 2009): 50–51.
23. William J. Reindl, "Mythbusters: The Facts Are in About Consumer-Driven Health Plans," *Benefits Quarterly* 26 (2010 First Quarter): 34–38.
24. Jena McGregor and Esme Deprez, "Health Care: GE Gets Radical," *BusinessWeek* (November 30, 2009): 30.
25. Jim Priebe and Karli Dunkelberger, "Employees Embrace Health Savings Accounts," *National Underwriter / Life & Health Financial Services* 113 (November 16, 2009): 18–30.
26. Kathy Klug and Lois Chianese, "Health Savings Accounts: Back to the Future," *Benefits Quarterly* 26 (2010 First Quarter): 12–23.
27. Amanda Gengler, "Three Moves to Make When Picking Health Benefits," *Money* 38 (November 2009): 17.
28. Whitney R. Johnson, "HSAs: Six Insights for Employees Leaving or Losing a Job," *Benefits & Compensation Digest* 46 (November 2009): 24–29.
29. Jon Olson, "A Tax-free Employee Benefit," *Surface Fabrication* 15 (July 2009): 7.
30. "Benefits Group Working to Preserve Pre-Tax Flexible Spending Accounts," *Managing Benefits Plans* 9 (October 2009): 13–15.
31. "Understanding HR's Role in the New Health Care Reform Law," *HR Specialist: Employment Law* 40 (May 2010): 7.
32. David Welch, "The Company Doctor Is Back," *BusinessWeek* (August 11, 2008): 48–49.
33. "On-site Health Centers a Boon for Highmark," *HR Specialist: Compensation & Benefits* 5 (January 2010): 7.
34. Lori Chordas, "On-the-Spot Care," *Best's Review* 110 (May 2009): 74–76.
35. "Benefits Cost Management: ROI for On-site Health Is 2-TO-1 After Two Years," *Controller's Report* 2009 (June 2009): 4–5.
36. Jeremy Smerd, "Work-Site Clinics Gaining Favor as Retail Locations Lag," *Workforce Management* 89 (April 2010): 8–10.
37. Beth Almeida and William Fornia, "Defined Benefit Plans: A Better Bang for the Buck," *Journal of Pension Benefits: Issues in Administration* 16 (Winter 2009): 11–15.
38. Michael C. Mikhitarian and John B. Wukitsch, "Revisiting Contributory Defined Benefit Plans: An Old Idea Whose Time Has Come (Again?)," *Benefits Quarterly* 26 (2010 Second Quarter): 13–19.
39. "Majority of Fortune 100 Employers Offer Only DC Plans to New Salaried Employees," *Pension Benefits* 18 (August 2009): 12.
40. Peter Coy, "Retirement, The Big Rethink," *BusinessWeek* (July 13, 2009): 36–41.
41. Stephen Gandel and Christopher Maag, "Why It's Time To Retire the 401(k)," *Time* 174 (October 19, 2009): 28–34.
42. "401(k) Sponsors Decrease Employer Matches, but Raise Benefits Budgets," *Managing 401(k) Plans* 2009 (November 2009): 4–7.
43. Coy, "Retirement, The Big Rethink."

44. Gandel and Maag, "Why It's Time To Retire the 401(k)."

45. Ira Langer, "Maximizing Owners' Benefits Under Qualified Retirement Plans," *Journal of Retirement Planning* 12 (September 2009): 11–22.

46. Raymond D. Berry, "Plan Design in the Balance," *Journal of Accountancy* 207 (January 2009): 40–43.

47. Jerry Geisel, "Coca-Cola Makes Move to Cash Balance Plan," *Business Insurance* 43 (February 23, 2009): 3.

48. John Koegel, "Is There an ESOP in Your Future?" *Community Banker* 17 (January 2008): 22–23.

49. Faith E. Ivery, "Best Practices for Maximizing Tuition Assistance Plans," *Chief Learning Officer* 9 (February 2010): 22.

50. Meredyth McKenzie, "Across the Globe," *Smart Business Atlanta* 6 (September 2009): 18.

51. Ann Pomeroy, "To Convince Executives To Relocate, Get Creative," *HRMagazine* 53 (January 2008): 10.

52. "Unusual Employee Benefits Attract, Retain," *Toledo Business Journal* 25 (August 2009): 17.

53. "Don't Cry! Babies at Work Easier than You Think," *HR Specialist: Compensation & Benefits* 5 (March 2010): 1–2.

54. Christopher Thaczyk, "Colgate-Palmolive," *Fortune* 161 (May 5, 2010): 39.

55. Mark Schoeff Jr., "Danger and Duty," *Workforce Management* 86 (November 19, 2007): 1–3.

56. John L. Bishow, "A Look at Supplemental Pay: Overtime Pay, Bonuses, and Shift Differentials," *Compensation & Working Conditions* (March 2009): 1.

57. Jennifer Parmelee Witt, "Now and Soon: The Changing Role of Voluntary," *National Underwriter / Life & Health Financial Services* 114 (March 15, 2010): 17–37.

58. Cathy Leibow, "A Shot in the Arm," *Employee Benefit News* 24 (February 2010): 42/57.

59. William Atkinson, "Filling In Around the Edges," *HRMagazine* 54 (November 2009): 55–58.

60. Gil Lowere and Bonnie Brazzell, "Worksite Benefits: The Latest Voluntary Benefits Trends," *National Underwriter / Life & Health Financial Services* 114 (March 15, 2010): 16–34.

61. "Top Trends in Voluntary Benefits: Survey Results," *Benefits & Compensation Digest* 47 (May 2010): 35.

62. Mike Simonds, "Better ROI from Benefits," *BusinessWeek Online* (February 11, 2010): 14.

63. Kenya McCullum, "The Retention Intention," *Office Pro* 69 (2009 Special Edition): 8–11.

64. *U.S. Statutes at Large* 88, Part I, 93rd Congress, 2nd Session, 1974: 833.

65. Ernest J. Guerriero, "Pension Protection Act of 2006: Effects on Defined-Benefit Plans," *Journal of Financial Service Professionals* 63 (March 2009): 58–70.

66. "Health Reform Law Means New Responsibilities for HR & Employers," *HR Specialist: Compensation & Benefits* 5 (May 2010): 6.

67. "What Health Reform Means For You and Your Company," *Payroll Manager's Letter* 26 (April 21, 2010): 1.

68. "The Power of Total Rewards in Any Economy," *Workforce Management* 88 (April 6, 2009): S7.

69. Dagmara Scalise, "Happy Workers," *H&HN: Hospitals & Health Networks* 80 (March 2006): 28–30.

70. Drew Robb, "Get the Benefits Message Out," *HRMagazine* 54 (October 2009): 69–71.

71. Adapted from Frederick Herzberg, *Work and the Nature of Man* (Cleveland: World, 1966): 91–106.

72. Adapted from Craig J. Cantoni, "Learn to Manage Pay and Performance Like an Entrepreneur," *Compensation & Benefits Review* 29 (January/February 1997): 52–58.

73. "Desperately Seeking Greater Employee Engagement," *HR Focus* 85 (June 2008): 13.

74. "Employee Satisfaction: Key to Recovery Success?" *HR Focus* 87 (April 2010): 1–15.

75. "Flex Work Heads List of Employer Retention Strategies," *HR Specialist: Compensation & Benefits* 5 (April 2010): 6.

76. "A Strategy To Retain Workers During Recession," *OfficePro* 70 (January/February 2010): 4.

77. "Work-Family Conflicts Affect Employees at All Income Levels," *HR Focus* 87 (April 2010): 9.

78. Cathy Leibow, "The Pursuit of Happiness," *Employee Benefit News* 24 (January 2010): 39–49.

79. Diane Domeyer, "Parental Perks at Work," *Office Pro* 68 (March 2008): 8.

80. Bridget Mintz Testa, "No Mere Perk: Flex-Work as a Strategic Tool," *Workforce Management* 89 (March 2010): 4.

81. Meredith Levinson, "Job Security: It's What Your Staff Wants," *CIO* 22 (September 15, 2009): 25.

82. "What to Cut and What to Keep in Your Organization's Benefits," *HR Focus* 86 (June 2009): 11–13.

83. "Flextime Does More Than Just Satisfy Employees," *HR Focus* 86 (September 2009): 12.

84. Carolyn Hirschman, "Share and Share Alike," *HRMagazine* 50 (September 2005): 52–57.

85. Jane Simms, "Who Job Shares Wins?" *Director* 59 (January 2006): 48–52.

86. "Long-Distance Employee Management Becoming the Norm," *HR Focus* 86 (March 2009): 9.

87. Iila A. Lipin, "A Practitioner's Guide to the Taxation of Telecommuting," *Tax Adviser* 41 (February 2010): 100–106.

88. "Out of Sight, Yes. Out of Mind, No," *BusinessWeek* (February 18, 2008): 60.

89. "Long-Distance Employee Management Becoming the Norm."

90. Jeffrey K. Guiler and Maryellen Kelly, "Don't Look for Me, I'll Be Working from Starbucks Today": A Review of Regulations That May Apply to Off-Site Workplaces," *SAM Advanced Management Journal* 74 (Spring 2009): 23–31.

91. Laura Fitzpatrick, "We're Getting Off the Ladder," *Time* 173 (May 25, 2009): 45.

92. Jenny Marlar, "Underemployment Rises to 20.3% in March," *Gallup Poll Briefing* (April 1, 2010): 1.

93. Rudy Bethea, Jr., "Global Benefits Management: Maintaining a Competitive Edge in Multiple Countries," *Employee Benefit Plan Review* 64 (November 2009): 22–23.

94. Lori Chordas, "Multiple Choice," *Best's Review* 109 (March 2009): 65–67.

95. Paul Shimer, "Looking for Land," *Employee Benefit News* 23 (June 2009): 30–32.

96. "Japanese Vie to be Family-friendliest," *Work-Life Newsbrief & Trend Report* (May 2008): 3.

97. Ibid.

CHAPTER

11 A Safe and Healthy Work Environment

HRM in Action: Smoke-free Workplaces: Dealing with the Low Hanging Fruit

An important health issue facing employers today is environmental tobacco smoke. Ann Skye, wellness manager at Quintiles Transnational Corporation, said, "Smoking is the number one culprit in poor health, and its negative effects are indisputable. It's the low hanging fruit in disease prevention, so to speak, and we feel it would be irresponsible for any employee wellness program not to aggressively address tobacco use."[1] Besides being a significant public health concern, smoking is an economic burden on employers, who are recognizing the value of providing smoking-cessation benefits.[2]

Employers have grown increasingly intolerant of smokers and many workplaces are smoke-free, although about 21 percent of adult Americans continue to smoke.[3] Even though some smoker advocates remain adamant that passive cigarette smoke is not harmful, the Surgeon General has concluded that there is no safe level of secondhand smoke exposure. The evidence that secondhand tobacco smoke causes serious harm becomes more concrete every day and may be the under-recognized cause of heart attack deaths.[4] Having smoke-free workplace policies helps to fulfill an employer's legal obligation to provide a safe workplace under OSHA's *general duty clause* (discussed later in this chapter). The policy also reduces the risk of litigation, potentially reduces workers' compensation premiums, and protects employees from harm.

Estimates are that exposure to secondhand smoke for individuals who have never smoked is responsible for about 3,000 lung cancer deaths and more than 35,000 coronary heart disease deaths in the United States annually.[5] A study released by the

After completing this chapter, students should be able to:

1. Describe the nature and role of safety and health.

2. Explain the role of the Occupational Safety and Health Administration.

3. Describe the economic impact of safety and explain the focus of safety programs.

4. Describe the consequences of repetitive stress injuries.

5. Explain the purpose of ergonomics.

6. Explain the effects of workplace and domestic violence on businesses.

7. Describe the nature of stress and means of managing stress.

8. Explain burnout.

9. Describe the purposes of wellness programs.

10. Describe the importance of physical fitness programs.

11. Explain substance abuse, describe substance-abuse-free workplaces, and describe how to implement a drug-testing program.

12. Describe employee assistance programs.

University of Minnesota Cancer Center revealed that nonsmoking employees had up to 25 times more nicotine in their bodies on days when they worked in restaurants and bars than on days they were not at work.[6]

Numerous studies have concluded that workplace smoking is not only hazardous to employees' health, but is also detrimental to the firm's financial health. Employees who smoke consume more health care resources, experience greater absenteeism, and tend to be less productive while at work. The CDC concluded that each employee who smokes costs employers $1,897 in lost productivity each year. Businesses pay an average of $2,189 in workers' compensation costs for smokers, compared with $176 for nonsmokers.[7] According to the American Lung Association, tobacco-related illnesses are the number one preventable cause of death in this country, claiming more than 393,000 lives every year and costing our nation $193 billion annually for health care and lost productivity. Another 50,000 people die from exposure to secondhand smoke, and there is no telling how many of us have been or will be affected by *third hand smoke*.[8] Third hand smoke is what you smell when a smoker gets in an elevator after going outside for a cigarette. Dr. Jonathan P. Winickoff at Harvard Medical School said, "Your nose isn't lying. The stuff is so toxic that your brain is telling you: 'Get away.'"[9]

According to the American Lung Association, smoking is banned in restaurants in 29 states and banned in bars in 25 states.[10] Anti-smoking ordinances also seems to improve heart health. A study found that there were 399 hospital admissions for heart attacks in Pueblo, Colorado, in the 18 months before the city's smoke-free ordinance took effect on July 1, 2003, compared with 237 heart attack hospitalizations from 18 months to three years after this date—a decline of 41 percent.[11]

Some business owners have taken a personal stand against smoking in general, not just smoking in the workplace. Four employees from Weyco, a firm that manages benefit plans for workers on behalf of other companies, were fired after refusing to take a nicotine test to determine whether they had smoked. President Howard Weyers said, "Some call this a violation of privacy, pointing to the principle that what you do in your own home is your own business. But they forget the part about so long as it doesn't harm anyone else."[12] Even so, 29 states and the District of Columbia have laws on the books elevating smokers to a protected class. However, Michigan, the state where Weyco is located, is not one of those states.[13]

This chapter begins by discussing smoke-free workplaces. Next, the nature and role of safety and health and the role of the Occupational Safety and Health Administration are discussed. The economic impact of safety and the focus of safety programs in business operations are presented next, and the consequences of repetitive stress injuries and the purpose of ergonomics are discussed. An explanation of the effect of workplace and domestic violence on businesses follows. The nature of stress is described and the means of coping with stress discussed. Then identity theft as a major stressor in today's environment and burnout are discussed. Following this, wellness programs and the importance of physical fitness programs are described. Substance abuse, substance-abuse-free workplaces, implementing a drug-free program, and the rationale for employee assistance programs are discussed. This chapter concludes with a global perspective entitled "Global Healthcare for Expats."

OBJECTIVE 11.1
Describe the nature and role of safety and health.

safety
Protection of employees from injuries caused by work-related accidents.

health
Employees' freedom from physical or emotional illness.

OBJECTIVE 11.2
Explain the role of the Occupational Safety and Health Administration.

Nature and Role of Safety and Health

In our discussion, **safety** involves protecting employees from injuries caused by work-related accidents. Included within the umbrella definition of safety are factors related to repetitive stress injuries and workplace and domestic violence. **Health** refers to employees' freedom from physical or emotional illness. Problems in these areas can seriously affect a worker's productivity and quality of work life. They can dramatically lower a firm's effectiveness and employee morale. In fact, job-related injuries and illnesses are more common than most people realize.

Occupational Safety and Health Administration

The Occupational Safety and Health Act of 1970 created the Occupational Safety and Health Administration (OSHA). OSHA aims to ensure worker safety and health in the United States by working with employers and employees to create better working environments. The Act requires employers to provide employees a safe and healthy place to work and this responsibility extends to providing *safe employees*. The courts have reasoned that a dangerous worker is comparable to a defective machine. Employers have a responsibility under the *general duty clause* of the Occupational Safety and Health Act to furnish a workplace free from recognized hazards that are causing or are likely to cause death or serious physical harm. In order to prove a violation of the general duty clause, OSHA has to demonstrate: 1) That a condition or activity in the workplace presented a hazard; 2) That the employer or its industry recognized this hazard; 3) That the hazard was likely to cause death or serious physical harm; and 4) That a feasible and effective means existed to eliminate or materially reduce the hazard.[14]

Since its inception, OSHA has helped to cut workplace fatalities by more than 60 percent and occupational injury and illness by 40 percent. At the same time, U.S. employment has more than doubled from 56 million workers at 3.5 million worksites to 147 million workers at 7.2 million sites. To handle this workload, OSHA has more than 2,220 employees, including 1,100 inspectors. However, death and injuries continue to occur. In 2008, 5,071 workers died on the job.[15]

The mission of OSHA is to promote and ensure workplace safety and health and reduce workplace fatalities, injuries, and illnesses. OSHA is committed to assuring—so far as possible—that every working man and woman in the nation has safe and healthful working conditions. OSHA believes that providing workers with a safe workplace is central to their ability to enjoy health, security, and the opportunity to achieve the American dream. Addressing safety and health issues in the workplace also saves the employer money and adds value to the business. Recent estimates place the business costs associated with occupational injuries at close to $170 billion—expenditures that come straight out of company profits.[16] To help small businesses, OSHA has expanded its assistance, reduced penalties, and put more of its informational materials in electronic formats such as DVDs and Internet sites. OSHA has emphasized that these firms will not be punished for violations if they seek OSHA's assistance in correcting problems. OSHA has formed agreements with a number of companies to promote increased safety education and outreach.

Even though OSHA would like a successful partnership relationship to exist, at times penalties must be given. Financial penalties serve as reminders to industry of the benefits of maintaining safe and healthy working conditions. Partly as a result of the Presidential election of 2008, there are likely to be changes in the way OSHA operates. Edward D. Foulke, co-chair of Fisher & Phillips' Workplace Safety and Catastrophe Management practice group in Atlanta, said that companies "need to realize that most likely there are going to be more inspections and increased penalty amounts, along with more scrutiny and less willingness to negotiate on penalties and classifications, with greater fines and increased penalty amounts that will likely result in more contests going to the review commission. You may also see an increase in possible criminal referrals to the U.S. Justice Department for safety and health violations."[17] In fact, in 2010, OSHA implemented the Severe Violator Enforcement Program that will increase inspections at worksites where "recalcitrant employers" have repeatedly violated safety regulations and endangered workers. It also requires a mandatory follow-up inspection to make sure the required changes were made.[18]

A serious hazard citation has a maximum penalty of $7,000. A willful citation might have a maximum amount of $70,000 per violation. Calculated instance by instance, if 10 employees were exposed to one hazard the employer intentionally did not eliminate, the penalty amount would immediately jump to $700,000.

OSHA has authorized stricter enforcement measures for manufacturers and other employers that repeatedly violate health and safety standards. In 2009, managers at more than 13,500 workplaces received letters notifying them that their rates of days away from work, restricted work, or job transfer injury and illness were higher than average based on a survey of 80,000 worksites' 2007 safety data. For every 100 full-time workers, the 13,500 employers had 5.0 or more injuries or illnesses that resulted in days away from work, restricted work, or job transfer. The national average is 2.1. The notice went on to say "OSHA recognizes that your elevated DART rate does not necessarily indicate a lack of interest in safety and health. Whatever the cause, a high rate is costly to your company in both personal and financial terms. In addition, you should be aware that OSHA may target up to 4,500 of the workplaces identified in the survey for inspection in the next year."[19] Recently, BP Products North America Inc. received the largest fine in OSHA's history, $87,430,000 for its failure to correct hazards faced by employees at its Texas City refinery.[20] However, this record may be broken as a result of the death and destruction caused by the oil well explosion and the resulting damage to the Gulf coast in 2010.

The average employer will not likely see an OSHA inspector unless an employee instigates an inspection. About 70 percent of OSHA inspections have resulted from employee complaints.

When OSHA inspectors come to a site, the employer has the option of denying the inspector access to the worksite. If the employer refuses access to view certain documents, OSHA must obtain an administrative subpoena.

The Act includes protection for workers who request inspections, refuse unsafe work, and complain about hazardous workplace conditions. Employers cannot retaliate against workers who exercise their rights and employers who do so may be subjected to fines and penalties.[21] Under the Occupational Safety and Health Act, an employee can legally refuse to work when the following conditions exist:

- The employee reasonably fears death, disease, or serious physical harm.
- The harm is imminent.
- There is too little time to file an OSHA complaint and get the problem corrected.
- The worker has notified the employer about the condition and requested correction of the problem, but the employer has not taken action.

OBJECTIVE 11.3

Describe the economic impact of safety and explain the focus of safety programs.

Safety: The Economic Impact

Job-related deaths and injuries of all types extract a high toll not only in terms of human misery, but also in economic loss. According to a recent Liberty Mutual Workplace Safety Index, the most disabling workplace injuries and illnesses cost U.S. businesses $53 billion in direct workers' compensation costs, an average of more than $1 billion per week.[22] The significant financial costs are often passed along to the consumer in the form of higher prices. Thus, job-related deaths and injuries affect everyone, directly or indirectly. Safety risks can be significant for employers. In addition to workers' compensation costs, OSHA can levy major fines. Indirect costs related to turnover and lost productivity add to the expense. The rate of growth in the cost of workplace injuries has slowed significantly. However, the cost remains high. The top leading cause of workplace injuries and their associated costs was overexertion (i.e., lifting, carrying, pushing, pulling, etc.), which accounted for 25.7 percent of direct workers' compensation costs to U.S. businesses.[23]

Companies have come a long way in recognizing the importance and cost benefits of safety. Workplaces are safer, thanks to efforts of employers, insurance companies, unions, and state and federal agencies. Safety professionals strive for lower workers' compensation costs, as do insurance companies, who work to keep both their clients' and their own costs down.

Focus of Safety Programs

Faulty management safety policies and decisions, personal factors, and environmental factors are the basic causes of accidents. These factors result in unsafe working conditions and/or unsafe employee actions. Every employer needs to have a comprehensive safety program in place regardless of the degree of danger involved. Safety programs may accomplish their purposes in two primary ways: one focusing on *unsafe employee actions* and the other on *unsafe working conditions*.

Unsafe Employee Actions

Training and orientation of new employees emphasizing safety is especially important. The early months of employment are often critical because work injuries decrease with length of service. The first approach in a safety program is to create a psychological environment and employee attitudes that promote safety. Accident rates decline when workers consciously or subconsciously think about safety. This attitude must permeate the firm's operations, and a strong company policy emphasizing safety and health is crucial. For example, a major chemical firm's policy states: "It is the policy of the company that every employee be assigned to a safe and healthful place to work. We strongly desire accident prevention in all phases of our operations. Toward this end, the full cooperation of all employees will be required." As the policy implies, no individual employee has the task of making the workplace safe. Although there is danger that everyone's responsibility will become no one's responsibility, a truly safe environment takes the effort of everyone from top management to the lowest-level employee. Although

ETHICAL DILEMMA

Illegal Dumping

You have just become aware that the company that disposes of your plant waste is not following Environmental Protection Agency guidelines. The firm is dumping toxic waste at night in a closed landfill six miles from the plant. To make matters worse, your brother-in-law operates the waste disposal company. You have already warned him once, and you have just learned that he is still illegally dumping. You confront him, telling him that you are going to use the hotline to report him if he illegally dumps waste one more time, but he threatens to implicate you if you blow the whistle.

What would you do?

every individual in a firm should be encouraged to come up with solutions to potential safety problems, the firm's managers must take the lead. Management's unique role is clear, since OSHA places primary responsibility for employee safety on the employer.

Unsafe Working Conditions

The second approach to safety program design is to develop and maintain a safe physical working environment. Here, altering the environment becomes the focus for preventing accidents. Even if Joe, a machine operator, has been awake all night with a sick child and can barely keep his eyes open, the safety devices on his machine will help protect him. Management should create a physical environment in which accidents cannot occur. It is in this area that OSHA has had its greatest influence.

Developing Safety Programs

Workplace accident prevention requires safety program planning. Plans may be relatively simple, as for a small retail store, or more complex and highly sophisticated, as for a large automobile assembly plant. Regardless of the organization's size, the support of top management is essential if safety programs are to be effective.

Table 11.1 shows some of the reasons for top management's support of a safety program. This information suggests that the lost productivity of a single injured worker is not the only factor to consider. Every phase of human resource management is involved. For instance, the firm may have difficulty in recruitment if it gains a reputation for being an unsafe place to work. Employee relations erode if workers believe that management does not care enough about them to provide a safe workplace. Firms will see an increase in compensation costs when they must pay a premium to attract and retain qualified applicants. Maintaining a stable workforce may become very difficult if employees perceive their workplace as hazardous.

JOB HAZARD ANALYSIS The main goal of safety and health professionals is to prevent job-related injuries and illnesses. Firms achieve this goal in several ways: by educating workers in

Table 11.1 Reasons for Management Support of a Safety Program

- **Personal loss.** The physical pain and mental anguish associated with injuries are always unpleasant and may even be traumatic for an injured worker. Of still greater concern is the possibility of permanent disability or even death.
- **Financial loss to injured employees.** Most employees are covered by company insurance plans or personal accident insurance. However, an injury may result in financial losses not covered by insurance.
- **Lost productivity.** When an employee is injured, there will be a loss of productivity for the firm. In addition to obvious losses, there are often hidden costs. For example, a substitute worker may need additional training to replace the injured employee. Even when another worker is available to move into the injured employee's position, efficiency may suffer.
- **Higher insurance premiums.** Workers' compensation insurance premiums are based on the employer's history of insurance claims. The potential for savings related to employee safety provides a degree of incentive to establish formal programs.
- **Possibility of fines or imprisonment.** Since the enactment of the Occupational Safety and Health Act, a willful and repeated violation of its provisions may result in serious penalties for the employer.
- **Social responsibility.** Many executives feel responsible for the safety and health of their employees. A number of firms had excellent safety programs years before OSHA existed. They understand that a safe work environment is not only in the best interests of the firm; providing one is the right thing to do.

the hazards associated with their work, installing engineering controls, defining safe work procedures, and prescribing appropriate personal protective equipment. **Job hazard analysis (JHA)** is a multistep process designed to study and analyze a task or job and then break down that task into steps that provide a means of eliminating associated hazards. It is an effective and useful tool to isolate and address safety issues and risks.[24]

JHA can have a major impact on safety performance. It results in a detailed written procedure for safely completing many tasks within a plant. A successful JHA program features several key components: management support, supervisor and employee training, written program, and management oversight. OSHA publication 3071, *Job Safety Analysis*, is a good primer on performing a JHA.

SUPERFUND AMENDMENTS REAUTHORIZATION ACT, TITLE III (SARA) SARA requires businesses to communicate more openly about the hazards associated with the materials they use and the produce and the wastes they generate. Although SARA has been around since 1986, some firms do not yet have a satisfactory program for it in place. The hazard communication standard often leads the list of OSHA violations, since the top category for OSHA citations is for no written hazard communication program. Dealing with this standard appears to be relatively simple and inexpensive, except when organizations ignore its provisions.

EMPLOYEE INVOLVEMENT One way to strengthen a safety program is to include employee input, which provides workers with a sense of accomplishment. To prevent accidents, each worker must make a personal commitment to safe work practices. A team concept, in which employees watch out for each other as a moral obligation, is a worthy goal. Supervisors can show support for the safety program by conscientiously enforcing safety rules and by closely conforming to the rules themselves. Participation in such teams helps form positive attitudes, and employees develop a sense of ownership of the program. Involved employees may become concerned with not only safety issues but also with ways to improve productivity.

SAFETY ENGINEER In many companies, one staff member coordinates the overall safety program. Titles such as *safety engineer* and *safety director* are common. One of the safety engineer's primary tasks is to provide safety training for company employees. This involves educating line managers about the merits of safety and recognizing and eliminating unsafe situations. Although the safety engineer operates essentially in an advisory capacity, a well-informed and assertive person in this capacity may exercise considerable influence in the organization. Some major corporations also have *risk management departments* that anticipate losses associated with safety factors and prepare legal defenses in the event of lawsuits.

Accident Investigation

Accidents can happen even in the most safety-conscious firms. Whether or not an accident results in an injury, an organization should carefully evaluate each occurrence to determine its cause and to ensure that it does not recur. The safety engineer and the line supervisor jointly investigate accidents. One of the responsibilities of any supervisor is to prevent accidents. To do so, the supervisor must learn, through active participation in the safety program, why accidents occur, how they occur, where they occur, and who is involved. Supervisors gain a great deal of knowledge about accident prevention by helping to prepare accident reports. OSHA Form 300 is a log of work-related injuries and illnesses (see Figure 11.1). Most employers will mail or electronically transmit records of occupational injuries and illnesses directly to OSHA.

Evaluation of Safety Programs

Perhaps the best indicator of a successful safety program is a reduction in the *frequency* and *severity* of injuries and illnesses. Therefore, statistics including the number of injuries and illnesses (frequency rate) and the amount of work time lost (severity rate) are often used in program evaluation. OSHA metrics currently in use are: total cases, nonfatal cases without lost workdays, total lost workday cases, cases with days away from work, and measure of fatalities. In addition to program-evaluation criteria, an effective reporting system helps to ensure that accidents are reported and receive attention. With the start of a new safety program, the number of accidents may decline significantly. However, some supervisors may fail to report certain

OSHA's Form 300

Log of Work-Related Injuries and Illnesses

You must record information about every work-related injury or illness that involves loss of consciousness, restricted work activity or job transfer, days away from work, or medical treatment beyond first aid. You must also record significant work-related injuries and illnesses that are diagnosed by a physician or licensed health care professional. You must also record work-related injuries and illnesses that meet any of the specific recording criteria listed in 29 CFR 1904.8 through 1904.12. Feel free to use two lines for a single case if you need to. You must complete an injury and illness incident report (OSHA Form 301) or equivalent form for each injury or illness recorded on this form. If you're not sure whether a case is recordable, call your local OSHA office for help.

Attention: This form contains information relating to employee health and must be used in a manner that protects the confidentiality of employees to the extent possible while the information is being used for occupational safety and health purposes.

U.S. Department of Labor
Occupational Safety and Health Administration

Form approved OMB no. 1218-0176

Year ____

Establishment name ____

City ____   State ____

						Classify the case							Check the "injury" column or choose one type of illness:				

Identify the person				Describe the case		Using these categories, check ONLY the most serious result for each case:				Enter the number of days the injured or ill worker was:		(M)				

(A) Case No.	(B) Employee's Name	(C) Job Title (e.g., Welder)	(D) Date of injury or onset of illness (mo./day)	(E) Where the event occurred (e.g., Loading dock north end)	(F) Describe injury or illness, parts of body affected, and object/substance that directly injured or made person ill (e.g. Second degree burns on right forearm from acetylene torch)	Death (G)	Days away from work (H)	Job transfer or restriction (I)	Other recordable cases (J)	On job transfer or restriction (days) (K)	Away from work (days) (L)	Injury (1)	Skin Disorder (2)	Respiratory Condition (3)	Poisoning (4)	All other illnesses (5)
						Page totals	0	0	0	0	0	0	0	0	0	0	0

Remained at work

Be sure to transfer these totals to the Summary page (Form 300A) before you post it.

	Injury (1)	Skin Disorder (2)	Respiratory Condition (3)	Poisoning (4)	All other illnesses (5)

Page ____ 1 of 1

Public reporting burden for this collection of information is estimated to average 14 minutes per response, including time to review the instruction, search and gather the data needed, and complete and review the collection of information. Persons are not required to respond to the collection of information unless it displays a currently valid OMB control number. If you have any comments about these estimates or any aspects of this data collection, contact: US Department of Labor, OSHA Office of Statistics, Room N-3644, 200 Constitution Ave, NW, Washington, DC 20210. Do not send the completed forms to this office.

Figure 11.1

OSHA's Form 300, Log of Work-Related Injuries and Illnesses

accidents to make the statistics for their units look better. Proper evaluation of a safety program depends on the accurate reporting and recording of data.

Organizations must use the conclusions derived from an evaluation for them to be of any value in improving the safety program. Gathering data and permitting this information to collect dust on the safety director's desk will not solve problems or prevent accidents. Accident investigators must transmit evaluation results upward to top management and downward to line managers in order to generate improvements.

Repetitive Stress Injuries

Repetitive stress injuries (RSIs) refer to a group of conditions caused by placing too much stress on a joint when the same action is performed repeatedly. The U.S. Bureau of Labor Statistics reports that repetitive stress injuries account for 25 percent of cases involving days away from work and that disorders associated with repetitive stress are responsible for nearly 60 percent of all work-related illness. Further, RSI represents 62 percent of all North American workers' compensation claims and results in between $15 billion and $20 billion in lost work time and compensation claims each year.[25]

A serious repetitive stress injury is **carpal tunnel syndrome (CTS),** caused by pressure on the median nerve that occurs as a result of a narrowing of the passageway that houses the nerve. People who have CTS may experience pain, numbness, or tingling in the hands or wrist, a weak grip, the tendency to drop objects, sensitivity to cold, and in later stages, muscle deterioration, especially in the thumb.

CTS tends to develop in people who use their hands and wrists repeatedly in the same way. Illustrators, carpenters, assembly-line workers, and people whose jobs involve work on personal computers are the ones most commonly affected. According to the National Council on Compensation Insurance, claims for carpal tunnel syndrome accounted for just 2 percent of all lost-time workplace injuries, but such injuries accounted for $1 billion in workers' compensation claim benefits, or an average of about $20,000 each.[26]

CTS is preventable, or at least its severity can be reduced. Managers can provide ergonomic furniture, especially chairs, and ensure that computer monitors are positioned at eye level and keyboards at elbow level. Employees can also cooperate by reporting early symptoms of CTS RSI and by taking the following actions:

- Rest the hand and wrist in a neutral position.
- Do not perform the exact activities that caused the syndrome.
- Take nonsteroidal anti-inflammatory drugs.
- Avoid any physical therapy aimed at exercising the hand muscle-tendon units until after symptoms have disappeared.

Other suggested actions include: keep wrists straight, take exercise breaks, alternate tasks, shift positions periodically, adjust chair height, work with feet flat on the floor, and be conscious of posture. Many of these actions suggest the need for ergonomics.

Ergonomics

A specific approach to dealing with health problems such as repetitive stress injuries and enhancing performance is ergonomics. **Ergonomics** is the process of designing the workplace to support the capabilities of people and job/task demands.[27] Through ergonomics, the goal is to fit the machine and work environment to the person, rather than require the person to make the adjustment. Ergonomics includes all attempts to structure work conditions so that they maximize energy conservation, promote good posture, and allow workers to function without pain or impairment. Failure to address ergonomics issues results in fatigue, poor performance, and repetitive stress injuries.

It is clear that there is an economic payoff in using ergonomics. The ergonomic initiatives of Schneider National, a provider of transportation, logistics, and related services, helped reduce workers' compensation costs by more than 9 percent. The injury-reduction strategy helps prevent the stress and discomfort of driving, reduced in-cab injuries, reduced back injuries outside of the cab, and lessened fatigue. After only six months, the percentage of drivers reporting discomfort dropped by more than 47 percent and the carrier also experienced 114 fewer lost-time injuries.[28] Other companies have also discovered that improving the work environment boosts morale, lowers injury rates, and yields a positive return on investment. A sound ergonomic approach to avoiding workplace injuries is prevention.[29] Employee input in the design and implementation of safety and health programs may well increase the chances for success of such programs.

Another threat to the safety and security of people on the job is workplace violence. The various ramifications of this phenomenon are discussed in the next section.

Workplace Violence

OBJECTIVE 11.6
Explain the effects of workplace and domestic violence on businesses.

workplace violence
Physical assault, threatening behavior, verbal abuse, hostility, or harassment directed toward employees at work or on duty.

OSHA defines **workplace violence** as physical assault, threatening behavior, verbal abuse, hostility, or harassment directed toward employees at work or on duty. ASIS International, an organization for security professionals, found that workplace violence affects more than 2 million workers each year. In the United States, 20 percent of all violent crimes occur in the workplace.[30]

According to a National Institute for Occupational Safety and Health publication, on average, 1.7 million workers are injured each year, and more than 800 die as a result of workplace violence.[31] Sadly, homicide is the second leading cause of death on the job, second only to motor vehicle crashes.[32] Regardless of who commits the crime, consider the horror of random workplace violence:

> Michael McDermott was a 42-year-old software programmer at Edgewater Technology in Wakefield, Massachusetts. He chose the day after Christmas 2000 for workforce catastrophe. After chatting with other employees until 11 a.m., he strolled through the high-tech firm's lobby with an AK-47 assault rifle, a shotgun, and a semiautomatic handgun. Bypassing the receptionist, he entered the Human Resources office, shot and killed three people; he then headed to accounting, where three employees had barricaded the door. Barging through, he shot and killed two accountants; the third escaped, hidden under her desk. What triggered McDermott's ire? The accounting department had garnished his wages to pay overdue taxes to the IRS.[33]

Homicide, as terrible as it is, accounts for only a small percentage of the overall incidence of workplace violence. There is no way to estimate the physical and psychological damage to other employees, who are only onlookers to the violent behavior. The issue facing most large employers is not *if* they will ever deal with an act of workplace violence, but *when*.

Although employers must take steps to reduce the potential for employee homicides, they must also take action against more pervasive problems that can inflict havoc day in and day out. These include bullying, verbal threats, harassment, intimidation, pushing, shoving, slapping, kicking, and fistfights. The vast majority of these types of assaults and other forms of aggression do not show up in the statistics, as they go unreported.

Vulnerable Employees

Employees at gas stations and liquor stores, taxi drivers, police officers, and convenience store managers working night shifts face the greatest danger from workplace violence. The National Census of Fatal Occupational Injuries reported that 35 deaths occurred in convenience stores in 2006.[34] Ninety percent of the time, armed criminals threaten these workers, not disgruntled co-workers.

No workplace is immune from violence. Hospital managers overwhelmingly say the biggest threat that emergency room workers face is patient violence. Most hospitals now have security guards stationed in their emergency rooms, particularly at times such as Saturday nights, when violence seems to escalate.

There are numerous reasons for violent acts committed by employees or former employees. Among the most common are personality conflicts, marital or family problems, drug or alcohol abuse, and firings or layoffs.

Legal Consequences of Workplace Violence

In addition to the horror of workplace violence, there is also the ever-present threat of legal action. Civil lawsuits claiming *negligent hiring* or *negligent retention* are a constant threat. Remember from Chapter 6 that negligent hiring is the liability an employer incurs when it fails to conduct a reasonable investigation of an applicant's background, and then assigns a potentially dangerous person to a position in which he or she can inflict harm. **Negligent retention** is the liability an employer may incur when a company keeps persons on the payroll whose records indicate a strong potential for wrongdoing and fails to take steps to defuse a possibly violent situation. If an employer ignores warning signs leading up to a violent incident, it could be held legally liable.[35] Perhaps many of the previously discussed forms of workplace violence could have been prevented if managers had paid more attention to potential problem employees. As previously mentioned, under OSHA's *general duty clause*, employers are required to furnish, to each employee, a place of employment that is free from recognizable hazards that are causing, or likely to cause, death or serious harm to the employee.[36]

negligent retention
Liability an employer may incur when a company keeps persons on the payroll whose records indicate a strong potential for wrongdoing and fails to take steps to defuse a possibly violent situation.

Individual and Organizational Characteristics to Monitor

Some firms that have had extensive experience with workplace violence are trying an alternative approach. Instead of trying to screen out violent people, they are attempting to detect employees who commit minor aggressive acts and exhibit certain behaviors. These individuals often go on to engage in more serious behaviors. Once identified, these people are required to meet with trained staff members for counseling as long as needed. This approach may require more commitment on the part of the firm, but the alternative cost of violence may make this expenditure reasonable in the long run.

While there are no sure signs an employee will commit an act of violence, certain behaviors can signal a problem such as: erratic behavior, increased irritability or hostility, reduced quality of work, poor organizational and time management skills, absenteeism, and a look of physical exhaustion. There are usually signs preceding workplace violence.[37] "We've never seen a case where someone just snapped," says Marc McElhaney, a psychologist and director of Critical Response Associates in Atlanta. "In every single one, there are a series of events that either someone ignored or did not respond to adequately."[38] One study found that workers who shoot and kill their co-workers are likely to be employees who recently experienced a negative change in employment status, including those who have been fired, whose contracts have not been renewed, or who have been suspended because of a dispute with management.[39] Remember the incident of Michael McDermott, previously mentioned. Payroll had garnished his wages to pay overdue taxes to the IRS.

Preventive Actions

The best protection employers can offer is to establish a zero tolerance policy for workplace violence against or by employees, according to the U.S. Labor Department's Occupational Safety and Health Administration. However, there is no way an employer can completely avoid risk when it comes to violence. Incidences of some unbalanced person coming in and shooting people happen randomly, and organizations can do little to anticipate or prevent them. However, there are things that can be done to reduce the risk. There are basically two parts to violence prevention. First, there must be a process in place to help with early detection of worker anger.[40] Second, supervisors and HR staff need to be trained in how to skillfully handle difficult employment issues. Firms should consider the following actions to minimize violent acts and to avoid lawsuits:

- Implement policies that ban weapons on company property, including parking lots.
- Under suspicious circumstances, require employees to submit to searches for weapons or examinations to determine their mental fitness for work.
- Have a policy stating that the organization will not tolerate any incidents of violence or even threats of violence.
- Have a policy that encourages employees to report all suspicious or violent activity to management.
- Develop relationships with mental health experts who will be available when emergencies arise.
- Equip receptionists with panic buttons to enable them to alert security officers instantly.

In spite of the human and financial costs of violence in the workplace, employers generally have not adequately trained employees in how to deal with potentially violent individuals. This is unfortunate, since research shows that providing workplace violence training to all employees, not just supervisors, may make a difference. Perhaps because of increased vigilance by organizations the number of homicides has declined from 1,080 in 1994 to 516 in 2008.[41]

Can the selection process predict applicants who will be prone to violence? The answer is "No." On the other hand, the profiles of individuals *not* prone to violence tend to have certain things in common. The most important markers for these people include:

- No substance abuse (one of the highest correlating factors).
- Being outwardly focused; having outside interests and friendships rather than being mainly self-involved.
- A good work history.

In order to confirm these characteristics, the firm must conduct a thorough background investigation.

Domestic Violence

Spillover from domestic violence is a threat to both women and their companies because after an abusive relationship is over, one of the easiest places to find them is at their workplace.[42] A recent study examined 500 assaults that occurred in the workplace as a result of domestic violence and just over half of the incidents they studied ended in at least one homicide.[43] Domestic violence has become an epidemic in this country. Robin Runge, director of the American Bar Association's Commission on Domestic Violence, said, "Beyond affecting the victim, domestic violence affects the victim's family members and co-workers—and that involves the workplace."[44] Domestic violence can have an impact on firms' bottom lines, costing about $5.8 billion each year in absenteeism, lower productivity, and turnover.[45] Employees miss an estimated 175,000 days of work each year because of domestic violence, according to the Family Violence Prevention Fund, a national nonprofit group. Business organizations have a huge stake in the problem of domestic violence.

Laws Related to Domestic Violence

Laws passed since the early 1980s recognize the seriousness of domestic violence. In 1984, the Family Violence Prevention and Services Act was passed to help prevent domestic violence and provide shelter and related assistance for victims. The Violence Against Women Act was passed in 1994, creating new federal criminal laws and establishing additional grant programs within the Department of Health and Human Services and the Department of Justice (DOJ). The Violence Against Women and DOJ Reauthorization Act of 2005 required a study to be prepared to determine the prevalence of domestic violence, dating violence, sexual assault, and stalking among men, women, youth, and children.[46] At least 29 states plus the District of Columbia have laws that allow people who leave jobs because of domestic violence to become eligible for unemployment benefits.[47] Also, some states such as Florida, California, Colorado, Hawaii, Illinois, Kansas, and Maine give domestic violence victims the right to take time off. Florida law permits employees to take up to three days leave from work in any 12-month period for a variety of activities connected with domestic violence issues.

Nature of Stress

stress
Body's nonspecific reaction to any demand made on it.

Stress is the body's nonspecific reaction to any demand made on it. It affects people in different ways and is therefore a highly individualized condition. Certain events may be quite stressful to one person but not to another. Moreover, the effect of stress is not always negative. For example, mild stress actually improves productivity, and it can be helpful in developing creative ideas.

Stress in the workplace is nothing new. One study found that 70 percent of workers reported that their employer does not do a good job of allowing them to balance their work life with their personal life.[48] In another study it found that one-third of Americans are living with extreme stress, and 48 percent believe their stress has increased over the past five years.[49] Several factors account for this rise, including increased workloads, terrorism, corporate scandals, and economic conditions. The recession of 2008/10 increased stress levels even among employees who still had jobs.[50] Although much of the world has reduced the number of hours worked each year per person over the past decade, Americans have done just the opposite. Each year, more than 275,000,000 working days are lost in the U.S. because of absenteeism resulting from stress.[51] If people work longer hours, they often do not have time to refresh, resulting in a deterioration of their personal lives.

Potential Consequences of Stress

Although everyone lives under a certain amount of stress, if it is severe enough and persists long enough, it can be harmful. In fact, stress can be as disruptive to an individual as any accident. It can result in poor attendance, excessive use of alcohol or other drugs, poor job performance, or even overall poor health. There is increasing evidence indicating that severe, prolonged stress is related to the diseases that are the leading causes of death—including cardiovascular disease, depression, immune system disorders, alcoholism, and drug addiction—plus the everyday headaches, back spasms, overeating, and other annoying ailments the body has developed in response to stress. Stress tops the list of changeable health risks that contribute to health care costs, ahead of other top risks such as current and past tobacco use, obesity, lack of exercise, high blood-glucose levels, depression, and high blood pressure.

Stressful Jobs

Stress and workload strains are very real challenges now, according to the findings of a CareerBuilder survey of more than 4,400 workers. Forty-seven percent of workers reported they have taken on more responsibility because of a layoff within their organization. Thirty-seven percent said they are handling the work of two people. Thirty percent feel burned out.[52] According to the "2008 Global Strategic Rewards Survey" conducted by Watson Wyatt Worldwide, workplace stress is one of the top reasons employees say they leave organizations.[53] NIOSH has studied stress as it relates to work and found that some jobs are generally perceived as being more stressful than other jobs. The 12 most stressful jobs are listed in Table 11.2. The common factor among these jobs is lack of employee control over work.[54] Workers in such jobs may feel that they are trapped, treated more like machines than people. Workers who have more control over their jobs, such as college professors and master craftspersons, hold some of the less stressful jobs.

The fact that certain jobs are identified as more stressful than others has important managerial implications. Managers are responsible for recognizing significantly deviant behavior and referring employees to health professionals for diagnosis and treatment. Telling signs of stress may include a reduction in the quantity and quality of work, frequent short periods of absence, increased alcohol consumption, poor time keeping, or becoming tearful or withdrawn. Under excessive stress, a person's dominant trait may become even more obvious. For example, if the individual is a private person, he or she withdraws from colleagues; if the person is upbeat, he or she becomes hyperactive. Ideally, stress should be dealt with before this occurs. To do so, managers must be aware of potential sources of stress. These sources exist both within and outside the organization. Regardless of its origin, stress possesses devastating potential.

According to Shelly Wolff, national practice director of health and productivity at Watson Wyatt, "Many companies don't appear to appreciate how stress is affecting their business. Too much stress from heavy demands, poorly defined priorities, and little on the-job flexibility can add to health issues."[55] In one survey, the single largest stress factor affecting on-the-job productivity was work overloaded.[56]

Table 11.2   Stressful Jobs

The 12 Jobs with the Most Stress

1. Laborer	7. Manager/administrator
2. Secretary	8. Waitress/waiter
3. Inspector	9. Machine operator
4. Clinical lab technician	10. Farm owner
5. Office manager	11. Miner
6. Supervisor	12. Painter

Other High-Stress Jobs (in Alphabetical Order)

Bank teller	Nurse's aide
Clergy member	Plumber
Computer programmer	Police officer
Dental assistant	Practical nurse
Electrician	Public relations worker
Firefighter	Railroad switchperson
Guard	Registered nurse
Hairdresser	Sales manager
Health aide	Sales representative
Health technician	Social worker
Machinist	Structural-mental worker
Meat cutter	Teacher's aide
Mechanic	Telephone operator
Musician	Warehouse worker

Source: From a ranking of 130 occupations by the federal government's National Institute for Occupational Safety and Health.

OBJECTIVE 11.7
Describe the nature of stress and means of managing stress.

Managing Stress

Only dead people are totally without stress, and experts emphasize that some stress is healthy. In fact, moderate stress is the key to survival. Yet, excessive, prolonged stress must be dealt with, and both the individual and organizations have a responsibility to take appropriate measures. There are a number of ways that individuals may control excessive stress. The following approaches are recommended:

- **Exercise.** One of the most effective means of dealing with stress is physical exercise. Stress results in chemical changes in the body, and exercise provides a means of returning the body to its normal state. Most people have a favorite form of exercise; it may be jogging, tennis, golf, racquetball, or walking.
- **Follow good diet habits.** A person under stress is burning up energy at a faster pace than normal. Proper eating habits are extremely important, but unfortunately, junk food often becomes the order of the day. Individuals must establish dietary goals that limit junk food and allow the maintenance of normal weight.
- **Know when to pull back.** Relaxation is essential to temper stress. Some people hold up well under stress for extended periods; others do not. But everyone should find time to pull back.
- **Put the stressful situation into perspective.** Some people tend to treat virtually all situations as a matter of life and death. Such an attitude can build up a tremendous amount of stress.
- **Find someone who will listen.** Finding someone who will listen can keep you from bottling up a problem that seems to eat away at your inner self.
- **Establish some structure in your life.** Stress often occurs when a person does not have control over a situation. In many instances, planning ahead is all that is needed to keep a person out of a stressful situation. Establishing structure may also mean leaving the job at the office. Most people need time away from the job to reduce stress levels.

TRENDS & INNOVATIONS

Identity Theft as a Major Stressor in Today's Environment

Identity theft is the mishandling or deceptive use of an individual's personal information.[58] It has become a harsh reality for today's employers, especially human resources professionals, since employment records contain just about everything an identity thief could want to know about an individual. A person's identity includes many different items, such as Social Security numbers, driver's license numbers, date of birth, home addresses, e-mail passwords, and ATM information. Gallup's Crime survey shows identity theft as Americans' top-ranked crime concern and a major stressor in today's society, as it can devastate a person's sense of security.[59] Sixty-six percent of U.S. adults say they worry "frequently" or "occasionally" about being a victim of identity theft, higher than the reported anxiety about 11 other types of crime.[60]

Identity theft artists at times contact job hunters who have posted résumés on career Web sites. They make a fake job offer and then ask for a Social Security number and birth date, saying that they need it to conduct a background check. Consider the case of Bob Knoe, a senior marketing executive with 22 years' experience, who had spent several months looking for a new position. He posted his résumé on the Web and one day he received a call from a person who said he was an HR director with a well-known company. The person said he was impressed with the résumé Bob had posted and wanted to meet with him as soon as possible since there appeared to be a perfect match. The HR person said that they needed to get the background check done quickly. A very detailed form was e-mailed to Bob with requests for Social Security number, date of birth, mother's maiden name, even a bank account number. Bob completed the form but did not hear back from the person and became nervous. He tried to get in touch with the individual and could not. Then he tried to use one of his credit cards and discovered that not only was the account maxed out, but several new accounts had been opened in his name and emptied. Certainly, Bob should not have given out this personal information until he was sure that he was dealing with a legitimate company.

James Van Dyke, president and founder of Javelin & Research, said, "Identity fraud is unique among crimes in that it involves at least two victims: the consumer plus an issuer, merchant, processor, or bank."[61] Employers have a duty to protect their employees from identity theft. That means making sure no unauthorized party can gain access to employees' Social Security numbers, banking information (that might show up on direct-deposit authorizations, for example), dates of birth, or any other data criminals could use to steal their money or compromise their privacy.[62] Congress passed the Identity Theft and Assumption Deterrence Act in 1988 that makes it a federal crime when anyone knowingly transfers or uses, without lawful authority, a means of identification of another person with the intent to commit, or to aid or abet, any unlawful activity that constitutes a violation of federal law. The Fair and Accurate Credit Transaction Act passed in 2003, but did not go into effect until 2010, required federal agencies to adopt regulations for financial institutions and creditors to address the act's "identity theft red flag" provision.[63] The Act says employers that negligently or purposely let employees' personally identifiable data fall into the wrong hands can face fines of up to $2,500 per infraction. It applies to customer data, too. But, identity theft crimes continue, and it seems to some that the thieves are getting better. In fact, survey released by Javelin Strategy & Research Inc. revealed that the number of identity fraud adult victims in the U.S. grew to 11.1 million in 2009, a 12 percent increase and the total annual fraud amount rose to 54 billion U.S. dollars, a 12.5 percent increase.[64]

---

identity theft
The mishandling or deceptive use of an individual's personal information.

- **Recognize your own limitations.** Probably among the most stressful conditions you can encounter is being placed in a situation where your limitations and inability to cope become quickly evident.
- **Be tolerant.** Learn to tolerate people for what they are. Being tolerant of others tends to keep you in touch with reality.
- **Pursue outside diversions.** Individuals need to establish a reasonable balance between work and family commitments and leisure.
- **Avoid artificial control.** It is true that loss or lack of control directly contributes to feelings of stress. However, the worst possible solution is to use artificial means to regain that sense of control.

To deal with stress associated with your job, isolate what is and is not important and do not worry about unimportant issues or issues beyond your control.[57]

OBJECTIVE 11.8
Explain burnout.

burnout
Incapacitating condition in which individuals lose a sense of the basic purpose and fulfillment of their work.

Burnout

Burnout, while rarely fatal, is an incapacitating condition in which individuals lose a sense of the basic purpose and fulfillment of their work. Individuals become exhausted either physically or mentally or both when burnout occurs. Seemingly the body or the mind can no longer handle the overwhelmingly high demands placed on it. Burnout differs from stress in that it causes people who have previously been highly committed to their work to become disillusioned and lose interest and motivation. Burnout is often associated with a midlife or midcareer crisis, but it can happen at different times to different people. When this occurs, they may lose their motivation to perform. Burnout is the most common factor leading to the decision to *check out* temporarily.

When burnout occurs, individuals seem to lose their enthusiasm for their job.[65] Burnout is frequently associated with people whose jobs require them to work closely with others under stressful and tension-filled conditions. However, any employee may experience burnout, and no one is exempt. The dangerous part of burnout is that it is contagious. A highly cynical and pessimistic burnout victim can quickly transform an entire group into burnouts. Virtual teams that exist over the long term (more than a year) often run a strong risk of declining performance due to team burnout.

Burnout's price tag is high: it results in reduced productivity, higher turnover, and generally lousy performance. According to the American Institute of Stress, employee burnout costs the U.S. economy about $300 million annually. People often become physically and psychologically weakened from trying to combat it. Although some employees try to hide their problems, shifts in their behavior may indicate dissatisfaction. They may start procrastinating or go to the opposite extreme of taking on too many assignments. They may lose things and become increasingly disorganized. Good-natured individuals may turn irritable. They may become cynical, disagreeable, pompous, or even paranoid. Their motivation toward a project may not be the same as it used to be, and they may dread doing work that they used to enjoy. It is very important that the problem be dealt with quickly. Some means of dealing with burnout include keeping expectations realistic, reducing workload, finding means to relax at work, and developing and maintaining interests outside work.

OBJECTIVE 11.9
Describe the purposes of wellness programs

Wellness Programs

Wellness programs are becoming more widespread as more employers become conscious of the impact employee health has on performance.[66] Despite the recession of 2008/10, more employers created and expanded wellness programs.[67] The traditional view that health is dependent on medical care and is the absence of disease is changing. Today, it is clear that optimal well-being is often achieved through environmental safety, organizational changes, and healthy lifestyles. There is growing evidence that in addition to containing direct medical costs, effective health programs boost productivity, reduce absenteeism, lower turnover and recruiting costs, and improve morale.[68] Infectious diseases, over which a person has little control, are not the problem they once were. From 1900 to 1970, the death rate from major infectious diseases dropped dramatically. However, the death rate from major chronic diseases, such as heart disease, cancer, and stroke, has significantly increased. Today, heart disease and stroke are the top two killers worldwide.[69] Chronic obstructive pulmonary disease and lung cancer are also growing threats to life. Healthy lifestyle measures such as not smoking, eating healthy foods, and exercising more may help prevent these diseases. Some companies offer specific forms of wellness programs that include weight management. BlueCross BlueShield provides an on-site Weight Watchers program, a "buddy system" for support, and a 35 percent discount on healthy options at its cafeterias.[70]

Chronic lifestyle diseases are much more prevalent today than ever before. The good news is that people have a great deal of control over many of them. These are diseases related to smoking, excessive stress, lack of exercise, obesity, and alcohol and drug abuse. Increased recognition of this has prompted employers to become actively involved with their employees' health and to establish wellness programs. Focusing on health care is inherently reactive; focusing on health is proactive and, potentially, a game changer.

There has been a shift toward an approach to improving health that includes involving workers in identifying problems and developing solutions. When Moen Inc., a home-care center supplier, opened its wellness center more than a decade ago, it was viewed primarily as a "soft benefit." Today, it definitely impacts the bottom line. Moen concluded that for every dollar spent on wellness initiatives, Moen adds $3 to $4 from the bottom line. Wellness programs often expand their focus to include other health issues, such as diet, stress, substance abuse, employee assistance programs, and smoking cessation.

In developing a wellness program, firms should first conduct a health-risk assessment (HRA) by surveying their employees to determining which workers could benefit from lifestyle change.[71] Then, a wellness program to address appropriate employee health needs can be implemented. Sometimes getting everyone on board to take a health risk assessment is difficult.

Once companies have identified high-risk employees and the health issues they face, they can determine what programs are needed and offer incentives for participation in activities such as smoking cessation classes or joining Weight Watchers. At Lincoln Plating, everyone gets quarterly health-risk appraisals that include blood-pressure screening and body weight, body fat, and flexibility measurements. Each employee reviews the quarterly results with the wellness manager or occupational nurse and sets individual wellness objectives. For supervisor level and above, it is also tied in with employees' compensation. Dan Krick, Lincoln Plating's vice president of human resources, said, "Last year, it cost me between $500 and a thousand dollars for missing my wellness objective, but I am working harder to meet my goals."[72]

Companies are increasingly using financial incentives to encourage employees to adopt healthier lifestyles either through a discount on premium contributions or cash.[73] Cigarette smokers who received money to quit were 2.9 times more likely to break the habit than those who just tried to do it for their health.[74] In fact, according to one survey of members of the ERISA Industry Council and the National Association of Manufacturers, approximately two-thirds of the employers currently offering wellness programs are using financial incentives to encourage participation. The most common incentive is health insurance premium reductions (40 percent) followed by cash or bonuses (30 percent). PepsiCo adds a $600 health insurance premium surcharge for smokers who do not join cessation programs. Participation increased and smoking quit rates jumped. IBM gives its employees up to two $150 payments each year for completing online family health assessments and for meeting goals for fitness, diet, and weight loss. It also offers financial incentives to employees in fitness programs.[75] A recent survey found that companies are also using penalties against workers for unhealthy behaviors. The most common penalty was higher premium benefits and increased deductibles.[76]

Physical Fitness Programs

OBJECTIVE 11.10
Describe the importance of physical fitness programs.

Physical fitness appears to be critical to career success and employers should be involved in promoting it. The most commonly offered in-house corporate wellness programs involve efforts to promote exercise and fitness. To understand the interest in such programs, consider the results of physical inactivity. They can include obesity, hypertension, heart disease, diabetes, anxiety, depression, and certain types of cancer.

From management's viewpoint, physical fitness programs make a lot of sense. Loss of productivity resulting from coronary disease alone costs U.S. businesses billions of dollars annually. Company-sponsored fitness programs often reduce absenteeism, accidents, and sick pay. There is increasing evidence that if employees stick to company fitness programs, they will experience better health, and the firm will have lower health costs.

Kenneth Cooper, who coined the term *aerobics* (which literally means *with oxygen*), had advice for those with or without access to fitness centers. To begin, he feels that moderate exercise is king. The basic recommendation is 30 minutes of exercise four to five days a week. People do not need to train for a marathon to be healthy; they just need to stop being couch potatoes.[77] He adds, "If you walk fast enough (12 minutes per mile) you can get the same benefits as running a 9-minute mile, without the strain on the joints." His studies also show that cardiovascular training is not enough. He advocated a heart-healthy diet and vitamin supplements like antioxidants. He felt that eliminating tobacco products and habit-forming drugs, controlling alcohol, keeping stress levels down, and getting periodic health exams round out everyone's fitness picture.[78]

Substance Abuse

Failure to test for drugs can sometimes have a disastrous effect on companies large and small. For instance, *Cake for You* is a small specialty bakery. Its service includes making and delivering wedding cakes to receptions. In hiring a delivery driver, *Cake for You* owners were always careful to determine that the potential candidate had a valid driver's license. The owners were quite pleased with their new employee, Mike. He was prompt, neatly attired, and seemed to have a pleasant demeanor. Unfortunately, while making a delivery one morning, Mike was involved in, and in fact caused, a four-vehicle accident that resulted in one fatality. The investigation revealed that Mike was high on marijuana. Had the owners of the firm included drug testing as part of their screening process, they might not be facing a huge lawsuit. In certain industries, such as transportation, for example, drug use on the job is especially hazardous and potentially devastating to the firm. Think of the damage that could be caused by a 40-ton truck careening out of control. Under ideal conditions, a fully loaded truck in daylight on a dry road cannot stop in less than 300 feet, or the length of a football field.

substance abuse
Use of illegal substances or the misuse of controlled substances such as alcohol and drugs.

Substance abuse involves the use of illegal substances or the misuse of controlled substances such as alcohol and drugs. The U.S. Department of Labor reports that the chances your organization employs one or more of the millions of American workers who abuse drugs or alcohol is greater today than ever. Safety consultant Craig Rapp of Utilicom Safety said that substance abusers have higher rates of absenteeism and employee turnover, creating management problems for their employers.[79] Research indicates that between 10 and 20 percent of the nation's workers who die on the job, test positive for alcohol or drugs.[80] Even so, few issues generate more controversy today than substance-abuse testing. Yet, alcohol and drug abuse are definitely workplace issues.

Alcohol Abuse

Although our society attaches a stigma to alcoholism, in 1956, the American Medical Association described it as a treatable disease. **Alcoholism** is a medical disease characterized by uncontrolled and compulsive drinking that interferes with normal living patterns. The National Council on Alcoholism & Drug Dependence (NCADD) reports that 40 percent of workplace fatalities and 47 percent of workplace injuries are related to alcohol consumption. Stress plays an important role in a person becoming an alcoholic. It is a significant problem that affects people at every level of society, and it can both result from and cause excessive stress. As a person starts to drink excessively, the drinking itself produces greater stress. A vicious cycle is created as this increased stress is dealt with by more drinking. Early signs of alcohol abuse are especially difficult to identify. Often the symptoms are nothing more than an increasing number of days absent from work.

alcoholism
Medical disease characterized by uncontrolled and compulsive drinking that interferes with normal living patterns.

Drug Abuse

According to the Substance Abuse & Mental Health Services Administration, more than 1 in 12 American workers report abusing drugs regularly. In industries such as food service and construction, nearly one in five employees admits to illegal drug use.[81] The National Institute of Drug Abuse cites that employees at risk for illegal on-the-job substance use have been shown to have three times more sick days, three times the tardiness rate, three times more accidents, and are five times more likely to file workers' compensation claims than individuals not engaging in illegal substance use.[82] Eighteen million people, ages 18 and older, are illicit drug users, and 79.4 percent (13.4 million) of these are employed.[83] Drug users are increasingly gravitating to the workplace, which is an ideal place to sell drugs. Since 95 percent of *Fortune* 500 companies conduct pre-employment drug screening, 60 percent of employed drug users work for smaller businesses, many of which do not use drug testing.

Web Wisdom

National Council on Alcoholism & Drug Dependence
http://www.ncadd.org/

Fights the stigma and the disease of alcoholism and drug addictions.

All illegal drugs have some adverse effects. Prescription drugs can also be as addictive, impairing, and destructive as common street drugs. According to drug enforcement agencies, at least 25–30 percent of drug abuse in the workplace involves prescription drugs. And standard drug screens do not always detect these drugs.

Substance-Abuse-Free Workplace

The Drug-Free Workplace Act of 1988 requires some federal contractors and all federal grantees to agree that they will provide drug-free workplaces as a condition of receiving a contract or grant from a federal agency (details of the Act may be seen in Table 11.3).

Table 11.3 Drug-Free Workplace Act of 1988

The Drug-Free Workplace Act of 1988 requires some Federal Contractors and all Federal grantees to agree that they will provide drug-free workplaces as a condition of receiving a contract or grant from a Federal agency.

Organizations, with contracts from any U.S. Federal agency, must comply with the provisions of the Act if the contract is in the amount of $100,000 or more. Organizations must do the following:

(A) publish a statement notifying employees that the unlawful manufacture, distribution, dispensation, possession, or use of a controlled substance is prohibited in the person's workplace. The statement should also notify employees of any punitive actions that will be taken.

(B) establish a drug-free awareness program to inform employees about
   (i)   the dangers of drug abuse in the workplace;
   (ii) the policy of maintaining a drug-free workplace;
   (iii) any available drug counseling, rehabilitation, and employee assistance programs; and
   (iv) the penalties that many be imposed upon employees for drug abuse violations.

(C) make it a requirement that each employee be given a copy of the workplace substance abuse policy.

If a contractor is found not to have a drug-free workplace, each contract awarded by any federal agency shall be subject to suspension of payments under the contract or termination of the contract, or both. The contractor may also be ineligible for award of any contract by any federal agency, and for participation in any future procurement by any federal agency, for a period not to exceed 5 years.

Source: http://workplace.samhsa.gov/FedPrograms/FedCntrsGrantee/DTWAct1988.htm, January 8, 2006.

The U. S. Department of Transportation (DOT) requires drug and alcohol testing for drivers of commercial vehicles.[84] Employees that perform "safety-sensitive duties," may be subject to the requirements of the U.S. DOT drug and alcohol testing regulations.[85] There are six situations where testing for alcohol or other drugs is required under federal transportation regulation standards, including: pre-employment, random, post-accident, reasonable suspicion, return-to-duty, and follow-up.[86] Many organizations that do not fall under the Act have opted for an alcohol- and drug-free policy. Drug testing as a component in an organization's selection process is one means of achieving this goal. However, since a large percentage of substance abusers are employed, this is obviously not the only solution to the problem. Firms have tackled the drug abuse problem head-on by establishing a drug-free workplace program. But, some cautions should be taken. Some philosophies and practices that can undermine the effectiveness of drug-free workplace programs may be seen in Table 11.4.

The steps for establishing a substance-abuse-free workplace may be seen in Figure 11.2. Note that the first step is to establish a drug- and alcohol-free policy.[87] The U.S. Department of Labor offers a Drug-Free Workplace Advisor that offers guidance on how to develop a drug- and alcohol-free workplace. At Texas Instruments, the policy is simple and straightforward: "There will be no use of any illegal drug."

The second step is to provide education and training for supervisors and workers. At a minimum, supervisor training should include a review of the drug-free workplace policy, the supervisor's specific responsibilities in implementing the policy, and ways to recognize and deal with employees who have job performance problems that could be related to alcohol and drug

Table 11.4 Philosophies and Practices That Can Undermine the Effectiveness of Drug-Free Workplace Programs

- Focusing only on illicit drug use and failing to include alcohol—the number one drug of abuse in our society
- Accepting drug use and alcohol abuse as part of modern life and a cost of doing business
- Overreliance on drug testing
- Focusing on termination of users rather than rehabilitation
- Reluctance of supervisors to confront employees on the basis of poor performance
- Reinforcing an individual's denial regarding the impact of his/her alcohol and drug use
- Restricting benefits and/or access to treatment of alcoholism and addiction
- Allowing insurers to restrict access to treatment programs

Source: http://www.dol.gov/elaws/asp/drugfree/drugs/screen5.asp?selection_list=, January 3, 2006.

Figure 11.2

Developing a Substance-Abuse-Free Workplace

use. Managers must learn to recognize impaired or intoxicated employees and those who may be addicted. Table 11.5 lists signs that *suggest* an employee may be a substance abuser. Many indicators of poor performance also may be signs of medical or mental health problems. The existence of these indicators alone is not adequate to determine the presence or absence of any condition. The supervisor should never try to diagnose, make accusations, or treat such problems. The indicators provide the supervisor a basis for making a referral to a person who can help the employee, such as an Employee Assistance Program.

Employees should also be educated as to the purpose and ramifications of the drug- and alcohol-free environment. The purpose of this training is to familiarize employees with the drug-free workplace program and provide general awareness education about the dangers of alcohol and drug abuse. Employees should be informed about the requirements of the organization's drug-free workplace policy, the prevalence of alcohol and drug abuse and their impact on the workplace, how to recognize the connection between poor performance and alcohol and/or drug abuse, the progression of the disease of alcohol and drug addiction, and what types of assistance may be available. The program should send a clear message that use of alcohol and drugs in the workplace is prohibited. Employees are encouraged to voluntarily seek help with alcohol and drug problems.

There are hundreds of substances that people abuse. These include marijuana, cocaine, amphetamines, heroin and other opiates, ecstasy, LSD, PCP, rohypnol, inhalants, alcohol, and steroids. As a supervisor, it is beneficial to have a basic knowledge of the most commonly abused drugs and their effects. The two most commonly abused drugs are marijuana and cocaine. Some signs of marijuana use include red eyes, dry mouth, slowed reaction time, increased hunger, paranoia, short-term memory loss, and a distorted sense of time. The most common signs of cocaine use are dilated pupils, increased energy and excited speech. Some cocaine users may also experience frequent nose bleeds.[88]

Table 11.5 Signs of Possible Substance Abuse

- Excessive absenteeism
- Radical mood swings
- Decline in personal appearance
- Smell of alcohol or other physical evidence of substance abuse
- Accident proneness and multiple workers' compensation claims
- Lack of coordination
- Psychomotor agitation or retardation. Alcohol, marijuana, and opioids can all cause fatigue. Cocaine, amphetamines, and hallucinogens can cause anxiety.
- Thought disturbances. Cocaine, alcohol, PCP, amphetamines, and inhalants often cause grandiosity or a subject sense of profound thought.
- Other indicators. Cocaine, PCP, and inhalants can all cause aggressive or violent behavior. Alcohol and other sedatives reduce inhibition. Marijuana increases appetite, whereas stimulants decrease it. Both types of drugs cause excessive thirst.

Sources: "Are You Prepared?" *Safety Management* (January 2003): 7; Deanna Kelemen, "How to Recognize Substance Abuse in the Workplace," *Supervision* 56 (September 1995): 4.

Implementing a Drug-Testing Program

The third step in establishing a substance-abuse-free workplace is to implement a drug-testing program. A drug-free workplace program should balance the rights of employees and the rights of employers, balance the need to know and rights to privacy, balance detection and rehabilitation, and balance the respect for employees and the safety of all. The difficulty is not in formulating the policy, but rather in implementing it. Also, remember that the Americans with Disabilities Act protects an employee in a substance-abuse rehabilitation program. Most of the larger corporations in the United States require some form of workplace drug testing. These proponents of drug-testing programs contend that they are necessary to ensure workplace safety, security, and productivity.

Urine, blood, oral fluids, or hair samples are possible drug testing methods, with most employers relying on urine testing. However, the majority regard blood tests as the forensic benchmark against which to compare others. The problem with this approach is that it is invasive and requires trained personnel for administration and analysis. The use of hair samples is unique in that drug traces will remain in the hair and will not likely diminish over time. Human hair samples are easy to collect, store, and transport, and they are difficult to change. Newer human hair drug tests said that 10 times as many job applicants and employees take cocaine and methamphetamines than found in urine tests. Although urine and blood testing can detect only current drug use, advocates of hair sample analysis claim it can detect drug use from 3 days to 90 days after drug consumption. This would prohibit an applicant from beating the test by short-term abstinence. [89]

When the oral fluid method is used, the collection pad is saturated and the individual places the swab in a collection vial, snaps off the handle, seals the container, and hands it over for analysis. Oral fluid testing is especially well-suited to cases of reasonable suspicion and post-accident testing. Oral fluid is a great deterrent because it can be done immediately in the workplace and it does not give an individual an opportunity to adulterate or substitute a urine specimen. From a prospective employee's viewpoint, oral fluid and hair testing may be less embarrassing than a urine test. For example, it is humiliating for a candidate to hear, "We're really happy to have you on board. But, will you take this cup and fill it?"

The final step in obtaining a substance-abuse-free workplace is the creation of an employee assistance program.

Employee Assistance Programs

OBJECTIVE 11.12
Describe employee
assistance programs.

**employee assistance
program (EAP)**
Comprehensive approach
that many organizations
have taken to deal with
burnout, alcohol and drug
abuse, and other emotional
disturbances.

The Drug-Free Workplace Act also requires federal employees and employees of firms under government contract to have access to employee assistance program services. An **employee assistance program (EAP)** is a comprehensive approach that many organizations have taken to deal with numerous problem areas such as burnout, alcohol and drug abuse, and other emotional disturbances.

As you would imagine, EAPs grew rapidly in number following that Act. Returns on investment in EAPs will vary but one estimate is that a mature, well-run program will return a minimum of three dollars for every dollar spent on it. Advantages claimed for EAPs include lower absenteeism, decreases in workers' compensation claims, and fewer accidents.

Whether managed in-house or outsourced, EAPs have traditionally focused first on mental health, including substance-abuse counseling. Today, companies are aware that the advantages of an EAP extend well beyond assistance for alcohol-related problems.[90] Many have expanded to include financial and legal advice, referrals for day care and elder care and a host of other services, including assistance with marital or family difficulties, job performance problems, stress, and grief. The recession of 2008/2010 caused some EAPs to move beyond mental health to serve recession-induced employee issues such as financial and legal challenges.[91] In an EAP, most or all of the costs (up to a predetermined amount) are borne by the employer. The EAP concept includes a response to personal psychological

A GLOBAL PERSPECTIVE

Global Healthcare for Expats

Healthcare coverage in the U.S., Australia, United Kingdom, and Western Europe are generally well established. But, a growing number of expats are being sent to emerging markets, including Central and Eastern Europe, the Far East, and Africa. Expats going to these countries expect to be supported with healthcare benefits such as private medical insurance, life insurance, and evacuation and repatriation coverage in the event of a medical emergency.[92] Michael Plaugmann, senior adviser on private medical insurance at Mercer, says, "Healthcare is a top priority whenever employees are sent overseas and, as a valuable attraction and retention tool, companies have to get that benefit right. However, what we have found is that although international markets are developing rapidly and new markets continue to emerge, employers are failing to update their expat benefit policies to ensure they are providing the best cover for a particular market or assignment."[93]

Although expats are usually covered by group international health plans, there is a trend to offer coverage tailored for specific destinations. For example, Bupa International has begun a European Health Plan, which provides Europe-wide cover for people working in Bulgaria, the Czech Republic, Estonia, Hungary, Latvia, Lithuania, Poland, Romania, Slovakia, and Slovenia. Tim Slee, global sales director at Bupa International, says, "Eastern Europe is a growth area economically, but medical provision and health systems are not always highly regarded compared to wider European standards. As international markets develop, we envisage a need for a more modular solution, and the provision of cover that is more appropriate for the market expats are working in."[94]

European healthcare systems vary in cost and quality. Further, a lot can depend on the exact location of the expat within a country. Although Slovakia is generally recognized as having adequate medical facilities in its major cities, outside these areas the standard of care is less reliable. There may also be language barriers to overcome. Most highly populated eastern European towns speak English but as one moves to less populated areas, there are fewer English-speaking medical staff.[95]

Matt Gales, regional sales consultant at Expacare, which recently begun a plan that provides coverage for companies with fewer than five employees, says, "If you are sending people to work in places where standards of local healthcare and medical treatment are uncertain, you have to provide insurance cover that gives them peace of mind." Sarah Dennis, international business consultant with Jelf Group, who has just returned from Hungary, says, "It was clear that while standards in some medical facilities were outstanding, in others they were poor. With such a lack of consistency, employers can't afford to provide anything less than a full international healthcare benefits package."[96]

Health care legislation is often different as a person goes from country to country. For example, Abu Dhabi has compulsory coverage for expatriates and requires a full refund for maternity costs and coverage for chronic conditions. Abu Dhabi imposes minimum health insurance requirements for expats. Any failure by international insurers to make sure their products comply could jeopardize the working visas of the expats they are covering.[97] In Switzerland, the rules vary between districts. Some require the expatriate to buy medical insurance from an organization in that district. The Dutch require any person who resides in the Netherlands to hold a health insurance policy that meets certain requirements, including preexisting and chronic conditions. On the other hand, France operates a system in which the state provides free health care, with individuals either paying for any shortfall or taking out insurance to cover it.[98] Legislation in Australia requires proof of insurance by all non-Australian citizens who do not have reciprocal healthcare agreements in place in the country.[99]

---

problems that interfere with both an employee's well-being and overall productivity. The purpose of assistance programs is to provide emotionally troubled employees with the same consideration and assistance given employees with physical illnesses. Just having an EAP sends a message that the employer cares, and this can provide considerable encouragement for employees.

A primary concern is getting employees to use the program. Some employees perceive that there is a stigma attached to *needing help*. Supervisors must receive training designed to provide specialized interpersonal skills for recognizing troubled employees and encouraging them to use the firm's employee assistance program. Addicted employees are often experts at denial and deception, and they can fool even experienced counselors.

Summary

1. *Describe the nature and role of safety and health.* Safety involves protecting employees from injuries due to work-related accidents. Health refers to the employees' freedom from physical or emotional illness.

2. *Explain the role of the Occupational Safety and Health Administration.* The role of the administration is to ensure a safe and healthful workplace for every American worker.

3. *Describe the economic impact of safety and explain the focus of safety programs.* Job-related deaths and injuries of all types extract a high toll not only in terms of human misery, but also in economic loss. The significant financial costs are often passed along to the consumer in the form of higher prices. Thus, job-related deaths and injuries affect everyone, directly or indirectly. Safety risks can be significant for employers. In addition to workers' compensation costs, OSHA can levy major fines.

   Safety programs may be designed to accomplish their purposes in two primary ways. The first approach is to create a psychological environment and attitudes that promote safety. The second approach to safety program design is to develop and maintain a safe physical working environment.

4. *Describe the consequences of repetitive stress injuries.* Repetitive stress injuries (RSIs) are a group of conditions caused by placing too much stress on a joint when the same action is performed repeatedly. The U.S. Bureau of Labor Statistics reports that repetitive stress injuries account for 25 percent of cases involving days away from work and that disorders associated with repetitive stress account for nearly 60 percent of all work-related illness.

5. *Explain the purpose of ergonomics.* Ergonomics is the study of human interaction with tasks, equipment, tools, and the physical environment. Through ergonomics, the goal is to fit the machine and work environment to the person, rather than require the person to make the adjustment.

6. *Explain the effect of workplace and domestic violence on businesses.* OSHA defines workplace violence as physical assault, threatening behavior, verbal abuse, hostility, or harassment directed toward employees at work or on duty. Workplace violence affects more than 2 million workers each year. In the United States, 20 percent of all violent crimes occur in the workplace. The National Institute for Occupational Safety and Health estimates that, in an average week, 20 workers are murdered and 18,000 others assaulted at U.S. workplaces. Homicide is the second leading cause of death on the job, second only to motor vehicle crashes.

   Spillover from domestic violence is a threat to both women and their companies. Domestic violence has become an epidemic in this country. Each year about 1,200 women are killed and 2 million are injured by their partners. The fastest-growing form of homicide is murder in the workplace. Homicide is the leading cause of on-the-job death for women and the number-two cause of death for men. Spillover from domestic violence is an unexpected threat to both women and their companies.

7. *Describe the nature of stress and means of managing stress.* Stress is the body's nonspecific reaction to any demand made on it. Three general areas from which stress may emanate include the organization (including the firm's culture), the jobs people perform, and working conditions. Personal factors focus on the family and financial problems. Finally, the general environment also contains elements that may produce stress.

   Stress may be coped with through numerous means, including exercise, following good diet habits, knowing when to pull back, putting the stressful situation into perspective, finding someone who will listen, establishing some structure in your life, recognizing your own limitations, being tolerant, pursuing outside diversions, and avoiding artificial control.

8. *Explain burnout.* Burnout, although rarely fatal, is an incapacitating condition whereby individuals lose a sense of the basic purpose and fulfillment of their work.

9. *Describe the purposes of wellness programs.* Wellness programs are becoming more widespread as more employers become conscious of the impact employee health has on performance. Today, the prevailing opinion is that optimal health can generally be achieved through environmental safety, organizational changes, and changed lifestyles.

10. *Describe the importance of physical fitness programs.* Many U.S. business firms have exercise programs designed to help keep their workers physically fit. These programs often reduce absenteeism, accidents, and sick pay.

11. *Explain substance abuse, describe substance-abuse-free workplaces, and describe how to implement a drug-testing program.* Substance abuse involves the use of illegal substances or the misuse of controlled substances such as alcohol

and drugs. The Drug-Free Workplace Act of 1988 requires some federal contractors and all federal grantees to agree that they will provide drug-free workplaces as a condition of receiving a contract or grant from a federal agency.

The first steps for establishing a substance-abuse-free workplace is to establish a drug- and alcohol-free policy. The second step is to provide education and training for supervisors and workers. The third step in establishing a substance-abuse-free workplace is to implement a drug-testing program. The final step in obtaining a substance-abuse-free workplace is the creation of an employee assistance program.

12. *Describe employee assistance programs.* An employee assistance program is a comprehensive approach that many organizations develop to deal with marital or family problems; job performance problems; stress, emotional, or mental health issues; financial troubles; alcohol and drug abuse; and grief.

Key Terms

safety   320
health   320
job hazard analysis (JHA)   324
repetitive stress injuries   326
carpal tunnel syndrome (CTS)   326

ergonomics   326
workplace violence   327
negligent retention   328
stress   329
identity theft   332

burnout   333
substance abuse   335
alcoholism   335
employee assistance program
  (EAP)   338

Questions for Review

1. What has been the impact of smoking and the workplace?
2. Define *safety* and *health.*
3. What is the purpose of the Occupational Safety and Health Act?
4. What are the primary ways in which safety programs are designed? Discuss.
5. What is the purpose of job hazard analysis?
6. What is the purpose of the Superfund Amendments Reauthorization Act, Title III (SARA)?
7. Why are companies concerned with repetitive stress injuries? What is carpal tunnel syndrome?
8. Define *ergonomics.* What is the purpose of ergonomics?
9. What effect does workplace and domestic violence have on an organization?
10. Why should a firm attempt to identify stressful jobs?
11. Why should a firm be concerned with employee burnout?
12. What are the purposes of wellness programs?
13. Why might physical fitness programs be established in organizations?
14. What is the purpose of substance-abuse-free workplaces in organizations?
15. What are the steps for establishing a substance-abuse-free workplace?
16. What is an employee assistance program?

HRM INCIDENT 1

What a Change!

"Just leave me alone and let me do my job," said Manuel Gomez. Dumbfounded, Bill Brown, Manuel's supervisor, decided to count to 10 and did not respond to Manuel's comment. As he walked back to his office, Bill thought about how Manuel had changed over the past few months. He had been a hard worker and extremely cooperative when he started working for Bill two years earlier. The company had sent Manuel to two training schools and had received glowing reports about his performance in each of them.

Until about a year ago, Manuel had a perfect attendance record and was an ideal employee. At about that time, however, he began to have personal problems, which resulted in a divorce six months later. Manuel had several times requested a day off to take care of personal business. Bill attempted to help in every way he could without getting directly involved in Manuel's personal affairs. But Bill was aware of the strain Manuel must have experienced as his marriage broke up, and he and his wife engaged in the inevitable disputes over child custody, alimony payments, and property.

During the same time period, top management initiated a push for improving productivity. Bill found it necessary to put additional pressure on all his workers, including Manuel. He tried to be considerate, but he had to become much more performance-oriented, insisting on increased output from every worker. As time went on, Manuel began to show up late for work, and actually missed two days without calling Bill in advance. Bill attributed Manuel's behavior to extreme stress. Because Manuel had been such a good worker for so long, Bill excused the tardiness and absences, only gently suggesting that Manuel should try to do better.

Sitting at his desk, Bill thought about what might have caused Manuel's outburst a few minutes earlier. Bill had suggested to Manuel that he shut down the machine he was operating and clean up the surrounding area. This was a normal part of Manuel's job and something he had been careful to do in the past. Bill felt the disorder around Manuel's machine might account for the increasing number of defects in the parts he was making. "This is a tough one. I think I'll talk to the boss about it," thought Bill.

Questions

1. What do you think is likely to be Manuel's problem? Discuss.
2. How might use of an employee assistance program help in this situation?

HRM INCIDENT 2

I'm Just Stressed Out!

Betty had always been the perfect employee. Her attitude was positive and she showed an understanding of all her colleagues at work. She spoke politely and fulfilled her tasks without any questions. Fun Fashions was a young, yet thriving business. The founder and owner, Samantha Wallace, had a well-established organization and most importantly, she was doing something she loved.

Samantha recruited Betty as her personal assistant ten years ago. Samantha trusted Betty completely because she had proven to be loyal and committed to Fun Fashions despite the many family problems Samantha knew she had. Still, Betty always had a smile on her face and this seemed to rub off on all other staff members, which resulted in a friendly work environment.

However, the last three weeks had revealed another side of Betty. She was late coming in and would rush off early. She now snapped at her co-workers and Samantha. What's more, the smile that made everyone's day had transformed into a frown. Samantha even noticed tears in Betty's eyes all the time.

"Without a doubt, something really terrible has happened to change her behavior," Samantha explained to John, the HR manager, who mentioned that the employees were complaining about Betty's attitude. "What do you want me to do?" John asked, "I didn't want to take action before discussing the matter with you."

"I'll talk to her," Samantha insisted. The following day, Samantha asked Betty to stay after everyone had left. Betty felt butterflies in her stomach and knew what to expect but "how do I respond?" she thought.

As soon as everyone had left, Samantha immediately addressed Betty by saying she was worried about her. "I know something is wrong. It's not like you to be angry and agitated at work and your productivity has really been bad. Talk to me, Betty."

As the tears swelled in her eyes, Betty thanked Samantha for being so patient. "I know I have been very negative lately and that this has reflected badly on the other employees and on my duties. But, I'm just so stressed out! I don't know what to do." Betty continued to explain that David, her husband, had left the house. As a result, she was left with three children and debts. "I'm so sorry, I didn't want to bring my problems to work but I had no choice."

"The stress is escalating and I just don't know how to manage it. Please help me, Samantha!"

Questions

1. How did Betty's attitude affect the work environment at Fun Fashions? Explain.
2. How would you describe Betty's change in character? Was it stress or burnout? Why?

Notes

1. "Even in Difficult Times, Employees See the Value of Smoking Cessation Programs," *Managed Care Outlook* 22 (June 1, 2009): 10–12.
2. Andrew Webber, "Tobacco-Cessation Efforts Are a U.S. Business Imperative," *Benefits & Compensation Digest* 46 (October 2009): 1/17.
3. Lydell C. Bridgeford, "Smoke Gets in Your Eyes," *Employee Benefit News* 22 (January 2008): 33–34.
4. "Smoking Ban Has Huge Heart Attack Impact," *Work-Life Newsbrief & Trend Report* (February 2009): 6–7.
5. Kathy Gurchiek, "Study: Smoking Ban Improved Air," *HRMagazine* 50 (January 2005): 34.
6. Paul McIntyre, "A Smoking Ban Isn't About Your Bottom Line, It's About Protecting Your Workers' Health," *Nation's Restaurant News* 39 (December 5, 2005): 24–34.
7. Ibid.
8. Katherine Harmon, "Carcinogens Detected from 'Thirdhand Smoke'," *Scientific American* 302 (April 2010): 29.
9. Joanne Wojcik, "President Should Light the Smoke-free Path," *Business Insurance* 43 (February 16, 2009): 6.
10. http://www.lungusa.org/ January 1, 2010.
11. "Study Shows Smoke-Free Policies Cut Hospitalization Costs," *HRMagazine* 54 (May 2009): 29.
12. Monica Dobie, "Quit Smoking or Lose Your Job," *World Tobacco* (May 2005): 20–21.
13. http://slati.lungusa.org/appendixf.asp
14. "Should Employer Have Recognized The Hazard?" *Safety Compliance Letter* February 1, 2010): 8.
15. http://www.osha.gov/ October 27, 2009.
16. http://www.osha.gov/dcsp/smallbusiness/index.html October 27, 2009.
17. Palema Babcock, "'A New Day' for Safety and Health," *HRMagazine* 54 (May 2009): 24.
18. Beth Mirza, "More Safety Inspections, More Enforcement, Civil Penalties," *HRMagazine* 55 (June 2010): 18.
19. "OSHA Flags High Injury and Illness Rates," *HRMagazine* 54 (June 2009): 24.
20. "OSHA $100,000 Club of Safety Citations," *EHS Today* 3 (February 2010): 33–34.
21. Jennifer Busick, "Whistleblower Protections Go Beyond Refusal to Perform Hazardous Work," *Safety Compliance Letter* (May 1, 2010): 5–6.
22. "The High Price of Injuries, Accidents," *Industrial Engineer* 42 (April 2010): 19.
23. Benjamin Treppa, "Perceived Trends in Ergonomics," *EHS Today* 2 (September 2009): 26–27.
24. Robert J. Miletsky, "Job Hazard Analysis Helps Contractors & Subcontractors Isolate & Address Risks," *Contractor's Business Management Report* 2009 (March 2009): 1/15.
25. "Ergo Claims & Costs Keep Climbing," *Industrial Safety & Hygiene News* 39 (March 2005): 12.
26. Milford Prewitt, "Workers' Comp for RSI-Related Injuries More Costly Overall," *Nation's Restaurant News* 39 (June 13, 2005): 1.
27. James Mellon, "Ergonomics—What's Real and What's Not," *EHS Today* 3 (January 2010): 18–19.
28. "Ergonomics Yield Benefits for Schneider," *Traffic World* 270 (April 10, 2006): 27.
29. Derek Timm, "Ergonomic Workplace Strategies Don't Have to Break the Bank," *Healthcare Purchasing News* 31 (2008): 86–87.
30. "Economic Crisis Raises Potential for Workplace Violence," *Teller Vision* (January 2009): 1–2.
31. Cassandra Dillenberger, "Avoiding Workplace Violence Incidents," *Contractor's Business Management Report* 2010 (February 2010): 1/13.
32. "Understanding and Preventing Violence in the Workplace," *Safety Compliance Letter* (March 1, 2009): 7–16.
33. Mariene Piturro, "Workplace Violence," *Strategic Finance Magazine* 82 (May 2001): 35.
34. Barbara Mulhern, Harlan Amandus, and Daniel Hartley, "History of Violence." *Convenience Store News* 43 (November 22, 2007): 151–156.
35. Michael Klaassen and Brian H. Kleiner, "Are You Risking a Negligent-Retention Lawsuit?" *Nonprofit World* 27 (March/April 2009): 17–19.
36. Cole A. Wist and Hugh C. Thatcher, "Workplace Violence: An American Secret," *Labor & Employment Law* 38 (Winter 2010): 6.

37. Dennis A. Davis, "Take a Proactive Approach to Prevent Workplace Violence," *HR Specialist: Texas Employment Law* 5 (January 2010): 6.

38. Todd Henneman, "Ignoring Signs of Violence Can Be a Fatal, Costly Mistake," *Workforce Management* 85 (February 27, 2006): 10–11.

39. "How to Predict and Prevent Workplace Violence," *HR Focus* 82 (April 2005): 10–11.

40. Libby John, "A Real Threat," *U.S. Business Review* 9 (April 2008): 112.

41. "Workplace Violence Update: What You Should Know Now," *HR Focus* 85 (June 2008): 7–11.

42. "Preventing Serious Domestic Violence Spillover Events," *Security Director's Report* 10 (January 2010): 1–13.

43. "What to Do When Domestic Violence Comes to Work," *HR Focus* 87 (January 2010): 10–11.

44. "How Domestic Violence Affects Workplaces—and What to Do," *HR Focus* 82 (January 2005): 9.

45. Lydell C. Bridgford, "Piercing the Veil of Silence: Domestic Violence and the Workplace," *Employee Benefit News* 20 (August 2006): 21.

46. "Services Provided to Victims of Domestic Violence, Sexual Assault, Dating Violence, and Stalking: GAO-07-846R," *GAO Reports* (July 19, 2007): 1–29.

47. Joanne Descheneaux, "Domestic Violence Victims Have Workplace Protection," *HRMagazine* 53 (March 2008): 32.

48. "Leading Productivity Killers in Today's Market: Overwork, Stress," *HR Focus* 85 (April 2008): 8.

49. "Will Stress Be Your Next Wellness Target?" *HR Focus* 85 (January 2008): 12.

50. "Employers Respond to Rising Workplace Stress," *HR Specialist: Illinois Employment Law* 4 (February 2010): 5.

51. Stephanie Schomer, "Under Pressure," *Fast Company* (April 2010): 112.

52. "Layoff 'Survivor' Stress: How to Manage the Guilt and the Workload," *HR Focus* 86 (August 2009): 4–6.

53. Leslie Stevens-Huffman, "It Pays to Reduce Stress," *Smart Business Northern California* 1 (November 2008): 22.

54. Katherine Hobson, "Beware: Your Job May Be Killing You," *U.S. News & World Report* 147 (February 2010): 50.

55. "Workplace Stress Taking a Harsh Toll," *Teller Vision* (April 2008): 4–5.

56. "Stress Craters Productivity and Your Retention Efforts," *Compensation & Benefits for Law Offices* 8 (April 2008): 4–6.

57. Shane R. Premeaux, R. Wayne Mondy, and Arthur Sharplin, "Stress and the First-Line Supervisor," *Supervisory Management* 30 (July 1985): 36–40.

58. Stephanie Shapson Peet, "Employers Are Stung with a Hefty Price When Employees Suffer an Identity Theft," *Supervision* 69 (July 2008): 10–12.

59. "Peer to Peer: Challenges for Trustees—Identity Theft and Fraud," *Benefits & Compensation Digest* 47 (May 2010): 24–25.

60. Lydia Saad, "Two in Three Americans Worry About Identity Theft," *Gallup Poll Briefing* (October 16, 2009): 1.

61. "Identity Fraud Down, Yet Cost to Consumer Rises, Javelin Finss," *CardLine* 8 (February 15, 2008): 18.

62. "Preventing Identity Theft: 6 Steps to Protect Employees' Data," *HR Specialist* 3 (September 2009): 4.

63. "FTC Red Flags Rule Checklist," *Health Care Registration: The Newsletter for Health Care Registration Professionals* 19 (March 2010): 3–5.

64. "Identity Fraud Reaches New High," *Teller Vision* (April 2010): 2–3.

65. Aiesha D. Little, "Beating Burnout," *Quill* 96 (May 2008): 34.

66. "Workplace Wellness: Getting the Best Return on Your Investment," *EHS Today* 3 (April 2010): 43–45.

67. Jennifer Schramm, "Wellness: Health's Keystone," *HRMagazine* 55 (January 2010): 68.

68. Nina Taggart, "A New Competitive Advantage: Connecting the Dots Between Employee Health and Productivity," *Benefits & Compensation Digest* 46 (June 2009): 20–23.

69. Ann D. Clark, "The New Frontier of Wellness," *Benefits Quarterly* 24 (2nd Quarter 2008): 23–28.

70. Pamela Babcock, "Getting the Weight Off," *HRMagazine* 53 (January 2008): 60–66.

71. Raymond Fabius, "Time to Take Better Care of Our Own," *Physician Executive* 35 (September/October 2009): 18–23.

72. Stephenie Overman, "Lincoln Plating Benefits from Strategic Wellness Program," *Employee Benefit News* 19 (October 1, 2005): 67–68.

73. Susan J. Wells, "Getting Paid for Staying Well," *HRMagazine* 55 (February 2010): 59–62.

74. Coco Ballantyne, "Quitters' Cash," *Scientific American* 300 (April 2009): 31.

75. "Wellness Incentives & Disincentives: 4 Case Studies," *HR Specialist* 8 (August 2009): 2.

76. "Growing Interest Among U.S. Employers to Penalize Workers for Unhealthy Behaviors," *Medical Benefits* 27 (April 30, 2010): 5–6.

77. Pamela Kufahl, "Success Requires the Facts," *Fitness Business Pro* 24 (September 2008): 6.

78. Jodi Schneider, "More Fit in Less Time," *U.S. News & World Report* 132 (May 13, 2002): 50–51.

79. Masha Zager, "Don't Abuse Substance-Abuse Testing," *Rural Telecom* 29 (January/February 2010): 46–49.

80. T. L. Stanley, "Workplace Substance Abuse: A Grave Problem," *Supervision* 70 (June 2009): 18–21.

81. Nancy N. Delogu, "Essential Elements of a Drug-Free Workplace Program," *Professional Safety* 52 (November 2007): 48–51.

82. Paul Meskanick, "Critical Success Factors for Recruitment Process Outsourcing (RPO)," *Offshore* 69 (June 2009): 8–11.

83. Mary M. Cox, "Workplace Substance Abuse Prevalent," *Toledo Business Journal* 25 (January 2009): 21–22.

84. David Kolman, "Drug Testing Compliance Testing Promotes Safety," *Beverage Industry* 100 (April 2009): 54.

85. "DOT Drug and Alcohol Testing," *Industrial Safety & Hygiene News* (June 2009): 70.

86. Sara Wesche, "Not on Your Watch: Behavioral Cues Can Flag Substance Abusers," *Industrial Safety & Hygiene News* 43 (June 2009): 60–61.

87. "Creating Drug-free Workplace: How to Draft a Policy, Conduct Legal Tests," *HR Specialist: Employment Law* 40 (May 2010): 4.

88. Ibid.

89. Del Jones, "Hair Tests Nail Drug Use at Work," *USA Today* (November 20, 2009): 3B.

90. Sean Fogarty, "EAPs New Role: A Core Strategic Element," *Employee Benefit Advisor* 8 (April 2010): 40–46.

91. Mike Garfield, "Silver Lining," *Benefits Selling* 8 (February 2010): 22–27.

92. "International Healthcare: Taking Care in New Regions," *Marketing Week* 32 (January 15, 2009): S9.

93. Ibid.

94. Ibid.

95. Ibid.

96. Ibid.

97. "International Healthcare: Taking Care in New Regions," *Marketing Week* 32 (January 15, 2009): S9.

98. Sam Barrett, "Keep Global Perks at a Healthy Level," *Employee Benefits* Special section (February 2008): 13–14.

99. Mark Coleman, "The Emperor's New Clothes or Global Healthcare Savvy?" *Employee Benefits* Special Section (January 2010): 2.

CHAPTER 12 Labor Unions and Collective Bargaining

HRM in Action: The Two-Tier Wage System Returns

In 1986, I was a coauthor of an article entitled, "The Two-Tier Wage System: A Major Breakthrough in the Reindustrialization of America?" for *Personnel Administrator,* now entitled *HRMagazine.* In the article we defined a **two-tier wage system** as "a wage structure where newly hired workers are paid less than current employees for performing the same or similar jobs."[1] We said that the trend in labor/management wage negotiations was this so-called two-tier wage system. At the time of the writing of the article, two-tier contracts had already been negotiated in the airline, copper, trucking, auto, and aerospace industries. Shortly afterwards, our projections proved to be incorrect and the two-tier wage system died.

But more than two decades later it has come back to life. UAW and General Motors negotiated a contract that included provisions for a two-tier wage system. The negotiated wage scale for any new *noncore employees* was $14 per hour which is half of what a typical worker would earn. Twenty percent of GM's employees are in this category. This category of workers will, however, receive traditional health care benefits and has the possibility to ultimately convert to a traditional job.[2] With the settlement between the UAW and General Motors, Chrysler and Ford were not far behind. But, there is a little difference. Ford makes no distinction between production and nonproduction workers for a new-hire wage; all new hires will be paid at the lower rate. Chrysler, however, followed GM's lead and paid nonproduction workers the lower wage.[3]

The automobile manufacturers are not the only U.S. companies to implement the two-tier wage system. Goodyear's contract with the United Steelworkers, covering 16 U.S. and Canadian sites, has a two-tier structure. [4]

After completing this chapter, students should be able to:

1. Describe the two-tier wage system.

2. Describe union objectives and explain the reasons why employees join unions.

3. Describe organized labor's strategies for a stronger movement and describe the basic structure of a union.

4. Define *collective bargaining* and identify the steps that lead to forming a bargaining unit.

5. Describe the collective bargaining process and explain collective bargaining issues.

6. Describe preparation for negotiations, negotiating the agreement, and breakdowns in negotiations.

7. Describe what is involved in reaching, ratifying, and administering the agreement.

8. Describe the grievance procedure in a union environment.

9. Explain recent/labor management legal trends and describe collective bargaining in the public sector.

10. Explain union decertification.

11. Describe the state of unions today.

The two-tier wage system is also being implemented in the U.S.-Mexican auto industry; unions are starting to agree to two-tier wages to win or keep auto plants in their nation. Ford Motor Co. agreed to build the Ford Fiesta at a factory in Cuautitlán, near Mexico City. However, even though the $3 billion project will employ 4,500 workers, some will be paid as little as $2.25 per hour, which is about half the current union rate.[5]

In recent negotiations between Precision Tube Co. and the United Steelworkers union, the company demanded mandatory overtime, reduction of vacation and personal days, more expensive family health insurance premiums and two-tiered wages that would have newly hired workers making around $9 per hour instead of the current $15.09 per hour.[6] Under the new labor management agreement, the union kept the personal days the company had tried to alter; and overtime was more restrictive than the original proposal. The union gave in on the company's request for a two-tier wage system, but no more than 25 percent of the work force will be paid the second-tier lower wages.[7]

The two-tier system has not received universal support. Some argue that the two-tier contracts have been associated with increased employee turnover, lower employee morale, and reduced productivity. However, it continues as a form of concessionary bargaining as organizations attempt to lower their compensation costs.[8]

This chapter begins by first discussing the two-tier wage system. Then, union objectives are discussed and the reasons why employees join unions are explained. Next, organized labor's strategies for a stronger movement are described and the basic structure of the union is described. Then, *collective bargaining* is defined followed by describing the steps that lead to forming a bargaining unit. Afterwards, collective bargaining and the collective bargaining process are described. After that, bargaining issues and preparation for negotiation are explained. Next, negotiating the agreement and ways to overcome breakdowns in negotiations are explained. Then, topics related to reaching, ratifying, and administering the agreement are presented. Subsequently, the grievance procedure in a union environment is discussed and recent/labor management legal trends are explained followed by describing collective bargaining in the public sector. The chapter concludes with sections on union decertification, the status of unions today, and a global perspective entitled "Union Organizing in the Global Environment Can Be Dangerous."

Union Objectives

The labor movement has a long history in the United States. Although each union is a unique organization seeking its own objectives, several broad objectives characterize the labor movement as a whole:

1. To secure and, if possible, improve the living standards and economic status of its members.
2. To enhance and, if possible, guarantee individual security against threats and contingencies that might result from market fluctuations, technological change, or management decisions.
3. To influence power relations in the social system in ways that favor and do not threaten union gains and goals.
4. To advance the welfare of all who work for a living, whether union members or not.
5. To create mechanisms to guard against the use of arbitrary and capricious policies and practices in the workplace.[9]

The underlying philosophy of the labor movement is that of organizational democracy and an atmosphere of social dignity for working men and women.

Why Employees Join Unions

Individuals join unions for many different reasons, which tend to change over time, and may involve job, personal, social, or political considerations. It would be impossible to discuss them all, but the following are some of the major reasons.

Dissatisfaction with Management

Every job holds the potential for real dissatisfaction.[10] Each individual has a boiling point that can cause him or her to consider a union as a solution to real or perceived problems. Union organizers look for arbitrary or unfair management decisions and then emphasize the advantages of union membership as a means of solving these problems. John Raudabaugh, a partner at Baker & McKenzie LLP in Chicago, says, "If you look at all the things that attract the employees to joining a union, it comes down to matters that can be replicated fully and satisfactorily by the corporation."[11] Some of the other common reasons for employee dissatisfaction are described in the following.

COMPENSATION Employees want their compensation to be fair and equitable. Wages are important because they provide both the necessities and pleasures of life. If employees are dissatisfied with their wages, they may look to a union for assistance in improving their standard of living. An important psychological aspect of compensation involves the amount of pay an individual receives in relation to that of other workers performing similar work (employee equity). If an employee perceives that management has shown favoritism by paying someone else more to perform the same or a lower-level job, the employee will likely become dissatisfied.

Union members know precisely the basis of their pay and how it compares with that of others. In the past, union members have accepted pay inequities if seniority was the criterion used.

JOB SECURITY   Historically, young employees have been less concerned with job security than older workers. The young employee seemed to think, "If I lose this job, I can always get another." But, if young employees witness management consistently terminating older workers to make room for younger, more aggressive employees, they may begin to think differently about job security. If the firm does not provide its employees with a sense of job security, workers may turn to a union.

ATTITUDE OF MANAGEMENT   People like to feel that they are important. They do not like to be considered a commodity that can be bought and sold. Thus, employees do not like to be subjected to arbitrary and capricious actions by management. In some firms, management is insensitive to the needs of its employees. In such situations, employees may perceive that they have little or no influence in job-related matters. Workers who feel that they are not really part of the organization are prime targets for unionization. Recently about 100 hourly workers at Smurfit-Stone Container Corp.'s corrugated box plant in North Tonawanda, New York voted to join the United Steelworkers union, claiming the company's disciplinary and promotional policies reflected favoritism.[12] Organizations that treat people with dignity and respect are typically difficult to organize.

Management's attitude may be reflected in even small actions. Employees may begin to feel they are being treated more as machines than as people. Supervisors may fail to give reasons for unusual assignments and may expect employees to dedicate their lives to the firm without providing adequate rewards. The prevailing philosophy may be: "If you don't like it here, leave." A management philosophy that does not consider the needs of employees as individuals makes the firm ripe for unionization. Management must keep in mind that unions will never gain a foothold if management is not abusive of its power. Companies that are pro-employees are not likely to be unionized.

Social Outlet

By nature, many people have strong social needs. They generally enjoy being around others who have similar interests and desires. Some employees join a union for no other reason than to take advantage of union-sponsored recreational and social activities that members and their families find fulfilling. Some unions now offer day-care centers and other services that appeal to working men and women and increase their sense of solidarity with other union members. People who develop close personal relationships, whether in a unionized or union-free organization, will likely stand together in difficult times.

Opportunity for Leadership

Some individuals aspire to leadership roles, but it is not always easy to progress into management. However, employees with leadership aspirations can often satisfy those aspirations through union membership. As with the firm, the union also has a hierarchy of leadership that begins with the union steward, and individual members have the opportunity to work their way up through its various levels.

Forced Unionization

right-to-work laws
Laws that prohibit management and unions from entering into agreements requiring union membership as a condition of employment.

In the 28 states without right-to-work laws, it is legal for an employer to agree with the union that a new employee must join the union after a certain period of time (generally 30 days) or be terminated. This is referred to as a "union shop agreement." **Right-to-work laws** prohibit management and unions from entering into agreements requiring union membership as a condition of employment. These laws are state statutes or constitutional provisions that ban the practice of requiring union membership or financial support as a condition of employment. They establish the legal right of employees to decide for themselves whether or not to join or financially support a union. Twenty-two states, located primarily in the South and West, have adopted such laws, which are a continuing source of irritation between labor and management. Oklahoma became the most recent right-to-work state.

Peer Pressure

Some individuals will join a union because they are urged to do so by other members of the work group. Friends and associates may constantly remind an employee that he or she is not a member of the union. In extreme cases, union members have threatened nonmembers with physical violence and sometimes have carried out these threats.

OBJECTIVE 12.3

Describe organized labor's strategies for a stronger movement and describe the basic structure of a union.

Organized Labor's Strategies for a Stronger Movement

Even though the labor movement has suffered setbacks over the past few decades, it is likely that union membership would have been even lower if the following strategies had not been used.

Strategically Located Union Members

The importance of the jobs held by union members significantly affects union power. For instance, an entire plant may have to be shut down if unionized machinists performing critical jobs decide to strike. Thus, a few strategically located union members may exert a disproportionate amount of power. The type of firm that is unionized can also determine a union's power. Unionization of truckers or dock workers can affect the entire country and, subsequently, enhance the union's power base. This is precisely what the longshoremen did in the West Coast strike of 2002, which affected commerce from San Francisco to Maine. Through control of key industries, a union's power may extend to firms that are not unionized.

Pulling the Union Through

One union tactic that has worked effectively at times is to put pressure on the end user of a company's product in order to have a successful organizing attempt. The United Automobile, Aerospace and Agricultural Implement Workers of America (UAW) authorized a strike against four Johnson Controls Inc. (JCI) factories in 2002 that made interior parts for some of the country's best-selling vehicles. The quick two-day strike cost workers little lost income, but it hurt General Motors Corporation and DaimlerChrysler Group by shutting down production of their popular Chevy TrailBlazer and Jeep Liberty sport-utility vehicles. Worried about lost sales in a profitable segment and desiring to preserve good relations with the UAW, GM and DaimlerChrysler played an active behind-the-scenes role by pressuring JCI to settle the dispute. The result was a major UAW victory. Not only did raises increase up to $6 an hour, but the strikers won a promise from JCI not to interfere with UAW efforts to organize some 8,000 workers at the 26 other JCI factories that supply the Big Three.[13]

Political Involvement

Committee on Political Education (COPE)
Political arm of the AFL-CIO.

The political arm of the AFL-CIO is the **Committee on Political Education (COPE)**. Founded in 1955, its purpose is to support politicians who are friendly to the cause of organized labor. The union recommends and assists candidates who will best serve its interests. In presidential and congressional elections, union support may have a significant impact. Union members also encourage their friends and families to support those candidates. Joshua Freeman, a professor of labor history at the City University of New York Graduate Center, said, "Unions have gotten weaker, but that weakness is not reflected in the political arena. They are very effective in mobilizing their members and families. It's now fairly common to have one out of four votes in an election coming from a union household."[14] The union's political influence increases as the size of the voting membership grows. With friends in government, the union is in a stronger position to maneuver against management. Political involvement now means more than endorsing candidates at all levels of politics, and then attempting to deliver the union membership's vote. Unions give money to candidates who pledge to help pass pro-labor legislation. In fact, in the 2008 election, organized labor contributed nearly $450 million toward the election of the President and a Democratic Congress.[15]

A 2010 Supreme Court decision ruled that corporations and labor unions can finance political advertising directly linked to political campaigns. The court ruled such limits are an unconstitutional violation of the First Amendment.[16] Previously, companies, unions, and other groups were prevented from directly paying for political ads during election campaigns. "This ruling strikes at our democracy itself," warned President Barack Obama. It "opens the flood-gates," he said, for corporations to "interfere with elections by running advertisements for or against candidates," such as himself. He vowed to fight for legal ways to undermine the ruling.[17] Only time will tell the result of this ruling.

Union Salting

union salting
Process of training union organizers to apply for jobs at a company and, once hired, working to unionize employees.

Union salting is the process of training union organizers to apply for jobs at a company and, once hired, working to unionize employees.[18] Although traditionally used by blue-collar labor unions within the construction and building industries, it is a strategy labor unions are also using in other sectors, such as the hotel and restaurant industries. The U.S. Supreme Court has ruled that employers cannot discriminate against "union salts" (*NLRB v Town & Electric Inc.*). Therefore, a company cannot terminate these employees solely because they also work for a union. However, if productivity suffers, the worker can be terrminated.

Flooding the Community

flooding the community
Process of the union inundating communities with organizers to target a particular business.

Flooding the community is the process of the union inundating communities with organizers to target a particular business in an organizing attempt. With their flooding campaigns, unions typically choose companies in which nonunionized employees have asked for help in organizing. Generally, organizers have been recruited and trained by the national union. They are typically young, ambitious, college-educated people with a passion for the American labor movement. Greg Denier, Change to Win director of communications, said, "We recruit from schools with labor centers such as Berkeley, Cornell, and Wisconsin. We also go to schools that are pipelines for employers, [schools] such as Wharton."[19] Organizers meet with employees in small groups and even visit them at home. They know every nuance of a company's operations and target weak managers' departments as a way to appeal to dissatisfied employees who may be willing to organize.

Public Awareness Campaigns

public awareness campaigns
Labor maneuvers that do not coincide with a strike or organizing campaign to pressure an employer for better wages, benefits, and the like.

Public awareness campaigns involve labor maneuvers that do not coincide with a strike or an organizing campaign to pressure an employer for better wages, benefits, and the like. Increasingly, these campaigns are used as an alternative to strikes because more employers are willing to replace their striking employees.[20] Employers have less recourse against labor campaigns that involve joining political and community groups that support union goals or picketing homes of a company's board of directors. They are also defenseless in dealing with the union's initiating proxy challenges to actions negative to labor, writing letters to the editors of the local newspapers, and filing charges with administrative agencies such as the Occupational Safety and Health Administration (OSHA), the Department of Labor, and the NLRB. These types of public awareness campaigns, which are not tied directly to labor gains, are often effective methods of developing union leverage. Also, fighting such campaigns is time consuming and costly for companies.

Building Organizing Funds

To encourage workers to come together, the AFL-CIO often asks its affiliates to increase organizing funds. The federation may also increase funding to its Organizing Institute, which trains organizers, and even launched an advertising campaign to create wider public support for unions. National unions are also creating organizing funds.

Unions Partnering with High Schools

Some high schools are pairing up with labor unions to prepare students for a career. Ten students from Saydel High School's construction shop class have entered a pilot program that allows them direct entry into United Association Plumbers and Steamfitters Local Union 33 once they

TRENDS & INNOVATIONS

Organizing Younger Workers, A Strategy Seriously Needed

A major strategy now being pursued by union organizers is to recruit younger workers and it may be coming at the right time since the lowest union membership rate is occurring among those ages 16 to 24 (4.7 percent).[22] However, in the past, younger organizers were often considered second-class citizens. Consider what Rachael Hunt, a young union organizer, recently said, "I have found young people like myself consistently treated as a lesser class. Young organizers today have a lot to offer the labor movement. But without years of dedicated service behind us, our role in organized labor is reduced to following orders, staying quiet, and repeating the failing strategies passed down the pike. Too many times, more experienced trade unionists have spoken to me as if I were a blank slate: ready to mold and be shaped to meet older organizers' viewpoints and goals. This same top-down, stale, bureaucratic organizational model that is crippling unions is also its biggest barrier to recruiting young people."[23]

A recent AFL-CIO study revealed that more than half of the young workers earn less than $30,000 annually and that 24 percent cannot afford their bills, which makes them reluctant to buy homes and start families. It revealed a lost decade for young workers in America. Not only have young workers lost financial ground over the past 10 years, they have also lost some of their

optimism.[24] Richard Trumka, AFL-CIO secretary treasurer, said, "A few years back a study found that young workers—white collar workers who really didn't want much to do with the labor movement—sat up and took notice when they heard about unions." He went on to say, "Winning protection for telecommuters...and bargaining for portable health care . . . and standing up to protect professional standards. When we talk about the problems facing contingent workers they really listen: and for good reason—after all, a man or woman working as a temp or a freelancer today may as well be walking a tightrope without a net. They know workers with unions make more money and have better benefits; they just don't think unions fit the way they work. And you can't blame them because we haven't really focused on the way they work. Well, we can't ask millennials to change the way they earn their living to meet our model for unionism; we have to change our approach to unionism to meet their needs."[25]

Trumka went on to say, "We need to address the fact that a lot of young people going to college today are drowning in a sea of debt by the time they come out. Now, fighting to make college affordable may not be a traditional union issue; but if we care about the economic security of young workers it has to become one! Now, I'm not suggesting that the labor movement ought to abandon all its traditions. But what I am saying is that nostalgia for the past is no strategy for the future. Tradition should always have a vote; we just can't let it have a veto."[26]

Young union members are certainly needed if the union is to achieve growth in the future. Surely, it is time for the union leaders to accept this.

---

graduate. As Local 33 apprentices, they receive training in plumbing, heating, air conditioning, medical gas, high purity piping, and water treatment. Greg Foshe, business manager of Local 33, said, "The goal of this program is to bring people into the union at a younger age. When students go from high school directly into their trade, they are going from learning situation to learning situation, creating a fast track educational experience."[21]

Organizing Through the Card Check

card check

Organizing approach by labor in which employees sign a card of support if they want unionization, and if 50 percent of the workforce plus one worker sign a card, the union is formed.

This organizing method is based upon management not objecting to the use of card check. The **card check** is an organizing approach by labor in which employees sign a nonsecret card of support if they want unionization, and if 50 percent of the workforce plus one worker sign a card, the union is formed. It permits workers to decide in a nonsecret election their union status. Essentially, organizations decide to remain neutral and peacefully permit their employees to decide if they wanted to unionize and not interfere as the union passes out authorization cards. In January 2008, the Teamsters launched its nationwide card-check campaign, a procedure in which workers sign cards to join a union instead of going through a secret voting process. A majority of workers in a bargaining unit must sign cards, which are then certified, before the company recognizes the union. Bargaining units from across the country signed authorization cards and were recognized as a union.[27] The largest was the Teamsters Drivers and Dockworkers employed by UPS Freight which added more than 9,900 members.[28]

ETHICAL DILEMMA

A Strategic Move

You are the plant manager for a medium-sized manufacturing company that has been experiencing growing employee tensions, and there has been a lot of talk among workers about forming a union. You have even seen what appear to be authorization cards being passed out around the plant. Sandy Marshall, one of the workers in your plant, has been seen talking to many of the workers, obviously about forming a union.

Sandy is very influential with the workers throughout the plant and appears to be a natural leader. You believe that if Sandy continues to promote the union, she will have a major impact among the workers in organizing the union. You have a supervisory position that has just come open. It pays a lot more than Sandy makes. You think, "If I make her a supervisor, she won't be able to use her influence to help get the union started." However, there is another worker in your department who is more qualified and has been with the firm several years longer than Sandy, although he is less influential with other workers throughout the plant.

What would you do?

Employee Free Choice Act

I rarely discuss a proposed law that as of this writing has yet to be passed and may not be passed. But, because of its potential impact on labor/management relations if passed, I will break with that tradition. In its present form, the Employee Free Choice Act (EFCA) proposes three major changes to the National Labor Relations Act. The EFCA would create a second method for workers to choose a union— the "card-check" provision—and impose tougher penalties against employers that violate laws on union organizing and negotiating. It also would mandate binding interest arbitration if an employer and a union cannot reach an agreement on a first contract within 120 days of good-faith bargaining.[29] Card checks are an expedited way of polling workers on union representation, but no secret-ballot election takes place.[30] The Employee Free Choice Act would eliminate the secret ballot in union organizing attempts. This highly contested act would affect much that is written in this chapter. For example, it would have a significant impact on establishing the collective bargaining relationship since it would eliminate the secret ballot. Also, the binding arbitration for the first contract affects the manner in which the labor/management agreement is formed. The Employee Free Choice Act would give an arbitrator immense authority to write the terms of the parties contract.[31]

Union Structure

The labor movement has developed a multilevel organizational structure. This complex of organizations ranges from local unions to the two principal federations—the AFL-CIO and the Change to Win Coalition.

Local Union

local union
Basic element in the structure of the U.S. labor movement.

craft union
Bargaining unit, such as the Carpenters and Joiners union, which is typically composed of members of a particular trade or skill in a specific locality.

The basic element in the structure of the American labor movement is the **local union** (or, the *local*). To the individual union member, it is the most important level in the structure of organized labor. Through the local, the individual deals with the employer on a day-to-day basis. A local union may fill a social role in the lives of its members, sponsoring dances, festivals, and other functions. It may be the focal point of the political organization and activity of its members.

There are two basic kinds of local unions: craft and industrial. A **craft union**, such as the Carpenters and Joiners union, is typically composed of members of a particular trade or skill in a specific locality. Members usually acquire their job skills through an apprenticeship-training program. An **industrial union** generally consists of all the workers in a particular plant or group of plants. The type of work they do and the level of skill they possess are not a condition for membership in the union. An example of an industrial union is the United Auto Workers.

The local union's functions are many and varied. Administering the collective bargaining agreement and representing workers in handling grievances are two very important activities. Other functions include keeping the membership informed about labor issues, promoting increased membership, maintaining effective contact with the national union, and, when appropriate, negotiating with management at the local level.

National Union

The most powerful level in the union structure is the national union. As stated previously, most locals are affiliated with national unions. A **national union** is composed of local unions, which it charters. As such, it is the parent organization to local unions. The local union, not the individual worker, holds membership in the national union. Each local union provides financial support to the national union based on its membership size. The Service Employees International Union (SEIU) is the largest and fastest-growing national union in North America, with 2.2 million members in the United States, Canada, and Puerto Rico.[32] The International Brotherhood of Teamsters has about 1.4 million members.[33]

The national union is governed by a national constitution and a national convention of local unions, which usually meets every two to five years. Elected officers, aided by an administrative staff, conduct the day-to-day operations of the national union. The national union is active in organizing workers within its jurisdiction, engaging in collective bargaining at the national level, and assisting its locals in their negotiations. In addition, the national union may provide numerous educational and research services for its locals, dispense strike funds, publish the union newspaper, provide legal counsel, and actively lobby at national and state levels.

American Federation of Labor and Congress of Industrial Organizations (AFL-CIO)

The **AFL-CIO** is the central trade union federation in the United States. The American Federation of Labor and Congress of Industrial Organizations (AFL-CIO) is a voluntary federation of 57 national and international labor unions. The AFL-CIO union movement represents 11.5 million members.[34] The AFL-CIO represents the interests of labor and its member national unions at the highest level. The federation does not engage in collective bargaining; however, it provides the means by which member unions can cooperate to pursue common objectives and attempt to resolve internal problems faced by organized labor. The federation is financed by its member national unions and is governed by a national convention, which meets every two years.

The structure of the AFL-CIO is complex. National unions can affiliate with one or more of the trade and industrial departments. These departments seek to promote the interests of specific groups of workers who are in different unions but have common interests. The federation's major activities include the following:

1. Improving the image of organized labor.
2. Extensive lobbying on behalf of labor interests.
3. Politically educating constituencies and others through COPE.
4. Resolving disputes between national unions.
5. Policing internal affairs of member unions.

The AFL-CIO is a loosely knit organization of national unions that has little formal power or control. The member national unions remain completely autonomous and decide their own policies and programs.

Change to Win Coalition

The **Change to Win Coalition** is a union federation consisting of unions that broke from the AFL-CIO and formally launched a rival labor federation representing about 6 million workers in 2005.

The Coalition, led by the Service Employees International Union, focuses its energies on new membership growth and not as much on lobbying. Also included in the new coalition are the International Brotherhood of Teamsters, the United Food and Commercial Workers International Union, Laborers' International Union of North America, and the United Farm Workers of America.[35] The Coalition wanted to direct its efforts at workers in industries in which employers could not easily outsource jobs. The primary targets for organizing included industries in cleaning, health care, hotels and restaurants, retailing, and transportation.[36]

Thus, the mission of the Change to Win Coalition is "to unite the 50 million workers in Change to Win affiliate industries whose jobs cannot be outsourced and who are vital to the global economy. We seek to secure the American Dream for them, and for all working people, including: a paycheck that supports a family, universal health care, a secure retirement, the freedom to form a union to give workers a voice on the job."[37]

OBJECTIVE 12.4

Define *collective bargaining* and identify the steps that lead to forming a bargaining unit.

collective bargaining

Performance of the mutual obligation of the employer and the representative of the employees to meet at reasonable times and confer in good faith with respect to wages, hours, and other terms and conditions of employment, or the negotiation of an agreement, or any question arising there under, and the execution of a written contract incorporating any agreement reached if requested by either party; such obligation does not compel either party to agree to a proposal or require the making of a concession.

bargaining unit

Group of employees, not necessarily union members, recognized by an employer or certified by an administrative agency as appropriate for representation by a labor organization for purposes of collective bargaining.

Establishing the Collective Bargaining Relationship

Before a union can negotiate a contract, it must first be certified. The primary law governing the relationship of companies and unions is the National Labor Relations Act, as amended. Collective bargaining is one of the key parts of the Act. Section 8(d) of the act defines **collective bargaining** as:

The performance of the mutual obligation of the employer and the representative of the employees to meet at reasonable times and confer in good faith with respect to wages, hours, and other terms and conditions of employment, or the negotiation of an agreement, or any question arising thereunder, and the execution of a written contract incorporating any agreement reached if requested by either party, but such obligation does not compel either party to agree to a proposal or require the making of a concession.

The Act further provides that the designated representative of the employees shall be the exclusive representative for all the employees in the unit for purposes of collective bargaining. A **bargaining unit** consists of a group of employees, not necessarily union members, recognized by an employer or certified by an administrative agency as appropriate for representation by a labor organization for purposes of collective bargaining.

A unit may cover the employees in one plant of an employer, or it may cover employees in two or more plants of the same employer. Although the act requires the representative to be selected by the employees, it does not require any particular procedure to be used so long as the choice clearly reflects the desire of the majority of the employees in the bargaining unit. The employee representative is normally chosen in a secret-ballot election conducted by the NLRB. When workers desire to become the bargaining representative for a group of employees, several steps leading to certification have to be taken (see Figure 12.1).

Prior to observing authorization cards passed out, there are usually signs of an upcoming union organizing attempt. Some indications might be: an increase in the number or intensity of employee complaints on wages, hours, working conditions, or management practices; unusual or more frequent employee challenges to management authority; and an increase in the number

Figure 12.1

Steps That Lead to Forming a Bargaining Unit

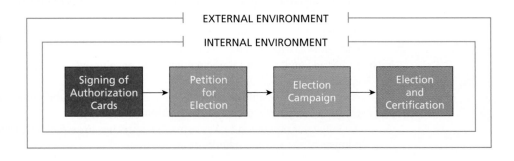

of formal complaints to government agencies such as, Occupational Health and Safety Administration, U.S. Department of Labor Wage and Hour, Wage and Hour Division, or state or federal equal employment agencies.[38]

Signing of Authorization Cards

authorization card
Document indicating that an employee wants to be represented by a labor organization in collective bargaining.

A prerequisite to becoming a recognized bargaining unit is to determine whether there is sufficient interest on the part of employees to justify the unit. Evidence of this interest is expressed when at least 30 percent of the employees in a work group sign an authorization card. The **authorization card** is a document indicating that an employee wants to be represented by a labor organization in collective bargaining. Most union organizers will not proceed unless at least 50 percent of the workers in the group sign cards.

Petition for Election

After the authorization cards have been signed, a petition for an election may be made to the appropriate regional office of the NLRB. When the petition is filed, the NLRB will conduct an investigation. The purpose of the investigation is to determine, among other things, the following:

1. Whether the Board has jurisdiction to conduct an election.
2. Whether there is a sufficient showing of employee interest to justify an election.
3. Whether a question of representation exists (for example, the employee representative has demanded recognition, which has been denied by the employer).
4. Whether the election will include appropriate employees in the bargaining unit (for instance, the Board is prohibited from including plant guards in the same unit with the other employees).
5. Whether the representative named in the petition is qualified (for example, a supervisor or any other management representative may not be an employee representative).
6. Whether there are any barriers to an election in the form of existing contracts or prior elections held within the past 12 months.[39]

HR Web Wisdom

National Labor Relations Board
http://www.nlrb.gov
The NLRB is a federal agency that administers the National Labor Relations Act.

If these conditions have been met, the NLRB will ordinarily direct that an election be held within 30 days. Election details are left largely to the agency's regional director.

Election Campaign

When an election has been ordered, both union and management usually promote their causes actively. Unions will continue to encourage workers to join the union, and management may begin a campaign to tell workers the benefits of remaining union-free. The supervisor's role during the campaign is crucial. Supervisors need to conduct themselves in a manner that avoids violating the law and committing unfair labor practices. Specifically, they should be aware of what can and cannot be done during the pre-election campaign period. Throughout the campaign, supervisors should keep upper management informed about employee attitudes.

Theoretically, both union and management are permitted to tell their stories without interference from the other side. At times, the campaign becomes quite intense. Election results will be declared invalid if the campaign was marked by conduct that the NLRB considers to have interfered with the employees' freedom of choice. Examples of such conduct include the following:

- An employer or a union threatens loss of jobs or benefits to influence employees' votes or union activities.
- An employer or a union misstates important facts in the election campaign when the other party does not have a chance to reply.
- Either an employer or a union incites racial or religious prejudice by inflammatory campaign appeals.
- An employer fires employees to discourage or encourage their union activities or a union causes an employer to take such an action.
- An employer or a union makes campaign speeches to assembled groups of employees on company time within 24 hours of an election.

Election and Certification

The NLRB monitors the secret-ballot election on the date set. Its representatives are responsible for making sure that only eligible employees vote, and for counting the votes. Following a valid election, the board will issue a certification of the results to the participants. If a union has been chosen by a majority of the employees voting in the bargaining unit, it will receive a certificate showing that it is now the official bargaining representative of the employees in the unit. However, the right to represent employees does not mean they have the right to dictate terms to management that would adversely affect the organization. The bargaining process does not require either party to make concessions; it only compels them to bargain in good faith in collective bargaining.

Collective Bargaining

Once the NLRB certifies the union, efforts can begin to negotiate a contract. The collective bargaining process is fundamental to union and management relations in the United States. Most union/management agreements in the United States are for a three-year period. Thus, on average, one-third of collective bargaining agreements occur each year. The bargaining structure can affect the conduct of collective bargaining. The four major structures are: one company dealing with a single union, several companies dealing with a single union, several unions dealing with a single company, and several companies dealing with several unions. Most contract bargaining is carried out under the first type of structure. The process can become quite complicated when several companies and unions are involved in the same negotiations. However, even when there is only one industry involved and one group of workers with similar skills, collective bargaining can be very difficult.

Collective Bargaining Process

Regardless of the current state of labor management relations, the general aspects of the collective bargaining process are the same and are illustrated in Figure 12.2. Depending on the type of relationship encountered, the collective bargaining process may be relatively simple, or it may be a long, tense struggle for both parties. Regardless of the complexity of the bargaining issues, the ability to reach agreement is the key to any successful negotiation.

As you can see, both external and internal environmental factors can influence the process. The first step in the collective bargaining process is preparing for negotiations. This step is often extensive and ongoing for both union and management. After the issues to be negotiated have been determined, the two sides confer to reach a mutually acceptable contract. Although breakdowns in negotiations can occur, both labor and management have at their disposal tools and arguments that can be used to convince the other side to accept their views. Eventually, however, management and the union usually reach an agreement that defines the rules for the duration of the contract. The next step is for the union membership to ratify the agreement. There is a feedback loop from "Administration of the Agreement" to "Preparing for Negotiation." Collective bargaining is a continuous and dynamic process, and preparing for the next round of negotiations often begins the moment a contract is ratified.

OBJECTIVE 12.5
Describe the collective bargaining process and explain collective bargaining issues.

Bargaining Issues

Because of the complex issues facing labor and management today, the negotiating teams must carefully prepare for the bargaining sessions. Prior to meeting at the bargaining table, the negotiators should thoroughly know the culture, climate, history, present economic state, and wage and benefits structure of both the organization and similar organizations. Because the length of a typical labor agreement is three years, negotiators should develop a contract that is successful both now and in the future. This consideration should prevail for both management and labor, although it rarely does. During the term of an agreement, the two sides usually discover contract provisions that need to be added, deleted, or modified. These items become proposals to be addressed in the next round of negotiations.

Figure 12.2

Collective Bargaining Process

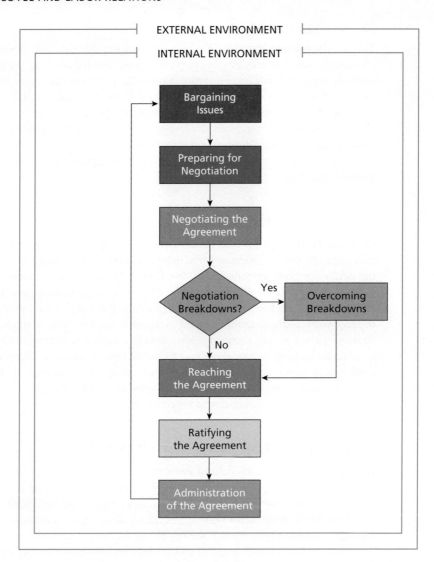

Bargaining issues can be divided into three categories: mandatory, permissive, and prohibited. **Mandatory bargaining issues** fall within the definition of wages, hours, and other terms and conditions of employment. These issues generally have an immediate and direct effect on workers' jobs. A refusal to bargain in these areas is grounds for an unfair labor practice charge. At times, collective bargaining toward new wage, rules, and benefits agreements may drag on for a long time. **Permissive bargaining issues** may be raised, but neither side may insist that they be bargained over. For example, management may want to bargain over health benefits for retired workers, but the union may choose not to bargain over the issue. Another permissive bargaining issue might be the union wanting child-care arrangements.

Prohibited bargaining issues, such as the issue of the closed shop, an arrangement whereby union membership is a prerequisite, are statutorily outlawed.

The Taft–Hartley Act made the closed shop illegal. However, the Act was modified 12 years later by the Landrum–Griffin Act to permit a closed shop in the construction industry. This is the only exception allowed. Despite much dissimilarity, certain topics are included in virtually all labor agreements. Each topic discussed in the following may be an issue in negotiations.

Recognition

This section usually appears at the beginning of the labor agreement. Its purpose is to identify the union that is recognized as the bargaining representative and to describe the bargaining

mandatory bargaining issues
Bargaining issues that fall within the definition of wages, hours, and other terms and conditions of employment.

permissive bargaining issues
Issues that may be raised, but neither side may insist that they be bargained over.

prohibited bargaining issues
Issues that are statutorily outlawed from collective bargaining.

unit—that is, the employees for whom the union speaks. A typical recognition section might read as follows:

> *The XYZ Company recognizes the ABC Union as the sole and exclusive representative of the bargaining unit employees for the purpose of collective bargaining with regard to wages, hours, and other conditions of employment.*

Management Rights

A section that is often but not always written into the labor agreement spells out the rights of management. If no such section is included, management may reason that it retains control of all topics not described as bargainable in the contract. The precise content of the management rights section will vary by industry, company, and union. When included, management rights generally involve three areas:

1. Freedom to select the business objectives of the company.
2. Freedom to determine the uses to which the material assets of the enterprise will be devoted.
3. Power to take disciplinary action for cause.

Basically management has the right to determine what work is to be done and where, when, and how it is to be done; to determine the number of employees who will do the work; to supervise and instruct employees in doing the work; to correct employees whose work performance or personal conduct fails to meet reasonable standards; and to hire, dismiss, and promote workers based on performance.

Union Security

closed shop
Arrangement making union membership a prerequisite for employment.

union shop
Requirement that all employees become members of the union after a specified period of employment (the legal minimum is 30 days) or after a union shop provision has been negotiated.

agency shop
Labor agreement provision requiring, as a condition of employment, that each nonunion member of a bargaining unit pay the union the equivalent of membership dues as a service charge in return for the union acting as the bargaining agent.

open shop
Employment on equal terms to union members and nonmembers alike.

Union security is typically one of the first items negotiated in a collective bargaining agreement. The objective of union security provisions is to ensure that the union continues to exist and perform its functions. A strong union security provision makes it easier for the union to enroll and retain members. Some basic forms of union security clauses are next described.

CLOSED SHOP   A **closed shop** is an arrangement whereby union membership is a prerequisite for employment.

UNION SHOP   A **union shop** arrangement requires that all employees become members of the union after a specified period of employment (the legal minimum is 30 days) or after a union shop provision has been negotiated. Employees must remain members of the union as a condition of employment. The union shop is generally legal in the United States, except in states that have right-to-work laws.

MAINTENANCE OF MEMBERSHIP   Employees who are members of the union at the time the labor agreement is signed or who later voluntarily join, must continue their memberships until the termination of the agreement, as a condition of employment. This form of recognition is also prohibited in most states that have right-to-work laws.

AGENCY SHOP   An **agency shop** provision does not require employees to join the union; however, the labor agreement requires that, as a condition of employment, each nonunion member of the bargaining unit pay the union the equivalent of membership dues as a kind of tax, or service charge, in return for the union acting as the bargaining agent. The National Labor Relations Act requires the union to bargain for all members of the bargaining unit, including nonunion employees. The agency shop is outlawed in most states that have right-to-work laws.

OPEN SHOP   An open shop describes the absence of union security, rather than its presence. The **open shop**, strictly defined, is employment on equal terms to union members and nonmembers alike. Under this arrangement, no employee is required to join or contribute to the union financially.

DUES CHECKOFF   Another type of security that unions attempt to achieve is the checkoff of dues. A checkoff agreement may be used in addition to any of the previously mentioned shop

checkoff of dues
Agreement by which a company agrees to withhold union dues from members' paychecks and to forward the money directly to the union.

agreements. Under the **checkoff of dues** provision, the company agrees to withhold union dues from members' paychecks and to forward the money directly to the union. Because of provisions in the Taft–Hartley Act, each union member must voluntarily sign a statement authorizing this deduction. Dues checkoff is important to the union because it eliminates much of the expense, time, and hassle of collecting dues from each member every pay period or once a month.

Compensation

This section typically constitutes a large portion of most labor agreements. Virtually any item that can affect compensation may be included in labor agreements. Some of the items frequently covered include the following:

WAGE RATE SCHEDULE   The base rates to be paid each year of the contract for each job are included in this section. At times, unions are able to obtain a cost-of-living allowance (COLA), or escalator clause, in the contract in order to protect the purchasing power of employees' earnings (discussed in Chapter 9).

OVERTIME AND PREMIUM PAY   Another section of the agreement may cover hours of work, overtime pay, hazard pay, and premium pay, such as shift differentials (discussed previously in Chapter 10).

JURY PAY   For some firms, jury pay amounts to the employee's entire salary when he or she is serving jury duty. Others pay the difference between the amount employees receive from the court and the compensation that would have been earned. The procedure covering jury pay is typically stated in the contract.

LAYOFF OR SEVERANCE PAY   The amount that employees in various jobs and/or seniority levels will be paid if they are laid off or terminated is a frequently included item.

HOLIDAYS   The holidays recognized and the amount of pay that a worker will receive if he or she has to work on a holiday is specified here. In addition, the pay procedure for times when a holiday falls on a worker's normal day off is provided.

VACATION   This section spells out the amount of vacation that a person may take, based on seniority. Any restrictions as to when the vacation may be taken are also stated.

FAMILY CARE   This is a benefit that has been included in recent collective bargaining agreements, with child care expected to continue to be a bargaining issue.

Grievance Procedure

grievance
Employee's dissatisfaction or feeling of personal injustice relating to his or her employment.

grievance procedure
Formal, systematic process that permits employees to express complaints without jeopardizing their jobs.

Virtually all labor agreements include some form of grievance procedure. A **grievance** can be broadly defined as an employee's dissatisfaction or feeling of personal injustice relating to his or her employment. A **grievance procedure** (discussed later in this chapter) is a formal, systematic process that permits employees to express complaints without jeopardizing their jobs.

Employee Security

This section of the labor agreement establishes the procedures that cover job security for individual employees. Seniority is a key topic related to employee security. *Seniority* is the length of time an employee has been associated with the company, division, department, or job. Seniority may be determined company-wide, by division, by department, or by job. Agreement on seniority is important because the person with the most seniority, as defined in the labor agreement, is typically the last to be laid off and the first to be recalled. The seniority system also provides a basis for promotion decisions. When qualifications are met, employees with the greatest seniority will likely be considered first for promotion to higher-level jobs.

Job-Related Factors

Many of the rules governing employee actions on the job are also included. Some of the more important factors are company work rules, work standards, and rules related to safety. This section varies, depending on the nature of the industry and the product manufactured.

OBJECTIVE 12.6
Describe preparation for negotiations, negotiating the agreement, and breakdowns in negotiations.

Preparation for Negotiations

The union must continuously gather information regarding membership needs to isolate areas of dissatisfaction. The union steward is normally in the best position to collect such data.[40] Because they are usually elected by their peers, stewards should be well informed regarding union members' attitudes. The union steward constantly funnels information up through the union's chain of command, where the data are compiled and analyzed. Union leadership attempts to uncover any areas of dissatisfaction because the general union membership must approve any agreement before it becomes final. Because they are elected, union leaders will lose their positions if the demands they make of management do not represent the desires of the general membership.

Management also spends long hours preparing for negotiations. All aspects of the current contracts are considered, including flaws that should be corrected. When preparing for negotiations, management should listen carefully to first-line managers. These individuals administer the labor agreement on a day-to-day basis and must live with errors made in negotiating the contract. An alert line manager is also able to inform upper management of the demands unions may plan to make during negotiations.

Management also attempts periodically to obtain information regarding employee attitudes. Surveys are often administered to workers to determine their feelings toward their jobs and job environment. Union and management representatives like to know as much as possible about employee attitudes when they sit down at the bargaining table.

Another part of preparation for negotiations involves identifying various positions that both union and management will take as the negotiations progress. Each usually takes an initially extreme position, representing the optimum conditions union or management would prefer. The two sides will likely determine absolute limits to their offers or demands before a breakdown in negotiations occurs. They also usually prepare fallback positions based on combinations of issues. Preparations should be detailed, because clear minds often do not prevail during the heat of negotiations.

A major consideration in preparing for negotiations is the selection of the bargaining teams. The makeup of the management team usually depends on the type of organization and its size. Normally, labor relations specialists, with the advice and assistance of operating managers, conduct bargaining. Sometimes, top executives are directly involved, particularly in smaller firms. Larger companies use staff specialists (a human resource manager or industrial relations executive), managers of principal operating divisions, and, in some cases, an outside consultant, such as a labor attorney.

The responsibility for conducting negotiations for the union is usually entrusted to union officers. At the local level, rank-and-file members who are elected specifically for this purpose will normally supplement the bargaining committee. In addition, the national union will often send a representative to act in an advisory capacity or even to participate directly in the bargaining sessions. The real task of the union negotiating team is to develop and obtain solutions to the problems raised by the union's membership.

Negotiating the Agreement

There is no way to ensure speedy and mutually acceptable results from negotiations. At best, the parties can attempt to create an atmosphere that will lend itself to steady progress and productive results. For example, the two negotiating teams usually meet at an agreed-on neutral site, such as a hotel. When a favorable relationship can be established early, eleventh-hour (or last-minute) bargaining can often be avoided. It is equally important for union and management negotiators to strive to develop and maintain clear and open lines of communication. Collective bargaining is a problem-solving activity; consequently, good communication is essential to its success. Negotiations should be conducted in the privacy of the conference room, not in the news media. Often in the media, the unions belittle management and naturally management strikes back. The media love it because it sells. The results are harmful, often to both sides. If the negotiators feel that publicity is necessary, joint releases to the media may avoid unnecessary conflict.

The negotiating phase of collective bargaining begins with each side presenting its initial demands. Because a collective bargaining settlement can be expensive for a firm, the cost of various proposals should be estimated as accurately as possible. Some changes can be quite expensive, and others cost little or nothing, but the cost of the various proposals being considered must always be carefully deliberated. The term *negotiating* suggests a certain amount of give-and-take, the purpose of which is to lower the other side's expectations. For example, the union might bargain to upgrade its members' economic and working conditions and the company might negotiate to maintain or enhance profitability.

One of the most costly components of any collective bargaining agreement is a wage increase provision. An example of the negotiation of a wage increase is shown in Figure 12.3. In this example, labor initially demands a 40-cent-per-hour increase. Management counters with an offer of only 10 cents per hour. Both labor and management, as expected, reject each other's demand. Plan B calls for labor to lower its demand to a 30-cents-per-hour increase. Management counters with an offer of 20 cents. The positions in plan B are feasible to both sides, as both groups are in the bargaining zone. Wages within the bargaining zone are those that management and labor can both accept, in this case, an increase of between 20 cents and 30 cents per hour. The exact amount will be determined by the power of the bargaining unit and the skills of the negotiators.

The realities of negotiations are not for the weak of heart and at times are similar to a high-stakes poker game. A certain amount of bluffing and raising the ante takes place in many negotiations. The ultimate bluff for the union is when a negotiator says, "If our demands are not met, we are prepared to strike." Management's version of this bluff would be to threaten a lockout. Each of these tactics will be discussed later as a means of overcoming breakdowns in negotiations. The party with the greater leverage can expect to extract the most concessions.

Even though one party in the negotiating process may appear to possess the greater power, negotiators often take care to keep the other side from losing face. They recognize that the balance of power may switch rapidly. By the time the next round of negotiations occurs, the pendulum may be swinging back in favor of the other side. Even when management appears to have the upper hand, it may make minor concessions that will allow the labor leader to claim gains for the union. Management may demand that workers pay for grease rags that are lost (assuming that the loss of these rags has become excessive). In order to obtain labor's agreement to this demand, management may agree to provide new uniforms for the workers if the cost of these uniforms would be less than the cost of lost rags. Thus, labor leaders, although forced to concede to management's demand, could show the workers that they have obtained a concession from management. Each side usually does not expect to obtain all the demands presented in its first proposal. Labor can lose a demand and continue to bring it up in the future. Demands for benefits that the union does not expect to receive when they are first made are known as **beachhead demands**.

beachhead demands
Demands that the union does not expect management to meet when they are first made.

Figure 12.3

Example of Negotiating a Wage Increase

Breakdowns in Negotiations

At times negotiations break down, even though both labor and management may sincerely want to arrive at an equitable contract settlement. Several means of removing roadblocks may be used in order to get negotiations moving again.

Third-Party Intervention

Often an outside person can intervene to provide assistance when an agreement cannot be reached and the two sides reach an impasse. The reasons behind each party's position may be quite rational, or the breakdown may be related to emotional disputes that tend to become distorted during the heat of negotiations. Regardless of the cause, something must be done to continue the negotiations. The two basic types of third-party intervention are mediation and arbitration.

mediation
Neutral third party enters the negotiations and attempts to facilitate a resolution to a labor dispute when a bargaining impasse has occurred.

MEDIATION   In **mediation**, a neutral third party enters the negotiations and attempts to facilitate a resolution to a labor dispute when a bargaining impasse has occurred. A mediator basically acts like a facilitator. The objective of mediation is to persuade the parties to resume negotiations and reach a settlement. A mediator has no power to force a settlement but can help in the search for solutions, make recommendations, and work to open blocked channels of communication. Successful mediation depends to a substantial degree on the tact, diplomacy, patience, and perseverance of the mediator. The mediator's fresh insights are used to get discussions going again. Mediation is voluntary at every step of the process. The mediator serves as an informal coach, helping to ensure that the discussions are fair and effective.

The principal organization involved in mediation efforts, other than some state and local agencies, is the Federal Mediation and Conciliation Service (FMCS). In 1947, the Taft–Hartley Act established the FMCS as an independent agency. Either one or both parties involved in negotiations can seek the assistance of the FMCS, or the agency can offer its help if it feels that the situation warrants it. Federal law requires that the party wishing to change a contract must give notice of this intention to the other party 60 days prior to the expiration of a contract. If no agreement has been reached 30 days prior to the expiration date, the FMCS must be notified.

arbitration
Process in which a dispute is submitted to an impartial third party for a binding decision; an arbitrator basically acts as a judge and jury.

ARBITRATION   In **arbitration**, a dispute is submitted to an impartial third party for a binding decision; an arbitrator basically acts as a judge and jury. There are two principal types of union management disputes: rights disputes and interest disputes. Disputes over the interpretation and application of the various provisions of an existing contract are submitted to **rights arbitration,** which will be discussed shortly under the heading of "Grievance Procedure in a Union Environment." This type of arbitration is common in the United States.

rights arbitration
Arbitration involving disputes over the interpretation and application of the various provisions of an existing contract.

The other type of arbitration, **interest arbitration**, involves disputes over the terms of proposed collective bargaining agreements. In the private sector, the use of interest arbitration as an alternative for impasse resolution has not been a common practice. Unions and employers rarely agree to submit the basic terms of a contract (such as wages, hours, and working conditions) to a neutral party for disposition. They prefer to rely on collective bargaining and the threat of economic pressure (such as strikes and lockouts), to decide these issues.

interest arbitration
Arbitration that involves disputes over the terms of proposed collective bargaining agreements.

For either rights or interest arbitration, the disputants are free to select any person as their arbitrator, so long as they agree on the selection. Most commonly, however, the two sides make a request for an arbitrator to either the American Arbitration Association (AAA) or the FMCS. The AAA is a nonprofit organization with offices in many cities. Both the AAA and the FMCS maintain lists of arbitrators. When considering potential arbitrators, both management and labor will study the arbitrator's previous decisions in an attempt to detect any biases. Obviously, neither party wants to select an arbitrator who might tend to favor the other's position.

After the arbitrator has been selected and has agreed to serve, a time and place for a hearing will be determined. The issue to be resolved will be presented to the arbitrator in a document that summarizes the question(s) to be decided. It will also point out any contract restrictions that prohibit the arbitrator from making an award that would change the terms of the contract.

At the hearing, each side presents its case. Arbitration is an adversarial proceeding, so a case may be lost because of poor preparation and presentation. The arbitrator may conduct the hearing much like a courtroom proceeding. Witnesses, cross-examination, transcripts, and legal counsel may all be used. The parties may also submit or be asked by the arbitrator to submit formal written statements. After the hearing, the arbitrator studies the material submitted and testimony given and is expected to reach a decision within 30 to 60 days. The decision is usually accompanied by a written opinion giving reasons for the decision.

The courts will generally enforce an arbitrator's decision unless: (1) the arbitrator's decision is shown to be unreasonable or capricious in that it did not address the issues; (2) the arbitrator exceeded his or her authority; or (3) the award or decision violated a federal or state law. In one arbitration case that ultimately went to the Supreme Court, the arbitrator's decision appeared to run counter to public policy, prohibiting workers who had tested positive for drugs from operating heavy machinery or being permitted to return to work. However, the Supreme Court wrote, "We recognize that reasonable people can differ as to whether reinstatement or discharge is the more appropriate remedy here. But both employer and union have agreed to entrust this remedial decision to an arbitrator."[41]

Union Strategies for Overcoming Negotiation Breakdowns

There are times when a union believes that it must exert extreme pressure to get management to agree to its bargaining demands. Strikes and boycotts are the primary means that the union may use to overcome breakdowns in negotiations.

STRIKES When union members refuse to work in order to exert pressure on management in negotiations, their action is referred to as a **strike**. A strike halts production, resulting in lost customers and revenue, which the union hopes will force management to submit to its terms. In recent times, strikes have rarely been part of 20,000 annual contract negotiation processes.[42] The number of strikes involving 1,000 or more workers in 2008 was 15; they idled 72,000 workers.[43] This is in comparison to the more than 200 strikes each year in the 1970s. The more than five-week work stoppage at Bell Helicopter Textron was the longest work stoppage of 2009 and involved approximately 2,500 unionized factory employees accumulating 67,500 days of idleness. Both employee and idleness numbers have declined significantly, reaching an all-time low in 2009.[44]

The timing of a strike is important in determining its effectiveness. An excellent time is when business is thriving and the demand for the firm's goods or services is expanding. However, the union might be hard-pressed to obtain major concessions from a strike if the firm's sales are down and it has built up a large inventory. In this instance, the company would not be severely damaged.

Contrary to many opinions, unions prefer to use the strike only as a last resort. During a strike, workers have little income. The strike fund may only pay for items such as food, utilities, and motor fuel. In recent years, many union members have been even more reluctant to strike because of the fear of being replaced. When a union goes on an economic strike and the company hires replacements, the company does not have to lay off these individuals at the end of the strike. For example, Edw. C. Levy Co., headquartered in Detroit, Michigan, hired permanent replacements for the 130 members of the International Union of Operating Engineers Local 150 who struck the contractor's operations at Mittal Steel Co.'s Burns Harbor plant.[45]

A union's treasury is often depleted by payment of strike benefits to its members. In addition, members suffer because they are not receiving their normal pay. Striking workers during one General Motors strike got paid about $150 a week strike pay instead of the roughly $1,000 a week that they might normally take home. Although strike pay helps, union members certainly cannot maintain a normal standard of living with these minimal amounts. Sometimes during negotiations (especially at the beginning), the union may want to strengthen its negotiating position by taking a strike vote. Members often give overwhelming approval to a strike. This vote does not necessarily mean that there will be a strike, only that the union leaders now have the authority to call one if negotiations reach an impasse. A favorable strike vote can add a sense of urgency to efforts to reach an agreement.

Successful passage of a strike vote has additional implications for union members. Virtually every national union's constitution contains a clause requiring the members to support and participate in a strike if one is called. If a union member fails to comply with this requirement, he or she can be fined be as high as 100 percent of wages for as long as union pickets remain outside the company. However, the Supreme Court has ruled that an employee on economic strike may resign from the union and avoid being punished by the union. In today's economy, union members are using more subtle measures, such as sick-outs and work slowdowns, to successfully avoid the impact of a strike while still bringing pressure on the company to meet union demands.

boycott
Agreement by union members to refuse to use or buy the firm's products.

BOYCOTTS   The boycott is another of labor's weapons to get management to agree to its demands. A **boycott** involves an agreement by union members to refuse to use or buy the firm's products.

A boycott exerts economic pressure on management, and the effect often lasts much longer than that of a strike. Once shoppers change buying habits, their behavior will likely continue long after the boycott has ended. At times, significant pressures can be exerted on a business when union members, their families, and their friends refuse to purchase the firm's products. This approach is especially effective when the products are sold at retail outlets and are easily identifiable by brand name. For instance, the boycott against Adolph Coors Company was effective because the name of the product, Coors beer, was directly associated with the company. Ultimately, the AFL-CIO signed an agreement with Coors that ended a labor boycott of the company.[46]

secondary boycott
Union attempt to encourage third parties (such as suppliers and customers) to stop doing business with a firm; declared illegal by the Taft-Hartley Act.

The practice of a union attempting to encourage third parties (such as suppliers and customers) to stop doing business with the company is known as a **secondary boycott**. The Taft–Hartley Act declared this type of boycott to be illegal.

Management Strategies for Overcoming Negotiation Breakdowns

There are times when management believes that it must exert extreme pressure to get the union to back away from a demand. The lockout and operating the firm by placing management and nonunion workers in the striking workers' jobs are the primary means that management may use to overcome breakdowns in negotiations.

lockout
Management decision to keep union workers out of the workplace and run the operation with management personnel and/or replacement workers to encourage the union to return to the bargaining table.

LOCKOUT   Management may use the lockout to encourage unions to come back to the bargaining table. In a **lockout**, management keeps employees out of the workplace and runs the operation with management personnel and/or replacements. Unable to work, the employees do not get paid; the fear of a lockout may bring labor back to the bargaining table. A lockout is particularly effective when management is dealing with a weak union, when the union treasury is depleted, or when the business has excessive inventories. The lockout is also used to inform the union that management is serious regarding certain bargaining issues.[47]

CONTINUE OPERATIONS WITHOUT STRIKING WORKERS   Another course of action that a company can take if the union goes on strike is to operate the firm by placing management and nonunion workers in the striking workers' jobs. The type of industry involved has considerable effect on the impact of this maneuver. If the firm is not labor-intensive and if maintenance demands are not high, such as at a petroleum refinery or a chemical plant, this practice may be quite effective. When appropriate, management may attempt to show how using nonunion employees can actually increase production. At times, management personnel will actually live in the plant and have food and other necessities delivered to them. This was the situation that occurred when the 900 members of local 470 of the International Association of Machinists struck the PPG Plant in Lake Charles, Louisiana, on May 26, 2006. Management continued to run the plant with management and contract labor personnel. The union members struck because of an increase in insurance payments and a new hiring-in rate for entry-level workers. Prior to the strike, the local had taken a strike vote, and an overwhelming number of workers had voted in favor of the strike. On August 9, 2006, the union permitted the workers to vote on whether to accept or reject management's proposal. It was rejected by a majority of the workers. Then management sent registered letters to all union members suggesting that they were not willing to maintain the current work situation, and the company was considering hiring replacement workers. Another vote was taken and the contract was accepted. Prior to the final vote, approximately 100 workers had resigned from the union and crossed the picket line.

OBJECTIVE 12.7
Describe what is involved
in reaching, ratifying,
and administering the
agreement.

Reaching the Agreement

The document that emerges from the collective bargaining process is known as a "labor agreement" or "contract." It regulates the relationship between employer and employees for a specified period of time. It is still an essential but difficult task because each agreement is unique, and there is no standard or universal model.

Ratifying the Agreement

Most collective bargaining leads to an agreement without a breakdown in negotiations or disruptive actions. Typically, agreement is reached before the current contract expires. After the negotiators have reached a tentative agreement on all contract terms, they prepare a written agreement covering those terms, complete with the effective and termination dates. The approval process for management is often easier than for labor. The president or CEO has usually been briefed regularly on the progress of negotiations. Any difficulty that might have stood in the way of obtaining approval has probably already been resolved with top management by the negotiators.

However, the approval process is more complex for the union. Until a majority of members voting in a ratification election approve it, the proposed agreement is not final. At times, union members reject the proposal and a new round of negotiations must begin. Many of these rejections might not occur if union negotiators were better informed about members' desires.

Administration of the Agreement

Negotiating, as it relates to the total collective bargaining process, may be likened to the tip of an iceberg. It is the visible phase, the part that makes the news. The larger and perhaps more important part of collective bargaining is administration of the agreement, which the public seldom sees. The agreement establishes the union–management relationship for the duration of the contract. Usually, neither party can change the contract's language until the expiration date, except by mutual consent. However, the main problem encountered in contract administration is uniform interpretation and application of the contract's terms. Administering the contract is a day-to-day activity. Ideally, the aim of both management and the union is to make the agreement work to the benefit of all concerned. At times, this is not an easy task.

Management is primarily responsible for explaining and implementing the agreement. This process should begin with meetings or training sessions not only to point out significant features but also to provide a clause-by-clause analysis of the contract. First-line supervisors, in particular, need to know their responsibilities and what to do when disagreements arise. In addition, supervisors and middle managers should be encouraged to notify top management of any contract modifications or new provisions required for the next round of negotiations.

The human resource manager or industrial relations manager plays a key role in the day-to-day administration of the contract. He or she gives advice on matters of discipline, works to resolve grievances, and helps first-line supervisors establish good working relationships within the terms of the agreement. When a firm becomes unionized, the human resource manager's function tends to change rather significantly, and may even be divided into separate human resource and industrial relations departments. In such situations, the vice president of human resources may perform all human resource management tasks with the exception of industrial relations. The vice president of industrial relations would likely deal with all union-related matters.

OBJECTIVE 12.8
Describe the grievance
procedure in a union
environment.

Grievance Procedure in a Union Environment

As previously defined, a *grievance procedure* is a formal, systematic process that permits employees to express complaints without jeopardizing their jobs. A grievance procedure under a collective bargaining agreement is normally well defined. It is usually restricted to violations of the terms and conditions of the agreement. There are other conditions that may give rise to a grievance, including the following:

- A violation of law.
- A violation of the intent of the parties as stipulated during contract negotiations.

- A violation of company rules.
- A change in working conditions or past company practices.
- A violation of health and/or safety standards.

Grievance procedures have many common features. However, variations may reflect differences in organizational or decision-making structures or the size of a plant or company. Some general principles based on widespread practice can serve as useful guidelines for effective grievance administration:

- Grievances should be adjusted promptly.
- Procedures and forms used for airing grievances must be easy to use and well understood by employees and their supervisors.
- Direct and timely avenues of appeal from rulings of line supervision must exist.

The multistep grievance procedure is the most common type. In the first step, the employee usually presents the grievance orally and informally to the immediate supervisor in the presence of the union steward. This step offers the greatest potential for improved labor relations, and a large majority of grievances are settled here. The procedure ends if the grievance is resolved at this initial step. If the grievance remains unresolved, the next step involves a meeting between the plant manager or human resource manager and higher union officials, such as the grievance committee or the business agent or manager. Prior to this meeting, the grievance is written out, dated, and signed by the employee and the union steward. The written grievance states the events, as the employee perceives them, cites the contract provision that allegedly has been violated, and indicates the settlement desired. If the grievance is not settled at this meeting, it is appealed to the third step, which typically involves the firm's top labor representative (such as the vice president of industrial relations) and high-level union officials. At times, depending on the severity of the grievance, the president may represent the firm. Arbitration is the final step in most grievance procedures. In arbitration, the parties submit their dispute to an impartial third party for binding resolution. Most agreements restrict the arbitrator's decision to application and interpretation of the agreement and make the decision final and binding on the parties. If the union decides in favor of arbitration, it notifies management. At this point, the union and the company select an arbitrator.[48]

When arbitration is used to settle a grievance, a variety of factors may be considered to evaluate the fairness of the management actions that caused the grievance. These factors include the following:

- Nature of the offense
- Due process and procedural correctness
- Double jeopardy
- Past record of grievant
- Length of service with the company
- Knowledge of rules
- Warnings
- Lax enforcement of rule
- Discriminatory treatment

The large number of interacting variables in each case makes the arbitration process difficult. The arbitrator must possess exceptional patience and judgment in rendering a fair and impartial decision.

Labor relations problems can escalate when a supervisor is not equipped to handle grievances at the first step. Since the union steward, the aggrieved party, and the supervisor usually handle the first step informally, the supervisor must be fully prepared. The supervisor should obtain as many facts as possible before the meeting, because the union steward is likely to have also done his or her homework.

The supervisor needs to recognize that the grievance may not reflect the real problem. For instance, the employee might be angry with the company for modifying its pay policies, even though the union agreed to the change. In order to voice discontent, the worker might file a grievance for an unrelated minor violation of the contract.

Figure 12.4

An Example of a Written Warning

Date: August 1, 2012

To: Wayne Sanders

From: Judy Bandy

Subject: Written Warning

We are quite concerned because today you were thirty minutes late to work and offered no justification for this. According to our records, a similar offense occurred on July 25, 2012. At that time, you were informed that failure to report to work on time is unacceptable. I am, therefore, notifying you in writing that you must report to work on time. It will be necessary to terminate your employment if this happens again.

    Please sign this form to indicate that you have read and understand this warning. Signing is not an indication of agreement.

_____

Name

_____

Date

Any disciplinary action administered may ultimately be taken to arbitration, when such a remedy is specified in the labor agreement. Employers have learned that they must prepare records that will constitute proof of disciplinary action and the reasons for it. Although the formats of written warnings may vary, all should include the following information:

1. Statement of facts concerning the offense.
2. Identification of the rule that was violated.
3. Statement of what resulted or could have resulted because of the violation.
4. Identification of any previous similar violations by the same individual.
5. Statement of possible future consequences should the violation occur again.
6. Signature and date.

An example of a written warning is shown in Figure 12.4. In this instance, the worker has already received an oral reprimand. The individual is also warned that continued tardiness could lead to termination. It is important to document oral reprimands because they may be the first step in disciplinary action leading ultimately to arbitration.

OBJECTIVE 12.9

Explain recent/labor management legal trends and describe collective bargaining in the public sector.

Recent Labor/Management Legal Trends

The NLRB reported that more than 20,000 unfair-labor-practice charges were filed in 2008, with a finding of merit in more than 40 percent of the cases. The NLRB ordered employers to pay out more than $70 million in back wages and offer reinstatement to 1,564 employees. The NLRB has recently been reconstituted and has resumed a full caseload. Employer practices in unionization drives are likely to fall under greater scrutiny.[49] In 2010, President Obama installed two new members, Craig Becker and Mark Pearce, to the five person National Labor Relations Board. Teamsters General President James P. Hoffa praised President Obama's recent appointments to the Board, saying the action "will allow the board to finally move forward." Becker is associate general counsel to both the Service Employees International Union and the AFL-CIO, while Pearce is a union-side labor lawyer for the Buffalo, N.Y., firm of Creighton, Pearce, Johnsen & Giroux.[50] The *Wall Street Journal* called Becker "labor's secret weapon."[51]

President Obama has signed four executive orders that will greatly impact federal government contractors. These orders require the following: (1) all federal contractors must post notices informing employees of their rights to form and join unions (EO 13496)[52]; (2) all federal contractors may not seek reimbursement for funds spent on influencing employees regarding unionization (EO 13494); (3) all federal contractors succeeding to a service contract must provide job opportunities to employees of the previous service contractor (EO 13495); and directing federal agencies taking bids for government construction projects in excess of $25 million to accept only those from contractors who agree in advance to a project labor agreement that requires a union workforce (EO 13502).[53]

EO 13494 impacts all federal contractors and mandates that costs associated with so called "persuader activities" designed to influence employees to join or not join a union are *not reimbursable* by the federal government under the government's contract with the employer. Examples of "unallowable" costs include (a) preparing and distributing materials; (b) hiring or consulting legal counsel or consultants; (c) holding meetings with employees; and (d) planning or conducting activities by managers, supervisors, or union representatives during work hours. Federal contractors are not prohibited from engaging in promotion activities, but they may not seek reimbursement for these expenses.[54]

Collective Bargaining in the Public Sector

More than half of the members of the two leading union federations (the AFL-CIO and Change to Win) are workers in government offices even though public-sector employment is only one-sixth of the overall workforce.[55] Executive Order 10988 established the basic framework for collective bargaining in federal government agencies. Title VII of the Civil Service Reform Act of 1978 regulates most of the labor management relations in the federal service. It establishes the Federal Labor Relations Authority (FLRA), which is modeled after the National Labor Relations Board. The FLRA has been relatively inactive lately but recently saw a resurgence of activities causing a large backlog of cases.[56] The intent of the FLRA is to bring the public-sector model in line with that of the private sector. Requirements and mechanisms for recognition and elections, dealing with impasses, and handling grievances are covered in the Act. Collective bargaining for federal unions has traditionally been quite different from private-sector bargaining because wages were off the table. Title V of the U.S. Code, the law that dictates rules for federal employees, did not allow bargaining over wage issues, except for the U.S. Postal Service.

There is no uniform pattern to state and local bargaining rights. More than two-thirds of the states have enacted legislation granting public-sector collective bargaining rights to some groups such as teachers, police, and firefighters. However, the diversity of state labor laws makes it difficult to generalize about the legal aspects of collective bargaining at the state and local levels.

In the public sector, most governmental jurisdictions prohibit their employees from striking. This was vigorously pointed out in the air traffic controllers (PATCO) strike of 1981 where President Ronald Reagan used replacement workers to end the first declared national strike against the federal government. PATCO sacrificed a substantial pay increase, a generous benefit package, and its very existence in its attempt to legitimize strikes in the public sector.[57] As a result, interest arbitration is used to a greater extent than in the private sector, although there is no uniform application of this method. A procedure used in the public sector is *final-offer arbitration,* which has two basic forms: package selection and issue-by-issue selection. In package selection, the arbitrator must select one party's entire offer on all issues in dispute. In issue-by-issue selection, the arbitrator examines each issue separately and chooses the final offer of one side or the other on each issue. Final-offer arbitration is often used to determine the salary of a professional baseball player. Both players and management present a dollar figure to an arbitrator. The arbitrator chooses one figure or the other.

Union Decertification

Until 1947, once a union was certified, it was certified forever. However, the Taft-Hartley Act made it possible for employees to decertify a union. **Decertification** is the reverse of the process that employees must follow to be recognized as an official bargaining unit. It results in a union losing its right to act as the exclusive bargaining representative of a group of employees. As union membership has declined, the need for decertification elections has also diminished.

The rules established by the NLRB spell out the conditions for filing a decertification petition; it is essentially the reverse of obtaining union recognition. At least 30 percent of the bargaining unit members must petition for an election. As might be expected, this task by itself may be difficult because union supporters are likely to strongly oppose the move. Also, although the petitioners' names are supposed to remain confidential, many union members are fearful that their signatures on the petition will be discovered. The timing of the NLRB's receipt of the decertification petition is also critical. The petition must be submitted between 60 and 90 days prior to the expiration of the current contract. When all these conditions have been met, the NLRB regional director will schedule a decertification election by secret ballot.

The NLRB carefully monitors the events leading up to the election. Current employees must initiate the request for the election. If the NLRB determines that management initiated the action, it will not certify the election. After a petition has been accepted, however, management can support the decertification election attempt. If a majority of the votes cast is against the union, the employees will be free from the union. Strong union supporters are all likely to vote. Thus, if a substantial numbers of employees are indifferent to the union and choose not to vote, decertification may not occur.

Unions Today

Labor unions have been in a continual decline for the past half-century.[58] In 2009, the union membership rate—the percent of wage and salary workers who were members of a union—was 12.3 percent, essentially unchanged from 12.4 percent a year earlier, the U.S. Bureau of Labor Statistics reported. The number of wage and salary workers belonging to unions declined by 771,000 to 15.3 million, largely reflecting the overall drop in employment due to the recession. More public sector employees (7.9 million) belonged to a union than did private sector employees (7.4 million) despite there being 5 times more wage and salary workers in the private sector. The union membership rate of 37.4 percent for public sector workers was substantially higher than the 7.2 percent rate for private industry workers (see Figure 12.5).[59]

Figure 12.5

Percentage of the Private Workforce That Is Unionized

Source: U.S. Department of Labor.

A GLOBAL PERSPECTIVE

Union Organizing in the Global Environment Can Be Dangerous

The International Trade Union Confederation (ITUC) is the world's largest trade union federation. It was formed on November 1, 2006, out of the merger of the International Confederation of Free Trade Unions (ICFTU) and the World Confederation of Labor (WCL). The ITUC represents 175 million workers through its 311 affiliated organizations' within 155 countries and territories. Guy Ryder is the current General Secretary.[64]

According to a study by the International Confederation of Free Trade Unions (now the ITUC), thousands of trade unionists were arrested, jailed, tortured, fired, or intimidated, and 223 were murdered or disappeared, across the world. The study, which draws on data from 132 countries, concluded that more than 4,000 trade unionists were arrested, 1,000 injured, and 10,000 fired. Violations were particularly severe in many export-processing zones. Ryder, said, "In places like Belarus, Zimbabwe and China, we find that undemocratic governments target trade unions first when their legitimacy is challenged."[65]

The report documents a long list of abuses, including many in textile and apparel plants in Asia, Africa, Latin America, and also in developed nations like the United States. Juan Somavia, director general of the International Labor Organization, said the report showed that while labor advocates have worked for decades to improve the treatment of workers, "the situation in many countries today shows that the struggle continues." The study alleged that management of JAR Kenya, a clothing maker in Nairobi, embarked on "a hostile attack on the Tailors and Textile Workers Union." It said active union members were "constantly harassed and intimidated. Some were locked up in the factory cell and handed over to the police on fabricated charges." The report added

that some were fired solely for joining the union. The survey pointed out that trade union rights are severely violated in many Far Eastern countries. It said police have attacked workers protesting in state-owned textile plants in China. "Any attempt to form a free trade union can be rewarded with huge prison sentences and even life imprisonment," it reported. The survey also documented harsh anti-union policies by management of garment and footwear factories in Indonesia and Pakistan, and fierce anti-union tactics in export-promotion zones in the Philippines, Sri Lanka, and other countries.[66] In Bangladesh, some of the mostly female employees at International Knitwear and Apparel who took part in actions for better working conditions lost their jobs, were threatened with death if they joined a union, and were beaten by hired thugs.[67]

With regard to the Americas, the report shows that hostility toward trade unions is a recurrent problem in many Central and South American countries. In Guatemala, it said, freedom of association "is virtually nonexistent," and added that employers in textile factories or the big multinationals refuse to recognize trade unions. No Guatemalan textile or apparel plants are currently unionized. In the case of the United States, the report estimated that "80 percent of employers engage consultants to assist in anti-union campaigning." Analysts alleged in the report that "some of the most extreme exploitation" takes place in territories controlled by the United States, such as the Northern Mariana Islands. The report argued the conditions there amount to a system of servitude: "Local authorities permit foreign-owned companies to recruit thousands of foreign workers, mainly young women from Thailand, China, the Philippines, and Bangladesh." The report contended workers in that region are forced to sign contracts that stipulate they must refrain from asking for wage increases, from seeking other work, or from joining a union. If they violate the contract, they face deportation, the report added.[68]

Likewise, organized labor in the capital-goods sector saw membership fall, as businesses cut capital-investment spending, prompting manufacturers to make layoffs. The reorganization of General Motors and DaimlerChrysler caused major cuts to be made in their labor force. The recession of 2008/10 battered two industries with high union density, manufacturing and construction.

The National Labor Relations Board (NLRB) conducted 1,579 elections in 2008 and unions won 66.8 percent of the representation elections, the highest win rate since 1984.[60] Jim Gray, a labor consultant for management, said, "unions are becoming more selective in where they go forward. But the win rate, though good, is not keeping up with what they're losing."[61] Today, there are only 2 million U.S. union manufacturing workers, which is down from 3.5 million a decade ago. However, there are more than 3 million workers in service and retail unions and more than 7 million in public-sector unions.[62] As compared with manufacturing, these are basically the low-wage jobs. John Schmitt, a senior economist with CEPR, said, "One of the most interesting developments is that the manufacturing workforce is less likely to be unionized than the rest of the workforce. That's something that's definitely new." Another change that has been occurring in organized labor is that women make up more than 45 percent of the unionized workforce—that is up from 35 percent in 1983.[63]

Remember my earlier discussion of "Recent Labor/Management Legal Trends" stated that significant changes affecting unions had been made by the new administration that came into office in 2008. The new NLRB had been reestablished with members who are pro labor. Also, four EOs that favored labor have recently been signed. Because of these and other pending measures, there are those who believe that labor will experience a membership surge.

Summary

1. *Describe the two-tier wage system.* The two-tier wage system is a wage structure where newly hired workers are paid less than current employees for performing the same or similar jobs.

2. *Describe union objectives and explain the reasons why employees join unions.* The underlying philosophy of the labor movement is that of organizational democracy and an atmosphere of social dignity for working men and women.

   Employees join unions because of dissatisfaction with management, the need for a social outlet, the need for avenues of leadership, forced unionization, and social pressure from peers.

3. *Describe organized labor's strategies for a stronger movement and describe the basic structure of a union.* Organized labor's new strategies for a stronger movement include strategically located union members, pulling the union through, political involvement, union salting, flooding the community, public awareness campaigns, building organizing funds, partnering with high schools, peacefully permitting employees to organize, and organizing through the card check.

   The basic element in the structure of the American labor movement is the local union. The national union is the most powerful level, and the American Federation of Labor and Congress of Industrial Organizations (AFL-CIO) is the central trade union federation in the United States.

4. *Define* collective bargaining *and identify the steps that lead to forming a bargaining unit.* Collective bargaining is "The performance of the mutual obligation of the employer and the representative of the employees to meet at reasonable times and confer in good faith with respect to wages, hours, and other terms and conditions of employment, or the negotiation of an agreement, or any question arising there under, and the execution of a written contract incorporating any agreement reached if requested by either party, but such obligation does not compel either party to agree to a proposal or require the making of a concession."

   The steps involved include signing authorization cards, petitioning for election, campaigning, winning the election, and being certified.

5. *Describe the collective bargaining process and explain collective bargaining issues.* The negotiating phase of collective bargaining begins with each side presenting its initial demands. The term *negotiating* suggests a certain amount of give-and-take. The party with the greater leverage can expect to extract the most concessions. Breakdowns in negotiations can be overcome through third-party intervention (mediation and arbitration), union tactics (strikes and boycotts), and management recourse (lockouts and continued operation without striking workers).

   Bargaining issues can be divided into three categories: mandatory, permissive, and prohibited. *Mandatory bargaining issues* fall within the definition of wages, hours, and other terms and conditions of employment. *Permissive bargaining issues* may be raised, but neither side may insist that they be bargained over. *Prohibited bargaining issues*, such as the issue of the closed shop, an arrangement whereby union membership is a prerequisite, are statutorily outlawed. Certain topics are included in virtually all labor agreements. These are: recognition, management rights, union security, compensation, grievance procedure, employee security, and job-related factors.

6. *Describe preparation for negotiations, negotiating the agreement, and breakdowns in negotiations.* The union must continuously gather information regarding membership needs to isolate areas of dissatisfaction. Management also spends long hours preparing for negotiations.

   The negotiating phase of collective bargaining begins with each side presenting its initial demands. The term *negotiating* suggests a certain amount of give-and-take. The party with the greater leverage can expect to extract the most concessions.

   Breakdowns in negotiations can be overcome through third-party intervention (mediation and arbitration), union tactics (strikes and boycotts), and management recourse (lockouts and continued operation without striking workers).

7. *Describe what is involved in reaching, ratifying, and administering the agreement.* The document that emerges from the collective bargaining process is known as a "labor agreement" or "contract."

   The approval process for management is often easier than for labor. The president or CEO has usually been briefed regularly on the progress of negotiations. Any difficulty that might have stood in the way of obtaining approval has probably already been resolved with top management by the negotiators. However, the approval process is more complex for the union. Until a majority of members voting in a ratification election approve it, the proposed agreement is not final.

   The larger and perhaps more important part of collective bargaining is administration of the agreement, which the public seldom sees. The agreement establishes the union–management relationship for the duration of the contract. Usually, neither party can change the contract's language until the expiration date, except by mutual consent. However, the main problem encountered in contract administration is uniform interpretation and application of the contract's terms.

8. *Describe the grievance procedure in a union environment.* A grievance procedure under a collective bargaining agreement is normally well defined. It is usually restricted to violations of the terms and conditions of the agreement.

9. *Explain recent/labor management legal trends and describe collective bargaining in the public sector.* The NLRB reports that more than 20,000 unfair-labor-practice charges were filed in 2008, with a finding of merit in more than 40 percent of the cases. The NLRB ordered employers to pay out more than $70 million in back wages and offer reinstatement to 1,564 employees. The NLRB has resumed its full caseload. Employer practices in unionization drives are likely to fall under greater scrutiny.

   Collective bargaining for workers in the public sector has traditionally been quite different from private-sector bargaining because wages have been off the table.

10. *Explain union decertification.* Decertification is essentially the reverse of the process that employees must follow to be recognized as an official bargaining unit.

11. *Describe the state of unions today.* Labor unions have been in a virtual continual decline for the past half-century. In 2009, the union membership rate—the percent of wage and salary workers who were members of a union—was 12.3 percent.

Key Terms

two-tier wage system   346
right-to-work
   laws   349
Committee on Political
   Education (COPE)   350
union salting   351
flooding the
   community   351
public awareness
   campaigns   351
card check   352
local union   353

craft union   353
industrial union   354
national union   354
American Federation of Labor
   and Congress of Industrial
   Organizations (AFL-CIO) 328
Change to Win Coalition   354
collective bargaining   355
bargaining unit   355
authorization card   356
mandatory bargaining
   issues   358

permissive bargaining
   issues   358
prohibited bargaining
   issues   358
closed shop   359
union shop   359
agency shop   359
open shop   359
checkoff of dues   360
grievance   360
grievance procedure   360
beachhead demands   362

mediation   363
arbitration   363
rights arbitration   363

interest arbitration   363
strike   364
boycott   365

secondary boycott   365
lockout   365
decertification   370

Questions for Review

1. What is the two-tier wage system?
2. What are the broad objectives that characterize the labor movement as a whole?
3. What are the primary reasons employees join labor unions?
4. What are organized labor's strategies for a stronger movement?
5. Define the following terms:
   a. Local union
   b. Craft union
   c. Industrial union
   d. National union
6. What steps must a union take in establishing the collective bargaining relationship? Briefly describe each step.
7. What are the steps involved in the collective bargaining process?
8. Distinguish among mandatory, permissive, and prohibited bargaining issues.
9. What are the primary means by which breakdowns in negotiations may be overcome? Briefly describe each.
10. What are the topics included in virtually all labor agreements?
11. Define each of the following:
    a. Closed shop
    b. Union shop
    c. Agency shop
    d. Maintenance of membership
    e. Checkoff of dues
12. What is involved for both management and labor in ratifying the agreement?
13. What is involved in the administration of a labor agreement?
14. How is the collective bargaining process different in the public sector?
15. Define *decertification*. What are the steps in decertification?
16. What is the status of unions today?

HRM INCIDENT 1

To Join Association of Maybank Class One Officer (A.M.C.O)

Jimmy had just graduated from university when he applied to join The Maybank Group, one of the largest banks in Malaysia, as a Management Trainee. This position would expose the new employee to various departments within the group after which he or she would become permanent staff at the bank.

It was during a training session that Jimmy got to know Tan, a trainer at a process session. After training, Tan approached Jimmy and they started talking about careers and their education backgrounds. Tan suggested Jimmy should join the union set up by officers and executives called the Association of Maybank Class One Officer (A.M.C.O). Initially, Jimmy was apprehensive about joining as he was afraid that it would jeopardize his chances at work. At university, his lecturers never really talked about unions. Jimmy asked, "What can A.M.C.O do for me?"

Tan replied, "A.M.C.O works hard to protect and improve working conditions for the members. A.M.C.O has won many benefits over the years that are now taken for granted as 'rights.'" These included: full medical coverage for the officer and his/her immediate family members, protection from workplace discrimination and harassment, and refreshment allowance.

Jimmy seemed somewhat unsure about joining A.M.C.O because he felt afraid about the prospects of putting his career in jeopardy. After the training, Jimmy met up with a few other senior colleagues. One of them asked, "Are you planning to join A.M.C.O? It's good, you know." Another worker commented that there were a lot of benefits to joining a union. He said, "If you join A.M.C.O, you can be protected from exploitation and discrimination in the workplace. Apart from that it can help you sort out any problems at work. Access to more opportunities for training will also be given to you."

Tan added, "Why not come to the meeting next week at A.M.C.O. I will email you the details. Maybe you should check out the A.M.C.O website for further information." Jimmy was still unsure but replied, "Alright, please email me the details."

Questions

1. Why would Jimmy have reservations about joining A.M.C.O?
2. What do you think would happen to Jimmy if he chooses not to join the A.M.C.O?
3. What are the other methods union members can use to recruit more members?

HRM INCIDENT **2**

You Are Out of What?

Marcus Ned eagerly drove his new company pickup onto the construction site. His employer, Kelso Construction Company, had just assigned him to supervise a crew of 16 equipment operators, oilers, and mechanics. This was the first unionized crew Marcus had supervised, and he was unaware of the labor agreement in effect that carefully defined and limited the role of supervisors. As he approached his work area, he noticed one of the cherry pickers (a type of mobile crane with an extendable boom) standing idle with the operator beside it. Marcus pulled up beside the operator and asked, "What's going on here?"

"Out of gas," the operator said.

"Well, go and get some," Marcus said.

The operator reached to get his thermos jug out of the toolbox on the side of the crane and said, "The oiler's on break right now. He'll be back in a few minutes."

Marcus remembered that he had a five-gallon can of gasoline in the back of his pickup. So he quickly got the gasoline, climbed on the cherry picker, and started to pour it into the gas tank. As he did so, he heard the other machines shutting down in unison. He looked around and saw all the other operators climbing down from their equipment and standing to watch him pour the gasoline. A moment later, he saw the union steward approaching.

Questions

1. Why did all the operators shut down their machines?
2. If you were Marcus, what would you do now?

Notes

1. Shane R. Premeaux, R. Wayne Mondy, and Art L. Bethke "The Two-Tier Wage System: A Major Breakthrough in the Reindustrialization of America?" *Personnel Administrator* 31 (November 1986): 92–100.
2. Thomas C. Graham, "The GM/UAW Contract: Winners, Losers, Lost Chances," *American Metal Market* 116 (December 2007): 98.
3. David Barkholz and Amy Wilson, "Ford: Benefits of Two-tier Wages Won't Come Until 2009," *Automotive News* 82 (February 11, 2008): 15.
4. "U.S. to Feel Impact of 2-tiered Wage System in Mexico," *Rubber & Plastics News* 37 (June 16, 2008): 8.
5. Ibid.
6. "Vote Eyed as Precision Tube, Union Reach Tentative Labor Agreement," *Metal Bulletin Daily* (September 11, 2009): 81.
7. "Precision Tube Contract Vote Ends Strike," *Metal Bulletin Daily* (September 18, 2009): 10.
8. Ken Jacobs, "A Tale of Two Tiers: Dividing Workers in the Age of Neoliberalism," *New Labor Forum* 18 (Winter 2009): 66–77.

9. Edwin F. Beal and James P. Begin, *The Practice of Collective Bargaining*, 5th ed. (Homewood, IL: Richard D. Irwin, 1982): 91.

10. Shari Lau, Erin Lee, Patton Lee, and Yvette Lee, "Performance-Based Discipline, Union Organizing, Bonus Taxation," *HRMagazine* 54 (September 2009): 27–28.

11. Robert J. Grossman, "On the Defense," *HRMagazine* 53 (January 2008): 38–39.

12. "SSCC Workers OK Deal to Unionize," *Official Board Markets* 86 (April 17, 2010): 16.

13. Joann Muller, "Has the UAW Found a Better Road?" *BusinessWeek* 3791 (July 15, 2002): 108.

14. Jessica Marquez, "As Elections Near, Unions Look to Sway Senate Races," *Workforce Management* 87 (April 21, 2008): 6.

15. Michael H. Schuster, "Obama and HR Strategy: Likely Impacts of the Administration's Employment and Labor Policies," *People & Strategy* 32 (2009): 18–25.

16. Michael Learmonth and Ira Teinowitz, "Court Ruling to Deliver $300M Boost to Media," *Advertising Age* 81 (January 25, 2010): 1–37.

17. "Unbound," *Economist* 394 (January 30, 2010): 39.

18. Daryll J. Neuser and Daniel D. Barker, "What Every Employer Should Know About the Law of Union Organizing," Employee Relations Law Journal 35 (Spring 2010): 3–45.

19. Robert Grossman, "Reorganized Labor," *HRMagazine* 53 (January 2008): 36–41.

20. Arthur B. Shostak, "PATCO's 1981 Strike," *Labor Studies Journal* 34 (June 2009): 149–158.

21. "Unions Takes Proactive Approach to Training," *Plant Engineering* 63 (October 2009): 8.

22. Rachel Haut, Natalie Kelly, and Max Mishler, "Youth Activism in the Labor Movement," *New Labor Forum* 18 (Winter 2009): 98–107.

23. Ibid.

24. Mark Schoeff, Jr., "Looking to Serve Youth," *Workforce Management* 88 (September 14, 2009): 1–3.

25. Richard. L. Trumka, "Selling Unions to Young Workers," *Vital Speeches of the Day* 75 (October 2009): 475–478.

26. Ibid.

27. "UPS Freight Workers Become Teamsters," *Toledo Business Journal* 24 (April 2008): 24–28.

28. "Teamsters Ratify UPS Freight Contract," *Florida Shipper* 33 (April 21, 2008): 13.

29. Josh Cable, "Is EFCA's Time Now," *Industry Week* 259 (April 2010): 26–28,

30. Mark Schoeff Jr., "NLRB'S Kirsanow Vows to Address Cases Objectively," *Workforce Management* 85 (February 13, 2006): 14.

31. "Interest Arbitration Under the Employee Free Choice Act: What Could This Mean for Employers?" *Venulex Legal Summaries* (2009 Q1, Special section): 2–6.

32. http://www.seiu.org/our-union/index.php, February 7, 2010.

33. http://www.teamster.org/content/fast-facts, February 7, 2010.

34. http://www.afl-cio.org/aboutus/thisistheaflcio/, January 3, 2010.

35. http://www.changetowin.org/about-us.html, July 16, 2008.

36. Grossman, "Reorganized Labor."

37. http://www.changetowin.org/about-us/mission.html, February 7, 2010.

38. "What Every Employer Should Know About the Law of Union Organizing."

39. *A Guide to Basic Law and Procedures under the National Labor Relations Act* (Washington, D.C: U.S. Government Printing Office, October 1978): 11–13.

40. T. L. Stanley, "Union Stewards and Labor Relations," *Supervision* 71 (February 2010): 3–6.

41. "Arbitrator's Decision Upheld," *Business Insurance* 34 (December 4, 2000): 2.

42. Arthur B. Shostak, "PATCO's 1981 Strike," *Labor Studies Journal* 34 (June 2009): 149–158.

43. Elizabeth A. Ashack, "Profiles of Significant Collective Bargaining Disputes of 2008," *Compensation & Working Conditions* (June 2009): 1.

44. Elizabeth A. Ashack, "Profiles of Significant Collective Bargaining Disputes of 2009," *Compensation & Working Conditions* (March 2010): 1.

45. Andrea Holecek, "Levy Co. Replaces Striking Steel Workers, Fires Others," *The Times* (March 29, 2006).

46. Heather Draper, "Coors Facing New Boycott: Workers at Brewer's Supplier Locked Out after Pact Expired," *Rocky Mountain News* (September 24, 2002): 6B.

47. Thomas Gnau, "AK: Production Will Go On and Improve," *Middletown Journal (OH)* April 26, 2006).

48. Charles A. Borell, "How Unions Can Improve Their Success Rate in Labor Arbitration," *Dispute Resolution Journal* 61 (February 2006): 28–38.

49. Fay Hansen, "Talking Union," *Workforce Management* 88 (November 16, 2009): 16–18.

50. John D. Boyd, "Teamsters Praise NLRB Appointments," *JoC Online* (March 30, 2010): 6.

51. "Obama Appoints Pro-union Attorney to NLRB," *HR Specialist: Employment Law* 40 (May 2010): 5.

52. "Fed Contractors Will Have to Post 'Right to Unionize' Notice," *HR Specialist: Texas Employment Law* 5 (March 2010): 1–5.

53. http://www.archives.gov/federal-register/executive-orders/2009-obama.html, May 5, 2010.

54. "New Executive Orders on Labor Relations Will Impact All Federal Contractors," *Venulex Legal Summaries* (2009 Q1, Special section): 1–2.

55. Samuel Estreicher, "'Think Global, Act Local': Employee Representation in a World of Global Labor

and Product Market Competition," *Labor Lawyer* 24 (Winter 2009): 253–265.

56. Alyssa Rosenberg, "Warming Trend," *Government Executive* 41 (November 2009): 44–52.

57. Michael R. Carrell and Christina Heavrin, *Labor Relations and Collective Bargaining: Cases, Practices, and Law* (Prentice Hall: Upper Saddle River, N.J.: 2010): 241.

58. John Godard, "The Exceptional Decline of the American Labor Movement," *Industrial & Labor Relations Review* 63 (October 2009): 82–108.

59. http://www.bls.gov/news.release/union2.nr0.htm, February 7, 2007.

60. "Union Win Rate Rose in 2008, & Number of Elections Increased," *HR Focus* (July 2009): 9.

61. Robert Grossman, "Reorganized Labor," *HRMagazine* 53 (January 2008): 36–41.

62. Ibid.

63. "Unions Trend Toward Female Majority," *Industry Week* 259 (January 2010): 21.

64. http://en.wikipedia.org/wiki/International_Trade_Union_Confederation

65. John Zarocostas, "Organizing in the Third World a Dangerous Job, Study Finds," *International Confederation of Free Trade Unions Reports* (June 25, 2002): 8.

66. Ibid.

67. Ibid.

68. Ibid.

12 History of Unions in the United States

Labor Movement Before 1930

Unions are not a recent development in American history. The earliest unions originated toward the end of the 18th century, about the time of the American Revolution. Although these early associations had few of the characteristics of present-day labor unions, they did bring workers in craft or guild-related occupations together to consider problems of mutual concern. These early unions were local in nature and usually existed for only a short time.[1]

Development of the labor movement has been neither simple nor straightforward; unionism has experienced as much failure as success. Employer opposition, the impact of the business cycle, the growth of American industry, court rulings, and legislation have exerted their influence in varying degrees at different times. As a result, the history of the labor movement has somewhat resembled the swinging of a pendulum. At times, the pendulum has moved in favor of labor and, at other times, it has swung toward the advantage of management.

Prior to the 1930s, the trend definitely favored management. The courts strongly supported employers in their attempts to thwart the organized labor movement. This was first evidenced by the use of criminal and civil conspiracy doctrines derived from English common law. A **conspiracy** is two or more persons who band together to prejudice the rights of others or of society (such as by refusing to work or demanding higher wages).

An important feature of the conspiracy doctrine is that an action, though legal when performed by one person, may become illegal when carried out by a group. In 1806, the year in which the conspiracy doctrine was first applied to labor unions, the courts began to influence the field of labor relations.[2] From 1806 to 1842, 17 cases charging labor unions with conspiracies went to trial. These cases resulted in the demise of several unions and certainly discouraged other union activities. The conspiracy doctrine was softened considerably by the decision in the landmark case *Commonwealth v Hunt* in 1842. In that case, Chief Justice Shaw of the Supreme Judicial Court of Massachusetts contended that labor organizations were legal. Thus, in order for a union to be convicted under the conspiracy doctrine, it had to be shown that the union's objectives were unlawful or the means used to gain a legal end were unlawful. To this day, the courts continue to exert a profound influence on both the direction and character of labor relations.

Other tactics used by employers to stifle union growth were injunctions and yellow-dog contracts. An **injunction** is a prohibited legal procedure used by employers to prevent certain union activities, such as strikes and unionization attempts. A **yellow-dog contract** was a written agreement between the employee and the company, made at the time of employment that prohibits a worker from joining a union or engaging in union activities. Each of these defensive tactics, used by management and supported by the courts, severely limited union growth.

In the latter half of the 19th century, the American industrial system started to grow and prosper. Factory production began to displace handicraft forms of manufacturing. The Civil War gave the factory system a great boost. Goods were demanded in quantities that only mass-production methods could supply. The railroads developed new networks of routes spanning the continent and knitting the country into an economic whole. Employment was high, and unions sought to organize workers in both new and expanding enterprises. Most unions during this time were small and rather weak, and many did not survive the economic recession of the 1870s. Union membership rose to 300,000 by 1872 and then dropped to 50,000 by 1878.[3] This period

conspiracy
Two or more persons who band together to prejudice the rights of others or of society (such as by refusing to work or demanding higher wages).

injunction
Prohibited legal procedure used by employers to prevent certain union activities, such as strikes and unionization attempts.

yellow-dog contract
Written agreement between an employee and a company made at the time of employment, that prohibits a worker from joining a union or engaging in union activities.

also marked the rise of radical labor activity and increased industrial strife as unions struggled for recognition and survival.[4]

Out of the turbulence of the 1870s emerged the most substantial labor organization that had yet appeared in the United States. The Noble Order of the Knights of Labor was founded in 1869 as a secret society of the Philadelphia garment workers. After its secrecy was abandoned and workers in other areas were invited to join, it grew rapidly, reaching a membership of more than 700,000 by the mid-1880s. Internal conflict among the Knights' leadership in 1881 gave rise to the nucleus of a new organization that would soon replace it on the labor scene.[5] That organization was the American Federation of Labor (AFL).

Devoted to what is referred to as either "pure and simple unionism" or "business unionism," Samuel Gompers of the Cigarmakers Union led some 25 labor groups representing skilled trades to found the AFL in 1886.[6] Gompers was elected the first president of the AFL, a position he held until his death in 1924 (except for one year, 1894–1895, when he adamantly opposed tangible support for the Pullman group strikers). He is probably the single most important individual in American trade union history. The AFL began with a membership of some 138,000 and doubled that number during the next 12 years.

In 1890, Congress passed the Sherman Anti-Trust Act, which marked the entrance of the federal government into the statutory regulation of labor organizations. Although the primary stimulus for this Act came from public concern over the monopoly power of business, court interpretations soon applied its provisions to organized labor. Later, in 1914, Congress passed the Clayton Act (an amendment to the Sherman Act), which, according to Samuel Gompers, was the Magna Carta of labor. The intent of this Act was to remove labor from the purview of the Sherman Act. Again, judicial interpretation nullified that intent and left labor even more exposed to lawsuits.[7] Nonetheless, as a result of industrial activity related to World War I, the AFL grew to almost 5 million members by 1920.[8]

During the 1920s, labor faced legal restrictions on union activity and unfavorable court decisions. The one exception to such repressive policies was the passage and approval of the Railway Labor Act of 1926. Passage of this legislation marked the first time that the government declared without qualification the right of private employees to join unions and bargain collectively through representatives of their own choosing, without interference from their employers. It also set up special machinery for the settlement of labor disputes. Although the Act covered only employees in the railroad industry (a later amendment extended coverage to the airline industry), it foreshadowed the extension of similar rights to other classes of employees in the 1930s.

Labor Movement After 1930

The 1930s found the United States in the midst of the worst depression in its history. The unemployment rate rose as high as 25 percent.[9] The sentiment of the country began to favor organized labor, as many people blamed business for the agony that accompanied the Great Depression. The pendulum began to swing away from management and toward labor. This swing was assisted by several acts and actions that supported the cause of unionism.

Anti-Injunction Act (Norris–LaGuardia Act), 1932

The Great Depression caused a substantial change in the public's thinking about the role of unions in society. Congress reflected this thinking in 1932 with the passage of the Norris–LaGuardia Act, which affirms that U.S. public policy sanctions collective bargaining and approves the formation and effective operation of labor unions. While this Act did not outlaw the use of injunctions, it severely restricted the federal courts' authority to issue them in labor disputes. It also made yellow-dog contracts unenforceable in the federal courts.[10]

National Labor Relations Act (Wagner Act), 1935

In 1933, Congress made an abortive attempt to stimulate economic recovery by passing the National Industry Recovery Act (NIRA). Declared unconstitutional by the U.S. Supreme Court in 1935, the NIRA did provide the nucleus for legislation that followed it. Section 7a of the

NIRA proclaimed the right of workers to organize and bargain collectively. Congress did not, however, provide procedures to enforce these rights.

Undeterred by the Supreme Court decision and strongly supported by organized labor, Congress speedily enacted a comprehensive labor law, the National Labor Relations Act (Wagner Act). This Act, approved by President Roosevelt on July 5, 1935, is one of the most significant labor management relations statutes ever enacted. Drawing heavily on the experience of the Railway Labor Act of 1926 and Section 7a of the NIRA, the Act declared legislative support, on a broad scale, for the right of employees to organize and engage in collective bargaining. The spirit of the Wagner Act is stated in Section 7, which defines the substantive rights of employees:

Employees shall have the right to self-organization, to form, join, or assist labor organizations, to bargain collectively through representatives of their own choosing, and to engage in other concerted activities, for the purpose of collective bargaining or other mutual aid or protection.

The rights defined in Section 7 were protected against employer interference by Section 8, which detailed and prohibited five management practices deemed to be unfair to labor:

1. Interfering with or restraining or coercing employees in the exercise of their right to self-organization.
2. Dominating or interfering in the affairs of a union.
3. Discriminating in regard to hire or tenure or any condition of employment for the purpose of encouraging or discouraging union membership.
4. Discriminating against or discharging an employee who has filed charges or given testimony under the Act.
5. Refusing to bargain with chosen representatives of employees.

The National Labor Relations Act created the National Labor Relations Board (NLRB) to administer and enforce the provisions of the Act. The NLRB was given two principal functions: (1) to establish procedures for holding bargaining-unit elections and to monitor the election procedures, and (2) to investigate complaints and prevent unlawful acts involving unfair labor practices. Much of the NLRB's work is delegated to 33 regional offices throughout the country.

Following passage of the Wagner Act, union membership increased from approximately 3 million to 15 million between 1935 and 1947.[11] The increase was most conspicuous in industries using mass-production methods. New unions in these industries were organized on an industrial basis rather than a craft basis, and members were primarily unskilled or semiskilled workers. An internal struggle developed within the AFL over the question of whether unions should be organized to include all workers in an industry or strictly on a craft or occupational basis. In 1935, 10 AFL-affiliated unions and the officers of two other AFL unions formed a new group. Called the Committee for Industrial Organization, its purpose was to promote the organization of workers in mass-production and unorganized industries. The controversy grew to the point that in 1938 the AFL expelled all but one of the Committee for Industrial Organization unions. In November 1938, the expelled unions held their first convention in Pittsburgh, and reorganized as a federation of unions under the name of Congress of Industrial Organizations (CIO). The new federation included the nine unions expelled from the AFL and 32 other groups established to recruit workers in various industries. John L. Lewis, president of the United Mine Workers, was elected the first president of the CIO.

The rivalry generated by the two large federations stimulated union-organizing efforts in both groups. With the ensuing growth, the labor movement gained considerable influence in the United States. However, many individuals and groups began to feel that the Wagner Act favored labor too much. This shift in public sentiment was in part related to a rash of costly strikes following World War II. Whether justified or not, much of the blame for these disruptions fell on the unions.

Labor Management Relations Act (Taft–Hartley Act), 1947

In 1947, with public pressure mounting, Congress overrode President Truman's veto and passed the Labor Management Relations Act (Taft–Hartley Act). The Taft–Hartley Act extensively revised the National Labor Relations Act and became Title I of that law. A new period began in the evolution of public policy regarding labor. The pendulum had begun to swing toward a more balanced position between labor and management.

Some of the important changes introduced by the Taft–Hartley Act included the following:

1. Modifying Section 7 to include the right of employees to refrain from union activity as well as engage in it.
2. Prohibiting the closed shop and narrowing the freedom of the parties to authorize the union shop.
3. Broadening the employer's right of free speech.
4. Providing that employers need not recognize or bargain with unions formed by supervisors.
5. Giving employees the right to initiate decertification petitions.
6. Providing for government intervention in national emergency strikes.

Another significant change extended the concept of unfair labor practices to unions. Labor organizations were to refrain from the following:

1. Restraining or coercing employees in the exercise of their guaranteed collective bargaining rights.
2. Causing an employer to discriminate in any way against an employee in order to encourage or discourage union membership.
3. Refusing to bargain in good faith with an employer regarding wages, hours, and other terms and conditions of employment.
4. Engaging in certain types of strikes and boycotts.
5. Requiring employees covered by union-shop contracts to pay initiation fees or dues in an amount which the Board finds excessive or discriminatory under all circumstances.
6. *Featherbedding,* or requiring that an employer pay for services not performed.

One of the most controversial elements of the Taft–Hartley Act is its Section 14b, which permits states to enact right-to-work legislation. The National Right to Work Committee, based in Springfield, Virginia, provides much of the impetus behind the right-to-work movement.

For about 10 years after the passage of the Taft–Hartley Act, union membership expanded at about the same rate as nonagricultural employment. But all was not well within the organized labor movement. Since the creation of the CIO, the two federations had engaged in a bitter and costly rivalry. Both the CIO and the AFL recognized the increasing need for cooperation and reunification. In 1955, following two years of intensive negotiations between the two organizations, a merger agreement was ratified, the AFL-CIO became a reality, and George Meany was elected president. In the years following the merger, the labor movement faced some of its greatest challenges.

Labor-Management Reporting and Disclosure Act (Landrum–Griffin Act), 1959

Corruption had plagued organized labor since the early 1900s. Periodic revelations of graft, violence, extortion, racketeering, and other improper activities aroused public indignation and invited governmental investigation. Even though the number of unions involved was small, every disclosure undermined the public image of organized labor as a whole.[12] Corruption had been noted in the construction trades, and in Laborers', Hotel and Restaurant workers', Carpenters', Painters', East Coast Longshoremen's, and Boilermakers' unions.

Scrutiny of union activities is a focal point in today's labor environment, but it began to intensify immediately after World War II. Ultimately, inappropriate union activities led to the creation in 1957 of the Senate Select Committee on Improper Activities in the Labor or Management Field, headed by Senator McClellan of Arkansas. Between 1957 and 1959, the McClellan Committee held a series of nationally televised public hearings that shocked and alarmed the entire country. As evidence of improper activities mounted, primarily against the Teamsters and Longshoremen/Maritime unions, the AFL-CIO took action. In 1957, the AFL-CIO expelled three unions (representing approximately 1.6 million members) for their practices. One of them, the Teamsters, was the largest union in the country.

In 1959, largely as a result of the recommendations of the McClellan Committee, Congress enacted the Labor-Management Reporting and Disclosure Act (Landrum–Griffin Act). This Act marked a significant turning point in the involvement of the federal government in internal union affairs. The Landrum–Griffin Act spelled out a *Bill of Rights for Members of Labor Organizations* designed to protect certain rights of individuals in their relationships with unions. The Act requires extensive reporting on numerous internal union activities and contains severe penalties for violations. Employers are also required to file reports when they engage in activities or make expenditures that might undermine the collective bargaining process or interfere with protected employee rights. In addition, the Act amended the Taft–Hartley Act by adding additional restrictions on picketing and secondary boycotts.[13]

In 1974, Congress extended coverage of the Taft–Hartley Act to private, not-for-profit hospitals. This amendment brought within the jurisdiction of the NLRB some 2 million employees. Proprietary (profit-making) health care organizations were already under NLRB jurisdiction. The amendment does not cover government-operated hospitals, only those in the private sector.

Key Terms

conspiracy   378
injunction   378
yellow-dog contract   378

Notes

1. *Brief History of the American Labor Movement,* Bulletin 1000 (Washington, DC: U.S. Department of Labor Statistics, 1970): 1.
2. Benjamin J. Taylor and Fred Witney, *Labor Relations Law,* 5th ed. (Englewood Cliffs, NJ: Prentice Hall, 1987): 12–13.
3. *Brief History of the American Labor Movement,* 9.
4. Foster Rhea Dulles, *Labor in America,* 3rd ed. (New York: Crowell, 1966): 114–125.
5. Ibid., 126–149.
6. James Ryan, "The Merger of the AFL & the CIO," *Merger of the AFL & the CIO* (2005): 1–2.
7. E. Edward Herman, Alfred Kuhn, and Ronald L. Seeber, *Collective Bargaining and Labor Relations* (Englewood Cliffs, NJ: Prentice Hall, 1987): 32–34.
8. *Brief History of the American Labor Movement,* 27.
9. *Historical Statistics of the United States, Colonial Times to 1970,* bicentennial ed. Part I (Washington, DC: U.S. Bureau of the Census, 1975): 126.
10. Taylor and Witney, *Labor Relations Law,* 78–81.
11. *Brief History of the American Labor Movement,* 65.
12. Dulles, *Labor in America,* 382–383.
13. *Brief History of the American Labor Movement,* 58–61.

13 Internal Employee Relations

HRM in Action: Worker Retention: It Costs Less to Keep Qualified Workers than to Replace Them

In the times of recession, it is easy to forget that retention of talented workers continues to be a critical concern. Smart organizations know that despite layoffs, voluntary turnover of the most talented workers can put an already challenged organization into an even more shaky position in terms of productivity and leadership. The 2008/10 recession caused a definite reduction in the workforce around the world. So, did organizations need to be concerned about employee retention? ABSOLUTELY! A poll of more than 22,400 Monster.com visitors found that 88 percent of U.S. respondents said they would be open to changing careers and 46 percent were actively seeking to change careers.[1] A recent survey by the Swiss outsourcing firm Adecco found that 54 percent of employed adults said that they are at least somewhat likely to look for new jobs once the economy turns around.[2] If this is so, companies must still show the remaining employees that they are valued because keeping the best employees productive, focused, and fully engaged is critical; top performers can usually find employment in any economy.[3] In fact, one of the best ways to improve a firm's financial position in difficult time is to retain their most valued employees.[4]

David Lacey, vice president of human resource business development at VIST Insurance, said, "The costs of replacing talented and effective employees far outstrip the expense of retaining and developing new employees. Recruiting and training new employees act as a drag on earnings from three to six months until the new employee is performing at the expected level. However, retained and highly motivated employees contribute to the company at a higher, more consistent and sustained level of

After completing this chapter, students should be able to:

1. Define *internal employee relations*.

2. Explain the concept of employment at will.

3. Explain discipline and disciplinary action.

4. Describe the disciplinary action process, discuss the various approaches to disciplinary action, and describe the problems in the administration of disciplinary action.

5. Describe terminations, explain termination of employees at various levels, and explain demotion as an alternative to termination.

6. Describe downsizing and explain the use of ombudspersons and alternative dispute resolution.

7. Describe transfers, promotions, resignations, and retirements as factors involved in internal employee relations.

performance."[5] It is much less expensive to retain and develop quality employees than it is to replace them.[6]

Most managers are keenly aware of the high cost of turnover, especially for their most productive employees.[7] Therefore, organizations need to constantly give these workers reasons to stay. Once a quality employee has been hired, half the battle has been won. The other half consists of finding ways to retain them. Sadly, many workers do not believe that their employers are putting forth much effort to retain them. A company needs to have an ongoing strategy to retain their valued employees. In fact, a recent survey found that higher-performing companies had substantially higher retention efforts than lower performers.[8]

Throughout this book, many topics have been discussed that, by themselves, may not appear to be a retention strategy. But, virtually every topic can be viewed in some manner as being a part of a total retention strategy. Let us see how some topics highlighted in your text might affect retention.

Chapter 1—A corporate culture or employer brand in which workers believe "it's fun to work at this company."

Chapter 2—Organizations that have a reputation for being ethically responsible.

Chapter 3—Organizations that encourage workplace diversity.

Chapter 4—Organizations that lets employees become aware of new job opportunities.

Chapter 5—Organizations that emphasize promotion from within.

Chapter 6—Employers that seek employees who "fit" into the organizational culture.

Chapter 7—Organizations that encourage employees to continue to grow and learn.

Chapter 8—Organizations that assess and reward employees based on their performance.

Chapter 9—Organizations that pay a fair wage based on employee productivity.

Chapter 10—Employers that create a balanced work–life environment.

Chapter 11—Organizations that provide employees with a safe and healthy work environment.

Chapter 12—Organizations that create a work environment where employees believe they do not need a union to represent them.

Chapter 13—Organizations with an internal employee administration program that is fair to all involved.

Managers play a pivotal role in an individual's retention decision. In all of the scenarios described, management either decided to do something or decided to do nothing. Throughout your text, the topic of metrics has been addressed. I propose at this point that the most important metric in HR today is the retention rate of your most qualified employees, the individuals who are capable of taking an organization to new heights.

In this chapter, employee retention is first discussed, followed by defining internal employee relations and discussing employment at will. Discipline and disciplinary action are then described, followed by a discussion of the disciplinary action process. Next, approaches to disciplinary action, problems in the administration of disciplinary action, and emotional intelligence as it relates to disciplinary action are presented. This is followed by a discussion of termination, termination of employees at various levels, and demotion as an alternative to termination. Next downsizing, the use of ombudspersons, and alternative dispute resolution are discussed. A discussion of transfers, promotions, resignations, and retirement follow. This chapter concludes with a global perspective entitled "Disciplinary Action in the Global Environment."

OBJECTIVE 13.1
Define *internal employee relations*.

internal employee relations
Those human resource management activities associated with the movement of employees within the organization.

OBJECTIVE 13.2
Explain the concept of employment at will.

Internal Employee Relations Defined

The status of most workers is not permanently fixed in an organization. Employees constantly move upward, laterally, downward, and out of the organization. To ensure that workers with the proper skills and experience are available at all levels, constant and concerted efforts are required to maintain good internal employee relations. **Internal employee relations** comprise the human resource management activities associated with the movement of employees within the organization. Some topics related to internal employee relations include terminations, demotions, downsizing, transfers, promotions, and resignations. Employment at will will first be discussed as a factor affecting internal employee relations.

Employment at Will

Employment at will is an unwritten contract created when an employee agrees to work for an employer but no agreement exists as to how long the parties expect the employment to last. In Chapter 3, numerous hiring standards to avoid were discussed. You learned that factors such as

employment at will
Unwritten contract created when an employee agrees to work for an employer but no agreement exists as to how long the parties expect the employment to last.

race, religion, sex, national origin, age, and disabilities should not be considered as a hiring standard unless the factor was a bona fide occupational qualification (BFOQ). Notwithstanding various employment standards to avoid that are based on laws, court decisions, and executive orders, approximately two of every three U.S. workers depend almost entirely on the continued goodwill of their employer. Individuals falling into this category are known as "at-will employees." Not included are individuals with a contract for a specified period of time such as with collective bargaining agreements. Teachers usually have an annual contract and are not at-will employees. Remember from Chapter 2, the Sarbanes–Oxley Act contained broad employee whistleblower protections. Thus, employees who report an illegal act, like whistleblowers, are not subject to employment at will. Generally, much of the U.S. legal system presumes that the jobs of such employees may be terminated at the will of the employer and that these employees have a similar right to leave their jobs at any time. Historically, because of a century-old common-law precedent in the United States, employment of indefinite duration could, in general, be terminated at the whim of either party.

The courts have made certain exceptions to the employment-at-will doctrine. Some of these include prohibiting terminations in violation of public policy, permitting employees to bring claims based on representations made in employment handbooks, and permitting claims based on the common-law doctrine of good faith and fair dealing. Employers can do certain things to help protect themselves against litigation for wrongful discharge based on a breach of implied employment contract.[9] Statements in documents such as employment applications and policy manuals that suggest job security or permanent employment should be avoided if employers want to minimize charges of wrongful discharge. Telling a person during a job interview that he or she can expect to hold the job as long as they want could be considered a contractual agreement and grounds for a lawsuit. A person should not be employed without a signed acknowledgment of the at-will disclaimer. In addition, the policy manual should have it clearly stated in bold, larger-than-normal print, so it is very clear to the employee that this is an at-will relationship. Other guidelines that may assist organizations in avoiding wrongful termination suits include clearly defining the worker's duties, providing good feedback on a regular basis, and conducting realistic performance appraisals on a regular basis.

Ethics was discussed in Chapter 2 and there are those who contend that even though an employer has a legal right to terminate an employee at will, there are ethical boundaries to be considered. Some of these include: terminate only as a last resort, after all other options have been exhausted; give as much notice as possible; provide as much severance pay and other help as one can; never terminate an employee for anything other than a legitimate business reason; never lie to an employee about the reason for his termination; always tell the truth; treat the employee with as much dignity and respect as possible. However, there is no law that says these ethical considerations have to be followed. Discipline and disciplinary action are next discussed.

OBJECTIVE 13.3
Explain discipline and disciplinary action.

discipline
State of employee self-control and orderly conduct that indicates the extent of genuine teamwork within an organization.

disciplinary action
Invoking a penalty against an employee who fails to meet established standards.

Discipline and Disciplinary Action

Discipline is the state of employee self-control and orderly conduct that indicates the extent of genuine teamwork within an organization. A necessary but often trying aspect of internal employee relations is the application of disciplinary action. **Disciplinary action** invokes a penalty against an employee who fails to meet established standards. Even though disciplinary action may be tense, unpleasant and fraught with conflict, at times it must be done.[10] Don Crosby, vice president of international and corporate HR at McDonald's, said, "It's the hardest thing a manager has to do. It's also rocky terrain for many executives, who simply do not know when or how to hold the stick, swinging it haphazardly and inconsistently, striking too hard, too soft, or not at all."[11]

Effective disciplinary action addresses the employee's wrongful behavior, not the employee as a person. Incorrectly administered disciplinary action is destructive to both the employee and the organization. Thus, disciplinary action should not be applied haphazardly. Disciplinary action is not usually management's initial response to a problem. Normally, there are more positive ways of convincing employees to adhere to company policies that are necessary to accomplish organizational goals. However, managers at times must administer disciplinary action when company rules are violated.

OBJECTIVE 13.4

Describe the disciplinary action process, discuss the various approaches to disciplinary action, and describe the problems in the administration of disciplinary action.

Disciplinary Action Process

The disciplinary action process is dynamic and ongoing. Because one person's actions can affect others in a work group, the proper application of disciplinary action fosters acceptable behavior by other group members. Conversely, unjustified or improperly administered disciplinary action can have a detrimental effect on other group members.

The disciplinary action process is shown in Figure 13.1. The external environment affects every area of human resource management, including disciplinary actions. Changes in the external environment, such as technological innovations, may render a rule inappropriate and may necessitate creating new rules. Laws and government regulations that affect company policies and rules are also constantly changing. For instance, the Occupational Safety and Health Act caused many firms to establish safety rules.

Changes in the internal environment of the firm can also alter the disciplinary action process. Through organization development, the firm may change its employer brand. As a result of this shift, first-line supervisors may begin to handle disciplinary action more positively. Organization policies can also have an impact on the disciplinary action process. Think how a new smoke-free workplace policy might impact the workplace and the possible need for disciplinary action.

The disciplinary action process deals largely with infractions of rules. Notice in Figure 13.1 that rules are established to better facilitate the accomplishment of organizational goals. Rules are specific guides to behavior on the job. The dos and don'ts associated with accomplishing tasks may be highly inflexible. For example, a company may forbid the use of tobacco products anywhere on company property.

Figure 13.1

Disciplinary Action Process

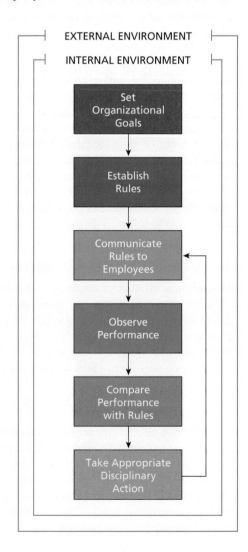

After management has established rules, it must communicate these rules to employees. All employees must know the standards in order to be disciplined persons. Individuals cannot obey a rule if they do not know it exists.[12] The manager then observes the performance of workers and compares performance with rules. As long as employee behavior does not vary from acceptable practices, there is no need for disciplinary action, but when an employee's behavior violates a rule, corrective action may need to be taken. Taking disciplinary action against someone often creates an uncomfortable psychological climate. However, managers can still sleep well at night after taking disciplinary action if the rules have been clearly articulated to everyone.

The purpose of disciplinary action is to alter behavior that can have a negative impact on achievement of organizational objectives, not to chastise the violator. The word *discipline* comes from the word *disciple,* and when translated from Latin, it means *to teach.* Thus, the intent of disciplinary action should be to ensure that the recipient sees disciplinary action as a learning process rather than as something that inflicts pain.

Note that the process shown in Figure 13.1 includes feedback from the point of taking appropriate disciplinary action to communicating rules to employees. When disciplinary action is taken, all employees should realize that certain behaviors are unacceptable and should not be repeated. However, if appropriate disciplinary action is not taken, employees may view the behavior as acceptable and repeat it.

Approaches to Disciplinary Action

Several approaches to the administration of disciplinary action have been developed. Three of the most important concepts are the hot stove rule, progressive disciplinary action, and disciplinary action without punishment.

Hot Stove Rule

According to the hot stove rule, disciplinary action should have the following consequences, which are analogous to touching a hot stove:

1. *Burns immediately.* If disciplinary action is to be taken, it must occur immediately so that the individual will understand the reason for it.
2. *Provides warning.* It is also extremely important to provide advance warning that punishment will follow unacceptable behavior. As individuals move closer to a hot stove, its heat warns them that they will be burned if they touch it; therefore, they have the opportunity to avoid the burn if they so choose.
3. *Gives consistent punishment.* Disciplinary action should also be consistent in that everyone who performs the same act will be punished accordingly. As with a hot stove, each person who touches it with the same degree of pressure and for the same period of time is burned to the same extent.
4. *Burns impersonally.* Disciplinary action should be impersonal. The hot stove burns anyone who touches it, without favoritism.

If the circumstances surrounding all disciplinary action were the same, there would be no problem with this approach. However, situations are often quite different, and many variables may be present in each disciplinary action case. For instance, does the organization penalize a loyal 20-year employee the same way as an individual who has been with the firm for less than six weeks? Supervisors often find that they cannot be completely consistent and impersonal in taking disciplinary action and they need a certain degree of flexibility.[13] Because situations do vary, progressive disciplinary action may be more realistic and more beneficial to both the employee and the organization.

Progressive Disciplinary Action

progressive disciplinary action
Approach to disciplinary action designed to ensure that the minimum penalty appropriate to the offense is imposed.

Progressive disciplinary action is intended to ensure that the minimum penalty appropriate to the offense is imposed. The progressive disciplinary model was developed in response to the National Labor Relations Act. The goal of progressive disciplinary action is to formally communicate problem issues to employees in a direct and timely manner so that they can improve their

Figure 13.2

Progressive Disciplinary Action Approach

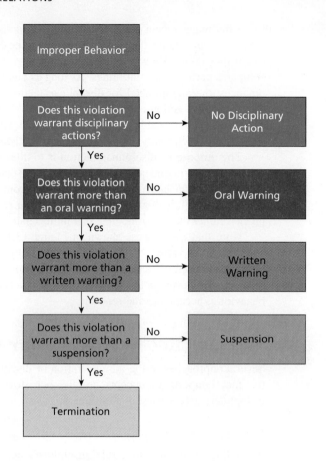

performance. Its use involves answering a series of questions about the severity of the offense.[14] The manager must ask these questions, in sequence, to determine the proper disciplinary action, as illustrated in Figure 13.2. After the manager has determined that disciplinary action is appropriate, the proper question is, "Does this violation warrant more than an oral warning?" If the improper behavior is minor and has not previously occurred, perhaps only an oral warning will be sufficient. Also, an individual may receive several oral warnings before a *yes* answer applies. The manager follows the same procedure for each level of offense in the progressive disciplinary process. The manager does not consider termination until each lower-level question is answered *yes*. However, major violations, such as assaulting a supervisor or another worker, may justify immediate termination of the employee. It is important for the worker to know what can result if improvement does not result.[15]

To assist managers in recognizing the proper level of disciplinary action, some firms have formalized the procedure. One approach is to establish progressive disciplinary action guidelines, as shown in Table 13.1. In this example, a worker who is absent without authorization will receive an oral warning the first time it happens and a written warning the second time; the third time, the employee will be terminated. Fighting on the job is an offense that normally results in immediate termination. Specific guidelines for various offenses should be developed to meet the needs of the organization. For example, the wearing of rings or jewelry for aircraft mechanics is strictly prohibited. There would likely be no such rule in an office environment. Basically, the rule should fit the need of the situation.

Disciplinary Action without Punishment

The process of giving a worker time off with pay to think about whether he or she wants to follow the rules and continue working for the company is called **disciplinary action without punishment**. The approach is to throw out formal punitive disciplinary action policies for situations such as chronic tardiness or a bad attitude in favor of affirming procedures that make employees want to take personal responsibility for their actions and be models for the corporate mission. When an employee violates a rule, the manager issues an oral reminder. Repetition brings a written

HR Web Wisdom

Progressive Disciplinary Action

http:// humanresources. about.com/od/ discipline/

Numerous articles related to disciplinary action and progressive disciplinary action.

disciplinary action without punishment
Process in which a worker is given time off with pay to think about whether he or she wants to follow the rules and continue working for the company.

Table 13.1   Suggested Guidelines for Disciplinary Action

Offenses Requiring First, an Oral Warning; Second, a Written Warning; and Third, Termination

Negligence in the performance of duties
Unauthorized absence from job
Inefficiency in the performance of job

Offenses Requiring a Written Warning and Then Termination

Sleeping on the job
Failure to report to work one or two days in a row without notification
Negligent use of property

Offenses Requiring Written Warning

Theft
Fighting on the job
Falsifying time cards
Failure to report to work three days in a row without notification
Offenses Requiring Immediate Discharge

reminder, and the third violation results in the worker having to take one, two, or three days off (with pay) to think about the situation. During the first two steps, the manager tries to encourage the employee to solve the problem. If the third step is taken, upon the worker's return, the worker and the supervisor meet to agree that the employee will not violate a rule again or the employee will leave the firm. When disciplinary action without punishment is used, it is especially important that all rules be explicitly stated in writing. At the time of orientation, new workers should be told that repeated violations of different rules will be viewed in the same way as several violations of the same rule. This approach keeps workers from taking undue advantage of the process.

Problems in the Administration of Disciplinary Action

As might be expected, administering disciplinary action is not a pleasant task, but it is a job that managers sometimes have to do. Although the manager is in the best position to take disciplinary action, many would rather avoid it even when it is in the company's best interest. Such reluctance often stems from breakdowns in other areas of human resource management. For instance, if a manager has consistently rated an employee high on annual performance appraisals, the supervisor's rationale for terminating a worker for poor performance would be weak. It would be embarrassing to decide to fire a worker and then be asked why you rated this individual so high on the previous evaluation. It could be that the employee's productivity has actually dropped substantially. It could also be that the employee's productivity has always been low, yet the supervisor had trouble justifying to upper-level management that the person should be terminated. Rather than run the risk of a decision being overturned, the supervisor retains the ineffective worker.

Occasionally, there may be suits involving members of protected groups who claim that the disciplinary action was taken against them because they are members of a protected group. One of the best ways for a company to protect itself against suits claiming discrimination or harassment is to ensure that it has proper, written policies barring unfair treatment of its staff, and a system for ensuring that the policies are followed. Disciplinary actions should be fully documented, and managers should be trained in how to avoid bias claims.[16] Also, although discrimination laws prohibit employers from making employment decisions based on an employee's membership in a protected class, basing decisions solely on performance helps prevent violation of these laws.[17]

A supervisor may be perfectly justified in administering disciplinary action, but there is usually a proper time and place for doing so. For example, taking disciplinary action against a worker in the presence of others may embarrass the individual and actually defeat the purpose of the action. Even when they are wrong, employees resent disciplinary action administered in public. By disciplining employees in private, supervisors prevent them from losing face with their peers.

ETHICAL DILEMMA

To Fire or Not to Fire

You are a first-line supervisor for Kwik Corporation, a medium-sized manufacturer of automotive parts. Workers in your company and also your department are quite close, and you view them as family. The work in your department can be quite dangerous. It is especially important that all workers wear their safety glasses, because in the past there have been some serious injuries. The company has a rule that states that any employee who does not follow the stated policy will receive a written reprimand on the first offense, and will be terminated on the second violation. You have had to terminate several workers in the past because of similar violations. The other day, Allen Smith, one of your best and most influential employees, violated the safety glasses rule and you gave him a reprimand. You hated to do that because he is by far your best worker and he often helps you if you have a problem with the other workers. He has also been with the company for a long time. You would really be lost without him. You walk up to Allen's workstation and observe him not wearing his safety glasses again. He knows that he has been caught and quickly puts his glasses on and says in a pleading voice, "Please don't fire me. I promise it will never happen again. I have just had a lot on my mind lately."

What would you do?

In addition, many supervisors may be too lenient early in the disciplinary action process and too strict later. This lack of consistency does not give the worker a clear understanding of the penalty associated with the inappropriate action. A supervisor will often endure an unacceptable situation for an extended period of time. Then, when the supervisor finally does take action, he or she is apt to overreact and come down excessively hard. However, consistency does not necessarily mean that the same penalty must be applied to two different workers for the same offense. For instance, managers would be consistent if they always considered the worker's past record and length of service.

Termination

Termination is the most severe penalty that an organization can impose on an employee; therefore, it should be the most carefully considered form of disciplinary action. The experience of being terminated is traumatic for employees regardless of their position in the organization. They can experience feelings of failure, fear, disappointment, and anger.[18] It is also a difficult time for the person making the termination decision. Knowing that termination may affect not only the employee but an entire family increases the trauma. Not knowing how the terminated employee will react also may create considerable anxiety for the manager who must do the firing. An individual who is terminated may respond with violence in the workplace or by being totally nonemotional in the matter.

When the decision is made to fire a worker, the employee should not really be surprised at the decision since he or she should have been given explicit warnings and counseling prior to being fired. The worker should have been advised of specific steps he or she needed to take to keep the job. Support should have been provided to show what needed to be done. The worker also should have been given a reasonable period of time to comply with the supervisor's expectations.

Web Wisdom

Emotional Intelligence Profile

http://www. myskillsprofile.com/ tests/eiq16

Take a test to determine your emotional intelligence.

Experts suggest that firings should be on Mondays because it lets the dismissed workers start looking for a job right away.[19] Further, firing a worker at the end of the day leaves little chance for discussion among the remaining staff that may interrupt the workplace. Managers should try to plan the termination and not make it based on emotions. Certain steps should be followed in the termination process. In the first place, the worker's manager normally should personally do the firing. Second, the firing process should be kept short and done so using nonaccusatory language. Third, the manager should not go into the reason for the dismissal and should not answer any

TRENDS & INNOVATIONS

Emotional Intelligence Needed in Disciplinary Action

Emotional intelligence is the ability to recognize and manage emotions. Daniel Goleman, psychologist and author of the book *Working with Emotional Intelligence,* describes emotional intelligence as the capacity for recognizing our own feelings and those of others, for motivating ourselves, and for managing emotions well in ourselves and in our relationships. Goleman believes that there are two distinct types of intelligence, intellectual and emotional. One might equate intellectual intelligence with "book smart," measured in terms of IQ, while emotional intelligence is usually known as "people smart" and has been measured in terms of EQ.[20] Goleman suggests that EQ levels determine up to 85 percent of leadership success. Some of the characteristics of individuals with high EQ include the "ability to cope successfully and proactively with life's demands and pressures, and to build and make use of rewarding relationships with others, while not being afraid to make tough decisions."[21] Individuals with high EQ are able to "maneuver their way through potentially volatile situations and walk away without feeling burned."[22] These are qualities managers definitely need should disciplinary action be necessary. Claire Hamon, CIO of Rok Group, said, "emotional insight is just as important as business and technical savvy. For me, it is important to legitimize emotion and bring in personality in order to help people understand the value of emotional intelligence alongside IQ and business acumen."[23]

Some organizations have credited emotional intelligence with increasing productivity. Coca-Cola, for instance, found that EQ had a major impact on productivity. Division leaders who developed EQ competencies exceeded their performance targets by 15 percent. However, those who did not expand their EQ missed their targets by 15 percent, a 30 percent difference. Likewise, Hallmark Communities discovered that sales representatives who developed EQ skills were 25 percent more productive than representatives with lower EQs. As another example, T-Mobile developed EQ skills in their customer service reps, and the company cut attrition in half and tripled their service representatives' productivity. Professor Jim Parker, a Trent University researcher of EQ measurement, says, "There is greater positive organizational impact if you can take people from the bottom 10 percent of an EQ scale to the bottom of the middle third of the scale, rather than focusing on self-actualized top performers."[24]

There are tests to determine a person's emotional intelligence. One of the most used, the Reuven Bar-On's EQ-I, has been endorsed by the American Psychological Association.[25] Some of the areas assessed include "self-regard, interpersonal skills, stress management and handling change to enable employees to play to their strengths and highlight areas to develop."[26] It is also possible to carry out team EQ testing to show the emotional intelligence of a team. Buckman Laboratories International, Inc. uses Thomas International's Personal Profile Analysis (PPA) during the hiring process. Catherine Walker, Vice President, Global Human Resources, says it "provides insight into the candidate's emotional intelligence, and helps "determine compatibility for the tasks and interpersonal relationships necessary to be successful within the hiring group." The test indicates the likelihood of fit within Buckman's corporate culture.[27]

Just what is the right amount of emotional intelligence for your organization? Experts say to "pick out a benchmark group by identifying those who inspire others, have leadership qualities, display a healthy work–life balance, and exemplify the qualities you would like to see in the organization." Benchmarking helps organizations to identify future leaders, as well as to recruit those who will fit into their corporate culture.[28]

emotional intelligence
Ability to recognize and manage emotions.

questions regarding the decision.[29,30] In some states, when an employee is involuntarily terminated, the employer must pay all earned and unpaid wages within 24 hours after the employee's demands it. To avoid any potential dispute over when a demand was made, most employers simply have the final paycheck available at the termination meeting. Also, select a location where there will be no interruptions. If the employee becomes argumentative, managers may need to get up and leave once the worker has been fired. For that reason, a manager's office should normally not be used.[31] Finally, most managers believe that it is best to have a witness since the person being fired may interpret your statements in the worst possible light.[32]

Termination of Employees at Various Levels

Regardless of the similarities in the termination of employees at various levels, distinct differences exist with regard to nonmanagerial/nonprofessional employees, executives, and middle and lower-level managers and professionals.

Termination of Nonmanagerial/Nonprofessional Employees

Individuals in this category are neither managers nor professionally trained individuals, such as engineers or accountants. They generally include employees such as steelworkers, truck drivers, salesclerks, and wait staff. If the firm is unionized, the termination procedure is typically well defined in the labor–management agreement. For example, drinking on the job might be identified as a reason for immediate termination. Absences, on the other hand, may require three written warnings by the supervisor before termination action can be taken.

When the firm is union-free, these workers can generally be terminated more easily since the worker is most likely an at-will employee. In most union-free organizations, violations justifying termination are often included in the firm's employee handbook. At times, especially in smaller organizations, the termination process is informal with the first-line supervisor telling workers what actions warrant termination. Regardless of the size of the organization, management should inform employees of the actions that warrant termination.

Termination of Executives

Unlike workers at lower level positions, CEOs do not have to worry about their positions being eliminated. Their main concern is pleasing the board of directors, because hiring and firing the CEO is a board's main responsibility. Often the reason for terminating a CEO is because the board of directors lost confidence in him or her. Tenure has become increasingly shaky for new CEOs, as the turnover in the *Fortune* 1000 companies is high. According to John Challenger, CEO to the outplacement firm of Challenger, Gray & Christmas, Inc., "If you're an executive, you may have noticed the revolving door."[33]

Executives usually have no formal appeal procedure. The reasons for termination may not be as clear as those for lower-level employees. Some of the reasons include the following:

1. *Economic downturns.* At times, business conditions may force a reduction in the number of executives.
2. *Reorganization/downsizing.* In order to improve efficiency or as a result of merging with another company, a firm may reorganize or downsize, resulting in the elimination of some executive positions.
3. *Philosophical differences.* A difference in philosophy of conducting business may develop between an executive and the Board. In order to maintain consistency in management philosophy, the executive may be replaced.
4. *Decline in productivity.* The executive may have been capable of performing satisfactorily in the past but, for various reasons, can no longer perform the job as required.

This list does not include factors related to illegal activities such as sexual harassment or insider trading. Under those circumstances, the firm has no moral obligation to the terminated executive.

An organization may derive positive benefits from terminating executives, but such actions also present a potentially hazardous situation for the company. Terminating a senior executive is an expensive proposition, often in ways more costly than just the separation package. The impact on the organization should be measured in relationships, productivity, strategic integrity, and investor confidence, as well as dollars. Many corporations are concerned about developing a negative public image that reflects insensitivity to the needs of their employees. They fear that such a reputation would impede their efforts to recruit high-quality managers. Also, terminated executives have, at times, made public statements detrimental to the reputation of their former employers.

Termination of Middle and Lower-Level Managers and Professionals

Typically, the most vulnerable and perhaps the most neglected groups of employees with regard to termination have been middle and lower-level managers and professionals. Employees in these jobs may lack the political clout that a terminated executive has. Although certainly not recommended, termination may have been based on something as simple as the attitude or feelings of an immediate superior on a given day.

OBJECTIVE 13.5
Describe terminations, explain termination of employees at various levels, and explain demotion as an alternative to termination.

demotion
Process of moving a worker to a lower level of duties and responsibilities, which typically involves a reduction in pay.

Demotion as an Alternative to Termination

Demotion is the process of moving a worker to a lower level of duties and responsibilities, which typically involves a reduction in pay. In the appendix to Chapter 7, demotion was discussed as a legitimate career option that had nothing to do with disciplinary action. In this section, demotion is addressed as a disciplinary action option. Emotions may run high when an individual is demoted. The demoted person may suffer loss of respect from peers and feel betrayed, embarrassed, angry, and disappointed. The employee's productivity may also decrease further. For these reasons, demotion should be used very cautiously. If demotion is chosen over termination, efforts must be made to preserve the self-esteem of the individual. The person may be asked how he or she would like to handle the demotion announcement. A positive image of the worker's value to the company should be projected.

The handling of demotions in a unionized organization is usually spelled out clearly in the labor–management agreement. Should a decision be made to demote a worker for unsatisfactory performance, the union should be notified of this intent and given the specific reasons for the demotion. Often the demotion will be challenged and carried through the formal grievance procedure. Documentation is necessary for the demotion to be upheld. Even with the problems associated with demotion for cause, it is often easier to demote than to terminate an employee. In addition, demotion is often less devastating to the employee. For the organization, however, the opposite may be true if the demotion creates lingering ill will and an embittered employee.

Downsizing, discussed next, is not the same as termination but the results for workers involved is the same; they no longer have a job.

OBJECTIVE 13.6
Explain downsizing, and explain the use of ombudspersons and alternative dispute resolution.

downsizing
Reverse of a company growing; it suggests a one-time change in the organization and the number of people employed (also known as restructuring or rightsizing).

Downsizing

Downsizing, also known as *restructuring* or *rightsizing*, is essentially the reverse of a company growing; it suggests a one-time change in the organization and the number of people employed. Typically, both the organizational structure and the number of people in the organization shrink for the purpose of improving organizational performance. One big lesson from research on downsizing is that when organizations resist or delay layoffs as long as possible, they tend to bounce back faster when the upturn hits.[34] This is especially true in organizations with skilled workers. This happens, in part, because these organizations save on recruiting and training costs when the demand for their people returns, and by keeping their experienced workforce around, they can move more effectively than their competitors that are scrambling to hire and train new employees with the right skills.[35]

Companies that have downsized should not forget about the workers who remain. Communication channels should be open to let those remaining workers know what and why the downsizing occurred. Often those who remain suffer *survivor's guilt* or *survivor syndrome* and open communication can do much to get by the feeling. Often it is a good idea to have a venting session where workers are allowed to express their concerns. Questions should be answered clearly and candidly.[36]

Planning is crucial as a company prepares for downsizing. Often there may be age and other discrimination claims if downsizing results in a disproportionately adverse impact upon members of a protected class. At times, older workers with higher salaries than their younger counterparts become targets for cost cutting measures and age discrimination claims occur. It is important to analyze the breakdown of downsized workers to ensure that all protected groups of workers are not disproportionately affected. It is equally imperative that an employer use objective, job-related criteria to decide which positions will be affected. Also, the downsizing organization should be prepared to deal with government requirements such as COBRA and ERISA (discussed in Chapter 10).

Workers should understand when they are hired how the system will work in the event of layoffs. When the firm is unionized, the layoff procedures are usually stated clearly in the labor–management agreement. Seniority usually is the basis for layoffs, with the least senior employees laid off first. The agreement may also have a clearly spelled-out *bumping procedure*. When senior-level positions are eliminated, the people occupying them have the right to bump workers from lower-level positions, assuming that they have the proper qualifications for the lower-level job. When bumping occurs, the composition of the workforce is altered.

Union-free firms should also establish layoff procedures prior to facing layoff decisions. In union-free firms, productivity and the needs of the organization are typically key considerations. When productivity is the primary factor, management must be careful to ensure that productivity, not favoritism, is the actual basis for the layoff decision. Therefore, it is important to define accurately productivity considerations well in advance of any layoffs.

Negative Aspects of Downsizing

When downsizing is chosen, companies typically describe the positive results, such as improving the bottom line. There may also be a negative side to downsizing.[37] Some of these are:

- During layoffs, employers and employees must realize that there is a natural grieving period, a desire to go back to the way things used to be. Friendships may be lost, and there is day-to-day uncertainty about the future. It is difficult to think about contributing to the bottom line when you do not know if tomorrow will be your day to be cut.[38]
- Layers are pulled out of a firm, making advancement in the organization more difficult. Thus, more and more individuals find themselves plateaued.
- Workers begin seeking better opportunities because they believe they may be the next in line to be laid off. Often the best workers find other jobs. Many retained employees go on to quit their jobs which further negatively impacts the organization.[39]
- Employee loyalty is often significantly reduced. For workers who remain after downsizing, the loyalty level is often low.
- Institutional memory or corporate culture is lost.
- Workers who remain after downsizing are also faced with the realization of having to do additional work (some call it "ghost work"). In a CareerBuilder survey, 47 percent of workers reported they have taken on more responsibility because of a layoff within their organization and 37 percent said they are handling the work of two people.[40]
- When demand for the products or services returns, the company often realizes that it has cut too deeply. It then begins looking for ways to get the job done.

Downsizing Software

Software applications are now available to assist management to downsize and restructure.[41] Matt Angello, founder of Bright Tree Consulting Group in Lancaster, Pennsylvania, says, "Organizations do themselves a disservice when they don't have a rigorous performance management system that supports HR decisions, particularly around layoffs."[42]

Some of the larger firms use these applications to identify and develop key employees. The same software tools can be used to help identify workers who should be kept and who should go during a downsizing. Software is available to compare employee performance and potential ratings. When annual reviews were stored in a filing cabinet, this was difficult to do. Rick Fletcher, president of technology consulting firm HRchitect, says, "Corporate America should have a lot more data than they had last time they did layoffs."[43]

Taleo Products provides software that assists companies with layoffs. The product is designed to help organizations assess employees according to factors such as skills and performance level. It facilitates involuntary job cuts as well as voluntary separations, such as early retirement. It allows firms to do "What if?" scenarios, showing how different hypothetical decisions would affect things such as costs and the diversity makeup of the workforce.[44] It even has a feature that makes sure the company computers get returned.

The application is useful not only in a crisis, but also as an aid to ongoing workforce pruning that may lessen the need for layoffs. If a company needs to curb costs, it can issue a voluntary retirement incentive program for a class of employees, where the number of people or total salary amount is capped at a certain level. By continuously "rightsizing" the organization, companies can maintain optimal labor costs and eliminate redundant positions.

Worker Adjustment and Retraining Notification Act (WARN)

The WARN Act requires covered employers to give 60 days advance notice before a plant closing or mass layoff that will affect a substantial number of workers. Covered employers generally include those with at least 100 full-time employees. As an example of of how the process works: Century Aluminum of West Virginia ceased operations on February 20, 2009. It had issued a federal WARN notice in December 2008 to its 679 employees.[45] Therefore, no penality was imposed on the company.

There are severe monetary sanctions for failing to comply with the requirements of WARN.[46] The penalties for WARN notice violations include liability to each affected worker for back pay and benefits for up to 60 days.[47] Approximately 1,650 former employees of Mortgage Lenders Network will divide a $2.7 million settlement. The company failed to provide the required 60-day warning notice to employees that it would close.[48] However, if an unforeseeable business circumstance causes a business to close earlier than 60 days, WARN does not apply. Such was the case with Hale-Halsell Company. Six days after the retailer United Supermarket, Hale-Halsell's biggest customer, severed ties with the company, the wholesaler announced 200 layoffs.[49]

Outplacement

As a result of downsizing, some organizations are assisting laid-off employees in locating jobs. The use of outplacement began at the executive level, but it has also been used at other organizational levels. In **outplacement**, laid-off employees are given assistance in finding employment elsewhere.

outplacement
A procedure whereby laid-off employees are given assistance in finding employment elsewhere.

Through outplacement, the firm tries to soften the impact of displacement. Barbara Barra, executive vice president of operations of the consulting firm Lee Hecht Harrison, said, "There is a strong correlation between how a company treats departing employees and its ability to attract and retain top talent now and in the future, particularly when the economy rebounds."[50] Some of the services provided by group outplacement include:

- A financial section that covers pension options, Social Security benefits, expenses for interviews, and wage/salary negotiations.
- Career guidance, perhaps using aptitude/interest and personality profile tests and software.
- Instruction in self-appraisal techniques, which helps in the recognition of the skills, knowledge, experience, and other qualities recruiters may require.
- Tutoring in personal promotional techniques, research, and gaining an entry to potential employers.
- Help with understanding the techniques that lead to successful interviews.
- Development of personal action plans and continuing support.

When organizational change takes place, there will be a psychological impact on both the individuals who were dismissed and those who remain. Companies use outplacement to take care of employees by moving them successfully out of the company. This proactive response will also likely have a positive influence on those who remain with the company after downsizing. More employers are offering outplacement help to preserve their employer brand and reputation. Labor and employment attorney Wendy Lane said, "Employers can go a long way toward increasing good will with just-released employees by offering to help them find alternative work."[51]

Severance Pay

severance pay
Compensation designed to assist laid-off employees as they search for new employment.

Severance pay is compensation designed to assist laid-off employees as they search for new employment. As of 2009, more than 80 percent of employers surveyed by Hewitt Associates conducted layoffs in the previous 24 months, and 45 percent intended to make further reductions in the next 12 months.[52] Although no federal law requires U.S. companies to pay severance, between 70–80 percent of employers say that they offer severance to terminated employees.[53] Even so, U.S. employees earn the least amount of severance pay worldwide, regardless of their job level or tenure.[54] When offered, they typically provide one to two weeks of severance pay for every year of service, up to some predetermined maximum. The employee's organizational level generally determines the amount of severance pay. For example, nonmanagers may get eight or nine weeks of pay even if their length of service is greater than eight or nine years. Middle managers may receive 12 to 16 weeks for the same number of years worked.

There are many compelling reasons to pay severance to employees who are involuntarily terminated. Many managers think that treating ousted workers well sends an important message to those who remain behind. There is also a feeling that "we all could be in that situation someday." But a major reason employers offer severance today is that they extract something in return. The departing worker must waive all rights to sue the company but the waiver has to be voluntary.[55] Mass layoffs in particular put companies at risk for age discrimination suits because cutbacks often target higher-paid workers, who tend to be older. In a recent survey, nearly three-quarters of some 400 human resource professionals answered "Yes" when asked if they required workers who were laid off to sign a form releasing their organization from liability for employment actions.[56] From the employee's viewpoint, severance is paid so that they will not sue the organization.[57] "It's not love; it's not a gift—it's a business transaction," notes Alan Sklover, author of *Fired, Downsized, or Laid Off.*[58]

Some companies are placing more emphasis on redeploying, rather than firing, workers. In one survey, 28 percent compared the cost of terminating with the cost of moving them somewhere else within the firm and chose redeployment. Redeployment is increasingly being used because of the pressure to improve retention, keep highly trained employees, and reduce turnover costs in the long run. The report cited one respondent, a high-tech firm, that has a goal of retaining 90 percent or more of its workforce scheduled for separation. "They conclude that to do otherwise is to, in effect, serve as a training ground for their competitors."[59]

All internal employee relations situations are not as severe as termination and layoffs and an ombudsperson or alternative dispute resolution may be used to resolve these disputes.

Ombudspersons

An **ombudsperson** is a complaint officer who has access to top management and who hears employee complaints, investigates, and recommends appropriate action. Employers use ombudspersons in their organizations to help defuse problems before they become lawsuits or scandals. "The more internal mechanisms a corporation has to deal with internal problems, the less likely these problems are to wind up in court," said Allan Weitzman, a partner with law firm of Proskauer Rose LLP. Ombudspersons are impartial, neutral counselors who can give employees confidential advice about problems ranging from abusive managers to allegations of illegal corporate activity.[60] Ombudspersons are used so that all workers may seek informal, confidential assistance to work through problems without losing control over how their concerns will be addressed. The ombudsperson is typically independent of line management and reports near or at the top of the organization.

Melissa Cameron is the ombudsman for Bayer Corporation North American operations. That means 16,600 employees can contact her confidentially to blow the whistle on bad behavior and discuss other workplace issues. She said, "Most of the calls that I get are HR matters. They might be questions regarding discrimination or performance reviews or pay issues. I can serve as another impartial person besides HR. Sometimes the employee just needs to vent." She further states that, "The ombudsman is a safety net, if you will. If you find even one or two cases a year that are substantiated, you have more than paid for my salary in terms of addressing a situation on the front end rather than going through litigation."[61]

Alternative Dispute Resolution

As the number of employment-related lawsuits increases, companies have looked for ways to protect themselves against the costs and uncertainties of the judicial system. **Alternative dispute resolution (ADR)** is a procedure whereby the employee and the company agree ahead of time that any problems will be addressed by agreed-upon means. Some of these include arbitration, mediation, mini-trials, and ombudspersons. Mediation is the preferred method for most people. ADR cases run the gamut from racial, gender, and age discrimination to unfair firings. The idea behind ADR is to resolve conflicts between employer and employee through means less costly and contentious than litigation. A successful program can save a company thousands of dollars in legal costs and hundreds of hours in managers' time. Just as important, perhaps, it can protect a company from the demoralizing tension and bitterness that employee grievances can spread through a workforce. Compared to litigation, ADR processes are less adversarial, faster and more efficient, relatively lower in cost, and private.

When parties agree to mediate, they are able to reach a settlement in 96 percent of the cases. A Presidential Executive Order requires federal agencies to: (1) promote greater use of mediation, arbitration, early neutral evaluation, agency ombudspersons, and other alternative dispute resolution techniques; and (2) promote greater use of negotiated rulemaking.

The Supreme Court rendered an opinion in *Circuit City v Adams* that greatly enhanced an employer's ability to enforce compulsory alternative dispute resolution agreements. The Court held that the ADR was valid and enforceable and made clear that ADR applied to the vast majority of employees and was available to employers seeking to enforce compulsory arbitration agreements.[62] A recent Supreme Court decision, *14 Penn Plaza LLC v Pyett*, upheld the enforceability of provisions contained in collective bargaining agreements mandating the arbitration of statutory claims, including claims based on employment discrimination. The ruling provides both employers and unions a procedure for how to preclude lawsuits and makes labor arbitration the exclusive remedy for such claims.[63]

Transfers

OBJECTIVE 13.7
Describe transfers, promotions, resignations, and retirements as factors involved in internal employee relations.

transfer
Lateral movement of a worker within an organization.

The lateral movement of a worker within an organization is called a **transfer**. A transfer may be initiated by the firm or by an employee. The process does not and should not imply that a person is being either promoted or demoted. Transfers serve several purposes. First, firms often find it necessary to reorganize. Offices and departments are created and abolished in response to the company's needs. In filling positions created by reorganization, the company may have to move employees without promoting them. A similar situation may exist when an office or department is closed. Rather than terminate valued employees, management may transfer them to other areas within the organization. These transfers may entail moving an employee to another desk in the same office or to a location halfway around the world.

A second reason for transfers is to make positions available in the primary promotion channels. At times, very productive but unpromotable workers may clog promotion channels. Other qualified workers in the organization may find their opportunities for promotion blocked. When this happens, a firm's most capable future managers may seek employment elsewhere. To keep promotion channels open, the firm may decide to transfer employees who are unpromotable but productive at their organizational level.

Another reason for transfers is to satisfy employees' personal desires. The reasons for wanting a transfer are numerous. An individual may need to accompany a transferred spouse to a new location or work closer to home to care for aging parents, or the worker may dislike the long commute to and from work. Factors such as these may be of sufficient importance that employees may resign if a requested transfer is not approved. Rather than risk losing a valued employee, the firm may agree to the transfer.

Transfers may also be an effective means of dealing with personality clashes. Some people just cannot get along with one another. Because each of the individuals may be a valued employee, a transfer may be an appropriate solution to the problem. But managers must be cautious regarding the "grass is always greener on the other side of the fence" syndrome. When some workers encounter a temporary setback, they immediately ask for a transfer before they even attempt to work through the problem.

Finally, because of a limited number of management levels, it is becoming necessary for managers to have a wide variety of experiences before achieving a promotion. Individuals who desire upward mobility often explore possible lateral moves so that they can learn new skills.

Promotions

promotion
Movement of a person to a higher-level position in an organization.

A **promotion** is the movement of a person to a higher-level position in the organization. The term *promotion* is one of the most emotionally charged words in the field of human resource management. An individual who receives a promotion normally receives additional financial rewards and the ego boost associated with achievement and accomplishment. Most employees feel good about being promoted. But for every individual who gains a promotion, there are probably others who were not selected. If these individuals wanted the promotion badly enough or their favorite candidate was overlooked, they may slack off or even resign. If the consensus of employees directly involved is that the wrong person was promoted, considerable resentment may result.

In Chapter 3, I discussed the numerous laws, court cases, and executive orders that apply when individuals are hired. These same hiring standards apply to promotion decisions. Promotion decisions should not discriminate against employees because of age, race, religion, national origin, color, sex, pregnancy, or disability.[64]

Resignations

Even when an organization is totally committed to making its environment a good place to work, workers will still resign. Some employees cannot see promotional opportunities, or at least not enough, and will therefore move on. A certain amount of turnover is healthy for an organization and is often necessary to afford employees the opportunity to fulfill career objectives. When turnover becomes excessive, however, the firm must do something to slow it. The most qualified employees are often the ones who resign because they are more mobile. On the other hand, marginally qualified workers never seem to leave. If excessive numbers of a firm's highly qualified and competent workers are leaving, a way must be found to reverse the trend.

Analyzing Voluntary Resignations

exit interview
Means of revealing the real reasons employees leave their jobs; it is conducted before an employee departs the company and provides information on how to correct the causes of discontent and reduce turnover.

When a firm wants to determine why individuals leave, it can use the exit interview and/or the postexit questionnaire. An **exit interview** is a means of revealing the real reasons employees leave their jobs; it is conducted before an employee departs the company and provides information on how to correct the causes of discontent and reduce turnover. They provide a company with valuable source of objective feedback.[65] Leigh Branham, author of *The 7 Hidden Reasons Employees Leave: How to Recognize the Subtle Signs and Act Before It's Too Late*, said, "Although employees will cite pay as the reason they quit their jobs, 60 to 80 percent of the time, his research indicates that only 12 to 15 percent of employees leave for this reason alone. The rest of the time, the primary reason is something other than salary; something often more personal and less tangible than the numbers on a pay stub."[66] Perhaps departing employees are reluctant to burn bridges by revealing the real reason for leaving because they may need a reference from their supervisor in the future and fear reprisal. However, only after determining the *real* reason for leaving can a firm develop a strategy to overcome the problem.

At times women who are on the fast-track are not candid about why they quit. A consulting firm was hired to discover why top-performing women were quitting in high numbers, saying in their exit interviews that they wanted to spend more time with their kids. But the employers later learned that these women had returned to work, some starting their own firms and working longer hours. In anonymous interviews, the women who had quit explained the problem. Most said they'd left their jobs because "they could not see a future for themselves there." The "more-time-with-kids" story was just cover—so they could maintain good relations with their former bosses.[67]

Often a third party, such as a person in the HR department or an outsource party, will conduct the exit interview. A third party may be used because employees may not be willing to air their problems with their former bosses. Outsourcing the exit interviews may be beneficial because employers believe that the person who is leaving will be more honest when he or she is not speaking to a company employee. The typical exit interview follows the following format:

- Establish rapport.
- State the purpose of the interview.
- Explore the employee's attitudes regarding the job.
- Explore the employee's reasons for leaving.
- Compare old and new jobs.
- Record the changes recommended by the employee.
- Conclude the interview.[68]

Over time, properly conducted exit interviews can provide considerable insight into why employees leave. Patterns are often identified that uncover weaknesses in the firm's management system. Knowledge of the problem permits corrective action to be taken. Also, the exit interview helps to identify training and development needs and identify areas in which changes need to be made.

postexit questionnaire
Questionnaire sent to former employees several weeks after they leave the organization to determine the real reason they left.

A **postexit questionnaire** is sent to former employees several weeks after they leave the organization to determine the real reason they left. Usually, they have already started work at their new companies. Ample blank space is provided so that a former employee can express his or her feelings about and perceptions of the job and the organization. Since the individual is no longer with the firm he or she may respond more freely to the questions. However, there are several major weaknesses in the use of the postexit questionnaire. Participation rates are usually low because former workers may not care enough to respond and they may be difficult to reach after they have departed.[69] Also, the interviewer is not present to interpret and probe for more information.

Attitude Surveys: A Means of Retaining Quality Employees

Exit and postexit interviews can provide valuable information for improving human resource management practices. The problem, however, is that these approaches are reactions to events that were detrimental to the organization. The very people you want to save may be the ones being interviewed or completing questionnaires.

attitude survey
Survey that seeks input from employees to determine their feelings about topics such as the work they perform, their supervisor, their work environment, flexibility in the workplace, opportunities for advancement, training and development opportunities, and the firm's compensation system.

An alternative, proactive approach is administering attitude surveys (survey feedback was described in Chapter 7). **Attitude surveys** seek input from employees to determine their feelings about topics such as the work they perform, their supervisor, their work environment, flexibility in the workplace, opportunities for advancement, training and development opportunities, and the firm's compensation system. Since some employees will want their responses to be confidential, every effort should be made to guarantee their anonymity. To achieve this, it may be necessary to have the survey administered by a third party. Regardless of how the process is handled, attitude surveys have the potential to improve management practices. For this reason, they are widely used throughout industry today. Joseph Cabral, senior vice president and chief human resources officer for the North Shore-LIJ Health System in Long Island, N.Y., says "North Shore has been surveying its 38,000 employees annually for the past three years, but it recently went to a quarterly survey to provide more real-time and actionable results and to allow comparisons across worksites and departments."[70]

Employees should be advised of the purpose of the survey. The mere act of giving a survey communicates to employees that management is concerned about their problems, wants to know what they are, and wants to solve them, if possible. Analyzing survey results of various subgroups and comparing them with the firm's total population may indicate areas that should be investigated and problems that need to be solved. For instance, the survey results of the production night shift might be compared to the production day shift. Should problems show up, management must be willing to make the suggested changes. It should be noted that if the survey does not result in some improvements, the process may be a deterrent to employees and future surveys may not yield helpful data. Basically, if you are not going to do anything as a result of the survey, do not bother to administer it.

Advance Notice of Resignation

Most firms would like to have at least a two-week notice of resignation from departing workers. However, a month's notice may be desired from professional and managerial employees who are leaving. When the firm desires notice, the policy should be clearly communicated to all employees. If they want departing employees to give advance notice, companies have certain obligations. For instance, suppose that a worker who gives notice is terminated immediately. Word of this action will spread rapidly to other employees. Later, should they decide to resign, they will likely not give any advance notice.

Recall from Chapter 5, on recruitment, that firms are now actively recruiting former employees. If the firm views a departing worker as eligible to return in the future, it should avoid treating that person like a second-class citizen. However, in some cases, permitting a worker to remain on the job once a resignation has been submitted may create some problems. If bad feelings exist between the employee and the supervisor or the company, the departing worker may be a disruptive force. On a selective basis, the firm may wish to pay some employees for the notice time and ask them to leave immediately.

A GLOBAL PERSPECTIVE

Disciplinary Action in the Global Environment

Previously, the discussion of disciplinary action was discussed as it related to managers in the United States. Moving into the international arena, often presents different situations. For instance, the punishment for a company employee who stole $10,000 in the U.S. would likely lead to termination. However, a Japanese judge ruled that the $10,000 was too small an amount to justify termination and the worker was reinstated.[71] It does not get any easier when terminating a worker for poor job performance. McDonald's' Don Crosby said, "It's unheard of." In fact, only a few years ago no performance appraisal system existed. In countries such as Japan, South Korea, and Taiwan, the government often sides with the employee. FedEx's Bianca Wong said, "There's always some gray area where some actions are tolerated," she explains. "It makes it more difficult for the employer because you don't know where to draw the line between right and wrong. It's very difficult to terminate a worker in Japan, both by law and by culture. Besides all sorts of government regulations, there's also a cultural notion of lifelong employment here. There are times when you have a mediocre employee whom you can't do anything about—you continue to try and try and try and try to develop him or improve his work, but if the person doesn't do anything really bad, there's little you can do."[72]

The concept of employment at will is generally accepted in the United States. Other governments such as Italy are more willing to protect employees in the loss of their jobs.

Mercer's Siobhan Martin-Wells said that Italy is, "a shining example of a place where it's really tough to discipline, because the second you do, the worker instantly calls out sick. Then you enter into a very protracted situation, because workers can go sick for up to twelve months without the company being able to do much." Siobhan went on to say, "While sick, and while the worker and the company argue over all sorts of details, the worker is still getting paid—and he can even work somewhere else at the same time if a doctor says that not working causes the worker mental distress or depression. Unfortunately, this is not that unusual."[73]

Europe may have the most employee-friendly laws. Citi's John Harker said, "When it comes to discharging a worker who is not performing, it's much harder to do in EU countries than in North America and other parts of the world." It is also difficult to discipline a worker for poor performance in China. Laws tend to come down on the side of the employees when addressing disciplinary action. According to Baxter's Elaine Lin, "I got a bad performance review because my boss doesn't like me is a perfectly acceptable employee defense."[74] In some ex-Communist European countries, disciplinary action can only occur once the worker has been convicted of a criminal offense. Because of the inconsistency in how government view disciplinary action in the global environment, it is very difficult for a global company to establish a standardized policy on disciplinary action.

Unions can also have an impact on how disciplinary action is administered. Calvin Tsang said this about taking disciplinary action in Sri Lanka, "You cannot terminate an employee without that employee's consent." Otherwise, the company must obtain the written approval to terminate from the labor commissioner's office, which can take up to three months."[75]

Offboarding

Offboarding involves exit interviews, removing access to company property, and other services involved in a former worker leaving the company. Topics such as the worker's 401(k) and COBRA need to be addressed. Teresa Grote, practice director of composite solutions for Ascendum, an information technology company, said, "I think that in our highly litigious society today, making sure that you go through proper offboarding is probably equally, if not more, important than proper onboarding." There are numerous risks in the termination process and it is important to establish a fair and uniform process as employees leave the company.[76]

Retirements

phased retirement
Any arrangement that allows people to move from fulltime work to retirement in steps.

Many long-term employees leave an organization by retiring. The majority of today's employees are not planning for a traditional retirement, in which they have an immediate and abrupt end to their working career at a specific age, such as 65. Most individuals expect to work in some capacity after retirement,[77] or plan to take a more gradual approach to transition into retirement. Many want to *phase-in* retirement by working fewer hours as they near 65, or after. **Phased retirement** is any arrangement that allows people to move from fulltime work to retirement in steps. A recent study found that retirees who transition from full-time work into a temporary or part-time job experience fewer major diseases and are able to function better day-to-day than people who stop working altogether.[78] Retirement is treated as a phased process rather than a sudden event marked by a sentimental speech and a gold watch.[79] About half of all American workers phase into retirement in some way.[80] In addition, 20 percent of employers say that phased retirement is critical to their company's HR strategy today; that number nearly triples, to 61 percent, when employers look ahead 5 years. Allen Steinberg, a principal at Hewitt Associates, said, "Employers will be losing key talent at a time when attracting and retaining skilled workers will be more important."[81]

The Pension Protection Act of 2006 (discussed in Chapter 10) permits limited phased retirement by allowing in-service pension plan withdrawals to begin at age 62 rather than 65. A benefit of phased retirement is that it permits a company to reduce labor costs without hurting morale. It also lets an organization hold on to its experienced workers so they can share their knowledge with a less experienced workforce.[82] Employees at Lee Memorial can work as few as 16 hours a week and still be eligible for benefits. Mercy Health's phased-retirement plan allows workers ages 50 and older to reduce the number of hours worked while keeping their benefits.[83] Home Depot has set up "snowbird" employment programs to retain valuable employees.

Sometimes employees will be offered early retirement before reaching the organization's normal length-of-service requirement. Historically, early retirement has been viewed as an attractive solution when workforce reductions had to be made. Early retirement plans, which gained popularity in the 1980s, appealed to older workers facing layoffs. Early retirement is still being used but companies reserve the right to reject a highly productive worker's request (Remember the Trends & Innovation, Chapter 4, Alternatives to Layoffs).

Summary

1. *Define internal employee relations.* Internal employee relations comprise the human resource management activities associated with the movement of employees within the organization.

2. *Explain the concept of employment at will.* Employment at will is an unwritten contract created when an employee agrees to work for an employer but no agreement exists as to how long the parties expect the employment to last.

3. *Explain discipline and disciplinary action.* Discipline is the state of employee self-control and orderly conduct present within an organization. It indicates the extent of genuine teamwork that exists. Disciplinary action occurs when a penalty is invoked against an employee who fails to meet established standards.

4. *Describe the disciplinary action process, discuss the various approaches to disciplinary action, and describe the problems in the administration of disciplinary action.* After management has established rules, it must communicate these rules to employees. The manager then observes the performance of workers and compares performance with rules. As long as employee behavior does not vary from acceptable practices, there is no need for disciplinary action, but when an employee's behavior violates a rule, corrective action may be necessary.

Three of the most important concepts are the hot stove rule, progressive disciplinary action, and disciplinary action without punishment.

As might be expected, administering disciplinary action is not a pleasant task, but it is a job that managers sometimes have to do. Although the manager is in the best position to take disciplinary action, many would rather avoid it even when it is in the company's best interest. Such reluctance often stems from breakdowns in other areas of human resource management.

5. *Describe terminations, explain termination of employees at various levels, and explain demotion as an alternative to termination.* Termination is the most severe penalty that an organization can impose on an employee; therefore, it should be the most carefully considered form of disciplinary action. Regardless of the similarities in the termination of employees at various levels, distinct differences exist with regard to nonmanagerial/nonprofessional employees, executives, and middle and lower-level managers and professionals.

Demotion is the process of moving a worker to a lower level of duties and responsibilities, which typically involves a reduction in pay. If demotion is chosen over termination, efforts must be made to preserve the self-esteem of the individual.

6. *Describe downsizing and explain the use of ombudspersons and alternative dispute resolution.* *Downsizing,* also known as *restructuring* or *rightsizing,* is essentially the reverse of a company growing; it suggests a one-time change in the organization and the number of people employed. Typically, both the organizational structure and the number of people in the organization shrink for the purpose of improving organizational performance.

An ombudsperson is a complaint officer with access to top management who hears employee complaints, investigates, and recommends appropriate action. Alternative dispute resolution (ADR) is a procedure whereby the employee and the company agree ahead of time that any problems will be addressed by an agreed-upon means.

7. *Describe transfers, promotions, resignations, and retirements as factors involved in internal employee relations.* The lateral movement of a worker within an organization is called a "transfer." A promotion is the movement of a person to a higher-level position in the organization. Even when an organization is totally committed to making its environment a good place to work, workers will still resign. One of the last phases of internal employee relations is retirement.

Key Terms

internal employee relations 386	emotional intelligence 393	transfer 399
employment at will 386	demotion 395	promotion 399
discipline 387	downsizing 395	exit interview 400
disciplinary action 387	outplacement 397	postexit questionnaire 401
progressive disciplinary	severance pay 397	attitude survey 401
action 389	ombudsperson 398	phased retirement 402
disciplinary action without	alternative dispute resolution	
punishment 390	(ADR) 398	

Questions for Review

1. Define *internal employee relations.*
2. What is meant by the term *employment at will?*
3. What is the difference between discipline and disciplinary action?
4. What are the steps to follow in the disciplinary action process?
5. Describe the following approaches to disciplinary action:
   a. hot stove rule
   b. progressive disciplinary action
   c. disciplinary action without punishment
6. What are the problems associated with the administration of disciplinary action?
7. How does termination often differ with regard to nonmanagerial/nonprofessional employees, executives, and middle and lower-level managers and professionals?

8. Define *downsizing.* What are some problems associated with downsizing?
9. What is the Worker Adjustment and Retraining Notification Act?
10. Define the following.
    a. outplacement
    b. severance pay
11. Define *ombudsperson.* Why might a firm want to use an ombudsperson?
12. Define *alternative dispute resolution (ADR).* Describe briefly.
13. Distinguish between demotions, transfers, and promotions.
14. Briefly describe the techniques available to determine the real reasons that an individual decides to leave the organization.

HRM INCIDENT 1

Should He Be Fired?

Toni Berdit is the Washington, D.C., area supervisor for Quik-Stop, a chain of convenience stores. She has full responsibility for managing the seven Quik-Stop stores in Washington. Each store operates with only one person on duty at a time. Although several of the stores stay open all night, every night, the Center Street store is open all night Monday through

Thursday but only from 6:00 A.M. to 10:00 P.M., Friday through Sunday. Because the store is open fewer hours during the weekend, money from sales is kept in the store safe until Monday. Therefore, the time it takes to complete a money count on Monday is greater than normal. The company has a policy that when the safe is being emptied, the manager has to be with the employee on duty, and the employee has to place each $1,000 in a brown bag, mark the bag, and leave the bag on the floor next to the safe until the manager verifies the amount in each bag.

Bill Catron worked the Sunday night shift at the Center Street store and was trying to save his manager time by counting the money prior to his arrival. The store got very busy, and, while bagging a customer's groceries, Bill mistook one of the moneybags for a bag containing three sandwiches and put the moneybag in with the groceries. Twenty minutes later, Toni arrived, and both began to search for the money. While they were searching, a customer came back with the bag of money. Quik-Stop has a general policy that anyone violating the money-counting procedure could be fired immediately. However, the ultimate decision was left up to the supervisor and his or her immediate boss.

Bill was very upset. "I really need this job," Bill exclaimed. "With the new baby and all the medical expenses we've had, I sure can't stand to be out of a job."

"You knew about the policy, Bill," said Toni.

"Yes, I did, Toni," said Bill, "and I really don't have any excuse. If you don't fire me, though, I promise you that I'll be the best store manager you've got."

While Bill waited on a customer, Toni called his boss at the home office. With the boss's approval, Toni decided not to fire Bill.

Questions

1. Do you agree with Toni's decision? Discuss.

HRM INCIDENT 2

It's the Best Thing to Do

The global economic crisis had really been a test of endurance for Maryam. With all the personal financial burdens that she had, she thought about the restaurant that she and her husband, John, had established. As a widow, she needed to reconsider her priorities. But, how could she lay off some of her employees? They had all been with them from day one and were loyal and committed to Maryam's Café.

However, Maryam realized that she had to explain the situation so she called a staff meeting. She started on a positive note of appreciation for all the efforts her staff had displayed.

"But…" Everyone looked at one another. Of course, they knew that things had been rough and they were aware of the economical situation but this did not stop their hearts sinking.

"… I can't keep up with my payments and I'm afraid I won't be able to pay your salaries this month. So, unfortunately and regretfully, I must let ten of you go," Maryam explained. "This is even more painful than John's death. I think the best way to do this is to go by seniority."

There was total silence and a few employees could not hold back their tears. The Café had been their second home and Maryam and John treated them with respect and created a family environment that was not only apparent among the staff but also among the customers.

Their thoughts were interrupted when Maryam said she would give the names to her accountant and that they would receive a modest gesture. She thanked them once more as she hurried out of the room, feeling like she was going to collapse.

No one knew what to say so they all huddled into a team hug.

Questions

1. Do you think Maryam handled the downsizing appropriately? Comment.

2. What are the problems associated with downsizing and how can they be approached?

Notes

1. Stacy Stracynski, "Workers Itch for Job Switch," *Incentive* 183 (November 2009): 9.
2. Pat Galagan, "Defection Alert!" *T+D* 64 (January 2010): 27–29.
3. "The Power of Total Rewards in Any Economy," *Workforce Management* 88 (April 6, 2009): S7.
4. T. K., "Retention: Your Most Important Recruitment Activity?" *CIO Insight* 106 (July 2009): 32.
5. Vasishtha Preeti, "Why You Need an Employee-Retention Program," *Advisor Today* 104 (August 2009): 60.
6. Amy M. Bladen, "Talent Management," *Leadership Excellence* 27 (April 2010): 18.
7. Manny Avramidis, "Retaining Employees," *Financial Planning* 38 (February 2009): 30.
8. Eileen McKeown, "Retention on the Upswing," *T+D* 64 (March 2010): 22–23.
9. Stephen D. Lichtenstein and Jonathan J. Darrow, "At-Will Employment: A Right to Blog or a Right to Terminate," *Journal of Internet Law* 11 (March 2008): 1–20.
10. "Disciplining Made Easy," *Managing People at Work* (January 2010): 5.
11. Vadim Liberman, "The Perfect Punishment," *Conference Board Review* 46 (January/February 2009): 32–39.
12. Angela Atkins, "The Poor Performance Disciplinary Dilemma," *Human Resources Magazine* 14 (October/November 2009): 30–31.
13. "Flying Pocketknife Cuts into Heart of Employer's Policy," *HR Specialist: North Carolina Employment Law* 4 (February 2010): 5.
14. "Progressive Discipline Keeps Staff on Track-and You Out of Court," *HR Specialist: New York Employment Law* 4 (October 2009): 4.
15. "What It Means to You," *Legal Alert for Supervisors* 5 (September 1, 2009): 2.
16. Cliffford M. Koen Jr. and Michael S. Mitchell, "Supervisor's Checklist for Termination/Discipline, *Supervision* 71 (January 2010): 3–6.
17. Shari Lau, Erin Lee, Patton Lee, and Yvette Lee, "Performance-Based Discipline, Union Organizing, Bonus Taxation," *HRMagazine* 54 (September 2009): 27–28.
18. Barry Shanoff, "Departing with Dignity," *Waste Age* 38 (September 2007): 26–28.
19. "Which Day of the Week Is Best to Fire, Hire and Give Reviews?" *HR Specialist: New York Employment Law* 7 (July 2009): 6.
20. Daniel C. Finley, "Develop Emotional Intelligence," *Advisor Today* 104 (November 2009): 58–59.
21. Jonathan Perks, "How to Develop Emotional Intelligence," *People Management* 14 (May 1, 2008): 42.
22. Martha McCarty, "Emotional IQ," *OfficePro* 70 (March/April 2010): 22–25.
23. Cath Jennings, "Dare to Be Different to Reach the Top," *Computer Weekly* (April 15, 2008): 14–16.
24. Joanne Reid, "The Resilient Leader: Why EQ Matters," *Ivey Business Journal* 72 (May/June 2008): 1–7.
25. Harvey Deutschendorf, "EQ Boost," *T+D* 63 (October 2009): 92–93.
26. Perks, "How to Develop Emotional Intelligence."
27. Margery Weinstein, "Emotional Evaluation," *Training* 46 (September 2009): 16.
28. Perks, "How to Develop Emotional Intelligence."
29. "Remind Managers: Never Discuss Reasons for Employee Terminations," *HR Specialist* 7 (May 2009): 3.
30. "Don't Pile on Reasons for Firing; You're Spoiling for Retaliation Fight in Court," *HR Specialist: Texas Employment Law* 5 (April 2010): 2.
31. "10 Steps to Stress-free, Lawsuit-free Termination Meetings," *HR Specialist: New York Employment Law* 7 (July 2009): 6.
32. "Three Keys to Keep Terminations from Turning into Lawsuits," *Legal Alert for Supervisors* 5 (March 15, 2010): 3.
33. Liz Wolgemuth, Kimberly Palmer, Katy Marquardt, Matthew Bandy, Rick Newman, Marty Nemko, "Career Guide 2008," *U.S. News & World Report* 144 (March 24, 2008): 45–61.
34. Geoff Colvin, "How Are Most Admired Companies Different? They Invest in People and Keep them Employed, Even in a Downturn," *Fortune* 161 (March 22, 2010): 82.
35. Robert Sutton, "Layoffs and Creativity: Are You Expelling the Innovators?" *Communication World* 26 (January/February 2009): 48.
36. "Forced to Lay Off People? Don't Forget Those Who Remain," *Legal Alert for Supervisors* 4 (May 4, 2009): 3.
37. Jeffrey Pfeffer, "Layoff the Layoffs," *Newsweek* 155 (February 15, 2010): 32–37.
38. Susan Storm Smith, "In a Time of Layoffs, Keep Human Resources Humane," *BusinessWeek Online* (March 19, 2009): 11.
39. Beverly Kaye and Eileen McDargh, "Leaders with ESP for Tough Times," *T+D* 63 (June 2009): 54–57.
40. "Layoff 'Survivor' Stress: How to Manage the Guilt and the Workload," *HR Focus* 86 (August 2009): 4–6.
41. Ed Frauenheim, "Software to Smooth Your Restructuring," *Workforce Management* 87 (April 7, 2008): 19.
42. Adrienne Fox, "Prune Employees Carefully," *HRMagazine* 53 (April 2008): 66–70.
43. Frauenheim, "Software to Smooth Your Restructuring."
44. Ibid.
45. "Century Closes W.Va. Smelter," *Metal Producing & Processing* 47 (March/April 2009): 4.
46. Olivia Goodkin and Wendy Lane, "Conducting Layoffs in a Recession," *Retail Merchandiser* 49 (January/February 2009): 37.
47. "Know Your Layoff Rules of Procedures," *HR Focus* 86 (February 2009): 2.

48. "Employees Get B&C Lender Settlement," *National Mortgage News* 33 (May 18, 2009): 15.
49. Lauren Williamson, "Grocer Gave Fair WARN-ing," *InsideCounsel* 20 (April 2009): 77.
50. "Severance, Outplacement Receive More Attention," *HR Focus* 86 (June 2009): 12.
51. Katherine Field, "Layoff Strategies," *Chain Store Age* 84 (December 2008): 58.
52. "U.S. Severance Remains Generous, Despite Recession," *HRMagazine* 54 (May 2009): 22.
53. Robert B. Jones, "12 Important Things Employers Should Be Doing With Severance Programs in Light of the Current Economy," *Benefits Quarterly* 25 (2009 Second Quarter): 29–37.
54. "Survey Finds Severance Pay Declines for U.S. Employees," *Report on Salary Surveys* 9 (January 2009): 4.
55. Anne E. Moran, "Waivers and Severance Arrangements: EEOC Announcement Offers Reminders for Employers," *Employee Relations Law Journal* 35 (2010): 72–80.
56. Rita Zeidner, "Most Employers Require Waivers for Severance Pay," *HRMagazine* 54 (January 2009): 27.
57. "How Employers Are Handling Severance," *Managing Benefits Plans* 10 (February 2010): 12–15.
58. "8 Keys to Negotiating Severance," *Executive Leadership* 24 (June 2009): 8.
59. "Severance, Outplacement Receive More Attention," *HR Focus* 86 (June 2009): 12.
60. "Ombuds Can Help Address Conflicts, Potential Lawsuits," *HR Focus* 82 (October 2005): 8.
61. "5 Questions: Melissa Cameron, Ombudsman, North American Operations, Bayer Corp," *Workforce Management* 88 (October 19, 2009): 8.
62. "Arbitration Agreements: The Way to Stop Employee Lawsuits Forever," *Supervision* 69 (February 2008): 14–15.
63. "U.S. Supreme Court Rules 5-4 that Union-Represented Employees Can be Forced to Arbitrate Statutory Employment Discrimination Claims," *Venulex Legal Summaries* (2009 Q2, Special section): 1–3.
64. "Choosing Employees for Promotion: A 6-step Legal Process," *HR Specialist: New York Employment Law* 4 (August 2009): 4.
65. Meredyth McKenzie, "Exit Interviews," *Smart Business Atlanta* 7 (March 2010): 24.
66. Kenya McCullum, "The Retention Intention," *Office Pro* 69 (2009 Special Edition): 8–11.
67. Sharon Meers and Joanna Strober, "When Women Don't Tell the Truth," *Conference Board Review* 46 (Summer 2009): 9–10.
68. Wanda R. Embrey, R. Wayne Mondy, and Robert M. Noe, "Exit Interview: A Tool for Personnel Development," *Personnel Administrator* 24 (May 1979): 46.
69. Terence E. Shea, "Getting the Last Word," *HRMagazine* 55 (January 2010): 24–25.
70. Lin Grensing-Pophal, "To Ask or Not To Ask," *HRMagazine* 54 (February 2009): 53–55.
71. V. L. "When You Don't Get to Make the Rules," *Conference Board Review* 46 (January/February 2009): 37.
72. Ibid.
73. Ibid.
74. Ibid.
75. Ibid.
76. Elizabeth Galentine, "Parting Ways Pleasantly," *Employee Benefit News* 23 (June 2009): 42–43.
77. Sally Hass and Steve Vernon, "Do the Downshift: A Win-Win Workforce Strategy," *Benefits & Compensation Digest* 47 (January 2010): 1–25.
78. "Working After Retirement May Lead to Better Health," *EHS Today* 2 (November 2009): 18.
79. "The Silver Tsunami," *Economist* 394 (February 6, 2010): 74.
80. Anna Rappaport, "Phased Retirement—An Important Part of the Evolving Retirement Scene," *Benefits Quarterly* 25 (2009 Second Quarter): 38–50.
81. Stephen Miller, "Phased Retirement Keeps Boomers in the Workforce," *HRMagazine* (December 2008): 61–62.
82. "Phased Retirement Can Benefit Baby Boomers, Employers Alike: Deloitte," *Money Management Executive* 17 (April 6, 2009): 3.
83. "Key Steps to Recruiting & Retaining Older Workers," *H&HN: Hospitals & Health Networks* 82 (January 2008): 55–56.

CHAPTER

14 Global Human Resource Management

HRM in Action: Getting Tougher to Bribe in the International Arena

The United States is rigorously enforcing the Foreign Corrupt Practices Act (FCPA), which prohibits U.S. firms from bribing foreign officials.[1] However, countries other than the United States face far fewer constraints when dealing with bribery. Although the 35 signatories of the Organization of Economic Cooperation and Development's 1997 convention made it a crime to bribe foreign officials, there has been little enforcement of laws by national governments, other than by the United States. Not having the ability to use bribery as a tool of doing business has been costly for American companies. In one survey, 43 percent of the companies surveyed reported that they had lost new business in the last five years because of bribery. According to a U.S. Commerce Department report, competition for 47 contracts worth $18 billion may have been affected by bribes that foreign firms paid to foreign officials. Because U.S. companies would not participate, the department estimates, at least eight of those contracts, worth $3 billion, were lost to them.[2]

The 9/11 attacks caused authorities to take a much closer look at financial data as they searched for terrorists' funds, and found bribery corruption in the process.[3] Under the FCPA, it is illegal to pay or attempt to pay bribes to foreign officials in connection with getting business, keeping business, or gaining an improper advantage over competitors. These provisions apply to any U.S. citizen, national, or resident wherever they are, as well as to any U.S.-based or U.S.-listed company.[4] Criminal penalties for individuals include fines of up to $250,000 per violation and imprisonment up to five years, or both. Business entities may be required to pay criminal fines up to $2 million per violation.[5] Whitney

After completing this chapter, students should be able to:

1. Describe the impact of global bribery in the international arena.

2. Describe the evolution of global business and global strategic human resource management.

3. Explain global staffing.

4. Describe global human resource development.

5. Explain global compensation.

6. Describe global safety and health.

7. Explain global employee and labor relations.

8. Describe legal and political factors affecting global human resource management.

9. Explain global EEO and sexual harassment.

Ellerman, a partner with law firm Katten Muchin Rosenman, said, "It's clear that we will see an increased number of FCPA prosecutions of companies and individuals in the next several years."[6]

The list of conviction under the FCPA continues to grow. Siemens agreed to pay $1.6 billion to settle enforcement actions in Germany and the United States implicating parties as high up the organizational chart as the CFO and the managing board. [7] Lucent recently paid a multimillion-dollar fine for "training" trips it had arranged for executives from state-owned telecommunications firms that involved visits to Las Vegas and Orlando, rather than factories. Baker Hughes paid $44 million in penalties to settle charges of bribery in Kazakhstan. There was a lot of corruption around the Iraq Oil for Food program and Chevron, Volvo, Flowserve, and Ingersoll-Rand paid major violations settlements. In 2009 KBR, a construction firm, and Halliburton, its former parent, were fined $579 million over bribes paid to obtain contracts in Nigeria.[8] DynCorp International, a military contractor, recently fired one of its top lawyers after an internal investigation into potential FCPA violations suggested payments totaling about $300,000 were made to speed up the visa and license process.[9] Conducting business globally exposes the United States and other companies to an environment that permits bribery, which is against the law in the United States. To ward against problems, some companies have started deploying internal audit teams to help their compliance and legal departments uncover potential FCPA breaches and improve processes and controls.[10]

Some have wondered if ethics can have any middle ground and if the middle ground where the answer of "maybe" would be appropriate. The specific culture of a country may answer that question. Western societies are based on the philosophies of Aristotle and Plato and are essentially black and white with no middle ground. On the other hand, Asians believe that ethics depend on the situation. Therefore, Asians may violate their company's code of ethics or even the Foreign Corrupt Practices Act without realizing anything is wrong. Confucian societies believe that "sometimes it's OK to cheat or steal, as long as it doesn't disturb social harmony by presenting a problem for the family," explains George Haley, author of *The Chinese Tao of Businesses: The Logic of Successful Business Strategy.*[11]

OBJECTIVE 14.1
Describe the impact of global bribery in the international arena.

The impact of global bribery is discussed first. Then the evolution of global business and global strategic human resource management is described. Global staffing, cyberwork in the global environment, and global human resource development are then explained. Global compensation and global safety and health are then examined, followed by a discussion of global employee and labor relations. This chapter concludes with a look at global legal and political factors.

OBJECTIVE 14.2
Describe the evolution of global business and global human resource management.

Evolution of Global Business

The growth of international businesses is no longer in doubt. "Organizations must either globalize or they will die" is an apt description of the 21st-century economy. The environment confronted by businesses today is so vastly different from doing business in one or two countries of only a few decades ago. The world is now one large marketplace consisting of 6.6 billion people speaking 6,700 languages, with thousands of governments all having different regulations and tax requirements. There are more than 900,000 organizations; the top 500 companies generate more than $21 trillion.[12] "When Willie Horton was asked why he robbed banks he said, 'Because that's where the money is!'" Such would be the case for going global; that is where the money is![13]

Jerome Carter, senior vice president of human resources for International Paper Co., said, "With globalization, everybody in the organization, and especially in the HR department, has had to change our focus, change our attitude and change our approach in the way we operate."[14] Much of the U.S. economy is based on exports and imports. Not long ago, Mercedes-Benz was still a "German" company, General Electric was "American," and Sony was "Japanese," but today these companies are truly global.[15] Years ago, a lot of U.S. multinational corporations had operations in Canada or perhaps Mexico, but not in many other countries. Now, U.S. firms such as Coca-Cola, Procter & Gamble, and Texas Instruments do most of their business and employ most of their workers outside the United States. Countless products of U.S. companies are made outside the country. Many non-U.S. companies make products here, such as Toyota American, which manufactures cars in Kentucky. Companies still regularly do business in Canada and Mexico, but many now have operations in Hong Kong, Singapore, Japan, the United Kingdom, France, Germany, and Southeast Asia, to name a few. More and more U.S. global corporations are doing business in former Eastern Bloc countries. Vietnam, a country with which the United States was at war throughout the 1960s until the mid-1970s, now has U.S. firms operating there. Today, globalization is not limited to only large organizations. It is now the main focus for both large and small firms.

Normally, companies evolve to the point of being truly global over an extended period. Perry Newman, founder and principal of the Atlantic Group, a consulting firm based on the East Coast that helps smaller businesses take their firms global, said, "Going global can provide a company with an assortment of rewards. There are a number of benefits for the small- to mid-sized business. First, of course, is that having a global customer base provides some protection against domestic business cycles. Companies that tend to export tend to be more profitable, better organized and more competitive than are companies that are exclusively domestically focused."[16]

exporting

Selling abroad, either directly or indirectly, by retaining foreign agents and distributors.

licensing

Arrangement whereby an organization grants a foreign firm the right to use intellectual properties such as patents, copyrights, manufacturing processes, or trade names for a specific period of time.

franchising

Option whereby the parent company grants another firm the right to do business in a prescribed manner.

multinational corporation (MNC)

Firm that is based in one country (the parent or home country) and produces goods or provides services in one or more foreign countries (host countries).

global corporation (GC)

Organization that has corporate units in a number of countries that are integrated to operate as one organization worldwide.

transnational corporation

Organization that moves work to the places with the talent to handle the job and the time to do it at the right cost.

Most companies initially become global without making substantial investments in foreign countries, by exporting, licensing, or franchising. **Exporting** entails selling abroad, either directly or indirectly, by retaining foreign agents and distributors. It is a way that many small businesses enter the global market. **Licensing** is an arrangement whereby an organization grants a foreign firm the right to use intellectual properties such as patents, copyrights, manufacturing processes, or trade names for a specific period of time. Licensing is usually limited to manufacturers. **Franchising** is an option whereby the parent company grants another firm the right to do business in a prescribed manner. Franchisees must follow stricter operational guidelines than do licensees. Franchising is popular with service firms, such as restaurants and hotels. Franchising possibilities are available in China, where the rapid emergence of a middle class, led by a growing population of educated professionals, is paving the way for franchise development.

Although exporting, licensing, and franchising are good initial entry options, in order to take full advantage of global opportunities, companies must make a substantial investment in other countries. Companies can vary greatly in their degree of global involvement. A **multinational corporation (MNC)** is a firm that is based in one country (the parent or home country) and produces goods or provides services in one or more foreign countries (host countries). A multinational corporation directs manufacturing and marketing operations in several countries; these operations are coordinated by a parent company, usually based in the firm's home country.

Many firms have evolved beyond being multinational to becoming **global corporations (GCs),** an organization that has corporate units in a number of countries that are integrated to operate as one organization worldwide. The global corporation operates as if the entire world were one entity. Global corporations sell essentially the same products throughout the world with components that may be made and/or designed in different countries. Expectations are that as the world becomes more globally open, the globalization of corporations will become much more commonplace. Not many years ago, Procter & Gamble was primarily a U.S. business investing heavily in food brands. Now it is a truly global corporation with more than 300 brands in more than 180 countries crossing the Americas, Europe, the Middle East and Africa, and Asia.[17] Its corporate leaders are an extremely diverse group, representing many cultures and backgrounds.

Today, global corporations are transforming themselves into transnationals. A **transnational corporation** moves work to the places with the talent to handle the job and the time to do it at the right cost. William J. Amelio, the CEO of Lenovo, the world's third-largest computer maker, calls his global workforce strategy "worldsourcing." Lenovo has executive offices in five cities worldwide and organizes its workforce around hubs of expertise, such as hardware designers in Japan and marketers in India. "You operate as if there's just one time zone," Amelio says. "And you're always on."[18]

The importance of human resource management in the global environment is illustrated by the fact that the Human Resource Certification Institute now has an international component. The Global Professional in Human Resources certification focuses on strategic HR management, global talent acquisition and mobility, global compensation and benefits, organizational effectiveness, talent development, workforce relations, and risk management.[19]

Global Strategic Human Resource Management

The world is experiencing an increasing global workforce. Global human resource problems and opportunities are enormous and are expanding. Individuals dealing with global human resource matters face a multitude of challenges beyond that of their domestic counterparts. These considerations range from cultural barriers to political barriers to international aspects such as compensation. Before upper management decides on a global move, it is vitally important that the critical nature of human resource issues be considered.

Companies that engage in the global economy place even greater emphasis on strategic HR. The global recession of 2008/10 illustrated the importance of strategic HR to Rio Tinto, a company involved in the mining and metals industries. Because of the global recession, the company announced a workforce reduction of 14,000 employees and contractors out of 100,000 employees and thousands of contractors worldwide. They used a "common global approach, regional severance policies, a comprehensive database, measurement tools to track the full impact of reductions and global providers for outplacement." Strategic HR helped them to early

Figure 14.1

Environment of Global Human Resource Management

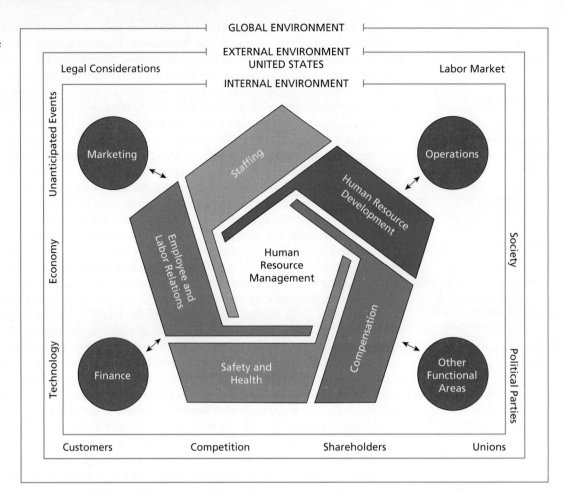

identify high-potential leaders and workers with critical skills and to retain as much talent as possible. The company also trained managers to help remaining employees stay focused.[20]

The functional areas associated with effective global human resource management are similar to the ones they experience domestically, as shown in Figure 14.1. Although the five functions are the same, the manner in which they are implemented may differ. Sound global human resource management practices are required for successful performance in each area. As with domestic human resources, the functional areas are not separate and distinct, but are highly interrelated.

OBJECTIVE 14.3
Explain global staffing.

Global Staffing

Before the staffing process for an international assignment begins, a thorough understanding of what is involved in the job should be developed (job analysis). A global organization must systematically match the internal and external supply of people with job openings anticipated in the organization over a specified period of time (human resource planning). Individuals should be recruited and selected based on the specific qualifications identified. Without proper identification of the qualities needed for an overseas assignment, an outstanding worker in the United States may fail on a global assignment.

expatriate
Employee who is not a citizen of the country in which a firm's operations are located, but is a citizen of the country in which the organization is headquartered.

Types of Global Staff Members

Companies must choose from various types of global staff members and may use specific approaches to global staffing. Global staff members may be selected from among three different types: expatriates, host-country nationals, and third-country nationals. An **expatriate** is an employee who is not a citizen of the country in which the firm operations are located, but is a citizen of the country in which the organization is headquartered. The U.S. expat population has grown rapidly largely because of the large numbers of workers who are being sent to China and

host-country national (HCN)
Employee who is a citizen of the country where the subsidiary is located.

India. A **host-country national (HCN)** is an employee who is a citizen of the country where the subsidiary is located. An example would be a U.S. citizen working for a Japanese company in the United States. Normally, the bulk of employees in international offices will be host-country nationals. Not only are companies staffed by locals less expensive, but they also offer advantages from a cultural and business standpoint. In most industries, host-country nationals comprise more than 98 percent of the workforce in the foreign operations of North American and Western European multinational companies. Hiring local people and operating the company like local companies whenever possible is good business. The ultimate goal of most foreign operations is to turn over control to local management. However, relying totally on local employees may, at times, pose problems. Chinese officials often think a foreign company (particularly a large multi-national) is not taking them seriously if a local represents them with no links to the decision makers in the home country. A **third-country national (TCN)** is a citizen of one country, working in a second country, and employed by an organization headquartered in a third country. An example would be an Italian citizen working for a French company in Germany.

third-country national (TCN)
Citizen of one country, working in a second country, and employed by an organization headquartered in a third country.

Approaches to Global Staffing

Using the three basic types of global staff, there are four major approaches to global staffing: ethnocentric, polycentric, regiocentric, and geocentric staffing.[21] These reflect how the organization develops its human resource policies and the preferred types of employees for different positions.

ethnocentric staffing
Staffing approach in which companies primarily hire expatriates to staff higher-level foreign positions.

ETHNOCENTRIC STAFFING   With **ethnocentric staffing**, companies primarily hire expatriates to staff higher-level foreign positions. This would be the case with Rich Products Corporation, based in Buffalo, New York, with $2.6 billion in annual sales. Rich sells food products in 73 countries and employs 7,300 workers worldwide. Judy Campbell, vice president, international human resources, said, "Our strategy has always been to focus on local talent development. We have never had more than six expats in any of our international locations. Our intent is to use local managers so that we learn about different ways of doing business and develop intimacy with customers."[22] This strategy assumes that home-office perspectives and issues should take precedence over local perspectives and issues and that expatriates will be more effective in representing the views of the home office. The corporate human resources department is primarily concerned with selecting and training managers for foreign assignments, developing appropriate compensation packages, and handling adjustment issues when managers return home. Generally, expatriates are used to ensure that foreign operations are linked effectively with parent corporations. However, the use of expatriate employees must be carefully considered, since the cost of an international assignment may be high.

polycentric staffing
Staffing approach in which host-country nationals are used throughout the organization, from top to bottom.

POLYCENTRIC STAFFING   When host-country nationals are used throughout the organization, from top to bottom, it is referred to as **polycentric staffing**. In developed countries such as Japan, Canada, and the United Kingdom, there has been more reliance on local executives, and less on traditional expatriate management. The ultimate goal of most foreign operations is to turn over control to local management. The use of the polycentric staffing model is based on the assumption that host-country nationals are better equipped to deal with local market conditions. Organizations that use this approach will usually have a fully functioning human resource department in each foreign subsidiary responsible for managing all local human resource issues. Corporate human resource managers focus primarily on coordinating relevant activities with their counterparts in each foreign operation. Most global employees are usually host-country nationals, because this helps to clearly establish that the company is making a commitment to the host country and not just setting up a foreign operation. Host-country nationals often have much more knowledge of the culture, the politics, and the laws of the locale, as well as how business is done. There is no standard format in the selection of host-country nationals.

regiocentric staffing
Staffing approach that is similar to the polycentric staffing approach, but regional groups of subsidiaries reflecting the organization's strategy and structure work as a unit.

REGIOCENTRIC STAFFING   **Regiocentric staffing** is similar to the polycentric approach, but regional groups of subsidiaries reflecting the organization's strategy and structure work as a unit. There is some degree of autonomy in regional decision making, and promotions are possible within the region but rare from the region to headquarters. Each region develops a common set of employment practices.

geocentric staffing
Staffing approach that uses a worldwide integrated business strategy.

GEOCENTRIC STAFFING **Geocentric staffing** is a staffing approach that uses a worldwide integrated business strategy. The firm attempts to always hire the best person available for a position, regardless of where that individual comes from. The geocentric staffing model is most likely to be adopted and used by truly global firms. Usually, the corporate human resource function in geocentric companies is the most complicated, since every aspect of HR must be dealt with in the global environment.

Selecting Expatriates

Expatriates are often selected from those already within the organization and the process involves four distinct stages: self-selection, creating a candidate pool, technical skills assessment, and making a mutual decision.

In stage one, self-selection, candidates determine whether they are right for a global assignment, whether their spouses and children are interested in relocating internationally, and whether this is the best time for a move. In the case of self-selection, the candidates assess themselves on all of the relevant dimensions for a job and then decide whether to pursue a global assignment. The self-assessment extends to the entire family. In a recent survey, 89 percent of those surveyed listed family concerns as the most common reason for assignment refusal. Spousal career concerns was listed by 62 percent.[23] Another survey found that 55 percent of employees facing dual career issues are less likely to put themselves forward as a candidate for a global assignment.[24] According to Rick Schwartz, president and chief executive officer of GMAC Global Relocation Services in Woodridge, Illinois, "when candidates are selected for expatriate assignments, spouses, partners and entire families also need to be 'selected.' Managers of international assignment programs can't approach an assignment as just another task. Instead, they must appreciate that they're managing an expatriate's future career, and that they face the possibility of early return and a possible doubling of the chances for employee attrition."[25] Basically, candidates must decide whether to go to the next step in the selection process.

Stage two involves creating a candidate database organized according to the firm's staffing needs. Included in the database is information such as the year the employee is available to go overseas, the languages the employee speaks, the countries the employee prefers, and the jobs for which the employee is qualified.

Stage three involves scanning the database for all possible candidates for a given global assignment; then the list is forwarded to the assigning department. There, each candidate is assessed on technical and managerial readiness relative to the needs of the assignment. In the final stage, one person is identified as an acceptable candidate based on his or her technical or managerial readiness and is tentatively selected.

If the decision is made to employ expatriates, certain selection criteria should be carefully considered in stages two and three. Cris Collie, chief executive officer of Worldwide ERC, said, "It takes a special blend of characteristics to add up to an outstanding expat who can be productive and accepted in an unfamiliar setting."[26] Expatriate selection criteria should include cultural adaptability, strong communication skills, technical competence, professional or operational expertise, global experience, country-specific experience, interpersonal skills, language skills, family flexibility, and country- or region-specific considerations. However, according to a recent survey by Cartus, a workforce development provider, when considering employees for international assignments, 72 percent of companies chose technical competence and 65 percent chose job experience.[27]

Background Investigation

I discussed in Chapter 6 the importance of conducting a background investigation on potential employees. Conducting background investigations when working in the global environment is equally, or even more, important but differences across cultures and countries often put up barriers. Each country has its own laws, customs, and procedures for background screenings. For instance, Japanese law covers a person working at the Tokyo office of a U.S.-based company and includes privacy statutes that prohibit criminal checks on Japanese citizens. The United Kingdom does not allow third parties such as background-checking firms to have direct access to criminal records held by local police. Instead, the job applicant and the recruiting organization must sign and submit a formal request to a specific agency responsible for handling criminal records. It can take up to 40 business days to get information back. Traci Canning, director of international operations for HireRight, a pre-employment screening company in Irvine, California, says, "It's important to

Web Wisdom

Worldwide ERC: The Workforce Mobility Association

http://www. worldwideerc.org/ about_us/Pages/ index.aspx

Association for professionals who oversee, manage, or support U.S. domestic and international employee transfer.

TRENDS & INNOVATIONS

Cyberwork in the Global Environment

Technology has created an assortment of possibilities that will be rewarding for some individuals, but not for others. Communication technology developments have significant implications for the job. Employees working in the global environment can communicate throughout the world virtually instantaneously. Wireless communication has created the potential for **cyberwork,** a possibility of a never-ending workday. BlackBerrys or iPhones, text messaging, e-mail, and around-the-clock computer access create endless possibilities for communication. The Blackberry literally makes a worker available for work 24 hours a day. Forgetting or losing your Blackberry produces anxiety. In his book, *Elsewhere, USA*, Dalton Conley calls the class of professionals who live this way "intraviduals." He defines his term: "a new breed of modern workers who struggles to manage multiple data streams and competing impulses and even selves."[28]

Everything has become blurred with technology. Some workers believe that their employer wants them available 24/7. What will employees scattered across the globe do when their managers need information from them at an inconvenient hour? Clients will not likely be content to wait until 8:00 a.m. (your time) for information. Obviously a worker could turn off their communication devices to prevent such inconvenient intrusions but that might be detrimental to career security. In one survey, a respondent said, "I am required to carry a cell phone 24/7. I am called any time there is a problem, and expected to answer. We have had people terminated for not answering phones." Others said they are expected to respond to cell phone calls and the "constant e-mail traffic, even on vacation." Another respondent said, "We are a worldwide company with customers and engineering staff all over the world. To accommodate and manage the time zones, I am expected to make myself available at any time. [For example,] answering e-mail and cell phone calls on Sunday to accommodate the 12-hour time difference in other countries is expected."[29] Even the cruise lines appear to be accommodating the 24/7 workday. They have the technology that permits passengers to use their cell phones and the Internet (although at a cost) while cruising. Perhaps the days of getting away from it all have ended.

understand the local context. In general, that means understanding how HR operations, law enforcement agencies, schools/universities and businesses operate outside the United States." HireRight tells the story of a person who had been in the United States for two years and had applied for a job with a multinational firm. There were no gaps in the individual's employment history that would suggest he had ever been in jail. However, further check revealed that he had been convicted of murder in his home country and in accord with a practice that was legal at the time, had paid a proxy to serve his prison term while he remained free and in the workforce.[30]

Hiring Temps in Japan

Employers in Japan have discovered a new way to find part-time workers in a hurry. They use global positioning systems in cell phones to find them. Tokyo's LocationValue is an online marketplace that lets stores who need cashiers or delivery companies in need of drivers search for qualified candidates in their vicinity.

LocationValue's Otetsudai Networks relies on Japan's wireless networks and GPS-enabled phones that are virtually everywhere. Job seekers click the "I'm free now" box from their mobile browsers, and the servers note the GPS location of the phone. Employers who are searching the site receive a list of candidates who are nearby and willing to work, even if only for an hour. Both parties get to evaluate each other later. This process tends to reduce both poor workers and bad employers. LocationValue has registered 54,000 job hunters and has a customer base of 3,000 businesses. Businesses pay fees for the service.[31]

OBJECTIVE 14.4
Describe global human resource development.

Global Human Resource Development

Many U.S. businesses operate under the assumption that American ways and business practices are standard across the globe. Similarly, some training and development professionals believe that training and development strategies that work for a U.S. audience can be equally effective abroad. Unfortunately, nothing could be further from the truth. Global training and development

Web Wisdom

*International HR
Organizations*

http://www.ifebp.org

International Foundation
of Employee Benefit Plans

http://www.ipma-hr.org

International Public
Management Association
for Human Resources

http://www.ipmaac.org

International Public
Management Association
for Human Resources

http://www.ihrim.org

International Association
for Human Resource
Information Management.
International HR
organizations are
identified.

is needed because people, jobs, and organizations are often quite different. Next, various aspects of global HR development will be discussed.

Expatriate Training and Development

The training of employees going on a global assignment has often been bleak, but appears to be improving. Lynn Rocafort, president of Relocation Counseling & Consulting, said, "60 percent of international assignments fail due to lack of cultural training and support. Difficulty in adjusting to a new environment greatly impacts an employee's work and home life."[32] The development process should start as soon as workers are selected—definitely before they begin the global assignment.

Organizations are recognizing that expatriate employees and their families face special situations and pressure that training and development activities must prepare them to deal with. Employees and their families must have an effective orientation program and a readjustment-training program. In addition, the employee must have a program of continual development. Figure 14.2 illustrates the ideal expatriate preparation and development program, which includes pre-move orientation and training, continual development, and repatriation orientation and training.

Pre-move Orientation and Training

Pre-move orientation and training of expatriate employees and their families are essential before the global assignment begins. The pre-move orientation needs to be aggressively undertaken so that the expatriate understands cultural dos and don'ts and is immersed in the language. Merely providing an expatriate a "cultural 'dummies' guide and a basic phrasebook for speaking with the locals won't be enough." [33] Continuing employee development, in which the employee's global skills are fitted into career planning and corporate development programs, makes the eventual transition to the host home country less disruptive. Marc Sokol, senior vice president at Personnel Decisions International, said, "The cost of failure is very high. If you leave it to self-study, then you're rolling the dice."[34]

Many organizations have established a formal *buddy system* to alleviate the stress new expatriates and their families normally endure, to reduce the time it takes for expatriates to operate at peak productivity. Buddies often inform expatriates of host-office norms and politics, invite them into their homes, introduce them to friends and networks, and help bolster their credibility in the office.

Continual Development: Online Assistance and Training

Companies now offer online assistance and training in areas such as career services, cross-cultural training, and employee assistance programs (EAPs). The Internet offers global employees assistance 24 hours a day, seven days a week. Technology is a time-saving and cost-effective solution for the stress experienced by employees who are on assignment or doing business travel. Even if the assignment is a short-term business trip, technology can be used to provide ongoing

Figure 14.2

**The Expatriate
Preparation and
Development
Program**

contact and support. For example, online career services can give expatriates and their spouses the opportunity to upgrade skills while on assignment.

Repatriation Orientation and Training

repatriation
Process of bringing expatriates home.

Orientation and training are also necessary prior to **repatriation,** which is the process of bringing expatriates home. However, returning expatriates have not always had a pleasant experience. Even though a company may spend considerable money in sending managers overseas, too many returning managers report dissatisfaction with the process.[35] Many companies do not specify in advance how the international experience will fit into an employee's career progression.[36] In fact, many expatriates were not even guaranteed a job upon their return.[37] Further, expats often come home to a company that has undergone significant change from such events as mergers, acquisitions, reorganizations, and workforce contraction or expansion which can create an unfamiliar environment.[38]

According to a study by a partnership between PricewaterhouseCoopers and Cranfield University School of Management, more than 25 percent of repatriated employees leave the company within one year after an international assignment ends.[39] Reasons given for leaving include they were not being properly prepared to return to their work and not being able to use skills that they learned abroad. Upon an expat's return from an international assignment, employers should make every effort to find a place in the organization that will use the experience gained during the assignment. Also, the returning expat should be given a job with at least the same degree of responsibility and authority.

To counter the challenges of repatriation, firms need to have a formal in-house repatriation program in place. A dialogue regarding expectations and career planning upon return will help to manage expectations. Also, the exchange should continue after the employee has returned home. In addition, acknowledgment and recognition of the significant overseas contribution is a courtesy that the returning employee has earned and richly deserves. Ideally, there should be a clear career path or position identified for the expatriate employee upon his or her return. Carolyn Ryffel, director of the training network and curriculum design at Cartus, says, "An effective repatriation training program will facilitate the assignees in clearly defining their new or strengthened skills and knowledge and coach them on how to position themselves in the corporate environment to which they've returned."[40]

Web Wisdom

Cartus

http://www.cartus.com/

Global mobility and workforce development support to organizations worldwide.

Global E-learning

Globalization has created a special need for e-learning and companies are embracing it to train the global workforce. In the past, a training program for a *Fortune* 200 company in the Far East would likely cost between $250,000 and $500,000 for travel and related expenses. Many believe that live, instructor-led training is still more effective, but the question that must be asked is, "how much more effective?" E-learning allows companies to keep the money and still receive a good training product.

The most obvious challenge for any global e-learning implementation is failure to recognize the impact of cultural differences on the programs' success. Without a culture analysis or failing to recognize cultural differences can seriously damage a global organization's success. A STD and i4cp's study found that only 25 percent addressed cultural differences that affect management. Cultural accessibility is required in that all learners are able to achieve the same learning outcomes by putting the same amount of effort to get the same knowledge without regard to culture or origin. A problem that evolves in implementing global e-learning is that the e-learning program is embedded with the culture of the person(s) who developed the program.[41] For example, in teaching graduate courses that had a large global population, I had to constantly be alert to not use colloquialisms and other forms of the English language that made it difficult to understand for students who spoke British English as a second language. I had to remember that everyone did not fully comprehend what I meant when I said something like "There is more than one way to skin a cat," or my southern roots saying "Y'all."

In Global English Corporation's "Globalization of English" research, 91 percent of employees of global corporations said that English is "required" or "important" in their jobs, and that the need is increasing dramatically. Eighty-nine percent of employees said they are more likely to climb the corporate ladder if they can communicate in English. Many companies offer courses only in English or in English and one other language, usually Spanish. An English-only focus works for firms that routinely conduct their business all over the world in English. But others need courses in more than one language. Companies that want to offer courses in several languages usually turn to translators. Financial services provider GE Capital relies on translation companies to offer Web-based courses in English, French, German, and Japanese.[42]

Hilton's team members are scattered the world over. In a sector that sees high turnover rates, it is also hard to imagine that a classroom trainer could keep up with the demands of hundreds of new workers requiring training. Hilton, along with many multinational companies, realized that it could save money through online courses. Hilton first introduced e-learning when the company launched its Hilton University with 60 generic business skills programs and 21 finance programs. Over the years, Hilton put in place an additional 40 business skills courses and significantly increased the number of generic online courses offered. Andrea Kluit, director of international learning and development at Hilton International, points out another huge plus of e-learning by saying, "Where a classroom course cannot be re-visited after its completion, an e-learning course can be used as a reference tool, returned to when team members feel the need to refresh their memories. We have found that in the case of systems training especially, this tool is invaluable in offering learners a re-usable resource and so is hugely popular."[43]

Virtual Teams in a Global Environment

Virtual teams are becoming commonplace in many organizations. Intel Corporation recently conducted a study that revealed that approximately two-thirds of their employees collaborated with team members located at different sites and in different regions.[44] With virtual teams, team members do not have to meet face-to-face to be effective, thereby eliminating "dead time" caused by traveling. These teams operate across boundaries of time and geography and have become a necessity of everyday working life.

Virtual teams enable companies to accomplish things more quickly and efficiently. The times when virtual team members are in one place are few, especially when members are located across the globe. This often makes global teams more difficult to manage effectively. Communication is the key to keeping teams working effectively together.[45] Some of the difficulties that virtual teams confront with regard to communication are discussed next. First, dispersed team members often do not feel as connected or committed to the team. There may be a feeling of disconnect caused by communicating by e-mail, instant messaging, audio conferencing, and other tools.[46] "Out of sight, out of mind" may apply suggesting that virtual team members need to get together from time to time. Second, communication problems between team members appear to be directly proportional to the number of time zones that separate them. Michael Kossler, senior enterprise associate for the Center for Creative Leadership, said, "An effective virtual leader rotates the time frames when conference calls for team meetings are going to be held so that the same people are not always inconvenienced."[47] If it is only a couple of zones, teammates will be in their offices earlier or later than one another, but their workdays still overlap enough to allow phone calls. If the distance stretches from 9 to 12 time zones, workdays do not overlap at all, and e-mail and voice mail must be used. Third, there is the language problem. Since English is becoming the world language, those for whom English is a second language may be at a disadvantage. Many Asians are concerned with saving face if they do not understand something. They may be hesitant to ask questions that would reveal their ignorance, thus widening the communication gap. Leading global virtual teams is certainly challenging.

Workers in virtual teams may experience a psychological concept called *fundamental attribution error*, which is the human tendency to credit other people's behavior to their personal characteristics rather than the situation they are in. For example, suppose that a colleague does not reply to your urgent email for days, so you say to yourself "that guy is just so arrogant and in their own little world" rather than "perhaps they didn't get my email: the server was down, they might be on leave, in meetings all day, etc." It is crucial not to be judgmental when working in virtual teams.[48] Giving virtual team members the benefit of the doubt is important to avoid misunderstandings.

Virtual team members do not have the luxury of getting together over lunch or just communicating informally in the office. To overcome this lack of informal getting to know each other, a community homespace such as MySpace and Facebook featuring pictures and profiles of team members, a discussion board, a team calendar, or a chat room might be beneficial. That way team members can connect with each other in ways other than meetings and establish stronger group bond.[49]

OBJECTIVE 14.5
Explain global compensation.

Global Compensation

Companies that are successful in the global environment align their human resources programs in support of their strategic business plans. A major component is the manner in which the human resources total compensation program supports the way the business is structured, organized, and operated both globally and regionally.

Compensation for Host-Country Nationals

Certainly, in compensation-related matters, organizations should think globally but act locally. One reason that organizations relocate to other areas of the world is probably the high-wage pressures in the home country that threaten their ability to compete on a global basis.[50] Globally, the question of what constitutes a fair day's pay is not as complicated as it is in the United States; normally, it is slightly above the prevailing wage rates in the area. The same is often true of benefits and nonfinancial rewards. Variations in laws, living costs, tax policies, and other factors all must be considered when a company is establishing global compensation packages. For example, Puerto Rico has laws requiring the paying of severance pay and a Christmas bonus.[51] Employers in Nigeria are required to provide a life insurance policy for employees at a rate of three times their salary. In Italy, a mandatory benefit is paid when an employee leaves an organization, regardless of whether this is due to resignation, termination, or retirement. In Belgium, employers offering a defined contribution pension scheme must provide a guaranteed investment return of 3.25 percent.[52]

The company will want to create a precise picture of employment and working conditions in order to establish appropriate practices in each country. Some of the factors that should be considered include: minimum wage requirements, which often differ from country to country and even from city to city within a country; working-time information such as annual holidays, vacation time and pay, paid personal days, standard weekly working hours, probation periods, and overtime restrictions and payments; and hiring and termination rules and regulations covering severance practices.

Culture often plays a part in determining compensation. North American compensation practices encourage individualism and high performance; continental European programs typically emphasize social responsibility; the traditional Japanese approach considers age and company service as primary determinants of compensation. In other countries, there is no guarantee that additional compensation will ensure additional output. In mainland China, workers who are paid by the hour often do not work hard. Under the communist system, working harder than anyone else did not result in additional pay. Therefore, there was no reason to do so. It has been found that, in some countries, additional pay has resulted in employees' working less. As soon as employees have earned enough to satisfy their needs, time spent with family or on other noncompany activities is perceived as more valuable than additional cash. In former communist countries, people were used to a system in which pay and performance were not related. Under the old system, good employees were paid the same as poor performers. With the collapse of the Iron Curtain, the idea that pay and performance should be related is now making its way into people's minds.

A country's culture can also impose significant constraints on the globalization of pay. In countries like France and Greece, where the best graduates often choose government positions with secure paychecks for life, it is quite difficult to attract good employees with pay schemes that include high bonuses for achieving specific objectives. In places like Hong Kong, where people value risk and are motivated by personal financial gains, employees who have achieved a significant professional result expect a financial form of recognition (raise, bonus, or commission) within a matter of weeks. They are likely to look for another employer if they have to wait until their next annual performance review. Whereas people in the United States derive great status from high pay, nations in large parts of Europe and Asia shun conspicuous wealth. In Italy, where teamwork is more valued than individual initiative, sales incentives for top sales professionals working in small teams can be demotivational. The recipient of a large award may feel awkward when receiving larger than a fair share of the reward pie.

Because of these and other cultural differences, it is difficult to design a global, one-size-fits-all pay scheme that attracts the best talent in all countries. In particular, pay-for-performance schemes often need to be adapted to local preferences, depending on whether income security or higher risks and returns are preferred.

Expatriate Compensation

Expatriate compensation provides exceptional challenges compared to home-country emp- loyment, such as developing packages that are reasonably cost-effective while still attractive and motivating. For expatriate managers and professionals, the situation is more complex than simply paying at or slightly above local host-country compensation rates. The largest expatri- ate costs historically has included overall remuneration, housing, cost-of-living allowances, and physical relocation.[53] Regarding tax-equalization payments, U.S. citizens living overseas were able to exclude up to $91,400 of gross income earned abroad in 2009 but the IRS adjusts the exclusion amount yearly for inflation.[54] Also, credits against U.S. income taxes are given for a portion of the foreign income taxes paid by U.S. expatriates beyond the $91,400 level.

In the past few years, additional challenges have hit companies as they have attempted to go global. First, the devaluation of the U.S. dollar has had a major impact on expat compensation. Also, there have been changes to the U.S. tax code that affect expatriate lifestyle. These chal- lenges come at a time when global business is expanding. Meeting these challenges will affect how effectively the United States competes in the global market.

Scott Sullivan, senior vice president of global sales and marketing with GMAC in Woodridge, Illinois, and a former expat, said, "For decades, being relocated to another country was a windfall for expats. They were getting paid in U.S. dollars and putting a lot of that money in the bank because dollars would go much further. Now the inverse of that is happening. Dollars don't go as far, meaning companies have to pay a lot more for U.S. citizens to go overseas."[55]

Kathy Trachta, director of global consulting for Paragon Global Resources in Rancho Santa Margarita, California, said, "Twenty years ago, a typical expat policy created a 'windfall' in that almost 100 percent of all living accommodations, expenses, schooling, transportation, and cost of goods and services was paid by the employer. Now, we have indexes that spell out the differ- ences between home and host country [and compensate] only for the differences plus a range or set dollar amount for housing—not an unlimited amount." In the past, expats regularly received a premium for taking an overseas assignment. Trachta noted, "This benefit is disappearing from more recent programs, with a hardship allowance remaining for specific locations where living is truly a difficult situation due to political unrest, adverse conditions or remote locations far from common conveniences."[56]

Achim Mossmann, managing director of KPMG LLP's International Executive Services in New York, said, "Organizations have moved away from the traditional expat programs. In the past, you had the typical U.S.-based balance-sheet approach with fully equalized employees and a strong focus on keeping employees on home-country compensation and benefits." Today, Mossmann says, "Instead of keeping employees on the home country's balance sheet, they're moved to the host country's compensation' package and treated like local employees. You still continue to pay a relocation allowance and moving costs, but strip away some of the allowances related to the home-country compensation packages." This trend has grown in the past three or four years.[57]

Mossmann also notes, "Typically, what you see is that on a more developmental level you apply the less generous package so the incentive for the employee is really related to personal and future development. For high-level employees and employees filling key positions, you typically still see companies utilize the fully equalized home-based packages." Still, pay packages are not being cut too much. Geoff Latta, executive vice president of ORC Worldwide in New York, a firm that provides consulting services primarily in the compensation area, says, "A lot of companies have hit the point where they'd love to be able to save money, but not at the direct expense of the assignee."[58]

OBJECTIVE 14.6
Describe global safety and health.

Global Safety and Health

U.S.-based global operations are often safer and healthier than host-country operations, but frequently not as safe as similar operations in the United States. Safety and health laws and regulations often vary greatly from country to country. Such laws can range from virtually nonexistent to as stringent as those in the United States. Also, health care facilities across the globe vary greatly in their state of modernization. Companies are attempting to overcome this problem. For example, global health care provider CIGNA International has teamed up with CIGNA Behavioral Health to offer an employee assistance program for expatriate employees of multinational firms. The EAP program allows CIGNA International participants to access a multilingual support and counseling network. Employees and their dependents can receive assistance through telephone or personal visits for a wide range of behavioral health and work–life concerns. The program is designed to help employees better manage stress and anxiety, depression and substance abuse, as well as to help them lead healthy lifestyles.

Additional considerations specific to global assignments are emergency evacuation services and global security protection. An international firm was preparing to evacuate 15 expatriate employees and dependents from a country that had suffered an earthquake. When it came time to meet at the departure point, 25 people showed up. Those arranging for the evacuation had not known that two technical teams were in the country supporting clients at the time.

Often, evacuation and care of injured employees is done through private companies. Medical emergencies are frightening under any circumstances, but when an employee becomes sick or injured abroad, it can be a traumatic experience. If the travelers are assigned to more remote or less developed areas, companies should be aware that in many medical facilities needles are often reused, equipment is not properly used, and there is a lack of basic medical supplies. Also, employees and their families living abroad must constantly be aware of security issues. Many firms provide bodyguards who escort executives everywhere. Some firms even have disaster plans to deal with evacuating expatriates if natural disasters, civil conflicts, or wars occur.

Global companies continue to face global safety risks. That is one of the lessons learned after the 1984 disaster in Bhopal, India, affected Union Carbide's worldwide operations. The Bhopal Disaster of 1984 was the worst industrial disaster in history. It was caused by the accidental release of 40 metric tons of methyl isocyanate (MIC) from a Union Carbide India, Limited (UCIL), pesticide plant located in the heart of the city of Bhopal, in the Indian state of Madhya Pradesh. UCIL was a joint venture between Union Carbide and a consortium of Indian investors. The accident in the early hours produced heavier-than-air toxic MIC gas, which rolled along the ground through the surrounding streets, killing thousands outright and injuring anywhere from 150,000 to 600,000 others, at least 15,000 of whom died later from their injuries. Some sources give much higher fatality figures.[59]

Health and safety professionals with international experience say one of the most important trends sweeping through successful multinational companies is the shift to a single safety management system that applies to all their operations throughout the world. Although the example of Bhopal revealed the risks of safety failures, experts emphasize that taking a global approach to safety and health is not only about avoiding problems. It also opens up a wealth of opportunities to improve performance.[60] Seiji Machida, coordinator of the occupational safety cluster at the International Labor Organization in Geneva, Switzerland, said, "Multinationals should have a policy applicable to all operations, regardless of the site. Such global systems don't have to be detailed, but there should be a framework or a set of principles."[61]

Although events on the scale of Bhopal are rare, many companies have discovered that the way they treat their workers anywhere on the planet can pose a risk to their corporate reputation. "On an ethical basis, it doesn't make sense to do one thing in one country and something different elsewhere," says Zack Mansdorf, senior vice president for safety, health, and environment at L'Oréal North America and Worldwide, a cosmetics company with operations in more than 200 countries and headquartered in Paris. "We're going to do it because it's the right thing to do." Mansdorf also notes the financial savings and morale and productivity improvements that always result from safety improvements. "In addition, the business argument is that for some companies, brand is everything." This rationale is especially powerful for consumer companies such as L'Oréal. A global system also offers many operational efficiencies, according to James Forsman, vice president and general manager of DuPont Safety Resources, a safety consulting business unit of the global chemical company based in Wilmington, Delaware. "The advantages are profound: You have a single set of standards now, as opposed to multiple standards, say one for Brazil, one for China and one for the U.S."[62] The result is a far simpler management process.

Understanding the local culture and how it affects safety is critical for success, and not always easy. "Take Italy, where drivers are known for driving too fast," says Mansdorf. "When they get in your factory and drive a forklift, you expect them to behave in a different fashion." It can be hard to find the right people in the right places with the right skills, and this sometimes requires difficult choices. Is it more important to know the local culture and language or to have safety and health expertise? It is easier to teach someone the company global standards than the local mores.[63]

Global Employee and Labor Relations

OBJECTIVE 14.7
Explain global employee and labor relations.

Obviously, the strength and nature of unions differ from country to country, with unions ranging from nonexistent to relatively strong. In fact, unionism in private companies is a declining phenomenon in nearly all developed countries.[64] Codetermination, which requires firms to have union or worker representatives on their boards of directors, is very common in European countries. Even though they face global competition, unions in several European countries have resisted changing their laws and removing government protections. Laws make it hard to fire workers, so companies are reluctant to hire. Generous and lengthy unemployment benefits discourage the jobless from seeking new work. Motorola paid a net pre-tax charge of about $83 million in related severance fees for jobs cut in Germany.[65] Wage bargaining remains centralized, and companies have little flexibility to fashion contracts that fit their needs. High payroll taxes raise labor costs, and their laws mandating cumbersome layoff procedures increase the cost of the product.

On the other hand, in some South American countries such as Chile, collective bargaining for textile workers, miners, and carpenters is prohibited. And unions are generally allowed only in companies of 25 workers or more. This practice has encouraged businesses to split into small companies to avoid collective bargaining, leaving workers on their own.

NAFTA and CAFTA

The North American Free Trade Agreement (NAFTA) between Canada, Mexico, and the United States facilitated the movement of goods across boundaries within North America. Although no agreement is perfect, NAFTA has opened markets and established a record of growth and success that could prove key to a strong recovery.[66] It forms a free-trade zone of more than 400 million people with a combined gross domestic profit of about $12 trillion dollars. Labor relations took a major step forward, with a side agreement on labor designed to protect workers in all three countries from the effects of competitive economic pressures. NAFTA established a Commission for Labor Cooperation with offices in each country, which is governed by a council made up of labor ministers of Canada, Mexico, and the United States. Each country is accountable for complying with its own labor laws when dealing with occupational safety and health; child labor; migrant workers; human resource development; labor statistics; work benefits; social programs for workers; productivity improvements; labor management relations; employment standards; the equality of men and women in the workplace; and forms of cooperation among workers, management, and government. A country that consistently fails to enforce its own labor laws could be fined up to $20 million per violation. There are also a number of principles identifying broad areas of common agreement to protect the rights and interests of each workforce. Since NAFTA was implemented, trade between the United States, Canada, and Mexico has grown dramatically as all three countries have seen increased volumes of trade.[67] Even so, the calls to renegotiate the treaty grew more intense as the economic condition of the member countries worsened because of the recession of 2008/10.[68]

CAFTA, the Central American Free Trade Agreement, was ratified by America's Congress after a long political battle, and signed into law in 2005. If increases like those that occurred in Mexico in the wake of the North American Free Trade Agreement (NAFTA) take place, it would provide a huge economic boost for a region whose infrastructure remains startlingly basic.[69] However, there are those who believe that CAFTA has failed to live up to expectations.[70] There are claims of fraud from textile executives who are calling on Congress and the Administration to overhaul the textile enforcement division of U.S. Customs & Border Protection and crack down on what they claim are soaring levels of fraud.[71]

OBJECTIVE 14.8
Describe legal and political factors affecting global human resource management.

Global Legal and Political Factors

The growing complexity of legal compliance in the global environment is one of the most important trend affecting global business. Managers working for global businesses have to contend with a growing tide of employment legislation that cuts across national boundaries. Legal and political forces are unique to each country, and sometimes, the laws of one contradict those of another. For instance, the French authorities acknowledge that their data-protection laws are in direct conflict with the U.S. Sarbanes–Oxley Act, but they insist that multinationals comply with French law. Further, the nature and stability of political and legal systems vary across the globe. U.S. firms enjoy relatively stable legal and political systems, and the same is true in many of the developed countries. In other nations, however, the legal and political systems are much less stable. Some governments are subject to coups, dictatorial rule, and corruption, which can substantially alter both the business and legal environments. Legal systems can also become unstable, with contracts suddenly becoming unenforceable because of internal politics.

HR regulations and laws vary greatly among countries. As previously mentioned, merely conducting a background check is different from one country to another. In many Western European countries, laws on labor unions and employment make it difficult to lay off employees. Because of political and legal differences, it is essential that a comprehensive review of the political and legal environment of the host country is conducted before beginning global operations.

Some have asked the question, "Does operating under local laws and customs free a company of all ethical considerations?" Yahoo! said it was obeying Chinese law when it turned an e-mail from a private Yahoo! e-mail account over to the Chinese government. The e-mail revealed the identity of Shi Tao, an editorial department head at *Contemporary Business News* in China's Hunan province, leading to his conviction and 10-year sentence. Shi's crime was sending an e-mail to a New York–based Web site regarding the Chinese government's warning to its representatives to watch for dissident activity during the 15th anniversary of the Tiananmen Square massacre. Yahoo!, in a statement read by spokeswoman Mary Osako, gave the following reasoning: "Just like any other global company Yahoo! must ensure that its local country sites must operate within the laws, regulations, and customs of the country in which they are based."[72] Each company will have to evaluate what it would do in instances such as Yahoo! encountered.

Americans may encounter laws that are routinely ignored by host countries, creating somewhat of a dilemma. For example, the laws in some countries that require a minimum age for factory workers are often not enforced. The U.S. Department of Labor report revealed continued child labor abuses in the apparel and textile industries.

Also affecting the environment in which global companies operate are certain tariffs and quotas that can greatly impact business profitability. **Tariffs** are taxes collected on goods that are shipped across national boundaries. For example, in 2005, Mexico imposed a tariff on U.S. exports because Congress had not repealed the Byrd amendment, formally known as the Continued Dumping and Subsidy Offset Act of 2000. Mexico imposed tariffs of $20.9 million in three product categories, including a 30 percent duty on dairy products, including baby formula, a 20 percent duty on wine, and a 9 percent duty on candy and chewing gum.[73] Recently, the United States ordered an additional tariff on Chinese tires of 35 percent the first year, 30 percent the second and 25 percent the third, on top of the 4-percent tariff the U.S. traditionally levies. The union said that more than 5,000 tire workers lost their jobs between 2004 and 2008 because of Chinese tire imports, with another 3,000 poised

tariffs
Taxes collected on goods that are shipped across national boundaries.

ETHICAL DILEMMA

Mordita

Your company, a distributor of heavy mining equipment, wants to trade in the Mexican market where cash under the table, *mordita* (a little bit), is part of doing business. This payoff practice is so ingrained in the Mexican culture that a business virtually cannot open a Mexican operation without going along. You have observed many companies that did not pay and they failed to enter the Mexican market, as well as those that paid and entered the market, and overall, did fairly well. You can continue to raise your stature with mining companies, farmers, and contractors, and encourage them to lobby the government to freely open the market, or you can pay the bribe.

What would you do?

to lose their jobs.[74] In 2010, U.S.-China trade relations heated again, this time over chicken. China, the largest market for U.S. chicken exports, planned to impose anti-dumping tariffs of up to 105.4 percent on U.S. broiler chicken imports saying that the poultry products were dumped at unfair prices onto the China market, causing "substantial damage" to domestic chicken producers.[75] There is much talk about eliminating tariffs around the world but actions directed at eliminating them have been limited. **Quotas** are policies that limit the number or value of goods that can be imported across national boundaries. The amount of textile that can be imported to the United States is often limited by quotas.

OBJECTIVE 14.9
Explain global EEO and sexual harassment.

quotas
Policies that limit the number or value of goods that can be imported across national boundaries.

Global EEO and Sexual Harassment

The global assignment of women and members of racial/ethnic minorities can involve legal issues, as these individuals may be protected by EEO regulations. American workers employed by American-controlled businesses operating overseas are still protected under the American employment laws. Women currently make up nearly 25 percent of expatriates, which is up from 14 percent not long ago.[76] Unfortunately, these gains in female expatriate participation rates have not been equally distributed worldwide. The gender gaps still exist in the Middle East, South Asia, and sub-Saharan Africa.[77] There are some countries in which the sexist culture is so ingrained that women would have extreme difficulty participating on equal footing with the majority population in the workforce. In fact, there are some cultures today that will not accept a woman as a boss.

Sexual harassment is also a global problem. A disproportionate number of cross-cultural sexual harassment complaints involve perpetrators and victims from different ethnic, racial, or national origin groups. When individuals from two different cultures interact, there is a potential for sexual harassment problems. Some behaviors that violate U.S. cultural norms may not be perceived as a problem in another culture. In many Mediterranean and Latin countries, physical contact and sensuality are a common part of socializing. The famous Cirque du Soleil, headquartered in Montreal, Canada, has had to adapt to the U.S. definition of sexual harassment when performing in the United States. While kissing good friends and co-workers on both cheeks is common in Montreal, such behavior could be considered a form of sexual harassment in the United States. Also, there are the semi-nude photos of Cirque performers hanging on the walls of the company's Montreal headquarters. Suzanne Gagnon, vice president of human resources, said, because of "America's stringent laws on pornography, sexual harassment and obscenity, those photos would never see the light of day in Las Vegas."[78]

Australia, Canada, the Netherlands, Sweden, and the United Kingdom are among jurisdictions that have laws specifying prohibited conduct and allowing employees to seek individual remedies. Italy, the Philippines, Taiwan, and Venezuela define sexual harassment as a criminal offense, and penalties and remedies are provided in special statutory penal codes. In Germany, Spain, and Thailand, sexual discrimination law is based on the concept of termination indemnity that allows employees to terminate their employment relationships due to discrimination or harassment. In turn, termination indemnity laws require employers to pay employees substantial severance pay if the cause of their termination is due to discrimination or harassment. In Japan, legislative initiatives are bolstered by U.S.-style regulations prohibiting sexual harassment.

Summary

1. *Describe the impact of global bribery in international business.* It is getting tougher to get by with bribery in the international arena these days.

2. *Describe the evolution of global business and global strategic human resource management.* Most companies initially become global without making substantial investments in foreign countries by exporting, licensing, or franchising. A multinational corporation is a firm that is based in one country (the parent or home country) and produces goods or provides services in one or more foreign countries (host countries). A global corporation has corporate units in a number of countries that are integrated to operate as one organization worldwide. A transnational corporation moves work to the places with the talent to handle the job and the time to do it at the right cost.

    The world is experiencing an increasing global workforce. Global human resource problems and opportunities are enormous and are expanding. Individuals dealing with global human resource matters face a multitude of challenges beyond that of their domestic counterparts.

3. *Explain global staffing.* Companies must choose from various types of global staff members and may use specific approaches to global staffing. Global staff members may be selected from among three different types: expatriates, host-country nationals, and third-country nationals. There are four major approaches to global staffing: ethnocentric, polycentric, regiocentric, and geocentric staffing.

4. *Describe global human resource development.* Many training and development professionals believe that training and consulting principles and strategies that work for a U.S. audience can be equally effective abroad. Nothing could be further from the truth. Global training and development is needed because people, jobs, and organizations are often quite different. The ideal expatriate preparation and development program includes pre-move orientation and training, continual development, and repatriation orientation and training.

5. *Explain global compensation.* Expatriate compensation provides exceptional challenges compared to home-country employment, such as developing packages that are reasonably cost-effective while still attractive and motivating. For expatriate managers and professionals, the situation is more complex than simply paying at or slightly above local host-country compensation rates.

    Globally, the question of what constitutes a fair day's pay for host-country nationals is not as complicated as it is in the United States; normally, it is slightly above the prevailing wage rates in the area. The same is often true of benefits and nonfinancial rewards.

6. *Describe global safety and health.* U.S.-based global operations are often safer and healthier than host-country operations, but frequently not as safe as similar operations in the United States.

7. *Explain global employee and labor relations.* The strength and nature of unions differ from country to country, with unions ranging from nonexistent to relatively strong.

8. *Describe legal and political factors affecting global human resource management.* Legal and political forces are unique for each country. The growing complexity of legal compliance in the global environment is one of the most important trends affecting global business. Mangers working for global businesses have to contend with a growing tide of employment legislation that cuts across national boundaries.

9. *Explain global EEO and sexual harassment.* The global assignment of women and members of racial/ethnic minorities can involve legal issues, as these individuals may be protected by EEO regulations. American workers employed by American-controlled businesses operating overseas are still protected under the American employment laws.

Key Terms

exporting   411
licensing   411
franchising   411
multinational corporation
    (MNC)   411
global corporation (GC)   411

transnational corporation   411
expatriate   412
host-country national (HCN)   413
third-country national (TCN)   413
ethnocentric staffing   413
polycentric staffing   413

regiocentric staffing   413
geocentric staffing   414
cyberwork   415
repatriation   417
tariffs   423
quotas   424

Questions for Review

1. What is meant by the statement, "Conducting business globally exposes U.S. companies to an environment involving bribery that they are not exposed to in the United States"?
2. Explain what is meant by the following quote: "Organizations must either globalize or they will die."
3. How has global business evolved?
4. Define the following terms:
   a. exporting
   b. licensing
   c. franchising
5. What are the various types of global staff members?
6. What are the approaches to global staffing?
7. Why is repatriation orientation and training needed?
8. What is the importance of e-learning in the global environment?
9. What difficulties do virtual teams have in the global environment?
10. What is meant by the statement with reference to compensation for host-country nationals, "Organizations should think globally but act locally"?
11. What is the status of expatriate compensation in recent years?
12. What are factors to consider in global health and safety?
13. What is the difference between NAFTA and CAFTA?

HRM INCIDENT 1

The Overseas Transfer

In college, Pat Marek majored in industrial management and was considered by his teachers and peers to be a good all-around student. Pat not only took the required courses in business, but he also learned French as a minor. After graduation, Pat took an entry-level management training position with Tuborg International, a multinational corporation with offices and factories in numerous countries, including the United States. His first assignment was in a plant in Chicago. His supervisors quickly identified Pat for his ability to get the job done and still maintain good rapport with subordinates, peers, and superiors. In only three years, Pat had advanced from a manager trainee to the position of assistant plant superintendent.

After two years in this position, he was called into the plant manager's office one day and told that he had been identified as ready for a foreign assignment. The move would mean a promotion. The assignment was for a plant in Haiti, a predominantly French-speaking country; but Pat wasn't worried about living and working there. He was excited and wasted no time in making the necessary preparations for the new assignment.

Prior to arriving at the plant in Haiti, Pat took considerable time to review his French textbook exercises. He was surprised at how quickly the language came back to him. He thought that there wouldn't be any major difficulties in making the transition from Chicago to Haiti. However, Pat found, on arrival, that the community where the plant was located did not speak the pure French that he had learned. There were many expressions that meant one thing to Pat but had an entirely different meaning to the employees of the plant.

When meeting with several of the employees a week after arriving, one of the workers said something to him that Pat interpreted as uncomplimentary. Actually, the employee had greeted him with a rather risqué expression but in a different tone than Pat had heard before. All of the other employees interpreted the expression to be merely a friendly greeting. Pat's disgust registered in his face.

As the days went by, this type of misunderstanding occurred a few more times, until the employees began to limit their conversation with him. In only one month, Pat managed virtually to isolate himself from the workers within the plant. He became disillusioned and thought about asking to be relieved from the assignment.

Questions

1. What problems had Pat not anticipated when he took the assignment?
2. How could the company have assisted Pat to reduce the difficulties that he confronted?
3. Do you believe the situation that Pat confronted is typical of an American going to a foreign assignment? Discuss.

HRM INCIDENT **2**

Was There Enough Preparation?

"Hi, Sam. How are the preparations going for your assignment in Japan?"

"Well, Elvis, I really feel prepared for the assignment, and the high level of apprehension I first experienced is gone."

"What exactly did the preparation program involve, Sam?"

"The experience was really exhaustive. First, I spent a good deal of time in a comprehensive orientation and training program. The program covered training and familiarization in the language, culture, history, living conditions, and local customs of Japan. Then, to make the transition back to home easier and better for my career, I have developed a plan with my boss that includes several trips back here to remain a key part of this operation. Also, my career development training will include the same training as the other managers in the home office. Finally, I was completely briefed on repatriation orientation and training that I would experience when I returned. Also, I was fully briefed on the compensation package, which appears to be fairly generous."

"That is great, Sam. Have you found a place to live yet?"

"Not yet, Elvis, but my wife and children are leaving in three days to meet with the company's relocation person to consider the various possibilities."

"How did the family like the orientation training, Sam?"

"Well, my wife ordered some Japanese language tapes, and I think she read all of the information that was covered in the class. She and the children will be fine because they have time to adapt; they don't have to hit the ground running like I do."

Questions

1. Do you believe that Sam's family is adequately prepared for the move to Japan? Why or why not?

2. Should the company's orientation program have included training for Sam's family?

3. Is repatriation orientation and training necessary for Sam's family on their return to the United States?

Notes

1. "Global Anticorruption Risks and Strategies for the Global Enterprise," *Compliance Week* 6 (October 2009): 18–19.
2. David M. Katz, "The Bribery Gap," *CFO* 21 (January 2005): 59–61.
3. "Ungreasing the Wheels," *Economist* 393 (November 21, 2009): 68–69.
4. "Global Anticorruption Risks and Strategies for the Global Enterprise."
5. Wendy Wysong, "New Attention On FCPA Investigations," *Financial Executive* 25 (October 2009): 52–54
6. Jaclyn Jaeger, "DoJ Expands Scope of Bribery Prosecutions," *Compliance Week* 6 (October 2009): 20.
7. "Global Anticorruption Risks and Strategies for the Global Enterprise."
8. "Ungreasing the Wheels."
9. Cathleen Flahardy, "FCPA Fallout," *Inside Counsel* 21 (January 2010): 15.
10. Matt Birk, "Prescription for FCPA Compliance," *Internal Auditor* 67 (February 2010): 53–57.
11. Gail Dutton, "Do the Right Thing," *Entrepreneur* 36 (May 2008): 92.
12. Charles Odell and Cheryl Spielman, "Global Positioning: Managing the Far-Reaching Risks of an International Assignment Program," *Benefits Quarterly* 25 (2009 Fourth Quarter): 23–29.
13. Elizabeth Galentine, "Going Global Is Really Not That Hard," *Employee Benefit Advisor* 7 (May 2009): 18–20.
14. Bill Leonard, "Earning His Papers," *HRMagazine* 53 (April 2008): 64–65.
15. Zachary Karabell, "Wake Up and Smell the Performance Gap," *Harvard Business Review* 84 (February 2006): 59–60.
16. Chris Petersen, "Going Global," *U.S. Business Review* 8 (September 2007): 16–17.

17. "Personal Care: Company Spotlight: Procter & Gamble," *MarketWatch: Global Round-up* 9 (March 2010): 112–118.

18. Jena McGregor and Steve Hamm, "Managing the Global Workforce," *BusinessWeek* (January 28, 2008): 34–35.

19. www.hcri.org, August 14, 2010.

20. Andrew Slentz, "Going Global to Last," *HRMagazine* 54 (August 2009): 36–38.

21. This section was developed based on Anne Marie Francesco and Barry Allen Gold, *International Organizational Behavior* (Upper Saddle River, NJ: Prentice Hall, 1998): 165.

22. Fay Hansen, "Looking South," *Workforce Management* 87 (April 21, 2008): 21–26.

23. Theresa Minton-Eversole, "Overseas Assignments Keep Pace, But Economic Conditions Hold the Reins," *HRMagazine* 53 (December 2008): 72–73.

24. Lorraine Bello and Galen Tinder, "Dual Career Implications on Workforce Mobility: The Evolution of the Relocating Spouse/Partner" *Benefits & Compensation Digest* 46 (September 2009): 36–39.

25. Minton-Eversole, "Overseas Assignments Keep Pace, But Economic Conditions Hold the Reins."

26. Theresa Minton-Eversole, "Best Expatriate Assignments Require Much Thought, Even More Planning," *HRMagazine* 53 (December 2008): 74–75.

27. Ann Pace, "Training for the Leap Overseas," *T+D* 63 (August 2009): 18.

28. Elisabeth Eaves, "The Elsewhere Man," *Forbes* 183 (February 16, 2009): 22–24.

29. Rick Merritt, "Working Harder in Tough Times," *Electronic Engineering Times* (August 22, 2005): 37–52.

30. Pamela Babcock, "Foreign Assignments," *HRMagazine* 50 (October 2005): 91–98.

31. Kenji Hall, "Keeping Temps on Tap," *BusinessWeek* (January 14, 2008): 56.

32. Gina M. Hernandez, "Cultural Training: Crucial to Relocation," *Caribbean Business* 35 (February 25, 2007): S2.

33. Michael Laff, "Offshore Acclimation," *T+D* 63 (May 2009): 22–23.

34. Ibid.

35. Avan R. Jassawalla and Hermant C. Sashittal, "Thinking Strategically About Integrating Repatriated Managers in MNCs," *Human Resource Management* 48 (September/October 2009): 769–792.

36. Ursula Wittig-Berman and Nicholas J. Beutel, "International Assignments and the Career Management of Repatriates: The Boundaryless Career Concept," *International Journal of Management* 26 (April 2009): 77–88.

37. Michelle V. Rafter, "Return Trip for Expats," *Workforce Management* 88 (March 16, 2009): 1–3.

38. Alice Andors, "Happy Returns," *HRMagazine* 55 (March 2010): 61–63.

39. Amy Maingaut, Lesa Albright, and Vicki Neal, "Policy Tips, Repatriation, Safe Harbor Rules," *HRMagazine* 53 (March 2008): 34–35.

40. Pace, "Training for the Leap Overseas."

41. Andrea Edmundson, "Culturally Accessible E-Learning: An Overdue Global Business Imperative," *T+D* 63 (April 2009): 40–45.

42. Deepak Desai, "Globalization and the English Skills Gap," *Chief Learning Officer* 7 (June 2008): 62–63.

43. Hanif Sazen, "Keeping It Fresh," *e.learning age* (June 2005): 28–29.

44. Jay F. Nunamaker Jr., Bruce A. Reinig, and Robert O. Briggs, "Principles for Effective Virtual Teamwork," *Communications of the ACM* 52 (April 2009): 113–117.

45. Lara Schlenkrich and Christopher Upfold, "A Guideline for Virtual Team Managers: the Key to Effective Social Interaction and Communication," *Electronic Journal of Information Systems Evaluation* 12 (2009): 109–118.

46. Rachael King, "How Virtual Teams Can Succeed," *BusinessWeek Online* (May 19, 2008): 27.

47. "Leading the Virtual Team," *Associations Now* (May 2008): 18.

48. Richard Naish, "In Teams We Trust," *e.learning age* (September 2009): 8.

49. Billie Williamson, "Managing Virtually: First, Get Dressed," *BusinessWeek Online* (June 17, 2009): 19.

50. Gina Ruiz, "Kimberly-Clark: Developing Talent in Developing World Markets," *Workforce Management* 85 (April 10, 2006): 34.

51. Lawson D. Thurston, "Severance Payment and Christmas Bonus Changes Increase Cost of Doing Business," *Caribbean Business* 34 (May 11, 2006): 58.

52. Vicki Taylor, "Benefits around the World," *Employee Benefits* (February 2006): Special Section, 8–9.

53. Virginia A. Hulme, "Short Staffed," *China Business Review* 33 (March/April 2006): 18–56.

54. http://www.irs.gov/publications/p54/ch04.html#en_US_publink100047498

55. Lin Grensing-Pophal, "Expat Lifestyles Take a Hit," *HRMagazine* 3 (March 2008): 5054.

56. Ibid.

57. Ibid.

58. Ibid.

59. http://en.wikipedia.org/wiki/Bhopal_disaster, February 14, 2010.

60. James L. Nash, "Managing Global Safety: The Power of One," *Occupational Hazards* 67 (September 2005): 28–32.

61. Ibid.

62. Ibid.

63. Ibid.

64. Samuel Estreicher, "'Think Global, Act Local': Employee Representation in a World of Global Labor and Product Market Competition," *Labor Lawyer* 24 (Winter 2009): 253–265.

65. Colleen Taylor, "Motorola Job Cuts Cost Company More Than $300M So Far," *Electronic News* 53 (October 8, 2007): 34.

66. Andrea MacDonald, "NAFTA: A Delicate Balance," *World Trade* 22 (October 2009): 30–33.

67. Adrienne Selko, "NAFTA: Learning to Love Thy Neighbor," *Industry Week* 258 (February 2009): 38–41.

68. Denise Bedell, "Revisiting NAFTA," *Global Finance* 23 (March 2009): 22–24.

69. "Nothing's Free in This World," *Economist* 376 (August 6, 2005): 30.

70. Leticia Lozano, "Hopes are High in Central America," *Florida Shipper* 34 (February 16, 2009): 11–13.

71. Kristi Ellis, "Textile Execs Claim CAFTA Fraud," *Women's Wear Daily* 197 (June 19, 2009): 128.

72. Ephraim Schwartz, "On Business and Ethics," *InfoWorld* 27 (October 10, 2005): 12.

73. "Mexico Hits U.S. Exports with Tariffs in Retaliation for Byrd Amendment," *Metal Center News* 45 (September 2005): 71.

74. Miles Moore, "WTO to Probe China Tire Tariffs," *Rubber & Plastics News* 39 (January 25, 2010): 3.

75. "Chicken Tariffs Escalate US-China Controversy," *Journal of Commerce* 11 (February 15, 2010): 8.

76. Shirley Puccino, "Worldwide Practices and Trends in Expatriate Compensation and Benefits," *Benefits & Compensation Digest* 44 (January 2007): 34–38.

77. Isobel Coleman, "The Global Glass Ceiling," *Foreign Affairs* 89 (May/June 2010): 13–20.

78. Cindy Waxer, "Life's a Balancing Act for Cirque du Soleil's Human Resources Troupe," *Workforce Management* 84 (January 2005): 52–53.

Glossary

Adverse impact: Concept established by the *Uniform Guidelines,* occurs if women and minorities are not hired at the rate of at least 80 percent of the best-achieving group.

Affirmative action: Stipulated by Executive Order 11246, it requires employers to take positive steps to ensure employment of applicants and treatment of employees during employment without regard to race, creed, color, or national origin.

Affirmative action program (AAP): Approach developed by organizations with government contracts to demonstrate that workers are employed in proportion to their representation in the firm's relevant labor market.

Agency shop: Labor agreement provision requiring, as a condition of employment, that each nonunion member of a bargaining unit pay the union the equivalent of membership dues as a service charge in return for the union acting as the bargaining agent.

Alcoholism: Medical disease characterized by uncontrolled and compulsive drinking that interferes with normal living patterns.

Alternative dispute resolution (ADR): Procedure whereby the employee and the company agree ahead of time that any problems will be addressed by an agreed-upon means.

American Federation of Labor and Congress of Industrial Organizations (AFL-CIO): Central trade union federation in the United States.

Applicant pool: Number of qualified applicants recruited for a particular job.

Applicant-tracking system (ATS): Software application designed to help an enterprise select employees more efficiently.

Apprenticeship training: Training method which combines classroom instruction with on-the-job training.

Arbitration: Process in which a dispute is submitted to an impartial third party for a binding decision; an arbitrator basically acts as a judge and jury.

Assessment center: Selection technique that requires individuals to perform activities similar to those they might encounter in an actual job.

Attitude survey: Survey that seeks input from employees to determine their feelings about topics such as the work they perform, their supervisor, their work environment, flexibility in the workplace, opportunities for advancement, training and development opportunities, and the firm's compensation system.

Authorization card: Document indicating that an employee wants to be represented by a labor organization in collective bargaining.

Availability forecast: Determination of whether the firm will be able to secure employees with the necessary skills, and from what sources.

Baby boomers: People born between just after World War II through the mid-1960s.

Bargaining unit: Group of employees, not necessarily union members, recognized by an employer or certified by an administrative agency as appropriate for representation by a labor organization for purposes of collective bargaining.

Beachhead demands: Demands that the union does not expect management to meet when they are first made.

Behavior modeling: T&D method that permits a person to learn by copying or replicating behaviors of others to show managers how to handle various situations.

Behavioral interview: Structured interview where applicants are asked to relate actual incidents from their past relevant to the target job.

Behaviorally anchored rating scale (BARS) method: Performance appraisal method that combines elements of the traditional rating scale and critical incident methods; various performance levels are shown along a scale with each described in terms of an employee's specific job behavior.

Benchmarking: Process of monitoring and measuring a firm's internal processes, such as operations, and then comparing the data with information from companies that excel in those areas.

Benefits (indirect financial compensation): All financial rewards that are not included in direct financial compensation (indirect financial compensation).

Board interview: An interview approach in which several of the firm's representatives interview a candidate at the same time.

Bonus: One-time annual financial award based on productivity that is not added to base pay.

Bottom-up forecast: Forecasting method in which each successive level in the organization, starting with the lowest, forecasts its requirements, ultimately providing an aggregate forecast of employees needed.

Boycott: Agreement by union members to refuse to use or buy the firm's products.

Broadbanding: Compensation technique that collapses many pay grades (salary grades) into a few wide bands in order to improve organizational effectiveness.

Burnout: Incapacitating condition in which individuals lose a sense of the basic purpose and fulfillment of their work.

Business games: T&D method that permits participants to assume roles such as president, controller, or marketing vice president of two or more similar hypothetical organizations and compete against each other by manipulating selected factors in a particular business situation.

Card check: Organizing approach by labor in which employees sign a nonsecret card of support if they want unionization, and if 50 percent of the workforce plus one worker signs a card, the union is formed.

Career: General course that a person chooses to pursue throughout his or her working life.

Career development: Formal approach used by the organization to ensure that people with the proper qualifications and experiences are available when needed.

Career path: A flexible line of movement through which a person may travel during their work life.

Career planning: Ongoing process whereby an individual sets career goals and identifies the means to achieve them.

Career security: Requires developing marketable skills and expertise that help ensure employment within a range of careers.

Caregiver (Family Responsibility) Discrimination: Discrimination against employees based on their obligations to care for family members.

Carpal tunnel syndrome (CTS): Common repetitive stress injury caused by pressure on the median nerve that occurs as a result of a narrowing of the passageway that houses the nerve.

Case study: T&D method in which trainees are expected to study the information provided in the case and make decisions based on it.

Cash balance plan: Retirement plan with elements of both defined benefit and defined contribution plans.

Central tendency error: Evaluation appraisal error that occurs when employees are incorrectly rated near the average or middle of a scale.

Change to Win Coalition: Union federation consisting of seven unions that broke from the AFL-CIO and formally launched a rival labor federation representing about 6 million workers in 2005.

Checkoff of dues: Agreement by which a company agrees to withhold union dues from members' paychecks and to forward the money directly to the union.

Classification method: Job evaluation method in which classes or grades are defined to describe a group of jobs.

Closed shop: Arrangement making union membership a prerequisite for employment.

Coaching: Often considered a responsibility of the immediate boss who provides assistance much as a mentor, but the primary focus is about performance.

Cognitive aptitude tests: Tests that determine general reasoning ability, memory, vocabulary, verbal fluency, and numerical ability.

Collective bargaining: Performance of the mutual obligation of the employer and the representative of the employees to meet at reasonable times and confer in good faith with respect to wages, hours, and other terms and conditions of employment, or the negotiation of an agreement, or any question arising there under, and the execution of a written contract incorporating any agreement reached if requested by either party; such obligation does not compel either party to agree to a proposal or require the making of a concession.

Committee on Political Education (COPE): Political arm of the AFL-CIO.

Comparable worth: Determination of the values of dissimilar jobs (such as company nurse and welder) by comparing them under some form of job evaluation, and the assignment of pay rates according to their evaluated worth.

Compensation: Total of all rewards provided employees in return for their services.

Compensation policy: Policies that provide general guidelines for making compensation decisions.

Compensation survey: A means of obtaining data regarding what other firms are paying for specific jobs or job classes within a given labor market.

Competencies: Broad range of knowledge, skills, traits, and behaviors that may be technical in nature, relate to interpersonal skills, or be business oriented.

Competency-based pay: Compensation plan that rewards employees for the capabilities they attain.

Compressed work week: Any arrangement of work hours that permits employees to fulfill their work obligation in fewer days than the typical five-day work week.

Conspiracy: Two or more persons who band together to prejudice the rights of others or of society (such as by refusing to work or demanding higher wages).

Construct validity: Test validation method that determines whether a test measures certain constructs, or traits, that job analysis finds to be important in performing a job.

Content validity: Test validation method whereby a person performs certain tasks that are actually required by the job or completes a paper-and-pencil test that measures relevant job knowledge.

Contingent workers: Described as the "disposable American workforce" by a former secretary of labor, have a nontraditional relationship with the worksite employer and work as part-timers, temporaries, or independent contractors.

Corporate career Web sites: Job sites accessible from a company homepage that list available company positions and provide a way for applicants to apply for specific jobs.

Corporate social responsibility (CSR): Implied, enforced, or felt obligation of managers, acting in their official capacity, to serve or protect the interests of groups other than themselves.

Corporate university: T&D delivery system provided under the umbrella of the organization.

Cost-of-living allowance (COLA): Escalator clause in a labor agreement that automatically increases wages as the U.S. Bureau of Labor Statistics cost-of-living index rises.

Country's culture: Set of values, symbols, beliefs, languages, and norms that guide human behavior within the country.

Craft union: Bargaining unit, such as the Carpenters and Joiners union, which is typically composed of members of a particular trade or skill in a specific locality.

Criterion-related validity: Test validation method that compares the scores on selection tests to some aspect of job performance determined, for example, by performance appraisal.

Critical incident method: Performance appraisal method that requires keeping written records of highly favorable and unfavorable employee work actions.

Customized benefit plan: Benefit plan that permits employees to make yearly elections to largely determine their benefit package by choosing between taxable cash and numerous benefits.

Cyberwork: Possibility of a never-ending workday.

Decertification: Reverse of the process that employees must follow to be recognized as an official bargaining unit.

Defined benefit plan: Retirement plan that provides the participant with a fixed benefit upon retirement.

Defined contribution plan: Retirement plan that requires specific contributions by an employer to a retirement or savings fund established for the employee.

Demotion: Process of moving a worker to a lower level of duties and responsibilities, which typically involves a reduction in pay.

Development: Learning that goes beyond today's job and has a more long-term focus.

Direct financial compensation: Pay that a person receives in the form of wages, salary, commissions, and bonuses.

Disciplinary action: Invoking a penalty against an employee who fails to meet established standards.

Disciplinary action without punishment: Process in which a worker is given time off with pay to think about whether he or she wants to follow the rules and continue working for the company.

Discipline: State of employee self-control and orderly conduct that indicates the extent of genuine teamwork within an organization.

Discretionary benefits: Benefit payments made as a result of unilateral management decisions in nonunion firms and from labor–management negotiations in unionized firms.

Disparate treatment: Occurs when an employer treats some employees less favorably than others because of race, religion, sex, national origin, or age.

Diversity: Any perceived difference among people: age, race, religion, functional specialty, profession, sexual orientation, geographic origin, lifestyle, tenure with the organization or position, and any other perceived difference.

Diversity management: Ensuring that factors are in place to provide for and encourage the continued development of a diverse workforce by melding these actual and perceived differences among workers to achieve maximum productivity.

Downsizing: Reverse of a company growing; it suggests a one-time change in the organization and the number of people employed (also known as restructuring or rightsizing).

Dual-career family: A situation in which both husband and wife have jobs and family responsibilities.

Dual-career path: Career path that recognizes that technical specialists can and should be allowed to contribute their expertise to a company without having to become managers.

E-learning: T&D method for online instruction.

Emotional intelligence (EQ): Ability to recognize and manage emotions.

Employability doctrine: Employees owe the company their commitment while employed and the company owes its workers the opportunity to learn new skills, but that is as far as the commitment goes.

Employee assistance program (EAP): Comprehensive approach that many organizations have taken to deal with burnout, alcohol and drug abuse, and other emotional disturbances.

Employee engagement: Level of commitment workers make to their employer, seen in their willingness to stay at the firm and to go beyond the call of duty.

Employee equity: Equity that exists when individuals performing similar jobs for the same firm receive pay according to factors unique to the employee, such as performance level or seniority.

Employee requisition: Document that specifies job title, department, the date the employee is needed for work, and other details.

Employee self-service (ESS): Processes that automate transactions that previously were labor-intensive for both employees and HR professionals.

Employee stock option plan (ESOP): Defined contribution plan in which a firm contributes stock shares to a trust.

Employer branding: Firm's corporate image or culture created to attract and retain the type of employees the firm is seeking.

Employment at will: Unwritten contract created when an employee agrees to work for an employer but no agreement exists as to how long the parties expect the employment to last.

Employment interview: Goal-oriented conversation in which an interviewer and an applicant exchange information.

Equity theory: Motivation theory that people assess their performance and attitudes by comparing both their contribution to work and the benefits they derive from it to the contributions and benefits of comparison others whom they select—and who in reality may or may not be like them.

Ergonomics: Process of designing the workplace to support the capabilities of people and job/task demands.

Essay method: Performance appraisal method in which the rater writes a brief narrative describing the employee's performance.

Ethics: Discipline dealing with what is good and bad, or right and wrong, or with moral duty and obligation.

Ethnocentric staffing: Staffing approach in which companies primarily hire expatriates to staff higher-level foreign positions.

Event recruiting: Recruiters going to events being attended by individuals the company is seeking.

Exclusive provider organization (EPO): Managed-care health organization that offers a smaller preferred provider network and usually provides few, if any, benefits when an out-of-network provider is used.

Executive: A top-level manager who reports directly to a corporation's chief executive officer or to the head of a major division.

Executive order (EO): Directive issued by the president that has the force and effect of law enacted by Congress as it applies to federal agencies and federal contractors.

Exempt employees: Employees categorized as executive, administrative, professional, or outside salespersons.

Exit interview: Means of revealing the real reasons employees leave their jobs; it is conducted before an employee departs the company and provides information on how to correct the causes of discontent and reduce turnover.

Expatriate: Employee who is not a citizen of the country in which the firm operations are located, but is a citizen of the country in which the organization is headquartered.

Exporting: Selling abroad, either directly or indirectly, by retaining foreign agents and distributors.

External environment: Factors outside an organization's boundaries that affect a firm's human resources.

External equity: Equity that exists when a firm's employees receive pay comparable to workers who perform similar jobs in other firms.

Factor comparison method: Job evaluation method that assumes there are five universal factors consisting of mental requirements, skills, physical requirements, responsibilities, and working conditions; and the evaluator makes decisions on these factors independently.

Financial equity: Perception of fair pay treatment for employees.

Flexible spending account (FSA): Health benefit plan established by employers that allows employees to deposit a certain portion of their salary into an account (before paying income taxes) to be used for eligible expenses.

Flextime: Practice of permitting employees to choose their own working hours, within certain limitations.

Flooding the community: Process of the union inundating communities with organizers to target a particular business in an organizing attempt.

Forced distribution method: Performance appraisal method in which the rater is required to assign individuals in a workgroup to a limited number of categories similar to a normal frequency distribution.

401(k) plan: Defined contribution plan in which employees may defer income up to a maximum amount allowed.

Franchising: Option whereby the parent company grants another firm the right to do business in a prescribed manner.

Free agents: People who take charge of all or part of their careers by being their own bosses or by working for others in ways that fit their particular needs or wants.

Gainsharing: Plans designed to bind employees to the firm's productivity and provide an incentive payment based on improved company performance.

Generalist: A person who may be an executive, performs tasks in a variety of HR-related areas.

Generation I: Internet-assimilated children born after the late 1990s.

Generation X: Label affixed to the 40 million American workers born between the mid-1960s and late 1970s.

Generation Y: Comprises people born between the late 1970s and late 1990s.

Genetic testing: Tests given to identify predisposition to inherited diseases, including cancer, heart disease, neurological disorders, and congenital diseases.

Geocentric staffing: Staffing approach that uses a worldwide integrated business strategy.

Glass ceiling: Invisible barrier in organizations that impedes women and minorities from career advancement.

Global corporation (GC): Organization that has corporate units in a number of countries that are integrated to operate as one organization worldwide.

Golden parachute contract: Perquisite that protects executives in the event that another company acquires their firm or the executive is forced to leave the firm for other reasons.

Graphoanalysis: Use of handwriting analysis as a selection factor.

Grievance: Employee's dissatisfaction or feeling of personal injustice relating to his or her employment.

Grievance procedure: Formal, systematic process that permits employees to express complaints without jeopardizing their jobs.

Group interview: Meeting in which several job applicants interact in the presence of one or more company representatives.

Halo error: Evaluation error that occurs when a manager generalizes one positive performance feature or incident to all aspects of employee performance, resulting in a higher rating.

Hay guide chart-profile method (Hay Plan): Refined version of the point method used by approximately 8,000 public and private-sector organizations worldwide to evaluate clerical, trade, technical, professional, managerial, and/or executive level jobs.

Hazard pay: Additional pay provided to employees who work under extremely dangerous conditions.

Health: Employees' freedom from physical or emotional illness.

Health maintenance organization (HMO): Managed-care health organization that covers all services for a fixed fee but control is exercised over which doctors and health facilities a member may use.

Health savings accounts (HAS): Tax-free health spending and savings accounts available to individuals and families who have qualified high-deductible health insurance policies as determined by IRS regulation.

Horn error: Evaluation error that occurs when a manager generalizes one negative performance feature or incident to all aspects of employee performance, resulting in a lower rating.

Host-country national (HCN): Employee who is a citizen of the country where the subsidiary is located.

Human capital metrics: Measures of HR performance.

Human resource development: Major HRM function consisting not only of training and development but also of career planning and development activities, organization development, and performance management and appraisal.

Human resource ethics: Application of ethical principles to human resource relationships and activities.

Human resource information system (HRIS): Any organized approach for obtaining relevant and timely information on which to base human resource decisions.

Human resource management (HRM): Utilization of individuals to achieve organizational objectives.

Human resource manager: Individual who normally acts in an advisory or staff capacity, working with other managers to help them deal with human resource matters.

Human resource planning (workforce planning): Systematic process of matching the internal and external supply of people with job openings anticipated in the organization over a specified period of time.

HR Outsourcing (HRO): Process of hiring external HR professionals to do the HR work that was previously done internally.

Identity theft: The mishandling or deceptive use of an individual's personal information.

In-basket training: T&D method in which the participant is asked to establish priorities for and then handle a number of business papers, e-mail messages, memoranda, reports, and telephone messages that would typically cross a manager's desk.

Indirect financial compensation (benefits): All financial rewards that are not included in direct financial compensation.

Industrial union: Bargaining unit that generally consists of all the workers in a particular plant or group of plants.

Injunction: Prohibited legal procedure used by employers to prevent certain union activities, such as strikes and unionization attempts.

Interest arbitration: Arbitration that involves disputes over the terms of proposed collective bargaining agreements.

Internal employee relations: Those human resource management activities associated with the movement of employees within the organization.

Internal equity: Exists when employees receive pay according to the relative value of their jobs within the same organization.

Internet recruiter: Person whose primary responsibility is to use the Internet in the recruitment process (also called cyber recruiter).

Internship: Special form of recruitment that involves placing a student in a temporary job with no obligation either by the company to hire the student permanently or by the student to accept a permanent position with the firm following graduation.

Job: Group of tasks that must be performed for an organization to achieve its goals.

Job analysis: Systematic process of determining the skills, duties, and knowledge required for performing jobs in an organization.

Job bidding: Procedure that permits employees who believe that they possess the required qualifications to apply for a posted position.

Job description: Document that provides information regarding the essential tasks, duties, and responsibilities of a job.

Job design: Process of determining the specific tasks to be performed, the methods used in performing these tasks, and how the job relates to other work in an organization.

Job enlargement: Increasing the number of tasks a worker performs, with all of the tasks at the same level of responsibility.

Job enrichment: Changes in the content and level of responsibility of a job so as to provide greater challenges to the worker.

Job evaluation: Process that determines the relative value of one job in relation to another.

Job evaluation ranking method: Job evaluation method in which the raters examine the description of each job being evaluated and arrange the jobs in order according to their value to the company.

Job fair: Recruiting method engaged in by a single employer or group of employers to attract a large number of applicants to one location for interviews.

Job hazard analysis (JHA): Multistep process designed to study and analyze a task or job and then break down that task into steps that provide a means of eliminating associated hazards.

Job-knowledge tests: Tests designed to measure a candidate's knowledge of the duties of the job for which he or she is applying.

Job posting: Procedure for informing employees that job openings exist.

Job pricing: Placing a dollar value on the job's worth.

Job rotation: Moves employees from one job to another to broaden their experience.

Job security: Implies security in one job, often with one company.

Job sharing: Two part-time people split the duties of one job in some agreed-on manner and are paid according to their contributions.

Job specification: A document that outlines the minimum acceptable qualifications a person should possess to perform a particular job.

Just-in-time training (on-demand training): Training provided anytime, anywhere in the world when it is needed.

Keyword résumé: Résumé that contains an adequate description of the job seeker's characteristics and industry-specific experience presented in keyword terms in order to accommodate the computer search process.

Keywords: Words or phrases that are used to search databases for résumés that match.

Labor market: Potential employees located within the geographic area from which employees are recruited.

Lateral skill path: Career path that allows for lateral moves within the firm, taken to permit an employee to become revitalized and find new challenges.

Learning organization: Firm that recognizes the critical importance of continuous performance-related T&D and takes appropriate action.

Leniency: Giving an undeserved high performance appraisal rating to an employee.

Licensing: Arrangement whereby an organization grants a foreign firm the right to use intellectual properties such as patents, copyrights, manufacturing processes, or trade names for a specific period of time.

Likes and dislikes survey: Procedure that helps individuals recognize restrictions they place on themselves.

Line managers: Individuals directly involved in accomplishing the primary purpose of the organization.

Local union: Basic element in the structure of the U.S. labor movement.

Lockout: Management decision to keep union workers out of the workplace and run the operation with management personnel and/or replacements.

Management development: Consists of all learning experiences provided by an organization resulting in upgrading skills and knowledge required in current and future managers.

Manager self-service (MSS): The use of software and the corporate network to automate paper-based human resource processes that require a manager's approval, record-keeping or input, and processes that support the manager's job.

Mandatory bargaining issues: Bargaining issues that fall within the definition of wages, hours, and other terms and conditions of employment.

Market (going) rate: Average pay that most employers provide for a similar job in a particular area or industry.

Mediation: Neutral third party enters the negotiations and attempts to facilitate a resolution to a labor dispute when a bargaining impasse has occurred.

Mentoring: Approach to advising, coaching, and nurturing, for creating a practical relationship to enhance individual career, personal, and professional growth and development.

Merit pay: Pay increase added to employees' base pay based on their level of performance.

Mission: Unit's continuing purpose, or reason for being.

Multinational corporation (MNC): Firm that is based in one country (the parent or home country) and produces goods or provides services in one or more foreign countries (host countries).

NACElink Network: An alliance among the National Association of Colleges and Employers, DirectEmployers Association, and Symplicity Corporation; a national recruiting network and suite of web-based recruiting and career services automation tools serving the needs of colleges, employers, and job candidates.

National union: Organization composed of local unions, which it charters.

Negligent hiring: Liability a company incurs when it fails to conduct a reasonable investigation of an applicant's background, and then assigns a potentially dangerous person to a position where he or she can inflict harm.

Negligent retention: Liability an employer may incur when a company keeps persons on the payroll whose records indicate strong potential for wrongdoing and fails to take steps to defuse a possible violent situation.

Network career path: Method of career progression that contains both a vertical sequence of jobs and a series of horizontal opportunities.

Niche sites: Web sites that cater to highly specialized job markets such as a particular profession, industry, education, location, or any combination of these specialties.

Nonfinancial compensation: Satisfaction that a person receives from the job itself or from the psychological and/or physical environment in which the person works.

Norm: Frame of reference for comparing an applicant's performance with that of others.

Objectivity: Condition that is achieved when everyone scoring a given test obtains the same results.

Ombudsperson: Complaint officer with access to top management who hears employee complaints, investigates, and recommends appropriate action.

Online higher education: Formal educational opportunities including degree and training programs that are delivered, either entirely or partially, via the Internet.

On-the-job-training (OJT): An informal T&D method that permits an employee to learn job tasks by actually performing them.

Open shop: Employment on equal terms to union members and nonmembers alike.

Organization development (OD): Planned and systematic attempts to change the organization, typically to a more behavioral environment.

Organizational fit: Management's perception of the degree to which the prospective employee will fit in with the firm's culture or value system.

Organizational stakeholder: Individual or group whose interests are affected by organizational activities.

Orientation: Initial T&D effort for new employees that inform them about the company, the job, and the workgroup.

Outplacement: A procedure whereby laid-off employees are given assistance in finding employment elsewhere.

Outsourcing: Process of hiring an external provider to do the work that was previously done internally.

Paid time off (PTO): Means of dealing with the problem of unscheduled absences by providing a certain number of days each year that employees can use for any purpose.

Salary compression: Situation that occurs when less experienced employees are paid as much as or more than employees who have been with the organization a long time due to a gradual increase in starting salaries and limited salary adjustment for long-term employees.

Pay followers: Companies that choose to pay below the going rate because of a poor financial condition or a belief that they do not require highly capable employees.

Pay grade: Grouping of similar jobs to simplify pricing jobs.

Pay leaders: Organizations that pay higher wages and salaries than competing firms.

Pay range: Minimum and maximum pay rate with enough variance between the two to allow for a significant pay difference.

Performance appraisal (PA): Formal system of review and evaluation of individual or team task performance.

Performance management (PM): Goal-oriented process directed toward ensuring that organizational processes are in place to maximize the productivity of employees, teams, and ultimately, the organization.

Permissive bargaining issues: Issues may be raised, but neither side may insist that they be bargained over.

Perquisites (perks): Special benefits provided by a firm to a small group of key executives and designed to give the executives something extra.

Personality tests: Self-reported measures of traits, temperaments, or dispositions.

Piecework: Incentive pay plan in which employees are paid for each unit they produce.

Phased retirement: Any arrangement that allows people to move from fulltime work to retirement in steps.

Point method: Job evaluation method where the raters assign numerical values to specific job factors, such as knowledge required, and the sum of these values provides a quantitative assessment of a job's relative worth.

Point-of-service (POS): Managed-care health organization that requires a primary care physician and referrals to see specialists, as with HMOs, but permits out-of-network health care access.

Polycentric staffing: Staffing approach where host-country nationals are used throughout the organization, from top to bottom.

Position: Collection of tasks and responsibilities performed by one person.

Postexit questionnaire: Questionnaire sent to former employees several weeks after they leave the organization to determine the real reason they left.

Preferred provider organization (PPO): Managed-care health organization in which incentives are provided to members to use services within the system; out-of-network providers may be utilized at greater cost.

Premium pay: Compensation paid to employees for working long periods of time or working under dangerous or undesirable conditions.

Profession: Vocation characterized by the existence of a common body of knowledge and a procedure for certifying members.

Professional employer organization (PEO): A company that leases employees to other businesses.

Profit sharing: Compensation plans that result in the distribution of a predetermined percentage of the firm's profits to employees.

Progressive disciplinary action: Approach to disciplinary action designed to ensure that the minimum penalty appropriate to the offense is imposed.

Prohibited bargaining issues: Issues that are statutorily outlawed from collective bargaining.

Promotion: Movement of a person to a higher-level position in an organization.

Promotion from within (PFW): Policy of filling vacancies above entry-level positions with current employees.

Psychomotor abilities tests: Tests that measure strength, coordination, and dexterity.

Public awareness campaigns: Labor maneuvers that do not coincide with a strike or organizing campaign to pressure an employer for better wages, benefits, and the like.

Quality circles: Groups of employees who voluntarily meet regularly with their supervisors to discuss problems, investigate causes, recommend solutions, and take corrective action when authorized to do so.

Quotas: Policies that limit the number or value of goods that can be imported across national boundaries.

Ranking method: Performance appraisal method in which the rater ranks all employees from a group in order of overall performance.

Rating scales method: Performance appraisal method that rates employees according to defined factors.

Realistic job preview (RJP): Method of conveying both positive and negative job information to the applicant in an unbiased manner.

Recruitment: Process of attracting individuals on a timely basis, in sufficient numbers, and with appropriate qualifications, to apply for jobs with an organization.

Recruitment methods: Specific means used to attract potential employees to the firm.

Recruitment sources: Where qualified candidates are located.

Reengineering: Fundamental rethinking and radical redesign of business processes to achieve dramatic improvements in critical, contemporary measures of performance such as cost, quality, service, and speed.

Reference checks: Validations from those who know the applicant that provide additional insight into the information furnished by the applicant and allow verification of its accuracy.

Regiocentric staffing: Staffing approach that is similar to the polycentric staffing approach, but regional groups of subsidiaries reflecting the organization's strategy and structure work as a unit.

Reliability: Extent to which a selection test provides consistent results.

Relocation benefits: Company-paid shipment of household goods and temporary living expenses, covering all or a portion of the real estate costs associated with buying a new home and selling the previously occupied home.

Repatriation: Process of bringing expatriates home.

Repetitive stress injuries: Group of conditions caused by placing too much stress on a joint when the same action is performed repeatedly.

Requirements forecast: Determining the number, skill, and location of employees the organization will need at future dates in order to meet its goals.

Results-based system: Performance appraisal method in which the manager and subordinate jointly agree on objectives for the next appraisal period; in the past a form of management by objectives.

Résumé: Goal-directed summary of a person's experience, education, and training developed for use in the selection process.

Reverse mentoring: A process where older employees learn from younger ones.

Right-to-work laws: Laws that prohibit management and unions from entering into agreements requiring union membership as a condition of employment.

Rights arbitration: Arbitration involving disputes over the interpretation and application of the various provisions of an existing contract.

Role-playing: T&D method where participants are required to respond to specific problems they may encounter in their jobs by acting out real-world situations.

Sabbaticals: Temporary leaves of absence from an organization, usually at reduced pay.

Safety: Protection of employees from injuries caused by work-related accidents.

Salary compression: Occurs when less experienced employees are paid as much as or more than employees who have been with the organization a long time due to a gradual increase in starting salaries and limited salary adjustment for long-term employees.

Scanlon plan: Gainsharing plan that provides a financial reward to employees for savings in labor costs resulting from their suggestions.

Secondary boycott: Union attempt to encourage third parties (such as suppliers and customers) to stop doing business with a firm; declared illegal by the Taft-Hartley Act.

Selection: Process of choosing from a group of applicants the individual best suited for a particular position and the organization.

Selection ratio: Number of people hired for a particular job compared to the number of individuals in the applicant pool.

Self-assessment: Process of learning about oneself.

Seniority: Length of time an employee has been associated with the company, division, department, or job.

Sensitivity training: Organization development technique that is designed to help individuals learn how others perceive their behavior (also know as T-group training).

Severance pay: Compensation designed to assist laid-off employees as they search for new employment.

Shared service center (SSC): Center that takes routine, transaction-based activities dispersed throughout the organization and consolidates them in one place (also known as a center of expertise).

Shareholders: Owners of a corporation.

Shift differential: Additional money paid to employees for the inconvenience of working less-desirable hours.

Simulators: T&D delivery system comprised of devices or programs that replicate actual job demands.

Skill-based pay: System that compensates employees for their job-related skills and knowledge, rather than his or her present job.

Social audit: Systematic assessment of a company's activities in terms of its social impact.

Social contract: Set of written and unwritten rules and assumptions about acceptable interrelationships among the various elements of society.

Specialist: Individual who may be an HR executive, a human resource manager, or a nonmanager who is typically concerned with only one of the five functional areas of human resource management.

Spot bonus: Relatively small monetary gift provided employees for outstanding work or effort during a reasonably short period of time.

Staffing: Process through which an organization ensures that it always has the proper number of employees with the appropriate skills in the right jobs, at the right time, to achieve organizational objectives.

Standardization: Uniformity of the procedures and conditions related to administering tests.

Stock option plan: Incentive plan in which executives can buy a specified amount of stock in their company in the future at or below the current market price.

Strategic planning: Process by which top management determines overall organizational purposes and objectives and how they are achieved.

Strength/weakness balance sheet: Self-evaluation procedure, developed originally by Benjamin Franklin, that assists people in becoming aware of their strengths and weaknesses.

Stress: Body's nonspecific reaction to any demand made on it.

Stress interview: Form of interview in which the interviewer intentionally creates anxiety.

Strictness: Being unduly critical of an employee's work performance.

Strike: Action by union members who refuse to work in order to exert pressure on management in negotiations.

Structured interview: Interviewer asks each applicant for a particular job the same series of job-related questions.

Substance abuse: Use of illegal substances or the misuse of controlled substances such as alcohol and drugs.

Succession planning: Process of ensuring that qualified persons are available to assume key managerial positions once the positions are vacant.

Survey feedback: Organization development method of basing change efforts on the systematic collection and measurement of a subordinate's attitudes through anonymous questionnaires.

Talent management: Strategic endeavor to optimize the use of human capital, which enables an organization to drive short- and long-term results by building culture, engagement, capability, and capacity through integrated talent acquisition, development, and deployment processes that are aligned to business goals.

Tariffs: Taxes collected on goods that are shipped across national boundaries.

Team building: Conscious effort to develop effective workgroups and cooperative skills throughout the organization.

Team equity: Equity that is achieved when teams are rewarded based on their group's productivity.

Telecommuting: Work arrangement whereby employees, called teleworkers or telecommuters, are able to remain at home (or otherwise away from the office) and perform their work using computers and other electronic devices that connect them with their offices.

Third-country national (TCN): Citizen of one country, working in a second country, and employed by an organization headquartered in a third country.

360-degree feedback evaluation method: Popular performance appraisal method that involves evaluation input from multiple levels within the firm as well as external sources.

Traditional career path: Employee progresses vertically upward in the organization from one specific job to the next.

Training: Activities designed to provide learners with the knowledge and skills needed for their present jobs.

Training and development (T&D): Heart of a continuous effort designed to improve employee competency and organizational performance.

Transfer: Lateral movement of a worker within an organization.

Transnational corporation: Moves work to the places with the talent to handle the job and the time to do it at the right cost.

Two-tier wage system: A wage structure where newly hired workers are paid less than current employees for performing the same or similar jobs.

Type I ethics: Strength of the relationship between what an individual or an organization believes to be moral and correct and what available sources of guidance suggest is morally correct.

Type II ethics: Strength of the relationship between what one believes and how one behaves.

Union: Employees who have joined together for the purpose of dealing with their employer.

Union salting: Process of training union organizers to apply for jobs at a company and, once hired, working to unionize employees.

Union shop: Requirement that all employees become members of the union after a specified period of employment (the legal minimum is 30 days) or after a union shop provision has been negotiated.

Unstructured interview: Interview in which the job applicant is asked probing, open-ended questions.

Validity: Extent to which a test measures what it claims to measure.

Vestibule system: T&D delivery system that takes place away from the production area on equipment that closely resembles equipment actually used on the job.

Virtual job fair: Online recruiting method engaged in by a single employer or group of employers to attract a large number of applicants.

Virtual reality: Extension of e-learning that permits trainees to view objects from a perspective otherwise impractical or impossible.

Vocational interest tests: Tests that indicate the occupation a person is most interested in and the one likely to provide satisfaction.

Voluntary benefits: Benefits which are 100 percent paid by the employee but the employer typically pays the administrative cost.

Wage curve: Fitting of plotted points to create a smooth progression between pay grades (also known as the pay curve).

Work standards method: Performance appraisal method which compares each employee's performance to a predetermined standard or expected level of output.

Workplace violence: Physical assault, threatening behavior, verbal abuse, hostility or harassment directed toward employees at work or on duty.

Work-sample tests: Tests that require an applicant to perform a task or set of tasks representative of the job.

Yellow-dog contract: Written agreement between an employee and a company made at the time of employment that prohibits a worker from joining a union or engaging in union activities.

Zero-base forecasting: Forecasting method that uses the organization's current level of employment as the starting point for determining future staffing needs.

Name Index

A

Achille, Roger S., 288
Aguilar, Melissa Klein, 67, 289
Aichlmayr, Mary, 233
Aiken, Penda, 223
Albright, Lesa, 428
Allen, Kristy, 221
Allen, Richard S., 289
Almeida, Beth, 315
Alpern, Peter B., 220
Alter, Michael, 196
Amandus, Harlan, 343
Amare, Nicole, 195
Amelio, William J., 411
Amour, Jeffrey St., 28
Amundsen, Phil, 138
Anand, Rohini, 233
Anderson, Barry, 59
Anderson, Cushing, 134
Anderson, Wayne, 221
Angello, Matt, 396
Ante, Spence, 161
Argyris, Chris, 214
Armstrong, Paul, 223
Arnold, Jennifer Taylor, 260
Arnsparger, Arlene, 231
Arnst, Catherine, 315
Ashack, Elizabeth A., 376
Asin, Barry, 139
Atkins, Angela, 406
Atkinson, William, 316
Austermuehle, Paul, 145
Avery, Christopher, 278
Avramidis, Manny, 406

B

Babcock, Pamela, 344, 428
Baca, Fidel, 47
Baird, Becca, 197
Baird, Mark, 146
Baker, Jennifer L., 68
Baker, Stephen, 160
Bakke, Allen, 89
Ballantyne, Coco, 344
Bandy, Matthew, 195, 406
Banham, Russ, 105
Bannon, Elisa, 150
Barker, Julie, 46, 47
Barkholz, David, 375
Barra, Barbara, 397
Barrett, Sam, 345
Barrington, Linda, 310
Barron, Monica, 128
Basso, Louis, 47
Bates, Steve, 47
Bauer, Christopher, 57, 68
Beagrie, Scott, 232
Beal, Edwin F., 376
Bedell, Denise, 429
Begin, James P., 376
Begley, Kathleen, 47
Bell, Ella, 75, 104
Bellinger, Alan, 47
Bello, Lorraine, 104, 428
Benezine, Kathryn, 195
Benko, Cathy, 228
Bennis, Warren, 214
Berg, Joel, 47
Berry, Raymond D., 316

Bersin, Josh, 233
Bethea, Rudy, Jr., 317
Bethke, Art L., 375
Beutel, Nicholas J., 428
Bharat, Mishra, 47, 196, 197
Bielski, Lauren, 221
Birger, Jon, 160
Birk, Matt, 427
Bishow, John L., 316
Blair, Lin, 60
Blake, Daniel J., 233
Bloch, Matt, 233, 289
Blockett, James, 46
Bobko, Philip, 134
Bolt, Robert, 69
Bolten, Randall, 288
Borell, Charles A., 376
Boseman, Glenn, 233
Boudreau, John W., 134
Boyd, John D., 376
Boyle, Matthew, 160, 161
Branham, Leigh, 303, 400
Brazeel, Stanna, 135, 232
Brazzell, Bonnie, 316
Brennan, Mike, 46
Bretz, Charles, 160
Briggs, Robert O., 428
Brittan, Michael, 104
Brockbank, Wayne, 135
Brown, Duncan, 293
Brown, Garrett, 69
Burke, Doris, 160
Burkhard, Laurie, 134
Burrows, Emma, 195
Burton, Jeremy, 35
Busick, Jennifer, 343
Buster, Maury A., 134
Butler, Kelly M., 104, 315
Button, Scott B., 134

C

Cable, Josh, 343, 376
Cabral, Joseph, 401
Cabrera, Elizabeth, 104
Cadrain, Diane, 315
Callahan, Sean, 161
Camarda, Tom, 220
Cameron, Melissa, 398
Campbell, Chris, 57
Campbell, Judy, 413
Canning, Traci, 415
Cantoni, Craig J., 316
Cappelli, Peter, 135
Carlson, Jennie, 231
Carpitella, Bill, 196
Carrell, Michael R., 377
Carroll, Lewis, 233
Carter, Jerome, 410
Caruth, Donald L., 105, 221
Caruth, Gail D., 221
Carvin, Beth N., 221
Case, Scot, 221
Cassidy, William, 160
Challenger, John, 394
Champy, James, 135
Chapman, Esther, 104
Charles, Joseph P., 68
Chatzky, Jean, 233
Chernin, Peter, 290
Cheung, Todd, 64

Chianese, Lois, 315
Chiang, Gordon, 160
Choe, Mok, 155
Chordas, Lori, 315, 317
Ciampi, Jon, 239
Cicero, 52
Civiello, Mary, 196
Claburn, Thomas, 161
Clark, Ann D., 344
Clarke, Nita, 234
Clausen, Thomas S., 260
Clonts, Cathy, 160
Coates, Michael, 54
Cobb, Liz, 289
Cohen, Evan, 160
Colarelli, Gina, 233
Cole, Wendy, 104
Coleman, Mark, 345
Collie, Cris, 414
Collins, Margaret, 289
Collinson, Simon, 190
Colvin, Geoff, 288, 406
Conley, Dalton, 415
Conlin, Michelle, 160, 221, 288
Conner, Marcia, 35
Cooper, Kenneth, 334
Cooper, Rory, 135
Corbett, Andrew, 233
Cordivari, Rich, 220
Cox, Mary M., 344
Coy, Peter, 160, 315
Crawford, Vicky S., 79
Crispin, Gerry, 188
Crosby, Don, 387, 402
Crouse, Abigail, 105
Crossland, Craig, 190
Crowell, Amber, 105

D

Dahl, Janice M., 68
Dail, Baljit, 291
Dale, Sarah Sturmon, 104
Danaher, Maria Greco, 105
Daniel, Diann, 47
Darrow, Jonathan J., 406
Daum, Julie Hembrock, 289
Davidson, Liz, 299
Davis, Dennis A., 344
Davis, Shirley A., 232
Dawson, Brad, 105
DeCapua, Clare, 47
Dehn, Guy, 100
Delogu, Nancy N., 344
Demos, Darryl, 135
Demos, Telis, 68
Denier, Greg, 351
Dennis, Sarah, 339
Deprez, Esme, 315
Derven, Majorie, 33, 47
Desai, Deepak, 428
Descheneaux, Joanne, 344
DeVries, Mike, 239
Digenan, John, 67
Dillenberger, Cassandra, 343
Dillon, Karen, 288
Dimon, James, 262
Dipper, Rick, 209
Dobie, Monica, 343
Docksai, Rick, 47
Dolezalek, Holly, 220

Domeyer, Diane, 308, 316
Donlin, Mike, 221
Donnellan, John, 68
Dorlington, Hank, 134
Doubleday, Diane, 289
Doughty, Susan, 289
Dowling, Donald, Jr., 156
Downey, Mark D., 105
Drakes, Sean, 260
Draper, Heather, 376
Drucker, Peter, 262, 265, 288
Duffy, Marcia Passos, 220
Dulles, Foster Rhea, 383
Dunkelberger, Karli, 315
Dutton, Gail, 220, 427
Dwyer, Timothy, 217
Dzierzak, Mark, 299

E

Earle, James E., 289
Eaves, Elisabeth, 428
Edmondson, Amy C., 220
Edmundson, Andrea, 428
Edwards, Ethan, 221
Edwards, Lisa Ann, 135
Edwards, Robert E., 46, 134, 161
Eibirt, Henry, 47
Einhorn, Bruce, 429
Elkeles, Tamar, 239
Ellis, Kristi, 429
Ellison, Larry, 29
Embrey, Wanda R., 407
(just) Engle, 67
Engle, 67
Epstein, Shoshanah D., 195
Eramo, Pat, 215
Estreicher, Samuel, 376, 428
Evans, Kelly, 104
Ewing, Jeff, 289

F

Fabius, Raymond, 298, 344
Falcone, Paul, 196, 243
Farkas, David, 160
Feldman, Debra, 170
Fernandez, Gerry, 147
Fernández-Aráoz, Claudio, 195
Ferracone, Robin A., 289
Ferris, Maria, 75
Field, Alan M., 135
Field, Ann, 233
Field, Katherine, 407
Fiester, Margaret, 135
Finch, J. Howard, 289
Finley, Bruce, 305
Finley, Daniel C., 406
Fischler, Lora A., 221
Fisher, Anne, 233, 260
Fisher, Sandra L., 135
Fishman, Nick, 184
Fitzpatrick, Laura, 233, 317
Flahardy, Cathleen, 68, 427
Flaherty, Kyle, 150
Fletcher, Rick, 396
Fogarty, Sean, 345
Fogel, Mark, 118
Fornia, William, 315
Forsman, James, 422
Forte, Jay, 134, 260
Foshe, Greg, 261
Foulke, Edward D., 321
Fox, Adrienne, 68, 135, 197,
   260, 406
Francesca, Gino, 220

Francesco, Anne Marie, 428
Franklin, Brenda, 289
Frase, Martha, 196, 315
Frase-Blunt, Martha, 196
Frauenheim, Ed, 47, 135,
   160, 196, 260
Freeman, Joshua, 350
Freivalds, John, 47
Fritz, Rita L., 220
Froschheiser, Lee, 134, 196

G

Gaddam, Soumya, 46
Gagnon, Suzanne, 424
Galagan, Pat, 47, 201, 220, 406
Galentine, Elizabeth, 407, 427
Gales, Matt, 339
Gallagher, Tracy, 260
Gallbraith, J. R., 135
Gandel, Stephen, 104, 315
Garcia, Stephen, 260
Gardner, Jennifer, 130
Garfield, Mike, 345
Garvin, David A., 220
Gates, Bill, 232
Gaudin, Sharon, 47
Gavin, Joanne H., 68
Gebavi, Andrew, 46
Gebler, David, 289
Geisel, Jerry, 316
Gengler, Amanda, 315
Gentile, Mary C., 67
Geoff, Colvin, 288, 406
Gerdes, Lindsey, 220
Gershkowitz, Todd M., 289
Ghosn, Carlos, 190
Giacalone, Katharine, 221
Giancola, Frank L., 288
Giancola, Frank, 289
Giannetto, David F., 260
Gibbons, Lisa, 38
Gilmore, Agatha, 196
Gnau, Thomas, 376
Gochman, Ilene, 244
Godard, John, 377
Gold, Barry Allen, 428
Goldberg, Betsy, 161
Goldstein, Alan M., 195
Goldstein, Andrew, 283
Goleman, Daniel, 393
Goodkin, Olivia, 406
Goodpaster, Kenneth E., 46
Gosier, Joan, 210
Gostanian, Greg, 233
Graham, Thomas C., 375
Greco, Susan, 195
Greene, Robert J., 236
Greengard, Samuel, 68
Greenwald, Judy, 104, 160, 288
Grensing-Pophal, Lin, 47, 407
Gresham, Lynn, 47
Grose, Thomas K., 197
Gross, Steve, 154
Grossman, Robert J., 196,
   289, 376
Grote, Dick, 250
Grote, Teresa, 402
Groysberg, Boris, 195
Guerriero, Ernest J., 316
Guiler, Jeffrek K., 317
Gully, Stanley M., 104
Gupta, Pankaj, 49
Gurchiek, Kathy, 343
Guttormson, Bonnie, 156

H

Hable, Shey Zeemer, 197
Hackett, Amy, 205
Haden, Stephanie S. Pane, 221
Hahn, David, 150
Hainer, Herbert, 64
Hale, Jamie, 121
Haley, George, 410
Hall, Kenji, 428
Hambrick, Donald, 190
Hamel, Leslie, 160
Hamilton, Michael, 57
Hamm, Steve, 428
Hammer, Michael, 135
Hamon, Claire, 393
Hansen, Fay, 288, 428
Hansen, Katharine, 196
Harker, John, 402
Harmon, Katherine, 343
Harned, Patricia J., 68
Harper, Roseanne, 160
Hart, Sally, 137
Hartley, Daniel, 343
Hartley, Darin E., 115, 134
Hartman, Neal, 190
Hass, Sally, 407
Haut, Rachel, 376
Hayley, Kathryn, 291
Hazard, Robert C., Jr., 288
Head, Joel, 28
Heath, Chip, 196
Heath, Dan, 196
Heavrin, Christina, 377
Hedger, Adrienne, 135, 195
Heineman, Ben W., Jr., 67
Helms, M.J., 301
Hempel, Jessi, 160
Hempel, Paul S., 261
Henderson, Richard I., 289
Hendrickson, Phil, 148
Henneman, Todd, 47, 344
Henricks, Mark, 160
Herbers, Angie, 288
Herbert, Ian, 47
Herbison, Gary, 233
Herbst, Moira, 160
Hernandez, Gina M., 428
Herrmann, Dominique J., 217
Herzberg, Frederick, 129, 135, 316
Heyman, Fredrik, 289
Hill, Jim, 260
Hill, Linda A., 190
Hirschheim, Rudy, 159
Hirschman, Carolyn, 316
Hite, Amanda, 150
Hobbs, Karen, 151
Hobson, Katherine, 344
Hoff, Ted, 220
Hoffman, Auren, 160
Hofman, Mike, 68
Hofmann, Jennifer, 220
Holecek, Andrea, 376
Holincheck, James, 127
Hollon, John, 233
Holmes, Sven Erik, 68
Horton, Willie, 410
Hoseman, Linda Lemel, 288, 289
Hossack, Richard, 135
Houghton, Andy, 260
Houston, George, 291
Huff, Charlotte, 220
Hulme, Virginia A., 428
Humphrey, John, 229
Hunt, Rachael, 352

I

Ickes, Linda, 195
Imberman, Woodruff, 289
Immelt, Jeff, 50
Israelite, Larry, 134
Ivery, Faith E., 316

J

Jacobe, Dennis, 160
Jacobs, Ken, 375
Jacobson, Louis S., 221
Jaeger, Jaclyn, 68, 427
Jager, Peter de, 105
James, Charles E., Sr., 171
Jansen, Julie, 225
Jasmin, Guerline, 233
Jassawalla, Avan R., 428
Jefferies, Michael, 262
Jefferson, Andy, 221
Jennings, Cath, 406
Jitendra, Mishra, 47, 196, 197
Johnson, Aleita, 221
Johnson, Dani, 135
Johnson, Gordon, 205
Johnson, Robert Wood, 60
Johnson, Whitney R., 315
Johnston, Dianna, 79
Jonathan, Katz, 220
Jones, Del, 345
Jones, Keith T., 260
Jones, Robert B., 407
Joyce, Susan, 151

K

Kahn, Sharon, 160
Kalwarski, Tara, 288, 289
Kamikow, Norm, 47
Kaplan, Michael, 196
Kaplan, Roger S., 105
Kapoor, Sanjay, 211
Karabatsos, Lew, 60
Karabell, Zachary, 427
Karel, David, 239
Karp, Melissa, 181, 244
Kaski, Toni, 28
Kaye, Beverly, 226, 406
Kazannian, Robert K., 135
Ke, Weiling, 135
Keefe, Jenny, 315
Kelly, Maryellen, 317
Kelly, Natalie, 376
Kensicki, Peter R., 68
Kesse, Charlene, 61, 261
Kiger, Patrick J., 160, 260
Kim, Dong-One, 289
Kincaid, Cynthia, 68
King, Andreas, 69
King, Martin Luther, Jr., 52
King, Rachael, 428
Kirpatrick, Donald, 213
Kisiel, Ralph, 195
Kiviat, Barbara, 161
Klaassen, Michael, 343
Klein, Adam, 197
Kleiner, Brian H., 343
Kleinsorge, Robert, 135
Kloberdanz, Lrostom, 104
Klug, Kathy, 315
Koegel, John, 316
Koen, Clifford M., Jr., 406
Koeppel, David, 160
Kolman, David, 345
Koppelman, Joel, 196

Kossler, Michael, 418
Kranz, Garry, 217, 220
Krattenmaker, Tom, 260
Kreicker, Noel, 217
Krell, Eric, 68, 221
Krick, Dan, 334
Kristie, James, 288
Kroc, Ray, 60
Krupp, Steve, 135
Kufahl, Pamela, 344
Kwicien, Jack, 195, 302

L

Lacey, David, 384
Laff, Michael, 68, 221, 428
Lalancette, Martial, 155
Lambert, A.G., 199
Lambert, Emily, 288
Lane, Wendy, 397, 406
Langer, Ira, 316
Larison, Robert J., 300
Larkin, Joseph M., 160
Lathrop, Lou Ann, 232
Latta, Geoff, 420
Lau, Shari, 221, 376, 406
Lawler, Edward E., III, 134, 249, 260
Lawrence, Dave, 293
Lay, Kenneth L., 53
Learmonth, Michael, 376
Ledbetter, Lilly, 78-79
Lee, Erin, 376, 406
Lee, Patton, 376, 406
Lee, Yvette, 376
Leibow, Cathy, 104, 316
Leinicke, Linda M., 67
Leipziger, Deborah, 59
Leonard, Bill, 104, 105, 195, 233, 427
Leondis, Alexis, 288, 289
Lermusi, Yves, 186
Levinson, Meredith, 316
Levitt, Arthur, 54
Lewis, John L., 380
Lewis, Kenneth D., 67
Leyes, Maggie, 233
Liberman, Vadim, 406
Lichtenstein, Stephen D., 406
Lichtman, Howard, 209
Lin, Elaine, 402
Lipin, Iila, A., 316
Little, Aiesha D., 344
Lloyd, Joan, 230, 260
Lojeski, Karen Sobel, 221
Lowere, Gil, 316
Lozano, Leticia, 429
Luscombe, Belinda, 221

M

Maag, Christopher, 315
MacDonald, Andrea, 428
Machida, Seiji, 421
Mackey, John, 288
MacMillan, Douglas, 161
Maginnis, Jerry, 68
Maingaut, Amy, 428
Malmquist, Warren, 55
Mandalson, Peter, 234
Mandes, Steve, 207
Manix, Sue, 309
Manning, Alan, 195
Mansdorf, Zack, 421
Marlar, Jenny, 417
Marler, Janet H., 135
Marquardt, Katy, 195, 406

Marquez, Jessica, 47, 220, 376
Martin, Lori Tansey, 105
Martin-Wells, Siobhan, 402
Mason, Barry, 289
Mathiason, Garry, 139
Matlack, Carol, 160
Matthews, John B., Jr., 46
Mauer, Roy, 195
Maylette, Tracy, 260
McCarty, Martha, 406
McClenahen, John S., 68
McCool, Joseph Daniel, 134, 220
McCormick, Carmen, 196
McCullum, Kenya, 316, 407
McDargh, Eileen, 406
McDermott, Michael, 327
McElhaney, Marc, 328
McGregor, Jena, 260, 315, 428
McIntyre, Paul, 343
McKee, Steve, 47
McKenzie, Meredith, 160, 196
McKeown, Eileen, 135, 406
McLeod, David, 234
McMichen, Caroline, 55
Meany, George, 381
Meers, Sharon, 407
Meisinger, Susan, 73, 104, 135, 260
Meister, Jeanne C., 35, 233
Mellon, James, 343
Merritt, Rick, 428
Meskanick, Paul, 344
Mikhitarian, Michael C., 315
Miletsky, Robert J., 343
Miller, Jody, 315
Miller, Matt, 315
Miller, Richard, 47
Miller, Ron, 68
Mills, D. Quinn, 190
Millstein, Sarah, 206
Miner, Nanette, 220
Minton-Eversole, Theresa, 159, 197, 428
Mishler, Max, 376
Mitchell, Michael S., 406
Moir, Stephen, 233
Mondy, Marianne, 208, 309
Mondy, R. Wayne, 46, 105, 134, 161, 196, 221, 232, 288
Mondy, Robert W., 232
Moore, Maggie, 220
Moore, Miles, 429
Moore, Philip S., 161
Moran, Anne E., 407
More, Sir Thomas, 63
Mossmann, Achim, 420
Mukherjee, Ajoy, 130
Mulhern, Barbara, 343
Muller, Joann, 376
Muller, Natalia, 220
Mullins, John, 233
Murphy, Mark, 196
McGill Murphy, Richard, 68
Muschewske, Robert C., 135
Mutch, Paula, 295

N

Nacherla, Aparna, 221
Nadler, Mark, 135
Naish, Richard, 428
Narang, Leenu, 160
Nash, James L., 428
Neal, Vicki, 221
Nelson, William A., 68

Nemko, Marty, 195, 406
Neuser, Daryll J., 376
Newman, Gary, 290, 291
Newman, Perry, 410
Newman, Rick, 195, 406
Nisbett, Richard, 183
Noe, Robert M., III, 46, 105, 134, 161, 407
Nohria, Nitin, 195
Nooyi, Indra, 190
Nugent, Anthony, 315
Nunamaker, Jay F., Jr., 428

O

O'Boyle, Karen, 211
O'Connor, James, 88–89
O'Connor, Sandra Day, 89
O'Keefe, Brian, 160
O'Leonard, Karen, 201
O'Neal, Pam, 150
O'Neil, Laurence, 135, 160
O'Reilly, Nancy, 221
Obama, Barack, 351
Obeng, Eddie, 135
Oberlin, Jeff, 107
Oberstein, Sophie, 221
Odell, Charles, 427
Oleniczak, Mary, 47, 196, 197
Oliphant, Becky J., 196
Oliphant, Gary C., 196
Olson, Jon, 315
Olsztynskin, Jim, 220
Onder, Amy, 104
Ordioni, Jody, 143
Osako, Mary, 423
Osborn, Sue, 310
Ostrosky, Joyce A., 67
Overman, Stephenie, 344
Owens, Donna N., 221

P

Pace, Ann, 104, 233, 428
Paetkau, Tyler M., 105
Pagano, Barbara, 315
Pagano, Elizabeth, 315
Palmer, Kimberly, 195, 233, 406
Paradise, Andrew, 134
Paradiso, Jane, 29
Park, Anna, 96
Parker, Jim, 393
Patel, Laleh, 221
Pearl, Mona, 135
Pease, David P., 221
Peloza, John, 69
Perks, Jonathan, 406
Petersen, Chris, 427
Pfeffer, Jeffrey, 260, 406
Philippe, Marie Y., 104
Phillips, Jack J., 221
Phillips, Jean M., 104
Phillips, Patti P., 221
Pierantozzi, Ron, 233
Pike, Charlie, 47, 196, 197
Pinola, Richard, 117, 135
Pinto, Consuela A., 105
Piturro, Mariene, 343
Plaugmann, Michael, 339
Poh, Timothy, 83
Pollock, Roy, 221
Pomerantz, Mary, 104
Pomeranz, Russell, 135
Pomeroy, Ann, 135, 316
Poor, W. Benjamin, 134
Pope, Byron, 221

Potemra, Michael J., 196
Potvin, Kyle, 195
Powell, Marci, 221
Prabhu, Jaideep, 190
Prager, Howard, 221
Pratt, Mary K., 232
Preeti, Vasishtha, 406
Premeaux, Shane R., 196, 221, 288, 344, 375
Prewitt, Milford, 343
Priebe, Jim, 315
Proctor, Bob, 188
Puccino, Shirley, 429

Q

Qualls, Robert A., 136
Quenqua, Douglas, 289

R

Rafter, Michelle V., 196, 428
Rai, Saritha, 221
Raju, Ramalinga, 48, 50
Ramakrishna G., 50
Ramos, Luis, 68
Randall, Iris, 260
Rappaport, Anna, 407
Rasbury, Angeli R., 232
Raudabaugh, John, 348
Rawe, Julie, 104
Ray, Emily Walls, 233
Raymond, Doug, 289
Rees, Dan, 64
Rehder, Sean, 188
Reid, Joanne, 406
Reilly, Richard R., 221
Reindl, William J., 315
Reinig, Bruce A., 428
Rexroad, W. Max, 67
Riboldi, Juan, 260
Rice, Anne Cumming, 221
Rich, Jay S., 260
Richter, Helene, 167
Rintels, Trish, 221
Robb, Drew, 161, 316
Robbins, McLean, 104
Roberts, Bill, 47, 135, 197, 233
Rocafort, Lynn, 416
Rodriguez, Robert, 46, 232
Roesler, Steve, 217
Roosevelt, Teddy, 53
Rosati, Giuseppe, 150
Rosato, Donna, 160
Rosen, Rich, 199
Rosenberg, Alyssa, 377
Ross, Judith A., 233
Rotella, Joe, 36
Roth, Philip L., 134
Rothman, Irv, 209
Rozenberg, Eric, 43
Rubiner, Betsy, 104
Ruge, Joanie, 139
Ruiz, Gina, 428
Runge, Robin, 329
Russell, Jeffrey, 260
Russell, Linda, 260
Ryan, James, 383
Ryan, Liz, 105, 195
Ryder, Guy, 371
Ryffel, Carolyn, 417

S

Saad, Lydia, 344
Saade, Renea I., 195

Salokas, Michael, 210
Sammer, Joanne, 260
Sartain, Libby, 41
Sashittal, Hermant C., 428
Savage, Marc, 159
Sawtell, Emily, 35
Sawyers, Arlena, 104
Scales, Melvin, 146
Scalise, Dagmara, 316
Scanlon, Joseph, 280
Schaffer, Greg, 195
Schiemann, William, 117
Schlenkrich, Lara, 428
Schmitt, John, 372
Schneider, Jodi, 344
Schneier, Craig E., 276
Schoeff, Mark, Jr., 105, 376, 316
Schomer, Stephanie, 344
Schooley, Claire, 209
Schotz, Andy, 68
Schramm, Jennifer, 135, 232, 288, 344
Schreiber, Barb Rosen, 130
Schullery, Nancy M., 195
Schullery, Stephen E., 195
Schumer, Charles, 162
Schuster, Michael H., 376
Schutzman, Charlotte, 309
Schwartz, Ephraim, 429
Schwartz, Rick, 414
Scoggin, Tareyece, 60
Selko, Adrienne, 428
Sensenig, Kevin J., 221, 260
Shanks, Hugh, 128
Shanoff, Barry, 406
Shapiro, Cynthia, 148
Sharplin, Arthur, 344
Shawstad, Taryn, 106
Shea, Terence E., 407
Shepherd, Leah Carlson, 160
Sherrard, Michael G., 105
Shimer, Paul, 317
Shorten, Barry, 47
Shostak, Arthur B., 376
Shulman, Barry, 160
Silver-Greenberg, Jessica, 288, 289
Silverman, Leslie, 97
Simmons, Neil, 233
Simms, Jane, 316
Simon, Mark, 220
Simonds, Mike, 315, 316
Sinegal, Jim, 51
Singh, Kuldeep, 232
Singh, Lakhwinder, 160
Sklover, Alan, 398
Skye, Ann, 318
Slentz, Andrew, 428
Sloan, Ken, 68
Smerd, Jeremy, 315
Smith, Allen, 104, 105, 161, 162
Smith, Anne Kates, 160
Smith, Brendan L., 196
Smith, David, 46
Smith, Susan Storm, 406
Snell, Roy, 55
Sokol, Marc, 416
Solganik, Howard, 147
Solis, Hilda, 269
Speers, Vic, 107
Speizer, Irwin, 160
Spielman, Cheryl, 427
Spray, Justin, 196

Stamper, Connie, 161, 197
Stanley, T. L., 67, 344, 376
Stebbins, Paul, 263
Steffee, S., 68
Steinberg, Allen, 403
Steinberg, Richard M., 289
Steiner, John E., Jr., 196
Stephen, Miller, 407
Stephens, Rex, 47
Steptoe, Sonja, 104
Stetz, Thomas A., 134
Stevens, Annie, 233
Stevens-Huffman,
    Leslie, 344
Stilels, Phillip, 47
Stock, Howard, 68
Stoddard, Nat, 135
Stolz, Richard, 289
Stracynski, Stacy, 406
Street, René, 221
Streit, Meghan, 289
Stringer, Howard, 190, 196
Stringer, Judy, 196
Strober, Joanna, 407
Stuart, Laurence, 156
Subervi, Ann, 56
Sullivan, John, 46
Sullivan, Scott, 420
Sutton, Robert, 406
Sweeney, Paul, 289
Swinford, David, 264

U

Taggart, Nina, 344
Tantillo, John, 47
Tanyeri, Dana, 161, 196
Tattanelli, Claudia, 207
Taylor, Benjamin J., 383
Taylor, Colleen, 428
Taylor, Vicki, 428
Teichman, Alysa, 221
Teinowitz, Ira, 376
Testa, Bridget Mintz, 316
Thaczyk, Christopher, 316
Thain, John, 262
Thatcher, Hugh C., 343
Thomas, R. Roosevelt, Jr., 73
Thomas, Dan, 38
Thompson, Kimberly, 196
Thornton, George C., III, 196
Thorpe, Norman, 47
Thurston, Lawson D., 428
Timm, Derek, 343
Tinder, Galen, 104, 428

Toossi, Mitra, 104
Tozzi, John, 160
Trachta, Kathy, 420
Tremayne, Jessica, 104
Treppa, Benjamin, 343
Trinka, Jim, 221
Truman, Harry S., 96
Trumka, Richard. L., 376
Trunk, Penelope, 47, 233
Tsang, Calvin, 402
Tyler, Kathryn, 68,
    233, 260

U

Ulrich, Dave, 135
Ulrich, Linda, 279
Upfold, Christopher, 428

V

Van Dam, Nick, 233
van Dyk, Deirdre, 104
Van Dyke, James, 332
Van Steenwyk, Jason, 195
Vassallo, Ron, 60
Verschoor, Curtis C., 67, 68

W

Wadhwa, Vivek, 67
Wagner, Janet, 233
Wagner, Jennifer, 289
Wagner, Kevin, 300
Wagner, Steve, 282
Wain, Daniel, 46
Walden, Dana, 290
Waldo, Mary Helen, 35
Walker, Catherine, 393
Wallace, J. D., III, 219
Wallace, Les, 221
Wallis, Claudia, 104
Walsh, Aidan, 43
Ward, Whitney, 196
Warner, Deborah, 223
Warren, James, 220
Wartzman, Rick, 47
Wash, Paul, 35
Waters, John K., 195
Watson, Hugh J., 260
Waugh, Skip, 260
Waxer, Cindy, 429
Webber, Andrew, 343
Webster, Lois, 134
Weeks, H. Shelton, 289
Weingarten, Rebecca, 233
Weinstein, Margery, 135, 406

Weirick, Kristen, 196
Weitzman, Allan, 398
Welch, John F., Jr., 260
Welch, David, 315
Welch, Jack, 244, 263
Wells, Penn, 135
Wells, Susan J., 104, 344
Wesche, Sara, 345
Weyers, Howard, 320
Whitney, Kellye, 68
Wick, Cal, 221
Wieczorek, Dave, 105
Wilkerson, Brian, 106
Wilkinson, Alec, 67
Wilkinson, Amanda, 315
Williams, Steve, 301
Williams, Susan, 310
Williamson, Billie, 428
Williamson, Lauren, 407
Willmer, Dave, 197
Wilson, Amy, 375
Winickoff, Jonathan P., 319
Witney, Fred, 383
Witt, Jennifer Parmelee, 316
Wittig-Berman, Ursula, 428
Wojcik, Joanne, 343
Wolff, Shelly, 330
Wolfinger, Pete, 221
Wolgemuth, Liz, 195, 406
Wong, Bianca, 402
Wortman, David, 85
Wright, Aliah D., 160, 195, 196, 260
Wukitsch, John B., 315
Wyatt, Watson, 29, 106, 121, 244, 283,
    297, 300, 330
Wyckoff, Claire, 135
Wysong, Wendy, 427

Y

Yang, Jai Lynn, 288
Yaquinto, Russell, 178
Yeaton, Kathryn, 233
Young, James R., 232

Z

Zachary, Louis J., 221
Zadek, Simon, 68
Zager, Masha, 344
Zalud, Bill, 105
Zarocostas, John, 377
Zeidner, Rita, 104, 105, 407
Zellers, Victoria, 105
Zickerman, Jason, 126
Zylich, Marjory, 305

Company Index

A

Abbott Laboratories, 300
Abercrombie & Fitch, 262
Aberdeen Group, 189
Accountantsworld.com, 149
Acquire, 123
Adarand Constructors, 89
Adecco Group North America, 139
Adidas, 64
Adolph Coors Company, 55, 365
Advanced Micro Devices, 59
Albemarle Paper Company, 87
Alcoa Inc., 59
AllFreelanceWork.com, 149
American Telephone & Telegraph Company, 82
American Tobacco Company, 88
AMR Research Inc., 128
Anglo Irish Bank, 48
Anticipatory Employment, 210
Aon Consulting, 291
Arkansas Blue Cross Blue Shield, 60
Aruspex, 123
Atlantic Coast Bank, 300
Atlantic Group, 410

B

B & Q, 70, 104
Baker & McKenzie LLP, 348
Baker Hughes, 409
Balfour Beatty, 217
Barking and Havering Authority, 310
Baxter International Inc., 59
Bayer Corporation North American, 398
Bear Stearns, 50
Bechtel Corporation, 54, 219
Bernard Hodes Group, 145
Bersin, 201
Bharti Airtel, 211
BIMA, 35
Biogen Inc., 276
Blackboard Learning System, 204, 205
BlueCross BlueShield, 333
BMW Manufacturing Co., 143
Breakingpoint systems, 150
Bright Tree Consulting Group, 396
Bristol-Myers Squibb, 199
Buck Consultants, 179
Buckman Laboratories International, Inc., 393
Bupa International, 339
Burger King, 59
Burlington Industries, Inc., 94

C

Capital One, 248
Career Development Partners, 223
CareerBuilder.com, 148
CareerXroads, 188
Cartus, 414, 417
Caterpillar, 248
CBOCS West Inc., 78
CBS, 57
Ceisel Masonry, 81
Century Aluminum of West Virginia, 397
CEPR, 372
Cfo.com, 149
Challenger, Gray & Christmas, Inc., 394

Charles Schwab & Co., 51
Checkster, 186
Chevron Corporation, 106, 409
Chrysler Corporation, 43, 120, 190, 290
Church's Chicken and Strategic Restaurants, Inc., 175
CIGNA Behavioral Health, 421
CIGNA International, 422
Cirque du Soleil, 424
Cisco Systems, 51, 57, 154, 209, 248, 290
Citi, 402
CLC Metrics, 188
Coca Cola Company, 59, 300
College.monster.com, 149
Competitive Technologies Inc., 54
Consolidated Coin Caterers Corp., 88–89
Contemporary Business News, 423
Coolworks.com, 149
Corragio Group, 126
Costco, 51
Cracker Barrel, 78
CreateHope, 60
Critical Response Associates, 328
CRM consultancy, 188
Cummins Mid-South, 239

D

Daimler-Benz, 43
DaimlerChrysler Corporation, 190, 290, 350
Daymark Advisors, 302
DDI, 182
Dell Inc., 59
Deloitte, 130, 138, 150, 282, 299, 312
Delphia Consulting LLC, 36
Delves Group, 283
Dice.com, 149
DirectEmployers Association, 148
Disney, 143, 298
Dollar Store, 175
Doosan, 156
DoubleClick, 155
Dow Chemical, 57, 300
Drake Beam Morin Inc., 211
Duke Power Company, 82, 87–88, 185
DuPont Safety Resources, 422

E

Eastbridge Consulting, 302
Eastman Kodak Company, 59
EBay, 57
Edgewater Technology, 327
EDS, 248
Edw. C. Levy Co., 364
EmployeescreenIQ, 184
Enron, 48, 53, 68, 300
Ernst & Young, 57, 68
Expacare, 339
Expertus, 205

F

Facebook, 35, 47, 149, 150, 185, 196, 226
Farah Manufacturing Company, 87
FedEx, 35, 143, 222, 300, 402
Fiat, 143
Financial Finesse, 299
Fisher & Phillips' Workplace Safety and Catastrophe Management, 321

Flowserve, 419
FMC Corporation, 62
Ford, 49, 248, 346, 347
Fortune, 29, 120, 126, 139, 190, 210, 228, 244, 277, 299, 302, 335, 394, 417
Forum Corporation, 229
FPL Group Inc., 59
Franciscan Health Systems, 301
Frederic W. Cook & Co., 283
Freelance.com, 149
Freudenberg-NOK, 83, 105

G

Gannett Co, Inc., 148
Gartner Inc., 127
GE Capital, 418
General Electric, 49, 146, 248, 297, 410
General Motors Corporation, 49, 120, 346, 350, 364, 371
Genzyme Corp., 59
Gifts in Kind, 59
Global Services, 217
GMAC Global Relocation Services, 414, 420
GMAC, 420
Gmail, 151
Goldman Sachs, 48, 59, 275
Goodyear Tire & Rubber Co., Inc., 78
Goodyear, 78, 248, 346
Google, 148, 153, 154, 155, 180, 181, 232, 244, 423
Greyhound, 84
Grote Consulting Corporation, 250
Guru.com, 149

H

Hale-Halsell Company, 397
Hallmark Communities, 393
Harrah's Entertainment, 298
Harris v Forklift Systems, Inc., 94
Headwinds Ltd., 28
Hewlett-Packard, 59, 143, 174, 209, 211, 248
Hill and Knowlton Canada, 54
Hilton, 418
Hime & Co., 311
HireRight, 414, 415
Home Depot, 59, 403
Honda, 73, 104, 168, 195
Hospitalsoup.com, 149
HotJobs, 148
Hotmail, 151
Hudson, 107
Human Productivity Lab, 209
HumanConcepts, 123
Hyatt, 143
Hyundai Mobis, 43

I

I4cp, 125, 417
IBM, 38, 47, 74–75, 301, 310, 334
IFCO Systems North America, 85
Ince&Tive, 43
Infohrm, 123
Ingersoll Rand Co., 156
Intel Corp., 59, 418
Intercontinental Hotels Group, 293
International Paper Co., 410
Internshipprograms.com, 149
I-trax Inc., 298

445

J

J.P. Morgan Chase, 262
JAR Kenya, 371
Javelin & Research, 332
Jeff Oberlin, Inc., 107
Jelf Group, 339
Job.com, 149
JobsInLogistics.com, 149
JobWhiz, 170
John Lewis, 235–236, 260
Johnson & Johnson, 60
Johnson Controls Inc., 350
Joyjobs.com, 149

K

Katten Muchin Rosenman, 409
KBR, 398, 409
Kellogg, 143
KPMG, 43, 57, 147, 217, 420
Kraft Foods Inc., 38,

L

L'Oréal, 155, 421, 422
Layover.com, 149
Lee Memorial, 403
Lehman Brothers, 50
Lenovo, 411
Liberty Mutual, 322
LifeSize, 209
Lincoln Plating, 334
LinkedIn, 35, 149, 150, 185, 226
Littler Mendelson, 139
Liz Claiborne, 167
LocationValue, 415
LRN, 57
Lucent, 409

M

Magnet Communications, 28
Marks and Spencer's, 71
Martin Marietta Corporation, 87
McDonald, 59, 60, 77
MeadWestvaco, 300
MedStar, 305
Mercedes-Benz, 410
Mercer, 154, 291, 305, 339, 402
Merrill Lynch, 262
Metrus Group, 117
Microsoft, 143, 148, 248, 274
Moen Inc., 333
Monster Worldwide, Inc., 148
Mortgage Lenders Network, 397
Motorola, 422
Mount Clemens General Hospital, 295–296

N

NACElink Network, 148
Nakisa, 123
National Football League, 174
National Patient Safety
    Agency, 310
Nestle, 49
New Learning Playbook, 35
NewsCorp., 291–292
Nickelodeon, 243
Nihon Shoken, 311
Nike, 59, 205
Nissan, 190, 298
Nortel, 209
Northwestern Mutual, 301

O

Oracle, 29
ORC Worldwide, 420
Owens-Illinois, 209

P

P.F. Chang's China Bistro, 291
Paragon Global Resources, 420
Pearl Meyer Partners, 264
Peet's Coffee & Tea, 41
Penna, 223
Pepsi, 190, 248, 334
Personnel Decisions International, 416
PG & E Corp., 59
PIFC, 293
Pinnacle West Capital Corp., 59
Polycom, 209
PPG, 365
Precision Castparts, 275
Precision Tube Co., 347
PricewaterhouseCoopers, 28, 49, 417
Procter & Gamble, 38, 59, 211, 411
Prologis, 59
Proskauer Rose, 97, 398

Q

Qualcomm, 239
Quintiles Transnational, 318

R

Raising Cane, 150
Relocation Counseling & Consulting, 416
Research in Motion, 291
Restogigs.com, 150
Reward Systems Inc., 236
Rich Products Corporation, 413
Right Management Consultants, 117, 178
Rio Tinto, 411
Ritz Carlton, 143
Robert Half Management Resources,
    30, 35, 166
Roesler Consulting Group, 217
Rok Group, 393
Ruby Tuesday, 205

S

Saba, 199, 296
Salesforce.com, 149
Santa Fe Trail Transportation Company, 92
Satyam, 48–50, 67
SAP, 123, 291
SBI Mutual, 49
Scotiabank, 130
Serena Software Inc., 35
Siemens, 57, 409
Sixfigurejobs.com, 149
Sony, 190, 275, 410
Southwest Airlines, 51, 143, 216, 243, 274
Sowela Technical Community College, 145
Spun Steak, 96
Staffing Industry Analysts, 139
Standard Parking, 60
Starbucks, 148
State Street Corp., 59
STD, 417
SuccessFactors, 239
SumTotal, 239
Sun Microsystems, 248
SunTrust Banks, 300
Symplicity Corporation, 148

T

Talbert Builders, 81
Talent Revolution, 150
Taleo Products, 396
Tandberg, 209
Target, 51, 59
Tata Consultancy Services, 130
Tech Mahindra, 50
Techjobbank.com, 149
Tesco, 71, 236, 260
The Alternative Board, 126
The Ashton Group, 301
The Hackett Group, 107
The McClatchy Company, 148
3M, 57
Time Warner, 211
TopCoder, 155
Towers Perrin, 128, 296
Toyota, 215, 221, 298, 410
Tribune Company, 148
Trivalent Benefits Consulting
    Inc., 38
TVjobs.com, 149
20th Century Fox Television, 290
TWA, 96
Twitter, 35, 47, 149, 150, 160, 185,
    205–206, 220, 226

U

U.S. Bancorp, 231
Union Carbide, 421
Union Pacific, 205
United Technologies Corp.,
    59, 301
University of Phoenix, 208
Universum Communications, 207
UPS, 222, 296, 352
US Bancorp, 51
US Cellular, 150
Utopia Communications, 56

V

Vemo, 123
Verizon Communications Inc., 310
VIST Insurance, 384
Volvo, 409

W

Wachovia, 127
Walgreen, 76, 298
Wal-Mart, 51, 55, 59, 146
Walt Disney Parks and
    Resorts, 298
Watson Wyatt Worldwide, 29, 297, 300, 330
Western Electric, 82, 238
Weyco, 320
Whirlpool, 143
World Bank, 49
World Fuel Services,
    263–264
WorldCom, 48
Worldwide ERC, 414

X

Xerox, 296
XING, 150

Y

Yahoo!, 148, 151, 423
YouTube, 150

Subject Index

A

Ability to pay, 267
Academic achievement, 177
Accident investigation, 324, 326
Accommodation, 76, 85, 96, 116, 182
Active job seeker, 140
Adarand Constructors v Pena, 89
Adding value to your career, 229
Adjusting pay rates, 274
Administrative employee, 269
Adverse impact, 79–80, 82, 87–88, 91–93, 172, 174, 182, 254, 395
Advertising, 84, 97, 143, 151–152, 154
Affirmative action
  defined, 97
  Executive Order 11246, 91, 96–97, 269
  Executive Order 11375, 96–97
Affirmative action program (AAP), 98–100
Age Discrimination in Employment Act (ADEA) of 1967, amended 1978, 1986, 77, 82–84, 86, 88–89, 269, 304
2006 Age Discrimination Act, 70
Agency shop, 359
Albemarle Paper Company v Moody, 87–88, 238
Alcohol abuse, 327, 335
Alcoholism, 330, 335
Alternative dispute resolution (ADR), 398–399
American Arbitration Association, 363
American Federation of Labor and Congress of Industrial Organizations (AFL-CIO), 350, 351, 352, 353, 354, 365, 369, 379, 381
American Institute for Managing Diversity, 73
American Lung Association, 319
American Medical Association, 335
American Society for Training and Development (ASTD), 58
American Tobacco Company v Patterson, 88–89
Americans with Disabilities Act Amendments Act of 2008, 85
Americans with Disabilities Act (ADA) of 1990, 82, 84–85, 97, 116, 187
Anti-Injunction Act (Norris-LaGuardia Act) of 1932, 379
Applicant pool, 92, 93, 143, 163
Applicant tracking system, 36, 166–167, 175, 181
Application, review of, 168
Apprenticeship training, 207
Arbitration, 353, 363–364, 367, 369, 398–399
Assessment center, 175
Assessment of employee potential, 238
Asynchronous learning, 208
Attitude survey, 401
At-will employees, 387
Automated reference checking, 36, 186–187
Availability forecast, 122–123

B

Baby boomers, 72, 230, 232
Background investigation, 85, 184–186, 187, 329, 414
Background investigation with social networking, 185
Bandwidth, 308
Bargaining unit, 352, 355, 356–357, 359, 362, 370
Base salary, 154, 282–283, 302
Beachhead demands, 362

Bechtel v Competitive Technologies Inc., 54
Behavior modeling, 205–206, 208
Behavioral interview, 179–180, 237
Behaviorally anchored rating scale (BARS) method, 248–249
Behaviors, 241
Benchmarking, 214
Benefits (indirect financial compensation)
  communicating, 305
  defined, 292
  disability protection, 300
  discretionary benefits, 292, 295
  employee services
    child care, 300
    educational assistance, 301
    food services/subsidized cafeterias, 301
    relocation, 301
    scholarships for dependents, 301
    unique employee services benefits, 301–302
  employee stock option plan, 300
  health care
    consumer-driven health care plans
      flexible spending account, 297–298
      health savings account, 297
    dental and vision care, 298
    major medical benefits, 298
    managed-care health organizations
      exclusive provider organizations (EPOs), 297
      health maintenance organizations (HMOs), 297
      point-of-service (POS), 297
      preferred provider organization (PPO), 297
    on-site health care, 298
  job environment as a nonfinancial compensation factor
    appropriate status symbols, 307
    capable managers, 307
    competent employees, 307
    congenial co-workers, 307
    sound policies, 306–307
    working conditions, 308
  job itself as a nonfinancial compensation factor, 305–306
  life insurance, 298
  mandated (legally required) benefits
    social security, 294
    unemployment compensation, 294
    workers' compensation, 294
  nonfinancial compensation, 32, 265, 305
  payment for time not worked, 295–296
    other types of payment for time not worked, 296
    paid vacations, 295
    sabbaticals, 296
    sick pay and paid time off, 295–296
  premium pay
    defined, 302
    hazard pay, 302
    shift differentials, 302
  retirement plans
    cash balance, 299–300
    defined benefits, 299
    defined contribution, 299
  workplace flexibility (work-life balance)
    compressed workweek, 309
    flextime, 308–309
    job sharing, 309–310

part-time work, 311–312
    telecommuting, 310
Biculturalism, 75
Biometric, 162–163
Blackboard learning system, 204–205
Board (or panel) interview, 180
Bona fide occupational qualification (BFOQ), 79, 83, 93, 99,387
Bonus, 32, 51, 55, 89, 124, 143, 154, 190, 227, 255, 262, 263–264, 275–276, 281–283
Bottom-up forecast, 122
Boycott, 365, 381–382
Bribery, 408
Broadbanding, 274
Building organizing funds, 351
Bumping procedure, 395
Burlington Industries, Inc. v Ellerth, 94
Burnout, 129, 223, 333, 338
Business games, 206
Business necessity, 82–83, 87, 93, 96, 116, 171

C

Candidate relationship management, 36, 188
Card check, 352, 353
Career (defined), 223
Career development
  defined, 226
  methods
    company material, 227
    discussions with knowledgeable individuals, 227
    manager/employee self-service, 227
    performance appraisal system, 228
    workshops, 228
Career paths
  adding value to your career, 229
  defined, 226
  demotion, 229–230
  dual-career path, 229
  free agents, 230
  lateral skill path, 229
  network career path, 229
  traditional career path, 228
Career planning
  defined, 223
    self-assessment, 223
    using the web for career planning assistance, 226
    using the web for self-assessment assistance, 225–226
Career security, 222
Caregiver discrimination, 97–98
Carpal tunnel syndrome, 326
Carpenters and Joiners Union, 353
Case study, 205
Cash balance plan, 229–230
CBOCS West Inc. v Humphries, 78
Central American Free Trade Agreement, 423
Central tendency error, 251
Change to Win Coalition, 353, 354–355
Checkoff of dues, 359–360
Cigarmakers Union, 379
Circuit City v Adams, 399
Civil Rights Act of 1866, 78, 82, 90, 92
Civil Rights Act of 1964—Amended 1972, 79–83, 87, 94–86, 97, 99, 143
Civil Rights Act of 1991, 82–83
Civil Service Reform Act, 369
Classification method, 271

Clawback contract provision, 284
Closed shop, 358, 359, 381
Coaching, 210–211
Code of ethics, 50, 54–55
Cognitive aptitude tests, 173
Collective bargaining
  administration of the agreement, 357, 366
  bargaining issues
    compensation
      family care, 360
      holidays, 360
      jury pay, 360
      layoff or severance pay, 360
      overtime and premium pay, 360
      vacation, 360
      wage rate schedule, 360
    employee security, 360
    grievance procedure, 360
    job-related factors, 360
    management rights, 359
    recognition, 358–359
    union security
      agency shop, 359
      closed shop, 359
      dues checkoff, 359–360
      maintenance of membership, 359
      open shop, 359
      union shop, 359
  breakdowns in negotiations
    management's strategies
      continue operations without striking
        workers, 365
      lockout, 362, 363, 365
    third-party intervention
      arbitration, 353, 363–364, 367, 369
      mediation, 363
    union strategies
      boycott, 364, 365, 381–382
      strikes, 351, 363, 364–365, 369, 378,
        380–381
  negotiating the agreement, 361–362
  preparing for negotiations, 357, 361
  ratifying the agreement, 366
Collective bargaining in the public sector, 369
Committee for Industrial Organization (CIO), 380
Committee on Political Education, 350–351
Commonwealth v Hunt, 378
Community colleges, 144, 208
Company-wide pay plans
  gainsharing, 280
  profit sharing, 279–280
Comparable worth, 79
Compensation
  defined, 32
  direct financial compensation, 32, 264
  indirect financial compensation, 32, 265
  nonfinancial compensation, 32, 265, 305
Compensation policy
  defined, 267
  market (going) rate, 267
  pay followers, 267
  pay leader, 267
Compensation survey, 268
Competencies, 277
Competency-based pay, 276–277
Competition, 34
Competitive games, 154–155
Compressed work week, 309
Concurrent Validity, 173
Congenial co-workers, 307
Congress of Industrial Organizations (CIO),
  354, 380
Consolidated Omnibus Budget Reconciliation
  Act of 1985, 303

Conspiracy, 378
Construct validity, 173
Consumer-driven health care plan
  flexible spending account, 297–298
  health savings account, 297
Consumer price index (CPI), 267
Content validity, 173
Contingent worker compensation, 282
Contingent workers, 139
Continuous background checks, 185
Contract workers' sites, 149
Core time, 308–309
Corporate and Auditing Accountability,
  Responsibility and Transparency Act
  of 2002, 53–54
Corporate career Web site, 147
Corporate social responsibility (CSR)
  defined, 34, 59
  implementing a corporate social responsibility
    program, 63–64
  stakeholder analysis and the social contract,
    60–63
    obligations to individuals, 62
    obligations to government, 62
    obligations to other organizations, 62
    obligations to society in general, 63
  strategic corporate social responsibility, 60
Corporate university, 207
Cost of living, 268
Cost-of-living allowance (COLA), 269
Country's culture, 43
Craft union, 353–354
Criterion-related validity, 172–173
Critical incident method, 247
Cross-training, 129
Crowd sourcing, 181
Cultural differences, 43, 75, 417, 420
Customer appraisal, 243
Customers, 34
Customized benefit plans, 303
Cyber recruiter, 147
Cyberwork, 415

D

Databases, 124
Davis-Bacon Act of 1931, 269
Decertification, 370, 381
Deductibles, 297–298, 334
Defense outplacement referral system
  (DORS), 146
Defined benefit plan, 299
Defined contribution plan, 299
Demotion, 229–230, 395
Dental care, 298
Department of labor job analysis schedule
  (JAS), 112
De-skilled, 77
Development (defined), 31
DirectEmployers Association, 148
Direct financial compensation
  company-wide pay plans
    gainsharing, 280
    profit sharing, 279–280
  contingent worker compensation, 282
  defined, 32, 264
  determinants of direct financial
    compensation, 266
  employee as a determinant of direct financial
    compensation
    competency-based pay, 276–277
    experience, 276
    luck, 278
    organization membership, 277

performance-based pay
  merit pay, 275–276
  piecework, 276
  variable pay (bonus), 276
political influence, 278
potential, 277
seniority, 277
skill-based pay, 276–277
equity in financial compensation
  employee equity, 265–266
  equity theory, 265
  external equity, 265
  financial equity, 265
  internal equity, 265
  team equity, 266
executive compensation
  are top executives paid too much?, 262–263
  base salary, 282
  bonuses and performance-based pay,
    282–283
  perquisites, 283
  stock-option plans, 283
global compensation
  compensation for host-country nationals,
    419–420
  expatriate compensation, 420
job as a determinant of direct financial
  compensation, 270
job evaluation
  classification method, 271
  defined, 270
  factor comparison method, 271–272
  Hay guide chart-profile, 272
  point method, 272
  ranking method, 271
job pricing
  adjusting pay rates, 274–275
  broadbanding, 274
  defined, 272
  pay grades, 272–273
  pay ranges, 273
  single-rate system, 274
labor market as a determinant of direct
  financial compensation
  compensation surveys, 268
  cost of living, 268
  economy, 269
  expediency, 268
  labor unions, 268
  legislation
    Davis-Bacon Act of 1931, 269
    Fair Labor Standards Act of 1938, as
      amended, 269–270
    Walsh-Healy Act of 1936, 269
organization as a determinant of direct
  financial compensation
  ability to pay, 267
  compensation policies
    market (going) rate, 267
    pay followers, 267
    pay leader, 267
  organizational level, 267
professional employee compensation, 280–281
sales representative compensation, 281
team-based pay, 278
Disability protection, 300
Disaster planning, 127–128
Disciplinary action
  approaches
    disciplinary action without punishment,
      390–391
    hot stove rule, 389
    progressive disciplinary action, 389–390
  defined, 387

problems, 391–392
process, 388–389
Disciplinary action without punishment, 390–391
Discipline, 387
Disciplinary action in the global environment, 386
Discretionary benefits
  employee services
    child care, 300
    educational assistance, 301
    food services/subsidized cafeterias, 301
    relocation, 301
    scholarships for dependents, 301
    unique employee services benefits, 301–302
  employee stock option plan, 300
  health care
    consumer-driven health care plans, 297
    dental and vision care, 298
    major medical benefits, 298
    managed-care health organizations, 297
    on-site health care, 298
Disparate impact, 82–83, 90
Disparate treatment, 91–92
Disposable American workforce, 139
Diverse workforce
  dual-career family, 75
  foreign workers, 76–77
  immigrants, 76
  mothers returning to the workforce, 74–75
  older workers, 75–76
  people with disabilities, 76
  single parents and working mothers, 74
  women in business, 74
  workers of color, 75
  young persons with limited education or skills, 77
Diversity, 73
Diversity management, 73–74
Domestic violence, 320, 329
Dothard v Rawlinson, 88
Downsizing
  defined, 395
  negative aspects, 396
  outplacement, 397
Downsizing software, 396
Drug abuse, 335
Drug-Free Workplace Act of 1988, 335–336, 338
Dual-career family, 75
Dual-career path, 229
Due process, 254
Dues checkoff, 359–360

E

E-learning, 204–205
Early retirement, 126, 304, 396, 403
EBSCOhost, 196
Economy, 36
Educational assistance, 301
EEO-27, 79
Election campaign, 356
Emergency Economic Stabilization Act of 2008, 270
Emotional intelligence, 393
Employability doctrine, 222
Employee enlistment, 143–144
Employee equity, 265–266
Employee leasing, 38, 139
Employee recording, 111
Employee referrals, 143
Employee services, 300–301

Employee as a determinant of direct financial compensation
  competency-based pay, 276–277
  experience, 276
  luck, 278
  organizational membership, 277
  performance-based pay
    merit pay, 275–276
    piecework, 276
    variable pay (bonus), 276
  political influence, 278
  potential, 277
  seniority, 277
  skill-based pay, 276–277
Employee assistance program (EAP), 338
Employee engagement, 234–235
Employee Free Choice Act , 353
Employee Polygraph Protection Act of 1988, 176
Employee requisition, 141
Employee Retirement Income Security Act of 1974, 303–304
Employee self-service, 128
Employee services
  child care, 300
  educational assistance, 301
  food services/subsidized cafeterias, 301
  relocation, 301
  scholarships for dependents, 301
  unique employee services benefits, 301–302
Employee stock option plans, 300
Employment at will, 386–387
Employment interview(s)
  candidate's role and expectations, 178
  concluding the interview, 184
  content
    academic achievement, 177
    interpersonal skills, 177
    occupational experience, 177
    organizational fit, 178
    personal qualities, 177
  interviewing problems
    contrast effect, 183
    inappropriate questions, 182
    interviewer domination, 183
    interview illusion, 183
    lack of training, 183
    nonverbal communication, 183
    premature judgment, 183
    permitting non-job-related questions, 182
  methods of
    board (or panel), 180
    group, 180
    multiple, 180
    one-on-one, 180
    realistic job previews, 181–182
    stress, 180–181
  planning, 177
  preliminary screening, 167–168
  types of
    behavioral, 179–180, 237
    structured, 179
    unstructured, 178–179
Employment tests
  cogitative aptitude, 173
  job-knowledge, 174
  personality, 174
  psychomotor abilities, 173–174
  vocational interest, 174
  work-sample, 174
Employer branding, 28–29
Employers Forum on Age, 71
Employment Eligibility Verification Form, 162
Equal Employment Opportunity Commission (EEOC), 79, 81–83, 93, 96, 140, 168

Equal Employment Opportunity (EEO)
  legislation
    Age Discrimination in Employment Act of 1967 as amended in 1978 and 1986, 77, 82–84, 86, 88,-89, 269, 304
    Americans with Disabilities Act Amendments Act of 2008, 85
    Americans with Disabilities Act (ADA) of 1990, 82, 84–85, 97, 116, 187
    Civil Rights Act of 1866, 78, 82, 90, 92
    Civil Rights Act of 1964—Amended 1972, 79–83, 87, 94–86, 97, 99, 143
    Civil Rights Act of 1991, 82–83
    Equal Pay Act of 1963, Amended in 1972, 78
    Illegal Immigration Reform and Immigrant Responsibility Act of 1996, 85–86
    Immigration Reform and Control Act of 1986, 85
    Lilly Ledbetter Fair Pay Act, 78–79
    Pregnancy Discrimination Act of 1978, 81–82
    Rehabilitation Act of 1973, 82, 84
    Uniformed Services Employment and Reemployment Rights Act of 1994, 86
    Veterans' Benefits Improvement Act of 2004, 86
  Supreme Court Decisions
    Adarand Constructors v Pena, 89
    Albemarle Paper Company v Moody, 87–88
    American Tobacco Company v Patterson, 88–89
    Burlington Industries, Inc. v Ellerth, 94
    CBOCS West Inc. v Humphries, 78
    Circuit City v Adams, 399
    Commonwealth v Hunt, 378
    Dothard v Rawlinson, 88
    Espinoza v Farah Manufacturing Company, 88
    Faragher v City of Boca Raton, 94
    14 Penn Plaza LLC v Pyett, 399
    Gratz v Bollinger, 89–90
    Griggs v Duke Power Company, 87, 116, 185
    Grutter v Bollinger, 89
    Harris v Forklift Systems, Inc., 94
    Ledbetter v Goodyear Tire & Rubber Co., Inc., 78
    Leonel v American Airlines, 84
    McDonald v Santa Fe Trail Transportation Company, 92
    Meritor Savings Bank v Vinson, 94
    O'Connor v Consolidated Coin Caterers Corp., 88–89
    Oncale v Sundowner Offshore Services, 95
    Phillips v Martin Marietta Corporation, 87–88
    Ricci v DeStefano, 90
    TWA v Hardison, 96
    University of California Regents v Bakke, 89
Equal Pay Act of 1963, Amended in 1972, 78
Equity in financial compensation
  employee equity, 265–266
  equity theory, 265
  external equity, 265
  financial equity, 265
  internal equity, 265
  team equity, 266
Equity theory, 265
Ergonomics, 326–327
Espinoza v Farah Manufacturing Company, 88
Essay method, 247

Ethics
  code of, 50, 54–55
  defined, 50
  human resource ethics, 56
  legislating ethics
    Corporate and Auditing Accountability,
      Responsibility and Transparency Act of
      2002, 53–54
    Federal Sentencing Guidelines for
      Organizations Act of 1992, 53
    Procurement Integrity Act of 1988, 53
  model of
    sources of ethical guidance, 52
    Type I ethics, 52
    Type II ethics, 52
  professionalization of human resource
    management
    American Society for Training and
      Development, 58
    Human Resource Certification Institute, 58
    profession defined, 58
    Society for Human Resource Management,
      54, 58
    WorldatWork, 58–59
Ethics training, 53, 56–58
Ethnocentric staffing, 413
Event recruiting, 154
E-verify, 85, 162–163
Evolution of human resource management, 40–41
Exclusive provider organization (EPO), 297
Executive, 39
Executive compensation
  base salary, 282
  bonuses and performance-based pay, 282
  perquisites, 283
  stock option plans, 283
Executive employee, 269
Executive job sharing, 309–310
Executive integration, 198–199
Executive order
  defined, 96
  9981, 96
  10988, 369
  11246, 91, 96, 97, 269
  11375, 96, 97
  13494, 369
  13495, 369
  13496, 369
  13502, 369
Executive orientation, 198–199
Executive search firms, 153
Exempt employee, 269
Exit interview, 399–400
Expatriate, 412
Expatriate compensation, 420
Exporting, 411
External environment
  competition, 34
  customers, 34
  defined, 33
  economy, 36
  labor market, 33
  legal considerations, 33
  political parties, 34
  shareholders, 34
  society, 34
  HR technology, 36
  unanticipated events, 36
  unions, 34
External equity, 265
External recruitment methods (traditional)
  comcompetitive games, 154–155
  event recruiting, 154
  executive search firms, 153
  internships, 153

  job fairs, 153
  media advertising, 151–152
  open houses, 154
  private employment agencies, 152
  professional associations, 154
  public employment agency, 152
  recruiters, 152
  sign-on bonuses, 154
  unsolicited applicants, 154
External recruitment sources
  colleges and universities, 145
  community colleges, 144, 208
  competitors in the labor market, 145
  ex-offenders, 146–147
  former employees, 145
  high school and vocational schools, 144
  military personnel, 146
  self-employed workers, 146
  unemployed, 146

F

Facebook, 35, 149–150, 185, 226
Factor comparison method, 271–272
Fair and Accurate Credit Transaction Act of
  2003, 332
Fair Credit Reporting Act of 1997, 185–186
Fair Labor Standards Act of 1938, as amended,
  269–270
Fair Pay Act, 78–79
Family and Medical Leave Act of 1993, 304
Faragher v City of Boca Raton, 94
Federal Labor Relations Authority, 369
Federal Mediation and Conciliation Service, 363
Federal Register, 99
Federal Sentencing Guidelines for
  Organizations Act of 1992, 53
Final-offer arbitration, 369
Financial scandal, 48–50
Flexible spending account, 297–298
Flexible time, 309
Flextime, 308–309
Flooding the community, 351
Food services/subsidized cafederias, 301
Forced distribution method, 248
Forecasting human resource requirements
  bottom-up forecast, 122
  relationship between volume of sales and
    number of workers required, 123
  zero-base forecasting, 123
Former employees, 145
401(k) plan, 299
14 Penn Plaza LLC v Pyett, 399
Franchising, 411
Free agents, 230
Frequency rate, 324
Fringe benefits, 293
Functional job analysis (FJA), 112

G

Gainsharing, 280
Garcia v Spun Steak, 96
Generalist, 39
Generation I, 232
Generation X, 230–231
Generation Y, 231
General duty clause, 318, 320, 328
General-purpose job boards
  careerbuilder.com, 148
  monster.com, 148
Genetic Information Nondiscrimination Act of
  2008, 176
Genetic testing, 176
Geocentric staffing, 413–414
Glass ceiling, 83

Glass ceiling commission, 83
Global compensation
  compensation for host-country nationals,
    419–420
  expatriate compensation, 420
Global corporation, 411
Global customized benefits, 311
Global e-learning, 417–418
Global employee and labor relations, 422
Global equal employment opportunity, 424
Global healthcare for expats, 339
Global human resource development
  continual development: online assistance and
    training, 416–417
  expatriate training and development, 416
  pre-move orientation and training, 416
  repatriation orientation and training, 416
Global legal and political factors, 423
Global safety and health, 421–422
Global sexual harassment, 424
Global staffing
  ethnocentric staffing, 413
  geocentric staffing, 414
  polycentric staffing, 413
  regiocentric staffing, 413
Global strategic human resource management
  background investigation, 414
  bribery, 408–409
  compensation
    compensation for host-country nationals,
      419–420
    expatriate compensation, 420
  defined, 411
  employee and labor relations, 422
  human resource development
    continual development: online assistance
      and training, 416–417
    e-learning, 417–418
    expatriate training and development, 416
    pre-move orientation and training, 416
    repatriation orientation and training, 416
  legal and political factors, 423
  selecting expatriates, 414
  staffing
    approaches
      ethnocentric staffing, 413
      geocentric staffing, 414
      polycentric staffing, 413
      regiocentric staffing, 413
    types of global staff members
      expatriate, 412
      host-country national (HCN), 412
      third-country national (TCN), 413
  virtual teams, 333, 418–419
Goals and timetables, 100
Golden parachute contract, 283
Graphoanalysis, 176
Gratz v Bollinger, 89–90
Graveyard shift, 302
Grievance, 360
Grievance procedure, 360
Griggs v Duke Power Company, 87, 116, 185
Group interview, 180
Grutter v Bollinger, 89
Guidelines-oriented job analysis (GOJA), 112
Guidelines on discrimination
  caregiver, 97
  national origin, 95–96
  religion, 96
  sexual harassment, 93–95

H

H-21B employment visa, 76–77
Halo error, 250

Handwriting analysis, 176
Harris v Forklift Systems, Inc., 94
Hay guide chart-profile method (Hay plan), 272
Hazard pay, 302
Health
  burnout, 129, 223, 333, 338
  defined, 32, 320
  employee assistance program, 338
  Occupational Safety and Health Act of 1970, 320
  Occupational Safety and Health Administration (OSHA), 320–323, 324, 327, 328, 351
  physical fitness programs, 334
  smoke-free workplaces, 318–319
  stress
    consequences, 330
    defined, 329
    managing, 331–332
    stressful jobs, 330
  substance abuse
    alcohol abuse, 327, 335
    defined, 335
    drug abuse, 335
    substance-abuse-free workplace, 335–337
  wellness programs, 333–334
Health care, 296
Health Insurance Portability and Accountability Act of 1996, 303
Health maintenance organizations (HMOs), 297
Health savings account, 297
High schools, 144, 207, 351
Hiring in rate, 273
Host-country national (HCN), 412
Hot stove rule, 389
Hourly workers' job sites, 149
HR outsourcing, 37
HR technology, 36
Human capital metrics
  defined, 188
  evaluating recruitment/selection effectiveness
    acceptance rate, 191
    cost/benefit of recruitment sources and methods, 191
    hiring manager overall satisfaction, 189
    new hire retention, 189
    quality of hire, 189
    recruiting costs, 189
    selection rate, 190
    time required to hire, 189
    turnover rate, 189
    yield rate, 191
  metrics for evaluating training and development
    benchmarking, 214
    bubusiness results derived from training, 212
    change of learner behavior, 213
    level of learning achieved, 213
    participant reaction, 213
    return-on-investment from training, 213
Human Resource Certification Institute, 58, 411
Human resource's changing strategic roles
  human resource manager, 37
  HR outsourcing, 37
  line manager, 39
  professional employer organization, 38–39
  shared service centers, 38
Human resource database, 124
Human resource designations
  executive, 39
  generalist, 39
  specialist, 39
Human resource development, 31
Human resource ethics, 56

Human resource information system (HRIS), 36
Human resource management (HRM)
  defined, 30
  environment
    competition, 34
    customers, 34
    economy, 36
    external environment defined, 33
    HR technology, 36
    labor market, 33
    legal considerations, 33
    political parties, 34
    shareholders, 34
    society, 34
    unanticipated events, 36
    unions, 34
  functions
    compensation, 32
    employee and labor relations, 32
    human resource development, 31
    safety and health, 32
    staffing, 30
Human resource management functions
  compensation, 32
  employee and labor relations, 32
  human resource development, 31
  safety and health, 32
  staffing, 30
Human resource manager, 30
Human resource outsourcing, 37
Human resource planning (HRP)
  defined, 30, 121
  forecasting human resource availability, 123
  forecasting human resource requirements, 122–123
  process, 121–122
  shortage of workers forecasted, 124
  surplus of workers forecasted, 125–126
Human resource research, 32
Hybrid programs, 208

Identity theft, 162, 332
Identity Theft and Assumption Deterrence Act of 1988, 332
Illegal Immigration Reform and Immigrant Responsibility Act of 1996, 85–86
Immediate supervisor appraisal, 242
Immigrants, 76
Immigration Reform and Control Act of 1986, 85
In-basket exercise (training), 175, 206
Indirect financial compensation, 32, 265, 294
Industrial relations, 32
Industrial union, 354
Injunction, 378, 379
Instructor-led training, 204
Interest arbitration, 353, 363, 369
Internal employee relations
  alternative dispute resolution (ADR), 398–399
  defined, 386
  demotion as an alternative to termination, 395
  disciplinary action
    approaches
      disciplinary action without punishment, 390–391
      hot stove rule, 389
      progressive disciplinary action, 389–390
    defined, 387
    problems, 391–392
    process, 388–389
  discipline, 387
  employment at will, 386–387

ombudsperson, 398
promotion, 399–400
resignation
  advance notice, 401
  analyzing voluntary resignation, 400–401
  attitude surveys, 401
  exit interview, 399–400
retirement, 402–403
termination
  executives, 394
  middle and lower-level managers and professionals, 394
  nonmanagerial/nonprofessional employees, 394
transfer, 399
Internal recruitment methods, 141–143
International Confederation of Free Trade Unions, 371
International Brotherhood of Teamsters, 352, 354, 355, 368, 381
Internet recruiter, 147
Internship, 153, 207
Interpretative guidelines (on)
  caregiver discrimination, 97
  discrimination because of national origin, 95–96
  discrimination because of religion, 96
  sexual harassment, 93–95
Interview illusion, 183
ISO 9027 quality assurance training standard, 214

J
Job, 108
Job analysis
  conducting, 109
  defined, 108
  information (types of), 110
  the law
    Americans with Disabilities Act (ADA) of 1990, 82, 84–85, 97, 116, 187
    Civil Rights Act of 1964, 79–83, 87, 94–86, 97, 99, 143
    Equal Pay Act of 1963, Amended in 1972,
    Fair Labor Standards Act of 1938, 269–270
    Occupational Safety and Health Act of 1970, 320
  methods
    combination, 111
    employee recording, 111
    interviews, 111
    observation, 111
    questionnaires, 111
  reasons for conducting
    compensation, 110
    employee and labor relations, 110
    legal considerations, 110
    performance appraisal, 110
    safety and health, 110
    staffing, 109
    training and development, 109
    team members, 115
    timeliness of, 115
Job analysis schedule (JAS), 112
Job bidding, 142–143
Job description
  date of the job analysis, 113
  defined, 100, 113
  duties performed, 113
  job identification, 113
  job specification, 109, 113–114
  job summary, 113
Job design
  defined, 129
  job enlargement, 129

Job design (*continued*)
  job enrichment, 129
  job rotation, 129
  reengineering, 129–130
Job enlargement, 129
Job enrichment, 129
Job environment as a nonfinancial
      compensation factor
  appropriate status symbols, 307
  capable managers, 307
  competent employees, 307
  congenial co-workers, 307
  sound policies, 306–307
  working conditions, 308
Job evaluation, 270–272
Job evaluation
  classification method, 271
  defined, 270
  factor comparison method, 271–272
  Hay guide chart-profile, 272
  point method, 272
  ranking method, 272
Job evaluation ranking method, 271
Job fair, 153
Job hazard analysis (JHA), 323, 324
Job identification, 113
Job-knowledge questions, 179
Job-knowledge tests, 174
Job posting, 142–143
Job pricing
  adjusting pay rates, 274–275
  broadbanding, 274
  defined, 272
  pay grades, 272–273
  pay ranges, 273
  single-rate system, 274
Job rotation, 129
Job-sample simulation questions, 179
Job sculpting, 115
Job search scams, 151
Job security, 222
Job security versus career security, 222
Job sharing, 309–310
Job specification, 109, 113–114
Job Training Partnership Act, 214
Jury pay, 296
Just-in-time training, 202

K

Keyword résumé, 169
Keywords, 169
Kirkpatrick/Phillips model, 213
KSAs, 203

L

Labor-Management Reporting and Disclosure
      Act (Landrum-Griffin Act) of 1959,
      381–382
Labor market, 33
Labor market as a determinant of direct
      financial compensation
  compensation surveys, 268
  cost of living, 268
  economy, 269
  expediency, 268
  labor unions, 268
  legislation, 269–270
Labor movement after 1930
  Anti-Injunction Act (Norris-LaGuardia Act)
      of 1932, 379
  Labor Management Relations Act
      (Taft-Hartley Act) of 1947, 380–381
  National Labor Relations Act (Wagner Act),
      1935, 379–380

Labor movement before 1930
  Commonwealth v Hunt, 378
  conspiracy, 378
  injunction, 378, 379
  yellow-dog contract, 378–379
Lack of objectivity, 250
Lateral skill path, 229
Layoff alternatives, 126
Learning organization, 200–201
*Ledbetter v Goodyear Tire & Rubber Co.,
      Inc.,* 78
Leniency, 250
Leonel v American Airlines, 84
Licensing, 411
Life insurance, 298
Likes and dislikes survey, 225
Lilly Ledbetter Fair Pay Act, 78–79
Line manager, 39
LinkedIn, 35, 149–150, 185, 226,
Local union, 353–354
Lockout, 362, 363
Luck, 278

M

Magna Carta of Labor, 379
Maintenance of membership, 359
Managed-care health organizations
  exclusive provider organizations (EPOs), 297
  health maintenance organizations
      (HMOs), 297
  point-of-service (POS), 297
  preferred provider organization (PPO), 297
Management by objectives, 249
Management development, 209–211
Management position description questionnaire
      (MPDQ), 112
Manager self-service, 39, 128
Mandated benefits, 293–294
Mandatory bargaining issues, 358
Manipulating the evaluation, 251–252
Market (going) rate, 267
*McDonald v Santa Fe Trail Transportation
      Company*, 92
Media advertising, 151–152
Mediation, 363
Medical examination, 84, 166, 187
Membership (organizational), 277
Mentoring, 210
Merit pay, 275–276
Meritor Savings Bank v Vinson, 94
Metrics for evaluating recruitment/selection
      effectiveness
  acceptance rate, 191
  cost/benefit of recruitment sources and
      methods, 191
  hiring manager overall satisfaction, 189
  new hire retention, 189
  quality of hire, 189
  recruiting costs, 189
  selection rate, 190
  time required to hire, 189
  turnover rate, 189
  yield rate, 191
Metrics for evaluating training and development
  benchmarking, 214
  business results derived from training, 212
  change of learner behavior, 213
  level of learning achieved, 213
  participant reaction, 213
  return-on-investment from training, 213
Military personnel, 146
Miller v Bank of America, 94
Minnesota Multiphasic Personality
      Inventory, 174

Mission, 118
Mistretta v Sandia Corporation, 238
Montes v Vail Clinic, Inc., 96
Mothers returning to the workforce, 74–75
Multigenerational diversity, 232
Multinational corporation (MNC), 411
Multiple interviews, 180

N

NACElink network, 148
National Association of Colleges and
      Employers, 54, 148
National Association of Manufacturers, 207
National Council on Alcoholism & Drug
      Dependence (NCADD), 335
National Council on Compensation
      Insurance, 326
National Institute for Occupational Safety and
      Health, 327
National Labor Relations Act (Wagner Act) of
      1935, 359, 379–380
National Labor Relations Board (NLRB), 351,
      355, 356, 357, 368, 369, 370, 371,
      372, 380
National Partnership for Women and Families, 97
National union, 351, 354
Negligent hiring, 186
Negligent retention, 254, 328
Negotiating the agreement, 361–362
Network career path, 229
Niche sites, 148–149
NLRB v Town & Electric Inc., 351
Nonexempt employee, 302, 311
Nonfinancial compensation, 32, 265, 305
Norms, 172
North American Free Trade Agreement, 422

O

Objectivity, 172
Observation, 111
Occupational Safety and Health Act of 1970, 320
Occupational Safety and Health Administration,
      320–323, 324, 327, 328, 351
O'Connor v Consolidated Coin Caterers Corp.,
      88–89
Office of Federal Contract Compliance
      Programs (OFCCP), 84, 93, 97, 98, 99,
      140, 141, 171
Offboarding, 402
Offshoring, 138
Older workers, 70–71, 75–76
Older Workers Benefit Protection Act
      of 1990, 304
Ombudsperson, 398
O*NET, 114
On-demand training, 202
On-the-job training (OJT), 206
*Oncale v Sundowner Offshore
      Services*, 95
One-on-one interview, 180
Online assessment, 175
Online higher education, 208
Online recruitment methods
  AllianceQ, 148
  contract workers' sites, 149
  corporate career Web site, 147
  general-purpose job boards
      careerbuilder.com, 148
      monster.com, 148
  hourly workers' job sites, 149
  Internet recruiter, 147
  NACElink network, 148
  niche sites, 148–149

social network recruiting, 149–150
virtual job fair, 147
weblogs, 148
Online synchronized study, 208
On-site health care, 298
Open houses, 154
Open shop, 359
Operation transition, 146
Order No. 40, 99
Organization as a determinant of direct financial
    compensation
  ability to pay, 267
  compensation policies
    market (going) rate, 267
    pay followers, 267
    pay leader, 267
  organizational level, 268
Organization development (OD)
  defined, 31, 214
  quality circles, 215
  sensitivity training, 216
  survey feedback, 215
  team building, 215–216
Organizational fit, 178, 180, 211
Organizational level, 267
Organizational stakeholder, 60
Orientation
  defined, 211
  purposes of
    company policies and rules, 211
    compensation, 211
    corporate culture, 211
    employee development, 211
    employment situation, 212
    socialization, 75, 212
    team membership, 212
Outplacement, 397
Outsourcing, 138

P

Paid time off, 295
Paid vacations, 295
Paired comparison, 247
Part-time work, 311–312
Passive job seeker, 140
PATCO, 369
Patient Protection and Affordable Care Act of
    2010, 298, 304–305
Pay followers, 267
Pay grade, 272–273
Pay leader, 267
Pay ranges, 273
Payment for time not worked, 295–296
Peer pressure, 350
Pension Protection Act of 2006, 304
People with disabilities, 76
Performance appraisal (PA)
  appraisal interview
    concluding the interview, 257
    employees' role, 256
    interview structure, 255
    scheduling the interview, 255
    use of praise and criticism, 255
  characteristics of effective appraisal system
    conduct performance reviews, 254
    continuous open communication, 254
    due process, 254
    job-related criteria, 253
    performance expectations, 253
    standardization, 253
    trained appraisers, 253
  defined, 31, 236
  environmental factors, 238

court decisions
  Albemarle Paper Company v Moody, 87, 238
  Mistretta v Sandia Corporation, 238
methods
  behaviorally anchored rating scale, 248–249
  critical incident, 247
  essay, 247
  forced distribution, 248
  ranking, 247–248
  rating scales, 245–247
  results-based system, 249
  360–degree feedback evaluation, 244–245
  work standards, 247
performance criteria
  behavior, 241
  competencies, 277
  goal achievement, 241
  improvement potential, 241
  traits, 240
period, 243
problems in
  appraisal discomfort, 249–250
  central tendency error, 251
  employee anxiety, 252
  halo/horn error, 250
  lack of objectivity, 250
  leniency/strictness, 250
  manipulating the evaluation, 251
  personal bias (stereotyping), 251
  recent behavior bias, 251
process, 239
responsibility for
  customer appraisal, 243
  immediate supervisor, 242
  peers and team members, 242–243
  self-appraisal, 227, 243
  subordinates, 242
uses of
  assessment of employee potential, 238
  career planning and development, 238
  compensation programs, 238
  human resource planning, 237
  internal employee relations, 238
  recruitment and selection, 237
  training and development, 237
Performance appraisal criteria
  behavior, 241
  competencies, 277
  goal achievement, 241
  improvement potential, 241
  traits, 240
Performance-based pay
  executive, 282
  merit pay, 275–276
  piecework, 276
  variable pay (bonus), 276
Performance management, 31, 236, 239
Permissive bargaining issues, 358
Perquisites, 283
Personal bias, 251
Personality tests, 174
Phased retirement, 402–403
*Phillips v Martin Marietta
    Corporation*, 87–88
Physical fitness programs, 334
Piecework, 276
Point-of-service (POS), 297
Point method, 272
Political involvement, 350–351
Political party, 34
Polycentric staffing, 413
Polygraph test, 176
Position, 108
Position analysis questionnaire (PAQ), 112

Postexit questionnaire, 401
Predictive validity, 172
Pre-employment screening: background
    investigation, 184–185
Pre-employment screening: reference check, 186
Preferred provider organization (PPOs), 297
Pregnancy Discrimination Act of 1978, 81–82
Preliminary screening, 167–168
Premium pay
  defined, 302
  hazard pay, 302
  shift differentials, 302
Prima facie, 78, 87, 88, 92, 185
Probable cause, 90
Probationary period, 91, 166, 243
Procurement Integrity Act of 1988, 53
Profession, 58
Professional associations, 154
Professional employee, 269–270
Professional employee compensation, 280–281
Professional employer organizations (PEOs),
    38–39
Professionalization of human resource
    management
  American Society for Training and
      Development, 58
  Human Resource Certification Institute, 58
  profession defined, 58
  Society for Human Resource Management, 58
  WorldatWork, 58–59
Profit sharing
  combination plans, 280
  current plans, 280
  deferred plans, 280
  defined, 279
Progressive disciplinary action, 389–390
Prohibited bargaining issues, 358
Promotion, 399–400
Promotion from within, 141
Psychomotor abilities tests, 173–174
Public awareness campaigns, 351
Public employment agency, 152
Pulling the union through, 350
Purpose ignorance, 94

Q

Qualified individuals with disabilities, 84–85
Quality circles, 215
Quality of hire, 189
Quotas, 424

R

Railway Labor Act of 1926, 379, 380
Ranking method of performance appraisal,
    247–248
Rating scales method, 245–247
Realistic job preview, 181–182
Reasonable accommodation, 85, 116, 182
Recent behavior bias, 251
Recruiters, 152
Recruitment
  alternatives
    contingent workers, 126, 139
    outsourcing, 138
    overtime, 139–140
    professional employer organizations
        (employee leasing), 139
  defined, 138
  external environment of,
    active or passive job seekers, 140
    labor market conditions, 140
    legal considerations, 140–141
  external recruitment sources

Recruitment (*continued*)
colleges and universities, 145
community colleges, 144
competitors in the labor market, 145
ex-offenders, 146–147
former employees, 145
high school and vocational schools, 144
military personnel, 146
self-employed workers, 146
unemployed, 146
internal methods of
employee referrals, 143
job posting and job bidding, 142–143
online recruitment methods
AllianceQ, 148
contract workers' sites, 149
corporate career Web site, 147
general-purpose job boards
careerbuilder.com, 148
monster.com, 148
hourly workers' job sites, 149
Internet recruiter, 147
NACElink network, 148
niche sites, 148–149
social network recruiting, 149–150
virtual job fair, 147
weblogs, 148
process, 141–142
promotion policies, 141
tailoring recruitment methods to sources, 155–156
traditional external recruitment methods
competitive games, 154–155
executive search firms, 153
internships, 153
job fairs, 153
media advertising, 151–152
open houses, 154
professional associations, 154
public employment agencies, 152
recruiters, 152
sign-on bonuses, 154
unsolicited applicants, 154
Recruitment methods, 142
Recruitment sources, 142
Red circle rate, 275
Reengineering, 129–130
Reeves v C.H. Robinson Worldwide, Inc., 95
Reference checks, 186
Regiocentric staffing, 413
Rehabilitation Act of 1973, 82, 84
Reliability, 172
Relocation benefits, 301
Repatriation, 417
Repetitive stress injuries, 320, 326
Requirements forecast, 122
Resignation, 400–421
Restoring American Financial
Stability Act of 2010, 263
Restricted hiring, 126
Restructuring, 395–396
Results-based system, 249
Résumés, 168–169
Retention (worker), 384–385
Retirement plans
cash balance, 299–300
defined benefits, 299
defined contribution, 299
Reverse mentoring, 211
Revised Order No. 30, 99
Ricci v DeStefano, 90
Right-to-work laws, 349, 359
Rights arbitration, 363
Rightsizing, 395

Risk management, 279, 324
Role-playing, 206

S

Sabbaticals, 296
Safety
defined, 320
domestic violence, 320, 329
economic impact, 322
ergonomics, 32, 326–327
focus
accident investigation, 324, 326
developing safety programs
employee involvement, 324
job hazard analysis, 323–324
safety engineer, 324
Superfund Amendments Reauthorization
Act of 1986, Title III, 324
evaluation of safety programs,
324, 326
unsafe employee actions, 322–323
unsafe working conditions, 323
Occupational Safety and Health
Act of 1970, 320
Occupational Safety and Health
Administration, 320–323, 324, 327,
328, 351
repetitive stress injuries, 320, 326
workplace violence
defined, 327
individual and organizational characteristics
to monitor, 328
legal consequences, 328
preventive actions, 328–329
vulnerable employees, 327
Safety director, 324, 326
Safety engineer, 324
Salary compression, 279
Sales representative compensation, 281
Sarbanes–Oxley Act, 53–54
Scanlon plan, 280
Secondary boycott, 365
Selection
assessment center, 175
concluding the interview, 184
decision, 187
defined, 30–31 164
employment interview
candidate's role and expectation, 178
content of the interview, 177–178
defined, 177
interview planning, 177
environmental factors of
applicant pool, 93, 140, 143, 165
legal considerations, 165
organizational hierarchy, 165
other HR functions, 165
probationary period, 91, 166, 243
speed of decision making, 165
type of organization, 166
interviewing problems
contrast effect, 183
inappropriate questions, 182
interviewer domination, 183
interview illusion, 183
lack of training, 183
nonverbal communication, 183
premature judgment, 183
permitting non-job related questions, 182
medical examination, 84, 166, 187
methods of interviewing
board (or panel), 180
group, 180
multiple, 180

one-on-one, 180
realistic job preview, 181–182
metrics for evaluating recruitment/selection
effectiveness
acceptance rate, 191
cost/benefit of recruitment sources and
methods, 191
hiring manager overall satisfaction, 189
new hire retention, 189
quality of hire, 189
recruiting costs, 189
selection rate, 190
time required to hire, 189
turnover rate, 189
yield rate, 191
negligent hiring, 186
notification of candidates, 188
pre-employment screening: background
investigation, 184–185
pre-employment screening: reference check, 186
preliminary screening, 167–168
process, 166
review of application, 168
review of résumés, 168–169
sending résumés via the Internet, 170
tests
advantages, 170
characteristics
norms, 172
objectivity, 172
reliability, 172
standardization, 171–172
validity, 172
online assessment, 175
potential problems, 170–171
types of employment tests
cogitative aptitude, 173
job-knowledge, 174
personality, 174
psychomotor abilities, 173–174
vocational interest, 174
work-sample, 174
unique forms of testing
genetic, 176
graphoanalysis, 176
polygraph, 176
types of interviews
behavioral, 179–180
structured, 179
unstructured, 178–179
types of validation studies
construct, 173
content, 173
criterion-related, 172–173
Selection process, 166
Selection ratio, 165–166
Selection tests
advantages, 170
characteristics
norms, 172
objectivity, 172
reliability, 172
standardization, 171–172
validity, 172
online assessment, 175
potential problems, 170–171
types of employment tests
cognitive aptitude, 173
job-knowledge, 174
personality, 174
psychomotor abilities, 173–174
vocational interest, 174
work-sample, 174
unique forms of testing

genetic, 176
graphoanalysis, 176
polygraph, 176
Self-appraisal, 227, 243
Self-assessment, 223
Self-directed teams, 215
Seniority, 277
Sensitivity training, 216
Severance pay, 397–398
Severity rate, 324
Service Employees International Union, 354, 355, 369
Sexual harassment, 93–95
Shared service center (SSC), 38
Shareholders, 34
Shift differential, 302
Shortage of workers forecasted
    compensation incentives, 124
    different selection standards, 124
    innovative inrecruiting, 124
    training programs, 124
Sick pay, 295–296
Sign-on bonuses, 154
Simulators, 209
Single parents, 74
Single-rate system, 274
Situational questions, 179
Skill-based pay, 276–277
Smoke-free workplaces, 318–319
Social audit, 53
Social contract
    defined, 61
    obligations to government, 62
    obligations to individuals, 62
    obligations to other organizations, 62
    obligations to society in general, 63
Social Network Recruiting, 149–150
Social networking, 35, 149–150, 185, 206, 211
Social Security Act of 1935, 294
Social Security Administration, 294
Socialization, 75, 212
Society for Human Resource Management, 58
Specialist, 39
Spot bonus, 276
Staffing, 30
Stakeholder analysis, 60–61
Standard Occupational Classification, 115
Standardization, 171–172
Status symbol, 307
Stereotyping, 94, 251
Stock option plan, 283
Straight commission, 281
Straight salary, 281
Strategic partner, 117–118
Strategic planning
    defined, 118
    process
        environmental assessment, 119
        mission determination, 118–119
        objective setting, 119–120
        strategy implementation, 120–121
        strategy setting, 120
Strategically located union members, 350
Strategy implementation
    human resources, 121
    information and control systems, 120
    leadership, 120
    organizational structure, 120
    technology, 120
Strength/weakness balance sheet, 224–225
Stress
    consequences, 330
    defined, 329
    managing, 331–332

stressful jobs, 330
Stress interview, 180–181
Strictness, 250
Strikes, 351, 363, 364–365, 369, 378, 380–381
Structured interview, 179
Subordinates appraisal, 242
Substance abuse, 335
Substance Abuse & Mental Health Services
    Administration, 335
Substance-abuse-free workplace
    employee assistance program, 338
    implementing a drug testing program, 338
Succession planning, 125–127
Superfund Amendments Reauthorization Act of
    1986, Title III, 324
Supreme Court Decisions
    Adarand Constructors v Pena, 89
    Albemarle Paper Company v Moody, 87–88
    American Tobacco Company v Patterson, 88–89
    Burlington Industries, Inc. v Ellerth, 94
    CBOCS West Inc. v Humphries, 78
    Circuit City v Adams, 399
    Commonwealth v Hunt, 378
    Dothard v Rawlinson, 88
    Espinoza v Farah Manufacturing Company, 88
    Faragher v City of Boca Raton, 94
    Gratz v Bollinger, 89–90
    Griggs v Duke Power Company, 87, 116, 185
    Grutter v Bollinger, 89
    Harris v Forklift Systems, Inc., 94
    Ledbetter v Goodyear Tire & Rubber Co., Inc., 78
    Leonel v American Airlines, 84
    McDonald v Santa Fe Trail Transportation Company, 92
    Meritor Savings Bank v Vinson, 94
    Phillips v Martin Marietta Corporation, 87–88
    O'Connor v Consolidated Coin Caterers Corp., 88–89
    Oncale v Sundowner Offshore Services, 95
    Ricci v DeStefano, 90
    TWA v Hardison, 96
    University of California Regents v Bakke, 89
    Vicky S. Crawford vs Metropolitan Government of Nashville and Davidson County, Tennessee, 79
Surplus of employees forecasted, 125
Survey feedback, 215
Swing shift, 302
SWOT analysis, 119

T

Talent management, 106–107
Tariffs, 423–424
Team building, 215–216
Team equity, 266
Teamsters, 352, 354, 355, 368, 381
Telecommuting, 310
Telepresence, 209
Teleworkers, 310
Termination, 392–394
Test anxiety, 171
Tests
    advantages, 170
    characteristics
        norms, 172
        objectivity, 172
        reliability, 172
        standardization, 171–172
        validity, 172

online assessment, 175
potential problems, 170–171
types of employment tests
    cogitative aptitude, 173
    job-knowledge, 174
    personality, 174
    psychomotor abilities, 173–174
    vocational interest, 174
    work-sample, 174
unique forms of testing
    genetic, 176
    graphoanalysis, 176
    polygraph, 176
Third-country national (TCN), 413
Third hand smoke, 319
360–degree feedback
    evaluation, 244–245
Title VII, 79–81, 143, 172
Total rewards, 293
Traditional career path, 228
Training (defined), 31, 200
Training and development
    defined, 200
    delivery systems
        colleges and universities, 145
        community colleges, 144, 208
        corporate university, 207
        online higher education, 208
        simulators, 209
        vestibule system, 208
        video media, 208
    determining needs
        organizational analysis, 203
        person analysis, 203
        task analysis, 203
    factors influencing
        learning styles, 201–202
        lifetime learning, 201
        other human resource functions, 202
        technological advances, 201
        top management support, 201
        world complexity, 201
    implementing programs, 212
    management development
        coaching, 210–211
        mentoring, 210
        reverse mentoring, 211
    methods
        apprenticeship training, 207
        behavior modeling, 205–206
        business games, 206
        case study, 205
        e-learning, 204–205
        in-basket exercise (training), 206
        instructor-led, 204
        internships, 207
        on-the-job training, 206
        role-playing, 206
    metrics for evaluating
        return on investment from training, 213
        business results derived from training, 213
        changes in learner behavior, 213
        benchmarking, 214
        level of learning achieved, 213
        participants reaction, 213
    objectives, 203–204
    organization development
        defined, 31, 215
        quality circles, 215
        sensitivity training, 216
        survey feedback, 215
        team building, 215–216

Training and development (*continued*)
  orientation
    defined, 211
    purposes, 211–212
    responsibility, 212
  process, 202
Training and development (defined), 200
Traits, 240
Transfer, 302, 399
Troubled Assets Relief Program (TARP) of
    2009, 270
Turnover rate, 189
TWA v Hardison, 96
Twitter, 35, 149–150, 185, 205–215, 226
Two in a box, 290–291
Two-tier wage system, 346–347
Type I ethics, 52
Type II ethics, 52

U

Underutilization, 100
Unemployment compensation, 294
*Uniform Guidelines on Employee Selection
    Procedures*, 81, 90–91, 110, 172, 253
Uniformed Services Employment and
    Reemployment Rights Act of 1994, 86
Union
  defined, 34
  establishing the collective bargaining
    relationship
    election and certification, 357
    election campaign, 356
    petition for election, 356
    signing of authorization cards, 356
  objectives, 348
  organized labor's strategies for a stronger
    movement
    building organizing funds, 351
    Employee Free Choice Act, 353
    flooding the community, 351
    organizing through the card check, 352
    partnering with high schools, 351–352
    political involvement, 350–351
    public awareness campaigns, 351
    pulling the union through, 350
    strategically located union
      members, 350
    union salting, 351

union decertification, 370
union structure
  AFL-CIO, 350, 351, 352, 353, 354, 365,
    369, 379, 381
  Change to Win Coalition, 353,
    354–355
  local union, 353–354
  national union, 351, 354
unions today, 370–371
why employees join unions
  dissatisfaction with management
    attitude of management, 349
    compensation, 348
    job security, 349
  forced unionization, 349
  opportunity for leadership, 349
  peer pressure, 350
  social outlet, 349
Union objectives, 348
Union salting, 351
Union shop, 359
Unions today, 370–371
United Auto Workers, 354
United Steelworkers, 346, 347, 349
Unique benefits, 301–302
*University of California Regents v
    Bakke*, 89
Unsolicited applicants, 154
Unstructured interview, 178–179
U.S. Employment Service, 152

V

Validation studies
  construct, 173
  content, 173
  criterion-related, 172–173
Validity, 172
Variable pay (bonus), 276
Vestibule system, 208
Veterans' Benefits Improvement Act of 2004, 86
*Vicky S. Crawford vs Metropolitan Government
    of Nashville and Davidson County,
    Tennessee*, 79
Video media, 208
Videoconferencing, 152, 209
Violence Against Women Act, 329
Violence Against Women and DOJ
    Reauthorization Act, 329

Virtual job fair, 147
Virtual teams, 333, 418–419
Vision care, 298
Vocational interest tests, 174
Voluntary benefits, 292, 302
Vulnerable employees (workplace violence), 327

W

*Wade v Mississippi Cooperative Extension
    Service*, 240
Wage curve, 273
Wage rate schedule, 360
Wagner Act of 1935, 379–380
Walsh-Healy Act of 1936, 269
Weblogs, 148
Wellness programs, 333–334
Whistle-blowing, 100
Women in business, 74
Worker Adjustment and Retraining Notification
    Act, 396–397
Work standards method, 247
Worker requirements questions, 179
Worker retention, 384–385
Workers of color, 75
Workforce Investment Act, 214
Workforce planning, 121
Working mothers, 74
Work-life balance, 308
Workplace flexibility
  compressed workweek, 309
  flextime, 308–309
  job sharing, 309–310
  part-time work, 311–312
  telecommuting, 310
Workforce planning software, 123
Workplace violence, 327–329
Family Violence Prevention and
    Services Act, 329
Work-sample tests, 174
WorldatWork, 58–59

Y

Yellow-dog contract, 378–379
Young persons with limited education or skills, 77

Z

Zero-base forecasting, 123